MARX IN THE AGE OF DIGITAL CAPITALISM

Studies in Critical Social Sciences Book Series

Haymarket Books is proud to be working with Brill Academic Publishers (www.brill.nl) to republish the *Studies in Critical Social Sciences* book series in paperback editions. This peer-reviewed book series offers insights into our current reality by exploring the content and consequences of power re- lationships under capitalism, and by considering the spaces of opposition and resistance to these changes that have been defining our new age. Our full catalog of *SCSS* volumes can be viewed at https://www.haymarketbooks .org/series_collections/4-studies-in-critical-social-sciences.

MARX IN THE AGE OF DIGITAL CAPITALISM

Edited by
CHRISTIAN FUCHS
VINCENT MOSCO

Haymarket
Books
Chicago, IL

First published in 2015 by Brill Academic Publishers, The Netherlands.
© 2016 Koninklijke Brill NV, Leiden, The Netherlands

Published in paperback in 2017 by
Haymarket Books
P.O. Box 180165
Chicago, IL 60618
773-583-7884
www.haymarketbooks.org

ISBN: 978-1-60846-709-9

Trade distribution:
In the U.S. through Consortium Book Sales, www.cbsd.com
In Canada, Publishers Group Canada, www.pgcbooks.ca
In the UK, Turnaround Publisher Services, www.turnaround-uk.com
In all other countries by Publishers Group Worldwide, www.pgw.com

Cover design by Jamie Kerry of Belle Étoile Studios and Ragina Johnson.

This book was published with the generous support of Lannan Foundation
and the Wallace Action Fund.

Printed in Canada by union labor.

10 9 8 7 6 5 4 3 2 1

Library of Congress Cataloging-in-Publication Data is available.

Contents

List of Figures and Tables

Figures

Tables

About the Authors

Editors

Christian Fuchs

is Professor at and Director of the University of Westminster's Communication and Media research Institute (CAMRI). He is co-editor of the open access online journal tripleC: Communication, Capitalism & Critique (http://www.triple-c.at). His research interests lie in the fields of Critical Information Society Studies, Critical Internet Research, critical social theory, media & society and the Critical Political Economy of Media, Communication & Society. He is author of numerous publications on these topics, including the monographs "Reading Marx in the Information Age: A Media and Communication Studies Perspective on Capital Volume 1" (Routledge 2016), "Digital Labour and Karl Marx" (Routledge 2014), "Social Media: A Critical Introduction" (Sage 2014), "Culture and Economy in the Age of Social Media" (2015), "OccupyMedia! The Occupy Movement and Social Media in Crisis Capitalism" (Zero Books 2014), "Foundations of Critical Media and Information Studies" (Routledge 2011), "Internet and Society: Social Theory in the Information Age" (Routledge 2008).

Vincent Mosco

is Professor Emeritus of Sociology at Queen's University where he was Canada Research Chair in Communication and Society and head of the Department of Sociology. His most recent books include To the Cloud: Big Data in a Turbulent World (2014), The Laboring of Communication (with Catherine McKercher, 2008), The Political Economy of Communication, second edition (2009), Getting the Message: Communication Workers and Global Value Chains (edited with Ursula Huws and Catherine McKercher, 2010), and Critical Studies in Communication and Society (edited with Cao Jin and Leslie Regan Shade, 2014).

Authors

Miriyam Aouragh

is Leverhulme fellow at the University of Westminster's Communication and Media Research Institute (CAMRI). Her research concerns the everyday implications of the internet for activists and qcyber warfare in the Arab-Israeli conflict. Her *Palestine Online: Transnationalism, the Internet and the Construction of Identity* came out in 2011 (IB Tauris). Miriyam is a socialist activist.

Brian A. Brown

is an Assistant Professor in the Department of Communication, Media & Film at the University of Windsor in Windsor, Ontario, Canada. His research is focused on the biopolitics of social media, autonomist theory, and visual culture studies.

Mattias Ekman

is working as a researcher at the Swedish Media Council and as a lecturer at the Department of Media Studies at Stockholm University. His research deals foremost with political mobilization and social media, right-wing extremism and the Internet, political communication and news media, and most recently, domestic media cultures. His latest publications include contributions in Ethnic and Racial Studies Journalism Practice, Celebrity Studies and Mediekultur.

Eran Fisher

is a senior Lecturer at the Department of Sociology, Political Science, and Communication, The Open University, Israel. He studies the intersection of new media and capitalism. His books include *Media and New Capitalism in the Digital Age* (2010, Palgrave), *Internet and Emotions* (2014, Routledge, co-edited with Tova Benski), and *Reconsidering Value and Labour in the Digital Age* (2015, Palgrave, co-edited with Christian Fuchs).

Katarina L. Gidlund

is associate Professor of Informatics at Mid Sweden University. Her main research interest is critical studies of digital technology and societal change. This involves issues such as critical and reflexive design, , the discursive level of design, and the interplay between rhetoric and practice (hegemonies and their material practices, power structures, the visualization of dominant stories, and embedded internationalities). She is co-coordinator of the Swedish eGovernment Research Network, programme committee member of the International EGOV conference and the Scandinavian Information Systems Conference, and appointed member in Användningsforum, the forum for usability and accessibility in the ICT domain iniated by the Swedish government.

Dal Yong Jin

is Associate Professor in the School of Communication at Simon Fraser University. He obtained his Ph.D. degree from the Institute of Communications Research at the University of Illinois at Urbana Champaign. He has taught in several institutions, including the University of Illinois in Chicago and the Korea Advanced Institute of Science and Technology (KAIST). His major research and teaching interests are on globalization and media, information technology policy, new media and game studies, transnational cultural studies, and the political economy of media and culture. He is the author of numerous books, including Digital Platforms, Imperialism and Political Culture (2015), *De-Convergence of Global Media Industries* (2013), *Hands On/Hands Off: The Korean State and the Market Liberalization of the Communication Industry* (2011), and *Korea's Online Gaming Empire* (2010).

Atle Mikkola Kjøsen

is a lecturer and doctoral candidate in the Faculty of Information and Media Studies at the University of Western Ontario where he researches Marxist value theory, media theory, logistics and supply chains, mobility, time-critical media and artificial intelligence.

Vincent Manzerolle

is an Assistant Professor in the Communication, Media & Film Department at the University of Windsor. He earned his PhD in Media Studies from the University of Western Ontario. His teaching and research focuses generally on the history, political economy, and theory of media. He has published on a range of topics including credit technologies, consumer databases, apps, wireless connectivity, mobile payment systems, and he is a co-editor of *The Audience Commodity in a Digital Age* (Peter Lang, 2014).

Katarina Giritli Nygren

is Associate Professor in Sociology and Director of the Forum for Gender Studies at Mid Sweden University. Her current research deals with the shifting governmentalities of and beyond neoliberalism in different contexts with a particular focus on the ways in which they produce inclusion as well as exclusion and how it intersects with class, gender and ethnicity. A particular attention has been paid to outline the theoretical arguments for developed analysis of the interconnections between risk, neo-liberal subjectivities and normalization processes.

Robert Prey

is an Assistant Professor in the Centre for Media and Journalism Studies at the University of Groningen, in the Netherlands. He earned his PhD from the School of Communication at Simon Fraser University in Canada. His research interests include the political economy of new media, popular music, global communication, and social and media theory. Robert's work has been published in numerous academic journals including *TripleC, Global Media Journal, The Information Society* and *The Asia-Pacific Journal*. Robert was a visiting researcher in the Department of Sociology at Sungkonghoe University in Seoul,

South Korea from 2007-2008. Prior to, and in between academic degrees he has worked in radio in Canada and with multicultural television in South Korea.

Jernej Amon Prodnik

is a post-doctoral researcher at the Institute of Communication Studies and Journalism at the Faculty of Social Sciences, Charles University in Prague (the PolCoRe group), and a researcher at the Social Communication Research Centre, Faculty of Social Sciences, University of Ljubljana (Slovenia). He defended his PhD in media and communication studies at the University of Ljubljana in 2013 under the title *Political Economy of Communication and Structural Transformations of Capitalism.* His principal research interests include critique of political economy (with a focus on media and communication) and the wider social context of technological changes and democratic potentials brought about by new technologies.

Anabel Quan-Haase

is Associate Professor of Sociology and Information and Media Studies at Western University. Her interests lie in social media, social networks, social capital, inequality, and serendipity.

Marisol Sandoval

is a Lecturer at the Department of Culture and Creative Industries at City University London. Her current research interests include alternative media, critical political economy of media and communication, the global division of labour in the culture industry, Corporate Social (Ir)Responsibility and worker co-operatives in the cultural sector. Marisol is co-editor of the open access journal tripleC – Communication, Capitalism and Critique and author of "From Corporate to Socail Media. Critical Perspectives on Corporate Social Responsibility in Media and Communication Industries" (Routledge 2014).

Jens Schröter

Prof. Dr. phil., is chair for media studies at the University of Bonn. He was director of the graduate school "Locating Media" in Siegen, see: http://www.uni-siegen.de/locatingmedia/. from 2008-2012 and is member of the DFG-graduate research center "Locating Media" at the University of Siegen since 2012. He was (together with Prof. Dr. Lorenz Engell, Weimar) director of the research project "TV Series as Reflection and Projection of Change" from 2010-2014, see: http://www.mediatisiertewelten.de/en/projects/tv-series-as-reflection-and-projection-of-change/. Main research topics are: Theory and history of digital media, theory and history of photography, theory and history of three-dimensional images, intermediality, copy protection, media theory in discussion with the critique of value, TV-series. April/May 2014: "John von Neumann"-fellowship at the University of Szeged, Hungary. September 2014: Guest Professor, Guangdong University of Foreign Studies, Guangzhou, People's Republic of China. Winter semester 2014/15: Senior-fellowship at the research group "Media Cultures of Computer Simulation", Leuphana-University Lüneburg. Recent publications: 3D. History, Theory and Aesthetics of the Transplane Image, New York/London/New Delhi/Sydney: Bloomsbury 2014; (Ed.) Handbuch Medienwissenschaft, Stuttgart: Metzler 2014. Visit www.medienkulturwissenschaft-bonn.de Visit www.theorie-der-medien.de email: schroeter@uni-bonn.de.

Sebastian Sevignani

studied media and communication, philosophy, and theology at the University of Salzburg. Currently, he holds a postdoctoral position at the University of Jena's Institute of Sociology and works on a re-actualisation of a critical sociology of needs. Sebastian is a member of the Unified Theory of Information Research Group (UTI) and member of the editorial board of tripleC: Communication, Capitalism & Critique. Journal for a Global Sustainable Information Society. Recent publications: "Privacy and Capitalism in the age of Social Media" (2016, with Routledge).

Andreas Wittel

is a Senior Lecturer at Nottingham Trent University (UK) and is currently interested in the interface between digital media and critical theory.

CHAPTER 1

Introduction: Marx is Back – The Importance of Marxist Theory and Research for Critical Communication Studies Today

Christian Fuchs and Vincent Mosco

'Marx is fashionable again,' declares Jorn Schutrumpf, head of the Berlin publishing house Dietz, which brings out the works of Marx and his collaborator Friedrich Engels. Sales have trebled – albeit from a pretty low level – since 2005 and have soared since the summer. [...] The Archbishop of Canterbury, Rowan Williams, gave him a decent review last month: 'Marx long ago observed the way in which unbridled capitalism became a kind of mythology, ascribing reality, power and agency to things that had no life in themselves.' Even the Pope has put in a good word for the old atheist – praising his 'great analytical skill.' (The Times, Financial crisis gives added capital to Marx's writings. October 20, 2008).

No one claims that we're all Marxists now but I do think the old boy deserves some credit for noticing that 'it's the economy, stupid' and that many of the apparently omniscient titans who ascend the commanding heights of the economy are not so much stupid as downright imbecilic, driven by a mad exploitative greed that threatens us all. Marx's work is not holy writ, despite the strivings of some disciples to present it as such (The Evening Standard, Was Marx Right All Along?. March 30, 2009).

Karl Marx is back. That, at least, is the verdict of publishers and bookshops in Germany who say that his works are flying off the shelves (The Guardian, Booklovers Turn to Karl Marx as Financial Crisis Bites in Germany. October 15, 2008).

Policy makers struggling to understand the barrage of financial panics, protests and other ills afflicting the world would do well to study the works of a long-dead economist: Karl Marx. The sooner they recognize we're facing a once-in-a-lifetime crisis of capitalism, the better equipped they will be to manage a way out of it (Bloomberg Business Week, Give Karl Marx a Chance to Save the World Economy. August 28, 2011).

Time Magazine showed Marx on its cover on February 2nd, 2009, and asked in respect to the crisis: "What would Marx think?" In the cover story, Marx was presented as the saviour of capitalism and was thereby mutilated beyond recognition: "Rethinking Marx. As we work out how to save capitalism, it's worth studying the system's greatest critic" (Time Magazine Europe, February 2nd, 2009).

In the golden, post-war years of Western economic growth, the comfortable living standard of the working class and the economy's overall stability made the best case for the value of capitalism and the fraudulence of Marx's critical view of it. But in more recent years many of the forces that Marx said would lead to capitalism's demise – the concentration and globalization of wealth, the permanence of unemployment, the lowering of wages – have become real, and troubling, once again (New York Times Online, March 30th, 2014).

These news clippings indicate that with the new global crisis of capitalism, we seem to have entered new Marxian times. That there is suddenly a surging interest in Karl Marx's work is an indication for the persistence of capitalism, class conflicts, and crisis. At the same time, the bourgeois press tries to limit Marx and to stifle his theory by interpreting Marx as the new saviour of capitalism. One should remember that he was not only a brilliant analyst of capitalism, he was also the strongest critic of capitalism in his time: "In short, the Communists everywhere support every revolutionary movement against the existing social and political order of things. In all these movements, they bring to the front, as the leading question in each, the property question, no matter what its degree of development at the time. Finally, they labour everywhere for the union and agreement of the democratic parties of all countries. The Communists disdain to conceal their views and aims. They openly declare that their ends can be attained only by the forcible overthrow of all existing social conditions. Let the ruling classes tremble at a Communistic revolution. The proletarians have nothing to lose but their chains. They have a world to win. Proletarians of all lands unite!" (Marx and Engels 1848/2004, 94).

In 1977, Dallas Smythe published his seminal article *Communications: Blindspot of Western Marxism* (Smythe 1977), in which he argued that Western Marxism had not given enough attention to the complex role of communications in capitalism. 35 years have passed and the rise of neoliberalism resulted in a turn away from an interest in social class and capitalism. Instead, it became fashionable to speak of globalization, postmodernism, and, with the fall of Communism, even the end of history. In essence, Marxism became the blindspot of all social science. Marxist academics were marginalized and it was increasingly career threatening for a young academic to take an explicitly Marxist approach to social analysis.

The declining interest in Marx and Marxism is visualized in Figure 1.1 that shows the average annual number of articles in the Social Sciences Citation

Index that contain one of the keywords Marx, Marxist or Marxism in the article topic description and were published in the five time periods 1968–1977, 1978–1987, 1988–1997, 1998–2007, 2008–2013. Choosing these periods allows observing if there has been a change since the start of the new capitalist crisis in 2008 and also makes sense because the 1968 revolt marked a break that also transformed academia.

Figure 1.1 shows that there was a relatively large academic article output about Marx in the period 1978–1987: 3659. Given that the number of articles published increases historically, also the interest in the period 1968–1977 seems to have been high. One can observe a clear contraction of the output of articles that focus on Marx in the periods 1988–1997 (2393) and 1998–2007 (1563). Given the historical increase of published articles, this contraction is even more severe. This period has also been the time of the intensification of neoliberalism, the commodification of everything (including public service communication in many countries) and a strong turn towards postmodernism and culturalism in the social sciences. One can see that the average number of annual articles published about Marxism in the period 2008–2013 (269) has increased in comparisons to the periods 1988–2007 (156 per year) and 1988–1997 (239 per year). This circumstance is an empirical indicator for a renewed interest in Marx and Marxism in the social sciences as effect of the new capitalist

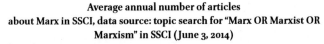

Average annual number of articles about Marx in SSCI, data source: topic search for "Marx OR Marxist OR Marxism" in SSCI (June 3, 2014)

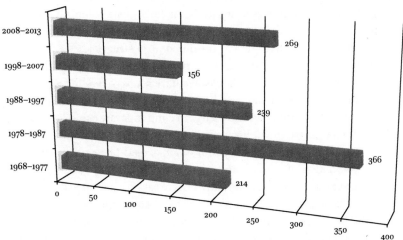

FIGURE 1.1 *Articles published about Marx and Marxism in the Social Sciences Citation Index*

crisis. The question is if and how this interest can be sustained and materiali-
wed in institutional transformations.

Due to the rising income gap between the rich and the poor, widespread precarious labour, and the new global capitalist crisis, neoliberalism is no longer seen
as common sense. The dark side of capitalism, with its rising levels of class conflict, is now recognized worldwide. Eagleton (2011) notes that never has a thinker
been so travestied as Marx and demonstrates that the core of Marx's work runs
contrary to common prejudices about his work. But since the start of the global
capitalist crisis in 2008, a considerable scholarly interest in the works of Marx has
taken root. Moreover, Žižek (2010) argues that the recent world economic crisis
has resulted in a renewed interest in the Marxian critique of political economy.

Communism is not a condition in a distant future, it is rather present in the
desires for alternatives expressed in struggles against the poverty in resources,
ownership, wealth, literacy, food, housing, social security, self-determination,
equality, participation, expression, healthcare, access, etc. caused by a system
of global stratification that benefits some at the expense of many. It exists
wherever people resist capitalism and create autonomous spaces. Communism
is "not a state of affairs which is to be established, an ideal to which reality
[will] have to adjust itself", but rather "the real movement which abolishes the
present state of things" (Marx and Engels 1844, 57). It is a revolution of the
propertyless, by those who do not own the economy, politics, culture, nature,
themselves, their bodies, their minds, their knowledge, technology, etc. Communism needs spaces for materializing itself as a movement. The contemporary
names of these spaces are not Facebook, YouTube or Twitter, but rather Tahrir
Square, Syntagma Square, Puerta del Sol, Plaça Catalunya, and Zuccotti Park.
The context of contemporary struggles is the large-scale colonization of the
world by capitalism. A different world is necessary, but whether it can be created
is uncertain and only determined by the outcome of struggles.

The capitalist crisis and the resulting struggles against the poverty of everything are the context for the two books. We have set ourselves the aim to contribute with this issue to the discussion about the relevance of Marx for
analyzing communication and knowledge in contemporary capitalism. Robert
McChesney (2007, 235f, fn 35) has accurately noted that while Marx has been
studied by communication scholars, "no one has read Marx systematically to
tease out the notion of communication in its varied manifestations". He also
notes that he can imagine that Marx had things to say on communication that are
of considerable importance. The task of the two books is to contribute to overcoming this lack of systematic reading of Marx on communication and media.

The chapter in the two books "Marx and the Political Economy of the Media"
and "Marx in the Age of Digital Capitalism" make clear that Baudrillard was

wrong to claim that "the Marxist theory of production is irredeemable partial, and cannot be generalized" to culture and the media and in also incorrect to insist that "the theory of production (the dialectical chaining of contradictions linked to the development of productive forces) is strictly homogenous with its object – material production – and is non-transferable, as a postulate or theoretical framework, to contents that were never given for it in the first place" (Baudrillard 1981, 214). Marshall McLuhan (1964/2001, 41) was wrong when he argued that Marx and his followers did not "understand the dynamics of the new media of communication". The two books demonstrate the enormous importance of Marx's theory for Critical Communication Studies today. If one wants to critically study communication and to use that research for social change, then the work of Marx provides an essential building block. Moreover, the chapters maintain that to critically examine communication we need to engage with the analysis and critique of capitalism, class, exploitation and with practical struggles for emancipation.

Most of the chapters in the two books are re-vised and updated editions of the special issue Marx is Back: The Importance of Marxist Theory and Research for Critical Communication Studies Today that was published in 2012 in the open access online journal tripleC: Communication, Capitalism & Critique (Vol. 10, No. 2, pp. 127–632, http://www.triple-c.at). The 28 updated chapters from the special issue are accompanied by updated version of three further articles published in tripleC (by Dal Yong Jin, Marisol Sandoval, and Christian Fuchs' Dallas Smythe-article) as well as a new chapter by Vincent Mosco ("Marx in the Cloud").

When putting together the tripleC special issue, we published a Call for Papers that much reflects the topics of the contributions in the two books and the special issue. It asked these questions:

* What is Marxist Media and Communication Studies? Why is it needed today? What are the main assumptions, legacies, tasks, methods and categories of Marxist Media and Communication Studies and how do they relate to Karl Marx's theory? What are the different types of Marxist Media/Communication Studies, how do they differ, what are their commonalities?
* What is the role of Karl Marx's theory in different fields, subfields and approaches of Media and Communication Studies? How have the role, status, and importance of Marx's theory for Media and Communication Studies evolved historically, especially since the 1960s?
* In addition to his work as a theorist and activist, Marx was a practicing journalist throughout his career. What can we learn from his journalism

about the practice of journalism today, about journalism theory, journalism education and alternative media?

* What have been the structural conditions, limits and problems for conducting Marxian-inspired Media and Communication Research and for carrying out university teaching in the era of neoliberalism? What are actual or potential effects of the new capitalist crisis on these conditions?

* What is the relevance of Marxian thinking in an age of capitalist crisis for analyzing the role of media and communication in society?

* How can the Marxian notions of class, class struggle, surplus value, exploitation, commodity/commodification, alienation, globalization, labour, capitalism, militarism and war, ideology/ideology critique, fetishism, and communism best be used for analyzing, transforming and criticizing the role of media, knowledge production and communication in contemporary capitalism?

* How are media, communication, and information addressed in Marx's work?

* What are commonalities and differences between contemporary approaches in the interpretation of Marx's analyses of media, communication, knowledge, knowledge labour and technology?

* What is the role of dialectical philosophy and dialectical analysis as epistemological and methodological tools for Marxian-inspired Media and Communication Studies?

* What were central assumptions of Marx about media, communication, information, knowledge production, culture and how can these insights be used today for the critical analysis of capitalism?

* What is the relevance of Marx's work for an understanding of social media?

* Which of Marx's works can best be used today to theorize media and communication? Why and how?

* Terry Eagleton (2011) maintains that the 10 most commonly held prejudices against Marx are wrong. What prejudices against Marx can be found in Media and Communication Studies today? What have been the consequences of such prejudices? How can they best be contested? Are there continuities and/or discontinuities in prejudice against Marx in light of the new capitalist crisis?

Thomas Piketty's (2014) book Capital in the Twenty-First Century shows empirically that the history of capitalism is a history of inequality and capital concentration. It has resulted in many responses and a public discussion of capitalism's problems (for an analysis of the reception of the book and its relevance for the political economy of the Internet see Fuchs 2014). Piketty's book is certainly not the 21st century equivalent of Marx's Capital because it lacks solid theoretical foundations. Piketty also misinterprets Marx (see Fuchs 2014), which is not a surprise because when being asked about Karl Marx, Piketty said: "I never managed really to read it".[1] Piketty's book has however stressed the importance of political measures that weaken capitalist interests and the capitalist class and especially the role that global progressive tax on capital and wealth could play in this context. This political debate should be welcomed by Marxists because Marx and Engels themselves called in the Communist Manifesto for a "heavy progressive or graduated income tax" (Marx and Engels 1968, 51). Marx and Engels would today embrace and radicalise the idea of a global progressive tax on capital.

A Marxist theory of communication should "demonstrate how communication and culture are material practices, how labour and language are mutually constituted, and how communication and information are dialectical instances of the same social activity, the social construction of meaning. Situating these tasks within a larger framework of understanding power and resistance would place communication directly into the flow of a Marxian tradition that remains alive and relevant today" (Mosco 2009, 44). A Marxist theory of communication sees communication in relation to capitalism, "placing in the foreground the analysis of capitalism, including the development of the forces and relations of production, commodification and the production of surplus value, social class divisions and struggles, contradictions and oppositional movements" (Mosco 2009, 94). Marxist Media and Communication Studies are not only relevant now, but have been so for a long time because communication has always been embedded into structures of inequality in class societies. With the rise of neoliberalism, Marxist communication theory has suffered a setback because it had become common to marginalise and discriminate against Marxist scholarship and to replace Marxism with postmodernism. So Marx was always relevant, but being Marxist and practicing Marxism were always difficult, in part because Marxist studies lacked a solid institutional base. What we can see today is a rising interest in Marx's work. The question is whether it will be possible to channel this interest into institutional transformations that challenge the predominant administrative character of media institutions and strengthen the institutionalization of critical studies of communication.

We can summarise the following areas of production, usage, and effects of media as they are found in Marx's works (for a detailed discussion of Marx on media communication in capitalism and explanation of a theoretical model, see: Fuchs 2010, 2011).

---

1 Chotiner, Isaac. 2014. "Marx? I never really managed to read it" – an interview with Thomas Piketty. *New Statesman Online* May 6, 2014: http://www.newstatesman.com/politics/2014/05/marx-i-never-really-managed-read-it-interview-thomas-piketty.

In commodity production:

· Specific: Media technology as rationalization technology in the media industry
· Specific: The process of capital concentration and centralization in the media sector
· Specific: The production of media capital, knowledge workers as wage labourers in media corporations
· General: Communication technologies for the spatial and temporal co-ordination of production in order to reduce constant and variable capital shares
· General: Communication technologies as means for the spatial expansion of capitalist production

In commodity circulation:

· Specific: Transmission technologies as means of accumulating media infra-structure capital
· Specific: Media as carriers of advertisements
· General: Communication technologies as means for reducing the circulation and turnover time of capital
· General: Media as means and outcomes of the globalization of world trade
· General: Media as means of the spatial centralization of capital

In the circulation and reception of ideas:

· Media as carriers and circulators of ideologies

In the production, circulation, and reception of alternative media:

· Alternative media that are alternatively produced, distributed, and inter-preted and function as means of class struggle and means of circulation of critical ideas

The model in Figure 1.2 summarises the connection of four aspects of the media, i.e., four roles of the media in the capitalist economy:

1) the commodity form of the media,
2) the ideological form of the media,
3) media reception, and
4) alternative media.

TABLE 1.1 *A systematic account of the role of media in the Marxian circuit of capital.*

Circulation	Production	Circulation	Consumption
M – C (Mp, L)	..P.. Media Technology as Means of Rationalization: $s/v\uparrow$ The process of capital concentration and centralization in the realm of the media	C' – M'	

Knowledge workers as wage labourers in media corporations

Media as means of inter-organizational corporate communication and co-ordination: $v\downarrow$, $c\downarrow$

Media for the spatial distribution and extension of capitalism

| | | Media as carriers of advertisements
Transmission media as forms of capital
Media and trade globalization
Media and spatial centralization of capital
Media as carriers & diffusion channels of ideologies | |

Alternative media as negating forces in media production, circulation, and consumption

It focuses on the role of the media in the production, circulation, and consumption processes of the economy, not on the relations to the political system (state, civil society, laws, etc.) and cultural institutions (education, family, religion, etc.). Capital accumulation within the media sphere takes place in both the media content sphere and the media infrastructure sphere. These two realms together form the sphere of media capital. The Marxian circuit of capital is shown for each of the two realms, which indicates that they are oriented to capital accumulation.

The commodity hypothesis can be visualized as the following processes that are shown in Figure 1.1: vertical and horizontal integration, media concentration, media convergence, media globalization, the integration of media capital and other types of capital, the rationalization of production, the globalization of production, circulation, and trade, and intra-company communication, advertising and marketing. The production of media content and the production of media technologies are shown as two different systems. They both belong to the media industry, but create different products. Processes of vertical integration make the boundaries between the two systems fuzzy. Concentration processes and horizontal integration, which are inherent features of capital accumulation, shape each of the two spheres. Media convergence is a specific feature of media infrastructure capital. The two realms together are factors that influence the globalization of the culture industry. The realm of the economy that is shown at the bottom right of Figure 1.2 represents capital accumulation in non-media industries and services. It is partly integrated with the media sector due to corporate integration processes. Media technologies advance the rationalization of production in this realm as well as in the media content industry. Furthermore, they advance the globalization of production, circulation, and trade. These globalization processes are also factors that, in return, promote the development of new media technologies. Media technologies are also used for intra-company communication. Rationalization, globalization, and intra-company communication are processes that aim at maximizing profits by decreasing the investment cost of capital (both constant and variable) and by advancing relative surplus value production (more production in less time). The media content industry is important for advertising and marketing commodities in the circulation process of commodities, which is at the same time the realization process of capital in which surplus value is transformed into money profit.

The ideology hypothesis is visualized in Figure 1.2 by media content capital and its relation to recipients. Media content that creates false consciousness is considered as ideological content. Media content depends on reception. The reception hypothesis is visualized in the lower left part of Figure 1.1. Reception is the realm wherein ideologies are reproduced and potentially challenged.

Alternative media is a sphere that challenges the capitalist media industry. The alternative media hypothesis is visualized in Figure 1.1 by a separate domain that stands for alternative ways of organizing and producing media whose aim is to create critical content that challenges capitalism. Media content depends on reception. Five forms of reception are distinguished in the left lower left part of Figure 1.2. Reception is the realm where ideologies are reproduced and potentially challenged. In some types and parts of media content capital, capital is accumulated by selling the audience, at a rate determined by its demographic characteristics, as a commodity to advertising clients. Dallas Smythe (1977) spoke in this context of the audience commodity. As advertising profits are not a general feature of all media capital, there is a dotted line in Figure 1.2 that signifies the audience commodity. In recent times, recipients have increasingly become an active audience that produces content and technologies, which does not imply a democratisation of the media, but mainly a new form of exploitation of audiences and users.

The use value of media and media technologies lies primarily in their capacity to provide information, enable communication, and advance the creation of culture. In capitalist society, use value is dominated by the exchange value of products, which become commodities. When the media take on commodity form, their use value only becomes available for consumers through exchanges that accumulate money capital in the hands of capitalists. Media and technologies as concrete products represent the use value side of information and

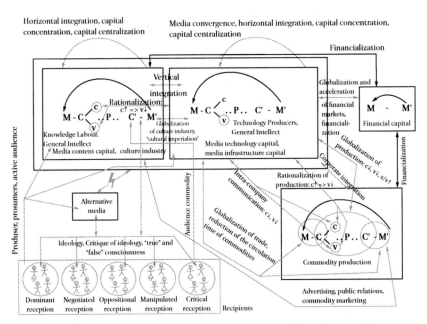

FIGURE 1.2   *The processes of media production, circulation, and consumption in the capitalist economy.*

communication, whereas the monetary price of the media represents the exchange value side of information and communication. The commodity hypothesis addresses the exchange value aspect of the media. The ideology hypothesis shows how the dominance of the use value of the media by exchange value creates a role for the media in the legitimatization and reproduction of domination. The two hypotheses are connected through the contradictory double character of media as use values and as exchange values. The media as commodities are in relation to money use values that can realize their exchange value, i.e., their price, in money form. Money is an exchange value in relation to the media. It realizes its use value – i.e. that it is a general equivalent of exchange – in media commodities. Consumers are interested in the use value aspect of media and technology, whereas capitalists are interested in the exchange value aspect that helps them to accumulate money capital. The use value of media and technology only becomes available to consumers through complex processes in which capitalists exchange the commodities they control with money. This means that the use value of media and technology is only possible through the exchange value that they have in relation to money. Commodification is a basic process that underlies media and technology in capitalism. Use value and exchange value are "bilateral polar opposites" (MEW 13, 72) of media and technology in capitalist society. By the time media and technology reach consumers, they have taken on commodity form and are therefore likely to have ideological characteristics. The sphere of alternative media challenges the commodity character of the media. It aims at a reversal so that use value becomes the dominant feature of media and technology by the sublation of their exchange value. Processes of alternative reception transcend the ideological character of the media – the recipients are empowered in questioning the commodified character of the world in which they live.

Marx's analysis of the media in capitalism visualized in Figure 1.1 can be summarized in the form of four major dimensions. The chapters in our two books reflect a categorisation of the role of the media in capitalism and study these dimensions each to a specific extent.

1) Media and commodities:
capital accumulation, media technology industry, media content industry/cultural industry, digital media industry, media and financialization, media and globalization, audience commodification, media concentration, media convergence, etc

2) Media and ideology:
media manipulation, media propaganda filters, advertising, public relations, commodity marketing, cultural imperialism, etc

3) Media reception and use:
ideological reception, critical reception, critical media use, etc

4) Alternative media:
alternative media production spheres, alternative public spheres, media
and social struggles, etc

The published and submitted contributions are predominantly in the areas of
media and commodification, media and ideology, and alternative media.
Media reception studies are not as well represented. This means that topics
like the audiences' interpretation of reality TV, popular music, soap operas,
sports, movies, quiz shows, or computer games are not so important for most
contemporary Marxist media and communication scholars in comparison to
topics like the exploitation of free labour on the Internet, the commodification
of research and education, Internet ideologies, socialist struggles about the
role of the media in various countries, the marginalization and discrimination
of Marxists and Marxism in Media and Communication Studies, capitalist crisis and the media, communication labour, critical journalism, the socialist
open access publishing, or alternative social networking sites. This demonstrates three key points:

* In the current situation of capitalist crisis and exploding inequality, a
focus on political economy topics, class struggle issues, the role of alternatives seems to be more important than the focus on cultural studies
topics (like fan culture) that can easily be accommodated into capitalist
interests and do not deal with the pressing problems such as precarious
living conditions and inequalities in the world.
* Classical audience studies has to a certain extent been transformed
into the study of the political economy of mediated play labour and
media prosumption, which is an area in which the study of production,
consumption and advertising converge. Marxist Media and Communication Studies have, as the two books show, welcomed this convergence
and related topics have become an important topic of this approach.
An important implication of this development is that the classical criticism that Marxist Media and Communication Studies is not particularly interested in reception and media consumption does not hold
because the issue has been taken up to a great degree with the rise of
consumption becoming productive, a development that has been
started by the audience commodification typical of the broadcasting
area and lifted to a new dimension of analysis by the rise of Internet
prosumption.

There is a pressing need for engaging with Marx and the critique of class and capitalism in order to interpret and change the contemporary world and contemporary media. The chapters in the two books show a deep engagement with and care about Marx's theory and it is natural that they do not align themselves with research streams that are critical of or ignore Marxist studies. They are predominantly grounded in Critical Political Economy and Critical Theory.

The chapters published in the 2 books *Marx and the Political Economy of the Media* and *Marx in the Digital Age* show the crucial relevance of Marx today for coming to grips with the world we live in, the struggles that can and should be fought, and the role of the media in capitalism, in struggles against it, and in building alternatives. It is encouraging to see that there is a growing number of scholars, who make use of Marx's works in Media and Communication Studies today. Whereas Marx was always relevant, this relevance has especially not been acknowledged in Media and Communication Studies in recent years. It was rather common to misinterpret and misunderstand Marx, which partly came also from a misreading of his works or from outright ignorance of his works. Terry Eagleton (2011) discusses ten common prejudices against Marx and Marxism and shows why Marx was right and why these prejudices are wrong. We have added to the following overview a media and communication dimension to each prejudice. This communication dimensions point towards common prejudices against Marx within Media and Communication Studies. The chapters in the two books show that these prejudices are wrong and that using Marx and Marxian concepts in Media and Communication Studies is an important and pressing task today. As a summary of the results provided by the chapters in the two books, we counter each of the anti-Marxian prejudices with a counter-claim that is grounded in the analyses presented in the two books show the importance of Marx for understanding society and the media critically.

1a) *Marxist Outdatedness!*
Marxism is old-fashioned and not suited for a post-industrial society.
1b) *Marxist Topicality!*
In order to adequately and critically understand communication in society, we need Marx.

2a) *Marxist Repression!*
Marxism may sound good in theory, but in practice it can only result in terror, tyranny and mass murder. The feasibility of a socialist society and socialist media are illusionary.

2b) *Capitalist Repression!*
Capitalism neither sounds like a good idea/theory nor does it work in practice, as the reality of large-scale inequality, global war, and environmental devestation shows. The feasibility of socialism and socialist media arises out of the crises of capitalism.

3a) *Marxism = Determinism!*
Marx believed in deterministic laws of history and the automatic end of capitalism that would also entail the automatic end of capitalist media.
3b) *Marxism = Dialectics and Complexity!*
Marxian and Hegelian dialectics allow us to see the history of society and the media as being shaped by structural conditioning and open-ended struggles and a dialectic of structure and agency.

4a) *Marxist Do-Goodism!*
Marx had a naïve picture of humanity's goodness and ignored that humans are naturally selfish, acquisitive, aggressive and competitive. The media industry is therefore necessarily based on profit and competition; otherwise it cannot work.
4b) *Capitalist Wickedness!*
The logic of individualism, egoism, profit maximization, and competition has been tried and tested under neoliberal capitalism, which has also transformed the media landscape and made it more unequal.

5a) *Marxist Reductionism!*
Marx and Marxism reduce all cultural and political phenomena to the economy. They do not have an understanding of non-economic aspects of the media and communication.
5b) *Marxist Complexity!*
Contemporary developments show that the economy in capitalism is not determining, but a special system that results in the circumstance that all phenomena under capitalism, which includes all media phenomena, have class aspects and are dialectically related to class. Class is a necessary, although certainly not sufficient condition for explaining phenomena of contemporary society.

6a) *Marxist Anti-Humanism!*
Marx had no interests in religion and ethics and reduced consciousness to matter. He therefore paved the way for the anti-humanism of Stalin and others. Marxism cannot ground media ethics.

6b) *Marxist Humanism!*

Marx was a deep humanist and communism was for him practical humanism, class struggle practical ethics. His theory was deeply ethical and normative. Critical Political Economy of the Media necessarily includes a critical ethics of the media.

7a) *The Outdatedness of Class!*

Marxism's obsession with class is outdated. Today, the expansion of knowledge work is removing all class barriers.

7b) *The Importance of Class!*

High socio-economic inequality at all levels of societal organisation is indicative of the circumstance that contemporary society is first and foremost a multi-levelled class society. Knowledge work is no homogenous category, but rather a class-structured space that includes internal class relations and stratification patterns (both a manager and a precariously employed call centre agent or data entry clerk are knowledge workers)

8a) *Marxists Oppose Democracy!*

Marxists favour violent revolution and oppose peaceful reform and democracy. They do not accept the important role of the media for democracy.

8b) *Socialism=Democracy!*

Capitalism has a history of human rights violations, structural violence, and warfare. In the realm of the media, there is a capitalist history of media support for anti-democratic goals. Marxism is a demand for peace, democracy, and democratic media. Marx in his own journalistic writings and practice struggled for free speech, and end to censorship, democratic journalism and democratic media.

9a) Marxist Dictatorship!

Marxism's logic is the logic of the party that results in the logic of the state and the installation of monstrous dictators that control, monitor, manipulate and censor the media.

9b) Capitalist Dictatorship!

Capitalism installs a monstrous economic dictatorship that controls, monitors, manipulates and censors the media by economic and ideological means. Marxism's logic is one of a well-rounded humanity fostering conditions that enable people to be active in many pursuits and includes the view that everyone can become a journalist.

10a) Non-class-oriented New Social Movements!
New social movements (feminism, environmentalism, gay rights, peace movement, youth movement, etc) have left class and Marxism behind. Struggles for alternative media are related to the new social movements, not to class struggles.
10b) Class-oriented New New Social Movements!
The new movements resulting from the current crisis (like the Occupy movement) as well as recent movements for democratic globalization are movements of movements that are bound together by deep concern for inequality and class. Contemporary struggles are class struggles that make use of a multitude of alternative media.

Overview of the Book *Marx in the Age of Digital Capitalism*

Christian Fuchs gives an overview of approaches to Critical Internet Studies and points out key concepts of this field. He argues that there is an ideological difference and struggle between "Critical" Cyberculture Studies and Critical Political Economy/Critical Theory of the Internet. He discusses the role of eleven Marxian concepts for Critical Internet Studies. Marxian concepts that have been reflected in Critical Internet Studies include: dialectics, capitalism, commodification, surplus value/exploitation/alienation/class, globalization, ideology, class struggle, commons, public sphere, communism, and aesthetics. He also gives an overview of important debates and concepts relating to digital labour.

Andreas Wittel presents the foundations of a Marxist political economy of digital media that focuses on the concepts of labour, value, property, and struggle. The author introduces the notion of digital media as distributed media. He suggests that the means of information production have become more accessible in the digital age, whereas the capitalist class controls the means of information distribution. Wittel discusses free online labour, debates about the measurability of labour in the age of knowledge and digital media, challenges to property that began with file sharing, and struggles over the digital commons.

Mattias Ekman discusses the role of the media and communication in capitalism's primitive accumulation. The author presents three examples: 1) The Swedish media representation of the global justice movement has focused on describing single acts of actual or potential violence and has rather ignored the political goals and causes of the struggles. 2) Swedish media and politicians presented the privatization of the Swedish telecommunication company Telia as an opportunity for the public to buy "people's shares". 3) The role of dispossession and violence in the commodification of users and their labour on social networking sites like Facebook.

Jens Schröter examines the idea that the Internet would bring about frictionless capitalism. He stresses that the Internet became popular during the time of neoliberalism and was a technology into which hopes and ideologies of endless economic growth without crisis were projected. He stresses that the dot.com crisis of the early years of this century shattered this ideology. The Internet would instead be enmeshed in the contradiction between the forces and relations of production.

Vincent Manzerolle and Atle Mikkola Kjøsen analyse changes in the cycle of capital accumulation that arise due to digitalization. The authors argue that personalization and ubiquitous connection are two important aspects of contemporary communicative capitalism that have impacted how the cycle of capital works. They point out that the critical analysis of capitalism and communication in capitalism should be based on the Marxian cycle of capital accumulation and that digital communication has resulted in a speed-up of the capital cycle and a facilitation of credit. They argue that the capital cycle is a communication process.

Eran Fisher analyses the role of alienation and exploitation in audience commodification on Facebook. Building on the work of Jhally and Smythe, he introduces the notion of audience alienation, suggesting that audiences of commercial media are not only exploited, but also do not control content and content production. The author sees Facebook asboth means of production and communication, as both a technology and a medium. Facebook would result in the exacerbation of exploitation and the mitigation of alienation, whereas commercial mass media would be based on low exploitation and high alienation.

Robert Prey analyses the role of the network concept in contemporary capitalism's ideological structures. The author discusses Castells' analysis of power in the network society, highlighting the importance Castells gives to exclusion. Drawing on Boltanski and Chiapello, he stresses the problems of basing social criticism on the network metaphor, especially the lack of focus on class and exploitation. The author acknowledges the importance of networks in contemporary capitalism and argues for a combination of this approach with Marx's theory of exploitation.

Jernej A. Prodnik discusses the role of the commodity in critical media and communication studies. He gives an overview of how Marx discussed the notion of the commodity and points out that it is a category that has been relevant in all of Marx's works. Related concepts, such as commodity fetishism and the commodification of everything, are discussed. The author especially discusses the role of the commodity in Dallas Smythe's works and Autonomous Marxism and criticizes contemporary criticisms of Smythe's, especially the points made by Brett Caraway.

Dal Yong Jin discusses the notion of cultural imperialism in the age of the Internet. He holds that this concept has continued importance for understanding how corporations dominate the Internet. He argues that predominantly Western and especially US companies dominate the Internet and that the only alternatives (such as Chinese platforms) are no alternatives because they use the same logic of capitalism and targeted advertising as Western capitalist platforms. Jin coins the notion of platform imperialism for understanding the structure of the contemporary Internet in the context of the new imperialism.

Marisol Sandoval shows that behind the clean surface of Apple computers, iPads and iPhones lies a dirty world of work and exploitation. She introduces based on Karl Marx's works a typology and systematic method for analysing dimensions of labour that she applies to the study of the labour involved in the production of Apple computers. Her analysis shows that the highly exploitative work conducted by Chinese workers in the Foxconn assemblage factories contradict how Apple presents itself. She deconstructs Apple's corporate ideology and shows how the company's imperialist and capitalist character makes Apple socially irresponsible. She grounds foundations of the Marxist concept of corporate social irresponsibility that can be opposed to the corporate ideology of corporate social responsibility (CSR).

Katarina Giritli Nygren and Katarina L Gidlund analyse the role of alienation in digital culture. They use Foucault's concept of pastoral power and Marx's notion of alienation. The authors draw on Foucault to describe the pastoral power of digital technology. It is a form of power that creates the illusion that digital technology allows individuality. Marx's notion of alienation is applied to the realm of digital technologies. Today traditional forms of alienation would be accompanied by digital alienation that is related to consumer culture, individualized self-expressions on platforms like Facebook, and a commodified Internet.

Sebastian Sevignani analyses the alternative social networking site Diaspora* in the context of discussions about privacy in capitalism. He stresses its connections to the free software movement and describes the origins of the privacy concept and its connections to the idea of private property. The author engages with the Marxist critique of the privacy concept, which has often been ignored by Marxist thinkers, and outlines the foundations of a socialist alternative. He applies this analysis to the case of Diaspora*.

Miriyam Aouragh provides a Marxist perspective on and analysis of social media in the Arab revolutions. The author connects the notion of mediation to Marxian theory and maintains that it is a connection between base and superstructure. The revolutions are framed in terms of capitalism, imperialism, and class. The author questions the Western-liberal framing of the revolutions and social media as Orientalism and presents a model of the revolution that situates social media in an online-offline dialectic of the revolutions.

Brian A. Brown and Anabel Quan-Haase's contribution deals with the question of which methodology is needed for studying the digital labour and digital labour conditions of social media prosumers. The methodology for the suggested Workers' Inquiry 2.0 is grounded in Marx's questionnaire for the Workers' Inquiry and the Italian Autonomist Marxist co-research method. The authors point out with the example of research conducted about Flickr how the methodology of the Workers' Inquiry 2.0 works. They point out the importance of artefacts, communities, and produsers in the Workers' Inquiry 2.0.

Vincent Mosco analyses the political economy of cloud computing and big data analysis. Cloud computing involves the external storage of users' data so that it can be accessed in a mobile manner. Mosco shows that cloud computing and big data's political economy involves an interlocking of digital capitalism and the surveillance state, is ideologically connected to digital positivism, has negative ecological impacts, is a threat to knowledge labour, and has resulted in new forms of cloud marketing and advertising. At the same time, new forms of reistance to capital accumulation in the digital age have emerged that pose the question of the Internet can be turned from a commercial profit machine into a democratic resource.

The two books *Marx and the Political Economy of the Media* and *Marx in the Age of Digital Capitalism* show the importance of Marxist theory for Critical Media and Communication Studies today. It makes clear that Media and Communication Studies should not just be critical in character, but that we need a Marxist Theory and Marxist Studies of Media and Communication today. The interest in and quality of the books as well as the large interest in other related activities in Marxist Communication Studies (as e.g. the Conference: Critique, Democracy and Philosophy in 21st Century Information Society. Towards Critical Theories of Social Media. Uppsala University. May 2nd–4th, 2012. See: Fuchs 2012; Fuchs and Sandoval 2014), especially among PhD students and younger scholars, shows that Marx is back. The deep interest in Marx's works shows the unease about capitalism and capitalist communications and the desire for alternatives.

References

Baudrillard, Jean. 1981. *For a Critique of the Political Economy of the Sign*. St. Louis: Telos Press.

Eagleton Terry. 2011. *Why Marx Was Right*. London: Yale University Press.

Fuchs, Christian. 2014. Thomas Piketty's Book "Capital in the Twenty-First Century", Karl Marx and the Political Economy of the Internet. *tripleC: Communication, Capitalism & Critique* 12 (1): 413–430.

Fuchs, Christian. 2012. New Marxian Times. Reflections on the 4th ICTs and Society Conference "Critique, Democracy and Philosophy in 21st Century Information Society. Towards Critical Theories of Social Media". *tripleC: Communication, Capitalism & Critique* 10 (1): 114–121.

Fuchs, Christian. 2011. *Foundations of Critical Media and Information Studies*. New York: Routledge.

Fuchs, Christian. 2010. Grounding Critical Communication Studies: An Inquiry into the Communication Theory of Karl Marx. *Journal of Communication Inquiry* 34 (1): 15–41.

Fuchs, Christian and Marisol Sandoval, eds. 2014. *Critique, Social Media and the Information Society*. New York: Routledge.

Marx, Karl and Friedrich Engels (MEW). *Werke*. Berlin: Dietz.

Marx, Karl and Friedrich Engels. 1844. *The German Ideology*. Amherst, NY: Prometheus Books.

Marx, Karl and Friedrich Engels. 1848/2004. *The Communist Manifesto*. Peterborough: Broadview.

Marx, Karl and Friedrich Engels. 1968. *Selected Works in One Volume*. London: Lawrence & Wishart.

McChesney, Robert W. 2007. *Communication Revolution. Critical Junctures and the Future of Media*. New York: The New Press.

McLuhan, Marshall 1964/2001. *Understanding Media: The Extensions of Man*. New York: Routledge.

Mosco, Vincent. 2009. *The Political Economy of Communication*. London: Sage. 2nd edition.

Piketty, Thomas. 2014. *Capital in the Twenty-First Century*. Cambridge, MA: Belknap Press.

Smythe, Dallas W. 1977. Communications: Blindspot of Western Marxism. *Canadian Journal of Political and Social Theory* 1 (3): 1–27.

Žižek, Slavoj. 2010. *Living in the End Times*. London: Verso.

CHAPTER 2

Towards Marxian Internet Studies

Christian Fuchs

1 Introduction

The Internet has become an important socio-technical system that shapes and is shaped by life in contemporary capitalism. Internet Studies has become a crucial field that is engaged in thinking about the transformations of society, individuality, politics, economy, culture, and nature (Fuchs 2008).

As some scholars have argued the third world economy crisis that started as housing and financial crisis, but soon became a world crisis of capitalism, has resulted in a renewed interest in approaches that label themselves as explicitly critical and anti-capitalist (for example: Harvey 2010, Žižek 2009, 2010b), it is an important task to reflect on the state of those approaches within Internet Studies that label themselves as being explicitly critical. The task of this chapter is therefore to provide a short overview of approaches to Critical Internet Studies, to point out key concepts of this field, and to reflect on critiques of Critical Internet Studies. The paper is divided into the discussion of the return of Marx (Section 2), Critical Cyberculture Studies (Section 3), Critical Political Economy/Critical Theory of the Internet (Section 4), a comparison of these two approaches (Section 5), a discussion of Critical Internet Studies concepts (Section 6), a discussion of digital labour (Section 7), critiques of Critical Internet Studies (Section 8). Finally, some conclusions are drawn (Section 9).

2 Marx is Back

Eagleton (2011) notes that never a thinker was so travestied as Marx and shows that the contrary of what the common prejudices claim about Marx is the core of his works. Žižek (2010b) argues that the recent world economic crisis has resulted in a renewed interest in the Marxian Critique of the Political Economy. This is shown by the attention recently paid to Marx in the mainstream media. *Time* magazine, for example, had Marx on its cover and asked about the global financial crisis: What would Marx think? (*Time Magazine*, February 2, 2009). Hobsbawm (2011, 12f) argues that for understanding the global dimension of contemporary capitalism, capitalism's contradictions and crises and the existence of socio-economic inequality we "must ask Marx's questions" (13). "Economic and political liberalism, singly or in combination, cannot provide the solution to the problems of the twenty-first century. Once again the time has come to take Marx seriously" (Hobsbawm 2011, 419).

One interesting thing about Marx is that he keeps coming back at moments, when people least expect it, in the form of various Marxisms that keep haunting capitalism like ghosts, as Derrida (1994) has stressed. It is paradoxical that almost 20 years after the end of the Soviet Union, capitalism seems to have intensified global problems, caused severe poverty and a rise of unequal income distribution, and as a result has brought a return of the economic in the form of a worldwide economic crisis and with it a reactualization of the Marxian critique of capitalism. Although a persistent refrain is "Marx is dead, long live capitalism", Marx is coming back again today.

There are especially six aspects of Marx's works that are relevant for the analysis of contemporary capitalism:

- The globalization of capitalism that is seen as an important characteristic of contemporary society by many social theorists is an important aspect in the works of Marx and Engels (for example: Callinicos 2003). Connected to this topic is also the Marxian theme of international solidarity as form of resistance that seems to be practiced today by the altermondialiste movement.
- The importance of technology, knowledge, and the media in contemporary society was anticipated by the Marxian focus on machinery, means of communication, and the general intellect (see for example: Dyer-Witheford 1999; Fuchs 2008, 2011; Hardt and Negri 2004; McChesney 2007).
- The immizerization caused by neoliberal capitalism suggests a renewed interest in the Marxian category of class (see for example: Harvey 2005).
- The global war against terror after 9/11 and its violent and repressive results like human casualties and intensified surveillance suggest a renewed interest in Marxian theories of imperialism (see for example: Fuchs 2011, Chapter 5; Hardt and Negri 2000; Harvey 2003).
- The ecological crisis reactualizes a theme that runs throughout Marxian works: that there is an antagonism between modern industrialism and nature that results in ecological destruction (see for example: O'Connor 1998).
- The new global economic crisis that started in 2008 has shown that Marxist crisis theory is still important today (Foster and Magdoff 2009, Foster and McChesney 2012, Harvey 2014, Kliman 2012, McNally 2011). Capitalism seems to be inherently crisis-ridden.

Žižek argues that the antagonisms of contemporary capitalism in the context of the ecological crisis, intellectual property, biogenetics, new forms of apartheid and slums show that we still need the Marxian notion of class and that there is a need to renew Marxism and to defend its lost causes in order to "render problematic the all-too-easy liberal-democratic alternative" (Žižek 2008, 6) that is posed by the new forms of a soft capitalism that promises and in its rhetoric makes use of ideals like participation, self-organization, and co-operation without realizing them. Therborn argues that the "new constellations of power and new possibilities of resistance" in the 21st century require retaining the "Marxian idea that human emancipation from exploitation, oppression, discrimination and the inevitable linkage between privilege and misery can come only from struggle by the exploited and disadvantaged themselves" (Therborn 2008, 61). Jameson argues that global capitalism, "its crises and the catastrophes appropriate to this present" and global unemployment show that "Marx remains as inexhaustible as capital itself" (Jameson 2011, 1) and makes *Capital. Volume 1* (Marx 1867) a most timely book.

The implication for Internet Studies is that it should give specific attention to the analysis of how capitalism shapes and is shaped by the Internet. This means that there is a need for rethinking Internet Studies and reorienting it as a Critique of the Political Economy and Critical Theory of the Internet that takes into account the specific character of Marxian analyses of media, technology, and communication, namely to analyze "how capitalist structures shape the media" (McChesney 2007, 79), the role of communication in the "structure of social relations and [...] social power" with a particular concern for the analysis of that role in the "system of social power called capitalism" (Garnham 1990, 7), and "the analysis of the relationship of media and capitalist society" (Knoche 2005, 105).

In 20th century Marxism, the critical analysis of media, communication, and culture has emerged as a novel quality due to the transformations that capitalism has been undergoing. Early 20th century approaches that gave attention to culture and ideology included the ones by Gramsci, Lukács and Korsch. The latter two thinkers have influenced Frankfurt School Critical Theory (Kellner 1989). Gramsci has had an important influence on British Cultural Studies (Turner 2003). Frankfurt School Theory and British Cultural Studies differ in a lot of respects, but have in common the interest in ideology critique. In addition, authors like Adorno, Horkheimer, Marcuse, Benjamin, Williams, or E.P. Thompson had a profound knowledge of, interest in and made thorough use of Marx's works. Cultural Studies has also been influenced by Althusser's theory of ideology (Turner 2003). The focus on ideology has been challenged by Critical Political Economy scholars like Smythe and Garnham, who stress the economic functions of the media, whereas other political economists like Schiller, Golding, Murdock, Herman, Chomsky, McChesney acknowledge the importance of the economic critique of the media, but have continued to also stress the role of media as producers of ideology (Mosco, 2009). More recent developments in Marxist theories of culture and communication have for example been approaches to integrate diverse approaches (for example: Kellner 1995), theories of alternative media that have been implicitly or explicitly inspired by Enzensberger's version of Critical Theory (for example: Downing 2001) and the emergence of the importance of Autonomist Marxism (for an overview see: Virno and Hardt 1996). Marxist Studies of the Internet can make use of this rich history of 20th century Marxism.

Critical Studies of the Internet have been influenced by various strands of Marxist Cultural and Media theory, such as Ideology Critique (see for example the concept of Net Critique: Lovink and Schultz 1997), Autonomist Marxism (Dyer-Witheford 1998; Fuchs 2008; Hakken 2003), Critical Political Economy (Andrejevic 2005, 2007, 2009; Fuchs 2009b, 2010a, 2011, 2014a, 2014b, 2014c, 2015, 2016; Hakken 2003), or Critical Theory (Andrejevic 2009; Fuchs 2008, 2011; Taylor 2009).

3   Cyberculture Studies and the Un-/Critical

We can distinguish two broad approaches in Internet Studies that describe themselves as critical. The first have a cultural studies background, the second a political economy background. The theoretical background of the first is, in broad terms, post-structuralist; that of the second is Marxist.

Critical Cyberculture Studies has been positioned explicitly as being an application of Cultural Studies and Postmodernism (Bell 2001, 65–91; Jones 2006, xv–xvi; Sterne 2006). David Bell (2006b) mentions in his introduction to his 4-volume collection Cybercultures. Critical concepts in media and cultural studies (Bell 2006a) 18 influences on Cyberculture Studies. Among them are for example cultural studies, the philosophy of science and technology, feminist studies, and policy studies, whereas approaches such as Critical Theory, Marxism, or critique of the political economy of the media and communication are conspicuous by their absence. The title of Bell's collection promises that one will find "critical concepts" of Internet Studies represented in the 1600 pages of the four volumes, but while reading the 69 chapters, one too often wonders why the critical dimension of the concepts is missing. Exploitation, surplus value, and class on the Internet are marginal issues, whereas topics such as the history of the Internet, research methods, virtual communities, online identities, bodies and minds in cyberspace, and cyborgs are prominently featured. Explicit discussions of Internet capitalism and exploitation, as in the contributions by Dwayne Winseck, Kevin Robins/Frank Webster, or Tiziana Terranova, are marginalized within this volume. The volume lives up to what Bell promises in the introduction – and does therefore not deserve the subtitle "critical concepts".

David Silver (2006b) characterizes "Critical Cyberculture Studies" as the third stage in Cyberculture Studies that followed after Popular Cyberculture Studies and Cyberculture Studies. He characterizes Critical Cyberculture Studies as:

(1)   exploring "the social, cultural and economic interactions that take place online" (Silver, 2006b, 67),
(2)   the analysis of discourses about cyberspace,
(3)   the analysis of access to the Internet,
(4)   focusing on participatory design (Silver 2006b, 67–73).

Silver advances a shallow notion of the critical. The first quality is extensively broad, the vast majority of analyses of the Internet focuses on social, cultural, or economic issues (except political and ecological analyses), so it remains unclear what shall be specifically critical about "Critical" Cyberculture Studies. When discussing the study of "online marginality", Silver stresses the importance of exploring "issues of race, ethnicity and sexuality" (Silver 2006b, 70). The category of class is not mentioned.

David Silver and Adrienne Massanari (2006) present in their collection *Critical cyberculture studies* 25 readings. In the introduction, Silver (2006a, 6f) mentions capitalism as one context of "Critical Cyberculture Studies", but a much stronger focus is on the "cultural differences" of "race and ethnicity, gender, sexuality, age, and disability" (Silver 2006a, 8). This is also reflected in the volume's contributions, where the analysis of class, surplus value, and exploitation on the Internet are marginal issues, whereas topics relating to "cultural difference" in cyberspace occupy a dominant position.

4   Critical Political Economy and Critical Theory in Internet Studies

The second typical approach that can be found in Critical Internet Studies is based on Critical Political Economy and Critical Theory. The sequence of presentation of the following approaches does not reflect an assessment of the importance of approaches, but is based on a chronological order of key works. Included are approaches that use distinctive terms related to critical theory and political economy to characterize themselves.

Geert Lovink and Pit Schultz (1997) argue that "Net Critique" analyzes the organization of power in the immaterial sphere (Lovink and Schultz 1997, 6) as well as imperialism and ideology on the Internet (Lovink and Schultz 1997, 11). The goal of Net Critique is free access to all media and all content (Lovink 1997). Net Critique would not be a theory, but a theory-praxis that stands for radical criticism within an exploding electronic public (Lovink and Schultz 1997). Since the *Call for Net Critique* (Lovink and Schultz 1997) has been published in 1997, a multitude of publications has emerged from the Net Critique Approach (for example: Lovink 2002; Lovink and Scholz 2005; Lovink and Zehle 2005; Jacobs, Janssen and Pasquinelli 2007; Lovink and Rossiter 2007; Rossiter 2006), which has more recently also included a critique of web 2.0 (for example: Lovink 2008; Lovink and Niederer 2008; Rossiter 2006). The Net Critique approach of Lovink and others does not understand itself as a systematic critical theory, but as a very practical form of critique that is therefore also closely related to media activism and media art.

Geert Lovink (2013) stresses in the introduction to the reader *Unlike Us: Social media monopolies and their alternatives* (Lovink and Rasch 2013) that in "contrast with social science scholars around Christian Fuchs discussing the (Marxist) political economy of social media, Unlike Us is primarily interested in a broad arts and humanities angle also called web aesthetics (as described by Vito Campanelli), activist use, and the need to discuss both big and small alternatives, and does not limit itself to academic research. We see critique and alternatives as intrinsically related and both guided by an aesthetic agenda" (Lovink 2013, 14). It is definitely the case that Geert Lovink's main achievement is that he has advanced the critical analysis of the Internet and social media with an aesthetic and arts-based focus. It is also understandable that he does not consider himself to be a social scientist and is not interested in using social science methods. But the separation between a social scientific Marxist political economy of social media on the one hand and a humanities-based critique on the other hand is artificial: Marxist political economy uses dialectical, philosophical and theoretical concepts that could be seen as the humanities side of political economy. The social sciences have in the form of social theory a humanities side themselves. In critical social sciences, critical social theories represent this dimension. Critical political economy also has a practical-political dimension and uses methods for critical empirical research.

In the formulation of the Unlike Us research agenda, Geert Lovink and Korinna Patelis (2013, 367) argue that what is "missing from the discourse is a rigorous discussion of the political economy of [...] social media monopolies". This means that a political economy agenda that Lovink (2013) positions in the book introduction as outside the Unlike Us universe has in the first instance been defined as part of the framework. The political economy framework propagated by the Unlike Us research agenda (Lovink and Patelis 2013) is of course somewhat crude and focuses on the power of monopolies without asking research questions about the exploitation of digital labour, the international and gender division of labour in the ICT/Internet/social media sector, value and surplus value, class, etc (the terms monopolies and monopoly are mentioned 7 times, terms such as class, surplus and value 0 times). So the logic of the argument is political economy yes and no, not if it is Marx or Fuchs, not if it is social science, yes if it is not-Marx and not-Fuchs and not-social science, etc. The whole argument is more than artificial and tries to construct a separation between two critical networks (the Unlike Us Network and the ICTs and Society-Network) that are in fact quite complementary and have no need to compete. I refuse to see these approaches and networks as competing and as being radically different. I am not interested in the politics of splintering typical for left-wing dogmatism that leave out seeing the power of the common enemy and that benefits can arise from synergies between networks and critical approaches.

Otherwise we might just end up the way Monty Python describe the paralysis of the left in *Life of Brian*: Reg: Right. You're in. Listen. The only people we hate more than the Romans are the fucking Judean People's Front. P.F.J.: Yeah... Judith: Splitters...P.F.J.: Splitters...Francis: And the Judean Popular People's Front. P.F.J.: Yeah. Oh, yeah. Splitters. Splitters...Loretta: And the People's Front of Judea...P.F.J.: Yeah. Splitters. Splitters...Reg: What? Loretta: The People's Front of Judea. Splitters. Reg: We're the People's Front of Judea! Loretta: Oh. I thought we were the Popular Front.

Nick Dyer-Witheford (1999) has suggested reinventing Marxism for the analysis of 21st century techno-capitalism. He terms this project cyber-Marxism. Dyer-Witheford's applies the approach of autonomist Marxism that is represented by scholars like Antonio Negri, Michael Hardt, Paolo Virno, Maurizzio Lazaratto, and others, to Internet Studies. Dyer-Witheford sees Autonomist Cyber-Marxism as an alternative to the techno-determinism of scientific socialism, the neo-Luddism of the Braverman-inspired technology-as-domination theories, and the techno-euphoria of many theorizations of post-Fordism (Dyer-Witheford 1999, 38–61).

Greg Elmer (2002) sees three characteristics of Critical Internet Studies:

(1)   the refutation and questioning of ideologies that claim the Internet is revolutionary,
(2)   the analysis of the "process of Internet corporatization and portalization" (Elmer 2002, x),
(3)   the focus on radical possibilities of the critical Internet community especially the cracks, fissures, and holes in the forms of domination that characterize the Internet.

David Hakken (2003) argues for a knowledge theory of value that is grounded in Marxian theory. He sees cyberspace as being shaped by "vast contradictions" (Hakken 2003, 393). New information- and communication technologies "are better viewed as terrains of contestation than as ineluctable independent forces. Technologies do have politics, but like all politics, they manifest multiple, contradictory tendencies" (Hakken 2003, 366).

Fuchs (2008, 2009a, b; 2010a, b; 2011; 2014a, b, c; 2015) speaks of Critical Internet Theory/Studies and the Critique of the Political Economy of the Internet. He argues that these approaches are grounded in more general approaches, especially Frankfurt School Critical Theory and Marx's Critique of the Political Economy that are both foundations for Critical Media and Information Studies (Fuchs 2011). He thereby undertakes an ontological and epistemological grounding of the critical analysis of the Internet by basing it:

(1)   on a general social theory level,
(2)   on the analysis of capitalism,
(3)   on the critical analysis of media, technology, and communication, and
(4)   on the specific analysis of the Internet in a critical inquiry that yields emergent qualities.

Fuchs defines Critical Internet Theory/Studies and the Critique of the Political Economy of the Internet as an approach that engages in "identifying and analysing antagonisms in the relationship of the Internet and society; it shows how the Internet is shaped and shapes the colliding forces of competition and cooperation; it is oriented towards showing how domination and exploitation are structured and structuring the Internet and on how class formation and potential class struggles are technologically mediated; it identifies Internet-supported, not yet realized potentials of societal development and radically questions structures that restrain human and societal potentials for cooperation, self-determination, participation, happiness and self-management" (Fuchs 2009b, 75). Fuchs (2011) defines this approach as a unity of philosophically grounded critical theory, empirical research, and praxis-oriented critical ethics.

For Mark Andrejevic (2009), "critical media studies 2.0" challenge the uncritical celebration of the empowering and democratizing character of contemporary media by showing how new media are embedded in old forms of domination. "Thus, when it comes to the revolutionary promise of participatory media, the challenge faced by the proponents and practitioners of a Critical Media Studies 2.0 is not to assert (in all too familiar rhetoric) that, 'everything has changed,' but rather to explain why, even in the face of dramatic technological transformation, social relations remain largely unaltered. To put it bluntly, Critical Media Studies is not interested in media for their own sake, but for society's sake" (Andrejevic 2009, 35). In an approach comparable to the one of Andrejevic, Paul A. Taylor (2009) speaks of Critical Theory 2.0 in order to "describe the manner in which traditional Critical Theory's (1.0) key insights remain fundamentally unaltered" (Taylor 2009, 93), which would be necessary for challenging web 2.0 optimism.

These approaches mainly differ in their understanding of theory, the role that is given to empirical research, the employment of different research methods (such as qualitative interviews, quantitative surveys, content analyses, statistical analyses, critical discourse analyses, or ethnography). For example Dyer-Witheford's cyber-Marxist approach is purely theoretical and based on a reconstruction of Marxian theory for cyberspace. Net Critique tends to discuss examples that are critically reflected upon from theory-inspired positions that are deliberately eclectic and sometimes personal or journalistic and do not form a systematic theoretical whole as in Adorno's prismatic method of exposition. Fuchs on the one hand is keen on basing his approach on a systematic Hegelian dialectical philosophy, in which every category has a clear place in the theoretical system and categories are dialectically developed from the abstract to the concrete level. On the other hand he applies dialectical philosophy at a concrete level as a foundation for empirical studies that make use of a whole range of methods.

Although there are vast theoretical, methodological, epistemological, and ontological differences between various approaches that advance a Critical Theory or the Critical Political Economy of the Internet, there are also commonalities that are especially relating to the normative understanding of criticism. One important commonality is the *normative understanding of critique*. Critical Internet scholars thereby reflect the old debate between the understanding of critique as epistemological/methodological and as normative procedure. This issue was already at the heart of the positivism debate in German sociology in 1961. Karl R. Popper (1962) argued that the method of the social consists of gaining and differentiating knowledge by testing solutions to problems. Popper considered this method as critical because scholars question the works of others in order to improve knowledge in trial and error processes. For Popper, critique was an epistemological method that shows logical contradictions. Theodor W. Adorno (1962) argued in contrast to Popper that contradictions are not only epistemological (in the relation of subject-object), but can be inherent in objects themselves so that they cannot be resolved by acquiring new knowledge (Adorno 1962, 551). Adorno stressed that Popper's ideal of value-free academia is shaped by the bourgeois concept of value as exchange value (Adorno 1962, 560). He said that positivism is only oriented on appearance, whereas critical theory stresses the difference between essence and appearance (Adorno 1969, 291). He pointed out that Popper's notion of critique is subjective and cognitive (Adorno 1969, 304). There is a fundamental difference between epistemological critique (Popper) and the critique of society (Adorno). Critical Internet scholars question the empiricist application of methods to studying the Internet without grounding the analyses in a thorough analysis in society and in a critical theory of society. This includes some who question all empirical research because they think that the normative falsehood of domination cannot be empirically tested, but only argued for. They all share Adorno's focus on the critique of society.

A second feature that Critical Internet Studies approaches share is the consideration of conventional Internet Studies that dominate the field as forms of instrumental and technological rationality that help legitimize and reproduce capitalism and other forms of domination within capitalism. Instrumental reason means that "ideas have become automatic, instrumentalized" that are not seen as "thoughts with a meaning of their own. They are considered things, machines" for the achievement of the reproduction and deepening of domination (Horkheimer 1974/1947, 15). Technological rationality is another term for instrumental reason, which stresses "elements of thought which adjust the rules of thought to the rules of control and domination" (Marcuse 1964b, 138). Technological rationality denies that reality could be other than it is today. It neglects alternative potentials for development. It aims at "liquidating the oppositional and transcending elements" (Marcuse 1964, 56). Technological rationality causes a one-dimensional thinking, in which "ideas, aspirations, and objectives that, by their content, transcend the established universe of discourse and action are either repelled or reduced to terms of this universe" (Marcuse 1964, 12). Critical Internet scholars consider conventional Internet Studies as ideological because they analyze the Internet as it is, without embedding the analysis into an analysis of structures of domination and without engaging in the struggle for a better world that abolishes domination.

A third commonality concerns the normative and practical levels. Critical Internet Study approaches criticize phenomena that they describe as exploitation, domination, oppression, or exertion of power and structural violence and seek to help advance practices that result in the liberation from these phenomena. Maria Bakardjieva (2010, 61) argues that Critical Internet Studies in contrast to statistical and interpretative approaches seeks answers to normative questions relating to the Internet's role in empowerment, oppression, emancipation, alienation and exploitation. Critical studies relate the analysis of the Internet to both domination and liberation. To a larger or lesser degree this involves explicitly the establishment of a post-capitalist society that is for example described as grassroots socialism, communism, participatory democracy, or sustainable information society. The normative dimension is described by such approaches as their emancipatory character.

The critical normative orientation is the central characteristic of Critical Internet Studies. It reflects Horkheimer's insight that critical theory aims at "a state of affairs in which there will be no exploitation or oppression" (Horkheimer 1937/2002, 241). Horkheimer in his essay on *Traditional and critical theory* reflects Karl Marx's critique of capitalism and reformulated Marxian theory as critical theory of society. One may therefore say that Critical Internet Studies is not only indebted to the Frankfurt School's understanding of critique, but also that the root of this understanding is the theory of Karl Marx. Marx summarized the normative dimension of critical analysis by saying that it grasps "the root of the matter", is based on "the teaching that *man is the highest essence for man*" and therefore ends "with the *categoric imperative to overthrow all relations* in which man is a debased, enslaved, abandoned, despicable essence" (MEW Vol. 1, 385). If we understand Marxian critique as the critique of all forms of domination and all dominative relationships, then all critical studies are Marxian-inspired. My argument is that this heritage should not be denied, but taken seriously and positively acknowledged.

The critical normative dimension Critical Internet Studies means that it does not operate in a vacuum, but is on a more general level related to various approaches in the analysis of media, communication, technology, culture, and information that also stress the normative critique of domination and the goal of emancipation. It is in this respect especially related to analyses of the critique of the political economy of media and communication, critical theory, and critical information systems research. The Critique of the Political Economy of the Media and Communication[1] studies the "the power relations,

---

1   Representatives of this approach, such as Peter Golding, Robert McChesney, or Graham Murdock, speak of a political economy approach, which is somewhat misleading because political economy is not necessarily critical as indicated by the subtitle of Marx's (1867) main work Capital: A Critique of Political Economy. Marx characterized uncritical political economy as approaches that systematize capitalism "in a pedantic way" by proclaiming capitalism and its constituents for "everlasting truths" (Marx 1867, 174–175). As those approaches that are normally discussed in the Anglo-American context under the heading of "political economy of the media and communication" do normally not naturalise and fetishise the specific capitalist form of the media and communicaiton, a self-description as critique of the political economy of the media and communication is in my view more appropriate. At the same time one has to see that terms such as "political economy" and "critical theory" are also useful terms in order to avoid being discriminated because of taking

that mutually constitute the production, distribution, and consumption of resources, including communication resources" (Mosco 2009, 2). This approach addresses "how the media system" interacts with and affects "the overall disposition of power in society" (McChesney 2007, 77), and asks "basic moral questions of justice, equity and the public good" (Murdock and Golding 2005, 61). A critical theory of media and technology analyzes "society as a terrain of domination and resistance and engages in critique of domination and of the ways that media culture engages in reproducing relationships of domination and oppression" (Kellner 1995, 4). It is "informed by a critique of domination and a theory of liberation" (Kellner 1989, 1; see also Feenberg 2002). Critical information systems research produces "knowledge with the aim of revealing and explaining how information systems are (mis)used to enhance control, domination and oppression, and thereby to inform and inspire transformative social practices that realize the liberating and emancipatory potential of information systems" (Cecez-Kecmanovic 2005, 19). Its task is the analysis of the role of information systems in disempowerment and empowerment and to help "overcome injustice and alienation" (Stahl 2008, 9).

5   Critical Cyberculture Studies and Critical Political Economy/
       Critical Theory of the Internet

The main difference that can be found in Critical Internet Studies is the one between Critical Cyberculture Studies and the Critical Political Economy of the Internet. The first approach focuses more on issues relating to the marginalization of identities online, whereas the second has a focus on issues relating to class, exploitation, and capitalism.

When reading "Critical" Cyberculture Studies books and collections, one should remember Nicholas Garnham's insights that "modern forms of racial domination are founded on economic domination" and that "forms of patriarchy have been profoundly marked by the way in which the capitalist mode of production has divided the domestic economy from production as a site of wage labor and capital formation" (Garnham 1998, 610). Critical Political Economy "sees class – the structure of access to the means of production and the structure of the distribution of the economic surplus – as the key to the structure of domination, while cultural studies sees gender and race, along with other potential markers of difference, as alternative structures of domination in

---

a Marxist approach, which unfortunately is a not infrequent reality in contemporary academia, politics, and society.

no way determined by class" (Garnham 1998, 609). The same difference can be found in Critical Internet Studies. The approach of "Critical" Cyberculture Studies tends to see gender and race in cyberspace as not being necessarily shaped by class. It tends to not see class as the key to understanding domination in cyberspace that has crucial influence on gender, race, and other lines of difference. It tends to ignore topics of class, capitalism, and exploitation. "Critical" Cyberculture Studies is therefore an approach that in its postmodern vein is unsuited for explaining the role of the Internet and communications in the current times of capitalist crisis. The crisis itself evidences the central role of the capitalist economy in contemporary society and that the critical analysis of capitalism and socio-economic class should therefore be the central issue for Critical Internet Studies.

Ernesto Laclau has in a trialogue with Judith Butler and Slavoj Žižek admitted that in postmodern approaches it is a common language game to "transform 'class' into one more link in an enumerative chain [...] "race, gender, ethnicity, etc. – and class" (Butler, Laclau and Žižek 2000, 297) and to put class deliberately as last element in the chain in order to stress its unimportance – Laclau speaks of "deconstructing classes" (Butler, Laclau and Žižek 2000, 296). Slavoj Žižek has in this context in my opinion correctly said that Postmodernism, Cultural Studies, and post-Marxism have by assuming an "irreducible plurality of struggles" accepted "capitalism as 'the only game in town'" and have renounced "any real attempt to overcome the existing capitalist liberal regime" (Butler, Laclau and Žižek 2000, 95). Subordinating or equalizing the category of class to other antagonistic categories (gender, ethnicity, age, capabilities, etc) poses the danger of burying the project and demand to establish participatory alternatives to the capitalist totality. The Butler-Laclau-Žižek debate implies for "Critical" Cyberculture Studies that its tendency of neglecting class, exploitation, and capitalism means that it will necessarily have a reformist political agenda and will not be able to conceptualize alternatives to a capitalist Internet in a capitalist society (Fuchs 2011).

All non-class antagonisms are articulated with class, whereas not all non-class antagonisms are articulated with each other. All antagonisms of contemporary society have class aspects and are conditioned by class. Class is the antagonism that binds all other antagonisms together; it prefigures, conditions, enables and constrains, and exerts pressure on possibilities for other antagonisms (Fuchs 2008). At the same time, non-class antagonisms influence the class antagonism so that complex dynamic relationships are present. If class is the super-antagonism of capitalism that does not determine or overdetermine, but condition other antagonisms, then it is important to give specific attention to this category.

According to its own self-descriptions, "Critical" Cyberculture Studies wants to help overcome "online marginalization". It does however very well in marginalizing critiques of how capitalism, class, and exploitation are related to the Internet. It therefore does not deserve the name "critical". "Critical" Cyberculture scholars should take very seriously Douglas Kellner's warning: "Neglecting political economy, celebrating the audience and the pleasures of the popular, overlooking social class and ideology, and failing to analyze or criticize the politics of cultural texts will make media/cultural studies merely another academic subdivision, harmless and ultimately of benefit primarily to the culture industry itself" (Kellner 2009, 19–20). It is time for cyberculture scholars to stop purely focusing on their heroes like Donna Haraway, Sherry Turkle, Howard Rheingold, Manuel Castells, and various postmodernists (Bell 2001, 74–88; Bell 2007; Silver 2006b, 65; Silver 2006a, 3) and to substantiate these approaches by reading and interpreting Karl Marx's works.

The number of and interest in analyses of the Internet that are focusing more on class and exploitation have been growing. In the current times of capitalist crisis and the end of postmodernism and culturalism, this development is likely to continue. My argument is that it is time to engage with pleasure in conducting Marxist Internet Studies. We have rather entered times, where it becomes increasingly a matter of explanation why you are not a Marxian scholar.

Truly critical Internet Studies have in common their opposition to positivistic Internet Studies, instrumental/technological rationality, the critique of domination, the struggle for emancipation, and the shared normative grounding in Marxian analysis and various critical analyses of the media, communication, technology, and information. My argument is not only that Internet Studies is in need of Marxian theory, but also that Internet Studies to a certain degree already makes use of Marxian categories and should therefore acknowledge its own Marxian roots.

The next section will focus on the analysis of specific Marxian categories of Critical Internet Studies.

6   Karl Marx and Critical Internet Studies Concepts

Critical Internet Studies to a certain degree already makes use of Marxian categories and should therefore acknowledge its own Marxian roots. With the help of examples this circumstance will now be shown especially for eleven Marxian concepts:

(1)   dialectics
(2)   capitalism
(3)   commodity/commodification
(4)   surplus value, exploitation, alienation, class
(5)   globalization
(6)   ideology/ideology critique
(7)   class struggle
(8)   commons
(9)   public sphere
(10) communism
(11) aesthetics

Vincent Mosco stresses that Marxian political economy decentres the media by "placing in the foreground the analysis of capitalism, including the development of the forces and relations of production, commodification and the production of surplus value, social class divisions and struggles, contradictions and oppositional movements" (Mosco 2009, 94). To this analysis, six additional crucial Marxian concepts are added: globalization, ideology, commons, public sphere, communism, and aesthetics.

The first relevant Marxian concept is *dialectics*. Marx applied the Hegelian method of dialectical thinking to the analysis of capitalism. Dialectics is "in its very essence critical and revolutionary" because "it regards every historically developed form as being in a fluid state, in motion, and therefore grasps its transient aspect as well. [...] the movement of capitalist society is full of contradictions" (Marx 1867, 103). Fuchs's approach has an epistemological and ontological focus on dialectical philosophy in order to conceptualize the relationship Internet/web 2.0 and society not as one-dimensional and techno-deterministic, but as complex, dynamic, and contradictory (Fuchs 2009b; Fuchs 2011, Chapters 2+3). Peter Lunenfeld (1999) and Michael Heim (1999) have spoken of the digital dialectic. Such approaches are related to the dialectical insight of the critical theory of technology that technology is "an 'ambivalent' process of development suspended between different possibilities" (Feenberg 2002, 15).

Marcuse (1941) wanted to avoid deterministic dialectics and to bring about a transition from a structural-functionalist dialectic towards a human-centred dialectic. Therefore he argued that capitalism is dialectical because of its objective antagonistic structures and that the negation of this negativity can only be achieved by human praxis. The Internet or specific Internet platforms have multiple, at least two, potential effects on society and social systems that can co-exist or stand in contradiction to each other (Fuchs 2008, 2011). Which potentials are realized is based on how society, interests, power structures, and struggles shape the design and usage of technology in multiple ways that are also potentially contradictory. One should therefore think about the Internet dialectically just like Marx thought about technology in capitalism as being shaped by an antagonism between productive forces and relations of production. Networked productive forces are in capitalism "antithetical forms", which are at the same time 'mines to explode' capitalism (Marx 1857/1858, 159) and governed by class relations that are 'no longer productive but destructive forces' (Marx and Engels 1846, 60). So for example the services created by Google anticipate a commons-based public Internet from which all benefit and create new potentials for human co-operation, whereas the freedom (free service access) that it provides is now enabled by online surveillance and user commodification that threatens consumer privacy and results in the economic exploitation of users. The solution is not to call for the abolition or replacement of Google, but to argue for its transformation into a publicly organized and controlled search engine (that could for example be run as collaborative project by public universities). The Internet holds at the same time potential for "capitalist spectacle and commodification" and the construction of "cyber-situations" that are "aimed at progressive change and alternative cultural and social forms" (Best and Kellner 2001, 237–238).

The second cluster of Marxian concepts that is reflected in Critical Internet Studies is *capitalism/capitalist mode of production/capitalist society*. For Marx, capitalism is a system of capital accumulation, in which the worker "has permission to work for his own subsistence, that is, to live only insofar as he works for a certain time gratis for the capitalist (and hence also for the latter's co-consumers of surplus value)" so that "the whole capitalist system of production turns on increasing this gratis labour" (Marx 1875, 310). Therefore this system "is a system of slavery" (Marx 1875, 310). The notion of capitalism/capitalist mode of production is reflected in Critical Internet Studies within concepts such as communicative capitalism, informational capitalism, the antagonism of the networked digital productive forces and the relations of production, digital capitalism, hypercapitalism, or new media capitalism.

The third important Marxian category is that of *commodity/commodification*. Marx argues that the fundamental element of capitalism is the commodity, a good that is exchanged in a certain quantitative relationship with money: x amount of commodity A = y units of money. "A given commodity, a quarter of wheat for example, is exchanged for x boot-polish, y silk or z gold, etc. In short, it is exchanged for other commodities in the most diverse proportions" (Marx 1867, 127). The commodity is for Marx the cell form of capitalism: "The wealth of societies in which the capitalist mode of production prevails appears as an 'immense collection of commodities'; the individual commodity appears as its elementary form" (Marx 1867, 125). Commodification is the transformation of a social relationship into an exchange relationship between buyer and seller. The notion of commodification has been used in Critical Internet Studies for example as the commodification of the Internet, the commodification of online privacy, the commodification of community in cyberspace, and the concept of profiling as online commodification machine of personal information.

Fourth, one finds the concepts of *class, surplus value, exploitation, and alienation* in Critical Internet Studies. These notions are inherently related for Marx. Their connection is neatly summarized in the following passage: "On the one hand, the process of production incessantly converts material wealth into capital, into means of creating more wealth and means of enjoyment for the capitalist. On the other hand, the labourer, on quitting the process, is what he was on entering it, a source of wealth, but devoid of all means of making that wealth his own. Since, before entering on the process, his own labour has already been alienated from himself by the sale of his labour-power, has been appropriated by the capitalist and incorporated with capital, it must, during the process, be realised in a product that does not belong to him. Since the process of production is also the process by which the capitalist consumes labour-power, the product of the labourer is incessantly converted, not only into commodities, but into capital, into value that sucks up the value-creating power, into means of subsistence that buy the person of the labourer, into means of production that command the producers. The labourer therefore constantly produces material, objective wealth, but in the form of capital, of an alien power that dominates and exploits him; and the capitalist as constantly produces labour-power, but in the form of a subjective source of wealth, separated from the objects in and by which it can alone be realised; in short he produces the labourer, but as a wage labourer. This incessant reproduction, this perpetuation of the labourer, is the sine quâ non of capitalist production" (Marx 1867, 716).

Examples for the usage of these Marxian categories in Internet Studies can be given. Fuchs (2010b) argues that capital accumulation is in the corporate 2.0 based on the infinite exploitation of prosumers, who are sold as Internet prosumer commodity to advertising clients. He sees users of the corporate web 2.0 as part of the proletarian class that is exploited by capital (Fuchs 2010b). He bases his analysis on Marx's surplus value concept and Dallas Smythe's notion of the audience commodity. Mark Andrejevic (2002) argues that the work of being watched in respect to the media is a form of exploitation and productive

labour. Discussions about value creation on digital media have become important. Andrejecvic speaks of "the interactive capability of new media to exploit
the work of being watched" (Andrejevic 2002, 239). Andrejevic (2009) employs
the term exploitation 2.0 in order to stress that exploitation remains a fundamental characteristic of the web 2.0 environment. In another work, Andrejevic
(2007) has connected the notion of the work of being watched to the category
of the digital enclosure. Terranova (2004) has advanced the concept of the
exploitation of free labour on the Internet. Digital labour-conferences like
"Digital labour: Workers, authors, citizens" (University of Western Ontario,
October 2009; see Burston, Dyer-Witheford and Hearn 2010), "The Internet as
Playground and Factory" (New School, November 2009; see the book Scholz
2012) and "Towards Critical Theories of Social Media. The Fourth ICTs and
Society-Conference" (Uppsala University, Sweden. May 2nd–4th, 2012, see the
collected volume Fuchs and Sandoval 2014) have achieved extraordinary interest in terms of contributions and attendance. A related question is the one of
how class relations have changed in the context of culture, the Internet, networks and information.

The fifth concept is that of *globalization*. Marx stressed that capitalism has
an inherent tendency to globalize because of "the entanglement of all peoples
in the net of the world-market" and "the international character of the capitalistic regime" (Marx 1867, 929). The world market, capital export and the global
organization of companies are aspects of this capitalist globalization process.
Kellner (2002) stresses the importance of Marx's dialectical and critical theory
in contemporary "technocapitalism" for understanding that globalization and
the Internet are contested terrains composed of oppositions. Harvey (1990),
reflecting Marx's insight that "capital by its nature drives beyond every spatial
barrier" and that "the means of communication and transport" are connected
to "the annihilation of space by time" (Marx 1857/1858, 524), says that the rise
of a flexible regime of accumulation in combination with new communication
technologies has brought about a new phase of time-space compression of
capitalism. The Internet has not caused, but enhanced the globalisation of
capitalist production, distribution and circulation. Communication technologies like the Internet are the medium and at the same time outcome of the
globalization tendency of capitalism (Fuchs 2008, 110).

The sixth concept is the one of *ideology/ideology critique*. For Marx, ideology
is inverted consciousness, consciousness that is manipulated so that it sees
reality other than it is. "In all ideology men and their circumstances appear
upside-down as in a camera obscura" (MECW Vol. 5, 14). It is "an inverted consciousness of the world" (MECW Vol. 3, 175). In *Capital,* Marx (1867) described
ideology as the fetishism of commodities that makes social relations appear as

characteristics of things and thereby creates "misty realms" of consciousness (Marx 1867, 165). In the 1990s, Internet ideology often presented the Internet as a new frontier for creating jobs, a prospering economy and enhancing democracy. The 2000 new economy crisis, in which a lot of high-risk venture capital based Internet companies went bankrupt, shattered these hopes. Around 2005, a new version of this ideology emerged: The assumption was now that "web 2.0" and "social media" advance creativity age, economic democracy and participatory culture because they allow users to share, engage and connect. However, corporate social media are based on the exploitation of digital labour and are therefore incompatible with economic democracy and participation (Fuchs 2014a, b). Eran Fisher (2010a, b) argues in this context that web 2.0 is shaped by a discourse that legitimates capitalism that he characterizes as the new spirit of networks. The rise of new technologies often creates an "eruption of feeling that briefly overwhelms reason" (Mosco 2004, 22). Technological determinism ignores the political economy of events. Social media determinism is an expression of the digital sublime, the development that "cyberspace has become the latest icon of the technological and electronic sublime, praised for its epochal and transcendent characteristics and demonized for the depth of the evil it can conjure" (Mosco 2004, 24).

The seventh Marxian category is *class struggle*. "The history of all hitherto existing society is the history of class struggle. Freeman and slave, patrician and plebeian, lord and serf, guild-master and journeyman, in a word, oppressor and oppressed, stood in constant opposition to one another, carried on an uninterrupted, now hidden, now open fight" (Marx and Engels 1968, 35–36). In Critical Internet Studies, the notion of class struggle is for example reflected in the concept of anti-capitalist Internet play struggles that help to "hack" capitalism or the notion of Internet as means for the circulation of class struggles. Related concepts are the electronic fabric of struggle and electronic civil disobedience. Hardt and Negri's (2004) concept of the struggle of the multitude has become of importance in such approaches. The multitude consists of "singularities that act in common" (Hardt and Negri 2004, 105), "all those who work under the rule of capital" (ibid., 106). It is shaped by immaterial labour, that is labour "that creates immaterial products, such as knowledge, information, communication, a relationship, or an emotional response" (ibid., 108).

The eighth Marxist category is that of *commons*. Commons are resources that are essential and basic for the survival of a society, that all need, and that are produced by all. Marx has stressed the common character of knowledge with his concept of the "General Intellect", which is the "power of knowledge, objectified", "general social knowledge" that becomes "a direct force of production" (Marx 1857/1858, 706). He pointed out that knowledge is "brought about partly by the cooperation of men now living, but partly also by building on earlier work" (Marx 1894, 199). Its common character is due to "communal labour, [that] however, simply involves the direct cooperation of individuals" (Marx 1894, 199). The concept of the commons has been applied to the context of knowledge on the Internet that is collectively produced and shared and appropriated by capital. *Discussions of Internet commons relate especially to free software, Wikipedia, and filesharing.*

The concepts of class struggle and the commons are in contemporary Marxism and in critical studies of the Internet especially grounded in Autonomist Marxism, a perspective that Žižek (2008, 354) criticizes (mainly in respect to Hardt and Negri) as celebrating the informational revolution as "the unique chance for overcoming capitalism" and as thereby ignoring the rise of a new frictionless soft capitalism that enabled by IT makes use of a rhetoric consisting of ideals like participation, self-organization, and co-operation without realizing them. Žižek however agrees with Hardt and Negri (2009) that the exploitation of the commons of society (such as knowledge on the Internet, education and culture) justifies at the political level as a form of resistance "the resuscitation of the notion of communism" (Žižek 2008, 429).

The ninth concept is the *public sphere*. Marx imagined alternatives to the bourgeois state that serves class interests when he described the Paris Commune as a specific kind of public sphere: The commune superseded class rule (Marx 1871, 274), it "was formed of the municipal councillors, chosen by universal suffrage in the various wards of the town, responsible and revocable at short terms" (Marx 1871, 274). "Public functions ceased to be the private property of the tools of the Central Committee. Not only municipal adminis-tration, but the whole initiative hitherto exercised by the State was laid into the hands of the Commune" (Marx 1871, 274). The Commune was "the self-government of the producers" (ibid., 275), who "administer their common affairs by an assembly of delegates" (ibid., 275), abolished "that class-property which makes the labour of the many the wealth of the few" (ibid., 277), and transformed "the means of production, land and capital, now chiefly the means of enslaving and exploiting labour, into mere instruments of free and associated labour" (ibid., 277) so that a "united co-operative" society (ibid., 277) emerges. Marx asks about such a true public sphere: "what else, gentlemen, would it be but Communism" (ibid., 277)? Habermas' original concept of the public sphere is grounded in this Marxian understanding (see: Habermas 1991, 122–129). Marx saw the bourgeois public sphere ironically (Habermas 1991, 123). "Marx denounced public opinion as false consciousness: it hid before itself its own true character as a mask of bourgeois class interests" (Habermas 1991, 124). Marx's "critique demolished all fictions to which the idea of the public sphere of civil society appealed. In the first place, the social preconditions for the equality of opportunity were obviously lacking, namely: that any person with skill and 'luck' could attain the status of property owner and thus the qualifications of a private person granted access to the public sphere, property and education. The public sphere with which Marx saw himself confronted contradicted its own principle of universal accessibility" (Habermas 1991, 124).

A number of authors has discussed how to apply the notion of the public sphere to the Internet and thereby has also taken into account Habermas' Marxist grounding by describing how the political economy of capitalism can colonize and thereby limit the potential of the Internet to act as a tool that advances the transformation towards a public sphere. However, many authors have ignored Marx's concept of the public sphere as communism that transcends the private control of the means of production and the acknowledgement of this dimension by Habermas. Taking both Marx's and young Habermas's concepts of the public sphere seriously must mean for Critical Internet Studies to discuss what a communist Internet is all about (Fuchs 2011). According to Habermas, the public sphere is not only a normative ideal, but also a concept that allows criticizing the political reality of the media. He has stressed in this context that the liberal public sphere limits its own value of freedom of speech and public opinion because citizens in capitalism do not have same formal education and material resources for participating in the public sphere (Habermas 1991, 227) and that it limits its own value of freedom of association and assembly because big political and economic organizations "enjoy an oligopoly of the publicistically effective and politically relevant formation of assemblies and associations" (Habermas 1991, 228). Critical Internet Studies should especially take a look at how freedom of speech and freedom of assembly are limited by unequal conditions of access (money, education, age, etc) and the domination of visibility and attention by big economic and political organizations.

The tenth concept considered here is *communism*. Marx and Engels did not mean by the term communism a totalitarian society that monitors all human beings, operates forced labour camps, represses human individuality, installs conditions of general shortage, limits the freedom of movement, etc. For them, communism is a society that strengthens common co-operative production, common ownership of the means of production, and enriches the individual sphere of activities and thereby individuality. The new crisis of capitalism has brought about an interest in the idea of communism (see for example: Žižek and Douzinas 2010). Marx spoke of "an association of free men, working with the means of production held in common, and expending their many different forms of labour-power in full self-awareness as one single social labour force"

(Marx 1867, 171). Communism is "a society in which the full and free development of every individual forms the ruling principle" (Marx 1867, 739). In Critical
Internet Studies, scholars have for example spoken about the goal of a communist Internet in a communist society (Fuchs 2011), 21st century communism
(Dyer-Witheford 1999, 4), cybernetic communism (Barbrook 2007), or dot.
communism (Moglen 2003), an alternative Internet (Atton 2004), a public-
service Net (Patelis 2000, 99) or public service and commons-based social
media (Fuchs 2014d). The notion of communism has for Internet Studies special relevance for the question to which extent the common sharing (like on
file sharing platforms) and co-operative production of knowledge (like on
Wikipedia or in the Free and Open Source Software movement) constitutes
foundations of a communist mode of production. Marx has stressed the common character of knowledge with his concept of the "General Intellect", which
is the "power of knowledge, objectified", "general social knowledge" that
becomes "a direct force of production" (Marx 1857/1858, 706). He pointed out
that knowledge is "brought about partly by the cooperation of men now living,
but partly also by building on earlier work" (Marx 1894, 199). Its common character is due to "communal labour, [that] however, simply involves the direct
cooperation of individuals" (Marx 1894, 199). The concept of the commons has
also been applied to the context of knowledge on the Internet that is collectively produced and shared and appropriated by capital (see for example:
Dyer-Witheford 1999, 4, 219ff; Fuchs 2010b, 2011; Hardt and Negri 2009, 282;
Žižek 2010a).

The eleventh concept is *aesthetics*. Marx pointed out that art should not be
organized as surplus-value generating labour, but in capitalism can be transformed into this kind of work and thereby can become an object of commodification (Marx 1863, 401). For Marx, communism meant the end of the division
of labour, so that all people could engage in artistic activities. "In a communist
society there are no painters but only people who engage in painting among
other activities" (Marx and Engels 1846, 418). Adorno pointed out based on
Marx the relationship of art, capitalism, and communism by arguing that
authentic art is non-identical with the logic of capitalism, it neglects instrumental reason: "the function of art in the totally functional world is its func-
tionlessness" (Adorno 1997, 320). In recent years, discussion abouts Marxist
aesthetics have been applied to the realm of the Internet, online play, and computer games (see for example: Kline, Dyer-Witheford and De Peuter 2003,
Andrejevic 2006, Dyer-Witheford and De Peuter 2009).

The eleven concepts discussed are some of the most frequently invoked
Marxian notions in Internet Studies. Others could be added and the discussion
extended, but the limited space of this article does not allow discussing these

issues at length. The examples given are, however, suggestive of the importance of Marxian theory for critical analysis of the Internet. Certainly such concepts are not only welcomed, but are also opposed. This phenomenon is discussed in the next section.

7   Digital Labour

The rise of "social media" that are based on targeted advertising combined with the rising interest in Marx's works in the course of the new world economic crisis has resulted in discussions about the political economy of the Internet and how Marx's works can be used in this context. In this context, especially the concept of digital labour has gained importance. New debates have emerged around the question if and how to use Marx for understanding digital media.

Authors have for example discussed the usefulness of Karl Marx's labour theory of value (Fuchs 2010b, Arvidsson and Colleoni 2012, Fuchs 2012), how the notion of alienation shall be used in the context of digital labour (Andrejevic 2012, Fisher 2012), or if and how Dallas Smythe's notion of audience labour can be used for understanding digital labour (for an overview discussion see my contribution in the companying volume "Marx and the Political Economy of Communication" to this book). My books *Social Media: A Critical Introduction* (Fuchs 2014b), *Digital Labour and Karl Marx* (Fuchs 2014a) and *Culture and Economy in the Age of Social Media* (Fuchs 2015) provide an introduction to as well as more advanced discussions of many of the involved issues. The general task has been how to best understand and conceptualise that users under real-time far-reaching conditions of commercial surveillance create a data commodity that is sold to advertising clients and who exactly creates the value that manifests itself in social media corporations' profits.

The digital labour debate has been accompanied by the question how feasible Karl Marx's labour theory of value is for understanding digital labour. This theory argues that the value of a commodity measured as the average number of hours it takes to produce it is a crucial economic category for the critical analysis of capitalism. It is connected to questions of productive and unproductive labour, surplus-value, exploitation and class. I have held and continue to hold the position that a digital labour theory of value is feasible and necessary. Some commentators have remarked that Marx's theory is out of date in the 21st century and that today value is determined by affects and reputation. They advocate a turn from Marx's objective concept of value to a subjective concept of value, much comparable to the neoclassical concept of value that postulates that "value depends entirely upon utility" and oppose the view that makes "labour rather than utility the origin of value; and there are even those who distinctly assert that labour is the cause of value" (Jevons 1871, 1). The claim that the labour theory of value is no longer valid implies that time plays no role in the contemporary capitalist economy. Attention and reputation can be accumulated and getting attention for social media does not happen simply by putting the information there – it requires the work of creating attention. The groups on Facebook and Twitter with the largest number of followers and likes are the ones of entertainers and companies who employ people such as social media strategists to take care of their social media presence. It is no accident that new job profiles such as social media editor, social media strategist, social media manager, social media consultant, social media community executive and social media analyst have recently emerged. Companies are willing to pay employees in order to invest time for creating and maintaining social media profiles. So we need to conceptualize value with a theory of time and need theories of time in society, capitalism and the media economy and the media.

For Marx, the creators of commodity values are productive workers exploited by capital. An important question that has arisen in the digital labour debate is who creates the value that materializes itself in the profits made by Facebook, Google and comparable companies. The crucial question is if the users of commercial social media are generating value and are exploited. One argument in the debate is that only wageworkers can create value and that Facebook users therefore are not exploited. Facebook would rather consume the value generated by the paid workers who are employed by those companies advertising on Facebook. Facebook would therefore not contribute to the exploitation of users, but the exploitation of wageworkers of companies that purchase social media ads. Some scholars make the related argument that Facebook rents out advertising space and that its profits therefore are a form of rent derived from ad clients' profits. Depending on the version of the digital rent argument, Facebook users are then considered as not being exploited or as being exposed to a secondary form of exploitation that is subsumed under the exploitation of wageworkers.

Most of these claims result in the assumption that wage-work is the crucial or only form of productive labour. The consequence of this argument is however not only that Facebook users are seen as unproductive and unexploited, but that also other forms of unpaid work constitutive for capitalism and pre-capitalist modes of production, especially housework and slave work, are unexploited and unproductive. They reproduce an argument against which Marxist feminism has struggled since decades, namely that only wageworkers are exploited by capital. Mariarosa Dalla Costa and Selma James (1972, 30) challenged the orthodox Marxist assumption that reproductive work is "outside social productivity". In contrast a socialist feminist position argues that "domestic work produces not merely use values, but is essential to the production of surplus value" and that the "productivity of wage slavery" is "based on unwaged slavery" in the form of productive "social services which capitalist organization transforms into privatized activity, putting them on the backs of housewives" (Dalla Costa and James 1972, 31). Zillah Eisenstein (1979, 31) argues that the gender division of labour guarantees "a free labour pool" and "a cheap labour pool". Maria Mies (1986, 37) says that women are exploited in a triple sense: "they are exploited [...] by men and they are exploited as housewives by capital. If they are wage-workers they are also exploited as wage-workers". The question who is a productive worker is not just a theory question, but a crucial political question because it is about the question who is an important political subject in the struggle against capitalism. Focusing only on wageworkers has patriarchal and racist implications.

An important question that has arisen within the digital labour debate is if it suffices to focus on the social media world and to limit the notion of digital labour to paid or unpaid work in the online realm (or even narrower to limit the term to users' unpaid labour on social media). We access social media on laptops and mobile phones that tend to be assembled in China. Hon Hai Precision (also known as Foxconn) is a Taiwanese company that was the 139th largest company in the world in 2014 (Forbes 2000, 2014 list[2]). In 2011, Foxconn had enlarged its Chinese workforce to a million, with a majority being young migrant workers who come from the countryside (SACOM 2011). Foxconn assembles e.g. the iPad, iMac, iPhone, Kindle, various consoles (by Sony, Nintendo, Microsoft). When 17 Foxconn workers attempted to commit suicide between January and August 2010 (most of them "successfully"), the topic of bad working conditions in the ICT assemblage industry became widely known. This circumstance was followed up with a number of academic works that show that workers' everyday reality at Foxconn includes low wages, working long hours, frequent work shift changes, regular working time of over 10 hours per day, a lack of breaks, monotonous work, physical harm caused by chemicals such as benzene or solder paste, lack of protective gear and equipment, forced use of students from vocational schools as interns (in agreement with the school boards) that conduct regular assembly work that does not help their studies, prison-like accommodations with 6–22 workers per room, yellow unions that are managed by company officials and whom the workers do not

2   http://www.forbes.com/global2000/list/, accessed on June 3, 2014.

trust, harsh management methods, a lack of breaks, prohibitions that workers move, talk or stretch their bodies, workers that had to stand during production, punishments, beatings and harassments by security guards, disgusting food (Chan 2013; Chan, Pun and Selden 2013; Pun and Chan 2012, Qiu 2012, Sandoval 2013). The Foxconn example shows that the existence and usage of digital media not just depends on the labour of software engineers and content producers. Digital labour covers a broad range of labour working under different conditions, including slave miners working in African conflict mines, smelters, hardware assemblers, software engineers, digital media content producers, eWaste workers, or users of commercial digital media.

Given the complex, networked and transnational reality of labour required for the existence and usage of digital media, a concept of digital labour is needed that can reflect these realities. One needs to go beyond cultural-idealist approaches that only focus on user-generated content and see how content production is grounded in industrial and agricultural labour and how the appropriation of nature in this respect interacts with culture. For adequately studying digital labour and digital media in general, a cultural-materialist approach is needed (Fuchs 2015).

Given these preliminary assumptions, one can provide a definition of digital work and digital labour:

· "Digital work is a specific form of work that makes use of the body, mind or machines or a combination of all or some of these elements as an instrument of work in order to organize nature, resources extracted from nature, or culture and human experiences, in such a way that digital media are produced and used. The products of digital work are depending on the type of work: minerals, components, digital media tools or digitally mediated symbolic representations, social relations, artefacts, social systems and communities. Digital work includes all activities that create use-values that are objectified in digital media technologies, contents and products generated by applying digital media" (Fuchs 2014a, 352).

· "Digital labour is alienated digital work: it is alienated from itself, from the instruments and objects of labour and from the products of labour. Alienation is alienation of the subject from itself (labour-power is put to use for and is controlled by capital), alienation from the object (the objects of labour and the instruments of labour) and the subject-object (the products of labour). Digital work and digital labour are broad categories that involve all activities in the production of digital media technologies and contents. This means that in the capitalist media industry, different forms of alienation and exploitation can be encountered. Examples are slave workers in mineral extraction, Taylorist hardware assemblers, software engineers, professional online content creators (e.g. online journalists), call centre agents and social media prosumers" (Fuchs 2014a, 351–352).

The digital labour debate has been accompanied a resurgent interest in Dallas Smythe's concept of audience labour and audience commodification for explaining the role of targeted advertising on social media. In this context notions such as prosumers labour have been used.

Prosumer labour on social media differs in a number of respects from audience labour in broadcasting:

· *Creativity and social relations*: Broadcasting audiences produce meanings of programmes, whereas social media prosumers not just produce meanings, but also content, communications with other users and social relations.
· *Surveillance*: Broadcasting requires audience measurements, which are approximations, in order to sell audiences as commodities. Social media corporations monitor, store and assess all online activities of users on their platforms and also on other platforms. They have very detailed profiles of users' activities, interests, communications and social relations. Constant real-time surveillance of users is an inherent feature of prosumers labour on capitalist social media. Personal data is sold as a commodity. Measuring audiences has in broadcasting and print traditionally been based on studies with small samples of audience members. Measuring and monitoring user behaviour on social media is constant, total and algorithmic.
· *Targeted and personalised advertising*: Advertising on capitalist social media can therefore more easily target user interests and personalise ads, whereas this is more difficult in commercial broadcasting.
· *Algorithmic auctions*: Algorithms organise the pricing of the user data commodity in the form of auctions for online advertising spaces on the screens of a specific number of users. The ad prices on social media vary depending on the number of auctioneers, whereas the ad prices in newspapers and on radio and TV are set in a relatively fixed manner and are publicly advertised. User measurement uses predictive algorithms (if you like A, you may also like B because 100 000 people who like A also like B).

The digital labour debate has been accompanied by the question how feasible Karl Marx's labour theory of value is for understanding digital labour. And often-overlooked aspect is that this theory is a theory of time in capitalism and that digital labour needs therefore to be situated in the temporalities of capitalism. One criticism brought forward against those who argue that users

of corporate social media platforms that use targeted advertising are exploited
has been that advertising as part of the sphere of circulation that only realises,
but does not create value, and that users' activities are one or several of the following (see for example: Bolaño and Vieira 2014, Comor 2014, Huws 2014, Reveley
2013, Rigi and Prey 2014): unproductive, no labour at all, less productive, a consumption of value generated by paid employees in sectors and companies that
advertise on social media, the realisation of value generated by paid employees
of social media corporations, or an expression of a system where what appears
as profits are rents derived from the profits of advertisers. These opinions are
not new, but just a reformulation of Lebowitz's (1986) criticism of Smythe.

The crucial category used in such discussions is Marx's notion of productive
labour. There are passages, where Marx argues that only wageworkers who produce surplus-value and capital that is accumulated is productive labour. For
example: "Every productive worker is a wage-labourer, but not every wage-
labourer is a productive worker. Whenever labour is purchased to be consumed
as a use-value, as a service and not to replace the value of variable capital with
its own vitality and be incorporated into the capitalist process of production
– whenever that happens, labour is not productive and the wage-labourer is no
productive worker" (Marx 1867, 1041). Or: "Productive labour, therefore, can be
so described when it is directly exchanged for money as capital, or, which is
only a more concise way of putting it, is exchanged directly for capital, that is,
for money which in its essence is capital, which is destined to function as capital, or confronts labour-power as capital. The phrase: labour which is directly
exchanged for capital, implies that labour is exchanged for money as capital
and actually transforms it into capital" (Marx 1863, 396–367).

Marx's thoughts on this topic are however inconsistent, so there cannot be
one "true" interpretation of what productive and unproductive labour is. The
interpretation of productive labour that I follow is one that stresses the notion
of the *Gesamtarbeiter* (collective worker).

Marx stresses that work is not an individual process. The more co-operative
and networked work becomes, which is the consequence of the technification
of capitalism and the rise of knowledge in production, the more relevant
becomes Marx's third understanding of productive labour: productive labour
as labour of the collective worker. The notion of the collective worker becomes
ever more important with the development of fixed constant capital and productivity (Marx 1857/58, 707). Marx has set out this concept both in *Capital,
Volume 1*, and the *Results of the Immediate Production Process*:

- "With the progressive accentuation of the co-operative character of the
  labour process, there necessarily occurs a progressive extension of the concept

of productive labour, and of the concept of the bearer of that labour, the productive worker. In order to work productively, it is no longer necessary for the individual himself to put his hand to the object; it is sufficient for him to be an organ of the collective labourer, and to perform any one of its subordinate functions. The definition of productive labour given above, the original definition, is derived from the nature of material production itself, and it remains correct for the collective labourer, considered as a whole. But it no longer holds good for each member taken individually" (Marx 1867, 643–644).

· "First, with the development of the real subsumption of labour under capital, or the specifically capitalist mode of production, the real lever of the overall labour process is increasingly not the individual worker. Instead, labour-power socially combined and the various competing labour-powers which together form the entire production machine participate in very different ways in the immediate process of making commodities, or, more accurately in this context, creating the product. Some work better with their hands, others with their heads, one as a manager, engineer, technologist, etc., the other as overseer, the third as manual labourer or even drudge. An ever increasing number of types of labour are included in the immediate concept of productive labour, and those who perform it are classed as productive workers, workers directly exploited by capital and subordinated to its process of production and expansion. If we consider the aggregate worker, i.e. if we take all the members comprising the workshop together, then we see that their combined activity results materially in an aggregate product which is at the same time a quantity of goods. And here it is quite immaterial whether the job of a particular worker, who is merely a limb of this aggregate worker, is at a greater or smaller distance from the actual manual labour. But then: the activity of this aggregate labour-power is its immediate productive consumption by capital, i.e. it is the self-valorization process of capital, and hence, as we shall demonstrate, the immediate production of surplus-value, the immediate conversion of this latter into capital" (Marx 1867, 1039–1040).

Figure 2.1 visualises the economic relationships of Facebook (and other corporate social media platforms using targeted advertising) and its advertising clients.

A commodity has a use-value, value and symbolic value. A company's production workers create the basic use-value that satisfies human needs. These activities take an average combined number of labour hours. Labour is the substance of value, labour time its measure and magnitude. In order to sell its

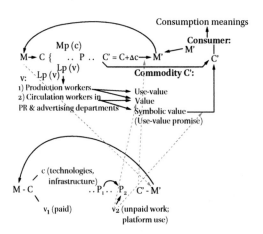

FIGURE 2.1   *The economic relationship of Facebook and its advertising clients*

commodity, a company tries to give positive meanings to it and to communicate these meanings to the public's members whom it tries to convince that this goods or service can enhance their lives and that they should therefore buy this commodity and not a comparable one offered by another company. Most commodities have independent from their physical or informational nature a cultural component that is created by cultural labour. The cultural dimension of a commodity is necessary ideological: it appeals to consumers' imagination and wants to make them connote positive images and feelings with the idea of consuming this commodity.

The creation of a commodity's symbolic ideology is a value-creating activity, but not a use-value generating activity. The use-value of a commodity can be physical and/or informational: we have cars for satisfying the need of driving from A to B, we listen to music for satisfying our aesthetic desires, etc. The exchange-value of a commodity is the relationship in which it is exchanged with another commodity, normally money: x commodity A = y commodity B (money). Symbolic value establishes a link and mediates between use-value and exchange-value, it helps accomplishing the exchange, in which consumers obtain use-values and capitalists money. Wolfgang Fritz Haug (1986) speaks in this context of the commodity's use-value promise: The sales and advertising ideology associated with a commodity promises specific positive life enhancement functions that the commodity brings with it and thereby conceals the commodity's exchange-value behind promises. The symbolic commodity ideology promises a use-value beyond actual consumption, an imaginary surplus and surplus enjoyment. These promises are detached from the actual use-value and are therefore a fictitious form of value.

Saying that the cultural labour of branding, public relations and creating commodity advertisements creates symbolic value is not detached from the notion of economic value. Rather value here precisely means that for the creation of this symbolic dimension of the commodity labour time is invested. It is therefore no wonder that almost all larger companies have their own public relations departments or outsource public relations and advertising to other companies. Paying the circulation workers employed in such departments or companies needs to be planned and calculated into the price of commodities.

Consumers give specific meanings to the commodities they buy and consume. They thereby construct consumption meaning and in doing so can react to use-value promises in different ways:

(1)   They can share these ideologies and buy the commodities because they hope the promise is an actual use value;
(2)   they can deconstruct the use-value promise as ideology and refuse buying the commodity;
(3)   they can deconstruct the use-value, but nonetheless buy the commodity for other reasons.

For communicating commodity ideologies to consumers, companies need to buy advertisement spaces in commercial media. Commercial media link commodity ideologies to consumers, they "transport" ideologies to consumers, although it is unclear and not determined how the latter react and if the confrontation with commodity ideologies results in actual purchases. Facebook and other corporate social media are advertising companies that sell advertising space and user data as commodities to clients who want to present commodity ideologies to users and hope that the latter buy their commodities. Facebook has paid employees that organise the development, maintenance and provision of its software platform. On December 31, 2012, Facebook had 4619 paid employees.[3] But Facebook cannot sell advertising space without its users. Without them, it would be a dead platform that would immediately cease to exist. On June 3, 2013, 42.513% of all Internet users had accessed Facebook within the preceding 3 months.[4] These were more than 1 billion people in the world.[5]

---

3   Facebook Inc., SEC Filings, Form 10-K 2012, http://www.sec.gov/Archives/edgar/data/1326801/000132680113000003/fb-12312012x10k.htm.
4   Data source: http://www.alexa.com.
5   According to http://www.Internetworldstats.com/stats.htm, the latest available world population count was 2 405 518 376 on June 3rd, 2013.

But are Facebook users productive workers? They are certainly not less important for Facebook's capital accumulation than its paid employees because without users Facebook would immediately stop making profits and producing commodities. Facebook's commodity is not its platform that can be used without charges. It rather sells advertising space in combination with access to users. An algorithm selects users and allows individually targeting ads based on keywords and search criteria that Facebook's clients identify. Facebook's commodity is a portion/space of a user's screen/profile that is filled with ad clients' commodity ideologies. The commodity is presented to users and sold to ad clients either when the ad is presented (pay-per-view) or when the ad is clicked (pay-per-click). The user gives attention to his/her profile, wall and other users' profiles and walls. For specific time periods parts of his/her screen are filled with advertising ideologies that are with the help of algorithms targeted to his/her interests. The prosumer commodity is an ad space that is highly targeted to user activities and interests. The users' constant online activity is necessary for running the targeting algorithms and for generating viewing possibilities and attention for ads. The ad space can therefore only exist based on user activities that are the labour that create the social media prosumer commodity.

Facebook clients run ads based on specific targeting criteria, e.g. 25–35 year old men in the USA who are interested in literature and reading. What exactly is the commodity in this example? It is the ad space that is created on a specific 25–35 year old man's screen interested in e.g. Shakespeare while he browses Facebook book pages or other pages. The ad is potentially presented to all Facebook users who fall into this category, which were 27 172 420 on June 3rd, 2013. What is the value of the single ad presented to a user? It is the average labour=usage time needed for the production of the ad presentation. Let's assume these 27 172 420 million users are on average 60 minutes per day on Facebook and in these 60 minutes 60 ads are presented to them on average. All time they spend online is used for generating targeted ads. It is labour time that generates targeted ad presentations. We can therefore say that the value of a single ad presented to a user is in the presented example 1 minute of labour/usage/prosumption time.

So Facebook usage is labour. But is it productive labour? Marx sees transportation labour that moves a commodity in space-time from location A to location B, which takes a certain labour time x, as productive labour: What "the transport industry sells is the actual change of place itself" (Marx 1885, 135). "The productive capital invested in this industry thus adds value to the products transported, partly through the value carried over from the means of transport, partly through the value added by the work of transport" (Marx 1885, 226–227).

The value generated by transporting a commodity from A to B is therefore x hours. The symbolic ideology of a commodity first needs to be produced by special ad and public relations employees and is in a second step communicated to potential buyers. *Advertising therefore involves production and transportation labour.* Advertising production does not create a physical commodity, but an ideological dimension of a commodity – a use-value promise that is attached to a commodity as meaning. Advertising transport workers do not transport a commodity in physical space from A to B, they rather organise a communication space that allows advertisers to communicate their use-value promises to potential customers. Facebook's paid employees and users are therefore 21st century equivalents of what Marx considered as transport workers in classical industry. They are productive workers whose activities are necessary for "transporting" use-value promises from companies to potential customers. Marx associated transport with communication as comparable forms of work. On Facebook and other social media platforms, transportation labour is communication labour.

Dallas W. Smythe argued that it is a specific feature of audience labour that audiences "work to market [...] things to themselves" (Smythe 1981, 4). Facebook users constantly work and constantly market things to themselves. Their usage behaviour constantly generates data that is used for targeting ads. All Facebook usage is productive labour, with the exception of those cases, where users block advertising with the help of ad block software, which probably only a minority does. Facebook usage labour ads value to the commodity that is sold by Facebook's ad clients. Practically this means that a lot of companies want to advertise on Facebook and calculate social media advertising costs into their commodity prices. Nielsen (2013) conducted a survey among advertisers and advertising agencies. 75% of the advertisers and 81% of the agencies that participated in the survey indicated that they buy targeted ads on social media. This shows the importance of social media for advertising today.

The production workers of Facebook's clients produce use-value and value. Their PR & advertising employees (or the workers in the companies to which this labour is outsourced) produce value and a use-value promise as symbolic value. Facebook's users produce the value and the communication of this use-value to themselves. They are productive workers. That they create value means that their labour time objectifies itself in commodities: the ad clients' employees objectify their labour in the commodity that is marketed to Facebook users, whereas Facebook users objectify their labour in the prosumer commodity that is sold to Facebook's clients. User labour is thereby also objectified in the commodity that is marketed and potentially sold to users themselves.

8   A Critique of the Critique of Critical Internet Studies

The use of Marxian concepts in Critical Internet Studies is opposed by two main strategies: (1) anti-Marxism, (2) the subsumption of Marxian concepts under the dominant ideology. Both aim at delegitimizing alternatives to the corporate control of the Internet.

The anti-communist strategy is represented by Andrew Keen and Josh Lanier. Andrew Keen, author of the book *The Cult of the Amateur: How Today's Internet is Killing Our Culture* (Keen 2007), argues that web 2.0 rhetoric has a political agenda and shares Marxist political goals (Keen 2006). Keen sees web 2.0 as a dangerous development and argues that a new web 2.0 communism will put an end to traditional culture and society. "Without an elite mainstream media, we will lose our memory for things learnt, read, experienced, or heard" (Keen 2006). The fear that haunts him seems to be the fear that capitalism and corporate interests are challenged and could somehow cease to exist. Josh Lanier (2006) argues that web 2.0 results in "digital Maoism", a form of collectivism that is as totalitarian as Maoism and negates individuality.

Such approaches advance the idea that Marxism is dangerous and anti-individualistic, which is an error. Whereas the individual was indeed not greatly valued by Mao or Stalin, it was highly important for Marx, who saw communism as the sublation of the class individual and the rise of the well-rounded individual. Communism is for Marx not the collectivization of life, but the creation of a highly productive post-scarcity economy that is based on wealth for all, the minimization of estranged labour, and the maximization of freely chosen labour. Maximizing self-determined labour has potentials for releasing creative capacities and fostering the maximization of the development powers of all humans. The precondition for Marx is the sublation of the private property of the means of production. "In the real community the individuals obtain their freedom in and through their association" (Marx and Engels 1846, 87). This real community would be the "re-integration or return of man to himself, the transcendence of human self-estrangement" (Marx 1844, 101f), "the *positive* transcendence of *private property* as *human self-estrangement,* and therefore as the real *appropriation* of the *human* essence by and for man" (Marx 1844, 102), and "the complete return of man to himself as a *social* (i.e., human) being" (Marx 1844, 102). Communist society enables the "all-round development of individuals, precisely because the existing form of intercourse and the existing productive forces are all-embracing and only individuals that are developing in an all-round fashion can appropriate them, i.e., can turn them into free manifestations of their lives" (Marx and Engels 1846, 464). For Marx, capitalism limits the development potentials of humans because the

lack of material resources does not allows them to fully develop their capacities. In communism, there is "the development of individuals into complete
individuals" (Marx and Engels 1846, 97). "The approporiation of a totality of
instruments of production is, for this very reason, the development of a totality
of capacities in the individuals themselves" (Marx and Engels 1846, 96).

For Marx, a communist society or socialist mode of production is based on
the principle: "From each according to his abilities, to each according to his
needs!" (Marx 1875, 306). This means that in a communist society all goods and
services are for free and human activities are self-chosen. The precondition is
that "the productive forces have also increased with the all-round development of the individual" and that "all the springs of common wealth flow more
abundantly" (Marx 1875, 306). Computer technology plays an important role in
achieving a communist society: it allows increasing productivity so that overall
wealth can be increased. If class relations are substituted by co-operative relations, these material conditions allow post-scarcity and wealth for all as a basis
for free labour (in the self of self-determined, not unpaid!) and free goods and
services (in the sense of gratis for all). A communist Internet is only possible in
such a communist society. In a communist society, digital goods and services
will be created in voluntary co-operative labour and will be available to all for
free. Digital commodities and commodities in general cease to exist. Self-
determined activities online and offline will create a well-rounded individuality that is not a form of digital Maoism, but a true form of freedom realized in
a dynamic and self-enhancing dialectic of individuality and collectivism.

The second strategy (ideological subsumption) is represented by Kevin Kelly,
who preached the neoliberal credos of liberalization, privatization, and commercialization in relation to IT in the 1990s (see for example: Kelly 1998), argues
that the "new web", where people "work toward a common goal and share their
products in common, [...] contribute labour without wages and enjoy the fruits
free of charge" (Kelly 2009, 118) constitutes a "new socialism" – "digital socialism". The new socialism is for Kelly a socialism, in which workers do not control
and manage organizations and the material output they generate. Therefore
this notion of socialism should be questioned. For Kelly, socialism lies in collective production, not in democratic economic ownership. If "socialism seeks to
replace capitalism by a system in which the public interest takes precedence
over the interest of private profit", "is incompatible with the concentration of
economic power in the hands of a few", and "requires effective democratic control of the economy" (*Frankfurt Declaration of the Socialist International*;
Socialist International 1951), then Kelly's notion of socialism that is perfectly
compatible with the existence of Microsoft, Google, Yahoo, and other web corporations (as indicated by the fact that he lists Google, Amazon, Facebook, and

YouTube in his history of socialism), is not at all a notion of socialism, but one of capitalism disguised as socialism. For Rosa Luxemburg, socialism was "a society that is not governed by the profit motive but aims at saving human labour" (Luxemburg 1913/2003, 301). She argued that the "aim of socialism is not accumulation but the satisfaction of toiling humanity's wants by developing the productive forces of the entire globe" (Luxemburg 1913/2003, 447).

Kelly's notion of socialism is incompatible with theoretical concepts of socialism, it is theoretically ungrounded and can be considered as the ideological attempt to redefine capitalism and capitalist exploitation as socialism.

9 Conclusion

The analysis of approaches in this chapter showed that there are methodological, ontological, and epistemological differences within Critical Internet Studies. Critical Cyberculture Studies is influenced by Cultural Studies, it rather ignores aspects of class and exploitation, and should therefore better be termed "Cyberculture Studies". Critical Theory and Critical Political Economy of the Internet are based on the insight that class is crucial for understanding the structures of exploitation and domination that express themselves on the Internet and in other media and that in capitalism, all forms of domination are related to and conditioned by forms of exploitation. Either implicitly or explicitly, a lot of Marxian concepts have been reflected in Critical Internet Studies: dialectics, capitalism, commodification, surplus value/exploitation/alienation/class, globalization, ideology, class struggle, commons, public sphere, communism, aesthetics. Anti-Marxism and subsumption are two strategies that attempt to neutralize the critical role of Marxian concepts in Internet Studies.

The outlined eleven Marxian concepts allow formulating an incomplete research agenda for Critical Internet Studies that includes the following questions:

(1) How can the creation, development and the contradictions of the Internet be understood by a dialectical and historical critical theory?

(2) What exactly is the role of the Internet in capitalism? How can this role be theorized and empirically measured? Which Internet-based capital accumulation models are there?

(3) Which forms of commodification do we find on the Internet and how do they work?

(4) Which different forms of surplus value creation are there on the Internet, how do they work? What do users think about them?

(5) How does the Internet interact with globalization processes?

(6)   Which myths and ideologies are there about the Internet? How can they be uncovered, analyzed, and criticized?

(7)   What is the role of the Internet in class struggles? What are the potentials, realities and limits of struggles for an alternative Internet?

(8)   What are Internet commons? How does the commodification of the Internet commons work? Which models for strengthening the Internet commons are there?

(9)   What are the potentials and limits of the Internet for bringing about a public sphere?

(10) What is a commons-based Internet? Which forms and models of a commons-based Internet are there? How can the establishment of a commons-based Internet be strengthened?

(11) How does the Internet change art and aesthetics? Are there potentials of online art and online aesthetics for challenging the logic of capitalism and to help advancing a different logic?

This chapter has attempted to show the importance of Marx for Critical Internet Studies. The results confirm the views of a number of critical media/ technology studies and information science scholars, who stress the importance of Marx for studying communication (see especially: Fuchs 2010a). Dallas Smythe called for a "Marxist theory of communication" (Smythe 1994, 258). Murdock and Golding (2005, 61) say that "Critical Political Economy of Communications" is "broadly marxisant". Andrew Feenberg has stressed that the critical theory of technology "originates with Marx" (Feenberg 2002, vii) and that Marx provided the first critical theory of technology (Feenberg 2002, 47). Robert McChesney has argued that Marx is of fundamental importance for communication science because he provided intellectual tools that allow:

1.   the critique of capital accumulation in the culture industry,
2.   the critique of commodity fetishism,
3.   the critique of ideologies that legitimate domination (McChesney 2007, 53–55). Furthermore 4. Marx's own journalistic practice would be a model for critical, independent quality journalism (McChesney, 2007 55–57).

Edward Herman (1998) has stressed that the following elements of Marx's analysis are important for an inquiry of contemporary capitalism and communication:

1.   the profit and accumulation drive,
2.   the role of technological change,

3. the creation of a reserve army,
4. globalization,
5. instability and crises,
6. the control of the state by dominating classes.

Gerald Sussmann (1999, 86) has emphasized in a special issue of the *Journal of Media Economics* on the topic of "Political Economy of Communication" that critical communication science is based on Marxian thinking: "Marx, one of the first to recognize modern communications and transportation as pillars of the corporate industrial infrastructure". Bernd Carsten Stahl (2008, 10, 32) has argued that Marx is the root of the critical intention of critical information systems research and critical studies in general.

If Internet Studies is a distinct highly interdisciplinary field (Ess 2011), then Critical Internet Studies can be characterized as a subfield of Internet Studies, which focuses on the analysis of dominative structures and practices on the Internet, Internet-based struggles against domination, and seeks to find ways of using the Internet for liberating humans from oppression, inequality, and exploitation. I have argued in this chapter that in the contemporary situation of capitalist crisis it is specifically important that Critical Internet Studies focuses on the analysis of the role of the Internet in capitalism and draws upon the Marxian roots of all critical studies. Some scholars in Critical Internet Studies acknowledge explicitly the importance of Marxian analysis for studying the Internet critically, whereas others refer implicitly to Marx. Authors in Critical Cyberculture Studies tend to bracket issues relating to class and capitalism. It is time to actively remember that Karl Marx is the founding figure of Critical Media and Information Studies and Critical Internet Studies (Fuchs, 2010a, 2011) and that Marxian analyses are crucial for understanding the contemporary role of the Internet and the media in society (see also: Fuchs and Winseck 2011).

Steve Macek (2006) has distinguished between two forms of digital media studies: (1) analyses "typically informed by Marxism, materialist feminism, radical political economy, critical sociology, and social movement theory", (2) "postmodernist and poststructuralist media scholarship" (Macek 2006, 1031–1032). The first approach is certainly "vastly superior to the other" (Macek 2006, 1038; see also the analyses in Artz, Macek and Cloud 2006). In addition, it needs to be stressed that the second approach is completely out of joint with the capitalist crisis times we have entered. Marx is back, capitalism is in crisis – therefore we require Marxist Internet Studies if we want to understand the role of the Internet in domination and exploitation and its potential for liberation.

References

Adorno, Theodor W. 1962. Zur Logik der Sozialwissenschaften. In *Soziologische Schriften I*, 574–565. Frankfurt/Main: Suhrkamp.

Adorno, Theodor W. 1969. Einleitung zum "Positivismusstreit in der deutschen Soziologie". In *Soziologische Schriften I*, 280–353. Frankfurt/Main: Suhrkamp.

Adorno, Theodor W. 1997. *Aesthetic Theory*. London: Continuum.

Andrejevic, Mark. 2002. The Work of Being Watched: Interactive Media and the Exploitation of Self-Disclosure. *Critical Studies in Media Communication* 19 (2): 230–248.

Andrejevic, Mark. 2005. The Work of Watching One Another: Lateral Surveillance, Risk, and Governance. *Surveillance & Society* 2 (4): 479–497.

Andrejevic, Mark. 2006. Apprehensions of the Future: Internet Aesthetics and Ideology. In *Ideologies of the Internet*, edited by Katharine Sarikakis and Daya Thussu, 19–34. London: Hampton Press.

Andrejevic, Mark. 2007. *iSpy: Surveillance and Power in the Interactive Era*. Lawrence: University Press of Kansas.

Andrejevic, Mark. 2009. Critical Media Studies 2.0: An Interactive upgrade. *Interactions: Studies in Communication and Culture* 1 (1): 35–51.

Andrejevic, Mark. 2012. Exploitation in the Data Mine. In Internet and Surveillance. The Challenges of Web 2.0 and Social Media. In *Internet and Surveillance. The Challenges of Web 2.0 and Social Media*, ed. Christian Fuchs, Kees Boersma, Anders Albrechtslund and Marisol Sandoval, 71–88. New York: Routledge.

Arvidsson, Adam and Eleanor Colleoni. 2012. Value in Informational Capitalism and on the Internet. *The Information Society* 28 (3): 135–150.

Artz, Lee, Steve Macek and Danah L. Cloud, eds. 2006. *Marxism and Communication Studies*. New York: Peter Lang.

Atton, Chris. 2004. *An Alternative Internet*. Edinburgh: Edinburgh University Press.

Bakardjieva, Maria. 2010. The Internet in Everyday Life: Exploring the Tenets and Contributions of Diverse Approaches. In *The Handbook of Internet Studies*, edited by Mia Consalvo and Charles Ess, 59–82. Chicester: Wiley.

Barbrook, Richard. 2007. *Imaginary Futures*. London: Pluto Press.

Bell, David. 2001. *An Introduction to Cybercultures*. New York: Routledge.

Bell, David, ed. 2006a. *Cybercultures. Critical Concepts in Media and Cultural Studies*. New York: Routledge.

Bell, David. 2006b. Introduction: Approaching Cyberculture. In *Cybercultures. Critical Concepts in Media and Cultural Studies, Volume I*, edited by David Bell, 1–10. New York: Routledge.

Bell, David. 2007. *Cyberculture Theorists*. New York: Routledge.

Best, Steven and Douglas Kellner. 2001. *The Postmodern Adventure*. New York: Guilford.

Bolaño, César R.S. and Eloy S. Vieira. 2014. The Political Economy of the Internet: Social Networking Sites and a Reply to Fuchs. *Television & New Media,* first published on April 2, 2014, doi: 10.1177/1527476414527137.

Burston, Jonathan, Nick Dyer-Witheford and Alison Hearn, eds. 2010, Digital Labour. Special issue. *Ephemera* 10 (3/4): 214–539.

Butler, Judith, Ernesto Laclau and Slavoj Žižek. 2000. *Contingency, Hegemony, Universality*. London: Verso.

Callinicos, Alex. 2003. *An Anti-Capitalist Manifesto*. Cambridge, UK: Polity.

Cecez-Kecmanovic, Dubravka. 2005. Basic Assumptions of the Critical Research Perspectives in Information Systems. In *Handbook of Critical Information Systems Research,* edited by Debra Howcroft and Eileen M. Trauth, 19–46. Cheltenham: Edward Elgar.

Chan, Jenny. 2013. A Suicide Survivor: The Life of a Chinese Worker. New Technology, Work and Employment 28 (2): 84–99.

Chan, Jenny, Ngai Pun and Mark Selden. 2013. The Politics of Global Production: Apple, Foxconn and China's New Working Class. New Technology, Work and Employment 28 (2): 100–115.

Comor, Edward. 2014. Value, the Audience Commodity, and Digital Prosumption: A Plea for Precision. In *The Audience Commodity in a Digital Age. Revisiting a Critical Theory of Commercial Media*, ed. Lee McGuigan and Vincent Manzerolle, 245–265. New York: Peter Lang.

Dalla Costa, Mariarosa and Selma James. 1972. The Power of Women and the Subversion of Community. Bristol: Falling Wall Press.

Derrida, Jacques. 1994. *Specters of Marx*. New York: Routledge.

Downing, John. 2001. *Radical Media*. London: Sage.

Dyer-Witheford, Nick. 1999. *Cyber-Marx. Cycles and Circuits of Struggle in High-Technology Capitalism*. Urbana, IL: Universiy of Illinois Press.

Dyer-Witheford, Nick and Greg De Peuter. 2009. *Games of Empire: Global Capitalism and Video Games*. Minneapolis, MN: University of Minnesota Press.

Eagleton, Terry. 2011. *Why Marx Was Right*. London: Yale University Press.

Eisenstein, Zillah. 1979. Developing a Theory of Capitalist Patriarchy and Socialist Feminism. In *Capitalist Patriarchy and the Case for Socialist Feminism*, ed. Zillah R. Eisenstein, 5–40. New York: Monthly Review Press.

Elmer, Greg, ed. 2002. *Critical Perspectives on the Internet*. Lanham: Rowman & Littlefield.

Ess, Charles 2011. Introduction to Part I. In *The Handbook of Internet Studies,* edited by Mia Consalvo and Charles Ess, pp. 11–15. Chicester: Wiley.

Feenberg, Andrew. 2002. *Transforming Technology: A Critical Theory Revisited*. Oxford: Oxford University Press.

Fisher, Eran. 2010a. Contemporary Technology Discourse and the Legitimation of Capitalism. *European Journal of Social Theory* 13 (2): 229–252.

Fisher, Eran. 2010b. *Media and New Capitalism in the Digital Age.* Basingstoke: Palgrave Macmillan.

Fisher, Eran. 2012. How Less Alienation Creates More Exploitation. *tripleC: Communication, Capitalism & Critique* 10 (2): 171–183.

Foster, John B. and Fred Magdoff. 2009. *The Great Financial Crisis. Causes and Consequences.* New York: Monthly Review Press.

Foster, John Bellamy and Robert McChesney. 2012. *The Endless Crisis. How Monopoly-Finance Capital Produces Stagnation and Upheaval from the USA to China.* New York: Monthly Review Press.

Fuchs, Christian. 2008. *Internet and Society. Social Theory in the Information Age.* New York: Routledge.

Fuchs, Christian. 2009a. A Contribution to the Critique of the Political Economy of Transnational Informational Capitalism. *Rethinking Marxism* 21 (3): 387–402.

Fuchs, Christian. 2009b. Information and Communication Technologies and Society. A Contribution to the Critique of the Political Economy of the Internet. *European Journal of Communication* 24 (1): 69–87.

Fuchs, Christian. 2010a. Grounding Critical Communication Studies: An Inquiry into the Communication Theory of Karl Marx. *Journal of Communication Inquiry* 34 (1): 15–41.

Fuchs, Christian. 2010b. Labour in Informational Capitalism and on the Internet. *The Information Society* 26 (3): 179–196.

Fuchs, Christian. 2011. *Foundations of Critical Media and Information Studies.* New York: Routledge.

Fuchs, Christian. 2012. With or without Marx? With or without Capitalism? A Rejoinder to Adam Arvidsson and Eleanor Colleoni. *tripleC: Communication, Capitalism & Critique* 10 (2): 633–645.

Fuchs, Christian. 2014a. *Social Media: A Critical Introduction.* London: Sage.

Fuchs, Christian. 2014b. *Digital Labour and Karl Marx.* New York: Routledge.

Fuchs, Christian. 2014c. *OccupyMedia! The Occupy Movement and Social Media in Crisis Capitalism.* Winchester: Zero Books.

Fuchs, Christian. 2014d. Social Media and the Public Sphere. *tripleC: Communication, Capitalism & Critique* 12 (1): 57–101.

Fuchs, Christian. 2015. *Culture and Economy in the Age of Social Media.* New York: Routledge.

Fuchs, Christian. 2016. Reading Marx in the Information Age: A Media and Communication Studies Perspective on "Capital, Volume 1". New York: Routledge.

Fuchs, Christian and Marisol Sandoval, eds. 2014. *Critique, Social Media and the Information Society.* New York: Routledge.

Fuchs, Christian and Dwayne Winseck. 2011. Critical Media and Communication Studies Today. A Conversation. *tripleC* 9 (2): 247–271.

Garnham, Nicholas. 1990. *Capitalism and Communication*. London: Sage.

Garnham, Nicholas. 1998. Political Economy and Cultural Studies: Reconciliation or Divorce? In *Cultural Theory and Popular Culture*, edited by John Storey, 600–612. Harlow: Pearson.

Habermas, Jürgen. 1991. *The Structural Transformation of the Public Sphere*. Cambridge, MA: MIT Press.

Hakken, David. 2003. *The Knowledge Landscapes of Cyberspace*. New York: Routledge.

Hardt, Michael and Antonio Negri. 2000. *Empire*. Cambridge, MA: Harvard University Press.

Hardt, Michael and Antonio Negri. 2004. *Multitude*. New York: Penguin.

Hardt, Michael and Antonio Negri. 2009. *Commonwealth*. Cambridge, MA: Belknap Press.

Harvey, David. 1990. *The Condition of Postmodernity*. Oxford: Blackwell.

Harvey, David. 2003. *The New Imperialism*. Oxford: Oxford University Press.

Harvey, David. 2005. *A Brief History of Neoliberalism*. Oxford: Oxford University Press.

Harvey, David. 2010. *A Companion to Marx's Capital*. London: Verso.

Harvey, David. 2014. *Seventeen Contradictions and the End of Capitalism*. Oxford: Oxford University Press.

Haug, Wolfgang Fritz. 1986. *Critique of Commodity Aesthetics*. Cambridge: Polity Press.

Heim, Michael. 1999. The Cyberspace Dialectic. In *The Digital Dialectic*, edited by Peter Lunenfeld, 24–45. Cambridge, MA: MIT Press.

Herman, Edward S. 1998. The Reopening of Marx's System. *New Politics* 6 (4): 131–135.

Hobsbawm, Eric. 2011. *How to Change the World. Marx and Marxism 1840–2011*. London: Little, Brown.

Horkheimer, Max. 1937/2002. Traditional and Critical Theory. In *Critical Theory*, 188–252. New York: Continuum.

Horkheimer, Max. 1947/1974. *Eclipse of Reason*. New York: Continuum.

Huws, Ursula. 2014. The Underpinnings of Class in the Digital Age: Living, Labour and Value. *Socialist Register* 50: 80–107.

Jacobs, Katrien, Marije Janssen and Matteo Pasquinelli, eds. 2007. *C'LICK ME. A Netporn Studies Reader*. Amsterdam: Institute of Network Cultures.

Jameson, Frederic. 2011. *Representing Capital*. London: Verso.

Jevons, W. Stanley. 1871. *The Theory of Political Economy*. London: Macmillan. Fifth edition.

Jones, Steve. 2006. Foreword. Dreams of a Field: Possible Trajectories of Internet Studies. In *Critical Cyberculture Studies*, edited by David Silver and Adrienne Massanari, ix–xvii. New York: New York University Press.

Keen, Andrew. 2006. Web 2.0. The Second Generation of the Internet Has Arrived. It's Worse Than You Think. *The Weekly Standard*, May 16.

Keen, Andrew. 2007. *The Cult of the Amateuer: How Today's Internet is Killing Our Culture*. New York: Currency.

Kellner, Douglas. 1989. *Critical Theory, Marxism and Modernity*. Baltimore, MD: Johns Hopkins University Press.

Kellner, Douglas 1995. *Cultural Studies, Identity and Politics between the Modern and the Postmodern*. New York: Routledge.

Kellner, Douglas. 2002. Theorizing Globalization. *Sociological Theory* 20 (3): 285–305.

Kellner, Douglas. 2009. Toward a Critical Media/Cultural Studies. In *Media/Cultural Studies: Critical Approaches,* edited by Rhonda Hammer and Douglas Kellner, 5–24. New York: Peter Lang.

Kelly, Kevin. 1998. *New Rules for the New Economy*. New York: Viking.

Kelly, Kevin. 2009. 009, 2009. The New Socialism. *Wired,* June 2009: 116–121.

Kliman, Andrew. 2012. *The Failure of Capitalist Production. Underlying Causes of the Great Recession*. New York: Pluto.

Kline, Stephen, Nick Dyer-Witheford and Greg De Peuter. 2003. *Digital Play: The Interaction of Technology, Culture and Marketing*. Montreal: McGill-Queen's University Press.

Knoche, Manfred. 2005. Kommunikationswissenschaftliche Medienökonomie als Kritik der Politischen Ökonomie der Medien. In *Internationale partizipatorische Kommunikationspolitik,* edited Petra Ahrweiler and Barbara Thomaß, pp. 101–109. Münster: LIT.

Lanier, Jaron. 2006. The Hazards of the New Online Collectivism. *Edge – The Third Culture.* Retrieved from http://www.edge.org/3rd_culture/lanier06/lanier06_index .html.

Lebowitz, Michael A. 1986. Too Many Blindspots on the Media. *Studies in Political Economy* 21: 165–173.

Lovink, Geert. 1997. Von der spekulativen Medientheorie zur Netzkritik. *Telepolis,* January 1.

Lovink, Geert. 2002. *Dark Fiber. Tracking Critical Internet Culture*. Cambridge, MA: MIT Press.

Lovink, Geert. 2008. *Zero Comments. Blogging and Critical Internet Culture*. New York: Routledge.

Lovink, Geert. 2013. A World Beyond Facebook. Introduction to the Unlike Us Reader. In Unlike Us Reader. Social Media Monopolies and their Alternatives, ed. Geert Lovink and Miriam Rasch, 9–15. Amsterdam: Institute of Network Cultures.

Lovink, Geert and Sabine Niederer, eds. 2008. *Video Vortex Reader. Responses to YouTube*. Amsterdam: Institute of Network Cultures.

Lovink, Geert and Korinna Patelis. 2013. *Unlike Us Research Agenda. July 15th, 2011*. In *Unlike Us Reader. Social Media Monopolies and their Alternatives,* ed. Geert Lovink and Miriam Rasch, 364–372. Amsterdam: Institute of Network Cultures.

Lovink, Geert and Miriam Rasch, ed. 2013. *Unlike Us Reader. Social Media Monopolies and their Alternatives*. Amsterdam: Institute of Network Cultures.

Lovink, Geert and Ned Rossiter, eds. 2007. *MyCreativity Reader. A Critique of Creative Industries*. Amsterdam: Institute of Network Cultures.

Lovink, Geert and Trebor Scholz, eds. 2005. *The Art of Free Cooperation*. New York: Autonomedia.

Lovink, Geert and Pit Schultz. 1997. Aufruf zur Netzkritik. In *Netzkritik*, edited by nettime, 5–14. Berlin: Edition ID-Archiv.

Lovink, Geert and Soenke Zehle, eds. 2005. *Incommunicado Reader*. Amsterdam: Institute of Network Cultures.

Lunenfeld, Peter. 1999. Introduction: Screen Grabs: The Digital Dialectic and New Media Theory. In *DigitalThe Dialectic*, edited by Peter Lunenfeld, xiv-xxi. Cambridge, MA: MIT Press.

Luxemburg, Rosa. 1913/2003. *The Accumulation of Capital*. New York: Routledge.

Macek, Steve. 2006. Divergent Critical Approaches to New Media. *New Media & Society* 8 (6): 1031–1038.

Marcuse, Herbert. 1941. *Reason and Revolution. Hegel and the Rise of Social Theory.* New York: Humanity Books.

Marcuse, Herbert. 1964. *One-Dimensional Man.* New York: Routledge.

Marx, Karl. 1844. *Ecomomic and Philosophic Manuscripts of 1844.* Mineola, NY: Dover.

Marx, Karl. 1857/1858. *The Grundrisse.* London: Penguin.

Marx, Karl. 1863. *Theories of Surplus Value.* Volume 1. London: Lawrence & Wishart.

Marx, Karl. 1867. *Capital: Critique of the Political Economy. Volume 1.* London: Penguin.

Marx, Karl. 1871. The Civil War in France. In *OneSelected Works In Volume*, 237–295. London: Lawrence & Wishart.

Marx, Karl. 1875. Critique of the Gotha Programme. In *OneSelected Works In Volume*, 297–317. London: Lawrence & Wishart.

Marx, Karl. 1885. *Capital: Critique of the Political Economy.* Volume 2. London: Penguin.

Marx, Karl. 1894. *Capital. Volume 3.* London: Penguin.

Marx, Karl and Friedrich Engels. 1846. *The German Ideology.* Amherst, NY: Prometheus.

Marx, Karl and Friedrich Engels. 1968. *Selected Works in One Volume.* London: Lawrence & Wishart.

McChesney, Robert W. 2007. *Communication Revolution.* New York: New Press.

McNally, David. 2011. *Global Slump. The Economics and Politics of Crisis and Resistance.* Oakland: PM Press.

MEW. 1962ff. *Marx-Engels-Werke.* Berlin: Dietz.

MECW. 1975ff. Marx-Engels-*Collected Works.* New York: International Publishers.

Mies, Maria. 1986. Patriarchy & Accumulation on a World Scale. Women in the International Division of Labour. London: Zed Books.

Moglen, Eben. 2003. *The dotCommunist Manifesto.* Retrieved August 8, 2010, from http://emoglen.law.columbia.edu/my_pubs/dcm.html#tex2html2.

Mosco, Vincent. 2004. *The Digital Sublime.* Cambridge, MA: MIT Press.

Mosco, Vincent. 2009. *The Political Economy of Communication*. London: Sage. 2nd edition.

Murdock, Graham and Peter Golding. 2005. Culture, Communications and Political Economy. In *Mass Media and Society*, edited by James Curran and Michael Gurevitch, 60–83. 4th Edition. New York: Hodder Arnold.

Nielsen. 2013. *Paid Social Media Advertising. Industry Update and Best Practices 2013*. New York: Nielsen.

O'Connor, James. 1998. *Natural Causes*. New York: Guilford.

Patelis, Korinna. 2000. The Political Economy of the Internet. In *Media Organisations in Society*, edited by James Curran, 84–107. London: Arnold.

Popper, Karl R. 1962. Zur Logik der Sozialwissenschaften. *Kölner Zeitschrift für Soziologie und Sozialpsychologie* 14 (2): 233–248.

Pun, Ngai and Jenny Chan. 2012. Global Capital, the State, and Chinese Workers: The Foxconn Experience. *Modern China* 38 (4): 383–410.

Qiu, Jack Lunchuan. 2012. Network Labor: Beyond the Shadow of Foxconn. In *Studying Mobile Media: Cultural Technologies, Mobile Communication, and the iPhone*, ed. Larissa Hjorth, Jean Burgess and Ingrid Richardson, 173–189. New York: Routledge.

Reveley, James. 2013. The Exploitative Web: Misuses of Marx in Critical Social Media Studies. Science & Society 77 (4): 512–535.

Rigi, Jakob and Robert Prey. 2014. Value, Rent, and the Political Economy of Social Media. The Information Society (forthcoming).

Rossiter, Ned. 2006. *Organized Networks*. Rotterdam: NAi.

Sandoval, Marisol. 2013. Foxconned Labour as the Dark Side of the Information Age: Working Conditions at Apple's Contract Manufacturers in China. *tripleC: Communication, Capitalism & Critique* 11 (2): 318–347.

Scholz, Trebor, ed. 2012. *Digital Labor. The Internet as Playground and Factory*. New York: Routledge.

Silver, David. 2006a. Introduction: Where is Internet Studies. In *Critical Cyberculture Studies*, edited by David Silver and Adrienne Massanari, 1–14. New York: New York University Press.

Silver, David. 2006b. Looking Backwards, Looking Forwards: Cyberculture Studies 1990–2000. In *Cybercultures. Critical Concepts in Media and Cultural Studies, Volume II*, edited by David Bell, 61–79. New York: Routledge.

Silver, David and Adrienne Massanari, eds. 2006. *Critical Cyberculture Studies*. New York: New York University Press.

Smythe, Dallas W. 1981. *Dependency Road*. Norwood, NJ: Ablex.

Smythe, Dallas W. 1994. *Counterclockwise*. Boulder, CO: Westview Press.

Socialist International. 1951. Aims and Tasks of the Socialist International. Retrieved August 8, 2010, from http://www.socialistinternational.org/viewArticle.cfm?ArticleID=39.

Stahl, Bernd C. 2008. *Information Systems: Critical Perspectives*. New York: Routledge.

Sterne, Jonathan. 2006. Thinking the Internet: Cultural studies versus the Millennium. In *Cybercultures. Critical Concepts in Media and Cultural Studies, Volume II*, edited by David Bell, 80–106. New York: Routledge.

Students & Scholars against Corporate Misbehaviour (SACOM). 2011. *iSlave behind the iPhone. Foxconn workers in Central China.* Available at: http://sacom.hk/wp-content/uploads/2011/09/20110924-islave-behind-the-iphone.pdf.

Sussman, Gerald. 1999. On the Political Economy of Communication. *Journal of Media Economics* 12 (2): 85–87.

Taylor, Paul A. 2009. Critical Theory 2.0 and Im/materiality: The bug in the Machinic Flows. *Interactions: Studies in Communication and Culture* 1 (1): 93–110.

Terranova, Tiziana. 2004. *Network Culture*. London: Pluto.

Therborn, Göran. 2008. *From Marxism to Post-Marxism?* London: Verso.

Turner, Graeme. 2003. *British Cultural Studies*. London: Routledge.

Virno, Paolo and Michael Hardt, eds. 1996. *Radical Thought in Italy*. Minneapolis, MN: University of Minnesota Press.

Žižek, Slavoj. 2008. *In Defense of Lost Causes*. London: Verso.

Žižek, Slavoj. 2009. *First as Tragedy, Then as Farce*. London: Verso.

Žižek, Slavoj. 2010a. How to Begin from the Beginning. In *The Idea of Communism*, edited by Žižek Slavoj and Costas Douzinas, 209–226. London: Verso.

Žižek, Slavoj. 2010b. *Living in the End Times*. London: Verso.

Žižek, Slavoj and Costas Douzinas, eds. 2010. *The Idea of Communism*. London: Verso.

CHAPTER 3

Digital Marx: Toward a Political Economy of Distributed Media

Andreas Wittel

1   Introduction

This is the claim: In the age of *mass media* the political economy of media has engaged with Marxist concepts in a rather limited way. In the age of *digital media* Marxist theory could and should be applied in a much broader sense to this field of research. For Marxist theorists this development is to be applauded, as it allows a broader inclusion and appropriation of his concepts. The article will provide a rationale for this claim with a two step approach.

The first step is to produce evidence for the claim that political economy of mass media engaged with Marxist theory in a rather limited way. It is also to explain the logic behind this limited engagement and to explain why digital media – or better: digital things – open up new and promising possibilities to incorporate a broader range of central Marxist concepts for an analysis of both, digital media (specifically) and (more generally) capitalism in the information age.

The second step – which really is the core objective of this article – is an exploration of key concepts of Marx's political economy – such as *labour, value, property and struggle* – and a brief outline of their relevance for a critical analysis of digital media or digital things. These key concepts are particularly relevant for a deeper understanding of phenomena such as non-market production, peer production, and the digital commons, and for interventions in debates on free culture, intellectual property, and free labour.

Part of this article is a critical inspection of the *free labour* concept, which was highly productive for an illumination of new developments in the social web but which suffers from a lack of analytical rigour and conflates a number of rather different practices. One of the key challenges in digital capitalism is the need to rethink labour for those human activities that blossom outside wage-based relations and other forms of commodified labour. In order to take the debate on free labour forward, I want to argue that we need to discuss labour. In order to think about labour we need to think about property, value and the value theory of labour.

Many of the conclusions I draw on in this article can only be achieved through struggle. A very brief remark on struggle points towards the relationship between digital media and social movements. In the digital age the political economy of media can occupy new territory with an inspection of direct action and its various forms of mediation.

2   The Political Economy of Mass Media

The political economy of media has been constituted as an academic field in the age of *mass media*, which are characterised by linear forms and one-way flows of communication, where content is being distributed from a small number of producers to a large number of recipients.

Outlining the key issues, questions, debates and findings of an academic field in a few paragraphs is always a difficult undertaking that leads to oversimplifications, questionable generalisations, and the privileging of a coherent narrative at the expense of a more nuanced perspective. This is also true for the field of political economy of media and communication. It is quite surprising however that there does exist a rather broad consensus of what this field is about. Comparing a number of introductions to this field (Mosco 1996; Devereux 2003; McQuail 2005; Durham and Kellner 2006; Laughey 2009; Burton 2010) it becomes rather obvious that there is not much disagreement about key issues, questions and findings that have been produced in the political economy of media and communication.

It starts with the observation that media institutions have increasingly become privatised and turned into businesses. This is seen as problematic as media industries are seen as not just any industry. To understand the unusual character of the media industries one has to examine the dual nature of the content being produced, which is simultaneously a commodity and a public good. It is a private good – a commodity – as media industries are using their products for the accumulation of profit. At the same time this content is a public good as it constitutes to some degree the public sphere. So on the one hand media institutions have a social, cultural, and political function, on the other hand they are driven by economic interests. It is this dual nature of media content which makes the assumption that media are an independent force, naturally safeguarding democracy and the public interest rather questionable. Equally doubtful is the assumption that mass media just mirror public opinion.

The political economy of media is based on the premise that media are powerful, that they are able to influence public opinion and shape public discourse. Therefore it is crucial to focus on the production of media content within a wider political and economic context. It is this focus on materiality and the political, economical, and technological conditions in which media content is being produced that distinguishes the political economy of media from other academic fields such as the more affirmative strands within cultural studies and audience studies, which generally locate power and control not with media institutions but with an active audience as the true producer of meaning.[1] The political economy of media is as much social analysis as media and communication analysis.

This field is mainly concerned with the following issues: Firstly with an understanding of the media market. How do media companies produce income and generate profits? Secondly with an inspection of questions of ownership of media organisations (public, commercial, and private non-profit organisations) and an analysis of the implications of ownership structures with respect to media products (obviously this is especially relevant for the production of news). Thirdly the field is concerned with changing dynamics of the media sector, in particular with developments such as internationalisation of media industries, concentration and conglomeration of media organisations, and diversification of media products. This leads into debates on cultural imperialism and media imperialism. The fourth issue is about media regulation, media policy, and media governance, originally on a national level but increasingly with a global perspective. It is important to note that these areas of inquiry are closely connected, in fact they overlap considerably.

In order to introduce the key claims of political economy of media in the shortest possible way, I will refer to a summary box in Denis McQuail (2005, 100). According to him, these are the core findings:

- Economic control and logic are determinant
- Media structure tends towards concentration
- Global integration of media develops
- Contents and audiences are commodified
- Diversity decreases
- Opposition and alternative voices are marginalised
- Public interest in communication is subordinate to private interests

Raymond Williams who is usually not portrayed as someone who is part of the inner circle of political economy of media was in fact among the first to develop such an approach. In an essay on the growth of the newspaper industry in England he starts with the observation that "there is still a quite widespread

---

1   For an analysis of the tensions between cultural studies and political economy see Kellner 1995 and Wittel 2004, for an analysis of the disagreements between political economy of media and active audience studies see Schiller 1989, 135–157.

failure to co-ordinate the history of the press with the economic and social history within which it must necessarily be interpreted" (Williams 1961, 194). He sets out to develop such a perspective, studying empirically a period of 170 years. His findings are highly sceptical:

> These figures do not support the idea of a steady if slow development of a better press. The market is being steadily specialised, in direct relation to advertising income, and the popular magazine for all kinds of reader is being steadily driven This does not even begin to look like the developing press of an educated democracy. Instead it looks like an increasingly organised market in communications, with the 'masses' formula as the dominant social principle and with the varied functions of the press increasingly limited to finding a 'selling point'.
>
> WILLIAMS 1961, 234

If we juxtapose this passage with the key claims in McQuail's summary box it becomes clear that Williams anticipated many of the themes and results that will be debated within this field over the next five decades. The quoted summary in his study is like a microcosm of the field.

3   Marx and the Political Economy of Mass Media

The theoretical roots of political economy of media – at least their critical tradition (which is all I am concerned with) – are usually located in Marxism. After all and as the name already indicates, this field within media studies explores communication from a political economy perspective. So how much engagement with Marx do we get in this academic field? The short answer: there is some engagement but it is fairly limited. In order to support this claim with some evidence I will check a number of texts that are generally considered to be important contributions.[2]

The first and rather surprising insight is that a considerable number of books (Herman and Chomsky 1988; Schiller 1989; Curran 1990; Herman and

---

2 To keep this analysis simple, I will ignore here German Marxist media theory (Brecht, Krakauer, Benjamin, Adorno, Enzensberger) at the beginning of the mass media age, a line of thought which – perhaps wrongly – is usually not included in the field of political economy of media. The texts I have chosen to consider are certainly not extensive, they are also not representative in any way, but they do provide a solid indication on the relation between this field and Marxist theory.

McChesney 1997; Curran and Seaton 1997; Grossberg et al 1998; Curran 2000; Nichols and McChesney 2006) have either no reference at all or less than a handful of references to Marx or Marxism. In the latter case these references function usually as signposts (such as to distinguish Marxists from liberal traditions of political economy). They do not engage with Marxist theory in a more profound manner.

Nevertheless they are all rooted in Marxist theory, or to be more precise, in one particular part of Marxist theory. They are all directly linked to the base and superstructure model. According to Marx human society consists of two parts, a base and a superstructure. The material base consists of the forces and relations of production, the superstructure refers to the non-material realm, to culture, religion, ideas, values and norms. The relationship between base and superstructure is reciprocal, however in the last instance the base determines the superstructure. This model has been developed in various writings of Marx and Engels, perhaps most famously in the preface to *A Contribution to the Critique of Political Economy* (Marx 1977) and in the *German Ideology* (Marx and Engels 1974).

> The mode of production of material life conditions the general process of social, political, and intellectual life. It is not the consciousness of men that determines their existence, but their social existence that determines their consciousness. (Marx 1977)
>
> The ideas of the ruling class are in every epoch the ruling ideas, i.e. the class which is the ruling material force of society, is at the same time its ruling intellectual force. The class which has the means of material production at its disposal, has control at the same time over the means of mental production, so that thereby, generally speaking, the ideas of those who lack the means of mental production are subject to it. The ruling ideas are nothing more than the ideal expression of the dominant material relationships, the dominant material relationships grasped as ideas; hence of the relationships which make the one class the ruling one, therefore, the ideas of its dominance [...] Insofar, therefore, as they rule as a class and determine the extent and compass of an epoch, it is self-evident that they do this in its whole range, hence among other things rule also as thinkers, as producers of ideas, and regulate the production and distribution of the ideas of their age: thus their ideas are the ruling ideas of the epoch.
>
> MARX AND ENGELS 1974, 64 F.

The texts mentioned above directly or indirectly apply the base and superstructure model to the media industry, which like no other industrial sector contributes to the production of the superstructure. However they apply this model in various ways and there is considerable disagreement about what some see as a deterministic model with a linear, non-dialectical, and reductionist perspective.

Durham and Kellner observe that "the focus in US-based political economy of communication tends to emphasize the economic side of the equation with focus on ownership, corporatization, and consumption, while in Britain there has been a spotlighting of the political dimension, with emphasis on public sector broadcasting, the importance of state-supported and regulated communication, and the politics of broadcasting." (Durham and Kellner 2006, 197) I would take this observation one step further: The US-based work on political economy of media is generally more in line with the base and superstructure model, whereas the research in Britain is slightly more critical of a material or economic reductionism. I would also suggest that these different positions are related to the media landscape in both countries, a free-market media landscape in the US and Britain still relying on a strong representation of public-sector broadcasting. It is no coincidence that the propaganda model (Herman and Chomsky 1988) has been developed in the US. Neither is it surprising that it is a US study that diagnoses a complete and systematic failure of critical journalism on the reporting of the Iraq war, and claims that the US media bring about a "destruction of democracy" that "a highly concentrated profit-driven media system...makes it rational to gut journalism and irrational to provide the content a free society so desperately requires." (Nichols and McChesney 2005, ix) Similar claims could not be found in British research with its rather critical position towards the base and superstructure model. Curran for example observes that "a sea change has occurred in the field," which is mostly about the "repudiation of the totalising explanatory frameworks of Marxism" (Curran 1990, 157 f.).

So far I have only referred to those texts with either no reference at all to Marxist theory or with only few references which then usually function like signposts. There are however texts that engage with Marx and in particular with his base and superstructure model in a more profound way. Mosco (1996) who provides perhaps the most detailed analysis of the literature in this field starts his books with an introduction to Marxist political economy. Murdock (1982) focuses in particular on the base and superstructure model and compares it with a more praxis-oriented perspective. Williams (1958, 265–284) engages in great detail with this model and argues that it is more complex than usually acknowledged (e.g. that this relation is reciprocal rather than a one way street). "The basic question, as it has normally been put, is whether the economic element is in fact determining. I have followed the controversies on this, but it seems to me that it is, ultimately, an unanswerable question." (Williams 1958, 280). Like Williams, Nicholas Garnham (1990) also counters charges of economic reductionism. He insists that Marx's model offers an adequate foundation for an understanding of the political economy of mass media. He moves away from a deterministic view of the relation between base and superstructure towards a model that is more anchored in reciprocity and a dialectic relation.

Let us conclude: Apart from some rare exceptions – most notably Dallas Smythe who will be discussed later – political economy of *mass media* incorporates Marxist theory in a rather limited way. This academic field refers predominantly to Marx's concept of base and superstructure (either directly or indirectly) to make claims about the relationship between ownership of means of production (and concentration of ownership, media conglomerates etc.) and questions of media content, ideology, manipulation, power and democracy.

To avoid any misunderstandings: This is not meant as a critique of political economists of *mass* media. I do not see this limited appropriation of Marxist concepts as a failure of this academic field. My point is very different. I want to argue that this limited appropriation made complete sense in the age of mass media. It has a logic to it that lies very much in mass media technologies. This will be discussed in more detail in the following section. It should also be noted, very much in line with my argument, that over the last decade, which marks the transition from mass media to distributed media, Marx has been rediscovered by political economists. Even more so, he has been rediscovered in ways that are not just rehearsals of the base and superstructure debate.[3]

4   Digital Technologies

What is the logic behind this rather restricted appropriation of Marxist theory? One might point out – referring again to the base and superstructure argument – that Marx was obviously more interested in the former and has thus neglected an analysis of the latter; that Marx did not have a lot to say about media and

---

3   Perhaps the first thorough appropriation of Marx's concepts for *distributed* media has been produced by Nick Dyer-Witheford (1999). He analyses how the information age, "far from transcending the historic conflict between capital and its laboring subjects constitutes the latest battleground in their encounter" (Dyer-Witheford 1999, 2). Since then other books have emerged with an explicit Marxist approach to theorise the Internet, e.g. Wayne 2003; Huws and Leys 2003; Stallabrass 2003; Wark 2004; Terranova 2004; Artz, Macek and Cloud 2006; Jhally 2006; Fuchs 2008; Mosco, McKercher, and Huws 2010; Kleiner 2010; Fuchs 2011, Fuchs et al. 2012).

communication. No doubt this is a persuasive argument. However this would not explain why in the age of digital media, so my claim, Marxist concepts could and should be applied in a much broader sense by political economists of communication.

We will probably get closer to an answer if we turn our attention to *media technologies*. In the age of mass media these technologies – the means of production – were expensive. Most people could not afford the ownership of all those assets necessary for print media or broadcast media. As a consequence there were only a limited number of media organisations which produced and disseminated media content to a huge number of consumers/recipients. Thus *mass media* are characterised by a small number of content producers and a large audience. For societies that perceive themselves as liberal democracies this is a rather problematic starting point. In fact no other issue about mass media is as problematic as the ownership of means of production and processes of media concentration, the ownership of media technologies and media organisations in the hands of increasingly fewer 'media moguls'. The limited appropriation of Marxist theory in the age of mass media results from a very specific *historic reality*, from historically unique concerns that were generated by *mass media technologies*.

Digital technologies have brought about a fundamentally different media landscape, where mass media are not the only show in town any more. They have been given company by *distributed media* and increasingly they seem to be replaced by this new kid on the block. Distributed media operate with a very different organisational logic. Whereas mass media are hierarchical, linear, with a control centre and one-way flow of media content from few producers to many recipients, distributed media are networked, non-linear, with multi-directional and reciprocal flows of media content from many producers to many consumers.

The terms *distributed* media and *digital* media are similar but not identical. I use the term *distributed media* to put an emphasis on the *social organisation* of media (even though this term also refers to Internet technologies), while the term *digital media* is used to refer to *technology only*. It is important to stress however that the social can never be fully separated from the technological. Every medium is simultaneously technological and social. Technological structures and relations between human beings are interlocked and mutually constitutive.

The logic of distributed media is profoundly shaped by the qualities and capabilities of digital technologies, which are superior to mass media technologies (say the printing press) in that they are much cheaper and much more efficient in a number of ways: (1) They can re-mediate older media forms such as text, sound, image and moving images as digital code; (2) they can integrate communication and information, or communication media (the letter, the telephone) with mass media (radio, television, newspaper); (3) digital objects can endlessly be reproduced at minimum costs; (4) they don't carry any weight, thus they can be distributed at the speed of light.

These phenomenological qualities of digital technologies, which rely largely on a distinction between bits and atoms, I want to argue, have profound implications for the social. Firstly the number of media producers increases dramatically in the digital age. Now everybody with access to a mobile phone or a laptop and access to a network is a potential producer of media content. Secondly digital technologies enable new social forms of media production and media distribution, for example large scale 'sharing' of media content[4] and large scale forms of collaboration and peer production such as open source code. Thirdly, as the number of media producers increases media themselves are becoming ubiquitous in that all aspects of the social world and our lives become mediated, from the global and public to the most intimate aspects of our existence (Livingstone 2009). Fourthly and perhaps most importantly digital technologies are not just media technologies. They are built into all productive processes (Castells 1996). The digital economy now is not just the ITC economy any more, it is simply the economy full stop. As a consequence of this process the digital does not just refer to the realm of media, but to new forms of production based on ICT s, and possibly (depending on the success of future struggles) to a new mode of production, to a 'commons-based peer production' (Benkler 2006). For this reason a political economy of digital media really is a political economy of digital things. It is this opening up of media from few professionals to many amateurs and from the state and markets to non-markets, and the blurring of boundaries between media industries and other industrial sectors, that suggest the possibility of a broader engagement with Marxist theory. In the digital age indeed all aspects of Marx's political economy become relevant for critical media theory.

A quick comment on *technological determinism*. This phenomenological analysis of digital things and their implications is not, in my view, an example of technological determinism. I do not want to suggest that all explanatory power lies with technologies and people are mere bystanders reacting to them. However I am also not very sympathetic to arguments on the opposite end that position all aspects of agency with people. Social determinism is as dangerous as technological determinism. My argument, which is broadly in line with Marx's thinking, is that technologies open up new possibilities for social production

---

4 For a critical analysis of sharing in the digital age see Wittel 2011.

and social organisation. They do not determine in any way the future of capitalism, which of course will solely be shaped by the struggles of the oppressed.

It is perhaps due to a rather strong aversion against technological determinism within the field of political economy of mass media that commentators have been a bit slow to acknowledge the profound difference between mass media and distributed media. Different responses and strategies have been employed to demonstrate that the new – meaning the so-called digital revolution – is highly overvalued. The first type of response (e.g. Murdock 2004) rejects any re-evaluation and argues that the digital age is not significantly different from the age of mass media and that historical continuities are more important than differences. Rather than falling for 'digital possibilities' political economists should study 'market realities'. The information society does not really exist, it is only 'presumed'. (Murdock and Golding 2001). The second type of response, the sitting-on-the fence approach (e.g. Curran and Seaton 2003, 235–293), is more cautious. It consists of a hesitation to take position and to make claims about changes with respect to digital technologies. A third type of response (e.g. Mosco 2004) consists of the deconstruction of this discourse, in particular of claims made by Internet-philiacs.

Indeed it would be naïve to ignore continuities. Equally dangerous however is a position that argues for business as usual. Let us explain this with an example. The issue of ownership of means of production, which largely dominated the discourse of political economy of mass media, will not lose any relevance in the age of distributed media. On the contrary, it will become an even more important topic as new concerns are emerging. However this issue needs to be re-conceptualised in two significant ways. *Firstly*: In the age of mass media the issue of ownership of means of production was only relevant with respect to media content. In the age of distributed media the issue of ownership of means of production is relevant with respect to media content, but also with respect to connectivity. This is not just about ideology and the manipulation of messages any more (base and superstructure), but also about the ownership of infrastructures, of networks and platforms that allow users to socialise, communicate, and collaborate. This is not just about meaning and representation, it is about the control of people's online interactions, it is ultimately about privileging certain forms of sociality and subjectivity. The *second* reason for a re-conceptualisation lies in the notion of 'means of production'. In the age of distributed media the means of production have become more democratic. Users with access to a computer and access to the Internet (which is more than one billion people) and some basic computer skills have the means necessary to produce media content. What they do not have however are the *means of distribution* and the *means of online storage* of media content. The means of distribution and the means of storage lie in the hands of few media conglomerates. They control the flows of information. They belong to what Wark describes as the vectoral class. "The vectoral class is driving the world to the brink of disaster, but it also opens up the world to the resources for overcoming its own destructive tendencies." (Wark 2004, 025) The analysis of this class struggle between capital and labouring subjects about the future framing of the Internet is also one of the key objectives of Dyer-Witheford (1999). To summarise this paragraph: With respect to means of production we can see important historical continuities but also some remarkable shifts.

Dmytri Kleiner starts his book with a bang: "What is possible in the information age is in direct conflict with what is permissible [...] The non-hierarchical relations made possible by a peer network such as the Internet are contradictory with capitalism's need for enclosure and control. It is a battle to the death; either the Internet as we know it must go, or capitalism as we know it must go." (Kleiner 2010, 7).

Of course this is a mildly exaggerated view. There is not just war going on, we can also see the development of new forms of co-operation and new models and arrangements between both sides. Still, I like this quote a lot as it is a pointed and condensed outline of the responsibility of political economy in the age of digital media and distributed networks. There is a technology that opens up new productive forces; there is a political-economic system with established relations of production. There is struggle between those who want to conserve existing relations of production and those who attempt to overcome them. And there is an indication of how to create a better world. Could the Internet in its more uncontrolled form teach us how to think about society at large?

We are already in the middle of Marx's political economy. In the following parts I want to discuss how some core concepts of his political economy become relevant for an analysis of media in the digital age. I will focus on four central terms, on *labour, value, property, and struggle*. Among these four concepts the notion of labour will be explored in more detail.

5   Labour

Throughout the last century labour has been analysed in the western hemisphere as wage labour only. Apart from the writings of very few Marxist theorists such as *André* Gorz (1999), alternatives to wage labour have hardly entered public discourse. It was a common perception that there was just no alternative to wage labour. Obviously this theoretical orientation was a reflection of an economic reality characterised largely by wage labour as the dominant form of production. This is how media production was organised in the age of mass media. No matter whether media institutions were public institutions or private companies, these institutions had employees who have received a wage in return for their work.

The contemporary media ecosystem looks profoundly different. Media content now is not only produced by employees working in and for companies, it is also created by the free labour of those who engage in peer production (the dissemination of content) and 'commons-based peer production', a term coined by Yochai Benkler (2002) to describe a new model of socio-economic production, in which large numbers of people work towards common goals without financial compensation for contributors. Media content now is not just produced for markets and paying audiences, there is also a rather significant non-market dimension to media production. This is a new situation. In fact the media and creative industries are at the moment the only industrial sector that is confronted with competition from free labour and non-market production.

The emergence of non-market production started in the 1980s with the open-source movement but has accelerated on an astonishing scale during the last decade with the social web. It has spread from the peer production of software and code to text, sound, images, and moving images. These digital commons are software commons, news commons, information commons, knowledge commons, education commons, art commons, and cultural commons.

Undeniably the digital whirlwind has created havoc in the creative industries. Newspaper journalism is in decline and struggling to find new business models. The title of a collection of essays on the collapse of journalism in the United States – "Will the last reporter please turn out the lights" (McChesney and Pickard 2011) – is an indication of the severity of this development. The music, film and publishing industries are also hit hard and are turning increasingly to legal enforcements of copyright infringement and to political lobbying for tighter regulations of the Internet (e.g. ACTA, SOPA, PIPA).

Many of the implications of this new media ecosystem however are not clear at all. Will this co-existence of corporate labour and free labour in the digital commons remain exclusively in the media industries and creative industries or will it spread to other industrial sectors as well? What are the relations between the media and creative industries and the digital commons? Are we in the middle of an 'immaterial civil war' (Pasquinelli 2007)? Or is such a perspective too one-dimensional as we can also see a number of collaborations between both sides, for example the corporate funding of open source software production? What are the long-term implications of this for the labour market in the media industries? It is likely that the rationalisation of media and cultural production due to digital technologies will lead to a shrinking of the market. But if it does, how dramatically will it shrink? Finally what does this mean for the rate of productivity in the media industries? Does capital profit from an exploitation of free labour or will the competition from the new kid on the block lead to a decline of productivity in the industry?

In order to better understand this new media ecology we need to focus on the concept of free labour. The first thing to note is that, while this term has recently been employed by Marxist theorists, Marx himself does not use the term free labour. Marx, partly in the tradition of classical political economy in the 18th and 19th century, partly developing a critique of this tradition, distinguishes between productive and unproductive labour. These are not neutral terms, they depend on class positions and they depend on specific types of society (feudal, capitalist etc.) and their specific relations of production. In capitalism productive labour is labour that is productive for capital. It produces commodities, exchange value, and profit (surplus value). Unproductive labour does not produce surplus value. To give an example: A person employed in a private household to perform tasks such as cooking and cleaning does not produce a commodity. While his or her labour-power is sold as a commodity, the product of this labour-power is not. Therefore this is unproductive labour. A cook working in as an employee in a restaurant however produces commodities, he or she produces meals that are sold to customers. Therefore this is productive labour. So productive and unproductive labour are not distinguished with respect to what people do (in both cases they cook), but with respect to their relation to capital and the commodity form. Applying the free labour of digital commoners to this concept it is obvious that according to Marx free labour is unproductive. Not very surprising this concept has received much criticism from Marxist feminists in the 1980s who argued that domestic labour, usually performed by women, would indeed create surplus value as this arrangement makes it possible to reduce wages even more for those who do not perform domestic labour. In my view this is a strong argument. Even more so it poses a real challenge to Marx's theory of surplus value.

Also relevant for the free labour concept is Marx distinction between labour and labour-process. Let us begin with labour:

> Labour is, in the first place, a process in which both man and Nature participate, and in which man of his own accord starts, regulates, and controls the material re-actions between himself and Nature. He opposes himself to Nature as one of her own forces, setting in motion arms and legs, head and hands, the natural forces of his body, in order to appropriate

Nature's productions in a form adapted to his own wants. By thus acting on the external world and changing it, he at the same time changes his own nature.

CAPITAL VOL. 1, 177

Labour is not merely an economic but a human activity. It is a universal category of human existence and it is independent of any specific economic or social forms. Labour is what keeps us alive and what makes us develop. This is a rather broad concept. Labour can be equated with action or with praxis. Labour is what we do.

In stark contrast to labour, his concept of labour-process refers to specific historic modes of production and to specific historic societies and economies. With this historical approach he wants to demonstrate that the labour-process, the specific organisation of work, is not inevitable. Existing labour-processes can always be overcome. Marx is particularly interested in the difference between a feudal and a capitalist labour-process. In capitalism the labour-process is based on wage-labour, on the fact that the worker sells his labour-power as a commodity to the capitalist. Comparing the feudal labour-process with the capitalist labour-process Marx highlights two things:

First, the labourer works under the control of the capitalist to whom his labour belongs; the capitalist taking good care that the work is done in a proper manner, and that the means of production are used with intelligence, so that there is no unnecessary waste of raw material, and no wear and tear of the implements beyond what is necessarily caused by the work. Secondly, the product is the property of the capitalist and not that of the labourer, its immediate producer. Suppose that a capitalist pays for a day's labour-power at its value; then the right to use that power for a day belongs to him, just as much as the right to use any other commodity, such as a horse that he has hired for the day [...] The labour-process is a process between things that the capitalist has purchased, things that have become his property.

CAPITAL VOL. 1, 184 F.

Here Marx has identified two forms of alienation that did not exist in feudalism or in any other mode of production before capitalism. The first form of alienation refers to the product of the worker's own work and the inability to use the product of this own work for his or her living. The second form of alienation refers to the inability to organise the process of work, which lies exclusively in the hands of the capitalist who owns the means of production. Let us apply again the concept of free labour to Marx distinction between labour and labour-process. Free labour then is always labour in the general sense of Marx concept. However the term does not refer to a specific historical labour-process. In a strictly Marxist framework the concept of free labour would only make sense if it would become the dominant mode of production and super-sede wage labour the same way that wage labour has superseded the labour of feudal serfs and pre-feudal slaves. We will revisit this issue in more detail.

The free labour debate is mostly initiated by autonomist Marxists close to the Italian operaismo school. It is connected to the writings of Maurizio Lazzarato and Michael Hart and Antonio Negri on immaterial labour, which is situated with the turn towards a Postfordist mode of production and its related processes such as the transformations in the organisation of work (the organ-isation of the labour process), the production of subjectivity and social rela-tions in work environments, and bio-political capitalism where capital ultimately captures life. This means that immaterial labour, which is both intellectual labour and affective labour, involves a number of activities that would not be considered work in Fordist work environments.

> It is not simply that intellectual labor has become subjected to the norms
> of capitalist production. What has happened is that a new 'mass intel-
> lectuality' has come into being, created out of a combination of the
> demands of capitalist production and the forms of 'self-valorization' that
> the struggle against work has produced.
>
> LAZZARATO 1998

The concept of immaterial labour is inspired by a few pages in the *Grundrisse*, where Marx (1973) writes about wealth creation and the production of value which is increasingly independent of labour.

> (T)he creation of wealth comes to depend less on labour time and on the
> amount of labour employed [...] but depends rather on the general state
> of science and on the progress of technology [...] Labour no longer
> appears so much to be included within the production process; rather
> the human being comes to relate more as watchman and regulator to the
> production process itself [...] He steps to the side of the production pro-
> cess instead of being its chief actor. In this transformation, it is neither
> the direct human labour he himself performs, nor the time during which
> he works, but rather the appropriation of his own general productive
> power, his understanding of nature and his mastery over it by virtue of
> his presence as a social body – it is, in a word, the development of the

social individual which appears as the great foundation-stone of production and of wealth.

MARX 1973, 704 F.

As Gorz has pointed out, Marx's language is a bit unstable and fluctuates
between a number of terms. What comes to replace labour is variably 'the general intellect', 'the general state of science and technology', 'general social
knowledge', 'the social individual', and the 'general powers of the human head'
(Gorz 2010, 2). The core claim made by Marx is very clear however: At some
stage in the development of capitalism knowledge, technology, and the general intellect firstly become somehow decoupled from labour and secondly
replace labour as the source for the creation of value. It is not hard to see why
these pages in the *Grundrisse* become so crucial for the concept of immaterial
labour. However these observations in the *Grundrisse* sit uneasy with the Marx
of *Capital Vol. 1*, who develops the labour theory of value and categorically
insists that labour is the only source for the creation of exchange value.

Tiziana Terranova (2004) is perhaps the first theorist who thoroughly
engaged with the concept of free labour. In an essay, which was first published
in 2000, before the arrival of the social web, before Wikipedia and social media
platforms, she conceptualises free labour as the "excessive activity that makes
the Internet a thriving and hyperactive medium" (Terranova 2004, 73). This
includes "the activity of building web sites, modifying software packages, reading and participating in mailing lists and building virtual spaces" (Terranova
2004, 74). Consistent with the operaismo discourse on immaterial labour, she
situates the emergence of free labour with Postfordism. "Free labour is the
moment where this knowledgeable consumption of culture is translated into
excess productive activities that are pleasurably embraced and at the same
time often shamefully exploited" (Terranova 2004, 78).

With this definition we have three features of free labour that are characteristic for most commentators in this debate. Free labour is firstly unpaid labour.
It is free in the sense of free beer; it is voluntarily given. Secondly it is free in the
sense of freedom. It is more autonomous and less alienating than wage labour.
It is not a factory but a playground. Thus it can be enjoyed. Thirdly it is exploited
by capital.

This dialectic between autonomy and exploitation is reflected in most
accounts of free labour, however with different interpretation of this tension.
Terranova is careful to avoid strong judgements and speaks of a 'complex relation to labour' (Terranova 2004, 73). Mark Andrejevic has explored the notion
of free labour in a number of studies on reality TV (Andrejevic 2008), YouTube
(Andrejevic 2009) and Facebook (Andrejevic 2011). These are all commodified

spaces and the core argument in each of these cases is a critique of accounts within media studies that celebrate participation and user generated content as an indication of a process of democratisation and an empowerment of users. He argues instead that the free labour invested in these commodified spaces is being exploited by capital. In his studies, the liberating, empowering and emancipatory potentials are clearly overshadowed by the negative dimensions of monetised communities. Matteo Pasquinelli (2008) goes one step further and critically engages with free labour and the commons. Obviously the commons is not captured or enclosed by capital, otherwise it would cease to be a commons. The various digital commons are not commodified spaces. Still Pasquinelli does not see any positive aspects about the digital commons. They are bad and dark spaces, as they are exploited by capital. This is a deeply asymmetrical relationship. Using Michel Serres' conceptual figure of the parasite and George Bataille's thoughts on excess, he writes about the 'bestiary of the commons', where capital behaves like vampires and sucks all the blood of the surplus energies of free labourers who seem to be too naïve to understand what is going on.

I have noted earlier that Dallas Smythe, one of the founding fathers of Canadian political economy of media, is one of the very few theorists in this field who does not merely engage with the base and superstructure concept but with other aspects of Marx's work. In fact he employs Marx's concept of labour-power. Smythe argues that media audiences are a commodity. They are made a commodity by media producers. The activity of watching television connects media audiences to advertisers. Thus media audiences perform labour. Even though Smythe did not use the term free labour he could be described as the founding father of the free labour debate. Like Andrejevic, Smythe studies media audiences in commodified environments. For Smythe this is a tragedy with three players: the two bad guys are media producers and advertisers; the victims are audiences. Media producers construct audiences. They also sell time to advertisers. Therefore they deliver audiences for advertisers. His argument why audiences perform labour is developed as follows: In modern capitalism there is no time left that it not work time. Capitalism makes "a mockery of free time and leisure" (Smythe 1977, 47). He explains how this observation relates to Marx's theory of labour power (labour power refers to the capacity to work).

> Under capitalism your labor power becomes a personal possession. It seems that you can do what you want with it. If you work at a job where you are paid, you sell it. Away from the job, it seems that your work is something you do not sell. But there is a common misunderstanding at

> this point. At the job you are not paid for all the labor time you do sell (otherwise interest, profits, and management salaries could not be paid). And away from the job your labor time is sold (through the audience commodity), although you do not sell it. What is produced at the job where you are paid are commodities...What is produced by you away from the job is your labor power for tomorrow and for the next generation: ability to work and to live.
>
> SMYTHE 1977, 48

This is certainly an innovative argument and Smythe deserves much credit for what was in the 1970s a rather unusual approach to media audiences. For two reasons however his argument is rather problematic. Firstly it is totalising as all time in the life of humans is work for a capitalist system, sometimes paid ('at the job') and sometimes unpaid ('away from the job'). This means that all reproductive time is time spent for work ('24 hours a day'). This is a much bigger claim than the claim of audience labour. For Smythe every single activity in our life becomes work for the capitalist system. This is maximum alienation and there is no way out. The second problem with this perspective is that it is based on a misinterpretation of Marx's concept of labour. Marx's distinction between concrete and abstract labour, between labour in productive use and labour power (the capacity to work) refers only to wage-based labour. It does not make much sense to use the concept of labour power for reproductive activities. The concept of labour power makes only sense in a context where labour power can be sold by the worker. This is precisely what distinguishes capitalism from other economic systems such as slavery or feudalism. Smythe's attempt to circumvent this problem by declaring that "away from the job your labour time is sold...although you do not sell it" is in my view an 'interpretation' of Marxist analysis that really goes against the fundamental ideas of Marx's theory of labour power.

David Hesmondhalgh has recently developed a critique of the free labour concept. He points out two things. Firstly he critically interrogates "the frequent pairing of the term with the concept of exploitation" which he sees as both, "unconvincing and rather incoherent" (Hesmondhalgh 2010, 276). Sometimes exploitation would refer to alienation, sometimes to ideology and manipulation, and in other cases to the fact that free labour is being captured and used by capital. However none of these things would really be about exploitation. I fully agree with this critique and would only add that according to the Marx of *Capital vol. 1* the exploitation of free labour is impossible. Exploitation refers to the surplus value that capitalists make from wage labour. Surplus value is the value created by workers in excess of their own labour-cost. It is the basis for profit and capital accumulation. For Marx of *Capital vol. 1* the idea that surplus value can be created outside the wage-relationship is nonsensical.

Secondly, Hesmondhalgh asks what political demands might flow from critiques of free labour. He points out that unpaid labour has always existed, using examples such as domestic labour and voluntary community labour (coaching football), and insists on the importance of prioritisation. Under what conditions, he asks, might we object to such unpaid labour, and on what grounds? Which forms of labour are particularly unjust? He also argues that throughout history most cultural production has been unpaid. Finally he points to the fact that those who undertake unpaid digital labour might gain other rewards, such as job satisfaction and recognition by peers.

It is indeed very important to question the claim that the emergence of free labour is somehow linked to Postfordism and to point out that unpaid labour has existed throughout the history of capitalism. It has existed as subsistence work (or domestic labour) and in the form of non-monetised activities, for example voluntary community work or mutual babysitting in the neighbourhood. However Hesmondhalgh is conflating the labour of an unpaid community football coach with the labour of users of profit-driven social media platforms. The former unpaid labour is labour in a non-commercial and thus non-profit environment. The latter is labour in a commercial environment that sells virtual or immaterial spaces to advertisers. This is an important distinction. Interestingly this is a distinction which remains rather nebulous within the free labour debate. Let us go back to the three authors I discussed earlier. For Terranova free labour refers to "the activity of building web sites, modifying software packages, reading and participating in mailing lists and building virtual spaces"; she does not make a distinction between the commercial and the non-commercial, between capital and commons (Terranova 2004, 74). Andrejevic writes only about free labour with respect to advertising spaces and profit-making. Pasquinelli writes only about free-labour and the exploitation of free labour with respect to the commons, with respect to digital sites that are non-profit sites.

All this is rather confusing. It is as confusing as Smythe's contradictory position: On the one hand he claims that exploitation happens 24 hours a day, that there is no time in our life that is not being exploited by capital, on the other hand he refers merely to those moments and spaces outside work that are advertised spaces and moments. All this is not just confusing, it is highly unsatisfactory with respect to exploitation, profit, and surplus-value, in short: with respect to the question of value. Clearly value can come from both, unpaid and paid labour. What is not clear at all however is the origin of exchange value and thus surplus value. Even Marx is sending different messages. In *Capital vol. 1* surplus value can only derive from wage labour, in *Grundrisse* Marx suggests that technology and the general intellect can also be exploited by capital. I find it difficult too to come up with a clear position how surplus value is being generated. In the next sub-chapter on value I will argue that what is valuable and why certain things are valuable is always a subjective category. Therefore it is impossible to decide where objectified value (exchange value, surplus value) really comes from.

Hesmondhalgh also addresses the question of political demands that could emerge in an age where wage labour co-exists with free labour. Again this is a very important point. However I would formulate this task in a different way. Let us go back to Marx's distinction between capitalist wage-based labour and his general take on labour (meaning: independent of particular historic economic modes of production) as a *"process in which both man and Nature participate," as something that transforms both the environment and human beings, as an activity that is not just an economic but a human activity. Labour in this sense can broadly be equated with practice or activity. It seems that this is a very contemporary definition of labour. Marx's general definition of labour corresponds very much with the points made by Lazzarato, Hardt and Negri, and other scholars associated with the operaismo school. All we need to do is to exchange the term practice for life. In bio-political capitalism work is life, work is our thoughts, our affects, our relationships, our subjectivities. It is becoming increasingly futile to distinguish work from leisure, communication, creativity, and play.*

What does this mean politically? In the digital age free labour and wage-based labour co-exist. This could be seen either as a broadly acceptable situation or it could be perceived, as I do, as utterly unjust and ultimately intolerable. This opens up two paths for critique. The first path is a critique of free labour and the political demand, as Hesmondhalgh indicates, would result in calls to integrate free labour in the wage-based system. However this is a dangerous road, as it would lead to an even more commodified world where every single human activity becomes measured in terms of exchange value. It should not become a political project to make the wage-based system and its insane measurements of value even stronger. The second path of critique would turn in the opposite direction. This would be a critique of the wage-labour economy itself. The search for alternatives to wage-labour has recently gained momentum. Demands for a minimum wage for every citizen are probably the most prominent model being discussed which could replace wage labour. The work of André Gorz is perhaps the most developed contribution to an outline of work "beyond the wage-based society" (Gorz 1999). Needless to say this is a radical approach, even utopian, with not much hope for realisation. On the other hand these are times that might need some radical rethinking of how we work, relate, create and live.

Undoubtedly the 'free labour' concept has proven to be highly productive for an illumination of new developments in the social web. It is one of the key challenges in digital capitalism to rethink labour for those human activities that blossom outside wage-based relations. However the concept of labour in 'free labour' suffers from a severe lack of analytical rigour. It conflates a number of rather different practices. Is the downloading of a song comparable with chatting to friends on a social networking platform? Are both activities comparable to either the reading of a mailing list post or the production of a Wikipedia entry? All these activities come under the label of free labour but surely they are very different things. Is watching a television series on a private channel the same as watching a series on a public TV channel that does not run commercials? Is there a difference between the free labour of commercial networking sites such as Twitter, Google+, and Facebook and users of open-source networking sites such as Diaspora? Why do we talk about free labour with respect to a post on a mailing list but not with respect to a material letter in an envelope and a stamp on it, that we send to friend? Would we, communicating on the phone, provide free labour for telecom companies? After all, the only difference between telecom companies and social media platforms such as Facebook or Twitter lies in a slightly different business model. Telecom companies so not use advertisers, so they need to charge customers for their service, whereas social media platform providers get their revenue from advertisers and are therefore able to offer their services for free.

Even more problematic is perhaps the use of the free labour concept for activities that are in fact not really based on free labour in the first place. It is usually assumed that free labour is labour which is not financially compensated. Things are more complicated however. The digital commons is created through a variety of forms of labour with respect to financial compensation. Let us look at the production of open source code. There is a growing tendency towards the funding of open-source projects by companies. Furthermore it is important to point out that an open-source software developer is usually not a shopkeeper during the day who starts producing code in her spare time. The overwhelming majority of open-source programmers are employed programmers, they are working for software companies. Often open source code is produced anyway but then made available to the open source community (Weber 2004). So the labour that goes into the development of open source software is often indirectly paid for. A similar argument could be made for the knowledge commons. A Wikipedia entry on, say 'modernity' is likely to be written by a specialist on this topic, a philosopher perhaps, likely by someone who is employed by a university.

This is the reason why some areas within the digital commons have developed with mind-blowing speed, whereas other areas remain largely underdeveloped.

The open-source commons and the knowledge commons are spearheading the digital commons for a good reason, as those who invest in building it often do get an income for their work. Other areas, for example the *education commons*[5] *and the arts commons stand in rather stark contrast to open-source and the knowledge commons. They remain largely underdeveloped as labour invested here is not paid for by other parties. These commons grow indeed with unpaid labour only, they rely on the passion, the love, and the enthusiasm by those who contribute and invest in it without any financial compensation.*

Postscript: A critique of free labour is important. A critique of the critique of free labour is equally important. However let us not get anal about this. If labour is life and labour is practice it will be difficult to develop a concept of free labour that is less nebulous than the concept of labour itself. This would turn out to be a futile enterprise, directing energies towards a project that is bound to fail. The true value of the free labour debate lies in the articulation not of a conceptual but a social problem. This social problem will only cease to exist when both, wage-based labour and free labour become just labour again, which will only be decided by the outcome of class struggle.

6   Value

In order to understand labour in its full complexity we have to turn towards value. Like labour, value is a vast area of social research. It is a term with many meanings and perspectives, a term that triggered numerous debates and it is easy to get distracted and lose sight of what matters most. So, what is valuable about value for the political economy of media? This is the first question that needs to be addressed. The second question refers to Marx and to the value that his concept of value has to offer for a better understanding of our contemporary media and communications ecosystem.

Economic anthropologist David Graeber (2001) distinguishes between three streams of thought with respect to value. Firstly there are values in the

---

5   I have written elsewhere (Wittel 2012) about contemporary attempts to create, as a result of the neo-liberal destruction of public universities and as a response to this, autonomous universities and autonomous cells of higher education. For this analysis I have made a conceptual distinction between a knowledge commons (e.g. sites such as Wikipedia) and an education commons. This distinction is much about labour and free labour. The knowledge commons grows with the growth of knowledge. It grows naturally; it just has to be uploaded to the Internet. In stark contrast, an education commons requires extra labour (real voluntary labour) that is not financially supported.

sociological sense. These are conceptions of what is ultimately good, proper, or desirable in human life. Secondly there is value in the economic sense. This is the degree to which objects are desired and how this desire is measured in quantitative terms. Thirdly there is value in the linguistic sense, which goes back to de Saussure's structural linguistics, where value is seen as meaningful difference. This is a concept that puts words (or things) in relation to other things. The value of some things can only be established in contrast to or in comparison with other things.

Within political economy of *mass* media the concept of value has received the same marginal attention as the concept of labour. In fact, as labour and value are so closely interrelated in Marxist theory, the same body of literature that is interested in labour is also interested in value.[6] One can only speculate why explorations on value have been largely ignored. My own explanation for this omission is rather simple: In a very general way and as a starting point mass media were perceived as valuable as a public good, as an independent force to safeguard democracy. However due to the increasing privatisation of mass media organisations and the economic interests of their owners the value of mass media as public good was under constant threat. Thus political economy of *mass* media never focuses on the potential value of mass media but on its opposite, on the dangers that economic interests and political regulation pose for democratic societies. Such a perspective made perfect sense. After all, political economy of mass media stands in the tradition of critical theory. It would have been odd indeed to praise media conglomerates and media moguls for their contributions to a shining public sphere.

If we apply Graeber's typology of value to the political economy of *mass* media we get a result that is very similar to the claim just made, but it is also a bit more nuanced. It is safe to say that there never was a concern about value in the economic sense; there were no attempts to measure the value of media products or media organisations in a quantitative way. It is also safe to say that the sociological dimension of value as values has not been explored in any meaningful way. This would have meant an engagement with the socially

---

6   It is not a coincidence that literature which incorporates concepts of labour and value is usually concerned with advertising. It is advertising which has inspired Smythe (1977) to develop the concept of the audience commodity. Most notably we find debates on value in the so called 'blindspot' debate (Murdock 1978; Smythe 1978; Livant 1979), which was triggered by Smythe's (1977) claim that TV audiences provide free labour for advertisers and for media producers. Value is also central to the work of Sut Jhally (1990), who makes a very similar argument about the advertising industry and about the labour of media audiences as Smythe (1977).

desirable values of media and communication. This would have been a debate about the utopian aspects of media and communication, how media should be organised, how they should work, what they should be. However an argument could be made that the political economy of *mass* media has something to say about value in the linguistic sense of de Saussure's structuralism, about the meaningful difference between comparable forms of media production and media organisation, notably about the difference between publicly and privately owned media organisation. Without referring to the notion of value explicitly, the British tradition of political economy of *mass* media does compare public media organisations with commercial media organisations and the result of this comparison is a positive assessment of state owned media organisations such as the BBC.

What is the relevance of these streams of thought for the age of *distributed* media? So far there are no signs that *value in the economic sense* is becoming an issue for intense debate. Indeed the measurement of value in calculable and quantifiable units would always have been a rather questionable objective for political economists of media in the first place. With the growing importance of immaterial labour this would turn into more than just a questionable objective – it would be a mad and utterly futile project. It has become increasingly obvious that the value of intellectual and affective things is beyond measure. "What has irreversibly changed however, from the times of the predominance of the classical theory of value, involves the possibility of developing the theory of value in terms of economic order, or rather, the possibility of considering value as a measure of concrete labor." (Negri 1999, 77 f.) Negri suggests instead to transform the theory of value from above to a theory of value "from below, from the basis of life" (Negri 1999, 78). Drawing on the work of Spinoza, Negri sees value as the power to act. We could add this to Graeber's typology as a fourth way to think about value: value is what empowers people to act.

In the age of distributed media, I would argue, debates on *value in the sociological sense* are blossoming. These are debates about the digital commons, about free labour and free culture, about openness, contribution, and sharing, about attention, about scarcity and abundance, about the gift economy, about property and access, about co-operation and collaboration as opposed to competition, about anonymous speech and anonymous action, about surveillance, privacy and transparency, about the value of experts and amateurs, about the Internet and democracy, about people and technology, about media and political action, about capitalism and exit strategies. These are attempts to make judgements about what is good and desirable.

I hope my argument comes across: In the age of *mass media* the value of media to safeguard democracy was under threat. In the age of *distributed* media this value is still under threat. But this is not the end of the story. Now questions on power, ideology, and manipulation (which of course will remain highly relevant) are being supplemented by new questions on agency, empowerment, potency, and possibilities. In the age of *mass* media there was not much discussion that connected media and inquiries on what is important about life. In the age of *distributed* media these debates are in full swing.

Can Marx's concept of value contribute to these debates? Let us rehearse quickly: In the labour theory of value (as outlined in *Capital vol. 1*) Marx rejects claims by liberal political economists that the value of commodities should be defined by markets, by people exchanging money and commodities. This liberal perspective oscillates between a position where value is either somehow intrinsic to commodities or it is defined by the desire of those who want to purchase a commodity. Marx argues that value emerges from the amount of labour (and the amount of time) that has been invested in the production of a commodity. The exchange of money and commodities hides the fact that it is the production of the commodity that gives it its value. From this dictum that value is the socially necessary labour-time embodied in a commodity Marx develops his concept of surplus value. Surplus value then refers to the difference between the cost of the labour power (the wages) and the value of labour that is congealed in commodities. Surplus value or profit is the difference between what the worker creates and what he or she receives in return. If value is created through labour, surplus value is created through the exploitation of labour.

Even within Marxist theory his labour theory of value has been subject to much controversy. For Slavoj Žižek it is "usually considered the weakest link in the chain of Marx's theory" (Žižek 2011, 205). Drawing on the work of Moishe Postone, Žižek argues that Marx's labour theory of value is not a trans-historical theory, but a theory of value in a capitalist society only. This poses an important question. How relevant is Marx's theory for our contemporary media ecosystem that is partly capitalist, partly publicly funded, and partly a digital commons? Does it make sense to apply his theory to what is sometimes called a 'gift economy' (Barbrook 1999) and sometimes an 'economy of contributions' (Siefkes 2007). And if so, how would this be possible? Let us consider for example a gift economy. Does it really help in a gift economy to locate the source of value specific objects in the production of these objects at the expense of the relationship between those who exchange objects as gifts? Such an approach would not make much sense. There is a need to broaden the horizon for theories of value that are exclusively developed for an understanding of capitalist economies only. The obvious place to find inspiration is the anthropological literature on value.

Graeber has produced an excellent review of the anthropological literature on value. He is searching for a concept that could overcome the dichotomy of gifts and commodities that could bridge a Maussean approach and a Marxist approach to value. He is especially impressed with the concept of value developed by Nancy Munn who has done extensive fieldwork in Melanesia. For Munn, value emerges in action. It is the process by which a person's capacity to act is transformed into concrete activity. Value is ultimately about the power to create social relationships.

> Rather than having to choose between the desirability of objects and the importance of human relations one can now see both as refractions of the same thing. Commodities have to be produced (and yes, they have to be moved around, exchanged, consumed...), social relations have to be created and maintained; all of this requires an investment of human time and energy, intelligence, concern [...] Framing things this way of course evokes the specter of Marx [...] We are clearly dealing with something along the lines of a labor theory of value. But only if we define 'labor' much more broadly.
>
> GRAEBER 2001, 45

One might add that such a concept of labour is pretty much identical with Marx general definition of labour as practice. And it is identical with what Negri and Spinoza describe as the power to act.

All this is theory and it might be hard to come up with a rationale as to why political economy of media needs to engage with value theory in the first place. In fact this is not the point I want to make. I do think however, that Marx's labour theory of value (understanding labour in this broad meaning of the term) would open up new paths for empirical research. If it makes sense to see *value as the power to act* and to see it as the power to create social relations, if value is about how people give meaning to their own actions, then a political economy of communication, a political economy of distributed media would be in a perfect position to redefine what political economy means and to establish what Negri (1999) calls a political economy from below. This would be research on value that is focused not on structures but on *subjectivities* and their desires to create, to connect, to communicate, to share, to work together and to give meaning to all these things.

7   Property

In the age of *mass media* property has always been significant with respect to the ownership of the means of production. However an interest on property in terms of media content was rather limited. Ronald Bettig (1996) is perhaps overly careful to say that the area of intellectual property and copyright in particular has been "relatively unexplored." He is one of very few political economists who examined the property of media content. Interestingly this is a study just at the beginning of the digital turn.

Bettig is interested in the difference between the normative principles of intellectual property and the actually existing system. The central normative justification for intellectual property is built on the assumption that the creators of intellectual and artistic work need an incentive to be creative. The copyright is meant to give the creator exclusive rights to exploit their work, which in turn will provide an income for the creator and motivate her to produce new work. However the actual copyright system does not operate according to this ideal. Most artistic and intellectual work relies on a process of production, reproduction, and distribution that involves many people and expensive technology. According to Bettig "ownership of copyright increasingly rests with the capitalists who have the machinery and capital to manufacture and distribute" (Bettig 1996, 8) the works.

> Precisely because the capitalist class owns the means of communication, it is able to extract the artistic and intellectual labor of actual creators of media messages. For to get 'published', in the broad sense, actual creators must transfer their rights to ownership in their work to those who have the means of disseminating it.
>
> BETTIG 1996, 35

This is a very correct analysis for the age of *mass media* that does not leave much room for hope. Still he states with astonishing foresight that "the enclosure of the intellectual and artistic commons is not inevitable or necessary, even though the emphasis on the logic of capital makes it seem as if it is." (Bettig 1996, 5). Bettig must have felt that times they are changing. In the mid 1990s when his book was published sharing cultures and the digital commons were largely restricted to the open source movement. There was no file-sharing software such as Napster, no legal experiments with copyright such as the Creative Commons, there was no social web. In the age of mass media the expansionary logic of capital has not left much room for an intellectual and artistic commons. An overwhelming part of media content was not common property but captured by capital. In this respect Bettig's statement has some prophetic qualities. By now it has become very clear that the enclosure of the intellectual and artistic commons is not inevitable at all. In fact this is the "battle to the death" which Kleiner refers to, the battle between artistic and intellectual labour and those who want to rescue the digital commons on one side of the battlefield and capital and those who aim for enclosure on the other side.

Bettig has developed a convincing argument with much empirical backup as to why the copyright arrangements – as legitimate as they are in an ideal normative sense – have not really supported the creators of intellectual and artistic work, but those who control the communication flows. With the digital turn this rather problematic arrangement is becoming even worse. As all digital objects can be reproduced endlessly and distributed with minimum additional costs they count as non-rival goods. In fact most intellectual property is non-rival, meaning they can be used by one person without preventing other people from using the same goods. Digital objects however are not only non-rival; they are also abundant by nature. Therefore all attempts to rescue the idea of copyright via digital rights are absurd in the sense that they create artificial scarcity. They turn objects that are abundant into legally scarce goods. To put it ironically: In the digital age only the creation of artificial scarcity can feed capitalist accumulation. It is exactly because digital things are not just non-rival but also abundant that the issue of intellectual property has moved from a sideshow to centre stage.

It is impossible to summarise the free culture debate in a few lines. I still want to make a few remarks, only to situate the key positions with respect to Marx. The first thing to note is that there is a relatively straightforward line between critical political economists and liberal political economists such as Yochai Benkler (2006) and Lawrence Lessig (2004). The latter celebrate free culture without giving up on the legitimacy of intellectual property. They merely suggest modifications to copyright law. They also applaud the digital commons as a progressive development without being overly concerned about the free labour that goes into the building of the digital commons. For Benkler (2006, 3) commons-based peer production enhances individual freedom and autonomy. This is where critical political economists take a different position. For them free labour is a problem that needs to be addressed.

The debates within the camp of critical political economists of digital media are not so clear-cut. While both positions exist, a passionate defence of free culture (e.g. Cory Doctorow 2008 or Kevin Carson 2011) and a passionate concern about free labour and the exploitation of this free labour by capital (Pasquinelli 2008; Kleiner 2010), in most accounts we find a general acknowledgement of this dilemma, a dilemma that is hard to crack, with many commentators sitting on the fence. One way out of the free culture dilemma resulted in the search for new models to guarantee the creators of artistic or intellectual work some income (e.g. Peter Sunde's 'Flattr' or Dmytri Kleiner's 'copyfarleft' and 'venture communism' suggestions).

Apart from some rare exceptions (notably Wark 2004 and Kleiner 2010), these debates circumvent however a discussion on property itself. Even those who passionately defend free culture support their position with rather pragmatic arguments, for example with the claim that free culture ultimately stimulates creative production and innovation, whereas copyright brings about a reduction of creative and innovative work. While these are important arguments I do find it astonishing that a fundamental critique of intellectual property itself has so far not been put on the table. Badiou asks a good rhetorical question: Why do we "keep tight controls on all forms of property in order to ensure the survival of the powerful?" (Badiou 2010, 5).

This is where Marx could come in rather handy. The first thing we can learn from Marx is that property is not a natural right. It is a historic product. Property relations are subject to specific historic conditions.

> The French Revolution, for example, abolished feudal property in favour of bourgeois property. The distinguishing feature of Communism is not the abolition of property generally, but the abolition of bourgeois property. But modern bourgeois private property is the final and most complete expression of the system of producing and appropriating products that is based on class antagonism, on the exploitation of the many by the few. In this sense, the theory of the Communists may be summed up in the single sentence: Abolition of private property.
>
> COMMUNIST MANIFESTO, 68

The second thing to note is that Marx's perspective on property is innovative and very distinct from liberal political theorists, as he does not focus on the relationship between a person and an object. Instead Marx conceptualises property as a relation that one person establishes to other people with respect to commodities. So fundamentally property relations are an expression of social relations. In capitalism property is based on the antagonism between capital and wage-labour. Is it is based on the accumulation of profit on the side of those who own the means of production.

> Self-earned private property, that is based, so to say, on the fusing together of the isolated, independent laboring-individual with the conditions of his labor, is supplanted by capitalistic private property, which rests on exploitation of the nominally free labor of others, i.e., on wage-labor. The capitalist mode of appropriation, the result of the capitalist mode of production, produces capitalist private property.
>
> CAPITAL VOL. 1, 762–63

As such capitalist private property is not so much about the ownership of things, but about the right to exclude others from using them. Dismantling the widespread myth that private property is justly earned by those who are intelligent and willing to work hard while the rest are 'lazy rascals', Marx comes up with an alternative explanation on the origin of property:

> Such insipid childishness is every day preached to us in defence of property [...] In actual history it is notorious that conquest, enslavement, robbery, murder, briefly force, play the greater part.
>
> CAPITAL VOL. 1, 713–14

Why does this quote resonate so well in a time when capitalism is facing its first global crisis? The third and for our purposes more important observation is Marx's distinction between *private and personal property*. In capitalism, *private* property is bad, it is not only the result of alienated labour (wage-labour) but worse, is it also the means that makes alienated labour possible in the first place and the means to maintain this unjust relation between capital and labour. Private property is productive property. It is property that is crucial for capitalist production. It is property that can be used for the creation of surplus value. It might be a bit simplistic but in general Marx equates private property with privately owned means of production. This is very different from *personal* property or property for consumption (for reproduction, for subsistence), which should not be socialised as there is no need for doing so. Unproductive property or property based on needs is rather harmless after all.

> When, therefore, capital is converted into common property, into the property of all members of society, personal property is not thereby transformed into social property. It is only the social character of the property that is changed. It loses its class character [...] The average price of wage-labour is the minimum wage, i.e. that quantum of the means of subsistence, which is absolutely requisite to keep the labourer in bare existence as a labourer [...] We by no means intend to abolish this personal appropriation of the products of labour, an appropriation that is made for the maintenance and reproduction of human life, and that leaves no surplus wherewith to command the labour of others.
>
> COMMUNIST MANIFESTO, 68 F.

No doubt intellectual property is not personal but *private* property. No doubt these are productive commodities. They produce surplus value and also lay the foundation for future commodities that produce even more surplus value.

Information produces more information, news produces more news, knowledge produces more knowledge, and art produces more art. Therefore intellectual property is an invention that in capitalism does not protect the creators of these immaterial objects. Instead it helps capitalist accumulation. Bettig has supported this claim in great detail with rich empirical evidence.

In my view the debate between those who support free culture and those who are concerned about the exploitative nature of free labour got stuck. Both positions should be supported from a Marxist point of view. They contradict each other but they do so in perfect harmony with what Marx sees as internal contradictions of capitalism. Furthermore, the development of new business models for intellectual and artistic workers does not look promising, neither theoretically nor practically. It all boils down to the simple fact that capitalists are not willing to support free labour for altruistic reasons and those who are exploited earn just enough to maintain their own subsistence.

The only way out of this dilemma is a debate on the legitimacy of private property itself. Property relations reflect social relations. Now we can close the circle. It will bring us back to value, to value in the sociological sense (what we appreciate about life) and to the fourth approach to value, the one that builds on Spinoza's theory of affect, to value as the power to act. It will also bring us back to labour. If free culture is good for society (which is a claim that never has been seriously contested) then society must find a way to support the creators of free culture. Society must find a way to support their unpaid contributions, their gifts to humanity. It is as simple as that. A global basic income is not the only possible solution to this problem, but it could be a good starting point.

A related debate that should be triggered from the free-labour-free-culture-dilemma refers to the division of labour. In a communist society "there are no painters; at most there are people who, among other things, also paint." (*Literature and Art*, 76).

If people use their power to act against the capitalist property regime, they will engage in struggle:

> The transformation of scattered private property, arising from individual labour, into capitalist private property is, naturally, a process, incomparably more protracted, violent, and difficult, than the transformation of capitalistic private property, already practically resting on socialised production, into socialised property. In the former case, we had the expropriation of the mass of the people by a few usurpers, in the latter we have the expropriation of a few usurpers by the mass of the people.
>
> CAPITAL VOL. 1: 764

Marx was perhaps a bit overly optimistic about this struggle. Then again, this optimism and the hope that goes with it are very much needed.

8   Struggle

There's class warfare, all right, but it's *my class, the rich* class, that's *making* war, and *we're winning*.
WARREN BUFFETT 2011

In the age of *mass* media political economists of communication have app-lied Marxist theory in a rather limited way. In the age of *digital and distrib-uted* media, so my main argument, political economy of communication can apply Marx's concepts in a broader way. I have used some key concepts of his political economy – in particular the concepts of labour, value, and property, which are all interlinked – to demonstrate their relevance for an analysis of our contemporary media ecology, which consists of an interesting mix of the state, the market, and the commons. Another concept which is obviously at the very heart of Marx's political economy is class struggle. Digital and dis-tributed media have opened up new possibilities for resistance and for the construction of alternatives to capitalism. None of these possibilities can be achieved without more fundamental changes enforced by the struggle of the oppressed.

Like labour, value and property, the concept of class struggle has featured within the political economy of *mass* media, but only at the margins (e.g. Mattelart and Siegelaub 1979). It never has been a key concept. Moreover, Dyer-Witheford is right to state that "while there are some studies of working class battles over digital machines and electronic media from a class struggle posi-tion, these have usually not offered any theoretical perspectives beyond...neo-Luddism." (Dyer-Witheford 1999, 64).

A theorisation of media and struggle is among the most important tasks for political economists of distributed media. How can we conceptualise class struggle in the 21st century, as there are so many practices associated with it? These are practices which refer to the agency of workers who resist exploita-tion at each point in the value chain, something political economists have recently addressed in detailed accounts (Huws and Leys 2003; Qui 2009; Mosco, McKercher and Huws 2010). Struggle in the information age also refers to hack-tivism and forms of resistance employed by loosely connected cyber 'groups' such as 'Anonymous'. Thirdly struggle refers to all those energies that are invested in the digital commons and the building of alternative goods and structures. Finally it refers to social movements. 2011 was the year of the first global uprising. While the specific relationship between social media and social movements does need to be studied in more detail, we can safely claim that social media can empower social movements and political activists. In the digital age the connection between media and struggle is complex but strong. Political economists of distributed media are expanding their research beyond a focus on media organisations or media industries; they are also studying what is happening in cyberspace; and they are studying what is happening in the real streets and squares.

Marx is back indeed and this time it's personal.

References

Andrejevic, Mark. 2008. Watching Television Without Pity. *Television & New Media* 9 (1): 24–46.

Andrejevic, Mark. 2011. Facebook als Neue Produktionsweise. In *Generation Facebook: Über das Leben im Social Net*, edited by Oliver Leistert and Theo Röhle, 31–50. Bielefeld: transcript Verlag.

Andrejevic, Mark. Exploiting YouTube: Contradictions of User-generated Labour. In *The YouTube Reader*, edited by Pelle Snickars and Patrick Vonderau, Stockholm: National Library of Sweden.

Artz, Lee, Steve Macek, and Dana Cloud (eds). 2006. *Marxism and Communications Studies: The Point is to Change It*. New York: Peter Lang.

Badiou, Alain. 2010. *The Communist Hypothesis*. London: Verso.

Barbrook, Richard. 1999. The High-Tech Gift Economy. In *Readme! Filtered by Nettime: ASCII Culture and the Revenge of Knowledge*, edited by Josephine Bosma, Pauline van Mourik Broekman, Ted Byfield Matthew Fuller, Geert Lovink, Diana McCarty, Pit Schultz Felix Stalder, McKenzie Wark, and Faith Wilding, 132–138. New York: Autonomedia.

Benkler, Yochai. 2002. Coase's Penguin, or, Linux and the Nature of the Firm. *The Yale Law Journal* 112 (3): 369–446.

Benkler, Yochai. 2006. *The Wealth of Networks. How Social Production Transforms Markets and Freedom*. New Haven and London: Yale University Press.

Bettig, Ronald V. 1996. *Copyrighting Culture: The Political Economy of Intellectual Property*, Oxford: Westview.

Burton, Graeme. 2010. *Media and Society: Critical Perspectives*. Maidenhead: Open University Press.

Carson, Kevin. 2011. How 'Intellectual Property' Imedes Competition. In *Markets Not Capitalism: Individualist Anarchism Against Bosses, Inequality, Corporate Power, and*

Structural Poverty, edited by Gary Chartier & Charles W. Johnson, 325–334. London, New York: Minor Compositions and Autonomedia.

Castells, Manuel. 1996. *The Rise of the Network Society*. Maldan, MA and Oxford: Blackwell.

Curran, James. 1990. The New Revisionism in Mass Communication Research: A Reappraisal. *European Journal of Communication* 5 (2): 135–164.

Curran, James. 2000. *Media Organisations in Society*. London: Arnold.

Curran, James and Jean, Seaton. 2003. *Power Without Responsibility: The Press, Broadcasting and New Media in Britain*. London: Routledge.

Curran, James and Jean Seaton. 1997. *Power Without Responsibility: The Press and Broadcasting in Britain*. London: Routledge.

Devereux, Eoin. 2003. *Understanding the Media*. London: Sage.

Doctorow, Cory. 2008. *Content*. San Francisco: Tachyon Books.

Durham, Meenakshi Gigi and Douglas Kellner. 2006. *Media and Cultural Studies: Keyworks*. Oxford: Blackwell.

Dyer-Witheford, Nick. 1999. *Cyber-Marx: Cycles and Circuits of Struggle in High-Technology Capitalism*. Urbana and Chicago: University of Illinois Press.

Fuchs, Christian. 2008. *Internet and Society: Social Theory in the Internet Age*. London: Routledge.

Fuchs, Christian. 2011. *Foundations of Critical Media and Information Studies*. New York: Routledge.

Fuchs, Christian, Kees Boersma, Anders Albrechtslund, and Marisol Sandoval (eds.). 2012. *Internet and Surveillance: The Challenges of Web 2.0 and Social Media*. New York: Routledge.

Garnham, Nicholas. 1990. *Capitalism and Communication: Global Culture and the Economics of Information*. London: Sage.

Gorz, André. 1999. *Reclaiming Work: Beyond the Wage-based Society*. Cambridge: Polity.

Gorz, André. 2010. *The Immaterial*. Calcutta: Seagull Books.

Graeber, David. 2001. *Toward an Anthropological Theory of Value. The False Coin of Our Own Dreams*. New York: Palgrave.

Grossberg, Lawrence, Ellen Wartella, and Charles Whitney. 1998. *Mediamaking: Mass Media in a Popular Culture*. Thousand Oaks, CA: Sage.

Herman, Edward and Noam Chomsky. 1988. *Manufacturing Consent: The Political Economy of the Mass Media*. London: Vintage.

Herman, Edward and Robert McChesney. 1997. *The Global Media: The New Missionaries of Corporate Capitalism*. London: Cassell.

Hesmondhalgh, David. 2010. User-generated Content, Free Labour and the Cultural Industries. *Ephemera* 10 (3/4): 267–284.

Huws, Ursula and Colin Leys. 2003. *The Making of a Cybertariat: Virtual Work in a Real World*. New York: Monthly Review Press.

Jhally, Sut. 1990. *The Codes of Advertising: Fetishism and the Political Economy of Meaning.* New York: Routledge.

Jhally, Sut. 2006. *The Spectacle of Accumulation: Essays in Culture, Media, & Politics.* New York: Peter Lang.

Kellner, Douglas. 1995. Media Communications vs. Cultural Studies: Overcoming the Divide. *Communication Theory* 5 (2): 162–177.

Kleiner, Dmytri. 2010. *The Telekommunist Manifesto.* Amsterdam: Institute of Network Cultures.

Laughey, Dan. 2009. *Media Studies: Theories and Approaches.* Harpenden: Kamera.

Lazzarato, Maurizio. 1998. Immaterial Labor. Accessed February 29, 2012. http://www.generation-online.org/c/fcimmateriallabour3.htm.

Lessig, Lawrence. 2004. *Free Culture: The Nature and Future of Creativity.* New York: Penguin Books.

Livant, William. 1979. The Audience Commodity: On the "Blindspot" Debate. *Canadian Journal of Political and Social Theory* 3 (1): 91–106.

Livingstone, Sonia. 2009. On the Mediation of Everything. *Journal of Communication* 59 (1): 1–18.

Marx, Karl. 1973. *Grundrisse: Foundations of the Critique of Political Economy.* London: Penguin Books.

Marx, Karl. 1977. *A Contribution to the Critique of Political Economy.* Moscow: Progress Publishers.

Marx, Karl. 1988. *The Communist Manifesto,* edited by Frederic Bender, New York: W. W. Norton.

Marx, Karl and Frederick Engels. 1974. *The German Ideology.* London: Lawrence and Wishart.

Marx, Karl and Frederick Engels. 1996. *Karl Marx Frederick Engels: Collected Works, Vol. 35: Karl Marx ; Capital, Vol. 1.* London: Lawrence and Wishart.

Marx, Karl and Frederick Engels. *Literature and Art.* New York: International Publishers.

Mattelart, Armand and Seth Siegelaub. 1979. *Communication and Class Struggle. An Anthology in 2 Volumes.* New York: Bagnolet.

McChesney, Robert and Victor Pickard, eds. 2011. *Will the Last Reporter Please Turn Out the Lights: The Collapse of Journalism and What Can Be Done to Fix It.* New York and London: The New Press.

McQuail, Denis. 2005. *McQuail's Mass Communication Theory.* London: Sage Publications.

Mosco, Vincent. 1996. *The Political Economy of Communication: Rethinking and Renewal.* London: Sage.

Mosco, Vincent. 2004. *The Digital Sublime: Myth, Power, and Cyberspace.* Cambridge, MA: MIT Press.

Mosco, Vincent, Catherine McKercher, and Ursula Huws. 2010. *Getting the Message: Communications Workers and Global Value Chains.* London: The Merlin Press LTD.

Murdock, Graham. 1978. Blindspots About Western Marxism: A Reply to Dallas Smythe. *Canadian Journal of Political and Social Theory* 2 (2): 109–119.

Murdock, Graham. 1982. Large Corporations and the Control of the Communications Industries In *Culture, Society and the Media,* edited by Michael Gurevitch, 118–150. London: Methuen.

Murdock, Graham. 2004. Past the Posts: Rethinking Change, Retrieving Critique. *European Journal of Communication* 19 (1): 19–38.

Murdock, Graham and Peter Golding. 2001. Digital Possibilities, Market Realities: The Contradictions of Communications Convergence. In *Register Socialist 2002: A World of Contradictions,* edited by Leo Panitch and Colin Leys, 111–129. London: Merlin Press.

Negri, Antonio. 1999. "Value and Affect." *Boundary* 2 26 (2): 77–88.

Nichols, John and Robert McChesney. 2005. *Tragedy and Farce: How the American Media Sell Wars, Spin Elections and Destroy Democracy.* New York: New Press.

Nichols, John and Robert McChesney. 2006. *Tragedy and Farce: How the American Media Sell Wars, Spin Elections and Destroy Democracy.* New York: New Press.

Pasquinelli, Matteo. 2007. ICW – Immaterial Civil War: Prototypes of Conflict Within Cognitive Capitalism. In *MyCreativity Reader: A Critique of Creative Industries,* edited by Geert Lovink and Ned Rossiter, 69–80. Amsterdam: Institute of Network Cultures.

Pasquinelli, Matteo. 2008. *Animal Spirits: A Bestiary of the Commons.* Amsterdam: NAi Publishers and Institute of Network Cultures.

Qui, Jack Linchuan. 2009. *Working-Class Network Society: Communication Technology and the Information Have-Less in Urban China.* Cambridge (MA): MIT Press.

Schiller, Herbert. 1989. *Culture, Inc: The Corporate Takeover of Public Expression.* N.Y.: Oxford U.P.

Siefkes, Christian. 2007. *From Exchange to Contributions: Generalizing Peer Production into the Physical World.* Berlin: Edition C. Siefkes.

Smythe, Dallas. 1977. *Dependency Road: Communications, Capitalism, Consciousness, and Canada.* Norwood: Ablex.

Smythe, Dallas. 1978. Rejoinder to Graham Murdock. *Canadian Journal of Political and Social Theory* 2 (2): 120–127.

Stallabrass, Julian. 2003. *Internet Art: The Online Clash of Culture and Commerce.* London: Tate Publishing.

Terranova, Tiziana. 2004. *Network Culture: Politics For the Information Age.* London: Pluto Press.

Wark, McKenzie. 2004. *A Hacker Manifesto.* Cambridge, MA: Harvard University Press.

Wayne, Mike. 2003. *Marxism and Media Studies: Key Concepts and Contemporary Trends.* London: Pluto.

Weber, Steven. 2004. *The Success of Open Source.* Cambridge, MA and London: Harvard University Press.

Williams, Raymond. 1958. *Culture and Society 1780–1950*. London: Chatto & Windus.

Williams, Raymond. 1961. *The Long Revolution*. London: Chatto & Windus.

Wittel, Andreas. 2004. Culture, Labour and Subjectivity: For a Political Economy from Below. *Capital & Class* 84 (Special Issue): 11–30.

Wittel, Andreas. 2011. Qualities of Sharing and Their Transformations in the Digital Age. *International Review of Information Ethics* 15.

Wittel, Andreas. Forthcoming 2012. Hochschulbildung als Gut: Vom öffentlichen Gut zur Ware zum Gemeingut? In *Wissensarbeit Und Arbeitswissen. Zur Ethnographie Des Kognitiven Kapitalismus*, edited by Gertraud Koch and Bernd Juergen Warneken, Frankfurt am Main: Campus.

Žižek, Slavoj. 2011. *Living in the End Times*. London, New York: Verso.

CHAPTER 4

The Relevance of Marx's Theory of Primitive Accumulation for Media and Communication Research

Mattias Ekman

1   Introduction

The current global crisis of capitalism has inspired numerous social theorists to both revitalize and reinvent many of the key arguments and trails within Marx's magnum opus *Capital*. Without any other comparison to the increasing body of literature that draws on *Capital,* this chapter will be yet one more attempt to connect to the seminal work that has been counted out so many times before by the apologetics of capitalism.

The purpose of this chapter is to discuss Marx's (1867/1990) theory of original/ primitive accumulation ("ursprüngliche Akkumulation"), described in the first volume of *Capital*, and its relevance for analysing the role of (mass) media, online communication and communication systems, in the process of capital accumulation. In order to revitalize Marx's argument in *Capital*, the theory of original/primitive accumulation is updated in relation to Harvey's (2003; 2006; 2010a) theory of "accumulation by dispossession." Harvey draws on Marx's discussion of primitive accumulation in order to unfold the neo-liberal shift within the development of global capitalism.

Following a basic theoretical understanding of primitive accumulation and accumulation by dispossession the chapter addresses two key aspects of news media content and media structures in relation to the processes of accumulation by dispossession. It examines the media representation of social struggle against capital accumulation, and how both news media content and news media systems facilitate capital accumulation in the finance sector. Furthermore the chapter taps into how surplus value is produced in the realm of Internet use, particularly Web 2.0. Here, some thoughts on how everyday Internet use could be understood as surplus labour and how users are transformed into commodities will be addressed. In relation to the discussion on everyday online activities, Marx's theory of original/primitive accumulation provides an understanding of new forms of exploitation by the appropriation of intellectual assets and creativity in the field of cultural production, distribution and communication in the Web 2.0. Here the chapter discusses how the commodification of free time, the self and social relations, plays a key part in the political economy of social media and the Internet. Included is also a short section that discusses if Internet surveillance, and the commercial gathering, owning and processing of personal information, could be understood as an underlying threat to citizens, and a part of what Žižek (2008) defines as the objective violence of capitalist exploitation.

The chapter combines the results of empirical research on news media with examples of how the everyday use of social media and intellectual assets and creativity in the field of cultural production/distribution could be explained through a Marxist theory of capital accumulation in a time of systemic crisis. Harvey's updated version of Marx's notion of original/primitive accumulation provides a strong argument for understanding the recent development of late capitalism.

2   The Process of Capital Accumulation

The immanent driving force of capitalism is the endless accumulation of capital, a process where capital is accumulated for the sake of accumulation, or as Marx (1867/1990, 595) put it "accumulation for accumulation's sake, production for production's sake." The very basic formula of capital accumulation, outlined by Marx (1885/1992) in the second volume of *Capital*, draws on how capital is circulated through several key phases:

$$M - C \ (Lp/Mp)...P \ (v/c)...C' - M'$$

To put it simple – the accumulation of capital is obtained by the circulation of capital, where money (M) is transformed into commodities (C) by the purchase of labour power (Lp) and means of production (Mp). To secure accumulation, the money needs to be greater in the end of the process than in the beginning, which means that the value of the produced commodity is higher than the value of the commodities used as inputs. In the production process the value of labour power and the means of production take the form of productive capital (P) when attached to the produced commodity. The value of labour force (v) equals the costs of the labour power bought (wages) and the value form of means of production (c) equals the cost of the means used (constant capital). So, surplus value is generated when the commodity is sold at a higher price than the costs of production, which is made possible by surplus labour (unpaid labour time). So what basically creates surplus value is the amount of labour time that is not paid for by the capitalists. When the produced commodity (C') is sold, capital once again enters the process of circulation in the form of (new) money (M'), and; the process of capital accumulation is thereby maintained (Marx 1867/1990; Harvey 1982/2006, 156ff; Fuchs 2011, 138).

Marx's theory of capital accumulation is highly complex and detailed (the whole second volume of Capital is basically an outline of the trails of capital accumulation), but it's still possible to simplify it in this manner without losing too much of its inner nature. Under ordinary circumstances, capital accumulation is secured through expanded reproduction.[1] In this process of reproduction, not only commodities and surplus value are reproduced, but also the whole relationship between capital and labour – between capitalists and wage labourers (Marx 1967/1990, 578). And since surplus value relies on the exploitative relation between capital and labour force, the circulation of capital is ultimately the reproduction of exploited wage labour by capitalists. The commodity labour power (Lp) is subordinated to processes of absolute or relative exploitation. The former refers to the extension of the amount of time each worker needs to put in, and the latter to the intensification of the labour process (Mosco 2009, 131).

The circulation of capital is an endless process, and given the inner contradictions of accumulation, capitalism eventually faces systemic crisis. The historical Marxist debates over what type of crises capitalism is undergoing tend to shift. Luxemburg (1913/2003) stresses the problems of under-consumption to explain systemic crises, but under-consumption is hardly a sufficient explanation of the crises within capitalism today. Harvey argues that capitalism is currently facing an over-accumulation crisis,[2] because we are experiencing a situation "when both surplus capital and labour exist but there are no way to bring them together" (Harvey 2006, 96). The over-accumulation crisis manifests itself when there are superfluous commodities, money and productive capacity form simultaneously with a surplus of labour power, but with the lack of "profitable opportunities" for capital to expand (Harvey 2003, 88). In order to deal with an over-accumulation crisis, capital tries to expand reproduction through temporal or spatial shifts. Harvey (2003, 89) calls these "spatio-temporal fixes." For example, by investing surplus capital and labour in long-term (large scale public) projects, or by relocating the surplus of capital and labour to other geographical spaces (Harvey 2006, 96). Capitalists have a tendency to expand

---

1 Marx (1867/1990, 711ff) distinguishes between "simple reproduction" and "expanded reproduction" (Marx 1867/1990; 1885/1992). Simple reproduction is basically the reproduction of capital-labour relations without any accumulation of capital.

2 The definition of what characterizes over-accumulation crises is highly simplified here, since systemic crises tend to inherit several dimensions (see Harvey 2003; 2006; 2010b, for a more in-depth analysis of systemic crises, & see Fuchs 2011, for an overview of different contemporary crises-explanations).

reproduction geographically by relocating the purchases of labour power or means of production elsewhere, and thus creating new spaces for the accumulation of capital. Since capitalism is a global system, expanded reproduction often results in a situation where crises are moved around geographically. The spatio-temporal fixes are reliant on and thrive from the advancement of communication technology and systems. Advancements in transport and communication that compresses time-space relations are therefore at the heart of temporal or spatial shifts. In search for new ways to invest surplus capital, capitalists also strive to appropriate new forms of labour and new resources, both material (such as natural resources), and immaterial (such as knowledge), into the circulation of capital. By doing so, it is possible to create surplus value from previously unexploited work and resources. One way to understand the process of appropriation of labour and resources, in contemporary over-accumulation crises is by looking back at the origins of the capitalist mode of production. In order to explain the relation between geographical imperialism and global capital, Harvey (2003; 2006; 2010a) draws on Marx's discussion of "ursprüngliche" or primitive accumulation in the first volume of *Capital*, in order to unfold the neo-liberal shift in our contemporary societies.

2.1   *Primitive Accumulation*

In Marx's (1867/1990, ch.26) discussion in *Capital*, primitive accumulation is the process in which pre-capitalist modes of production are transformed into capitalism – it is the starting point of the capitalist mode of production. Thus it is also the process, in which the producers are separated from their means of production and where they are transformed into wage labourers that are sold on the market (i.e. labour power becomes a commodity). So primitive accumulation also constitutes the very process, in which the working class is formed:

> The capital-relation presupposes a complete separation between the workers and the ownership of the conditions for the realization of their labour. As soon as capitalist production stands on its own feet, it not only maintains this separation, but reproduces it on a constantly extending scale. The process, therefore, which creates the capital-relation can be nothing other than the process which divorces the worker from the ownership of the conditions of his own labour; it is a process which operates two transformations, whereby the social means of subsistence and production are turned into capital, and the immediate producers are turned into wage-labourers. So-called primitive accumulation, therefore, is nothing else than the historical process of divorcing the producer from the means of production. It appears as 'primitive', because it forms the

pre-history of capital and of the mode of production corresponding to capital.

MARX 1867/1990, 874–875

In Marx's depiction of how the old feudal system was transformed into capitalism, the liberal version of capitalism mounting like a natural evolution of capital is confronted by a much blunter version of reality. The transformation of the feudalist system was a process marked by a brutal and often violent expropriation of capital. The enclosure of the commons, the colonial system, imperialism, the use of slave labour, the expulsion of peasant populations forced into industrial wage labour, etc., were often violent. So in Marx's version of the "ursprüngliche" or primitive accumulation, violence plays a central part. As Marx (1867/1990, 875) argues in a famous statement in *Capital*; "...the history of this, their expropriation, is written in the annals of mankind in letters of blood and fire." Undoubtedly Marx's depiction of the historical process of capital is only partly true; there were also peaceful or at least less violent transformations (Harvey 2010a, 304f). Nevertheless, Marx exposed the liberal myth, painting a picture of a smooth transformation originated from the shoulders of hardworking men with specialized labour skills that became employers – that story was anything but true.

For the labourer, the process of primitive accumulation was double sided, workers were set free from the feudal oppression system, slavery, etc. just to become entrapped in a new relation of exploitation, the system of wage labour – indirect forced labour. Or as Marx argues in *Grundrisse*, in a comment on the indignation of a former slave master on the fact that slaves were freed from bondage, but did *not* become wage labourers in the plantations owned by the latter:

> They have ceased to be slaves, but not in order to become wage laborers, but, instead, self-sustaining peasants working for their own consumption. As far as they are concerned, capital does not exist as capital, because autonomous wealth as such can exist only either on the basis of direct forced labour, slavery, or indirect forced labour, wage labour.
>
> MARX 1857/1993, 326

We will return to some contemporary examples of how self-sufficient peasantry and collectively owned and organized agricultural production (mobilized in the form of social movements such as Movimento dos Trabalhadores Rurais Sem Terra [MST] and Via Campesina) is fighting the expulsion and enforcements of populations into wage-labour, and how media plays a crucial part in justifying the expulsions in the name of economic development.

So, if primitive accumulation is the starting point of the capitalist mode of production, how could it help us understand processes of capital accumulation in contemporary late capitalism? Harvey (2003; 2005; 2006; 2010a) argues, inspired by Luxemburg (1913/2003), that many of the specific features of primitive accumulation are highly visible in today's modern neo-liberal capitalism. For Marx the 'normal' process of accumulation is expanded reproduction, but Luxemburg (1913/2003) argued that the continuous accumulation of capital also inherited a "primitive" feature. This formed one key argument in her theory of imperialism – capital always creates new geographical spaces of exploitation, or "capitalism's penetration of non-capitalist societies" (Callinicos 2009, 40). Luxemburg's theory can also be used for understanding how other milieus outside the circulation of capital are colonised by capital. Marxist feminists have attached Luxemburg's idea of colonialism to the reproductive work done by women in the household (Hartsock 2006). Reproductive work constitutes "an inner colony and milieu of primitive accumulation," by ensuring the reproduction of (male) wage labourer (Fuchs 2011, 282).

Harvey (2006) argues that current accumulation of capital inherits characteristics from the original process as well. In fact, accumulation through expanded reproduction and by dispossession "are organically linked, dialectically intertwined" with each other (Harvey 2003, 176). There are at least two key arguments that locate specific features of primitive accumulation (embedded) in modern capitalist reproduction. First there are numerous examples of population expulsion and appropriations of land (particularly in Latin America and Asia), there are violent extractions of natural resources (all over the global south); and there is systematic and sometimes extreme violence against those who struggle against these processes all over the global south. The level of violence has also been intensified in some instances (Harvey 2010a, 308). Secondly, it seems that the ongoing reproduction of capitalism continues to involve some of the characteristics of primitive accumulation, such as increasing national debt and what Marx (1867/1990, 777ff) identified as the growing credit system. The whole endeavour of the financial credits and loans handed out by IMF and the World Bank have a striking resemblance to the emerging credit system and the state as actor in processes of privatization several hundred years ago. Harvey (2003; 2005; 2006; 2010a) describes these features of primitive accumulation as "accumulation by dispossession." It could be described as the (futile) neo-liberal answer to a continuous decline in global growth (Harvey 2003, 145; 2006, 42). Accumulation by dispossession is characterized by four key elements: *privatization, financialization, the management and manipulation of crises* and *state redistributions* (Harvey 2006).

2.1.1   Privatization

Accumulation by dispossession is manifested by the privatization of public assets – the appropriation of the commons. These privatizations include everything from natural resources (water, land, air), infrastructure (public transport, telecommunications, energy supplies), social systems of redistribution, social services, healthcare, education, public institutions, public housing, warfare, and so on, basically anything that is not already included in the circulation of capital. There is also a privatization of immaterial assets such as knowledge, genetic material, and reproduction processes. All these areas, which previously were outside capital accumulation because they were regarded as commons, public services, of national interest, etc., are appropriated to different degrees in the neo-liberal model of capitalism. By adding them to the circulation of capital they are incorporated into capitalist property relations, thus they also transform the social relations of subjects in society. Students, patients, water drinkers, citizens, etc., are transformed into clients, customers and buyers of goods and services as commodities. The process of accumulation by dispossession is therefore ultimately a process of social exploitation. The contemporary process of privatization has been defined by Indian writer and activist Arundhati Roy (2001 in Harvey 2006, 44–45) as a "barbaric dispossession on a scale that has no parallel in history."

Processes of privatization can be swift and clean without any particularly struggle or use of force, this is predominantly the case in the global north where the state has been the main propagator of privatizations. But the processes of dispossession in the global south are often followed by harsh or violent expulsions of rural populations and appropriations of everyday natural resources (Harvey 2006, 45). Sometimes the outcome of dispossessions is open social struggle and sometimes capital even loses. This was the case during the water wars in Cochabamba, Bolivia, in the late 1990s. During a wave of privatizations orchestrated by the IMF, the city's public drinking water was sold to the US-owned company Bechtel, which resulted in increasing water prices and a limitation of supplies. The dispossession of water resulted in a hard struggle for the right to water as basic human asset, which ultimately forced the city to re-buy the water rights (Olivera and Lewis 2004). So processes of privatization can also sharpen class struggle and class-consciousness in various ways.

Privatization also includes warfare. War is in fact an increasingly commodified endeavour, where private companies make huge profits in security and torture. Warfare is simply a process in which huge transfer of government funding to private owned capital takes place. Luxemburg's (1913/2003, 434) discussion of "militarism as a province of accumulation" of the early 20th-century could basically be an explanation of today's late capitalist imperialism, in which the military-industrial complex plays a key role in facilitating expanded reproduction of capital and 'creating' new spaces of exploitation by violence and destruction (Žižek 2009).

The appropriation of public assets by dispossession creates the appearance of a growing accumulation because new areas of exploitation and processes of surplus value are added to the circulation of capital.

2.1.2   Financialization

The second characteristic of accumulation by dispossession is financialization. The enormous increase in financial capital is intertwined with deregulations of markets, a rapid development of information and communication technology and the processes of privatization. Speculation in the capitalist financial system has contributed to an apparent economical growth through major capital redistributions. The financial system holds a particularly important position in the "thievery" of public assets such as pensions (Harvey 2006, 45). The on-going build-up of fictitious capital, through hedge funds, ponzi schemes and asset stripping, together with an overall emphasis on stock value, generates an apparent economical growth. These processes were depicted as one main factor when the global economic crisis set in 2008. Financialization, and the increasing importance of the financial sector, also marks the stagnation phase in the so-called Kondratiev cycles that distinguish growth and stagnation within the capitalist world system over historical periods (Arrighi 2010). Marx (1867/1990, 920) stressed the importance of the credit system in order to understand the growing power of capital over states and the rapid (spatial) centralization of capital. As an example the IMF and the World Bank are doing the job by setting "up micro-credit and micro-finance institutions to capture what is called 'the wealth at the bottom of the pyramid' and then suck out all that wealth to support ailing international financial institutions…and use that wealth to pay the asset and merger games…" (Harvey 2010a, 272). Media researcher Almiron (2010) highlights the growing relationship between financial capital and news media organizations. News media are increasingly dependent on financial actors, such as banks, and therefore financialization has profound consequences on news practices and content (Almiron 2010).

2.1.3   The Management and Manipulation of Crises

Third, the neo-liberal turn in capitalism has resulted in orchestrated economic crises. Crises permit rapid redistribution of assets and economic shock therapy in the form of structural adjustment programs. Orchestrated crises were more or less the rule in Latin America during the 1980s and the 1990s. Debt crisis in single countries enabled quick changes to the IMF's structural adjustment programs, and thereby transformed the national economies according to the neo-liberal model propagated by transnational institutions such as IMF and the World Bank. These provoked crises resulted in a massive relocation of capital and created an apparent accumulation of capital. The crises produced a large population of unemployed labour force that created "a pool of low wage surplus labour convenient for further accumulation" (Harvey 2006, 47). These crises also expose the use of violence that is applied in order to secure the interest of capital. The violence emanating in the intersection of capital and states is manifested through brutal suppression of protests, labour organizing and social movements all over the global south.

2.1.4   State Redistribution

In neo-liberal capitalism, the state is transformed into the most central actor in the redistribution (privatization) of public assets. The privatization of the public sector, or large cuts in the funding of public services, constitutes the fourth key element in accumulation by dispossession (Harvey 2006, 48). There are numerous examples of how the state, despite the political character of the ruling government, has played a key role in processes of privatization. For example; the privatization of the pension system under fascist dictatorship (in Chile in the early 1980s), during social-democratic governments (in Sweden in the late 1990s) and during the Peronist rule in Argentina (in the 1990s), privatization of public housing in the UK during Thatcher's government in the 1980s, during both social-democratic and centre-right wing (local) governments in Sweden over the past fifteen years, and the privatization of agricultural land during the nationalist rule (PRI) in Mexico in the 1990s. The list of privatizations is almost endless. In the greater perspective, state redistributions spawn massive relocations of public assets to private ownership. The transfer of public assets into the private sector is not only about the privatization of social services such as education, health care, social work, infrastructure, pensions, etc., but it also involves pure money transfers to the business sector in the form of bank rescue programs and government investment in the private sector. In the U.S. the "corporate welfare programs," which signify the neo-liberal turn, have resulted in an enormous redistribution of taxpayer's money into the hands of the private sector (Harvey 2006, 49).

The effects of state redistribution are sometimes violent. There are several cases of direct warfare against social mobilization, for example against social movements in Chiapas and Oaxaca, Mexico, trade unionists in Colombia, the organized landless rural workers in the MST in Brazil, the Adivasi in India, and so on. State redistribution may also involve a more latent symbolic violence against people who are forced from their homes due to property speculation that surfaced in the aftermath of the large privatization of public housing (as in London), or the expulsion of large populations caused by the private expropriation of natural resources (everywhere in the global South). The formation of such indirect violence is a key attribute in several processes in late capitalism. We will now tap into what distinguishes the violence of original/primitive accumulation in relation to our contemporary era of new imperialism through accumulation by dispossession.

2.2   *The Role of Violence in the Process of Accumulation*

In order to understand the neo-liberal turn in capitalist accumulation and the processes that mark the global expansion of capital, we must consider how global capital is connected to territorial geo-politics in a neo-imperialist manner. Primitive accumulation or accumulation by dispossession is basically a form of imperialism (Harvey 2003). Capitalism inherits a contradiction between the global expansion of capital, and a territorial logic of power (geopolitical behaviour of nation states) (Harvey 2006, 105). Harvey's (2003) analysis of imperialism shows that geopolitical rivalry and global capital accumulation coincide and reshape the basis of accumulation. The analysis of capital accumulation and the geopolitical development that consists of both primitive accumulation and expanded reproduction reveal that violence plays a central role in the expansion of the capitalist world system. Violence is simply part of the inner logic of accumulation, it surfaces when its needed as a necessary component in securing the "right" of capital. Wallerstein (2001, 29) argues that the problems of expansion in a period of systemic crisis will be accompanied with potentially more violent capital expansion. Parallel to the political decline due to the weakening position of nation states in relation to transnational institutions such as the IMF/WB, the process will undoubtedly increase the amount of daily violence in the world system. Violence emerges at the intersection of global capital accumulation, especially in the accumulation by dispossession, and the territorial geopolitics of the U.S. as the leading hegemon in the world. So violence is inevitably part of a system that breeds further economic and social inequality, and thus it can be understood as an intra-systemic necessity.

Let us now turn to the specific role of violence in the accumulation by dispossession. The capitalist system relies on both active and underlying violence, as means of securing accumulation and the private control over the means of production. Žižek (2008) distinguishes between subjective and objective violence. Subjective violence, such as interpersonal aggression, crime, terror or the repressive apparatus of the state, is overt and exercised with a specific intent of some sort (pathological, political, patriarchal, etc.). Objective violence is on the other hand built into the practices of capitalism, and manifested in overt discrimination, structural racism, economic destitution, or other forms of more subtle exploitation. The two forms of violence are relational. Subjective violence, for example the suburban riots in cities like Paris and London, can be comprehended in its relation to objective violence, the annihilation of social trust caused by economic exploitation, expulsion, racism and discrimination. Subjective violence is just the more visible of the two (Žižek 2008). As objective violence could be viewed as a consequence of the exploitative social relations in capitalism, it also appears as an underlying threat of violent acts against those who contest it. In this sense, the objective violence is part of what Gramsci defines as the consent of hegemony, a form of violence that intertwines the two forms of capitalist dominance, force and consent, or to put it in Gramsci's (1929–35/1971, 263) words: "hegemony protected by the armour of coercion." Subjective and objective violence are two different manifestations of systemic violence constituted in relation to sociopolitical power and economic exploitation. The global capitalist accumulation by dispossession is often marked with overt systemic violence in the form of crisis therapy, physical destruction of traditional means of production, and material expropriation through warfare and occupation, as we have seen in Iraq (Žižek 2009, 17), and by an increasingly violent, economic impoverishment of subjects in the global South (Ekman 2011). Violence becomes a common feature of capitalist exploitation processes, much so because the system tends to increase an extreme asymmetry in the distribution of assets during processes of expropriation. Objective violence also includes symbolic violence, or what Galtung (1990) defines as "cultural violence." It refers to those aspects of culture that "can be used to justify or legitimize direct or structural violence" (Galtung 1990, 291). So in relation to Žižek's model, cultural violence could include those aspects of news media that legitimize the use of force against social mobilization and protests, or to news media that justifies war.

So, in conclusion, we can view the historical processes of primitive accumulation preceding the capitalist mode of production, i.e. as a historical formation, characterized by colonialism, imperialism, mass expulsions of populations, the creations of mass industries, the working class and capitalists. But we can also consider primitive accumulation as a continuation of characteristics that are embedded in the capitalist mode of production. The never-ending appropriation of labour and recourses through time and space, forced into capitalist property relations, are undoubted tainted by many of the features described by Marx (1867, 1990). At the end, the main feature of primitive accumulation is the forced separation of means of production from the producers.

3   The General Role of Media and Communication in the
     Accumulation of Capital

There is a bundle of theoretical and empirical work that draws on Marx's theory of capital in order to understand the role of media and communication in
the accumulation of capital (cf. Mosco 2009). Fuchs (2011, 141ff) distinguishes
between several aspects, both internal to media and communication (as industries) and external to media and communication (as general accounts) that
might illuminate its specific role in the processes of capital accumulation.
I will only touch upon a couple of aspects that could be useful in order to
understand media and communication in relation to primitive accumulation
or accumulation by dispossession. The first aspect deals with the ideological
dimension of media content and the structural relations between news systems and the financial sector. The ideological element is crucial to the reproduction of capitalism in various ways, economically, politically, juridical and so
forth. For example, the media have a powerful position in reifying social relations by normalizing and facilitating the privatization of everyday life. For
example, media content produces the audiences as consumers of goods and
services. The aim here is not to evoke too much of the historical discussion of
ideology critique, but to distinguishes some core ideological elements in relation to accumulation by dispossession. Second, the discussion on how the free
time of individuals is appropriated and transformed into surplus labour,
touches upon the notion of how social media work as an infrastructure for
advertisement that advances capital accumulation (cf. Fuchs 2011, 149). Social
media and modern information technology are crucial in the compression of
time and space in the everyday circulation of commodities. We are, when using
smart-phones, going online, and so on, constantly targeted as consumers. In
fact, most parts of the Internet have been commercialized, and processes of
commodification constantly subjugate users. There is not much that separates
commercial from non-commercial content on the Internet (Hesmondhalgh
2007, 259).

3.1   *News Media and the Naturalization of Accumulation
       by Dispossession*

I would like to address a couple of cases, in which both structural and ideological dimensions of news media could be pinpointed in relation to processes of
primitive accumulation and accumulation by dispossession. The first case discusses the role of news in relation to the privatization of public services and
how news media coincide with the interest of, and facilitates the practices of,
the financial sector (cf. Almiron 2010; Hope 2010). The second example deals

with the media representation of the global justice movement, global protests and the World Social Forum in Swedish mass media (Ekman 2011).

3.1.1   Endorsing Privatization and Facilitating Financialization

In the 1980s and the 1990s most of the countries in the world were swept along the wave of privatizations that mark the neo-liberal turn in the global capitalist system. In Sweden, where the public sector previously was well developed and economically prioritized, processes of deregulation and privatization transpired in an increasing speed. The situation in Sweden reflected, more or less, the tendencies that were visible in the rest of Western Europe. In correspondence to the rapid wave of privatization in the 1990s the noun "market" emerged as one of the most prominent agents in the news on economical matters (cf. Mårtenson 2003; Viscovi 2006). The representation of the "market" as a unified actor, which reacts on political decisions, declares which political actors are good or bad, and decides on how to view the overall economic condition, changed the discourse of news reporting on economical matters (Mårtenson 2003). The mediated notion of the "market" emerged as an ideological element to the neo-liberal turn and the massive deregulation of the capitalist economy. In correspondence to the emergence of the "market," news turned to the financial sector, and the stock market became a prevailing feature. This also meant that actors from the financial sector tended to dominate as experts in the everyday news flow. The representation of economic issues was signified by a shift from labour markets, unions, etc. to the financial sector and the construction of the mediated citizen as a private-economic subject (as opposed to wage-labourer, a citizen, or someone outside the realm of finance speculation) (Viscovi 2006). Almiron's (2010, 167) study on two leading Spanish newspapers in 2006 shows a similar result. Financial actors and indicators dominate the news, and Almiron (2010, 167) conclude that: "the lack of independent journalistic investigation in most of the information was almost absolute." The paradigm shift within the news, identified by Mårtenson (2003) and Viscovi (2006), corresponded with the process of financialization in accumulation by dispossession.

Let's consider one specific Swedish case that signifies the role of news media in endorsing privatization by facilitating the transfer of ordinary people's savings into the financial market, and one truly global phenomenon that shows how news flows become intertwined with financial flows and how the interests of financial news coincide with the interests of financial actors.

In June 2000 the publically owned telecommunication company Telia was partly privatized (30 percent was sold to the public). Almost one million Swedes became shareholders after substantial commercial advertising (in television, newspapers and in the public space) and after a political campaign (the whole privatization was endorsed on a personal level by the minister of finance) aided by news media. In the process of privatizing part of the company, the stock was promoted as a "people's-share"[3] in the news. This ideological noun was used in order to smoothen out the fact that the public now could buy something that was already in their possession, and with the opportunity to make a profit.[4] For example, a couple of weeks prior to the privatization, the second largest tabloid, Expressen, published several articles endorsing the readers to purchase shares. One article used the luring headline: "Eight reasons in favor of Telia...This is why the share might become a winner" (Bolander 2000a). Articles, both in tabloids and dailies, used financial actors to boost the privatization and the opportunity to make a quick profit: "Stock market experts believe in a killing on the market" (headline in Bolander 2000b), "Telia is predicted a good start. Experts advise to purchase the new people's-share" (headline in Magnusson 2000). Some articles were just plain buyers guides: "How to purchase Telia – the new people's-share" (headline in Norlin 2000), "How you can purchase the people's-share" (headline in Wendel 2000). The list of articles aiding the privatization could be extended. The whole construction of a "people's-share" is very much a media phenomenon interlinked to the increasing focus on the financial sector. When searching the largest Swedish press archive *Mediearkivet*, it reveals that the term "people's-share" appeared in a total of 186 articles prior to the privatization of Telia. But from the year 1999, when the privatization process started, and onwards, it has appeared 1113 times, peaking at 400 articles in the year 2000. The seven biggest Swedish newspapers published 220 articles containing the word "people's-share" in the year 2000 alone.

The privatization of public infrastructures such as telecommunication services corresponds to similar processes of marketization within news production (Almiron 2010). The mounting commercialization of news and the increasing symbiosis between financial news and the financial sector, paralleled by limited economic recourses and increasing time limits within journalistic production, results in a very uncritical journalism (of course with notable exceptions). The harsher conditions of news journalism as a result of increasing demands of higher profit margins (obtained from what Marx defines as

---

3   The noun "people's-share", corresponds to the concept of the "people's-home", a term used to explain the Swedish welfare model that prevailed in Swedish society during the post ww II-period. The concept of a people's-home, was first used in 1928 in a speech by Swedish Prime Minister Per Albin Hansson (Meidner 1993, 212).

4   However, this was not the case. The share became a huge disappointment, and by 2010 the value was reduced to half the launching price in 2000 (Dalarnas Tidningar 2010).

relative surplus value, 1867/1990, 429ff), simultaneously with a decrease in sales, make financial news an easy target for economically well-situated actors in the financial markets. So apart from the obvious role of information and communication technology in facilitating the circulation of capital in the financial markets, the equivalent role of traditional news media should not be overlooked (cf. Hope 2010).

So, let us now look at a more global phenomenon where news media coincide with the interest of, and facilitates the practices of, financial markets. We now move to the accumulation of capital that Marx defines as M-M', money generated out of money (Marx 1867/1990, 248). The relationship between news media and the financial sector is not new; on the contrary it goes back to the very first European newspaper, owned by a banking family (Almiron 2010, 68). However, as a consequence of the massive deregulations of the financial sector (banking, credit flows, etc.) and the emergence of new means for financial speculation through information and communication technology in the 1990s, information within news media flows and financial flows started to overlap in real time (Hope 2010, 654). Broadcasters such as Bloomberg and CNBC became engines in the mounting flow of asset transfers within the financial sector, generating a massive speculative financial economy. In the 1980s and 90s large television networks fused with the world of financial transactions, providing vast amounts of financial information to journalists all over the world (Hope 2010). One could argue that finance broadcasting provided the raw material (in the form of digits, index, rates, financial "expert" discourses, etc.) to news outlets all over the world. This raw material was then used in producing news in different media settings in different economic and geographical contexts. A rapid movement on the stock markets somewhere in the global financial system had a direct impact on both actors in the financial sector as well in the media sector. In the mid-1990s these media/finance flows of information were also transferred online, creating an instant flow of financial information on the Internet. The merger of interests between the field of finance capital and news journalism that was visible to a certain extent in the 1980s became more or less standard after the rapid development of information and communication technologies in the 1990s (Hope 2010). In the beginning of the 21st century "most of the top news-media conglomerates have experienced a huge increase in their financial links and dependencies" (Almiron 2010, 152). So considering the instant flow of information through communication systems, the growth within the financial sector exploded in the first years of the past decade. The increase in Web-based financial actors flourished alongside computer generated algorithmic trading, secrete hedge funds, derivative trading, asset-stripping, and so on, creating an enormous build-up of fictitious capital. In all this, the relationship between actors within news media organisations and in the financial sector became even more blurred, both in case of ownership and personal interests among journalists. For example, high-prolific journalists became advisers on financial blogs and the blogosphere "helped to constitute the informational environments of financial print media and business television channels" (Hope 2010, 660).

The mutual interest between news and the financial sector was a great factor in the (almost) total failure of journalism in the build up to the economic crisis in 2008 (Almiron 2010). The general oblivious attitude among journalists and news producers towards the preceding financial break down in 2008 have rendered some internal criticism (see for example Schechter 2009; Fraser 2009), but the overall discussion of the political economy of financial news is still marginal outside critical media research.

So considering the role of financial news outlets and economical journalists, news media have without a doubt contributed to the increasing speculation in the financial system, by aiding the processes of financialization. The 'superfluousness' of financial information, instantly transferred through communication systems, has together with an increasing dependency on, and ownership by, financial actors, contributed to uncritical news flows on economic issues. You could even argue that a major part of the financial news is mere an informational infrastructure of finance capital interests. In relation to what Marx (1867/1990, 920) identified as the emerging credit system (what is basically today's finance system), the role of banks, credit institutions and other financial actors could not be understated in relation to the compression of time and space through communications systems. Undeniably, the function of ICT's and financial news flows in facilitating the rapid centralization of capital in the hands of financial institutions, establishes them as key actors much as the banks and the credit system in the historic processes of primitive accumulation (Marx 1867/1990).

3.1.2 The Global Justice Movement: Violence and Politics

The global justice movement is at the forefront of the struggle against accumulation by dispossession. It is a diverse but socially and politically coherent movement of movements that addresses the specific relation between capital and processes that resemble the features of primitive accumulation described by Marx. The struggles fought by different social movements are aimed at ongoing processes of peasant expulsions, privatization of natural recourses, the thievery of land and means of production, the suppression of indigenous people, the financial system of debts and structural adjustment programs, all coerced by national and global capital aided by brute state power. In conclusion, the global justice movement could be seen as a social and political reaction to the processes that constitute capital accumulation by dispossession (Harvey 2010a, 313).

The mobilizations against a series of global summits towards the end of the last millennium became visible to a transnational public during the WTO-meeting in Seattle in late November 1999. Following an explosion of protests around the world at similar events, the Global Justice Movement made headline news all over the world (Klein 2001). Through the creation of the World Social Forum (WSF) in 2001, the diverse political resistance generated by the dispossession of labour, resources and land, constituted a common ground. The World Social Forum facilitates a unique space for discussions, meetings, seminars, and social contacts that generates diverse political collaborations, platforms, campaigns, and decisions (Sen and Waterman 2009). In short – the WSF and the global justice movement represent the first step in organizing global resistance against capital in an age that has been characterized as post-political (Mouffe 2008).

So, how did the social mobilizations of the global justice movement come to the fore in (Swedish) mainstream news? On the one hand, the more moderate political issues connected to the features of accumulation by dispossession such as debt relief, financial speculation and the consequences of deregulations, did make it into the news flow. The demand for debt relief, taxes on financial speculation and the right to certain basic goods (particularly water), *were* addressed in the mainstream, and sometimes even endorsed by political commentators and actors outside the global justice movement. On the other hand, at the end, it also became clear that most of the representation focused on the social and political impossibilities of achieving any larger changes within the global economic system. When political action was represented in the news media, such as in the mobilization for a total debt relief, the framing neglected the long-going struggle among social movements against the structural adjustment programs of the IMF and the World Bank. Instead representatives of Western governments were given credit for putting the issue on the agenda of global summits (Ekman 2011). A similar conclusion could be drawn from research made on US news media. As Lance Bennett and colleagues conclude from their study on US news media: "Perhaps the greatest irony in the journalistic construction of the globalization debate is that WEF elites were given disproportionate credit for issues that activists had long before defined and attempted to get into the news on their own terms" (Bennett et al. 2004, 450). The struggles of large social movements against accumulation by dispossession were mostly ignored and when they did come to the fore in the news, their struggles were often depicted as obsolete. In the dominating liberal discourse on globalization, peasant mobilization and struggle were framed as something that stalled wider economic progress and prosperity in the global south. At least this was the case in the mainstream reporting on the political agenda of the World Social Forum (Ekman 2011).

More radical political issues that confronted the very rationale of global economic and political structures were less visible; instead much of the news coverage tended to focus either on what was framed as a political and social incoherence of the global justice movement or at the violence occurring during the protests. In the case of the global protests against summits, the political dimension in the news flow was totally subordinated to reports about violence, or even reports about *potential* violence. The latter was manifested by news reports on upcoming protests as violent threats, as unavoidable violent confrontations, and even as non-present violence (through comments on the surprisingly peaceful character of demonstrations) (Ekman 2011, 136). When political matters were addressed, the global justice movement was described negatively in relation to the dominant institutional practices and processes in summits (Ekman 2011).

A closer look at the representation of violence reveals that it constitutes one of the primary expectations in the news reporting. The focus on violence forms an element in a far-reaching historical understanding of protests, which is naturalized in the discursive practices between journalism and state/police institutions (cf. Halloran, Elliot and Murdock 1970; Murdock 1981; Carter and Weaver 2003; Doyle 2003; Cottle 2006). Mediated violence tends to reproduce a police-based law and order discourse, and works as a rationalization of power, in which journalism first and foremost reproduces the image of systemic violence as necessary for protecting citizens and for maintaining general order in relation to organized violent protests (cf. Wahl-Jorgensen 2003). So, mediated violence could be viewed as a double-edged sword in relation to the social mobilization of the global justice movement. On the one hand, news media dismiss part of the protests and the protesters for being violent. On the other hand, news media legitimize and justifies systemic violence by mainly disseminating a police discourse of law and order (cf. Galtung 1990). For example, in the news representation of the mobilization against the wTO-meeting in Cancún 2003, news media naturalized the militarization of the meeting by framing it as an issue of "security" (Ekman 2011). Several news articles depicted the massive presence of military and police (more than 20.000), military helicopters, military vessels and police barriers as "protection" for the wTO-delegates (Ekman 2011, 157). Simultaneously, the demonstrations were depicted as threats to "free trade" (Ekman 2011, 156). This form of objective violence emerges at the intersection of state/capital militarization and news media (cf. Zizek 2008).

In conclusion, the news representation of the global justice movement is dominated by hegemonic discourses on globalization, economics, social protests and politics. The rationale of neo-liberal ideology is manifested in the dominant discourse of "globalism" (cf. Fairclough 2006). It holds a preferential position in explaining how social change takes place in mediated public political debates during the period of contested neo-liberal hegemony (Ekman 2011). News coverage of global mobilization and resistance are ultimately reified as a result of the absence of any larger discussions or explanations of the global economic system that are not intra-systemic. Instead the reality is truncated, simplified and packaged, and complex social relationships are reified in relation to dominant discourses of the global economy (Ekman 2011). As media scholar Berglez (2006, 180) argues: journalism "partly embraces and 'shows understanding' for the political struggle against the capitalist system, although in terms of *neutralizing* the radical dimension of the political struggle (making it less leftist and class-located), thereby paving the way for the transformation of the radical political struggle into another (normal) *everyday life practice*." So, huge global social mobilizations against accumulation by dispossession, do not gain any significant political legitimization through conventional media exposure.

3.2   *Dispossession of Everyday Online Activity*
The second part, in which Harvey's theory of accumulation by dispossession could be used in relation to media and communication research, is by examining the specific role of online communication systems and platforms. Here Marx's (1867/1990, 668ff) discussion on how surplus value is generated could explain how work performed by users of social media are appropriated by capital and transformed into surplus labour. So here we will tap into the ongoing discussion of how to understand the activity performed by everyday users of social media on Web 2.0 (often refer to as prod*users*) in relation to capitalist interests (cf. Fuchs 2009; Jakobsson and Stiernstedt 2010). The production of surplus value by exploiting the activity performed on social media sites such as Facebook, YouTube, etc. is made possible by selling users, and more specifically, the output of their work, to advertisers. The concept of media audiences as commodities is well debated within the research field of political economy of communication (cf. Smythe 1982/2006; Mosco 2009, 136ff). The main element in Smythe's (1982/2006) argument is that the audience constitutes the main commodity of the mass media (Mosco 2009, 136). Smythe's concept highlighted the role of media producers in the construction of audiences in relation to advertisers. The idea of audience commodification also located media organizations into the "total capitalist economy" (Mosco 2009, 137), as an integrated

part in the circulation of capital. However, the idea of audiences performing work for media owners, for example by watching television, have been largely debated within the field of political economy (Mosco 2009, 137). Media scholar Bolin (2011, 37) suggests that viewing television could be understood as "a part of the recreation of the worker's labour power." Watching TV is not an activity that produces something, but instead a process that could be defined as a *raw material* in the production process undertaken by advertisers and media companies. Thus, watching television is part of the means of production (viewer as statistics), but it can't be considered labour (Bolin, 2011, 37). In the first phase of the circulation of capital, when the capitalist acts as a buyer of commodities, companies purchases statistic on viewer demographics (Mp) used in producing advertisements (cf. Marx 1867/1990). However, Mosco (2009, 137) argues that whether Smythe's idea of audiences constituting labour is useful or not could be left aside. Instead the main insight of the materialist approach in Smythe's theory is the concept of a reciprocal relationship in the triad of "media company-audience-advertiser" (Mosco 2009, 137). The idea that mass media are not only ideological producers or transmitters, but also totally integrated in the circulation of capital is unquestionably useful when analyzing the political economy of mass media. Moreover, since Internet use is different from the 'work' of traditional mass media audiences, by the concrete activity of users, Smythe's theory proves to be more fruitful when considering everyday online activity, compared to traditional television watching or newspaper reading.

As Fuchs (2010; 2011) points out, social values are continuously quantified, measured, aggregated and reified in digital social networks. Commercial developers of social media services continuously develop more advanced (and detailed) surveillance systems to appropriate and refine what Marx's (1867/1990, 274) defined as the 'peculiar commodity' – labour power – sold to advertisers. Audience labour consists of both the labour time and the meta-data generated from user interaction, and since digital labour is 'free' (Terranova 2013), capital's "immanent drive...towards increasing the productivity of labour" (Marx 1867/1990, 436f) does not depend on the relative reduction of variable capital, but on the extension of the appropriated (surplus) labour in time and intensity (i.e. productivity). The work dispossessed by capital is everything users do when they are communicating through various commercial platforms and sites on the Internet. For example, in the case of Facebook and other networking platforms, this process of transferring surplus labour of online activity by everyday users into the circulation of capital, is refined by providing to advertisers specific segments of users, based on the information obtained from Web traffic, preferences and activities on networking sites and other places on the

Internet. Here the appropriated labour consists of everything we do when we are online. Most parts of the work performed by users are monitored and enclosed by different networking sites, search engines, e-mail services, etc. Here you could actually speak about a process that separates the means of production (intellectual, communicative and creative) from the worker (pro-dusers) (Marx 1867/1990, 875). It is not a direct forced separation, but an indirect one. The indirect forcing factors are basically the disadvantages that you might experience when being outside a network platform such as Facebook, for example the loss of job-opportunities, personal connections, social relations, and other immaterial assets. The price of being outside could be measured against the fact that you "sell" all your information and activities to a commercial actor to be able to participate. As a consequence, everyday online activity constitutes a dynamic field of potential surplus labour ready to be transformed into surplus value. This is refined by surveillance systems that track user behaviours and monitor activity by categorizing what is uploaded, "liked" (in the case of Facebook), what your e-mails contains (in the case of Gmail), what Websites you visit on a regular basis, and basically everything that you do when surfing the corporate part of the World Wide Web (Fuchs 2011; Jakobsson and Stiernstedt 2010).

However it is not only the time and the work, in the form of texts, images, videos, and other aspects of personal information (in the form of unpaid labour) that are dispossessed by capital. Network sites such as Facebook also transform the social relations between users and business corporations. When users integrate companies, brands, and other commodities into their everyday social networks, the producer-consumer relationship becomes just another personal relationship, much like the one you have in your everyday social life. For example, Coca Cola has almost 40 million fans on its Facebook page.[5] Since companies, brands and products have their own pages in networking sites such as Facebook, the interaction between business and consumers is, potentially, instant and never ending. The activities on social networks sites also advance commodified individualism by transforming inter-personal communication in relation to products and consumption (cf. Fuchs 2011, 315). The marketing strategies of big multi-national companies aim to captivate the social being in itself, creating milieus that colonize every lasting part of private and personal life. This reflects, or indeed advances, what Jhally (2000, 29) refers to as the "overwhelming...commercial colonization of our culture." The most ultimate appearance of this reification process is probably the ideology and practice that indulges the construction of the individual self as a brand, or as a platform

---

5   In the form of "likes" (Facebook 2012).

for commercial branding. This is a phenomenon that is highly visible in the blogosphere. In the anticipation of catching the eye of advertising firms, in order to get some revenue from the business sector, thousands of bloggers act like advertising posters for brand names and products by incorporating and mediating their consumption in communication platforms in Web 2.0. Consequently communication platforms and infrastructures constitute a highly dynamic arena for dispossession of labour and the "life" outside ordinary wage-labour. When free time and the social conditions of every-day life become integrated in the production-consumption relation of capital accumulation, users are reified simply by being unpaid producers of images, texts, videos, stories, etc., that transform them into commodities that are sold to advertisers and companies. All the user-generated content on commercial platforms such as Facebook are owned, stored and processed with the purpose of generating surplus value, this is of course the whole idea of corporate investments. In fact, the Internet is overflowed by capital interests, so you could primarily characterize it as a "space...dominated by corporations" (Fuchs 2011, 337).

The rapid development of information and communication technology also has implications for the commodification of public space. For example, in relation to the research on the privatization of public space (cf. Harvey 1989; Sennett 1992), contemporary mobile phone technology has new and dynamic ways of luring subjects into the production-consumption relation of capital accumulation. The traditional debate on the privatization processes of public space has focused on how public spaces are transformed into shopping malls, corporatized areas, gated communities and so on, creating what Sennett (1992) refers to as "dead public spaces." These sanitized and corporately controlled commodified spaces are increasingly visible all over the globe. The most striking feature of these spaces is how they affect social relations and behaviours, by incorporating and naturalizing patterns of consumption into the organization of everyday life.

However, with the rapid development of mobile phone technology, *all* public spaces become potentially commodified. The mere fact that a person may well be constantly logged in to her/his Facebook account through the mobile phone opens up for a whole new dimension of the commodification of public space. This suggests that you are, at least potentially, submitted to constant corporate surveillance, monitored by several actors integrated in your online networks, and thus performing unpaid labour that is appropriated by capital. This has serious implications for the very idea of privacy (cf. Fuchs 2011, 313) and in fact the whole notion of what constitutes free time, what constitutes work and public space. Since smart phones enable the interaction between conventional advertisement (billboards, posters, etc.) and online activities by the use of

Quick response-codes (QR) etc., the activities in physical public space (whether in the subway on your way to work, or at the billboard posted on the wall in your neighbourhood) are integrated with your activities in your virtual space. Moreover. the "apps" that seems to facilitate individual communication patterns, also colonize private subjects and alter patterns of social behaviour in everyday life by transferring them into the production-consumption relation of capital accumulation. The "apps" have a double-commodified character, they are goods that users are purchasing, and they also engage users in more consumer-based activities. Furthermore, since users increasingly rely on smartphone apps, they also expose themselves to intricate technological systems of surveillance. Smartphone apps' transmit sensitive personal data, such as usernames and passwords, the physical location of the phone/user, information on sex, age, personal contacts, and sent and received text messages, to the company that owns the app, and also to third parties (Wall Street Journal 2010).

Needless to say, the development of mobile phones and the massive dislocation of space when performing online communication also open up for a more positive and creative non-commercial communicative behaviour. It can enable political and social mobilization and resistance to capital and the political structures that uphold the exploitation of labour (Fuchs 2011). The problem is of course not rapid development of communication technology, but the colonization of communicative social relations by capital.

In relation to the features of accumulation by dispossession, the surveillance and invasion of privacy by corporate Internet owners such as Facebook, Google, Yahoo, and so on, could be understood as means to expand the reification of social relations and the self. But I will also like to stress the possibilities of one other factor immanent in the processes of primitive accumulation – violence. If we accept Žižek's (2008) idea of systemic violence as inherited by a subjective (physical) and an objective (structural or symbolic) dimension, we could argue that corporate surveillance of private subjects through technologies that monitor the information we upload, and the activities we participate in our online activities, constitute a potential objective violence. The ownership of such a great amount of information on the private being of individuals and groups, without any transparency of how this huge bundle of information is stored or used, could be comprehended as a potential threat to subjects. Besides the fact that advertised based networks and platforms already censor and forbid certain content and activities in order to satisfy advertisers (Fuchs 2011), the information of private subjects could potentially be sold to anyone. This implies that information regarding political issues or other socially sensitive oriented matters (how private the user may think they are in respect to privacy settings and person-to-person communication) could be gathered and used for purposes other than commercial advertising. So, in this respect, the surveillance of the corporate Internet could be comprehended as a potential threat simply because there is no guarantee what the information will be used for, who is buying it and to what extent private/personal information is circulated. Sensitive information, owned, gathered and processed by companies like Facebook, could be sold as commodities to actors within the military-industrial complex, or to political actors. Since surveilled subjects, and the constant flow of information emanating from users, are commodities in the market place, objective violence appears as an underlying threat to those whose personal/private information contests the current interests of the ruling political and economic powers.

4   Conclusion

In order to identify the role and function of news media and communication systems in the ongoing accumulation of capital, I have argued that Marx's (1867/1990) concept of primitive accumulation and Harvey's (2003; 2006; 2010) theory of accumulation by dispossession could contribute to critical media and communication research. The concept of primitive accumulation as a continuing set of characteristics within the expanded reproduction of capital is useful in order to understand some distinctive elements in contemporary news media content, news flows and news media systems, and within the development of online communication platforms. The processes that distinguish capital accumulation in the time of neo-liberal global expansion coincide with many of Marx's descriptions of how pre-capitalist modes of production were transformed into capitalism. The ongoing global crisis reveals that expanded reproduction of capital is facing many constrains, and thus the search for new ways to secure the accumulation of capital indicate that more and more aspects of our societies are, and will continue to be, relocated into capital property relations. In these transformation processes, new areas of commodification are located and new ways of appropriating unpaid (free time) labour are developed. In these processes news media systems and online communication play a considerable dynamic part. This chapter has targeted two areas in which primitive accumulation/accumulation by dispossession could contribute to the research field of the political economy of media and communication.

First, I have addressed the specific ideological dimension of news and the function of financial news flows and systems in relation to capital accumulation. Second, I have discussed various aspects of how surplus value is produced in relation to everyday Internet use and in relation to the rapid advancement of communication technology.

The first aspect that can be summarized here is how news media facilitate the privatization of the commons, endorse the transfer of public assets into private property relations and depoliticize and delegitimize social mobilization against capital. Furthermore the chapter shows how news flows and news media systems coincide and interlink with financial flows and actors, thus constituting a close relationship between financial news and the finance sector. This relationship is also attached to the rapid changes within information and communication technology and the compression of time and space in capital accumulation.

The second aspect dissects the political economy of Web. 2.0 with a specific focus on how prod*users* are commodified and sold to advertisers and how the work performed by users in social network platforms such as Facebook is appropriated by capital. The commodification of social media and Internet use has potentially far-reaching possibilities. The colonization of free time, the total commercialization of recreation, personal social relations and even the self, by capital, is made possible by the corporate control over the user dimension in social networks and other social media platforms. Internet surveillance, in which commercial gathering, owning and processing of private information, is one of the major assets in the circulation of capital and could be viewed as a potentially threat to users, and even a part of the objective violence constituted in capitalist exploitation.

Undeniably this chapter has focused on the negative aspects of how mainstream news media facilitates and reproduces the exploitation of capital, how the use of new information/communication technology become colonized by capital, and how commodification processes tend to dominate the flow of information in global media and communication systems. However, there are also several aspects of media production and communication technology that point in an opposite direction and open up for counter-hegemonic formations in a global context. The dynamic production and circulation of alternative and radical media and the ongoing struggle for a commons-based Internet are important aspects to highlight within critical media and communication research. The realm of news media production and communication technologies is never monolithic, thus it also needs to be theorized and analysed from the perspective of emerging alternatives (cf. Fuchs 2011). After all, the groundbreaking theory of Marx on capitalism also points out alternatives to the total exploitation of capital.

References

Almiron, Núria. 2010. *Journalism in Crisis. Corporate Media and Financialization*. New Jersey: Hampton Press.

Arrighi, Giovanni. 2010. *The Long Twentieth Century.* London: Verso.

Bennett, W. Lance, Victor W. Pickard, David P. Iozzi, Carl L. Schroeder, Taso Lagos and C. Evans Caswell. 2004. Managing the public sphere: Journalistic construction of the great globalization debate. *Journal of Communication* 54 (3): 437–455.

Berglez, Peter. 2006. *The Materiality of Media Discourse – On Capitalism and Journalistic Modes of Writing.* Örebro: Örebro Studies in Media and Communication 4.

Bolander, Hans. 2000a. Åtta skäl som talar för Telia. Expressens Hans Bolander: Därför kan aktien bli en vinnare. *Expressen* May 21. 6.

Bolander, Hans. 2000b. Börsexperterna tror på klipp. *Expressen* May 31. 6.

Bolin, Göran. 2011. *Value and the Media.* Farnham and Burlington: Ashgate.

Callinicos, Alex. 2009. *Imperialism and Global Political Economy.* London: Polity Press.

Carter, Cynthia and C. Kay Weaver. 2003. *Violence and the Media.* Buckingham and Philadelphia: Open University Press.

Cottle, Simon. 2006. *Mediatized conflict: developments in media and conflict studies.* New York: Open University Press.

Dalarnas Tidningar. 2010. Så mycket har Teliaaktien fallit. Dalarnas Tidningar 14 June 2010. Accessed 25 February 2012. http://www.dt.se/nyheter/dalarna/1.3086140-sa -mycket-har-teliaaktien-fallit.

Doyle, Aaron. 2003. *Arresting Images: Crime and Policing in Front of the Television Camera.* Toronto: Toronto University Press.

Ekman, Mattias. 2011. *Den globala rättviserörelsen i svenska medier.* Stockholm: JMK.

Facebook CocaCola. 2012. Accessed 20 February 2012. http://www.facebook.com/ cocacola.

Fairclough, Norman. 2006. *Language and Globalization.* New York: Routledge.

Fraser, Matthew. 2009. Five reasons for crash blindness. *British Journalism Review* 20 (4): 78–83.

Fuchs, Christian. 2009. Some reflections on Manuel Castells' book Communication Power. *tripleC – Cognition, Communication, Co-operation: Open Access Journal for a Global Sustainable Information Society* 7 (1): 94–108. Accessed 27 February 2012. http://www.triple-c.at/index.php/tripleC/article/view/136/90.

Fuchs, Christian. 2010. Labor in Informational Capitalism and on the Internet. *The Information Society: An International Journal* 26 (3): 179–196.

Fuchs, Christian. 2011. *Foundations of Critical Media and Information Studies.* New York: Routledge.

Galtung, Johan. 1990. Cultural Violence. *Journal of Peace Research* 27 (3): 291–305.

Gramsci, Antonio. 1929-35/1971. *Selections from the Prison Notebooks.* New York: International Publishers.

Halloran, James. D., Philip Elliot and Graham Murdock. 1970. *Demonstrations and Communication: A Case Study.* Harmondsworth, England: Penguin Books.

Hartsock, Nancy. 2006 Globalization and Primitive Accumulation: The Contributions of David Harvey's Dialectical Marxism. In *David Harvey. A Critical Reader,* ed. Noel Castree and Derek Gregory. Malden, MA: Blackwell.

Harvey, David. 1982/2006.*The Limits to Capital.* London: Verso.

Harvey, David. 1989. From Managerialism to Entrepreneurialism: The Tansformation of Urban Governance in Late Capitalism. *Geografiska Annaler* 71 (B): 3–17.

Harvey, David. 2003. *The New Imperialism.* Oxford: Oxford University Press.

Harvey, David. 2005. *A Brief History of Neoliberalism.* Oxford: Oxford University Press.

Harvey, David. 2006. *Spaces of Global Capitalism: A Theory of Uneven Geographical Development.* London: Verso.

Harvey, David. 2010a. *A Companion to Marx's Capital.* London: Verso.

Harvey, David. 2010b. *The Enigma of Capital: And the crises of Capitalism.* London: Profile Books.

Hesmondhalgh, David. 2007. *The Cultural Industries.* London: Sage.

Hope, Wayne. 2010. Time Communication, and Financial Collapse. *International Journal of Communication* 4 (2010): 649–669.

Jakobsson, Peter and Fredrik Stiernstedt. 2010. Pirates of Silicon Valley: State of exception and dispossession in Web 2.0. *First Monday* 15 (7). Accessed February 25, http://firstmonday.org/htbin/cgiwrap/bin/ojs/index.php/fm/article/view/2799/2577.

Jhally, Sut. 2000. Advertising at the edge of the apocalypse. In *Critical studies in media commercialism,* ed. Robin Andersen and Lance Strate. New York: Oxford University Press.

Klein, Naomi. 2001. Reclaiming The Commons. *New Left Review* 9: 81–89.

Luxemburg, Rosa. 1913/2003. *The Accumulation of Capital.* London: Routledge Classics.

Magnusson, Karl. Erik. 2000. Telia spås en bra start. Experterna råder till köp av den nya folkaktien. *Göteborgs-Posten* May 22. 35.

Marx, Karl. 1857/1993. *Grundrisse: Foundations of the critique of political economy.* London: Penguin Classics.

Marx, Karl. 1867/1990. *Capital: Volume 1: A Critique of Political Economy.* London: Penguin Classics.

Marx, Karl. 1885/1992. *Capital: Volume 2: A Critique of Political Economy.* London: Penguin Classics.

Mediearkivet. 2012. Accessed on February 25. https://web.retriever-info.com/.

Meidner, Rudolf. 1993. Why did the Swedish Model Fail? *Socialist Register* 29: 211–228.

Mosco, Vincent. 2009. *The Political Economy of Communication. Second Edition.* London: Sage Publications.

Mouffe, Chantal. 2008. *Om det politiska.* Hägersten: Tankekraft.

Murdock, Graham. 1981. Political Deviance: the press presentation of a militant mass demonstration. In *The Manufacture of News: social problems, deviance and the mass media,* ed. Stanley Cohenand Jock Young.London: Constable.

Mårtenson, Bo. 2003. *Den televiserade ekonomin- Nyheter om statsbudgeten 1980–1995.* Stockholm: JMK.

Norlin, Arne. 2000. Så köper du Telia – Den nya folkaktien. *Aftonbladet* April 15. 5.

Olivera, Oscar and Tom Lewis. 2004. *Cochabamba! Water Rebellion in Bolivia.* Boston: South End Press.

Schechter, Danny. 2009. Credit crisis: How did we miss it? *British Journalism Review* 20 (1): 19–26.

Sen, Jai and Peter Waterman. (eds.) 2009. *World Social Forum Challenging Empires.* Montreal/New York/London: Black Rose Books.

Sennett, Richard. 1992. *The Fall of Public Man.* New York: W.W. Norton.

Smythe, Dallas. W. 1982/2006. On the Audience Commodity and its Work. In *Media and Cultural Studies Keyworks,* ed. Meenakshi Gigi Durham and Douglas M. Kellner, 230–256. Malden, MA: Blackwell.

Terranova, Tiziana. 2013. Free Labor. In *Digital Labor: Internet as Playground and Factory,* ed. Trebor Scholz, 33–57. New York, NY: Routledge.

Viscovi, Dino. 2006. *Marknaden som monster och monster. Ekonomiska experter och nyheter om ekonomi i Rapport 1978–1998.* Göteborg: JMG.

Wallerstein, Immanuel. 2001. *Liberalismens död.* Stockholm: Vertigo.

Wall Street Journal. 2010. What They Know- Mobile. *WSJ Blogs.* Accessed 22 February, 2014. http://blogs.wsj.com/wtk-mobile/.

Wahl-Jorgensen, Karin. 2003 Speaking Out Against the Incitement to Silence: The British Press and the 2001 May Day Protests. In *Representing Resistance- Media, Civil Disobedience and The Global Justice Movment,* ed. Andy Opel and Donnalyn Pompper. 130–148. Westport/CT: Praeger Publishers.

Wendel, Per. 2000. Så köper du folkaktien. *Expressen* May 21. 6.

Žižek, Slavoj. 2008 *Violence. Six sideways reflections.* New York: Picador.

Žižek, Slavoj. 2009 *First as Tragedy, Then As Farce.* London: Verso.

CHAPTER 5

The Internet and "Frictionless Capitalism"

Jens Schröter

1   Introduction

Following 1989/90, hardly any "new media" gained as much importance as the Internet did – on two parallel levels simultaneously: firstly, the Internet became and remains the central vehicle of transnational economy, and secondly, the new technology became the focus of mythical tales: "Hardly had the social utopia been banished than the bourgeois media began to revel in unsocial technical utopias" (Haug 2003, 68; cf. Mosco 2004; Schröter 2004a; Flichy 2007). After the Cold War between Eastern Stalinism and Western capitalism, it seemed the next stage of history would be the solution to all problems, a capitalism rendered "frictionless" (Bill Gates) by the Internet. Gates' formulation by the way implied that capitalism up to that point was still full of friction, despite all official assertions to the contrary.

As early as 1981, Lyotard had observed that "[e]ven capitalism, the liberal or neo-liberal discourse [...] ha[s] little credibility in the contemporary situation", for "it no longer knows how to legitimate itself". However, capitalism can exploit "information technologies" in order to achieve "the computerization of all of society [...]. That is today's capitalist horizon; and it is clear this will be what brings capitalism out of the crisis" (Lyotard 1986, 210). Lyotard takes completely for granted that information technologies will be able to solve the diagnosed crisis – rather than exacerbating it.

However, at this time "the Internet" as such did not yet exist, only some of its predecessor networks which were hardly used by corporations. The *Arpanet*, one of the more important predecessors of the Internet (cf. Campbell-Kelly/ Swartz-Garcia 2013), resulted from the overlapping of military (communication that would still function in case of a thermonuclear war) and academic (sharing computer resources, which were scant at this time) discursive practices. For a long time, it was seen emphatically as a non-commercial, non-economic medium (cf. Abbate 1999; Schröter 2004a, 20–148). Only in the 1990s did the net become more widely used, particularly following the 1991 lifting of the ban on commercial activity and opening of the www in 1994. And today, in 2011, it literally seems to have become the "net of the world market" (Marx 1991, 929).

The Internet is a prime example of how technologies do not automatically bring about social change on their own, but how they are "redesignated" by hegemonic discursive practices,[1] meaning by capitalism dominated by "neoliberalism" from 1973 onwards, but especially so since 1989/90. Hence, neither the conditions of production nor the forces of production can be considered the individual cause; rather, the cause is always to be found in their complex interaction. Thus "transnational business", the growing trend to outsource whole sections of companies, was accelerated or indeed only made possible by the net, itself increasingly incorporated into hegemonic capitalist discourse: "The local, organisational, institutional and legal *unity* hitherto covered by the term 'business' is now *disintegrated, dismantled* and *dispersed*. Business is now only a virtual entity [...]" (Kurz 2005, 88). Precisely this "molecularisation" of business units can only function due to an "immediate global flow of information in real time" (ibid., 89). It is possible to enumerate many further levels on which the Internet slotted into the structures of neoliberalist capitalism, thus enabling its global dislocation in the first place: for example, how email communication renders individuals permanently available, how new forms of teleworking and ostensible self-employment are made possible, how new distribution channels are opened up, how personalized advertising and the collection of information about consumers is made possible and above all, how the gigantic and de-substantialised finance sector was only able to grow to this extent because of data networks (cf. ibid., 220–298). This complex process is of course not without its contradictions, but its various aspects cannot be considered in detail here (cf. Dyer-Witheford 1999; Haug 2003, 67–96).

Rather, the question arises of whether the net does not paradoxically *also constitute* the prime example of the "revolt of modern productive forces against modern conditions of production" (Engels and Marx 2009, 10). To put this another way: the Internet could be an example of how hegemonic capitalist discourse attempts to transform a new, initially underdetermined technology into a hegemonic operational technology, but finds itself limited precisely by this attempt, for the "true barrier to capitalist production is capital itself" (Marx 2006, 358). To put this yet another way: the initial euphoria over the web's potential – still present in the capitalist periphery where the Internet is still spreading, as Alzouma (2011) shows using the example of Niger – and the related (attempted) sedimentation of hegemonic structures in it can also be frustrated by the net. And this is not due to the fact that there are "resistant" subcultures on the web, as will be shown later, but precisely because of the web's "success". There are hegemonic "adjustments" ("Zurechtmachungen", in

---

1   On the concept of hegemony, cf. Laclau & Mouffe (1985).

Nietzsche's original German) of new media, but there is no guarantee that they will develop as originally anticipated.

The following section will outline some parts of the discourse on the Internet that developed during the 1990s. We are concerned in particular with those arguments that, hardly had the "user-friendly" *World Wide Web* platform become popular, sought to transform the Internet into a medium of the global neoliberal economy.

2   Frictionless Capitalism

The Internet was only cleared for commercial activity in 1991, and soon afterwards began to expand rapidly due to the spread of the www and browsers after 1994. Politics reacted quickly. As early as 1994, the U.S. Vice-President Al Gore gave his speech *Building the Information Superhighway*, in which he coined the metaphor of the *information superhighway*. Gore invokes the utopian model of the "universal archive" that developed alongside the earliest forms of the Internet: "We now have a huge quantity of information available with respect to any conceivable problem that is presented" (1994). And as the Vice-President makes abundantly clear, this information should be placed primarily at the disposal of "business people" so that they can succeed in their tasks. However, the problem is how to find one's way around this vast mass of information: "As we confront this huge quantity of information, we see the appearance of these new devices that can sort through it quickly, organize it, and apply it". These "new devices" are of course none other than the personal computers (with installed browsers allowing access to search engines etc.) that spread rapidly from the beginning of the 90s. They are able to provide valuable services in economic problem-solving, as they do in politics: "Probably 90 percent of the work I do when I'm in my office in the West Wing of the White House is on a computer terminal". But in order for all of this information to be available, the machines need to be connected. Gore stresses that the development of the *National Information Infrastructure* is mainly the task of private enterprise – despite the fact that the development of data networks was primarily supported by the military and universities, and thus at least partly by public funds.

Naturally, Europe did not want to lag behind the USA. The "Bangemann Report" titled *Europe and the Global Information Society* hurriedly composed by the EU Commission only refers back to Gore's transport metaphor in passing, but sounds even more optimistic: "The information society has the potential to improve the quality of life of Europe's citizens, the efficiency of our social and economic organisation and to reinforce cohesion" (Bangemann et al. 1998, 7). Five years after the collapse of the Eastern Bloc networks are perceived not only as a new means of creating social cohesion, but also as a way of increasing productivity. However: "There is a danger that individuals will reject the new information culture and its instruments" (ibid., 7). Despite frequently invoking "pluralism" (ibid., 19), the report appears to consider dissenters prone to "rigidity, inertia and compartmentalisation [sic!]" unacceptable – a "great deal of effort must be put into securing widespread public acceptance and actual use of the new technology" (ibid., 7). For the "market-driven revolution" – similarly to Al Gore, a market-ideological repression of the highly subsidised nature of data network development by universities and the military is conspicuous here – demands and encourages "full competition", from which the tautological inference follows: "Since information infrastructures are borderless in an open market environment, the information society has an essentially global dimension" (ibid., 12, 16). The a priori assumption is a global market, which the new medium is to cosy up to and serve. And so these programmatic statements continued.[2]

The *Magna Charta for the Knowledge Age* was published in 1994. This manifesto of the conservative thinkers centred around Newt Gingrich repeatedly demands "universal access" to cyberspace, the "bioelectric environment that is literally universal" (Dyson et al. 1994, 27). Although – with blatant disregard for large parts of the earth – it proclaims that "[t]oday we have, in effect, universal access to personal computing" (ibid., 33–34), on the other hand it states: "Creating the conditions for universal access to interactive multimedia will require a fundamental rethinking of government policy" (ibid., 34). It is evident from the contradiction between the statement that everyone is already networked and the demand that everyone should be networked that the *Charta* has no clear concept of or policy on the information society. Rather, this manifesto – in line with the changing role of the state in the transition to neoliberal capitalism (cf. Kurz 1999, 642–667) – is full of classical liberalism simply dressed up in new costumes. The mantra-like demand is for a "cyberspace marketplace" (Dyson et al. 1994, 31), free from all (social) state constraints, that everyone will supposedly have access to: due to their scepticism

---

2   Discussing the question of whether and how hegemonic discursive practices are inscribed in technologies and thus try to operationalise them is particularly relevant in the case of computers, as this technology is by definition open and programmable, waiting like a sponge to soak up discursive practices in the form of programmes; cf. Schröter (2004a, 7–17, 279–292; 2005). This pro-gramming process has nothing in common with the simple, unsustainable instrumentalism advocated by Kellner (2004) in regard to the "information superhighway."

towards government, the authors reject the metaphor of the information superhighway – the building of highways frequently being a state matter. The utopia of universal accessibility implied in the *Magna Charta* by no means refers to information as such, but to marketable information.

The manifesto states: "The meaning of freedom, structures of self-government, definition of property, nature of competition, conditions for cooperation, sense of community and nature of progress will each be redefined for the Knowledge Age" (ibid., 26–27). Due to pressure from digital media, these terms require redefinition: phenomena such as the (former) music file sharing service *Napster* or even the simple copying of music CDs with commercially available CD burners show that the traditional notion of intellectual property or copyright ("definition of property") is in danger of being undermined by the digital code and its potentials for reproduction. As the authors themselves write: "Information [...] can be replicated at almost no cost – so every individual can (in theory) consume society's entire output" (ibid., p. 28). However, in order to prevent this theory becoming reality, the authors of the *Magna Charta* fall back upon a more traditional definition of property and demand decisive action on the part of the state that is otherwise much maligned in neoliberal discourse: "Clear and enforceable property rights are essential for markets to work. Defining them is a central function of government" (ibid., 29). The use of digital Internet technology on file sharing sites such as *Napster* has since been curtailed by policing so that compatibility with the imperatives of the music industry ("clear and enforceable property rights") is ensured.[3] This example in particular shows clearly that effort at least is always made to shape new media and the new ways they are used to existing social structures – with police force if needs be.[4] In this sense it is simply absurd and cynical to persist in talking of a "digital revolution"[5] – for the term "revolution", whether for better or for worse, has always been historically connected to the idea of changing existing social structures.

In any case, proclamations of the new perspectives of the Knowledge Age and the supposedly upcoming "knowledge society" that have proliferated since the 1990s simply repeat familiar neoliberal demands: withdrawal of the state, expansion of a market "characterized by dynamic competition consisting of easy access and low barriers to entry" (ibid., 30) resulting – as the constant

---

3   The portal still exists (www.napster.com), but the free sharing of music files is no longer possible.

4   Or with massive threats and intimidation – as evident in the respective poster, cinema and television campaigns. These function like instruction manuals, driving home a conservative usage of data networks, that is to say a usage compatible with capitalism.

5   As, for example, in pseudo-futurological works of propaganda such as Tapscott (1996).

insistence on "universal access" suggests – in *compulsory* participation in the market. The point however is that cyberspace (only four years after having been opened up to commercial exchange) is seen as the "prototypical competitive market" (ibid., 34) ultimately promising one thing: "the renaissance of American business and technological leadership" (ibid., 30). This kind of cyber-libertarianism with its concurrent anti-state impulses has also become known under the catchphrase "Californian ideology" (cf. Barbrook and Cameron 1995). John Perry Barlow's *Declaration of the Independence of Cyberspace* (cf. Barlow 1996) is informed by the same ideology. It is based on Jefferson's Declaration of Independence of the USA and similarly rejects any state interference in cyberspace – even though without explicit reference to a liberal understanding of the market.[6]

Nearly all of the texts mentioned here demand a reduction of monopolies, which seems absurd considering the role played by *Intel* and particularly *Microsoft* in today's computer market (not to mention *Google* or *Facebook* nowadays). Bill Gates, the founder and former CEO of *Microsoft*, rejects the metaphor of the information superhighway, as the "real problem of the highway metaphor is that is emphasizes the infrastructure rather than its applications" (Gates 1996, 6). However, the reference to applications shows that presumably Gates rejects the metaphor mainly because it is not commercial enough. Gates's writing reveals a notion that can only be termed utopian: "The interactive network will be the ultimate market" (ibid.). He goes on to explain:

> [I]f every buyer knew every seller's price and every seller knew what every buyer was willing to pay, then everyone in the 'market' would be able to make fully informed decisions and society's resources would be distributed evenly. To date we haven't achieved Smith's[7] ideal because would-be buyers and would-be sellers hardly ever have complete information [...] The Internet will extend the electronic marketplace and become the ultimate go-between, the universal middleman [...] It will be a shopper's heaven.
>
> IBID., 180–181

That is to say that the universal communication between buyers and sellers made possible by the Internet and the universal access that home PCs give to all ranges of goods will prevent that participants in the market have only

---

6   With the exception that "the wealth of our marketplaces" in cyberspace is referred to, which appears to assume an understanding of the Internet as a market.

7   Gates is here referring to Adam Smith, one of the masterminds of market economy.

"imperfect and limited information" (ibid., 180).[8] Universal communication and access results in "broad, efficient competition" (ibid., 205; on the history of the fantasy of "universal communication" and "universal access", cf. Schröter 2004a). This is how the market can finally develop fully (Gates's real-life models are the stock markets as "healthy [...] electronic markets" – as if there were no such things as crashes...). This universal competition has several components: thus Gates repeatedly mentions the attention (cf. ibid., 197, 211, 216, 224 etc.) a product must be able to command from potential customers on the Internet. Then Gates emphasises the possibilities for radically individualised advertising and production opened up by the net: besides a (somewhat oxymoronic) individual newspaper, it is the individual tailoring of clothes that seems to hold particular appeal for him. If everyone could "indicate [their] measurements" (ibid., 189) electronically, customised tailoring via the Internet would become possible. His shopper's heaven is defined more clearly:

> At a growing number of [Levi Strauss & Co.] outlets, customers pay about $10 extra to have jeans made to their exact specification – any of 8,448 different combinations of hip, waist, inseam, and rise measurements and styles.
>
> IBID., 189

It is a strange idea of "freedom" that consists of a choice between 8,448 nearly identical alternatives, without it being clear how an overview of this amount of choice is to be achieved (cf. Schröter 2004b). This kind of concept is a perfect "fit" for the www, the main problem of which lies precisely in its lack of central directories and mechanisms for the reduction of complexity, presenting the user with a vast quantity of possible information, a quantity often lauded as proof of its plurality of opinions and wealth of information. However, "a search that brings up 12,000 results has delivered not wealth, but white noise" (Winkler, 1997, p. 176). As is well known, search engines provided a historical solution to this problem (cf. Haigh 2008; see Mager 2011 for an analysis that shows the capitalist construction of search engines).

Moreover, Gates's text reveals a disconcerting shift. The main focus is no longer upon how users can access market-based information, but how advertising and production can access customers in their turn. Consumers are not only

---

8   It might even be possible to trace the emergence of "Big Data" back to the trial to implement the "perfect market" in reality, because "perfect markets" are possible only – according to neoclassical ideology – when having perfect transparency. This idea will be developed in another essay soon.

supposed to register their measurements electronically – rather, Gates formulates the long-term objective that "software agents" will be able to commercialise the subconscious also:

> The questionnaire might include all sorts of images in an effort to draw subtle reactions out of you. Your agent might make the process fun by giving you feedback on how you compare with other people.
> GATES 1996, 191

This totalitarian order – including driving home "how you compare" with others, i.e. what counts as standard – enables a huge rise in consumption efficiency; the PC serves as an efficiency machine not just in terms of Al Gore's work, but also in terms of buying – indeed, it seems possible to suggest products to consumers that they themselves do not (yet) know they want.

This "techno-eschatology" combines "free-market visions of endless expansion, and an abiding faith in technology" (Dery 1996, 8, 10). It is possible to enumerate countless further similar web manifestos: thus Dertouzos (1997, 9) also writes: "It seemed natural and inevitable to me that the future world of computers and networks would be just like the Athens flea market – only instead of physical goods, the commodities would be information goods".

In all of the texts discussed here, barriers are broken, global expansion (of markets) is predicted, and limitless, universal competition and concurrent unlimited access to the Internet is not only demanded, but more or less commanded – often in the name of an anonymous "we" or "us". This seems to blend in perfectly with the structure of the www: "Internet protocol enables almost unlimited expansion and thus accommodates the pressure of capital to accumulate and expand" (Altvater 1998, 60; cf. Schiller 1999).

And thus, around 1999, a new magic word dreamed up around the mid-1990s began to circulate: *New Economy*. The constant conjuration of the Internet as the medium of a new capitalism seemed to have reached its goal. As if from nowhere, the shares of dot.com start-ups shot sky high, and the Internet seemed to have become a veritable money-making machine. However, as it is well known, this bubble soon burst with a loud bang.

3   The Productive Force of the Internet and the Relations of Production

The discussions dating from the 1990s reveal the programme for programmable machines: They are to serve the complete and utter expansion of capitalism to every corner of the world, including individual subjects' inner selves. With the advent of *eBay*, every flat becomes part of the global market, and every private homepage creates a shop window for marketing one's own self. Paul Treanor remarked quite early on that the neoliberal discourse on the Internet proliferating during the 1990s had totalitarian characteristics:

> This logic says in effect: 'no one is free to stay outside the free market'. [...] Net-ism does not want a choice: it wants the Net, one Net, one global Net, one Net everywhere, one universal cyberspace, and nothing less. It seems that, as with the ideology of the free market (and as with liberalism in general), no co-existence is possible with the Net.
>
> TREANOR 1996

But as has already been suggested several times, there are reasons to doubt – following Marx – whether this rededication and readjustment of the Internet is in fact really *frictionless*. The burst of the *New Economy* bubble already indicates this.

It appears as if the spread of digital media, the "third industrial revolution", is actually conflicting with capitalism – as suggested by the legal and police disputes over file sharing sites such as *Napster* and other phenomena such as CD burning, illegal sharing of films etc.[9] Intimations of this sort are already to be found in one of the sources of today's digital media culture. In his 1948 book on cybernetics, Norbert Wiener wrote of the coming potential of the "ultra-rapid computing machine[s]":

> The automatic factory and the assembly line without human agents are only so far ahead of us as is limited by our willingness to put such a degree of effort into their engineering as was spent, for example, in the development of the technique of radar in the Second World War. [...] It may very well be a good thing for humanity to have the machine remove from it the need of menial and disagreeable tasks, or it may not. [...] It cannot be good for these new potentialities to be assessed in the terms of the open market [...] There is no rate of pay at which a United States pick-and-shovel laborer can live which is low enough to compete with the work of

---

9 Cf. Hartmut Winkler, who states: "One is almost reminded of the Marxist contradiction between productive forces and the conditions of production: the technical potential of technical reproduction and its societal constitution – copyright – are directly opposed to one another" (Winkler 2004, 29). See also Kurz (2007) for a polemic, but detailed discussion if digital products disrupt the commodity form.

a steam shovel as an excavator. The modern industrial revolution is similarly bound to devalue the human brain, at least in its simpler and more routine decisions. [...] [T]aking the second [industrial] revolution as accomplished, the average human of mediocre attainments or less has nothing to sell that is worth anyone's money to buy.

WIENER 1961, 26–28

In his 1964 classic of media theory *Understanding Media*, Marshall McLuhan complained of the "folly of alarm about unemployment" (McLuhan 2003, 464). Sixteen years earlier, Wiener apparently already was aware that the third (he calls it the second) industrial revolution would result in a large-scale rationalisation of workplaces due to cost-cutting competition – McLuhan himself calls it "competitive fury" (McLuhan 2003, 455). And one hundred years earlier than McLuhan, Marx also knew this: for when to work will mean only to behave as "a watchman and regulator to the production process", then (for most people at least) "labour [...] cease[s] to be the great well-spring of wealth". The less production depends on "direct labour time spent" than on "the general state of science and on the progress of technology", the more "production based on exchange value breaks down" (Marx 2005, 705). This goes for example for industrial robots that have made millions of workers redundant, from the car industry to the fully automated video rental store. The current much lamented mass unemployment, which is still growing in spite of continually sinking real wages and has resulted in a sluggish domestic market, is a direct consequence of this. Even the supposedly up and coming "service society", "information society" or "knowledge society"[10] cannot be the solution, for it is in this sector in particular – and here we return to the Internet – that work can be made redundant by digital technology (cf. Frey and Osborne 2013): *online*, one can buy train and plane tickets, books, CDs, clothing, wallpaper, wardrobes (see *eBay*) and so forth; one can bank, search through numerous archives and even get hold of the wine tasted in the shop round the corner at a cheaper price. Countless salespeople and advisors thus also become superfluous:

In the same way that production work was thinned out or completely abolished by industrial robots, office work and services are now being

---

10 Marx already knew that science and technology have caused "general social knowledge [to] become a *direct force of production*" (Marx 2005, 706) – however, this debate is in precisely that section of the *Grundrisse* concerned with the "contradiction between the foundation of bourgeois production (value as measure) and its development. Machines etc." (ibid., 704).

thinned out or abolished by the Internet. The first wave or stage of the microelectronic revolution had already made far more of the workforce redundant than the capitalist exploitation process could reabsorb by lowering the cost of products and the market expansion thus made possible. If the compensatory mechanism in the capitalist development of productive forces of earlier [industrial] revolutions was no longer effective during the first stage of the microelectronic revolution, it is even less so during its second, Internet-determined stage. The result can only be further, significant growth in structural mass unemployment: in the Federal Republic of Germany, there will simply then be eight or ten million unemployed instead of four million.

    KURZ 2000

And when the RFID chips currently hailed as the newest great achievement network products in supermarkets, warehouses and so on, then most warehouse and supermarket workers will end up on the street (and this, rather than data protection, is the new chip's real problem).[11] Around 2005, the world's largest 200 businesses encompassed more than 25% of global economic activity, but were only able to employ 0.75% of humanity (cf. Kurz 2005, 81). Even though simulation, automatisation and networking cause productive forces' potential to soar, more and more people seem to be excluded from the cycle of work[12] – earning money – consumption, which in the end plunges the entire

---

11   Cf. the online RFID journal as the richest source of information: http://www.rfidjournal .com, retrieved November 9, 2011. The best introduction to this technology and the possibilities it offers is an article under the following link: http://www.rfidjournal.com/article/ articleview/1339/1/129/, retrieved November 9, 2011. Here it states explicitly: "Some auto-ID technologies, such as bar code systems, often require a person to manually scan a label or tag to capture the data. RFID is designed to enable readers to capture data on tags and transmit it to a computer system – without needing a person to be involved." Another job lost!

12   This argument has been criticized. There has been a discussion around the so-called ‚productivity paradox' (f.E. Brynjolfsson 1992): It seemed as if the increasing use of computers didn't increase productivity and so didn't erase work (for critiques of this position see some of the contributions in Wilcocks and Lester 1999 and Trenkle 2011). But even some of the most passionate advocates of this argument, f.E. Erik Brynjolfsson, have to admit in a recent publication with the telling title 'Race against the Machine' (Brynjolfsson and McAfee 2011) that digital technology is erasing work and therefore leads to serious problems for economic reproduction. Of course affirmative writers like Brynjolfsson come not even close to the insight that capitalism and digital technology might not be compatible – and it's absurd that he and his co-author praise their insight that digital technology might erase work as a new discovery (see the quote in Brokaw 2011: "But there has been

structure of the market economy into crisis. For those who do not work do not consume and do not pay taxes,[13] meaning that neither can the products generated be sold (leading to a crisis of the domestic market), nor can the state responsible for the legal, education-political etc. framework of the market continue to function – the ever deeper debt of a lots of European states are common knowledge. Consumers, who lose their jobs or have to do mini-jobs, take credits to maintain their standard of living. At the same time businesses are forced to go into debt in order to keep up with increasingly rapid leaps in productivity. The consumers, the state and the businesses need credits. The simultaneity between the spread of digital technology, increasing structural mass unemployment and the inflation of the (credit-based) financial markets since the 1970s is surely no coincidence – rather, it is a sign of the conflict between capitalist conditions of production and digital or networked forces of production.

The obvious counterargument that new technologies create new industries and new jobs (if only for the people delivering the products ordered on *eBay*) unfortunately does not hold water. At present, far fewer new jobs are being created (and if so, they are often only in the precarious low-pay sector) than are being cut.

---

relatively little talk about role of acceleration of technology"), as if there hadn't been the whole Marxian discussion or at the least the work of Jeremy Rifkin (1995). See also the recent book by Constanze Kurz and Frank Rieger (2013) and especially the study of Frey and Osborne (2013), who argue that 47% percent of all jobs in the US are threatened by computerisation in the next years. For a historical account of the discussion on 'technological unemployment' in the US see Bix (2000). See also the differentiated discussion in Cortada (2004, 30–40).

13   Not to mention the transnational molecularised businesses granted tax cuts due to frantic location competition (cf. Kurz 2005, 135–144). When speaking about global economy one point has to be made: One reviewer of this text asked: "How does uneven development fit the conclusions drawn from the work of Wiener and Marx?" If I understand correctly the question was directed at the Chinese growth, without which the global crisis would be even deeper. This implies that China proves that capitalism is still working well, at least in some parts of the world. Doesn't the growth rate of Chine prove this? This question is interesting, but to answer it in detail there is not enough space here (especially because this is not the central topic of this chapter). But to give a short answer: Chinas seeming "successes" are in no way a counterargument to the diagnosis of (perhaps terminal) capitalist crisis (see Kurz 2005, 180–186; see the short comments on China in Kurz 2010). On the contrary: Chinas growth is completely dependent on the fictive capital generated by credits (mostly) in the US. The Chinese economy is completely oriented on export (mostly) in the US. When the credit-chains in the US collapse the Chinese growth will end – not to mention the disruptive social and ecological problems.

Thus digital technologies by no means lead to "frictionless capitalism" and the "ultimate market" (Bill Gates); rather, they cause the market economy currently considered our only option to function less and less efficiently (Kurz takes a particularly strong position on this, cf. Kurz 1999, 602–780; see also Ortlieb 2008; Haug 2003, 293 is slightly more cautious when stating that "high-technology with the computer as its leading productive force has pushed [capitalism] to its limits"; cf. also Rifkin 1995). Thus it may come to a "conflict [...] between the material development of production and its social form" (Marx 2006, 1024). This shows that Marx speaks neither of technological[14] nor social determinism – instead, he is concerned with the relationship between the technological forces of production and social form:

> At a certain stage of their development, the material productive forces of society come into conflict with the existing relations of production [...] From forms of development of the forces of production these relations turn into their fetters. Then comes the period of social revolution.[15]
>
> MARX 1904, 12

This is the real meaning of the catchphrase "digital revolution", one that usually remains unconscious. The leading thinker on cybernetics Norbert Wiener

---

14   Even though it occasionally sounds like this in Marx's writing, for example when he writes: "Social relations are closely bound up with productive forces. In gaining new productive forces, human beings change their methods of production, and by changing their methods of production, the way they earn their living, they change all of their social conditions. The hand-mill gives you society with the feudal lord; the steam-mill society with the industrial capitalist" (Marx 2009, pp. 48–49).

15   In Castoriadis' brilliant discussion of Marx, this particular aspect of Marxian analysis appears to have been misinterpreted. Castoriadis states that Marx accuses the capitalist conditions of production of "a slow-down in the development of the productive forces," while this has actually "instead accelerated in proportions that were unimaginable in an earlier time" (Castoriadis 1998, 15). While the ideological whips of the overdue modernisation in the former Eastern Bloc did in fact assert that their so-called "socialism" liberated the development of the productive forces, Marx's point – particularly in the *Grundrisse* – is that capitalism develops the forces of production to an inconceivable extent and that *precisely that* limits it – for this development does away with the work that accumulation of value is based upon. The *Communist Manifesto* states: "Modern bourgeois society with its relations of production, of exchange and of property, a society that has conjured up such gigantic means of production and of exchange, is like the sorcerer who is no longer able to control the powers of the nether world whom he has called up by his spells" (Marx and Engels 2009, 10). This does not sound like a slowing down of productive forces by the conditions of production, rather the latter have been forced into a tight spot by the former.

seems already to have anticipated this: "The answer, of course, is to have a society based on human values other than buying and selling" (Wiener 1961, 28).

It is surprising that the conflict Wiener anticipates between the potential of computer technology and the capitalist social form of reproduction makes no appearance at all in the current debate on cybernetics in media studies (cf. Bergermann 2004) – despite the fact that this conflict is the *crucial* effect of the programmable technologies connected to the science of cybernetics. It seems as if the analysis of media and communication would benefit a lot from re-reading Marx (see Mosco 2009). For example, Claus Pias writes:

> For the – definitely problematic – theory of non-deterministic teleology carries huge political implications that impinge not only upon ideas of how a society where cybernetic technologies have been installed is able to bring itself into the desired form more or less on its own (though by which means is unclear) and stabilise itself in that form. [...] Cybernetic arrangements are able to capture every aberration and render deviant unrest productive for their purposes. Cybernetics is a government that thrives on disturbance and permanent crisis, for this is how it stabilises itself.
>
> PIAS 2004, 323, 325

The possibility that cybernetic arrangements, their knowledge and the digital media connected to them could actually have a *destabilising* effect on the market-based form of Pias's underdetermined notion of 'society' is not taken into consideration, similarly to Lyotard's *grand récit* of 1981.[16] In contradiction to Wiener, the "redundancy of utopia" (Pias, 2004, p. 325) can only be diagnosed if one is not yet affected by this destabilisation. Since 2008, we seem to have been experiencing it more clearly than ever.

4   Conclusion

It is interesting that after the year 2000 we witnessed a little bit of history repeating. At the end of the 1990s Gates' optimistic notion of 'frictionless capitalism' was ridiculed by the subsequent collapse of the dot-com-crash. Before

---

16   Pias does admit, however, that cybermetics might be "definitely problematic." Pircher only mentions that "in Western market economies automatisation was perceived as a threat" (2004, 93) – even though it was not just "perceived" as such, but actually was and is a threat to many jobs.

the crisis beginning of 2008 there was a similar optimistic discourse, this time on the 'Web 2.0' (see Leister and Röhle 2011 for critical analyses of the optimistic discourses around *Facebook*). Again it seemed that the new Internet applications, the 'social media', could be the source of new kinds of work, value and wealth. But this didn't work – despite all the usages of social media as new technologies of control, discipline and the commercialization of the unconscious (see Fuchs 2010a; 2010b; 2011). Perhaps this shows again that digital media are not compatible with capitalism and that there is no way to make them compatible. Perhaps they are simply – with Marx – the productive forces that clash with the relations of production. This does of course not lead by itself to a new post-capitalist form of society, but it seems to heighten the awareness that something has to be done.

References

Abbate, Janet. 1999. *Inventing the Internet*. Cambridge, MA: MIT Press.

Altvater, Elmar 1998. Kehrseiten der Globalisierung. *Telepolis. Die Zeitschrift der Netzkultur* 4 (5): 54–61.

Alzouma, Gado. 2011. Young People, Computers and the Internet in Niger. *Journal of African Media Studies* 3 (2): 277–292.

Bangemann, Martin et al. 1994. Europe and the Global Information Society. Retrieved November 5, 2011, from http://www.umic.pt/images/stories/publicacoes200801/raport_Bangemanna_1994.pdf.

Barbrook, Richard and Andy Cameron. 1995. The Californian Ideology. Retrieved November 8, 2011 from http://www.hrc.wmin.ac.uk/theory-californianideology-main.html.

Barlow, John Perry 1996. A Declaration of the Independence of Cyberspace. Retrieved November 8, 2011 from https://projects.eff.org/~barlow/Declaration-Final.html.

Bergermann, Ulrike. 2004. Von Schiffen und Schotten: Der Auftritt der Kybernetik in der Medienwissenschaft. *Medienwissenschaft Rezensionen* 1: 28–40.

Bix, Amy Sue. 2000. *Inventing Ourselves Out of Jobs? America's Debate Over Technological Unemployment*, 1929–1981. Baltimore: John Hopkins University Press.

Brokaw, Leslie. 2011. How the Digital Revolution is Affecting Employment. Retrieved March 6, 2012 from http://sloanreview.mit.edu/improvisations/2011/10/26/brynjolfsson-and-mcafee-book-looks-at-digital-revolution-and-its-transformation-of-employment/#.T1imVpi9Zdo.

Brynjolfsson, Erik. 1992. The Productivity Paradox of Information Technology: Review and Assessment. Retrieved March 6, 2012 from http://ccs.mit.edu/papers/CCSWP130/ccswp130.html.

Brynjolfsson, Erik and Andrew McAfee. 2011. *Race Against The Machine: How the Digital Revolution is Accelerating Innovation, Driving Productivity, and Irreversibly Transforming Employment and the Economy* (Kindle-Book).

Campbell-Kelly, Martin and Daniel D. Swartz-Garcia. 2013. The History of the Internet: The Missing Narratives. *Journal of Information Technology* 28: 18–33.

Castoriadis, Cornelius. 1998. *The Imaginary Institution of Society*. Cambridge, MA: MIT Press.

Cortada, James W. 2004. *The Digital Hand, How Computers Changed the Work of American Manufacturing, Transportation and Retails Industries*. Oxford: Oxford University Press.

Dertouzos, Michael. 1997. *What Will Be. How the New World of Information Will Change our Lives*. New York: Harper.

Dery, Mark. 1996. *Escape Velocity: Cyberculture at the End of the Century*. New York: Grove.

Dyer-Witheford, Nick. 1999. *Cyber-Marx. Cycles and Circuits of Struggle in High Technology Capitalism*. Urbana: University of Illinois Press.

Dyson, Esther et al. 1994. A Magna Charta for the Knowledge Age. *New Perspectives Quarterly* 11 (4): 26–37.

Engels, Friedrich and Karl Marx. 2009. *The Communist Manifesto*. Teddington: Echo.

Flichy, Patrice. 2007. *The Internet Imaginaire*. Cambridge, MA: MIT Press.

Frey, Carl Benedikt and Michael A. Osborne. 2013. The Future of Employment. How Susceptible are Jobs to Computerisation. Retrieved November 15, 2014 from http://www.oxfordmartin.ox.ac.uk/publications/view/1314.

Fuchs, Christian. 2010a. Labor in Informational Capitalism and on the Internet. *The Information Society* 26 (3): 179–196.

Fuchs, Christian. 2010b. Facebook, Web 2.0 und ökonomische Überwachung. *Datenschutz und Datensicherheit* 7: 453–458.

Fuchs, Christian. 2011. The Contemporary World Wide Web. Social Medium of New Space of Accumulation? In *The Political Economies of Media. The Transformation of the Global Media Industries*, edited by Dwayne Winseck and Dal Yong Jin, 201–220. London: Bloomsbury.

Gates, Bill. 1996. *The Road Ahead*. Rev. ed. London: Penguin.

Gore, Al. 1994. Building the Information Superhighway. Retrieved November 8, 2011 from http://s93894098.onlinehome.us/Mine/WilliamGibson/Source/gorespeech .html.

Haigh, Thomas. 2008. The Web's Missing Links: Search Engines and Portals. In *The Internet and American Business*, edited by William Aspray and Paul E. Ceruzzi, 159–199. Cambridge, MA: MIT Press.

Haug, Wolfgang Fritz. 2003. *High-Tech-Kapitalismus. Analysen zu Produktionsweise, Arbeit, Sexualität, Krieg und Hegemonie*. Hamburg: Argument.

Kellner, Douglas. 2004. Marxism and the Information Superhighway. Retrieved November 8, 2011 from http://www.gseis.ucla.edu/faculty/kellner/essays/marxisminformationsuperhighway.pdf.

Kurz, Constanze and Frank Rieger. 2013. *Arbeitsfrei. Eine Entdeckungsreise zu den Maschinen, die uns ersetzen.* München: Riemann.

Kurz, Robert. 1999. *Schwarzbuch Kapitalismus: Ein Abgesang auf die Marktwirtschaft.* Frankfurt am Main: Eichborn.

Kurz, Robert. 2000. Euphorie um die New Economy: Das Internet als Traumfabrik des neuen Marktes. Retrieved November 8, 2011 from http://www.exit-online.org/html/link.php?tab=schwerpunkte&kat=Kritik+%40+Krise+des+Werts+und+des+Geldes&ktext=Euphorie+um+die+New+Economy.

Kurz, Robert. 2005. *Das Weltkapital. Globalisierung und innere Schranken des modernen warenproduzierenden Systems.* Berlin: Bittermann.

Kurz, Robert. 2007. Der Unwert des Unwissens. Verkürzte 'Wertkritik' als Legitimationsideologie eines digitalen Neo-Kleinbürgertums. Retrieved March 6, 2012, from http://www.exit-online.org/link.php?tabelle=aktuelles&posnr=264.

Kurz, Robert. 2010. Interview, conducted by Peter Jellen. *Telepolis.* Retrieved March 6, 2012, from: http://www.exit-online.org/link.php?tabelle=schwerpunkte&posnr=204.

Laclau, Ernesto and Chantalle Mouffe. 1985. *Hegemony and Socialist Strategy. Toward a Radical Democratic Politics.* London Verso.

Leistert, Oliver and Theo Röhle, 2011. *Generation Facebook. Über das Leben im Social Net.* Bielefeld: Transcript.

Lyotard, Jean-François. 1986. Rules and Paradoxes and Svelte Appendix. *Cultural Critique* 5: 209–219.

Mager, Astrid. 2011. Algorithmic Ideology. How Capitalist Society Shapes Search Engines. Retrieved November 8, 2011 from http://papers.ssrn.com/sol3/papers.cfm?abstract_id=1926244.

Marx, Karl. 1904. *Contribution to the Critique of Political Economy.* Chicago: International Library Publishers.

Marx, Karl. 1991. *Capital* (Vol. 1). London: Penguin.

Marx, Karl. 2005. *Grundrisse. Foundations of the Critique of Political Economy.* London: Penguin.

Marx, Karl. 2006. *Capital* (Vol. 3). London: Penguin.

Marx, Karl. 2009. The Poverty of Philosophy. Retrieved November 9, 2011, from http://www.marxists.org/archive/marx/works/download/pdf/Poverty-Philosophy.pdf.

McLuhan, Marshall. 2003. *Understanding Media.* Berkeley: Gingko.

Mosco, Vincent. 2004. *The Digital Sublime. Myth, Power and Cyberspace.* Cambridge, MA: MIT Press.

Mosco, Vincent. 2009. *The Political Economy of Communication.* London: SAGE. 2nd Edition.

Ortlieb, Claus Peter. 2008. Ein Widerspruch von Stoff und Form. Zur Bedeutung der Produktion des relativen Mehrwerts für die finale Krisendynamik. Retrieved March 6, 2012, from http://www.math.uni-hamburg.de/home/ortlieb/WiderspruchStoffForm Preprint.pdf.

Pias, Claus. 2004. Unruhe und Steuerung. Zum utopischen Potential der Kybernetik. In *Die Unruhe der Kultur. Potentiale des Utopischen*, edited by Jörn Rüsen, 301–325. Weilerswist: Velbrück.

Pircher, Wolfgang. 2004). Markt oder Plan? Zum Verhältnis von Kybernetik und Ökonomie. In *Cybernetics – Kybernetik. The Macy Conferences 1946–1953, Vol. 2, Essays und Dokumente*, edited by Claus Pias, 81–96. Berlin: diaphanes.

Rifkin, Jeremey 1995. *The End of Work*. New York: Putnam.

Schiller, Dan. 1999. *Digital Capitalism. Networking the Global Market System*. Cambridge, MA: MIT Press.

Schröter, Jens. 2004a. *Das Netz und die Virtuelle Realität. Zur Selbstprogrammierung der Gesellschaft durch die universelle Maschine*. Bielefeld: transcript.

Schröter, Jens. 2004b. 8448 verschiedene Jeans. Zu Wahl und Selektion im Internet. In *Paradoxien der Entscheidung*, edited by Friedrich Balke, Gregor Schwering and Urs Stäheli, 117–138. Bielefeld: transcript.

Schröter, Jens. 2005. World Brain – Electronic Brain – Global Brain. Plädoyer für De-Sedimentierung statt Organizismus. *Paragrana. Zeitschrift für historische Anthropologie* 14 (2): 283–303.

Tapscott, Don. 1996. *The Digital Economy*. New York: McGraw-Hill.

Treanor, Paul. 1996. Internet as Hyper-Liberalism. Retrieved November 8, 2011 from http://web.inter.nl.net/users/Paul.Treanor/net.hyperliberal.html.

Trenkle, Norbert. 2011. Massenausfall. Wie der Kapitalismus an seiner eigenen Produktivität erstickt. Retrieved March 6, 2012 from http://www.streifzuege.org/2011/massenausfall/print/.

Wiener, Norbert. 1961. *Cybernetics or Control and Communication in the Animal and the Machine*. Cambridge, MA: MIT Press.

Willcocks, Leslie P. and Stephanie Lester, eds. 1999. *Beyond the IT Productivity Paradox*. Chichester: Wiley.

Winkler, Hartmut. 1997. *Docuverse. Zur Medientheorie der Computer*. München: Boer.

Winkler, Hartmut. 2004. *Diskursökonomie. Versuch über die innere Ökonomie der Medien*. Frankfurt am Main: Suhrkamp.

CHAPTER 6

Digital Media and Capital's Logic of Acceleration*

Vincent Manzerolle and Atle Mikkola Kjøsen

Since the publication of our original article (Manzerolle and Kjøsen 2012) there have been a number of developments in the field of telecommunications, payment technologies and banking that support our original argument, but also require that we address them and update accordingly. When we wrote our original piece the widespread adoption of near-field communication (NFC) as a mobile payment standard was still uncertain. At that time it served more as a useful probe with which to introduce and discuss the relationship between capital's logic of acceleration and digital media. While the certainty of NFC as an industry standard is yet to be determined, it has benefited most recently from the support of Apple and its Apple Pay service. Apple, now one of the largest companies in the world with respect to market capitalization, has provided a crucial endorsement of NFC by incorporating the standard into its iPhone 6 and Apple Watch devices. The incorporation of NFC as a mobile payment standard is itself only one, albeit important, component of the Apple Pay ecosystem which involves strategic partnerships with retailers, but most crucially, credit card companies and banks. NFC, and mobile payment generally, is now benefitting from Apple's considerable marketing and advertising prowess.[1] As the promotional literature for Apple Pay proclaims:

> Paying in stores or within apps has never been easier. Gone are the *wasted moments finding the right card. Now payments happen with a single touch.* Apple Pay will change how you pay with breakthrough contactless payment

---

* Thanks to Nick Dyer-Witheford, Edward Comor, and Bernd Frohmann for their various contributions to the intellectual development of this chapter. Thanks are also due to Veronica Manzerolle for offering her time and editorial skills, and to Lee McGuigan for reading and commenting on a draft of the paper. Finally, thanks to Jordan Coop for his help in designing the figure of the circuit of capital.

1 Apple's marketing and advertising efforts are an important intervention in socializing consumers to accept and adopt mobile payment technologies and services. As a 2013 Accenture report notes, "Some 41 percent of North American smartphone users are highly aware that their phones can be used as payment devices at retail counters, yet only 16 percent have done this" (Accenture 2013, 4).

technology and unique security features built right into the devices you
have with you every day. So you can use your iPhone, Apple Watch, or
iPad to pay in a simple, secure, and private way.[2]

Apple Pay combines NFC payment technology with its own thumbprint scan-
ner built into each new device to create a level of security and simplicity for
the transaction process, and allows both online and offline purchases to be
integrated into one platform. Although still a mostly unproven service, Apple
Pay is a further harbinger of the convergence of ubiquitous digital media platforms with the flows of financial data. However, Apple's alignment with credit
card companies, and the closing off of access to valuable transactional data by
retailers (Freed-Finnegan and Wall, 2014), has spawned some resistance from
banks and retailers and has led to a competing mobile payment system, for
example the CurrentC payment platform developed by the MCX consortium,
led by Walmart.[3] Beyond Apple, NFC continues to be adopted as a standard
supported by major corporations across the mobile ecosystem: from software
developers (Google, Microsoft), to handset designers (Samsung, Research In
Motion), semiconductors (Qualcomm, Broadcom, and NXP), to credit card
companies (Visa and Mastercard). For example, the Softcard[4] payment
network, which is now rolling out in the United States, has similarly
brought together major telecommunications companies (Verizon, AT&T, and
T-Mobile) and credit card companies (Visa, Mastercard, and American Express)
around the NFC standard. Perhaps what is most notable for media researchers
is the broad convergence between telecommunications and finance institutions and infrastructures.[5] That very convergence is evidenced by
Canada's Rogers Communications' successful application to become a bank

---

2   https://www.apple.com/apple-pay/. Emphasis added.

3   http://currentc.com.

4   http://www.gosoftcard.com/.

5   More recently, pressure from credit card and banking companies on retailers to upgrade pay
    terminals to accept the inclusion of NFC compatibility. "Merchants are facing heavy pressure
    to upgrade their payment terminals to accept smart cards. Over the last several months, Visa,
    Discover and MasterCard have said that merchants that cannot accept these cards will be
    liable for any losses owing to fraud... While updating the terminals for smart cards, VeriFone
    also plans to upgrade for smartphone wallets, providing the capability for near-field com-
    munication, the technology used by the Google and Isis wallets, the two biggest smartphone
    wallet projects" (Brustein, 2012b). This pressure may help NFC reach a critical mass for wide-
    spread adoption of mobile payment by consumers and retailers.

and creditor.[6] Indeed, its Suretap mobile payment technology uses NFC as a central mechanism.[7]

NFC not only demonstrates a new political economic configuration for media and finance industries, but at a more micro level, NFC points to two of the most defining characteristics of contemporary digital media: personalization and ubiquitous connectivity.[8] These qualities are not simply autonomous expressions of technological change, but as we will argue, they reflect a teleology of digital media itself – one largely shaped by the barriers existing in capital's sphere of circulation. We hope to situate these new phenomena within Marx's theorization of circulation, but to also suggest new theoretical modes of analysis.

We argue that NFC is just one small example of a more general evolution of digital media in line with capital's *logic of acceleration*. It represents this logic in two key ways. First, it accelerates the actual moment of exchange by reducing latency and minimizing "wasted moments"; second, it produces transactional data that can be used as a logistical resource to accelerate the circulation of commodities (Manzerolle and Kjøsen, 2014). It is precisely this logic we will address by examining and situating the place of media within the overall circuit of capital. Media enable capital to move as an iterative process and are therefore key in circulating capital; they are the means by which capital communicates itself in and through society.

This chapter argues that questions of circulation are central to the study of contemporary and future media under capitalism. Moreover, it argues that such questions – questions that evidence strong parallels with those of media theorists and historians largely outside of the Marxist tradition – have been central to Marx's

---

6 "The [Rogers] bank would likely primarily deal in credit and mobile payment services, as opposed to bricks and mortar bank branches that take traditional savings and loan accounts" (Evans 2011). See www.rogersbank.com.

7 http://www.rogers.com/web/content/suretap.

8 There have been a number of alternative mobile payment systems proposed, reflecting a diversity of interests; for example, PayPal is seen as a potential competitor of NFC (Barr 2012). Startup company Square has also offered a mobile payment service using a card reading adaptor that plugs into a mobile device (https://squareup.com/). Hedging its bets, Visa has invested heavily in Square (Barth, 2011). Moreover, even social media networks are moving quickly to incorporate peer-to-peer payment and transactional functions into their platforms, most notably Facebook Messenger, Twitter and Snapchat. It is uncertain to what extent NFC will play in these services, but they are representative of a broad pursuit by new digital media companies to embed payment-like features in their platforms.

analysis of the reproduction and acceleration of capital. Marx's concepts of the circuit and circulation of capital imply a theory of communication (Parker 1981; 137–138; Mattelart 1996:101; Peters 2001:125; Manzerolle and Kjøsen 2012). Thus the purpose of our paper is to outline the logistical mechanisms that underlie a Marxist theory of media and communication that foregrounds the role new media play in reducing circulation time.

Few authors have approached media from the perspective of the circuit or the circulation of capital, though there are notable exceptions (Parker 1981; Garnham 1990; Martin 1991; Fuchs 2009). Nicholas Garnham calls for an approach to Marxist theories of communication that eschews the vertical base-superstructure approach for one that treats capitalism as a horizontal "process which is continuous, circular and through time" (Garnham 1990, 45). According to Garnham, the circulation of capital – in essence classical Marxist value theory – is the "crucial starting point for any political economy of mass communication" because it refocuses analyses of communication on capital's physical, spatial and temporal moments of its self-realization (Garnham 1990, 45). He suggests that a comprehensive analysis of most media phenomena can be gained from circuit and circulation-centric analyses (Garnham 1990, 45–53). Although Garnham made his suggestion decades ago, Marxist media studies is dominated by production-centric or base-superstructure analyses. Christian Fuchs (2009) is one of the few exceptions. He argues that for a "systematic location of the media in capitalism, one can take as a starting point the Marxian circuit of commodity metamorphosis and the accumulation of capital as it is described in Vol. 2 of *Capital*" (Fuchs 2009, 377). The benefit of Fuchs' approach is that he is able to treat capitalism as a system of production, circulation and consumption of both commodities and ideologies.

The necessity of theorizing communication from a circuit and circulation-centric point of view stems from the emergence of a number of new technological phenomena that intensify capitalist logic of acceleration. The convergence of telecommunications and finance industries in the form of mobile payment systems and technologies like NFC allude to a broader conceptualization of communication media as a moment in which both circulation and exchange are re-commodified and sold to consumers. Mobile payment systems allow a logistical efficiency (through personalization) in both the communication of marketing messages *and* in the realization of value, fused together in one ubiquitously connected technology.

For the purposes of understanding the implementation of such technologies that are ostensibly employed to accelerate the circulation of capital, measured in reduced circulation times, we need to pay attention to *Capital Volume 2*, and key sections in the *Grundrisse*.[9] It is here that we find clues to capital's logic of acceleration that determine the evolution and rollout of contemporary

---

9   See Marx 1973, 401–423, 516–549, 618–690, 717–735.

and future digital media. Our goal is to situate the ongoing evolution of contemporary media within an existing logic identified by Marx. We add to his analysis a focus on the formal and material qualities of specifically *digital* media. We ground the logic of acceleration within the materiality of contemporary digital media, and in so doing uncover prospectively new tensions and contradictions.[10] The newness of our contemporary moment lies in the maturation (in complexity, sophistication, profitability) of digital media and the development and convergence of the finance, telecommunications, and media industries. Out of this convergence, the digital form allows the moment of exchange to become ubiquitous and immediate. Indeed our opening example of Apple's NFC-enabled service encapsulates this convergence.

Digital media not only offer an acceleration of circulation in time and space, but through personalization, provide new vectors for capital; finding the shortest route between the point of production and exchange, and producer and consumer. Thus in addition to its acceleration, circulation becomes diagrammatic through personalization (Elmer 2004, 41–48).[11] What we identify as new is how the drive to accelerate is taken to its logical end in the conditions of ubiquity and immediacy engendered through digital media.

1   The Circuit of Capital

Garnham (1990) and Fuchs (2009) argue that media and communication should be systematically located within the circuit of capital. We take their

---

10   It is beyond the scope of this chapter to consider resistance and class struggle in relation to circulation. Revealing how capital can be short circuited, however, is the ultimate goal of our exploration of the increasing importance of circulation. Research (for example, Bonachich and Wilson 2008, 239–243) suggests that labour has been generally weakened by the recent logistics revolution. However, the streamlining and rationalization of the supply chain have given workers that are strategically positioned in the distribution network more potential class or bargaining power (Silver 2003, 100–103; Bonachich and Wilson 2008: 244–249). Similarly, unionized and non-unionized workers in the telecommunications industry have repeatedly demonstrated that capital's circulatory infrastructure can become a site for class struggle (see Mosco and McKercher 2008).

11   D.N. Rodowick describes diagrammatics as "the cartography of strategies of power," and thus the figure of the diagram helps depict "a historical image of how strategies of power attempt to replicate themselves in forms of surveillances, documentation, and expression on the one hand, and in the spacial organization of collective life on the other" (quoted in Elmer 2004, 41–42). Greg Elmer writes, "In the realm of contemporary infomatics, the diagram therefore allows us to trace the everyday data economy in which habits, routines, rhythms, and flows are digitized, coded, and diagnosed for the purposes of control" (2004, 47).

argument one step further and argue that what capital communicates is value, that the circuit of capital (M − C...P...C' − M) can be understood as a schematic for this communication of value and that consequently the circulation of capital can be understood as a theory of communication.[12] After all, capital is "value-in-process" (Marx 1973:536).

The circulation of capital incorporates the circulation of commodities on the market (C-M-C) as a moment of its own process. It is important to bear in mind, however, that the circulation of commodities is wider than an individual circuit of capital; C-M-C can also refer to general circulation, in which all individual circuits of capital interact. "The circulation of capital...contains a relation to general circulation, of which its own circulation forms a moment, while the latter likewise appears as posited by capital" (1973, 619–620). The sphere of circulation refers to more than simply market exchange. Nicholas Garnham argues that within the sphere of circulation "we need to look at what Marx called the locational and temporal moments, referring to the problems both of the actual spatial extensions of the market (the physical transport of goods) and the time expended in commercial transactions (this time refers not to any labour time used in commercial transactions, but to the actual lapsed time expended in transforming a commodity into money and vice-versa...)" (1990, 46).

As Marx explains in *Volume 2*, capital is a circuit because it enables a quantity of value to pass through a sequence of three mutually connected metamorphoses. As it passes through these stages, value both maintains itself and increases its magnitude. Once it has moved through each of these stages, capital has completed one turnover and can repeat the process anew. The circuit has three stages: the sphere of production (stage 2) and circulation (stages 1 and 3); and the three particular forms of capital (money [M], commodity [C] and productive-capital [P]). When the social function of a particular form is fulfilled, capital completes a stage and assumes the next form. Stage 1 is

---

12   Importantly, because capital is a circuit or a closed feedback loop, capital can be understood as both the subject and purpose of the communication of value. In *Grundrisse*, Marx argues that when the circulation of commodities is incorporated into the life process of capital, it gives the process the content of value (1973, 626). Marx writes that capital is the "predominant" subject of the metamorphoses of value (1973, 620; see also 1976, 255). We argue that capital is an non-human subject that seeks to transmit value-content through the circuit, which can only occur by forcing the content to assume and discard the three forms of capital. In this communication process, other actors, such as workers and capitalists, are reduced to mere relays (transmitters and receivers) or a data source in the case of living labour. Kjøsen (2013) takes this argument to its logical extreme, comparing the circuit of capital to a general communications system as defined by Claude Shannon, argues that economic behaviour is a form of programming by economic forms, and that therefore so-called human actors are reduced to mere relays for value.

completed by the capitalist using money's function as means of payment and/
or purchase to acquire labour-power and means of production. When these
commodities are set in motion as productive capital (P), and are productively
consumed, the second stage is completed. The result of the production stage is
a mass of commodities (C') with a higher quantity of value than originally
advanced. The third stage is completed when the commodity's function of
being bought and sold is fulfilled, thereby realizing the surplus value created in
production, and making capital accumulation possible in the first stage (Marx
1978, 132–133).

The circuit is Marx's concept of capital (see Figure 6.1). It is the universal
form within which the particular forms of capital are internally related. The
identity of capital can thus be found in its unity and in the difference to itself
as unity. This *negative unity* is found when capital exists in either of its stages
or forms (Arthur 1998, 102–116). Capital is found in two aspects: "first as the
unity of the process, then as a particular one of its phases, itself in *distinction*
to itself as unity" (Marx 1973, 622). Capital is unified in the movement from its
universal to particular forms. Although the forms of money-, productive- and
commodity-capital are necessary for the existence of capital, the particular
forms are not in and for themselves capital. Outside the circuit they simply
function as money, commodities and a production process. Only in the circuit
do they also have the social form of capital (Arthur 1998, 107). The three forms
are only capital insofar as they are internally related to each other in the totality of the circuit as the functional forms of circulating capital (Arthur 1998, 102;
Marx 1978, 133). In other words, they are forms of capital because each form is
the possibility of assuming the next form and completing and moving to the
next stage of the circuit (Marx 1978, 112). When capital is in negative unity, it is

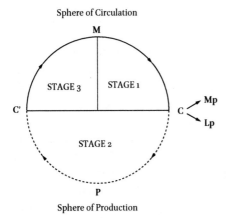

FIGURE 6.1
The circuit of capital

only potentially capital and perpetually becoming – it is capital if, and only if, it can discard its current form and metamorphose into the next form, which occurs only when the associated function is fulfilled. Money-capital is latently productive capital, which is the possibility of commodity capital that in turn is the becoming of money-capital.

For accumulation to take place, capital must constantly move between the two spheres of production and circulation; although surplus value is created in the sphere of production, it must be *realized* and accumulated in the sphere of circulation. This realization is a necessary condition and moment of the entire motion of capital: capital is the unity-in-process of production and circulation (Marx 1973, 405–6, 535, 620; 1978, 205). Effectively, capital must always be in motion in order to *be* capital; when capital is not in movement, it is stuck in a particular form and stage and is therefore negated as capital and devalued as value (Marx 1973, 621). To reduce these periods of negation and devaluation, capital must increase its velocity thus decreasing the time spent in circulation. To accelerate, however, capital must develop or adopt media that allows it to bind space and time, and thereby progressively overcome the barriers capital posits to its functioning (see below). It is never a guarantee, however, that an individual capitalist will complete a turnover:

> The three processes of which capital forms the unity are external; they are separate in time and space. As such, the transition from one into the other, i.e. their unity as regards the individual capitalists, is accidental. Despite their inner unity, they exist independently alongside one another, each as the presupposition of the other. Regarded broadly and as a whole, this inner unity must necessarily maintain itself to the extent that the whole of production rests on capital, and it must therefore realize all the necessary moments of its self-formation, and must contain the determinants necessary to make these moments real.
>
> MARX 1973, 403

In other words, the formal circulation of capital (inner unity) contradicts its *real* circulation process (external unity), in which capital assumes a *material* form alongside its particular economic forms. Capital "*risks* getting tied up for certain intervals," because it must invest itself in matter that exists in geophysical space; it is therefore never guaranteed that it will metamorphose into its next form (Arthur 1998, 117, 133). Consequently, circulation must be considered from both its formal and real moments. Real circulation refers to the actual circulation of matter, i.e. the movement at a given speed, of commodities and money through space and time. Real circulation thus includes transportation, infrastructure, vehicles, packaging, warehouses, banking, and so on. Consequently, the circulation of capital is inherently a logistical affair that requires a specific organization of space and time. This affair has always been about accelerating capital's movement and has been done through progressive re-organizations of space and time and the adoption of newer and faster media such as jet transportation, containers and intermodal transportation, and digitization together with telecommunications.

There are benefits to increase capital's velocity: because the sum and mass of surplus value created within a period is negatively determined by the velocity of capital the faster capital moves through the sphere of circulation, the more surplus value will be created and validated. The rate of surplus value and profit may be increased by acceleration when speed contributes to reduce circulation costs (Marx 1973, 518; 1978, 124, 389). In a given period, the velocity of turnover substitutes for the volume of capital (Marx 1973, 518–519, 630). It is also a competitive advantage for individual capitalists to reduce their turnover in relation to the social average turnover time (Harvey 1989, 229).

2   On Barriers: Space and Time

In *Grundrisse*, Marx argues that capital posits barriers in contradiction to its tendency to function freely and expand boundlessly, delaying the transition of capital from one form and phase to the next and/or limit the quantity of surplus value produced and realized within a given period (1973, 421, 538). He identifies necessary labour as a barrier in the sphere of production; and need/use-value, availability of equivalents (money), space and circulation time as barriers belonging to the sphere of circulation (Marx 1973, 404–405, 542–543).

To "release its own potency" capital constantly tries to overcome its barriers (Negri 1984, 115). We posit that capital relies on various media technologies to overcome these barriers. The function of machinery in the sphere of production is to manipulate time, i.e. decrease the necessary labour of the worker. Media have a similar function of manipulating time, but belonging to the sphere of circulation media may manipulate circulation time rather than labour time. Media are employed in the sphere of circulation in order to reduce circulation time and/or the costs associated with circulation (e.g. storage and exchange). More importantly, media can reduce circulation time by enabling capital to overcome the barriers of need, money, space and time. Larger and faster vehicles enable capital to overcome these barriers by extending markets in space, annihilating space with time or reducing absolutely the time capital circulates from a given place to the other. Credit is an example of a medium that enables capital to overcome the barrier of money, but as we will explain below, it also acts to increase the speed *and* vector of capital's circulation. What is peculiar about mobile devices is that they open up for dealing with these barriers simultaneously as we discuss in the following section.

The circulation of capital proceeds in space and time. As capital extends itself in space and strives to make the earth into a market, capital tries to "annihilate this space with time, i.e. to reduce to a minimum time spent in motion from one place to another" (Marx 1973, 539). That space is annihilated with time means that spatial distance is reduced to temporal distance; spatial extension folds into circulation time. Thus the annihilation of space becomes identical to abbreviating the circulation time of capital. Circulation time is a barrier to capital because the time spent in circulation is time that could be used for the valorization of value. The barriers around use-value and equivalents are also significant, but will be addressed later in the paper.

Circulation time is a deduction from production time, specifically a deduction of surplus labour time (Marx 1973, 538–539). The maximum number of repetitions is reached when the velocity of circulation becomes *absolute,* i.e. when circulation time is zero. If this occurs there would be no interruption in production resulting from circulation and overall turnover time would be equal to production time (Marx 1973, 544–45, 627). It is the "necessary tendency of capital to strive to equate circulation time to 0; i.e. to suspend itself, since it is capital itself alone which posits circulation time as a determinant moment of production time" (Marx 1973, 629).[13] The closer circulation time comes to zero, however, "the more capital functions, and the greater is its productivity and self-valorization" (Marx 1978, 203). It is in this tendency that capital seeks new methods of communicating value at ever-greater velocities. Capital's increasing attention to logistics or supply chain management – as evidenced in the rapid development of telecommunications and transportation infrastructure – is determined by its need for speed.

As an example of the apotheosis of this drive consider recent investments in fiber-optic trans-Atlantic cables purporting to shave off six milliseconds of transmission time. Scheduled to be completed in September 2015, cable company Hibernia Atlantic is currently building the

---

13   Although capital is working towards the elimination of circulation time, if it was to achieve this, it would negate itself. Absolute velocity is represented as a circulation time of zero, which is nothing but the suspension of the sphere of circulation. Without the moment of exchange, surplus value cannot be realized and capital is therefore negated. If circulation time is suspended, it would be the same as to "suspend the necessity of exchange, of money, and of the division of labour resting on them, hence capital itself" (Marx 1973, 629). Digital piracy is an example of such a suspension (see Kjøsen, 2010).

first new trans-Atlantic cable in a decade. By shortening the cable length by approximately 310 miles, the four-fiber pair optical cable system promises to reduce transmission time between London and New York by six milliseconds from the current 65-millisconds. In the world of high-frequency trading, time is not measured according to the human scale, but the non-human scale of algorithms and software bots with the salient unit of time being the milli-, micro- or even the nanosecond. For human action and perception, the milli-seconds saved means nothing, but for high-frequency financial trading houses that rely on algorithms to execute buy and sell orders, a single millisecond could result in as much as $100 million to the annual bottom line (Hecht 2011; Williams 2011). Fifty-nine milliseconds between London and New York is, how-ever, not fast enough for the world of algorithmic finance capital.

Although for so-called humans the world shrinks to nothing when our elec-tromagnetic media operate at speeds of 60 to 90 percent of the speed of light, the expanse of the globe is massive for non-human subjects that reckon time in microseconds. The fastest fiber-optic route between New Jersey and Chicago is approximately 16 milliseconds. In the world of algorithmic trading, accord-ing to Donald MacKenzie (2011), it's "a huge delay: you might as well be on the moon." Indeed, Andrew Bach head of network services at NYSE Euronext said that "[t]he speed of light limitation is getting annoying" (in Hecht 2011). More recently, researchers are exploring the possibility of further shortening the time distance between financial centres by shooting neutrinos *through* the earth. The use of neutrinos to communicate financial transactions is signifi-cant because "neutrinos travel at the speed of light" thus "traders using the technology would on average have a nearly 30 millisecond time advantage, with participating London and Sydney brokerages garnering a full 44 millisec-onds" (Dorminey, 2012). Through the unfolding *telos* of capitalist media, circu-lation time is reduced to the point of elimination, or at least to a time so intensive that it has no meaning to humans.

3   Media of Buying and Selling

"Money as such has become a pseudo-event – information only"
MCLUHAN AND NEVITT 1972, *78*

The ability of capital to be transported or transmitted depends on both the economic and material form that capital takes – this materiality also includes electromagnetic waves and the encoding of digital data. For example, the mobility of commodity capital depends on the means of communication and the natural qualities of the commodity, such as weight, size, fragility and perishability. It is in this process that capital relies upon various media to bind space and time in ways commensurable to its logic of acceleration. The digital form takes this logic to its natural end.

To situate the development of specifically *capitalist* media within a broader history of media change (which allows us to foreground formative, material, and technical differences in different media), we turn to the medium theory tradition (Innis, McLuhan) to get a sense of how this logic is reflected in the material and technical composition of media. Specifically, we find an analysis of how media are central to the organization of space and time that bridges phenomenology and political economy. As Harold Innis (1964; 1995) argues, media organize space and time and thereby contribute to the reproduction (or disintegration) of social/power structures.

Analyzed comparatively, different media emphasize different space/time ratios, reflecting the relative bias of a given medium. In comparison to media that emphasize their persistence through time (architecture, stone engraving, religious rituals and institutions), media that emphasized the control of space are said to possess a *spatial bias*. For Innis, spatial bias refers to media, such as the price system and the market that break up time into "discrete, uniform, measurable chunks that can be valuated in money terms" (Babe 2000, 73; Innis 1995, 66–87). For example, Innis notes that the spatial bias of the price system in Western political economies "facilitated the use of credit, the rise of exchanges, and calculations of the predictable future essential to the development of insurance" as a way to predict the future and minimize risk (Babe 2000, 72; see Innis 1964, 33–34). Moreover, the concept of bias is also a reflection of a medium's capacity to bind space and time in accordance with the reproduction of a given political economic configuration.

In the effort to overcome the physical, spatial and temporal barriers to circulation, digital code is one of the dominant forms in which capital now invests itself because digitization *is* acceleration. In digital form, capital's real circulation approaches its formal ideal. Indeed, digital data appears to be the perfect medium for self-valorizing value. When something is digitized it exists only conceptually or symbolically, which represents the primacy of images and signs over material objects. Any object rendered digitally is a numerical representation (Manovich 2001, 52).

Most importantly, however, is that capital in the form of bits is less resistant to circulation than when it is comprised of atoms; in digital form, capital can circulate at the speed of electromagnetic waves. There is no need for a real metamorphosis of qualitatively different material forms; what is left of the circulation of commodities on the integrated circuit are mere differences in voltage and a proliferation of digital data. At the speed of electromagnetic waves the expanse of the earth is reduced to nothing. Without having to traverse real space, the time capital spends in the commodity form due to transportation is eliminated. Capital in digital form has little dead time compared to physical commodities; it spends literally no time negated and devalued in its commodity form because the same copy is able to spawn endless copies of itself.

We should be under no illusions that this is exactly what has happened with financial exchanges. M – M' is the archetypal commercial exchange as movement of information. With technologies such as NFC, this process occurs with the traditional metamorphosis of commodities as well. However, we now consider how a technology like NFC can reduce circulation time with reference to the difficulty of the sale in the more mundane setting of a retail environment.

Marx divides the circulation process of capital into the two separate, opposing moments of sale (C' – M') and purchase (M – C). In the sphere of circulation capital goes through these antagonistic moments in whichever order. Consequently, the circulation time of capital – the measure of its velocity – can also be broken down into two parts. Selling-time represents the time needed to convert commodity-capital into money, while purchasing-time reflects the time needed to convert money-capital into the elements of production (Marx 1978, 204). C' – M' and M – C may also transpire separately in space, meaning that selling and buying occurs at different locations (Marx 1978, 205). As discussed above, it is accidental whether capital in any of its forms can actually *assume* the next form and stage in the circuit. The difficulty comes in part from where and when capital in commodity form is sold. The purchase of the elements of production may take longer time if, for example, the necessary means of production cannot be found in the market, needing their production first, or if they are bought from distant markets the time it takes for their transportation to the point of production would form an element of purchasing-time. Marx argues, however, that in normal circumstances, the sale "is the most difficult part of [capital's] metamorphosis, and thus forms the greater part of the circulation time" (1978, 204).

There are a number of reasons for why the sale is more difficult than the purchase, the chief reason being their different forms and associated social functions (i.e. whether it is the commodity or the money that is the point of departure for the movement). The commodity onto which the character of universal equivalent has been imposed is money; it being the visible incarnation of all human labour. Money is the "form assumed in common by the values of

all commodities" and "it is therefore directly exchangeable with all other commodities" (Marx 1976, 159). In other words, in the form of money, "value exists
in its ever convertible form" and is in "constant readiness for action" (Marx
1978, 204). Formally, the movement M – C, the sale, therefore has low latency.
Thus apart from the problem associated with "sourcing" the correct quantity of
the means of production and labour-power from the market, the purchase, for
analytical reasons, can be treated as if it occurs automatically. In commodity-
form, however, value is not in the direct form of exchangeability and this fact
alone is what makes the sale more difficult and its duration longer relative to
the purchase. The commodity must pass the "test of use-value" before its price
can be realized in money (Marx 1976, 179). That is, someone must have a need
for the commodity's use-value, but there is never any guarantee that in a given
market there is *in fact* a need for its particular use-value or, if there is need, that
this need is backed up with "hard" cash; need and equivalents are thus barriers
to capital (see below). Marx therefore refers to the sale, "the leap taken by value
from the body of the commodity into the body of the [money]," as the commodity's "*salto mortale*" (Marx 1976, 200).

There is a further distinction to be made between the movements C' – M' and
M – C, which "has nothing to do with the difference in form between commodities and money, but derives from the capitalist character of production" (Marx
1978, 205). While both movements represent a change in the form of value, "C'
– M' is at the same time the realization of the surplus-value contained in C'"
(Marx 1978, 205). This is not the case with M – C. Marx therefore argues that "the
sale is more important than the purchase" (Marx 1978, 205). Thus while it is
important to reduce both selling- and purchasing-time there is an added pressure to sell as fast as possible because the commodity is impregnated with surplus-value. While buying and selling formally represents movements of
commodities and money as a change of form, from a material point of view they
are also supported by the real movements of commodities and money as physical objects, and also by the human gestures involved in buying and selling.

Marx refers to exchange, the twinned acts of buying and selling, as a "changing of hands." The physical movement of exchange is thus a transfer of commodities from the seller into the hands of the buyer, money going in the
opposite direction. It is in reference to this material changing of hands that we
should understand how payment technologies, for example those backed by
NFC, can increase the velocity of capital, i.e. reduce its overall circulation-time
by specifically reducing selling-time.

A sale is at the same time a purchase because for someone to sell another
person has to buy (Marx 1976, 205). This intimate connection means that accelerating either the sale or the purchase will reduce the time it takes to exchange

commodities for money. Capital is a phenomenon in movement. At the market, say a retail store, the last leg of commodity-capital's movement is the checkout process whereby money and commodities, moving in opposite direction of one another, finally by changing hands. The implication is that while Apple Pay and NFC payment terminals abbreviates the time a customer takes to buy commodities, it also reduces the selling-time of the commodity-capital. Although the time saved with one customer is minimal, in aggregate through a given period there are many customers that fiddle with payment terminals and their many different menus and choices, cannot remember pin numbers, have to swipe cards many times over due to worn magnetic strips, and so on. By solving these aggregate issues, NFC-enabled devices can potentially lead to considerable reductions in selling-time. Such payment media should, however, be understood next to other revolutions at the checkout counter, such as the barcodes, RFID and sensor networks. Scanning a barcode takes considerably less time than punching in individual prices of commodities (Brown 1997). Together payment and checkout technologies not only increases the velocity of capital through the third stage of its circuit and the metamorphosis of commodities into money, but it also makes the labour of the checkout worker more productive (and the technique of buying more efficient), thereby reducing costs of circulation considering that all labour involved in the positing of value in its form does not create value (Marx 1978, 208).

The acts of buying and selling can be both physical or virtual gestures, and will take longer or shorter time based on how money changes "hands," which in part depends on what material form money takes and how this money is transferred. Money's natural form can be metallic or paper as notes, checks and money orders. Today, however, money is almost purely electronic, and our purchases are done with credit or debit cards often in connection with pin numbers (and/or signatures) entered into a payment terminal whose system (e.g. VISA, Mastercard, Interac) extends via modems, telephone lines, fiber optic cables, satellites, servers and so on back to banks and corporate headquarters.

While paying for something is mundane in capitalist societies, it is an act that is learned and routinized from a young age. Historically, we have had to be able to calculate correct change and how to receive it as coins and paper, but increasing technical sophistication instead now requires remembering pin-numbers, knowing how to generally manipulate screens, buttons and the particular menus and options of very diverse payment technologies. Hence, in terms of material practice, buying with cash is different from paying with a credit card. Arguably, the former takes longer than the latter. If you pay with money as coins and/or paper, you will first have to take your wallet or money directly out of your pocket, count up the right amount, hand it over to the sales representative, receive (if any) the correct change back, and then place this change back into your wallet and/or pocket whereby you can walk out with your purchases and bring them into the sphere of consumption. With credit/ debit cards and their associated payment terminal and ecosystem, you first have to take your wallet and/or card out of your pocket, find the right card, wait for the moment the payment terminal is ready to accept your swipe or the insertion of your card, choose between various options such as paying from checking or savings, cash back, and in the end entering your pin number to authorize a transfer of money.

In the introduction we cited promotional literature on Apple Pay. What is interesting about this quote is that it specifically addresses the latency of exchange, but addressed to the money-owning buyer: "Gone are the wasted moments and finding the right card." The moments Apple refers to include the time it takes to complete some of the payment gestures just described (see Figure 6.2, which shows a NFC-enabled device). With NFC-enabled devices or credit/debit card most of these wasted moments are eliminated; all you have to do is to tap a phone (or other device) on a payment terminal, and in the case of Apple Pay, authorize the transaction with a fingerprint scan (or other nominal authenticating action).

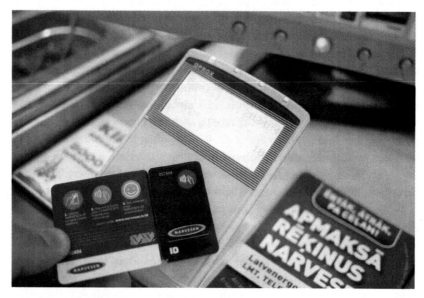

FIGURE 6.2 *NFC terminal*
CREATIVE COMMONS ATTRIBUTION 2.0 LICENSE, NARVESEN NFC ID, BY KĀRLIS DAMBRĀNS, SOURCE: HTTPS://WWW.FLICKR.COM/PHOTOS/ JANITORS/8725959338/IN/SET-72157633462217992/.

This basic ease of use is an essential component of the NFC standard itself which is essentially a set of technical specifications for short-distance transmission of data, similar to *tap-to-pay* features of some credit and debit cards. NFC allows for the secure transmission of personal data, with limited read-write abilities integrated into an NFC chipset. This technology builds on existing contactless standards with the goal of creating global interoperability across systems and devices; it "enables devices to share information at a distance of less than 4 centimeters with a maximum communication speed of 424 kbps."[14] According to the NFC Forum (www.nfc-forum.org), a lobbying and standardization group,

> Near Field Communication is based on inductive-coupling, where loosely coupled inductive circuits share power and data over a distance of a few centimeters. NFC devices share the basic technology with proximity (13.56 MHZ) RFID tags and contactless smartcards, but have a number of key new features.... An NFC-enabled device can operate in reader/writer and peer-to-peer mode, and may operate in card emulation mode. An NFC tag is typically a passive device (for example, integrated in a smart poster) that stores data that can be read by an NFC-enabled device.

Although NFC based-technologies have a range of uses – including healthcare, transportation, and general information collection and exchange – commercial attention has been increasingly fixated on creating mobile payment systems that would effectively eliminate the need for debit or credit cards, indeed, any kind of personal identification that might slow the purchasing act (showing redundant secondary ID) for, indeed: "Moments are the elements of profit" (Marx 1976, 352).

4   Consumption Capacity and the Communication of Capital

For capital, communication constitutes a spectrum that spans logistics and cultural production (including ideology). It is from this communicative spectrum that we can reveal capital's logic of acceleration within the evolution of

---

14   "Users can share business cards, make transactions, access information from smart posters or provide credentials for access control systems with a simple touch" http://www
.nfcforum.org/aboutnfc/nfc_and_contactless/).

contemporary digital media. Yet as we initially noted, personalization and connectivity enhance the *vector* of capital's circulation. Acceleration becomes diagrammatic as capital's circulation is overlaid onto the ubiquitous flows of personalized data.

We argue that qualities of ubiquitous personalization and connectivity offer clear evolutionary examples directed at overcoming two crucial, yet interconnected, barriers binding space and time in accordance with the needs of circulation. In a lucid passage from the *Grundrisse*, we might refer to as the "Fragment on Communication" (Marx 1973, 398–423), Marx explicates capital's communicative spectrum in light of two significant barriers. The first barrier is a cultural barrier involving the expansion of needs, use values and desires; the second involves the means to pay. As Marx writes: "Its first barrier, then, is *consumption itself* – the *need for it*.... Then, secondly, there has to be an equivalent for it" (Marx 1973, 404–405). Taken together these two barriers reflect a specific consumption *capacity* or *magnitude*. While the first barrier traces the entire evolution of the advertising and marketing apparatus (and its migration onto digital platforms), the latter has been overcome by the creation of credit and crediting mechanisms (whose expansion has been directly related to digital media and infrastructure; see Manzerolle 2010). What we find increasingly with digital and new media are the converging poles of capitals' communicative spectrum in the articulation of consumption capacity. Cultural and logistical barriers find their articulation, and prospective panacea, in the proliferation of personalized and networked devices. Moreover, we might assess how consumption capacity articulates a very specific organization (and production) of space and time.

It is significant that the fragment on communication is preceded by a brief passage on the creation of free time in society.

> It is a law of capital...to create surplus labour, disposable time; just as it is equally its tendency to reduce necessary labour to a minimum...it is equally a tendency of capital to make human labour (relatively) superfluous, so as to drive it, as human labour, towards infinity.
>
> MARX 1973, 399

As more free time is created, so too are the productive capacities of the social individual. Importantly, free time gives way to the more full development of the social individual, and of culture generally, a process of enculturation that creates an ever-greater diversity of needs. As culture grows in complexity and sophistication, so does the individual.

> [T]he cultivation of all the qualities of the social human being, produc-
> tion of the same in a form as rich as possible in needs, because rich in
> qualities and relations – production of this being as the most total and
> universal possible social product, for, in order to take gratification in a
> many-sided way, he must be capable of many pleasures, hence cultured
> to a high degree – is likewise a condition of production founded on
> capital.
>
> MARX 1973, 409

Because surplus value relies on the production of free time to increase the ratio
between necessary and surplus labour, capital also creates free time generally,
allowing for the expansion of cultural activities. As a result capital can circulate more freely as the realization of surplus value is potentially linked to the
expanding set of needs variously produced by the converging media, telecom,
and culture industries.

Consequently, the consumption associated with this expanding bundle of
needs comes to reproduce "the individual himself in a specific mode of being,
not only in his immediate quality of being alive, and in specific social relations" (Marx 1973, 717). The social being of the individual and the circulation of
capital are tied to the perpetual modulation of consumption. It is for precisely
this reason that free time can be mobilized to serve the circulatory needs of
capital, particularly through the advancement of information and communication technologies (ICTs) (Webster and Robins 1999; Manzerolle 2011). Both
the cultural sphere of consumption (use values) and the political economic
development of ICTs reproduce a *social being* whose capacities develop in line
with the requirements of circulation.

The development of free time is important for another reason: It creates
new moments within daily life that can be subsumed into, and is an expansion
of, circulation itself. On this note, Dallas Smythe identified the productive
capacity of attentional forms and the mobilization of audiences towards an
expanding array of new use values (Smythe 1981, 40; McGuigan 2012). The colonization of everyday life by digital and networked devices has opened up new
pores, cracks, and crevices of daily life into possible moments of communicative utility in service of capital's logic of acceleration (Manzerolle and Kjøsen
2014). As Leopoldina Fortunati has suggested, mobile ubiquitous media help
fill the pauses and downtime of everyday life with potentially new moments of
"communicative use" (2002, 517). The intensifying technological mediation of
human capacities by digital media give way to the "exploitation" of free (often
enthusiastic) labour of users (Zwick et al. 2009).

The rise of web 2.0 (and its various corollaries) evidences the growing, increasingly necessary, input of free labour to capital's circulation. The unpaid work in free, or unwaged, time is constantly a point at which capital seeks to harness capital's spiralling algorithm of accumulation. Capitalism here requires a cultural exteriority as a source for future commodification. As Marx tacitly suggests, capital creates greater free time in order to subsume that time for the purposes of circulation (Marx 1973, 401). Using an analogy Marx deploys to understand the necessary work of circulation, this creative and communicative labour "behaves somewhat like the 'work of combustion' involved in setting light to a material that is used to produce heat" (Marx 1978, 208). In free time, produced and/or enabled by ICTs, human capacities (creative, cognitive, attentional and affective) act as fuel speeding up the circulation of capital (see Stiegler 2010; Manzerolle and Kjøsen, 2014). Of specific importance is the creation, whether explicitly or implicitly, of a mass of personal data (Manzerolle and Smeltzer 2011).

Thus in trying to overcome the various barriers to circulation, capital's specific organization and management of space and time is crucial, but only insofar as this management coincides with the production of an expanding bundle of needs and the related ability to purchase commodities. This is where the capitalist development and application of ICTs – including a wide variety of ubiquitous, personalized, mobile digital media – becomes so crucial to the overall circulation of capital, but specifically the transformation of commodity-capital into money (C' – M'). Similarly, the ubiquity and instantaneity of personalized digital media offers the possibility of precisely coordinating production and consumption, replacing the traditionally accidental and ideally anonymous moments of exchange with over-determination that comes from the ability to identify and pin-point consumers in space and time. It is by this very process that capital enhances the vector of its circulation and makes the circuit diagrammatic (Manzerolle and Kjøsen 2014).

The twinkling of an eye becomes a metaphor for the electronic pulses that encompass all cultural and economic information. We take as emblematic of this process the current evolution of mobile payment systems, but perhaps more generally, the convergence of communication media and crediting or transactional mechanisms. Consumption capacity is increasingly articulated in and through digital media, and we can situate the development of mobile payment technologies like NFC within the process to generally heighten consumption capacity while offloading costs onto consumers for their means of consumption – in this case the convergence of telecommunications and finance opens up new areas of commodification through digital data, in addition to the general expansion of consumption capacity.

The digital devices that enable our articulation as communicating subjects also act to absorb and translate our behaviour into usable flows of data. As many recent commentators have suggested, we live in an era of *big data* in which the production of data is no longer a competitive obstacle for capital (Hardy 2012; Lohr 2012); now it is the ability to store, process, and mine an immense accumulation of personalized or scalable data. The collection of this data then becomes of paramount importance, and their collection occurs at the moment of exchange, i.e. at the point of sale (POS). This confirms what the prophet Marshall McLuhan observed: there is a "steady progression of commercial exchange as the movement of information itself"(1964, 149). The cybernetic actualization of this potential is the diagrammatization of capital. As we have argued elsewhere, data about consumers, become vectors:

> pregnancy is a vector. By statistically analyzing point-of-sale [data], the Target Corporation is able to "predict" who is pregnant, because pregnant women buy specific commodities during each trimester. Using [data] from such purchases, Target's marketers can send vouchers for commodities that they know a consumer will need as her pregnancy progresses.
>
> MANZEROLLE AND KJØSEN 2014, 154–155

As we argue, this process is the most advanced in its articulation by the apps ecosystem, through which "capital has gained a targeting system. This targeting system has the function of predicting who will buy what, where, and when. The system thus calibrates its predictive targeting by aggregating and processing [data] extracted from the devices of individual consumers" (Manzerolle and Kjøsen, 154).

Thus in the same way that industrial machinery absorbed the physical and intellective capacities of the worker in the sphere of production, so too, our networked environment absorbs the digital streams produced by the very nature of personalization and connectivity in the sphere of circulation. For this reason, it is not surprising that such processes are *baked* into the design, technical composition and functionality of smartphones – particularly in light of the rapid global adoption of these devices in both so-called developed and developing markets (ITU 2011). Indeed, such surveillance operates on at least three levels – operating systems, carriers, and third-party applications – creating a torrent of personal data flowing to and from these connected devices. This invisible dataveillance is an embedded component of our social lives and relationships as they are increasingly mediated by digital networked technologies. Social networks like Facebook leverage the social work of users to subsume them, turning them into a means of piggybacking the circulatory requirements of capital onto the personal relationships (and unpaid cultural labour) of communicating subjects.

In this respect, the purported value of transactional and payment data becomes crucial as a logistical resource accelerating the coordination of commodities and consumption capacity. Personalized mobile devices are vital in this respect both at point of sale and during the shopping process. Apple's efforts reflect not only the potential profitability of controlling the adoption of mobile payment devices and services, but also in acting as crucial gatekeepers in the usage and monetization of transaction data. Walmart's competitive CurrentC payment standard was developed in order that it can retain precious transaction data to feed its logistical dominance in retail. In addition, it is employing Bluetooth beacons and other wireless tracking techniques to monitor the movement of consumers through physical stores and online.

Unlike the previous era, in which personal data was segregated in silos by institution specific databases, the era of personalization and ubiquitous connectivity not only provides exponential growth in the quality and quantity of personal data, but also allows that data to be automatically indexed by user and location (primarily through mobile services). To what end? Digital media help transform our very social being into multiplying nodes in the process and vectorization of circulation. As Marx notes, the overall effect on social being is to turn individuals into independent centers of exchange, ever-more subjected to the rhythms of this intensifying circulation process.

> Consumption is mediated at all points by exchange.... To each capitalist, the total mass of all workers, with the exception of his own workers, appear not as workers, but as consumers, possessors of exchange values (wages), money, which they exchange for his commodity. They are so many centres of circulation with whom the act of exchange begins and by whom the exchange value of capital is maintained.
>
> MARX 1978, 419

Indeed with the rise of ubiquitous media, the body itself becomes inseparable from a steady stream of digital data. The combination of personalization and ubiquity makes the intensifying extraction of information a resource in the diagrammatic expansion and intensification of capital's vector of circulation.

As we have described in the preceding section, digital media are premised on a homogenization of all information into digital code and given form as electronic pulse. This is the same for all information regardless of actual content; the formative existence is the same. In the rise of financial capitalism – or the financialization of the economy, particularly its application of ICTs networked globally – the irresistible impulse is towards employing the means of communication for a total abbreviation of the transformations within the circulation process that gives rise to the abbreviated formulation M – M' – the circuit of finance capital. It takes less time to complete a turnover when capital does not need to pass into the material forms of productive-capital and commodity-capital. But the pressure to shorten circulation time is nevertheless there for the same reason as a normal circuit, as the example of the new transatlantic cable demonstrates.

The problem of credit, a topic, which prior to Volume 3, Marx regularly brings up only to defer his analysis (Marx 1973, 519, 535, 542, 549; 1978, 192, 330, 420–421, 433), reflects a similar problem with digital data; its nominal existence is interchangeable with all other types of information. As credit overcomes a recurring lack of equivalents available for purchase while capital expands its production of surplus value, it multiplies the use of abstractions in circulation. "Where does the extra money come from to realize the extra surplus-value that now exists in the commodity form?" (Marx 1978, 419). "The storing up of money on the one side can proceed even without cash, simply through the piling up of credit notes" (Marx 1978, 422). Throughout Marx's explication of the sphere of circulation, particularly in *Grundrisse*, there is a constant reference to the *deus-ex-machina* of the entire system, namely, credit. At various points, he raises the spectre of credit to suggest how it overcomes barriers, or artificially bypasses circulation, precipitating crises of circulation in the creation of fictitious or virtual money capital. "The entire credit system, and the over-trading, over-speculation etc. connected with it, rests on the necessity of expanding and leaping over the barrier to circulation and the sphere of exchange" (Marx 1973, 416). All information becomes homogeneous and interchangeable. For capitalism's accumulative algorithm this is problematic precisely because its logic is based on a process of transforming value and is validated step by step through its metamorphoses.

Although his analysis is not developed in *Volume 2*, Marx explains that the *credit economy* is merely an extension of the money economy, but that each represents "different stages of development of capitalist production" in contrast to the *natural economy* "what is emphasized in the categories money economy and credit economy, and stressed as the distinctive feature, is actually not the economy proper, i.e. the production process itself, but rather the mode of commerce between the various agents of production or producers that corresponds to the economy" (Marx 1978, 195–196). It is precisely the personalization of our media represented in the credit economy that qualitatively changes the mode of commerce between agents of production. Through personalization, crediting mechanisms generally become intertwined with media and, in fact, it is precisely this integration that Apple Pay seeks to exploit and profit from.

Credit is not only a medium by which to accelerate the circulation of capital and its turnover time (Marx 1981, 567), but is also a system of abstractions for personalizing, and prospectively commodifying the various moments of exchange which can be accomplished through the collection and processing of transactional data. Credit overcomes temporal boundaries by allowing the identity and character of the creditor to act as leverage against future payment (for example, see credit reporting and rating agencies; Manzerolle and Smeltzer 2011). By credit, we include not only the lending of money but also the technical mechanisms that allow credit to be granted so as to reduce circulation time. Digitization has enabled the expansion of credit, sometimes for pernicious or predatory purposes (Manzerolle 2010). As such, digital media systems increasingly produce greater and greater abstractions, and these become *real* abstractions through the consumption of materials and labour time (Cheney-Lippold, 2011).

This speed-up via abstractions and crediting mechanisms cannot occur on its own, but requires infrastructure to actually transmit and expand the range of financial and personal data and thus fuel the creation of ever-more sophisticated abstractions. Although the creation and provision of credit is important, it is equally important to provide crediting mechanisms that leverage personalized data to speed up transactions (whether of credit or real money). NFC technologies are only one small example of the broader credit apparatus. Our digital media are increasingly functioning as means of either facilitating credit or making credit more efficient (credit ratings, credit cards, virtual goods, mobile payments). Increasingly, these flows of data are being treated as a kind of pseudo currency, or at least ascribe some nominal value for their marketing importance. Indeed, consumers are willing to hand over personal information in exchange for coupons, discounts, and other rewards (Accenture 2013, 5). The production of abstractions, like those emerging from the credit system for example, function as mediators of value approaching zero circulation time. This mirrors similar considerations that have suggested that personal data itself be transformed into currency (Brustein 2012a; Zax 2011).

Conclusion: The Cybernetic Imagination of Capitalism

As we have demonstrated, recent developments in mobile payment systems and fiber-optic cables provide evidence of capital's logic of acceleration. These media reflect the evolution of digital media under capitalism as a search for overcoming barriers of use-value, equivalents, space and time. Marx's description of circulation describes the communication of capital as a spectrum tuned to overcoming different barriers. At one end we find the logistical circulation of capital (commodities, labour and money); at the other, we find questions of need and desire as shaped by cultural practices and institutions.

The personalization of media mimics the liberal market ideal of matching consumers with commodities. The evolution of mobile devices with integrated NFC capabilities will turn these devices into tools for providing/automating a whole range of personalized services. This evolution has important implications for post-industrial, service based economies. Personalization of this sort will make obsolete a whole mass of service sector jobs as they are either automated or replaced by the unpaid labour of these ubiquitously connected users, which is a process that offloads costs associated with circulation onto the consumer, while expanding the range of data that can be offered commercially, by telecoms and other third parties (for example, mobile application developers). We can think of the growth of personalization in the era of ubiquitous connectivity as a feedback mechanism that flows through our personalized media, part of a much broader algorithmic expanding and speeding-up through the growing torrent of digital data (whether financial, logistical, personal, or increasingly, all of them together).

According to Otto Mayr (1971), the concept of self-correcting/self-regulating system was one of the chief metaphors for the free market, in which the flows of goods, money and prices would create a self-correcting system that could maximize social welfare for the largest number of people. Personalization of the sort we are now seeing falls closely in line with the beliefs and values of typical liberal market theories; using both personalization and ubiquitous connectivity as a means of efficiently and instantaneously matching services and products with consumers. Our media systems have largely evolved within "the cybernetic imagination of capitalism" (Webster and Robins 1999, 111). Although we are inundated with a quantitative increase in human communication, there is infinitely more expansive network of machinic communication governing the communication of capital and its logic of acceleration. In an early form it expresses Shannon's mathematical theory of communication, which is itself a feedback system (Shannon and Weaver 1949). In both, it is the search for perfect information – the elimination of noise – that constitutes a mathematically perfect, but impossible, communication system. It is no surprise then that our means of communication and our means of exchange (including both money and information over a network) are converging. Within the cybernetic imagination of capitalism, digital media offer capital the vectors through and by which the logic of acceleration is articulated *diagrammatically*.

References

Accenture. 2013. *Driving Value and Adoption of Mobile Payments – Consumers Want More.*

Arthur, Christoper. J. 1998. The Fluidity of Capital and the Logic of the Concept. In *The Circulation of Capital: Essays on Volume Two of Marx's Capital,* edited by Christopher J. Arthur and Geert Reuten, 95–128. London: Macmillan.

Babe, Robert E. 2000. *Canadian Communication Thought: Ten Foundational Writers.* Toronto: University of Toronto Press.

Barr, Alistair. 2012. Paypal execs woos big retailers with pricing, data, *Reuters*, February 10. Accessed February 27, 2012. http://www.reuters.com/article/2012/02/10/paypal -kingsborough-idUSL2E8D8AE720120210.

Barth, Chris. 2011. Visa and Square: Why Goliath is investing in David, *Forbes*, April 27. Accessed May 3, 2012. http://www.forbes.com/sites/chrisbarth/2011/04/27/visa-and -square-why-goliath-is-investing-in-david/.

Bonachich, Edna, and Jake B. Wilson. 2008. *Getting the Goods: Ports, Labor and the Logistics Revolution.* Ithaca, NY: Cornell University Press.

Brown, Stephen A. (1997). Revolution at the Checkout Counter: The Explosion of the Bar Code. Cambridge, MA: Harvard University Press.

Brustein, Joshua. 2012a. Start-ups Seek to Help Users Put a Price on Their Personal Data, *The New York Times*, February 12. http://www.nytimes.com/2012/02/13/ technology/start-ups-aim-to-help-users-put-a-price-on-their-personal-data.html.

Brustein, Joshua. 2012b. Many Competing Paths on the Road to the Phone Wallet, *The New York Times, May* 6. http://www.nytimes.com/2012/05/07/technology/many -competing-paths-on-the-road-to-a-phone-wallet.html.

Cheney-Lippold, John. 2011. A New Algorithmic Identity: Soft Biopolitics and the Modulation of Control, *Theory, Culture, Society* 28(6): 164–181.

Dorminey, Bruce. 2012. Neutrinos to Give High-frequency Traders the Millisecond Edge, *Forbes*, April 30. Accessed May 3, 2012. http://www.forbes.com/sites/brucedorminey/ 2012/04/30/neutrinos-to-give-high-frequency-traders-the-millisecond-edge/.

Elmer, Greg. 2004. Profiling Machines: Mapping the Personal Information Economy. Cambridge, Mass.: MIT Press.

Evans, Peter. 2011. Rogers Wants to Start Bank, *CBC News*, September 6. Accessed February 8, 2012. http://www.cbc.ca/news/business/story/2011/09/06/rogers-bank.html.

Fortunati, Leopoldina. 2002. The Mobile Phone: Towards New Categories and Social Relations. *Information, Communication & Society* 5 (4): 513–528.

Freed-Finnegan, Marc, and Jonathan Wall. 2014. Apple Pay 'No-Data-Collection' Isn't a Feature. It's a Prob lem. *VentureBeat*, October 27. http://venturebeat.com/2014/10/27/ apple-pay-no-data-collection-isnt-a-feature-its-a- problem/.

Fuchs, Christian. 2009. Some Theoretical Foundations of Critical Media Studies: Reflections on Karl Marx and the media *International Journal of Communication* 3: 369–402.

Garnham, Nicholas. 1990. *Capitalism and Communication: Global culture and the Economics of Information*. London: Sage.

Hardy, Quentin. 2012. I.B.M.: Big Data, Bigger Patterns. *New York Times*, February 15. Accessed February 11, 2012. http://bits.blogs.nytimes.com/2012/02/15/i-b-m-big-data-bigger-patterns/.

Harvey, David. 1989. *The Condition of Postmodernity. An Enquiry into the Origins of Cultural Change*. New York: Blackwell.

Hecht, Jeff. 2011. Light is Not Fast Enough For High-speed Trading. *New Scientist*, October 1. Accessed March 10. http://www.newscientist.com/article/mg21128324.700-light-is-not-fast-enough-for-highspeed-stock-trading.html.

Innis, Harold Adams. 1964. *The Bias of Communication*. Toronto: University of Toronto Press.

ITU. 2011. *The World in 2011: ICT Facts and Figures*. International Telecommunications Union.

Kjøsen, Atle Mikkola. 2010. *An Accident of Value: A Marxist-Virilian Analysis of Digital Piracy*. MA Thesis. University of Western Ontario, London, Canada. Available from http://uwo.academia.edu/Kjøsen/Papers/387636/An_Accident_of_Value_A_Marxist-Virilian_Analysis_of_Digital_Piracy.

Kjøsen, Atle Mikkola. 2013. Human Material in the Communication of Capital. Communication + 1, 2 (3).

Lohr, Steve. 2012. The Age of Big Data, *New York Times*, February 12. Accessed February 13, 2012. http://www.nytimes.com/2012/02/12/sunday-review/big-datas-impact-in-the-world.html?_r=1&pagewanted=1&ref=technology.

MacKenzie, Donald. 2011. How to Make Money in Microseconds. *London Review of Books* 33 (10): 16–18.

Manovich, Lev. 2001. *The Language of New Media*. Cambridge, Mass.: The MIT Press.

Manzerolle, Vincent. 2010. The Virtual Debt Factory: Towards an Analysis of Debt and Abstraction in the American Credit Crisis. *tripleC – Cognition, Communication, Co-Operation* 8 (2); 221–236.

Manzerolle, Vincent. 2011. Mobilizing the Audience Commodity: Digital Labour in a Wireless World. *Ephemera* 10 (3/4): 455–469.

Manzerolle, Vincent and Kjøsen, Atle Mikkola. 2012. The Communication of Capital: Digital Media and the Logic of Acceleration. *Triple C* 10(2): 214–229.

Manzerolle, Vincent, and Atle Mikkola Kjøsen. 2014. Dare et Capere: Virtuous Mesh and a Targeting Diagram. In *The Imaginary App*, eds. Paul D. Miller and Svitlana Matviyenko. Cambridge, MA: MIT Press: 143–162.

Manzerolle, Vincent, and Sandra Smeltzer. 2011. Consumer Databases and the Commercial Mediation of Identity: A Medium Theory Analysis. *Surveillance and Society* 8 (3).

Martin, Michele. 1991. Communication and Social Forms: The Development of the Telephone, 1876-1920. *Antipode* 23 (3): 307–333.

Marx, Karl. 1973. *Grundrisse: Foundations of the Critique of Political Economy* (Martin Nicolaus, Trans.). London: Penguin.

Marx, Karl. 1976. *Capital: A Critique of Political Economy, volume 1* (Ben Fowkes, Trans.). London: Penguin.

Marx, Karl. 1978. *Capital: A Critique of Political Economy, volume 2* (David Fernbach, Trans.). London: Penguin.

Marx, Karl. 1981. *Capital: A Critique of Political Economy, volume 3* (David Fernbach, Trans.). London: Penguin.

Mattelart, Armand. 1996. *The Invention of Communication*. Minneapolis, MN: Minnesota University Press.

Mayr, Otto. 1971. Adam Smith and The Concept of the Feedback System: Economic thought and technology in 18th-century Britain. *Technology and Culture* 12 (1): 1–22.

McGuigan, Lee. 2012. Consumers: The Commodity Product of Interactive Commercial Media, Or, Is Dallas Smythe's Thesis More Salient Than Ever? Journal of Communication Inquiry 36 (4): 288–304.

McLuhan, Marshall. 1964. *Understanding Media: The Extensions of Man*. New York: McGraw-Hill.

McLuhan, Marshall, & Nevitt, Barrington. 1972. *Take Today: The Executive As Dropout*. Don Mills, Ont.: Longman Canada.

Mosco, Vincent, and Katherine McKercher. 2008. *The Labouring of Communication: Will Knowledge Workers of the World Unite?* New York: Lexington Books.

Negri, Antonio. 1984. *Marx Beyond Marx*. South Hadley, MA: Bergin & Garvey Publishers Inc.

Parker, Ian. 1981. Innis, Marx, and the Economics of Communication: a Theoretical aspect of Canadian Political Economy. In *Culture, Communication and Dependency. The Tradition of H. A. Innis*, eds. Melody, William H, Salter, Liora and Heyer, Paul. Norwood, NJ: Ablex Publishing Press: 127–143.

Peters, John Durham. 1999. *Speaking into the Air: A History of the Idea of Communication*. Chicago, IL: University of Chicago Press.

Silver, Beverly. 2003. *Forces of Labor: Workers' Movements and Globalization Since 1870*. New York, NY: Cambridge University Press.

Shannon, Claude Elwood, and Warren Weaver. 1949. *The Mathematical Theory of Communication*. Urbana: University of Illinois Press.

Smythe, Dallas Walker. 1981. *Dependency Road: Communications, Capitalism, Consciousness and Canada*. Norwood, NJ: Ablex Pub.

Stiegler, Bernard. 2010. *For a New Critique of Political Economy*. Cambridge, UK ; Malden, MA: Polity.

Webster, Frank, and Kevin Robins. 1999. *Times of the Technoculture*. New York: Routledge.

Williams, Christoper. 2011. The $300 m Cable That Will Save Traders Milliseconds, *Telegraph*, September 11. Accessed March 2, 2012.http://www.telegraph.co.uk/technology/news/8753784/The-300m-cable-that-will-save-traders-milliseconds.html.

Zax, David. 2011. Is Personal Data the New Currency. *Technology Review*, November 30. Accessed March 1, 2012. http://www.technologyreview.com/blog/helloworld/27377/.

Zwick, Detlev, Samuel Bonsu, and Aaron Darmodt. 2009. Putting Consumers to Work. *Journal of Consumer Culture* 8 (2): 163–196.

CHAPTER 7

How Less Alienation Creates More Exploitation? Audience Labour on Social Network Sites*

Eran Fisher

1 Audience Work in the Mass Media

The contribution of Marxist theory to communication studies runs wide and deep (see, for example, Hardt 1992, Artz, Macek, and Cloud 2006). Two analytical coordinates to the study of media, however, stand out as particularly influential: a cultural analysis and a materialist analysis.[1] The two approaches offer quite a different perspective on what it is precisely that audience does. A cultural analysis focuses on the superstructure and uncovers the ideological role of media content in the reproduction of capitalism. Such an analysis of cultural studies (Holmes 2005, 23–24) includes, for example, an investigation into the ideological content of books (Radway 1984), journals (Lutz and Collins 1993, Stevenson, Jackson, and Brooks 2001) advertisements (du Gay et al. 1997, Section 1), movies (Wasko 2001), television shows (Liebes and Katz 1994), and news (Said 1981) (see: Akass and McCabe 2007). Analyzing the undercurrent ideologies of media content could pertain to capitalist concerns, such as class, consumerism, and inequality, as well as to other concerns, such as gender, nationalism, and race (see: hooks 1996, Hall 1995).

Two intellectual legacies have been particularly central in the development of this analytical coordinate: the Frankfurt school (Adorno 2001, Horkheimer and Adorno 1976) and the Birmingham school (Hall 1980, 1995). The two schools differ in their interpretation of the workings of ideology and in the role of the audience. The Frankfurt School views ideological messages as forced down on passive audiences. This has led to study how ideology is coded into media messages. The Birmingham School attributes audience with an active

---

* Thanks to Uri Ram for his invaluable help formulating the argument. I would also like to thank Christian Fuchs and Vincent Mosco for their constructive remarks.

1 I use the distinction between cultural studies and political economy as ideal types, referring to categories of analysis, rather than to actual coherent schools, or individual researchers, which always tend to be more nuanced. Thus, for example, I do not argue that the Frankfurt School has dealt merely with ideology, but rather that the ideal type of cultural studies and its focus on ideology is well epitomized in the thrust of the School's work.

capacity to decode, or "read" ideological messages in the media and resist them (Hall 1980, Mathijs 2002), leading to a theorization of audiences as participants in the construction of multiple meanings of media texts (Ang 1985, Morley 1992). Generally, then, whether assuming that ideological content is propagated top-down to audiences, or whether audiences are seen as actively participating in the process of meaning-making, this strand of Marxist research contributes to the analysis of the media as an ideological site.

A second dominant contribution of Marxist theory to communication studies is a materialist analysis, focusing on the "base". Such analysis of political economy uncovers the relations of production entailed in media institutions. Here, too, one can discern two dominant approaches. Predominantly, the political economy of the media focuses on media ownership. This approach analyzes media as a means of production, investigating issues of media monopoly, media corporation's mergers and consolidations, links between government and the media, and employment arrangements of media workers (Mosco 2009; Mosco and McKercher 2009; Schiller H. 1991; Schiller D. 2010; McChesney 2008; Herman and Chomsky 1988). In the 1970–80s, the political economy of the media was greatly revised by analyzing media as a site of production in and of itself, thus highlighting the productivist role of audience in the creation of media value, both as a commodity and as labour power. This approach was pioneered by Dallas Smythe's groundbreaking work on the audience commodity (Smythe 1981). Smythe suggested that what goes on in mass communication is not primarily audience consumption of media content – produced by media corporations – but, in fact, the selling of audience attention to advertisers. This formulation rendered the audience as active participant in the political economy of mass communication. Smythe's notion of the work of the audience revolves particularly on cognitive and emotional work: learning to desire and buy particular brands and commodities. His was a critique of what he considered to be a "blindspot" in the aforementioned Marxist culturalist analysis, which tended to focus exclusively on the content of media products.

Rather than viewing the media merely as an ideological, superstructural apparatus, that supports relations of production in the economic base – presumably located elsewhere (for example, in the factory) – Smythe positioned the media as a vital component in the chain of capital accumulation. Smythe suggested that the media sells the audience commodity to advertisers. In return for the bait of programing, audience remains glued to the television screen, thus watching advertisements, which become an ever-important driving motor for consumption. For the first time, then, Smythe assigned the mass media and the audience central roles in advanced capitalism, arguing that the "mass media produce audience as commodities for sale to advertisers", and that "audience-power" is put to work by advertisers by "getting audiences to market commodities to themselves" (Jhally and Livant 1986, 129). In some respects, Smythe transplanted the Birmingham School's notion of the active audience, from the realm of meaning-making to that of money-making.

Further developments in this strand of Marxist political economy analyzed media as a site for the production of value in and of itself. Jhally and Livant (1986) argued that Smythe's focus on the contribution of audience labour for manufacturers of branded commodities "has tended to deflect the specificity of the analysis away from communications to the ensuing consumption behavior of the audience" (Jhally and Livant 1986, 129). "Ultimately" they say, "Smythe was concerned with drawing attention to the place of communications in the wider system of social reproduction of capital" (ibid., 129). Criticizing Smythe's heavy reliance on the use-value of messages (as motivating consumption), Jhally and Livant explore the blindspot that is "located more firmly *within* the media industries" (ibid., 129, emphasis in original). They therefore analyze watching as a form of working since it harnesses human "capacities of perception" (ibid., 126) to the creation of value. The creation of surplus-value in the media is based on "extra watching" of commercials, on watching more ads than are necessary to pay for programming. This "surplus watching time" (ibid., 127), then, suggests that audience, in fact, work for programmers, not advertisers.

Such analysis constructs the media as a dynamic site of struggle between audience (labour) and media providers (capital), a struggle that revolves on time. Jhally and Livant (1986) do that by employing Marx's distinction between extensive and intensive exploitation. Marx insisted that capitalist struggles ultimately revolve around time, since surplus-value can only arise from workers working more time than is actually needed to reproduce their lives. This extra working creates surplus-value which, rather than being exchanged for its equivalent, is rendered into capital and is introduced to the process of accumulation (for example, by investing in new technology). Since this entails the creation of value by one class of people (workers) and its uncompensated transference to another class (capitalists), Marx refers to that as exploitation. The problem, inherent to capitalist accumulation, is that surplus-value tends to diminish over time, dwindling away the source of capital accumulation (Marx 1993, Ch. 13). To expand, or even just conserve the rate of surplus-value, capital strives to find ways to enlarge the scope of exploitation. This is done by either of two forms: extensive exploitation and intensive exploitation. Extensive exploitation refers to techniques and arrangements by which more time is dedicated to work, for example, by elongating the working day or by cutting down on lunch breaks and vacation time. Intensive exploitation is achieved by having workers produce more in less time, for example, by accelerating the rhythm of work or making the work process more efficient.

Jhally and Livant (1986) argue that both these processes of exploitation have been occurring in the mass media. The audience has been asked to work more and harder over the course of history. The extension of exploitation was achieved by introducing audience with more advertisements, thus making them watch (i.e., work) more time. The intensification of exploitation, or the increase in relative surplus-value was achieved in two ways: "reorganizing the watching population, and...reorganizing the watching process" (Jhally and Livant 1986, 133). The first involves all sorts of techniques, from media market research to the rating system, all of which are aimed at helping media corporations target a specific audience with a specific ad; such market segmentation leads to increase in the value of advertisement. As Jally and Livant put it: "Specification and fractionation of the audience leads to a form of 'concentrated viewing' by the audience in which there is...little wasted watching" (133). Since highly targeted advertising costs more, "we can say that the audience organized in this manner watches 'harder' and with more intensity and efficiency" (Jhally and Livant 1986, 133–134). The other way by which relative surplus-value is exerted is through the division of time, accomplished mainly by shorter commercials.

2 Mass Media Alienation

While Marxist political economy of the media has been concerned since the 1970s with the question of exploitation in the media, little attention has been given to the notion of alienation within this framework; an oddity, considering that Marx conceived an inextricable link between the two. Marx's conception of alienation is complex and multi-layered, pertaining to a process as a well as a result. Alienation pertains to the separation of the worker from vital life processes and objects, as well as to the resulting state of estrangement from these objects. It is the estrangement of workers from the labour process, from other workers, from the finished product, and ultimately from their selves, their species-being (Marx 1978). Rather than work being an activity that workers control and navigate, rather than the real essence of a person be objectified in what he does, rather than work be a means of self-realization and authentic expression, rather than work help a person connect, communicate, and collaborate with other human beings, work under capitalism results instead in alienation.

I use the term alienation somewhat leniently, to highlight the humanist aspects in Marx's critique of capitalism and distinguish it from his more structural and economic critique. In Marxist critique, alienation and exploitation are inextricably linked, and may even be thought of as complementary tenets. Alienation is both a pre-condition for exploitation and the result thereof. Both are corollaries of the very foundations of capitalism – private property and the commodification of labour; one problem cannot be resolved without resolving the other. They do, however, point to two different aspects in Marx's critique of capitalism. The distinction is often made (following Althusser) between the young and mature Marx, the former offering a more humanist analysis of capitalism, the latter a more economistic one. While the empirical accuracy of this distinction is questionable (the mature Marx of Capital still insists on the relevance of alienation as a central cause and effect of capitalism), it does capture two distinct thrusts in Marx's critique of capitalism.

Alienation entails not only a social-economic condition whereby "value" and the product are separated from their real producers and are transferred from one class to another. More than that, alienation signals an existential state of not being in control over something (the labour process, the product, etc.), of being estranged from something (one's humanity, etc.). The thrust of this concept and the reason to introduce it over and above exploitation is precisely to highlight the contradictions of capitalism from a humanist viewpoint.

Another liberty I take with the notion of alienation is that I use the term to refer to a condition whereby work, the work process, the product of labour, and one's essence are more or less alienated. Such compromise of Marxist theoretical purity is justified in the name of historical reality. As Boltanski and Chiapello (2005) have shown, the social and political history of industrial capitalism has been one of mitigating one problem over the other, rather than eliminating both. Hence their distinction between the humanist artistic critique and the economistic social critique. In the context of this chapter, less alienation refers to a greater possibility to express oneself, to control one's production process, to objectify one's essence and connect and communicate with others. Thus, for example, working on one's Facebook page can be thought of as less alienating than working watching a television program.

Watching the media is constructed as a leisure activity in liberal discourse. Media consumption is depicted as the opposite of the alienation that dominates production; a time away from the alienation of the workday, and a chance for de-alienation (as the case is for example in the prominent uses and gratifications theory; see Katz, Blumler, and Gurevitch 1973–1974). Constructing audiencing as a consumerist activity, positions the audience in an active capacity of choice. As opposed to the work process, of which workers had no control, watching television supposedly puts the control in the hands of the viewer (literally so, with the advent of the remote control). Watching the mass media, then, is constructed in liberal discourse as a consumerist, irrational, fun, and fulfilling practice.

While Marxist political economy of the media ignored the question of alienation, the culturalist-ideological analysis did pay attention to some core aspects of alienation, even if not attending to the concept per se. If watching – in the capitalist media environment – is a form of working, then the process and content of that labour are also alienated from the audience. In fact, both advertisements and programs (which support the content of the advertisements) feed into and thrive on audience alienation, suggesting that self-fulfilment and objectification should and will arrive from consumption and leisure activities, rather than from work. Such themes are most extensively explored in the work of the Frankfurt School on the culture industry (Adorno 2001, Ch.6). But such analysis does not explicitly link audience exploitation to audience alienation. According to Marx, alienation and exploitation are inextricably linked and are a corollary of the very foundations of capitalism – private property and the commodification of labour. One problem cannot be resolved without resolving the other.

3   Audience Work on Social Networking Sites: The Case of Facebook

Recently, there has been a renewed interest in the notion of audience work in light of a changing media environment, particularly the emergence of web 2.0 and social network sites (SNS). Some features of this new media environment makes a revisiting of the concept of audience labour particularly important. As opposed to mass media, SNS is characterized by high levels of participation, by user-generated content, and by the ability to create varied channels of communication: one-to-one, one-to-many, and many-to-many.

Marxist-inspired research on this new media environment has focused almost exclusively on audience exploitation. Simultaneously, mainstream (liberal) research has tended to reaffirm the common-sense and ideological construction of SNS as facilitating de-alienation by offering users opportunities for self-expression, authenticity, communication, collaboration with others, and deep engagement with, and control over cultural, social, and economic ventures.

My argument is that both these trends – seemingly contradictory – are in fact dialectically linked. Exploitation and de-alienation are not simply two contrasting interpretations of SNS; rather, Marxist theory encourages us to accommodate them within a single analytical framework. SNS give audience more opportunities for objectification by allowing self-expression, authenticity, and communication and collabouration with others. As the communication and sociability of users are commodified, so does their labour become a source for exploitation. In what follows I consider the dialectics of exploitation and alienation on SNS by taking a closer look at Facebook.

4   Facebook as a Means of Communication

What is the work that SNS users do? What is it precisely that they produce? And how are they exploited? To accommodate a dialectical analysis of Facebook we should be looking at it as both a means of communication and a means of production. That is, not only as a new form of media which allows for new modes of communication (Napoli 2010), but also as a technology that facilitates a new mode of production. This should help up overcome the shortcoming of previous Marxist analysis, which offers two divergent analyses of the media as *either* a means of communication or a means of production. While such dialectical approach is appropriate to any form of mass media it becomes particularly important in the new media environment, which can be defined precisely as tying communication and production more closely together. Indeed, the unique character of web 2.0 has encouraged researchers to look more carefully at the dialectics of these two coordinates (Scholz 2010, Lee 2011).

Facebook, the world's most popular SNS, was launched in February 2004 and had 845 million monthly active users at the end of December 2011 (Facebook 2012b). Facebook offers a platform where users can create personal profiles to present themselves and communicate in varying degrees of detail and complexity about their whereabouts, thoughts, feelings, and actions. Users may add other Facebook users as friends, exchange messages with them, and follow after their public messages and their whereabouts. Users may also create communities, or sub-networks, based on shared interests. The profile allows users to characterize themselves along various personal categories, such as gender and education history, as well as through lifestyle choices, such as favorite artists and hobbies.

Users communicate with friends through various private and public tools such as "Status", which allows users to inform their friends of their whereabouts and actions; "Wall", which is the a space on every user's profile page that allows friends to post messages for the user to see; and "Chat", which allows private, synchronic communication with friends. Users may also create and join interest groups and "Like" pages, initiated and operated primarily by governmental, commercial, and non-governmental organization as means of advertisement, sale, and mobilization. The plethora of networks and communities of which Facebook users are part can generate social action – political, economic, communal, or societal – by mean of communication and organization. Facebook is reported to have an increasingly central role in facilitating and organizing social movements and political upheavals from the Anti-Globalization movement to the Arab Spring.

Facebook is inherently "biased" to communication so that even some personal activities on one's own profile automatically translate into communication. Such is the case of photo "tagging" in the Photos application, one of the most popular applications on Facebook, where users can upload albums and photos. If an uploaded photo features a user's friend, he may tag the photo. This sends an automatic notification to the tagged friend, containing a link to the photo. Thus, posting a photo may roll into a communication event.

Such banal description highlights the communication facet of Facebook, and the opportunities it facilitates for users' de-alienation, especially, as opposed to the limited opportunities facilitated by mass media. The age of mass- media was dominated by broadcast television and radio, print newspapers, and film. It was centralist, allowing only a uni-directional flow of information from few to many, and from top down. Mass-media created a hierarchical dichotomy between active producers and passive consumers, content was prepackaged and thus limited in variety, at once assuming and constructing a relatively homogenous audience. Social media, in contrast, facilitates varied communication forms: few to few, few to many, many to many. It is interactive, allowing users more engagement, and rendering the passive, homogeneous audience of mass-media into an active and engaged audience. Communication on the Internet allows individuals to narrate their lives (e.g. blogs), make their views public (talkbacks), and express their creativity (YouTube). It also allows Internet users to collabourate among themselves in an increasingly participatory culture (Jenkins 2009, Burgess and Green 2009). Indeed, most research looks at the communication facet of Facebook, and at its ability to empower individuals by contributing to their objectification.

Thus, Internet research tends to construct communication – multiple, democratic, trespassing boundaries of space and time – as an ideal, most fully materialized by means of the Internet. It tends to focus on user's experience with Facebook, emphasizing individual agents' purposeful use of Facebook for communication. Such "methodological individualism" (Popper 1971: Ch. 14), where individual users are the point of departure for the analysis, leads much research to focus on users' satisfaction (Bonds-Raacke and Raacke 2010, Quan-Haase and Young 2010), or on the consequences of communicating on Facebook to user's subjectivity and psychological well-being (Gonzales and Hancock 2011, Ong et al. 2011). Lastly, studies in the tradition of virtual ethnography too emphasize the communication facet of Facebook, with privacy and the dissolution of the private sphere toping research concerns (West, Lewis, and Currie 2009, Brandtzaeg, Luders, and Skjetne 2010).

These studies, then, take Facebook's mission statement – to "giv[e] people the power to share and make the world more open and connected...Millions of people use Facebook everyday to keep up with friends, upload an unlimited number of photos, share links and videos, and learn more about the people they meet" (Facebook 2012). – at face value, and see it as a virtual space of communication, sociability, and community.

5   Facebook as a Means of Production

Having predominantly conceived as a means of communication, the public and academic discussion on Facebook tends to highlight its capacity to contribute to (or hamper) de-alienation among users. As aforementioned, my goal here is to point out how this capacity for objectification is linked with an empowered capacity for exploitation. This demands that we recall that being a commercial company, Facebook's primary mission is to accumulate capital, and that we analyze Facebook as technology and see it as galvanizing social relations. Such analysis of Facebook as a capitalist technology that facilitated and exacerbates exploitation, should then be linked to the dominant analysis of Facebook as a media for communication allowing de-alienation.

Facebook's accumulation strategy can be appreciated by proxy of its staggering market value. While Facebook's market value is highly unstable and speculative, but it can nevertheless be determined to be in the neighbourhood of US$75–100 billion. What precisely in Facebook is worth $100 billion? Where does the value of Facebook emanate from? And at a more sociological level: what are the relations of production upon which SNSs are founded? We can thus begin to outline a political economy of SNS by conceptualizing Facebook not merely as a means of communication but also as technology, as embodying social relations.

A full answer to these questions should tie both facets of Facebook: as a means of communication and a means of production; to understand Facebook as technology, we need to understand Facebook as being also a media. This dialectical link of media and technology, of communication and production, is in fact a key feature of contemporary capitalist society; Facebook epitomizes a new form of production relations, where value is created not primarily by workers of the company, but by the audience. And the most important thing that Facebook users produce – the primary source of Facebook's value – is communication and sociability.

The value of Facebook is derived from Facebook's unprecedented ability to have access to information, store, own, process, and analyze it, and deliver it to its customers. Metaphorically, then, Facebook might be mistakenly seen as a warehouse of information. But the term barely begins to uncover the novelty of Facebook. To better understand the political economy of Facebook we must ask what this information consists of, how it comes into being, and by whom. To do that I will distinguish between five different types of information, which are to some extent layered one on top of the other: demographic, personal, communicative, performativite, and associational. Such typology suggests that rather than a warehouse, a more apt metaphor for Facebook is a factory, where *information is produced through communication and sociability*, rather than simply stored. What is new and unique about Facebook, and crucial to its political economy, is that much of the information in SNS emanates from the very practice of using it, from being a media of communication and sociability. Here it is that Facebook as a means of communication (media) and a means of production (technology) converge.

Communication between Facebook users generates a plethora of personal and social information about users, information which is becoming increasingly valuable for companies in virtually all consumer industries, and which is eagerly sought after by advertising, public relations, and marketing professionals. Some of that information is quite "lean" and can be described as demographic. SNS become key sites where demographic information is written, recorded, aggregated, and organized. The availability of demographic information on SNS is based on either users' self-disclosure (for example, in the case of age, gender, marital status, or education), or the location of servers (in the case of geographical location). While this kind of information "precedes" Facebook, it is not completely independent of Facebook, since SNS encourage their users to self-disclosure. This has a formal manifestation in Facebook's terms of use, which forbid users to "provide any false personal information on Facebook", and directs them to "keep...contact information accurate and up-to-date" (Facebook 2011a). Indeed, Facebook's privacy settings have been persistently designed to keep users' information as open as possible for public viewing (Fuchs 2011a, 2011b). More subtly and fundamentally, the ethics and norms that developed on SNS put premium on a genuine representation of the self. This signifies a turn from the culture of anonymity, promulgated during the early years of online sociability in forums, chat rooms, and MUDS (Turkle 1997).

This brings us to a second, 'thicker' layer of information, which pertains to the identity and authenticity of users. The ethics of SNS call for publicness, for defining and identifying oneself to oneself and to others. Users are encouraged to reveal and present their true self and define who they are through profiling. Such a demand puts users in a position of forced reflexivity, an obligation to think about, define, and present themselves. Such reflexivity is built into the website's design, which encourages users to self-disclose abundantly and systemically. As Illouz (2007, Ch. 3) has shown, profile-based websites (such as dating sites) encourage users to think about themselves in particular terms and identify themselves according to preconceived and pre-packaged categories, thus rationalizing self-disclosure. For example, when constructing a personal profile on Facebook users are asked to define their "philosophy" with the following categories: "religion", "political views", "people who inspire you", and "favourite quotes". Even though this kind of personal information presumably precedes engagement with Facebook, it cannot really be thought of as pre-existing information that Facebook merely harvests, but as information which gets articulated within the specific context of social networks, i.e., that of communication and sociality.

The third layer of information is further dependent on the engagement of users with Facebook: information based on the communication content of users, on their conversations with each other. In economic terms, this is arguably the most valuable information produced by users. Indeed, the attention of companies, professionals, and applications engages in the endeavour of monetizing SNS is primarily focused on communication content. Such endeavour employs quantitative and qualitative methods to analyze the content of interpersonal and social communication in order to decipher what people are talking about and in what way. The analyzed trends, keywords, themes, and narratives can then be associated with demographic information (such as gender, geographical location, or age) or with behavioural information (such as consumption behaviour), and yield valuable commercial information. Such information is also highly individualized, allowing it to make a definite connection between a specific content and a specific person.

Commercial interests not only listen in to the conversation of users, but also use the SNS to initiate, engage with, and shape the conversation. They can participate in the conversation by propagating messages, creating a buzz, and designing fashions and fads. An exemplar of that is the viral message (or the meme), often originating and promulgated by public relations professionals (see: Downes 1999, Green 2010: Ch. 11). In such cases, users become the media through which messages are propagated.

While communication content on Facebook covers virtually every aspect of human communication, it is worthy to note two particular types of information that SNS is especially conducive in allowing their articulation and organization, and that are of increasing value in contemporary capitalism: mundane information, and emotional queues. Mundane information pertains to everyday expressions of lived experience, such as photos taken on a trip, or reports about one's whereabouts (Beer and Burrows 2010). These scraps of information about everyday life experiences were hitherto perceived as too fragmented, insignificant, and personal to be noticed or reported on in public. SNS is especially fit to host this kind of information, which in turn opens up a capillary gaze at the way people live. Emotional queues pertain to subjective emotional expressions, and to emotional characterizations which accompany the communication. Emotional queues are usually tied to some activity done by users, such as reading a news story, or waiting in line at the supermarket. The ever-presence and immediacy of social media through mobile devices means that sentiments are registered and expressed almost as they occur, rather than reported upon in retrospect. SNS – because they are personal, interpersonal, and social; because they are associated with leisure activities and sociability; because they encourage people to be expressive, frank, and above all communicative – are particularly apt for the production and extraction of such types of information.

The forth layer of information is performativite, pertaining to quantitative and qualitative characteristics of users' activities on SNS, such as the number of friends they have, the dynamics of the sub-networks of which they are part, their level of engagement with Facebook, time spent on Facebook, type of activities (number of posts, number of photos posted, number and nature of "likes" clicked) and so forth.

The fifth and last layer of information, closely related to the previous one, is associational. This refers to the very formation of sub-networks within the SNS: a user's link to other profiles, to commercial and political pages, to news stories, brands, and so forth. By forming networks of associations, users are producing webs of meaning, symbolic universes, and semantic fields. Association information is valuable in further identifying and characterizing individuals. In a postmodern culture, where identity is constructed through signs, the web of "Likes" that users form serves as an indicator of their identity. Associational information may therefore be valuable in uncovering correlations between indicators. Moreover, the sub-networks that are formed are highly valuable since they are likely to have an identifiable character; in public relations terms, sub-networks are highly segmented groups, because opt-in is voluntary and based on some manifest characteristic. Thus, associational information allows public relations professional to identify (as well as construct) groups based on their positive attitudes towards a material, service, or cultural product, follow the different layers of information they produce, and engage these groups directly (for example, by creating a buzz).

Beginning from the most basic demographic information to the most sophisticated, it is not merely pre-existing personal information that SNS now make easier to collect. More dramatically, the existence of much of this information is dependent on the very use of SNS, on people joining them and conducting large parts of their life in them; it is information that comes into being in the very act of communicating and socializing. In sum, my argument is that such types of information – which are of increasing value in contemporary economy – are dependent on a means of communication to be produced.

6   The Dialectics of Exploitation and Alienation on SNS

Marxist theory, then, introduced two coordinates to the analysis of the media: a culturalist, ideology approach, and a materialist, political economy approach. In more abstract terms, these two coordinates refer to two distinctive facets of media as either a means of communication or a means of production. Notwithstanding Marx's insistence on a dialectical analysis of society, Marxist studies of the media commonly employ either of these two coordinates (Fenton 2007). This is not to say that such studies are flatly undialectical, but rather, that dialectics is not internalized into the analysis of media. Thus, for example, culturalist analysis shows how media products such as television programs work ideologically to support relations of production in general, not in the media particularly.

Scholarship on the political economy of new media, and on audience labour in particular, also tended to be relatively one-sided, highlighting SNS as a site of exploitation of "free labour" (Terranova 2004, Ch. 3). Such approach has been criticized as over-deterministic, structuralist, and functionalist (Caraway 2011). Rather than underscoring media as a site of struggle between labour and capital, such approach gives a one-sided analysis, that of capital. The crux of Smythe's argument is that with mass communication all time becomes productive time, an argument later to be much developed with the notions of the social factory, and immaterial labour. Caraway argues that such framework is unable to distinguish leisure time from work time, coerced labour from free labour, and capacity to work from willingness to work. This lack of distinctions, says Caraway, obfuscate the Marxist category of labour. He questions Smythe's historical narrative, according to which a decrease in factory labour time was complemented by an increase in labour time in front of media advertisements. Caraway suggests an alternative version which endows labour with agency. According to the alternative version, the reduction in working hours, and the corollary expansion of leisure time were a result of a persistent and bloody struggle of workers at the beginning of the 20th century. More theoretically, then, Caraway (2011) argues that the critical potentials of the notions of the social factory and immaterial labour are absent from contemporary accounts. And Scholz has emphasized the dialectical relations between Facebook as playground and as factory (Scholz 2010).

Following this line of inquiry, this chapter has attempted to explore the dialectics of production and communication within contemporary media forms, both building on the work of Smythe (1981) and Jhally and Livant (1986), and updating it. It argues that the extension and intensification of exploitation of audience labour in the mass media ran into relatively low barriers. The extension of exploitation was limited by the capacity of viewers to watch advertisements. Watching television ads is not something that audience commonly enjoys. The media cannot therefore screen too many ads from fear of losing viewers' attention (which is the actual labour power that it sells to advertisers). New technologies of television viewing which allow audience more control over viewing (such as TIVO) are setting further limits on exploitation since they allow audience to skip over ads.

The intensification of exploitation is also fairly limited by two parameters. First, the monitoring, rating, and segmentation system of mass media is highly expensive.[2] Moreover, it is imbued in a paradox: the more accurate the information on viewers is, the more the surplus-value of watching increases (Jhally and Livant 1986). However, such increase in value is somewhat undermined by the price of collecting more accurate information. Moreover, viewers' monitoring techniques are based on statistical analysis, and are hence inaccurate and unreliable by definition. The desires, personality, and behaviour of each and every individual in the audience of the mass media are hard to gauge. The second parameter which sets limits to the intensification of exploitation in the mass media is that the intensification of exploitation requires media corporations to create programs that provide the appropriate "bait" for the desired audience. They can fail miserably achieving this task, either by not attracting enough audience, or not attracting a desired segment of the audience.

---

2 For example, the 2011 revenues of Nielsen, the largest global media rating company, were over $5.5 billion (Nielsen 2012).

SNS offer a transcendence of these limitations, allowing the extension and intensification of exploitation to go beyond the limits that the mass media set. The extension of exploitation is achieved by having users spend more time on SNS. The work of Facebook users is done incessantly. In January 2010 Facebook became the site where U.S. web users spend most time (Parr 2010). The average web user spends more time on Facebook than on Google, Yahoo, YouTube, Microsoft, Wikipedia and Amazon combined (Parr 2010). The Nielsen rating for that month revealed that the average American user spends more than seven hours a month on Facebook, or 14 minutes per day. And American Facebook users are not even the heaviest users. An industry study of the monitoring and analysis firm Experian from September 2011 found that Facebook is most heavily used in Singapore, where the average visit to the social network lasts more than 38 minutes (Emerson 2011).

Moreover, thanks to the ubiquity of mobile devices (from laptops to smartphones) and wireless networks (from Wi-Fi to 3G) users are almost always accessible to Facebook. Compared with television watching, which is spatially fixed and temporally limited, Facebook offers a much more flexible usage patterns. More time, than, in more parts of the day (work day, leisure time) can be spent communicating and socializing on Facebook. Self-surveillance technologies, such as Foursquare or Facebook Places (or: Location) also put users at an arms-length from their friends, extending the duration they are likely to be active on the social network.

SNS allow also the intensification of exploitation. Rather than mass media corporations allocating resources to monitor and segment their audience, it is users of SNS that segment themselves in a manner that can only be dreamt of for television audience. Such procedure is much cheaper, as it is in effect "outsourced" to users, who act as produsers (Bruns 2008). Moreover, the information gathered about the audience is also much more accurate and thick. Whereas the mass media knew its audiences as statistical entities, as aggregates and abstract segments, Facebook knows its users as individuals. The capillary reach of SNS, then, facilitates the intensification of exploitation; a biopolitical nervous system which harnesses the immaterial labour of users.

This puts into question a central tenet of the Autonomist interpretation of Marxism. The notions of immaterial labour and general intellect suggest a process of deterritorialization of knowledge, the prime means of production of contemporary capitalist accumulations. Virno speaks of "a repository of knowledges *indivisible* from living subjects and from their linguistic co-operation" (Virno 2001, quoted in Dyer-Witheford 1999, 222, emphasis mine). Such knowledges are hard to locate, localize, and collect, since they are "produced" during leisure time, within private spaces, and within the communicative space between individuals, as part of their everyday lives. The analysis presented here suggests we should think about SNS as a technology for the reterritorialization of the kind of labour that produces such knowledges – immaterial labour – and the kind of knowledges that are produced – general intellect (Peterson 2008).

Hence, the extension and intensification of exploitation in social media compared with mass media relies on the unprecedented ability to harness new forces of production to the accumulation process, particularly the production of information through communication and sociability. The audience of SNS creates value simply by audiencing, by using the media platform to express itself, communicate, and socialize. Such exploitation, then, is conditioned by a promise for de-alienation. SNS offer a media environment where audience work can potentially lead to objectification: users have much more control over the work process and the product (although not owning it legally); work entails communication that helps users connect with others and objectify more facets of their species being. SNS is a space for self-expression, for making friends, constructing communities, and organizing a political, cultural, social, or economic action.

The two processes that SNS facilitates – the exacerbation of exploitation and the mitigation of alienation – are not simply co-present but are dialectically linked. SNS establishes new relations of production that are based on a dialectical link between exploitation and alienation: in order to be de-alienated, users must communicate and socialize: they must establish social networks, share information, talk to their friends and read their posts, follow and be followed. By thus doing they also exacerbate their exploitation. And vice-versa, in order for Facebook to exploit the work of its users, it must contribute to the de-alienation of their users, propagating the ideology that de-alienation can in fact (and solely) be achieved by communicating and socializing on SNS, an ideology of communication, networking, and self-expression (Dean 2010), which sees network technology and social media in particular as the golden route to de-alienation. In such ideology, alienation is linked with a lack of communication and with social isolation, a malady promised to be cured through communication and through SNS. And so, the more users communicate and socialize, the more they post photos and follow their friends, the more they "Like" – in short, the more they engage in authentic self-expression and interpersonal communication – the more they objectify and de-alienate. Put differently, the more they work, the more they create surplus-value, and the more they are exploited.

7   A Closed-Circuit of Communication and Production

The case of Facebook alludes to new relations of production, emerging within a new environment of social media. The new relations of production are markedly different from those crystallized in the mass media, and theorized by Smythe (1981) and Jhally and Livant (1986). They are based on a new trade off between exploitation and alienation. In comparison with mass media, and television in particular, SNS can be conceptualized as a technology that is able to extend and intensify exploitation, while at the same time alleviating alienation. Audience work on SNS is both more exploitative and more de-alienating. In fact, the capacity of SNS to exploit audience work is dependent on its capacity to alleviate alienation. SNS users work harder – producing more information, communication, and sociability – the more they perceive this work to be de-alienating.

Recently, there has been an emerging interest in the question of audience work and exploitation. In two complementary chapters, Andrejevic (2011a, 2011b) examines the application of the categories of exploitation and alienation, respectively, to analyze the political economy of social media. Andrejevic suggests that social media users can be thought of as alienated from their media labour only to the extent that they do not control the product on which they labour (Andrejevic 2011b). He distinguishes between two types of information that are subject to exploitation on social media: intentional/unintentional information. The former pertains to data extracted from intentional actions of users (such as posting a photo, or tweeting), while unintentional information pertains to data that users produce unintentionally, while doing something else. The generation of unintentional data can be described, according to Andrejevic, "as the alienated or estranged dimension of their activity" (2011b, 85). My suggested categorization of the types of information produced by users suggests that such distinction is hard to make, and is therefore a problematic basis to discern alienated labour from unalienated one. Most data that users produce has a dual character: while being intentional, posting a photo also produces unintentional information such as the web of users that are exposed to the photo or comment on it.

My contentions in this chapter rely on a different understanding of alienation as a relative entity, arguing that *within* capitalism workers can be more or less alienated. Hence, I suggest that the relations of production entailed by social media are based on an implicit social contract which allows media companies to commodify the communication produced by users (i.e., exploiting them) in return for giving them control over the process of producing communication, and expanding their opportunity for de-alienation.

Andrejevic does point to the complexity of the relations between social media users and companies. Indeed he defines the challenge of employing the notion of exploitation in the context of social media as being about explaining "the relationship between willing participation and commercial exploitation" (2011a, 83). And suggests that to account for exploitation on social media we must also appreciate that the work of the audience is a source for enjoyment for users, and a way to "overcome alienation in the realm of consumption" (Andrejevic 2011b, 80). But he does not suggest a direct link between the two.

The dialectical link between media as a means of communication and media as a means of production in SNS and web 2.0 has been most productively theorized with the notion of immaterial labour (Virno and Hardt 2006). Indeed, Smythe's analysis forestalls this concept by pointing to the commodification of audience attention, i.e., the mobilization of its cognitive faculties for capitalist accumulation. Immaterial labour (and in other contexts: general intellect [Virno 2001]) pertains to a creative force of cognitive, emotional, and communicative capacities that are located within individuals, not factories. One of the key tenets of this analytical category, developed by the Italian Autonomist Marxist School, is that such productive potentials of human life and lived experience is extremely difficult to be harness, contain, or structure by capital. Hence, the increased reliance of capitalism on immaterial labour holds a revolutionary potential.

The dialectical analysis of the media presented here, however, suggests another interpretation, by taking into account the media within which such labour is carried out. Such analysis suggests that SNS offer precisely that space, that factory, which allows the extraction of these human potentialities and their subsumption by capital. As Napoli puts it, "the creative work of the audience is an increasingly important source of economic value for media organizations" (Napoli 2010, 511). Revisiting the notion of audience work on web 2.0, Napoli theorizes new media as mass communication, arguing that the term is flexible enough to account for audiences in contemporary media environment. The revolutionary nature of web 2.0 lies not in the ability of ordinary individuals to generate content, but in their newfound ability to distribute their content widely through the web (Napoli 2010). Napoli, then, directs us at circulation, not production, as the lynchpin of audience work in contemporary media environment, circulation that, as we have seen, is part and parcel of capital accumulation on SNS. If, as Napoli suggests, new media is mass communication, with the distinction that now more individuals are able to reach mass audience, then new media can be thought of as media which allows for far greater quantities of information (content) to be produced freely by far more people, and run over far greater numbers of channels of communication.

What is particularly unique in SNS is that they create an autarchic economic system, a closed-circuit of communication and production in a way that was fairly limited in the mass media age. Lee (2011) shows how Google's advertising program creates a self-propelling mechanism for the creation of exchange-value. The company "vertically integrates the search engine, the advertising agency, and the rating system" (434). Thus, for example, Google sells keywords for advertisers, allowing them to feature ads when particular words are searched. Such keywords, Lee notes, have no use-value, and in fact only have exchange-value within the Google universe, "*within* Google AdWords" (Lee 2011, 440, emphasis in original). Cohen (2008) and Fuchs (2011a, 2011b) also highlight the integration of few distinct moments along the circulation of capital within SNS. Their respective works shows how, within the context of SNS, surveillance becomes a means of commodifying the information that users produce. Fuchs (2011a) offers a Marxist political economy perspective to understand surveillance over SNS users conducted by companies as an alternative to the liberal "civilian" perspective. Such surveillance is not aimed primarily at political control by states, but is rooted in a capitalist desire to commodify information. Fuchs (2011a) highlights the contradictory nature of surveillance and privacy in contemporary society. While capitalism is conditioned by the requirement for privacy (for ex., of bank accounts and holdings) to legitimate wealth inequality, it also promotes surveillance of workers in order to tighten control over them and render the accumulation process more efficient.

Indeed, the political economy of SNS is unique in allowing the integration and conflation of previously distinct processes of production, circulation, and consumption. Not only are they taking place at the same site, but they are also feeding into each other. The production of information by users is monitored, aggregated, analyzed, and rendered into information commodities which are further consumed by users, and so on.

Immaterial labour, the productive force that propels the valorization of SNS, embodies this dual character of exacerbating exploitation and enabling de-alienation. On the one hand, immaterial labour, in comparison with material labour, has a greater potential to be enjoyable, involve personal, idiosyncratic components, carried out during leisure time or even be perceived as a form of leisure activity, playful, emotional and communicative. On the other hand, to the extent that such labour is performed on SNS, it is also commodified and entails the creation of surplus-value.

As we have seen, Facebook, too, operates as a closed system that is able to commodify communication and sociability. Thus, for example, exchange-value arises from the links created between users by users. Such links become informational commodities because companies can learn from them about consumers' behaviours. But they also serve as channels of communication (i.e., as media) for the propagation of commercial messages. In summary, the audience in SNS is a commodity (sold to advertisers), a labour power (producing communication), and media (a means of communication) through which commercial messages are distributed.

Conclusion

Table 7.1 summarizes the argument. In the mass media the exploitation of audience work is fairly limited. The nature of the exchange between media corporations and their working audience is programming (which acts as "wages") for watching advertisements ("labour"). Surplus-value arises from extra-watching (Jhally and Livant 1986), from producing value that exceeds that value needed to produce the programming. In comparison, the level of exploitation in social media is more intensive and extensive. Here, the media itself, i.e., the platform ("wages") is exchanged for the audience work of communicating and socializing ("labour"). Surplus-value arises from extra-communicating, from producing thicker, more textured information than is possible for individual users to use.

Alienation of the working audience in the mass media is relatively high. Television audience remains unidentifiable and anonymous to media corporations. Such audience is principally passive, merely choosing the programs it watches. The mass media also constructs a clear hierarchy between the producers of content and its consumers. Alienation of the working audience in social media is lower. The audience is actively engaged in the production of

TABLE 7.1   *Shifts in levels of exploitation and alienation in different media environments*

	Exploitation	Alienation
Mass media	Low exchange: programming for advertisement	High Anonymity Passivity Hierarchy
Social media	High exchange: platforms for communication	Low Engagement Authenticity

media content. Audiencing entails deep engagement with the media, opening up the opportunity for authentic self-expression, and for communication and collaboration with others. Lastly, a high level of exploitation of audience work enabled by social media is dialectically linked with a low level of alienation. Higher levels of exploitation are dependent on high intensity of communication and sociability, which, in turn, are dependent on the affordances that SNS allow for de-alienation.

References

Adorno, Theodor. 2001. *The Culture Industry: Selected Essays on Mass Culture*. New York: Routledge.

Adorno, T.W. 1976. Television and the Patterns of Mass Culture. In *The Critical View of Television*, edited by Horace Newcomb. New York: Oxford University Press.

Akass, Kim, and Janet McCabe. 2007. Analysing Fictional Television Genres. In *Media Studies: Key Issues and Debates* edited by Eoin Devereux, 283–301. London: Sage.

Andrejevic, Mark. 2011a. Social Network Exploitation. In *A Networked Self: Identity, Community, and Culture on Social Network Sites*, edited by Zizi Papacharissi, 82–101. New York: Routledge.

Andrejevic, Mark. 2011b. Exploitation in the Data Mine. In *Internet and Surveillance: The Challenges of Web 2.0 and Social Media*, edited by Christian Fuchs, Kees Boersma, Anders Albrechtslund, and Marisol Sandoval, 71–88. New York: Routledge.

Ang, Ien. 1985. *Watching Dallas: Soap Opera and the Melodramatic Imagination*. London: Methuen.

Artz, Lee, Steve Macek, and Dana Cloud, eds. 2006. *Marxism and Communication Studies: The Point is to Change It*. New York: Peter Lang Publishing.

Beer, David, and Roger Burrows. 2010. Consumption, Prosumption and Participatory Web Cultures, *Journal of Consumer Culture* 10 (1): 3–12.

Boltanski, Luc and Ève Chiapello. 2005. *The New Spirit of Capitalism*. New York: Verso.

Bonds-Raacke, Jennifer, and John Raacke. 2010. MySpace and Facebook: Identifying Dimensions of Uses and Gratifications for Friend Networking Sites. *Individual Differences Research* 8 (1): 27–33.

Brandtzaeg, Petter, Marika Luders, and Jan Haavard Skjetne. 2010. Too Many Facebook "Friends"? Content Sharing and Sociability Versus the Need for Privacy in Social Network Sites. *International Journal of Human-Computer Interaction* 26 (11–12): 1006–1030.

Bruns, Axel. 2008. *Blogs, Wikipedia, Second Life, and Beyond: From Production to Produsage*. New York: Peter Lang.

Burgess, Jean and Joshua Green. 2009. *YouTube: Online Video and Participatory Culture*. Oxford: Polity.

Caraway, Brett. 2011. Audience labour in the new media environment: A Marxian revisiting of the audience commodity, *Media, Culture, and Society* 33 (5): 693–708.

Cohen, Nicole. 2008. The Valorization of Surveillance: Towards a Political Economy of Facebook. *Democratic Communiqué* 22 (1): 5–22.

Dean, Jodi. 2010. *Blog Theory: Feedback and Capture in the Circuits of Drive*. Cambridge: Polity.

Downes, Stephen. 1999. Hacking Memes, *First Monday* 4 (10), available at http://firstmonday.org/htbin/cgiwrap/bin/ojs/index.php/fm/article/view/694/604.

du Gay, Paul, Stuart Hall, Linda Janes, Hugh Mackay, and Keith Negus. 1997. *Doing Cultural Studies: The Story of the Sony Walkman*. London: Sage.

Dyer-Witheford, Nick. 1999. *Cyber-Marx: Cycles and Circuits of Struggle in High Technology Capitalism*. Urbana: University of Illinois Press.

Economist, The. 2012. The Value of Friendship. February 4. http://www.economist.com/node/21546020.

Emerson, Ramona. 2011. Facebook Use By Country: See Who Spends The Most Time Social Networking. *The Huffington Post*. October 1. http://www.huffingtonpost.com/2011/09/30/facebook-use-by-country_n_987722.html#s379259&title=1_Singapore.

Facebook. 2012a. Information page. http://www.facebook.com/facebook?v=info.

Facebook. 2012b. Newsroom. http://newsroom.fb.com/content/default.aspx?NewsAreaId=22.

Fenton, Natalie. 2007. Bridging the Mythical Divide: Political Economy and Cultural Studies Approaches to the Analysis of the Media. In *Media Studies: Key Issues and Debates*, edited by Eoin Devereux, 7–31. London: Sage.

Fuchs, Christian. 2011a. An Alternative View of Privacy on Facebook. *Information* 2: 140–165.

Fuchs, Christian. 2011b. Web 2.0, Prosumption, and Surveillance. *Surveillance and Society* 8 (3): 288–309.

Gonzales, Amy, and Jeffrey Hancock. 2011. Mirror, Mirror on my Facebook Wall: Effects of Exposure to Facebook on Self-Esteem. *CyberPsychology, Behavior & Social Networking* 14 (1/2): 79–83.

Green, Andy. 2010. *Creativity in Public Relations* (4th ed.). London: Kogan.

Hall, Stuart. 1980. Encoding/decoding. In *Culture, Media, Language*, edited by Stuart Hall, A. Lowe, and P. Willis. London: Hutchinson.

Hall, Stuart. 1995. The Whites of their Eyes: Racist Ideologies and the Media. In *Gender, Race and Class in Media*, edited by Gail Dines and Jean Humez, 18–23. London: Sage.

Hardt, Hanno. 1992. *Critical Communication Studies: Essays on Communication, History and Theory in America*. New York: Routledge.

Herman, Edward, and Noam Chomsky. 1988. *Manufacturing Consent: The Political Economy of the Mass Media*. New York: Pantheon.

Holmes, David. 2005. *Communication Theory: Media, technology, Society*. London: Sage.

hooks, Bell. 1996. *Reel to Real: Race, Sex, and Class at the Movies*. New York: Routledge.

Horkheimer, Max, and Theodor Adorno. 1976. *Dialectics of enlightenment*. New York: Continuum.

Illouz, Eva. 2007. *Cold Intimacies: The Making of Emotional Capitalism*. Cambridge: Polity.

Jenkins, Henry. 2009. *Confronting the Challenges of Participatory Culture: Media Education for the 21st Century*. Cambridge: MIT Press.

Jhally, Sut, and Bill Livant. 1986. Watching as Working: The Valorization of Audience Consciousness, *Journal of communication* 36 (3): 124–143.

Katz, Elihu, Jay G Blumler, and Michael Gurevitch. 1973–1974. Uses and Gratifications Research, *The Public Opinion Quarterly* 37 (4): 509–523.

Liebes, Tamar, and Elihu Katz. 1994. *The Export of Meaning: Cross-Cultural Readings of Dallas*. Cambridge: Polity.

Lee, Micky. 2011. Google Ads and the Blindspot Debate. *Media, Culture, and Society* 33 (3): 433–447.

Lutz, Catherine, and Jane Collins. 1993. *Reading National Geographic*. Chicago: The University of Chicago Press.

Marx, Karl. 1978. Economic and Philosophical Manuscripts of 1844. In *The Marx-Engels Reader*, edited by Robert Tucker, 70–91. New York: Norton & Company.

Marx, Karl. 1993. *Capital*, Vol. 3. New York: Penguin Books.

Mathijs, Ernest. 2002. Big Brother and Critical Discourse: The Reception of Big Brother Belgium. *Television and New Media* 3 (3): 311–322.

McChesney, Robert. 2008. *The Political Economy of Media: Enduring Issues, Emerging Dilemmas*. New York: Monthly Review Press.

Mosco, Vincent. 2009. *The Political Economy of Communication*. Thousand Oaks: Sage.

Mosco, Vincent, and Catherine McKercher. 2009. *The Labouring of Communication: Will Knowledge Workers of the World Unite?* Lanham, MD: Lexington Books.

Morley, David. 1992. *Television, Audiences and Cultural Studies*. New York: Routledge.

Napoli, Philip. 2010. Revisiting 'Mass Communication' and the 'Work' of the Audience in the New Media Environment, *Media, Culture and Society* 32 (3): 505–516.

Nielsen. 2012. Financial Information: Income Statement. http://ir.nielsen.com/reports .aspx?keyreport=592&iid=4260029.

Ong, Eileen, Rebecca Ang, Jim Ho, Joyclynn Lim, Dion Goh, Chei Lee, and Alton Chua. 2011. Narcissism, Extraversion and Adolescents' Self-Presentation on Facebook. *Personality & Individual Differences* 50 (2): 180–185.

Parr, Ben. 2010. Facebook is the Web's Ultimate Timesink. *Mashable*, February 17. http:// mashable.com/2010/02/16/facebook-nielsen-stats/.

Peterson, Soren Mork. 2008. Loser Generated Content: From Participation to Exploitation. *First Monday* 13 (3).

Popper, Karl. 1971. *The Open Society and its Enemies*, Vol. 2. Princeton: Princeton University Press.

Quan-Haase, Anabel, and Alyson Young. 2010. Uses and Gratifications of Social Media: A Comparison of Facebook and Instant Messaging. *Bulletin of Science, Technology & Society* 30 (5): 350–361.

Radway, Janice. 1984. *Reading the Romance: Women, Patriarchy, and Popular Literature*. Chapel Hill: University of North Carolina Press.

Said, Edward. 1981. *Covering Islam: How the media and the experts determine how we see the rest of the world*. New York: Pantheon Books.

Schiller, Dan. 2010. *How to Think about Information*. Chicago: University of Illinois Press.

Schiller, Herbert. 1991. *Culture, Inc.: The Corporate Takeover of Public Expression*. New York: Oxford University Press.

Scholz, Trebor. 2010. Facebook as playground and factory. In *Facebook and Philosophy: What's on Your Mind?*, edited by D.E. Wittkower, 241–52. Chicago: Open Court.

Smythe, Dallas. 1981. *Dependency Road: Communication, Capitalism, Consciousness and Canada*. Norwood: Ablex.

Stevenson, Nick, Peter Jackson, and Kate Brooks. 2001. *Making Sense of Men's Magazines*. Cambridge: Polity Press.

Terranova, Tiziana. 2004. *Network Culture: Politics for the Information Age*. London: Pluto Press.

Turkle, Sherry. 1997. *Life on the Screen: Identity in the Age of the Internet*. New York: Simon & Schuster.

Virno, Paolo. 2001. General Intellect. In *Lessico Postfordista*, edited by Adelino Zanini and Ubaldo Fadini. Milano: Interzone [Italian, translated by Arianna Bove]. http://www.generation-online.org/p/fpvirno1.htm.

Virno, Paolo, and Michael Hardt. 2006. *Radical Thought in Italy: A Potential Politics*. Minneapolis: University of Minnesota Press.

Wasko, Janet 2001. *Understanding Disney: The Manufacture of Fantasy*. Cambridge: Polity.

West, Anne, Jane Lewis, and Peter Currie. 2009. Students' Facebook 'Friends': Public and Private Spheres. *Journal of Youth Studies* 12 (6): 615–627.

CHAPTER 8

The Network's Blindspot: Exclusion, Exploitation and Marx's Process-Relational Ontology

Robert Prey

1   Introduction

From the terrorist networks that brought down the twin towers to the financial networks that brought about the credit crunch, today, as Hardt and Negri (2004, 142) put it, "we see networks everywhere we look." As the key isomorphism and central metaphor of our times, the idea of the network has become the new "organizing framework" (Cavanagh 2007, 24) for how we understand social interaction in contemporary society.

This of course raises some important questions for social critique. The metaphors, narratives, and frames we draw on for meaning perform into being both forms of power and our ability to imagine critiques of power. Thus, this chapter begins by asking what should be an obvious question: how does the network metaphor shape our understanding of power?

In what follows, I argue that the network metaphor provokes a one-dimensional understanding of power, one that fixates on an inclusion/exclusion binary and is largely blind to relations of exploitation. The reasons for the homology between network thinking and the critique of exclusion will be discussed, as will the inadequacy of thinking about power solely in such terms. I then turn to an examination of how Marx can provide us with richer critique of power in a world that – while increasingly connected – remains resolutely wedded to the exploitation of surplus value. However, instead of carpet-bombing the network metaphor from the heights of ideological critique, this chapter takes a reconstructive approach by first acknowledging a common ontological basis – what I call a "process-relational ontology" – that is shared by both network theorists and Marx. By starting from this common position it becomes possible to reconstruct the distinctive path Marx takes by materializing 'process' and internalizing 'relations'. These critical differences, I argue, explain the importance of exploitation in Marx's work and its neglect in the work of most network theorists.

Before network thinkers and Marx can be brought together in conversation however, let us first turn our attention to the network metaphor, its ubiquity, and the mode of critique it engenders.

1.1   *The Network Metaphor*

The incessant use of 'network' or 'networking' in the media may give the impression that these are simply superficial faddish terms. However, in some academic circles the study of 'networks' is regarded as the new super-science (Barabasi 2003; Watts 2004) and "a leading contender for the basis of a long hoped for 'theory of everything'" (Cavanagh 2007, 25). For Manuel Castells, one of the leading theorists of 'the network society', "network theory could provide a common language, a common approach toward the understanding of nature and society through the fundamental shared networks of biological networks, neural networks, digital networks, and human communication networks" (Castells 2011b, 795).[1] Regardless of how we judge the soundness of such statements it is certainly true, as Duncan Watts points out, that "a mutual investment in networks as a research agenda has united researchers in the physical and social sciences, and has brought together mathematicians and sociologists, psychologists and biologists in the search for understanding" (Cavanagh 2007, 25).[2]

For media and communication theorists, the network form is widely understood to be one of the key characteristics of 'new media' (Gane and Beer 2008). Indeed 'networks' are one of the information revolution's 'hurray' words as Allison Cavanagh (2007, 9) puts it. The Internet in particular is taken as the "gold standard" (ibid., 48) of what a network is, emerging in recent years as "the world's hardest-working metaphor" (ibid., 23).

Of course, it is a particularly impoverished perspective that reduces the idea of 'the network' to a recent technological form. Networks are certainly not a contemporary invention.[3] They can be recognized in all societies throughout

---

1   In discussing network theory in this chapter I will primarily focus on Manuel Castells' notion of networks and his thesis of the 'network society'. I do this because his is arguably the most prominent and familiar version of network theory within Communication and Media Studies. While Castells presents an original theory of networks, much of my analysis and critique can be understood to apply to network theory in general.

2   In part this has to do with how broad the definition of networks is. As Watts observes: "In a way, nothing could be simpler than a network. Stripped to its bare bones a network is nothing more than a collection of objects connected to each other in some fashion. On the other hand, the sheer generality of the term network makes it slippery to pin down precisely" (Watts 2004, 27). The myriad ways of understanding the 'network metaphor' as it is used in social theory has resulted in a situation whereby "even within a discipline it would be serendipity rather than design if two theorists were talking about the same concept at the same time" (Cavanagh 2007, 9).

3   The attempt to understand society through the study of networks is not new either (see Quandt 2008). In Communication and Media Studies, Mattelart and Mattelart (1998) describe

history. However, Castells and other contemporary scholars believe that "contemporary social circumstances provide, for the first time, a unique basis for [the] pervasive expansion [of networks] throughout the whole social structure" (Hepp, Krotz, Moores, and Winter 2008, 4). This basic argument – that a unique combination of technological, political and cultural factors have coalesced so that networks have emerged from under the shadow of previously dominant hierarchical forms of organization – accounts for "the rise of the network metaphor" (Cavanagh 2007).

Yet, if we accept the idea that metaphors do not just describe but also prescribe – that metaphors actively constitute the world we attempt to understand – then we must be willing to accept that there are direct political implications for the metaphors we choose. This is not an argument against the use of metaphors. Indeed as John Urry writes: "social scientific work depends upon metaphors and much theoretical debate consists of contestation between different metaphors" (Urry 2003, 42). However, we must think carefully about the type of metaphors we employ and their effects on shaping our perceptions of social reality.[4]

Precisely how the network metaphor shifts our understanding of social and political critique will be examined in the following section. I will argue that the network metaphor orientates critique towards a binary focus on inclusion and exclusion. In doing so it simultaneously orients critique away from the problem of exploitation.

1.2   *The Network Metaphor and 'Exclusion': A Homology*

It is almost conventional wisdom amongst contemporary social and political theorists that relations of power and inequality today operate more through exclusion than through exploitation. The sociologist Scott Lash, for example, argues that exploitation has ceased to be the locus of power, having been replaced by exclusion, including the self-exclusion of "relatively disembeded"

---

how pioneering communications scholar Everett Rogers drew from the work of Gregory Bateson, Georg Simmel and Jacob L. Moreno to update his theories of innovation by foregrounding communication network analysis. However, while network analysis has never been more than a marginal endeavor Castells and other contemporary proponents of the 'network society' thesis believe that it is more applicable than ever.

4   Castells is certainly aware of this issue; indeed it is a central part of his theory of "communication power." In his most recent book he draws on neuroscience and cognitive linguistics to argue that we are made up of neural networks connected to an outside world of networks through the metaphors, narratives, and frames we draw on to make meaning. As Castells (2009, 145) puts it "[p]ower is generated in the wind mills of the mind" and thus "the fundamental form of power lies in the ability to shape the human mind" (ibid., 3).

elites (Lash 2002, 4). Similarly, in his latest book *Communication Power*, Castells argues:

> There is a fundamental form of exercising power that is common to all networks: exclusion from the network [...] there is one form of exclusion – thus, of power – that is pervasive in a world of networks: to include everything valuable in the global while excluding the devalued local.
>
> CASTELLS 2009, 50

We can see from this quote that not only does Castells see exclusion as "a fundamental form of exercising power," but 'exclusion' and 'power' actually appear to morph into one concept. According to Castells and other social theorists, if networks and connectivity are the dominant logic or morphology of life, then oppression is defined by disconnection from these networks. As the British geographer and theorist Nigel Thrift puts it matter-of-factly, "new forms of connection produce new forms of disconnection" (Thrift 2002, 41).

For Castells, the emergence of the new spatial logic that characterizes the network society is expressed through the fragmentation of physical space in a variable geography of hyperconnection and structurally induced "black holes" – what he refers to as "the Fourth World." This "new geography of social exclusion" includes much of Sub-Saharan Africa, American inner-city ghettos, French banlieues and Asian mega-cities' shanty towns (Castells 2000c, 168). Exclusion thus becomes the predominant side effect of contemporary 'informational capitalism'. For Castells, according to one commentator,

> [...] large sections of the world population are not so much repressed – rather they are abandoned, declared worthless, and bypassed [...] by the global flows of wealth and power [...] The intense, if repressive, attention totalitarian regimes paid to their citizens has been replaced by the extensive neglect of informational capitalism, which also declared entire populations to be "redundant," to be ignored or treated as undesirable migrants if they show up at the gated communities of the rich.
>
> STALDER 2006, 131

Power in 'the network society' is exercised through network gatekeeping (Barzilai-Nahon 2008). Social actors establish their positions of power "by constituting a network that accumulates valuable resources and then by exercising their gatekeeping strategies to bar access to those who do not add value to the network or who jeopardize the interests that are dominant in the network's programs" (Castells 2011, 774). "If a node in the network ceases to perform a useful function it is phased out from the network, and the network rearranges itself – as cells do in biological processes" (Castells 2000b, 15). Enrolling all that is useful and required for the continued survival of the network and expunging all that is considered useless or detrimental, the network "works on a binary logic: inclusion/exclusion" (ibid.).

What is most important to take away from such a conceptualization of power is that power is not enacted through personalized decisions but rather through the protocols that a network sets. A protocol is a mechanism that binds seemingly autonomous agents together so that they are able to interact and form a network.[5] "Without a shared protocol, there is no network" (Galloway 2004, 75).[6] Protocol allows power to become disassociated from the acts of individual agents and instead embeds power in the rules and regulations that make up the system.

Exclusion is perfectly situated to assume pole position as the dominant political critique in a society that seemingly coheres around networks; where being connected in constantly shifting links of affinity becomes the ultimate aim and where power is never manifested in a fixed 'class', individual, or institution.[7] As Daniel Béland explains:

---

5   In the world of digital computing, the term 'protocol' refers to the standards governing the implementation of, and the communication between, specific technologies. However protocol is not a new word. A protocol may be technical, legal, financial, or cultural in nature. As Alexander Galloway notes, "[p]rior to its usage in computing, protocol referred to any type of correct or proper behaviour within a specific system of conventions. It is an important concept in the area of social etiquette as well as in the fields of diplomacy and international relations" (Galloway 2004, 7).

6   For example, the highway system, like any system held together by protocols, allows "interdependence on the basis of independence" (Stalder 2006, 134). To be denied entry, or to be excluded from the system – to be refused a driver's license for example – represents the gravest threat. Thus, unlike traditional command-and-control hierarchies, which monitor the content of interaction, power operates in a network through the protocols that set the 'rules of engagement'. As Felix Stalder notes, "[t]his is precisely the point where we can locate the transformation of power operating through repression to power operating through exclusion" (Stalder 2006, 135).

7   The post-Marxist critique of the idea that power emanates from an identifiable centre has almost become a new academic orthodoxy. When Castells describes power as operating in a 'space of flows' he is building on and adding to a diverse tradition that includes Foucault, Laclau and Mouffe and other influential post-Marxist theorists. In a different way, the recent work of Hardt and Negri (2000, 2004, 2009), which I will be discussing in more detail later on, also builds on this tradition. The contribution of Castells, and Hardt and Negri, is in providing the perfect metaphor for the diffuse, de-centred world of post-Marxists, because "[b]y definition, a network has no centre" (Castells 2000b, 15).

[...] social exclusion is based on a horizontal, spatial metaphor rather than a vertical model of inequality focusing mainly on income disparities. From the perspective of the social exclusion paradigm, people are more 'in' or 'out' of mainstream society than 'up' or down' the class or the income distribution structure.

BÉLAND 2007, 127

The network metaphor is also a horizontal, spatial metaphor. The "world is flat" because it is increasingly networked. This is the source of the homology between the network metaphor and "the theme of exclusion" (Boltanski and Chiapello 2006, 347). In their groundbreaking text *The New Spirit of Capitalism* French academics Luc Boltanski and Ève Chiapello argue persuasively that "the theme of exclusion" is "clearly based on a representation of society constructed around the network metaphor" (Boltanski and Chiapello 2005, 348):

In our view, the very rapid diffusion of a definition of the social world in terms of networks that accompanied the establishment of the connexionist world makes it possible to understand how the dynamic of exclusion and inclusion – initially associated with the fate of marginal groups – was able to take the place previously assigned to social classes in the representation of social misery and the means of remedying it.

BOLTANSKI AND CHIAPELLO 2005, 349

Thus, according to Boltanski and Chiapello, the increased focus on networks during the 1980s and 1990s helped shift social and political debate away from class inequality and income redistribution. The relative success of individuals or groups instead becomes dependent on their ability to tap into networks: to be judged to be 'of value' to the network. Failure to do so results in exclusion. If the success of an argument is determined by its simplicity and coherence then this binary model of inclusion/exclusion would certainly win the day.

1.2.1   The Problem with 'Exclusion'
While recognizing that exclusion is a worthy target of critique in our "connexionist" world, Boltanski and Chiapello take issue with the dominant, almost single-minded focus on exclusion in much of contemporary social theory.[8]

---

8   Likewise, in this chapter I am not attempting to deny the existence of exclusion. I am arguing that it has become too hegemonic. We thus find ourselves in a very different intellectual moment compared to what Raymond Murphy (1985) was describing when he tried to overcome the limitations of the then-dominant voice of critique – Marxist theories of exploitation – with an appeal to Weber's social closure theory of exclusion.

This is because 'exclusion', in their opinion, exhibits numerous shortcomings as the central locus of critique.

First of all, 'exclusion' defines the excluded as those who lack something, or possess negative characteristics. Boltanski and Chiapello describe how the discourse of exclusion originally emerged in the 1970s as a way to discuss the marginality of those with physical or mental handicaps, but it has since grown to include those 'at risk' populations who are considered to have social handicaps.[9] A lack of qualifications is the explanation most frequently given for the exclusion of certain populations. "It is precisely this link between poverty and fault – or, to be more precise, between poverty and personal properties," Boltanski and Chiapello (2005, 354) recognize, "that can easily be converted into factors of individual responsibility." This is clearly a step backward as blaming the victim, in whatever guise it assumes, was something "the notion of class, and especially that of the proletariat, had succeeded in breaking" (ibid).

> Unlike the model of social classes, where explanation of the 'proletariat's' poverty is based upon identifying a class (the bourgeoisie, owners of the means of production) responsible for its 'exploitation', the model of exclusion permits identification of something negative without proceeding to level accusations. The excluded are no one's victims, even if their membership of a common humanity (or 'common citizenship') requires that their sufferings be considered and that they be assisted.
>
> BOLTANSKI AND CHIAPELLO 2005, 347

Thus 'exclusion' is for Boltanski and Chiapello a "topic of sentiment" rather than a "topic of denunciation." This shifting of responsibility onto the backs of the oppressed seriously weakens the political force of critique; leaving the critic with little choice of weaponry save for appeals to generosity and compassion.[10] Exclusion, Boltanski and Chiapello recognize, is presented as "someone's

---

9   In an essay entitled "The Social Exclusion Discourse" Daniel Béland documents the French origins of the concept. He writes "[a]s early as 1965, social commentator Jean Klanfer published a book entitled *L'Exclusion sociale: Étude de la marginalité dans les sociétés occidentales* [Social exclusion: The study of marginality in western societies]. In this moralistic book emphasising personal responsibility, the term 'social exclusion' refers to people who cannot enjoy the positive consequences of economic progress due to irresponsible behavior" (Béland 2007, 126).

10   Béland writes "the dominant political discourse about social exclusion has done little more than legitimise modest social programmes that seldom challenge the liberal logic seeking to limit social spending while encouraging citizens to become increasingly dependent on market outcomes (ie. 'recommodification')" (Béland 2007, 134).

misfortune (to be struggled against), not as the result of a social asymmetry from which some people profit to the detriment of others" because "exclusion, unlike exploitation, profit[s] no one" (Boltanski and Chiapello 2005, 354).

Finally, reintegration becomes the only recourse in a world where injustice is understood as being about exclusion from the system. If this is the solution though, how do we then assess oppression that occurs through the inclusion of subjects into exploitative networks or systems? Modern regimes of power – as critical thinkers from Marx to Foucault have recognized – work through modes of incorporation. Modern power is productive, Foucault concluded in his study *Discipline and Punish,* because "its aim is to strengthen the social forces – to increase production, to develop the economy, spread education, raise the level of public morality; to increase and multiply" (Foucault 1991, 207). 'Panopticism' for Foucault, or capitalism for Marx, fuses the economic with the political – the creation of value with the organization of power. Any attempt to update theories of power for the contemporary era must not forget that the creation, extraction and circulation of value is fundamentally an exercise and an expression of power; it both requires asymmetries of power in order to occur and it produces new power relations in the process. It is not very clear in Castells' work, for example, how 'exclusion' as the fundamental form of exercising power in the network society increases economic productivity. It should instead be asked, as Marcuse puts it, "whether the excluded are really excluded from the system, or whether they are in fact quite useful for it but simply excluded from its benefits" (Marcuse 2002, 139).

Common to all of the shortcomings of "the theme of exclusion" is an implicit assumption: that the world is made up of an inside/outside binary. In such a world the traditional critique of exploitation makes little sense if "on one side, we have highly prosperous strong people and, on the other, little people in a miserable state, but there is no link between them and they move in completely different worlds" (Boltanski and Chiapello 2005, 360). Can this really describe the social world we live in? The answer is of course no.

This is where the problem with the single-minded focus on exclusion by network thinkers gets interesting; for isn't the 'network' the form *par excellence* for understanding the world as shared and common? Isn't "the science of networks" a super-science for "the connected age" (Watts 2003)? Here we arrive at what seems to be a contradiction: the network metaphor posits a connected and relational world while at the same time conceiving of power as operating predominantly through exclusion and disconnection.

The limitations acknowledged call out for a reintroduction of 'the theme of exploitation' into contemporary social critique. This is certainly not a groundbreaking realization. However, when it has been acknowledged we have usually been presented with one of the following two options. The most common response taken by Marxian scholars has been that of *'ideologiekritik'*: all talk of networks is deemed ideological and a return to the analysis of class and exploitation is called for (Garnham 2004; Callinicos 2006). Alternatively, following Boltanski and Chiapello's (2005) lead, we can largely accept the network discourse and attempt to generate a new theory of exploitation more suitable for our "connexionist" world.

In what follows, I attempt to offer a third approach; one that leaves behind metaphors and narratives of networks and instead examines the common ontological framework that I argue guides the thinking of both network theorists and Marx. Clearly Marx was not a 'network' theorist as conventionally understood. Nevertheless, his discussion of capital as a relation and as value-in-motion shares deep affinities with network thinking.[11] This is no mere coincidence. In this chapter, I argue that this affinity stems from a shared *process-relational* ontology. By locating a common position from which to begin, it becomes possible to reconstruct the distinctive path Marx took in conceptualizing 'process' and 'relations', and in turn, understand how this path leads us not into the inclusion/exclusion cul-de-sac but rather to a critique of exploitation *writ large*.[12]

---

11   Scott Kirsch and Don Mitchell develop in detail the affinities between Marx and network theory – in particular actor-network theory: "Marx, of course, did not write in the language of networks. But he did write in the language of circuits, showing in great detail how capital – as value in motion – travels a set of circuits, from, for example, the hands of the capitalist, into the machines and buildings of the work place, and on into the produced commodity. He shows how capital precisely *because* it is a relation, becomes "frozen" for greater or lesser duration as the means of production or the produced commodity, only to be returned to the capitalist when the commodity is exchanged on the market. Commodities "stabilize" social relations in technologies and "things as such," and commodity circulation in this sense is a network" (Kirsch and Mitchell 2004, 696).

12   Although my focus in this chapter is on exploitation and exclusion in the economic field, it is important to point out that Marx's theory of exploitation need not be limited to this field. Buchanan (1979, 122) argues that Marx's work includes "three distinct but related conceptions of exploitation: (a) a conception of exploitation in the labor process in capitalism, (b) a transhistorical conception of exploitation which applies not only to the labor process in capitalism but to the labor processes of all class-divided societies', and (c) a general conception of exploitation which is not limited to phenomena within the labor process itself." Marx's most general conception of exploitation appears in one of his earliest works, *The German Ideology*, where he describes the bourgeois view of interpersonal relations which sees all human relations *in general* as exploitable:

> [...] all [...]activity of individuals in their mutual intercourse, eg., speech, love, etc., is depicted (by the bourgeois) as a relation of utility and utilization. In this case the utility relation has a quite different meaning, namely that I derive benefit for myself by

2 Network Ontology

Let us now leave behind the network metaphor and work our way down to the level of ontology. Once we do so we will quickly realize that this metaphor is no more than a contemporary version of a much older philosophical position which can be traced back to the pre-Socratic Greek philosopher Heraclitus. This "process-relational ontology," as I will call it, has found new life in network analysis. I will begin by explicating what is meant by 'process'.

2.1 *Process*

Network thinkers emphasize processes. Social reality is composed not of static things, but of activity, of change, of flows. The idea that process precedes substance has been the primary argument of process philosophers from Heraclitus to Alfred North Whitehead.

How does this relate to networks? Networks are *dynamic* patterns of processes. The physicist Fritjof Capra, a former colleague of Castells at Berkeley, has been a tireless popularizer of the new science of complexity and autopoeisis, which places networks at the center of all life processes. Capra, drawing on the seminal work of the Chilean biologists Humberto Maturana and Francisco Varela, argues that what makes life a dynamic process and not a static system is the characteristic of renewal and recreation. "[L]iving networks continually create, or recreate, themselves by transforming or replacing their components. In this way, they undergo continual structural changes, while preserving their web-like patterns of organization" (Capra 2004, 10). Thus, networks are not determined by one individual component (contra the genetic blueprint argument for example), nor are they characterized by the static and stable organization of relations. Instead, it is the entire *process* of interactions and the continuous bringing into being of emergent properties through interactions with the surrounding environment, which prevents a network from entering a state of decay.

Networks are also not characterized by one-off interactions but rather by enduring, recurrent, re-creative patterns of interaction over time. Thus, a focus

---

doing harm to someone else (*exploitation de l'home par l'home*) [...] All this actually is the case with the bourgeois. For him only one relation is valid on its own account – the relation of exploitation; all other relations have validity for him only insofar as he can include them under this one relation, and even where he encounters relations which cannot be directly subordinated to the relation of exploitation, he does at least subordinate them to it in his imagination. The material expression of this use is money, the representation of the value of all things, people and social relations. (Marx 1974, 110).

on process necessarily draws our attention to the importance of temporality. From a process perspective, "how we make ourselves as beings is how we make ourselves in time, how we are time, and how time is us" (Pomeroy 2004, 108). Being *is* time because being is always becoming.

It is true that many network theorists often slip back into substantialism. The ubiquitous web diagrams that seem to accompany every discussion of networks often privilege spatiality over temporality. However, as Mustafa Emirbayer (1997) points out, this can be blamed on the hegemony of substantialism in everyday thought patterns. Its very embeddedness in Western languages forces us to reduce processes to static conditions.[13] What is important to remember though is that network thinking (if not always its representation) conceives of networks as always-in-the-process of becoming.

2.2 *Relations*

Relations, writes the Dutch network theorist Jan van Dijk, are "the prime focus of attention in a network perspective"[14] (van Dijk 2006, 25). Relations can be understood as the most basic form inherent to any network and a network can be said to exist whenever two or more linked relations are present.

Rather than attempting to understand actors by looking at the institutions and structures under which they live, or through the individual traits and characteristics they posses, network thinkers believe that we can learn far more about someone or something through the relations they are embedded within. This argument is based on an ontology which sees the world as constituted by forms instead of substances. Relational ontology posits that relations *between* entities are ontologically more important than the entities in and of themselves (Wildman, 2010). In any network, Felix Stalder points out, "it makes no sense to argue that nodes come first and then they begin to create connections. Rather it is through the connections that nodes create and define one another.

---

13   We can only express change by adding a verb to a thing. Emirbayer quotes Norbert Elias for an example of this: "We say "The wind is blowing," as if the wind were actually a thing at rest which, at a given point in time, begins to move and blow" (Elias 1978, 111f. cited in Emirbayer 1997, 283).

14   While Castells is well known for not providing clear definitions of the concepts he uses – preferring instead to let definitions emerge organically through their usage – Jan van Dijk provides a very useful definition of networks in his book *The Network Society*. "A network can be defined as *a collection of links between elements of a unit*. The elements are called nodes. Units are often called systems. The smallest number of elements is three and the smallest number of links is two. A single link of two elements is called a relation(ship)" (van Dijk 2006, 24).

Nodes are created by connections, and without nodes there can be no connections" (Stalder 2006, 177).

Network thinkers can be situated along a spectrum in terms of how they conceptualize the relative importance of relations to nodes. Jan van Dijk adopts what he calls a "moderate network approach" by focusing not solely on relations, but "also on the characteristics of the units (nodes) that are related in networks (people, groups, organizations, societies)" (van Dijk 2006). Other network theorists take relational ontology to its logical extreme, arguing that there are no essences (units or nodes) at all. Actor-Network theorists Bruno Latour and John Law call their approach "radical relationality." This is the principle that "[n]othing that enters into relations has fixed significance or attributes in and of itself. Instead, the attributes of any particular element in the system, any particular node in the network, are entirely defined in relation to other elements in the system, to other nodes in the network" (Law, 2003, 4).[15] It is not necessary to go to this extreme though in order to accept the central argument agreed upon by all network theorists; that "[a]ll entities [...] achieve their significance by being in relation to other entities" (ibid.).

Finally, process and relation must be understood as co-dependent because "a universe driven by the movement of process is necessarily a relational universe. In fact, the processive movement itself is the self-generation of relationality" (Pomeroy 2004, 143). As I will demonstrate in the following sections, a process-relational perspective is also the key to understanding Marx's philosophy, and in particular his theory of exploitation.

3   Marx's Process-Relational Ontology

How is Marx also a process-relational thinker? How does Marx's process-relational ontology differ from that of network theorists such as Manuel Castells? In what follows, I will attempt to answer these questions by demonstrating how Marx materializes process philosophy through his category of 'production' and how Marx does not simply emphasize relations, but *internal* relations. Finally, I will elaborate on the importance that 'contradiction' plays in generating the dynamic nature of Marx's ontology.

---

15   Just as in the idea, first proposed by de Saussure, that all words only achieve meaning when they are juxtaposed with other words – ie. father and son, day and night etc. – radical relationality extends this insight beyond language to all things and beings.

3.1   *Materializing Process*

As Bertell Ollman argues, Marx consistently prioritizes movement over stability in his writings:

> With stability used to qualify change rather than the reverse, Marx – unlike most modern social scientists – did not and could not study why things change (with the implication that change is external to what they are, something that happens to them). Given that change is always a part of what things are, his research problem could only be *how, when,* and *into what* they change and why they sometimes appear not to (ideology).
>
> OLLMAN 2003, 66

However, while Marx shares this predilection with network theorists, process nevertheless takes on a whole new meaning in his writings. This is because, as the philosopher Anne Fairchild Pomeroy argues, Marx materializes process through his foundational category of 'production'.[16] Pomeroy compares Marx to the process-relational philosopher Alfred North Whitehead, illustrating how the category of 'production' in Marx is the "functional equivalent" of the category of 'process' in Whitehead's metaphysics (Pomeroy 2004, 44).[17] A brief overview of what Marx means by 'production' may be helpful to demonstrate how it informs his process-relational ontology.

'Production' is for Marx a highly complex term that serves as a necessary abstraction. Just as 'process' for Whitehead performs multiple levels of analysis, Marx's concept of 'production' functions on numerous levels from the most

---

16   Since process is a temporal concept it may be helpful to give a brief overview of Marx's theory of time. Against Kant Marx argues that time is not an a priori form of perception, nor is it an objective sequence that is located purely outside collective subjectivity (à la Newton). Instead, Marx argued, human time-consciousness emerges out of the very labouring activity, which objectifies our world. This is because it is only through labouring activity (production) that real novelty comes into being. While Heidegger posits the activity of 'Being' as the source of temporality, Marx regards this activity (labour) as introducing time into things (objects, institutions etc). In turn the 'objectified' form of labour introduces objective time (see Gould, 1978, 56–68, for a much more detailed explanation).

17   It is possible to sum up Pomeroy's argument for the equivalence of 'production' and 'process' as follows. Firstly, "[b]oth Marx and Whitehead use their respective terms to refer both to the general abstract character of all productive processive activity and to any specific concrete instance or moment of that activity." Second of all, "[p]roduction and process both refer to and serve to explicate the movement of becoming that is the temporal or historical world..." and finally "[b]oth process and production are affected by socially related individuals..." (Pomeroy 2004, 60).

abstract and general to the most concrete and specific. In Marx's writings 'production' operates:

> (1) on the level of the general conditions found in all production as the interchange between, indeed identity between, human life and nature; (2) on the many levels of historical forms of production: communal, feudal, capitalist, (3) within each of these, on the levels of different branches of production, and (4) on the levels of the activity of the social subjects who are 'active in a greater or sparser totality of branches of production'.
>
> MARX 1973, 86; cited in Pomeroy 2004, 46

It is important to first nail down the most general characteristics of production because as Marx says "[n]o [specific mode of] production will be thinkable without them" (Marx 1973, 85).

Most importantly, Marx conceives of production as a temporal process. Production in general involves three analytically distinct but unified moments: *appropriation* (of the social-natural world), *productive activity* (creative re-creation by and of the subject) and *objectification* (of a novel relational being or object). Whether one is building a house or reading a magazine one is always engaged in this production process. Importantly, the subject engaging in the productive activity is also changed by and through this activity. "[P]roductive activity not only makes "things" or objects in the natural world, but also objectifies the form of the subjective activity itself. It is a production of a certain kind of individual" (Pomeroy 2004, 54). As Marx put it in *Capital*, "He acts upon external nature and changes it, and in this way he simultaneously changes his own nature" (Marx 1990, 283). Thus, "[t]he processive or productive individual *is what it does*" (Pomeroy 2004, 70). This is made very clear in *The German Ideology* where Marx and Engels write that the mode of production:

> [...] must not be considered simply as being the production of the physical existence of the individuals. Rather it is [...] a definite *mode of life* on their part. As individuals express their life, so they are. What they are, therefore, coincides with their production, both with *what* they produce and with *how* they produce.
>
> MARX and ENGELS 1974, 42

While bourgeois economists distinguish between production, distribution and consumption, Marx argued that all were specific moments in the productive process. While clearly not identical they are distinctions within a unity. They all serve to drive the productive process forward. When I 'consume' a meal I am also 'producing' my being. "Consumption as a moment, production as a moment, are occurring for the sake of the movement itself, process itself" (Pomeroy 2004, 53).

Production as process is necessarily also production as relation. As Pomeroy expresses it, "the processive movement itself is the self-generation of relationality" (Pomeroy 2004, 143). Thus, at the centre of this production process stands not the independent, isolated producer – the Robinson Crusoe character celebrated by bourgeois thinkers – but the individual as the ensemble of social relations, or as Carol Gould (1978) phrases it, "individuals-in-relations."

> [T]he *social* character is the general character of the whole movement: *just as* society itself produces *man as man*, so is society *produced* by him. Activity and consumption, both in their content and in their *mode of existence*, are *social*: *social* activity and *social* consumption.
>
> MARX 1988, 104

Thus, for Marx, each human being is what he or she does, and what he or she does, constantly, is produce. We are continuously re-producing ourselves as we produce something new.

Earlier I described how network thinkers regard the processes of renewal and recreation as crucial to how networks are able to sustain themselves. Marx's conception of 'production' performs much the same function, but for "individuals-in-relations" and the objective world produced into being. In Castells' theory of "the network society," the locus of production is transformed from individuals-in-relations to knowledge-in-networks. This is because for Castells the key source of productivity in the network society is not the knowledge worker, but knowledge itself. The tendency by network theorists to naturalize knowledge represents the continuation of a long trend in economic thought of bestowing innate qualities of value on factors of production. Marx criticized this fallacy vehemently in his day and would no doubt concur that knowledge or information "is not inherently valuable but that a profound social reorganization is required to turn it into something valuable" (Schiller 1988, 32, cited in Jessop 2003, 2).

A network approach does not necessarily preclude a material view of process. Like Castells, Hardt and Negri (2000, 2004, 2009) posit the network as the dominant form power takes in contemporary society. Unlike Castells and most other network theorists though, Hardt and Negri understand power as operating through processes of *inclusion*. The logic of capital, what they call "Empire," is best understood as a "universal republic, a network of powers and counterpowers structured in a boundless and inclusive architecture" (Hardt and Negri

2000, 166). Hardt and Negri understand this logic to be one that necessitates constant movement and expansion outwards. Echoing Marx, Hardt and Negri write, "the capitalist market is one machine that has always run counter to any division between inside and outside. It is thwarted by barriers and exclusions; it thrives instead by including always more within its sphere" (Hardt and Negri 2000, 190). By focusing on inclusion, Hardt and Negri are able to better conceive of power as productive.

Who is the source of this production that 'Empire' seeks to include? In Hardt and Negri's Spinoza-influenced language, it is the 'multitude'. The multitude is a conception of class that extends beyond the wage-labourer to include all those who labour to produce "the common." It follows from this that Hardt and Negri re-evalute exploitation to be about the expropriation of the common. We could think of this as 'network exploitation' whereby the common which is produced through the networked activity of the multitude is simultaneously exploited by Empire. Capital is therefore dependent on the multitude's production.

Hardt and Negri thus follow Marx in understanding human agency to be generative of a surplus: life as a process of production. This represents an advance over network theories that can only conceive of power as working through exclusion. As discussed earlier in this chapter, the theme of exclusion tends to focus attention on deficiencies or handicaps, broadly construed. The excluded are those who lack proper educational qualifications for example. Exclusion thus emerges as a problem of *lack*. Exploitation on the other hand is a problem of *excess*. 'Exploitation' defines the exploited as those who *have* something, for why else would they be exploited? As Hardt and Negri (2004, 333) write in *Multitude*, " '[t]he oppressed' (or excluded) may name a marginal and powerless mass, but 'the exploited' is necessarily a central, productive, and powerful subject."

By shifting the focus of critique from exclusion to inclusion, Hardt and Negri are better able to address more complex modes of power, including contemporary processes of exploitation. At the same time their adherence to the network metaphor generates some problems that I will be addressing in more detail later. First, let us move on to a discussion of how Marx's process-relational ontology can be distinguished by its understanding of relations as internal.

3.2   *Internal Relations*

In his widely cited "Manifesto for a Relational Sociology," Mustafa Emirbayer (1997, 290) describes Marx as a "profoundly relational thinker" whose relational ontology is revealed through his "analyses of alienation [...] his discussion of

commodity fetishism, his keen insights in the internal relations among production, distribution, exchange, and consumption, and, indeed his understanding of the capital/wage-labour relation itself." It has also been said that
"[p]erhaps no word appears more frequently in Marx's writings than *Verhältnis*
(relation)" (Ollman 2003, 73).[18]

But to simply state that Marx was a relational thinker does not tell us very
much. The question should instead be what kind of a relational thinker was
Marx?

Marx's relationality is generated from a philosophy of internal relations –
what Ollman considers to be "the much-neglected foundation of his entire
dialectical method" (Ollman 2003, 116). While Marx draws inspiration from
Hegel, the philosophy of internal relations traces its origins to the Greek philosopher Parmenides, reappearing in the modern period as a central tenet of
Spinoza's thought.

To say that all relations are internal is to imply that everything has some
relation, however distant, to everything else and that these relations are *necessary*. To say that relations are necessary is to argue that they are essential to the
characteristics of the *relata*. "Internal relations are those in which the individuals are changed by their relations to each other, that is, where these relations
between individuals are such that both are reciprocally affected by the relation" (Gould 1978, 37). Contrarily, external relations serve to link up *relata* but
"each *relatum* is understood to be a separate self-subsistent entity, which exists
apart from the relation and appears to be totally without change in their nature
or constitution" (Gould 1978, 38).

The importance of distinguishing between a relationality composed of
internal relations and one made up of *external* relations becomes clear
when we look at Castells' thesis of the network society. What allows Castells
to posit the emergence of a novel social formation – a "network society" – is
the distinction he makes between "modes of production" and "modes of
development."[19] The current mode of production is still capitalist, according to
Castells, but with a new mode of development that fuels its productivity:

---

18   Ollman (2003, 73) also acknowledges though that "the crucial role played by *Verhaltnis* in
      Marx's thinking is somewhat lost to non-German-language readers of his works as a result
      of translations that "...often substitute 'condition', 'system', and 'structure' for 'relation'."

19   According to Castells, modes of production are characterized by "[t]he structural princi-
      ple under which surplus is appropriated and controlled" (Castells, 2000a, 16). The "net-
      work society" is still founded on the capitalist mode of production, however the causal
      force which gives the network society its defining characteristics is its specific "mode of
      development." Modes of development are distinguished by the main source or "element"
      that generates their productivity.

"*informationalism.*"[20] However, Castells does not sufficiently anchor this mode of development within the mode of production. 'Informationalism' appears to act as an external causal force. As already mentioned, knowledge or information is naturalized as a factor of production (like land, capital or labour) obscuring the conditions under which it is produced. Value is thus erroneously attributed to the immanent qualities of things *brought into* the production process rather than to a process generated *out of* particular social relations.

The problem, as Wayne realizes is "[h]ow can we assess the continuities and differences *within* a mode of production that is oriented toward the perpetual transformation of technological forces and social relations?" (Wayne 2004, 141). As Marx writes in *The Economic and Philosophical Manuscripts*, bourgeois political economy is unable to understand the internal dynamics and connections that drive capitalist development. Instead this development is attributed to "external and apparently accidental circumstances" (Marx 1972, 106, cited in Wayne 2004, 139). This is precisely the problem with Castells' analysis.

For Castells, network relations are external. The network society represents the emergence of a new social morphology resulting from the development of new (technological) relations between pre-existing *relata.*[21] Castells is careful to acknowledge that technology does not *cause* the transformation to a network society, but he insists that it is "the indispensable *medium*" (Castells 2000b, 14). In other words, for Castells (technological) networks provide the means through which individuals are brought into relation.

Much of the commentary on this aspect of Castells' theory revolves around accusations of technological determinism (see Webster 1995; van Dijk 1999). However, I would argue that any such determinism is itself a direct result of an ontological focus on *external* rather than *internal* relations. In other words, technological determinism, or any form of determinism for that matter, is but one symptom of a philosophy constructed around external relations.

As different as Hardt and Negri's employment of the network metaphor is from Castells', it too offers a form of determinism that emerges out of an external

---

20   While the industrial mode of development was based on new forms and uses of energy, the current "informational mode of development" locates its source of productivity in "the technology of knowledge generation, information processing, and symbol communication" (ibid., 17). Castells acknowledges that knowledge and information is key to all modes of development throughout history, his argument is instead that specific to the informational mode of development "is the action of knowledge upon knowledge itself as the main source of productivity" (ibid.).

21   This is even more evident in Jan van Dijk's work when he proposes that in the network society "basic units are held to be individuals, households, groups and organizations *increasingly linked by social and media networks*" (van Dijk, 2006, 28).

relation. As autonomist Marxists, Hardt and Negri see capital as dependent on the productivity of the multitude. Indeed, the position that labour is the active subject which capital attempts to domesticate represents the single most innovative idea put forward by autonomist Marxists. It stands on its head the orthodox Marxist position that capital unfolds according to some automatic, self-contained logic. But it is just as one-sided.

The problem is that while Hardt and Negri foreground production as the networked process that capital feeds off of, the 'multitude' and 'Empire' – are not *internally* related. The multitude is conceived of as *autonomous* from Empire. Hardt and Negri (2004, 225) insist that the multitude must not be understood as Empire's "dialectical support." "Empire and the multitude are not symmetrical: whereas Empire is constantly dependent on the multitude and its social productivity, the multitude is potentially autonomous and has the capacity to create society on its own" (ibid.).

Thus, it could be said that what network technology is to Castells' theory of the "network society," network struggle is to Hardt and Negri's "commonwealth." The theories of both Castells, and of Hardt and Negri, can be considered essentialist to the extent that they isolate a single external causal force.

This is not to say that the influence of network technology or network forms of struggle are false explanations. Essentialist explanations are not so much false as they are partial. As Resnick and Wolff put it "…each essentialist moment is understood to be true – it illuminates a connection – *and* false – it obscures other connections that, if and when considered, will show all previously elaborated connections to have been true and false in this sense" (Resnick and Wolff 2006, 83). In other words, technological determinism and what could be called "class struggle determinism" are partial explanations, or in Marx's terminology "abstractions." According to Carol Gould, "an external relation is only an appearance for Marx in the sense that they are the way internal relations appear from a one-sided or abstract point of view" (Gould 1978, 38).

A theory of internal relations means for Marx that "interaction is, properly speaking, *inneraction* (it is "inner connections" that he claims to study)" (Ollman 2003, 27). This means that, for Marx, relationality is always already there. It does not require network technology to be brought into existence. It is an a priori *condition of possibility* for such technology. While the pervasiveness of network technology may serve to intensify and highlight this intrinsic relationality, it does not invent it. Facebook, for example, is an ingenious way of capturing the connective desires and practices that are internal to human relationality. Mark Zuckerberg though did not invent social networking; he simply organized sociability under one domain.

To make such an argument is certainly not to say that that network technologies and new network forms of organization have no impact on social
development. Of course they do. But these technologies and forms of organization do not appear from outer space. They emerge from within, reifying and
abstracting from internal social relations. Consider money, the most powerful
and pervasive network 'technology'. At first glance it may appear to be an external relation that influences and distorts almost all realms of life. However Marx
regards money as an abstraction of internal relations. This is most forcefully
(and humorously) demonstrated in the final chapter of *Capital: Volume 1*, "The
Modern Theory of Colonization." Marx tells the story of the British politician
E.G. Wakefield who discovered in the colonies the truth about capitalist
relations – that money has no meaning if there is no wage-labourer to buy:

> A Mr. Peel, he (Wakefield) complains, took with him from England to the
> Swan River district of Western Australia means of subsistence and of pro-
> duction to the amount of £50,000. This Mr. Peel even had the foresight to
> bring besides, 3,000 persons of the working class, men, women, and chil-
> dren. Once he arrived at his destination, 'Mr. Peel was left without a ser-
> vant to make his bed or fetch him water from the river'. Unhappy Mr. Peel,
> who provided for everything except the export of English relations of
> production to Swan River!
>
> MARX 1990, 932F.

Here Marx is substantiating his well-known argument that "capital is not a
thing, but a social relation between persons which is mediated through things"
(ibid.). Exploitation describes the terms of this relationship under capitalism.

Exploitation for Marx is a *necessarily* relational concept. It could only have
emerged from a philosophy of internal relations. While the exploiters require
the exploited in order to generate surplus value, the exploited in the capitalist
system also require the exploiters in order to sell their labour power – in order
to survive. Marx's theory of exploitation is more than simply the observation
that the success of certain individuals or groups is causally related to the depri-
vation of others. Marx's theory of exploitation begins from the observation
that the *existence* of a certain class in society is dependent on the *existence* of
another class. Indeed, as with the two ideal categories in Hegel's master/slave
dialectic, exploiters and the exploited need each other in order to retain their
identity. In other words Marx's theory of exploitation presupposes the existence of a necessarily shared world composed of internal relations.

When network theorists such as Castells acknowledge the existence of
exploitation they do so with an understanding of exploitation as an *external*

relation – an event rather than a process – which one prefigured entity or relata performs on another. In certain times and spaces this event occurs more frequently than in others but exploitation is not considered necessary to the existence of the relata.

However, it would be insufficient to end our argument here. Marx's process-relational ontology and the theory of exploitation that emerges from it cannot be understood without discussing the importance of 'contradiction'. It is to the concept of 'contradiction' that we now turn to.

3.3 *Contradiction*

Contradiction offers the ability to understand *how* and *why* change occurs. Contradiction, of course, describes the existence of two structural principles within a system which simultaneously depend upon and negate each other. It is commonly acknowledged that capitalism is defined by contradictions and its relative success or failure in managing them.[22] Contradiction is also the principle that unites Marx's understanding of process and internal relations, as process is instigated through internal *contradictory* relations.

The importance of contradiction to Marx's process-relational ontology and his theory of exploitation is perhaps best revealed by contrasting it with Castells' approach. Castells offers up a model of power that minimizes contradiction. As Mike Wayne recognizes, at times Castells' mode of development even "sounds suspiciously like a new mode of production which has transcended the antagonistic contradictions of capitalism" (Wayne 2004, 142). By introducing a mode of development/mode of production duality Castells downplays the origin of all knowledge within specific class relations. In turn this flattens the dialectical contradictions which exist within Marx's mode of production argument – between the forces and relations of production.

Remember that power, for Castells, circulates through the 'space of flows' which by definition contains no centre. Instead it works through inclusion and exclusion; enrolling what is of value and rejecting all else. Castells does not shy away from critiquing the injustices that emerge from such an account of power,

---

22   Bob Jessop (2001, 4) describes some of the main contradictions within capitalism:

> For example, the commodity is both an exchange-value and a use-value; the worker is both an abstract unit of labour power substitutable by other such units (or, indeed, other factors of production) and a concrete individual with specific skills, knowledge, and creativity; the wage is both a cost of production and a source of demand; money functions both as an international currency and as national money; productive capital is both abstract value in motion (notably in the form of realised profits available for re-investment) and a concrete stock of time – and place – specific assets in the course of being valorised; and so forth.

such as the aforementioned 'black holes'. However, such a critique offers only *description*, not *explanation*. Massimo De Angelis captures this problem well:

> When we understand power as a flow, however insightful the metaphor may be, until we pose this 'flow' in terms of a flow of social relations and the *mode* of their exercise, power remains a thing (a fluid thing, but a thing nevertheless), since it is not explained how its exercise as a *relation* makes it move. Thus, I can understand capital flows as a thing in terms of interest rate differentials across countries, but until I have related this movement to the broad problematic of how livelihoods in the two countries are systemically pitted against each other *by virtue* of this capital movement or the threat of this movement, and until I have understood and problematised the *rationale* of this, my concept of power is quite useless from the perspective of radical alternatives.
>
> DE ANGELIS 2007, 172

No matter how highly sophisticated and detailed Castells' theory of the transition to a society constructed around networks is, at its core it is still based on a traditional cause-and-effect chain of description. Such an account of social change is what Hegel referred to as "bad infinity": an endless series of causes generated from effects caused by previous effects that never arrives at an explanation of the *how* or the *why* (Rees 1998, 7).

As discussed earlier, this is due to the tendency to understand 'cause' as something *external* rather than *internal* to the system. As Ollman (2003, 18) writes:

> [w]hereas nondialectical thinkers [...] are involved in a nonstop search for the 'outside agitator', for something or someone that comes from outside the problem under examination and is the cause for whatever occurs, dialectical thinkers attribute the main responsibility for all change to the inner contradictions of the system or systems in which it occurs.

It is this legacy of Hegel's dialectical philosophy that most clearly distinguishes Marx's process-relational ontology from the ontology of network theorists such as Castells. For it is through relations of exploitation that Marx was able to materialize Hegel's idealist concept of contradiction. Under capitalism, exploitation is simultaneously a central source and expression of contradiction as "the worker is both an abstract unit of labour power...and a concrete individual with specific skills, knowledge, and creativity" (Jessop 2003, 4).

However contradiction should not be understood to work itself out in a predictable teleological fashion. Contradiction necessarily implies "overdetermination" meaning that "an individual, an event, a social movement, and so on – is constituted by all the other aspects of the social and natural totality within which it occurs" (Resnick and Wolff 2006, 80). Every entity, every aspect of history is contradictory in that it is constantly being pushed and pulled in multiple different directions by all its overdeterminants. Indeed history can be conceived of as "a dense network of overdeterminations" or in Althusser's famous phrase, "a process without a subject" (ibid).

Resnick and Wolff (2006) develop Althusser's concept of "overdetermination" to highlight the role contradiction plays in Marx's process-relational ontology. The "contradictoriness of any existent impels it to change (i.e. makes every existent a process), which thereby alters how it overdetermines all existents" (ibid.). Marx's conceptualization of process thus achieves its dynamism through the contradictions inherent within and between internal relations. Leaving behind the language of 'cause' and 'effect' we thus enter the "logic of overdetermined constitutivity" (ibid.).

Hardt and Negri, with their invocation of the network metaphor to describe the constitution of the 'multitude' and 'Empire', do recognize that "[i]nformational networks aggravate the capitalist contradiction between the collective production and the individual appropriation of goods" (Fuchs and Zimmerman 2009, 107). Indeed this contradiction forms the core of the antagonistic relationship between 'Empire' and the 'multitude'. However, while this may be a central contradiction at the heart of informational capitalism, it can also be considered an *'under*determined' contradiction. This is because Hardt and Negri fail to interrogate the complex class dynamics and contradictions within both capital understood as 'Empire' and labour understood as the 'multitude'. When critics point out the subjectivist and overly optimistic tone of Hardt and Negri's work, they are really pointing out the absence of overdetermination.

Certainly, as I've repeated throughout this chapter, capital is a relation that through exploitation "both presupposes and reproduces the mutual interdependence of capital and wage-labour" (Callinicos 2006, 200f.). However, as Alex Callinicos points out "the capital-relation also necessarily includes 'many capitals' because it is through the competitive struggle among rival firms that the characteristic tendencies of the capitalist mode become operative" (Callinicos 2006, 201). Following Robert Brenner, Callinicos argues that we can understand the capitalist mode of production as constituted by two contradictory relations: the 'vertical relationship' between capitalists and labour and the 'horizontal relationship' between 'many capitals'.

Pointing this out serves to reintroduce contradiction into the flattened category of 'Empire'. The same must be done for the 'multitude'. For instance, the exploited multitude, as Fuchs and Zimmerman (2009, 93) remind us, "is

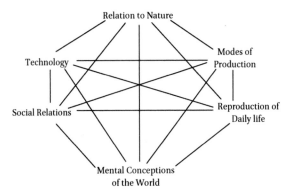

FIGURE 8.1 *Based on Harvey (2010, 195)*

itself antagonistically constituted by exploiting and exploited classes and class fractions." What is needed is an accounting of the myriad transnational networks of production and the *"contradictory class positions"* (*Wright 1985*) that make up the 'multitude'.[23] By ignoring the exploitative relations that operate *within* the multitude the network metaphor's flattening trick is allowed to work its magic once again.

A better, more "overdetermined," approach may be visualized through a diagram David Harvey uses to explain Marx's dialectical method (see Figure 8.1). Each of these 'hubs' in Harvey's diagram can be isolated as the determining force in social change but in order to get the full picture all must be taken into consideration – relationally, dialectically – as dynamic moments within an "ecological totality" (Harvey 2010, 196). This process of explanation is ongoing; there is no completion, closure, or final destination.

It is with the recognition that all internal relations are contradictory, and in turn overdetermined, that we can finally see how Marx's process-relational ontology achieves its dynamic form. In turn, such a process-relational approach breathes new life into Marx's theory of exploitation, permitting us to understand its contemporary relevance.

---

23   Of course contradictions between differentially situated workers do not necessarily have to provoke division and antagonism. However, unity is also not automatic; it must be worked at. For example, in their study of the trends in the trade union movement in both the developed and developing world Catherine McKercher and Vincent Mosco describe "the consolidation of small and narrowly-focused unions into larger and more diverse organisations, representing not simply workers in a specific trade, or even within a single industry but in a broad sector of the economy, such as the converging communications, culture, and information sector" (McKercher and Mosco 2010, 3).

4   Conclusion: Networks and Exploitation

This chapter has attempted to accomplish two main tasks. The first task was to demonstrate that the overwhelming popularity of the network metaphor, like all metaphors, is useful as a heuristic device but not innocent of power effects. How we choose to describe the world we inhabit has direct political implications. I argue that while the network metaphor may illuminate new organizational forms throughout contemporary society it also serves to focus social critique on the problem of exclusion to the neglect of processes of exploitation.[24] While exclusion is an important and obvious injustice, it is not, as Castells (2009, 33) and others (ie. Lash 2002, 4) argue, the preeminent mode of injustice in 'the network society', nor is exploitation a derivative form of exclusion (Murphy 1985). At the same time, while the purpose of this chapter has been to highlight exploitation – the network's 'blindspot' – this should not be taken to mean that 'exclusion' is a mirage. Instead, what we need is a better understanding of the *internal relations* between processes of exclusion and exploitation.

'Exclusion' though, as I argued, leaves much to be desired as the central theme of social critique. 'Exploitation' in fact seems to do a better job of reminding us of the shared and dynamic basis of social reality. However, instead of following Boltanski and Chiapello's lead and generating a new theory of exploitation more suitable for a 'connexionist' world, this chapter argues that we already have a theory of exploitation for such a world – Marx's theory of exploitation.

The second task of this chapter was to demonstrate why Marx's theory of exploitation is still relevant for critiquing power within contemporary 'informational capitalism'. I first reveal how network theories are rooted in a process-relational ontology that shares much with Marx's ontology. Marx's particular understanding of *process* and *relation*, and his recognition of *contradiction*, is contrasted with that of contemporary network theorists, particularly Manuel Castells but also Hardt and Negri. It is this common *process-relational* perspective that allows us to understand Marx's contemporary relevance. At the same time, it is the key distinctions which promise to reinvigorate critique.

---

24   While I critique the network metaphor for its 'blindspot', I am mostly in agreement with
       Felix Stalder's assessment that the network society thesis signals "the return of sociologi-
       cal macrotheory after years of postmodern pessimism about the possibility, or even desir-
       ability, of such a project" (Stalder 2006, 1). This is generally something to be welcomed but
       I attribute it largely to the process-relational ontology that guides this thesis, which brings
       our attention back to structural forms and the relational processes that enact these forms.

Peter Marcuse critiques Castells for presenting "the excluded without the excluders" (cited in Stalder, 2006 140). However, my argument is that this is not a criticism that can be limited to Castells. Rather, it appears to be inherent to all social critique built around the network metaphor. This is because network theorists conceive of power as a de-centered 'flow', operating through the protocols that set the network's "rules of engagement." This Foucaultian conception of power – whereby power permeates society in constantly morphing formations of interlinked networks – is often contrasted with the supposed Marxist idea of power as a 'resource', emanating from a fixed external location. I hope though that this chapter's explication of Marx's process-relational ontology and his concomitant theory of exploitation makes it clear that such an interpretation is wrong-headed.

In conclusion, Bertell Ollman neatly summarizes the purpose behind Marx's process-relational ontology:

> Marx's quest [...] is never for why something starts to change (as if it were not already changing) but for the various forms this change assumes and why it may *appear* to have stopped. Likewise, it is never for how a relation gets established (as if there were no relation there before), but again for the different forms it takes and why aspects of an already existing relation may *appear* to be independent.
>
> OLLMAN 2003, 14

As we look out of our windows, at a world that appears to be both ever more in flux and ever more interconnected, it is all too easy to be captured by appearances. We really *can* see networks everywhere we look. The question we need to ask though is why does the world reveal itself to us through certain forms and not others? Are these forms really new, and if so, where did they come from? Asking these questions gives us the chance to realize that Marx's theory of exploitation, contrary to popular perception, is no relic of a hierarchical world of industrial capitalism but rather a theory of social relations that is highly suited to critiquing power within contemporary informational capitalism.

References

Barabási, Albert-László. 2003. Linked: The New Science of Networks. *American Journal of Physics* 71 (4): 409–410.

Barney, Darin. 2004. *The Network Society*. Cambridge.

Barzilai-Nahon, Karine. 2008. Towards a Theory of Network Gatekeeping: A Framework for Exploring Information Control. *Journal of the American Society for Information Science and Technology* 59 (9): 1493–1512.

Béland, Daniel. 2007. *The Social Exclusion Discourse: Ideas and Policy Change. Policy & Politics* 35 (1): 123–139.

Boltanski, Luc and Ève Chiapello. 2006. *The New Spirit of Capitalism.* London: Verso.

Buchanan, Allen. 1979. Exploitation, Alienation, and Injustice. *Canadian Journal of Philosophy* 9 (1): 121–139.

Callinicos, Alex. 2006. *The Resources of Critique.* Cambridge: Polity.

Capra, Fritjof. 2004. *The Hidden Connections: A Science for Sustainable Living.* New York: Anchor Books.

Castells, Manuel. 2000a. *The Rise of the Network Society, the Information Age: Economy, Society and Culture Vol. I.* Second Edition, Cambridge, MA; Oxford, UK: Blackwell.

Castells, Manuel. 2000b. Materials for an Exploratory Theory of the Network Society". *British Journal of Sociology* 51 (1): 5–24.

Castells, Manuel. 2000c. *End of Millennium, the Information Age: Economy, Society and Culture Vol. III.* Second Edition, Cambridge, MA; Oxford, UK: Blackwell.

Castells, Manuel. 2009. *Communication Power.* Oxford University Press, USA.

Castells, Manuel. 2011a. A Network Theory of Power. *International Journal of Communication* 5: 773–787.

Castells, Manuel. 2011b. Introduction to the Workshop: The Promise of Network Theory. *International Journal of Communication* 5. 794–795.

Cavanagh, Allison. 2007. *Sociology in the Age of the Internet.* Berkshire: McGraw-Hill International.

De Angelis, Massimo. 2007. *The Beginning of History: Value Struggles and Global Capital.* London: Pluto Press.

Elias, Norbert. 1978. "*The civilising process: The history of manners.*" New York:

Emirbayer, Mustafa. 1997. *Manifesto for a Relational Sociology. The American Journal of Sociology* 103 (2): 281–317.

Foucault, Michel. 1991. *Discipline and Punish: The Birth of the Prison.* London: Penguin Books.

Fuchs, Christian. 2009. Some Reflections on Manuel Castells' Book Communication Power. *tripleC – Cognition, Communication, Co-operation: Open Access Journal for a Global Sustainable* Information *Society* 7 (1): 94–108. Accessed November 3, 2011. http://www.triple-c.at/index.php/tripleC/article/viewFile/136/90.

Fuchs, Christian and Rainer E. Zimmermann. 2009. *Practical Civil Virtues in Cyberspace: Towards the Utopian Identity of Civitas and Multitudo.* Munich Series in Design Science, Volume 5. Aachen: Shaker.

Galloway, Alexander. 2004. *Protocol, or, How Control Exists after Decentralization.* Cambridge: The MIT Press.

Gane, Nicholas and David Beer. 2008. *New Media: The Key Concepts.* Oxford: Berg.

Garnham, Nicholas. 2004. Information Society Theory as Ideology. In *The Information Society Reader*, edited by Frank Webster, 165–184. London: Routledge.

Gould, Carol C. 1978. *Marx's Social Ontology: Individuality and Community in Marx's Theory of Social Reality.* Cambridge: The MIT Press.

Hardt, Michael and Antonio Negri. 2000. *Empire.* Cambridge, MA: Harvard University Press.

Hardt, Michael and Antonio Negri. 2004. *Multitude: War and Democracy in the Age of Empire.* New York: The Penguin Press.

Hardt, Michael and Antonio Negri. 2009. *Commonwealth.* Cambridge, MA: Belknap Press.

Harvey, David. 2010. *A Companion to Marx's Capital.* Vol. 1. Verso Books.

Hepp, Andreas, Friedrich Krotz, Shaun Moores and Carsten Winter, eds. 2008. *Connectivity, Networks and Flows: Conceptualizing Contemporary Communications.* Cresskill, New Jersey: Hampton Press, Inc.

Jessop, Bob. 2001. The State and the Contradictions of the Knowledge-Driven Economy, Published by the Department of Sociology, Lancaster University, Lancaster LA1 4YN. Accessed March 25, 2012. http://www.comp.lancs.ac.uk/sociology/papers/ Jessop-State-and-Contradictions.pdf.

Jessop, Bob. 2003. The State and the Contradictions of the Knowledge-Driven Economy, Department of Sociology, Lancaster University.

Kirsh, Scott., & Mitchell, Don. 2004. *The nature of things: dead labor, nonhuman actors, and the persistence of Marxism.* Antipode 36 (4), 687–705.

Lash, Scott. 2002. *Critique of Information,* London: Sage.

Law, John. 2003. *Networks, Relations, Cyborgs: On the Social Study of Technology.* Published by the Centre for Science Studies, Lancaster University: Lancaster. Accessed December 30, 2011. http://www.comp.lancs.ac.uk/sociology/papers/Law -Networks-Relations-Cyborgs.pdf.

Marcuse, Peter. 2002. Depoliticizing Globalization: The Information Age and the Network Society of Manuel Castells. In *Investigating the City: Contemporary and Future Perspectives,* edited by John Eade and Christopher Mele, 131–158. Oxford: Blackwell.

Marx, Karl. 1972. *Economic and Philosophical Manuscripts of 1844.* New York: International Publishers.

Marx, Karl. 1973. *Grundrisse: Foundations of the Critique of Political Economy.* Translated by Martin Nicolaus. London and New York: Penguin Books.

Marx, Karl. 1990. *Capital: A Critique of Political Economy, Volume 1.* London: Penguin.

Marx, Karl and Friedrich Engels. 1974. *The German Ideology,* edited by Chris J. Arthur. New York: International Publishers.

Mattelart, Armand and Michèle Mattelart. 1998. *Theories of Communication. An Introduction.* London: Sage Publications.

McKercher, Catherine and Vincent Mosco. 2010. Getting the Message: Communications Workers and Global *Value* Chains. *Work Organisation, Labour & Globalisation.* 4 (2): 1–9.

Murphy, Raymond. 1985. Exploitation or Exclusion? *Sociology* 19 (2): 225–243.

Ollman, Bertell. 2003. *Dance of the Dialectic: Steps in Marx's Method.* Urbana: University of Illinois Press.

Pomeroy, Anne Fairchild. 2004. *Marx and Whitehead: Process, Dialectics, and the Critique of Capitalism.* Albany: State University of New York.

Quandt, Thorsten. 2008. Network Theory and Human Action: Theoretical Concepts and Empirical Applications. In *Connetivity, Networks and Flows: Conceptualizing Contemporary Communications*, edited by Andreas Hepp, Friedrich Krotz, Shaun Moores, and Carsten Winter, 111–133. Cresskill, New Jersey: Hampton Press, Inc.

Rees, John. 1998. The Algebra of Revolution: The Dialectic and the Classical Marxist Tradition. Routledge, London and New York.

Resnick, Stephen A. and Richard D. Wolff. 2006. New Departures in Marxian Theory Routledge, NY.

Schiller, Dan. 1988. "How to think about information." The political economy of information: 27–43.

Stalder, Felix. 2006. *Manuel Castells and the Theory of the Network Society.* Oxford: Polity Press.

Thrift, Nigel. 2002. A Hyperactive World. In *Geographies of Global Change: Remapping the World,* edited by R.J. Johnston, Peter J. Taylor, and Michael J. Watts, 29–42. Malden, MA: Blackwell Publishers.

Urry, John. 2003. *Global Complexity.* Cambridge: Polity Press.

Van Dijk 1999. The One-Dimensional Network Society of Manuel Castells. New media & society, 1(1), 127–138.

Van Dijk, Jan A.G.M. 2006. *The Network Society: Social Aspects of New Media.* 2nd ed. London: Sage Publications Ltd.

Watts, D.J. 2003. *Six Degrees: The Science of a Connected Age.* New York: Norton.

Watts, D.J. 2004. The New Science of Networks. *Annual Review of Sociology* 30: 243–270.

Webster, Frank.1995. *Theories of the Information Society.* London: Routledge.

Wayne, Mike. 2004. Mode of Production: New Media Technology and the Napster File. *Rethinking Marxism: A Journal of Economics, Culture and Society.* 16 (2) 137–154.

Wildman, Wesley J. 2010. An Introduction to Relational Ontology. In *The Trinity and an Entangled World: Relationality in Physical Science and Theology*, edited by John Polkinghorne and John Zizioulas, 55–73. Grand Rapids: Eerdmans.

CHAPTER 9

3C: Commodifying Communication in Capitalism

Jernej A. Prodnik

1   Introduction

It is a tendency of informational flows to spill over from whatever network they are circulating in and hence to escape the narrowness of the
channel and to open up to a larger milieu.

TIZIANA TERRANOVA (2004, 2)

Commodity-form and commodification have played an important, if often overlooked, role in critical studies of capitalist societies. Authors such as Adorno
(2001/1991), Debord (1970, ch. 2), Lukács (1971), Sohn-Rethel (1972; 1978), Mattelart
(1978), Cleaver (2000/1979), Wallerstein (1983, ch. 1), Mosco (1989; 2009), Huws
(2003), Murdock (2000; 2006a), Postone (2003/1993), Dan Schiller (1988; 2007)
and Wittel (2013) have focused their attention on this so-called "cell-form of
capitalism," as the commodity has been characterised in Marx's writing.
Commodity-form[1] was a key category in Marx's work. It played a crucial role
throughout his whole *oeuvre*, from his early writings on political economy to
his latter conceptualisations that included full development of the role it car-
ries in constitution and reproduction of the capitalist societies (Marx and
Engels 1976; 1987; Marx 1993/1858; 1990/1867; see also Murdock 2006a; Barbalet
1983, 90f.). Even in post-modernity, commodification process can be seen as
being amongst crucial preconditions for the general preservation of capitalist
social relations and continuing expansion of capital. Historically speaking,
processes of transforming literally *anything* into a privatized form of (fictitious) commodity that can be exchanged in the market are thus of critical
importance for both the rise and continuing reproduction of capitalism. It is
only via the production of commodities for exchange that capitalists can extract
surplus value from labour (Huws 2003, 61).

---

1   Sohn-Rethel takes a close look at the term "form," which he defines as being time-bound: "It
    originates, dies and changes with time" (1978, 17). This supposedly distinguishes Marx and his
    dialectical thought from all other schools of thinking. For Jameson (2011, 35) the word "form"
    prevents "thingification" or reification of money, exchange-value etc., that are first and fore-
    most social relations.

The process of commodification often very directly influences the immediate experiences of individuals on the subjective and inter-subjective level, while it also has a strong influence on the wider society and relations within it. Expansion of the commodity–form throughout social spheres always produces an observable transformation of our social reality and by a rule makes possible a further increase in economic inequality. It radically transforms social bonds and values that were not based on the market exchange (Thompson 1991, ch. 4, ch. 5; Harvey 2009, 55–56, 62–64; Wittel 2013, 314) and also necessarily contributes to an enhanced individualization of (and within) society. At the same time, market operates independently and beyond direct control of human beings (Barbalet 1983, 89–92). One of the key points made by Marx (1990/1867, 163–177) in his *theory of commodity fetishism* was not only that commodities take on a life of their own, beyond the immediate control of human beings, but that they also claim mastery over people. In the capitalist social formation, "the process of production has mastery over man, instead of the opposite," claims Marx (1990/1867, 175). As summed up by Harvey (2010, 42), "market forces, which none of us individually control, regulate us."

In this chapter, I aim to contribute to a large body of academic work dealing with commodification and commodity-form by directing focus on the field of communication in the widest sense of this word. Commodity-form and commodification are analysed from a theoretical, conceptual and historical point of view, whilst the main consequences of the global universalisation of the commodity-form for society and social relations are emphasized as well. In the following section of this chapter (Section 2), I first look closely at how the commodity-form was analysed by Marx throughout his *oeuvre* and how this corresponds to the wider constitution of capitalist society. How different critical authors following Marx analysed these processes helps me to clarify the role commodification plays in the emergence of commodity fetishism and how capitalist production and exchange contribute to human individualisation.

In Section 3 of the chapter this analysis is further extended by demonstrating there is now an enduring global commodification of everything, including culture, creativity, information, and diverging types of communication; these social categories are becoming fundamental in what could also be called capitalist informational societies. I identify historical dialectical approach as the only possible way of making sense of the on-going contradictory social transformation, which manifests itself simultaneously as continuity of capitalist social relations and discontinuity of the means of production. In this part the analysis is carried out by using different methods of historicizing. *Firstly*, through the Braudelian *longue durée* approach (Braudel 1980), which is used to analyse the long-term changes in communication, information, and culture, as they have been slowly transformed into commodities produced for market exchange since the fifteenth century. *Secondly*, by defining fundamental political and economic processes occurring in recent decades that help with an explanation of the rise in the influence of communication and information in the current historical epoch. In Section 3 of the chapter, commodification of communication and information is therefore analysed in a deeply historical manner by looking at how these resources have been subjugated to capitalist market relations since the capitalist economic system first emerged several centuries ago. It is pointed out their commodification was part-and-parcel of the developing capitalism, accompanied by recurring conflicts, contradictions and antagonistic struggles. It was especially political incentives and interventions (policymaking, funding of research and development, etc.), however, that led to the increasing social, economic and political significance of the information and communication systems and resources we have been witnessing in the last few decades.

Furthermore, I am interested in how commodification was approached at in the (critique of) political economy of communication (Section 4). The latter will – first and foremost – be done through a reappraisal of the "blind spot debate" (and the concurring "audience commodity" thesis), which also played a crucial role in the development of political economy of communication as such.[2] Section 5 helps me to clarify how commodification, with the help of digitalisation, is able to penetrate into communication processes and thus construct new commodities. These findings are connected to some of the recent neo-Marxist approaches, especially to the authors coming from the autonomist/post-operaist movement (Section 5). I demonstrate how insights into this intellectual strand can provide an understanding of the ongoing commodification processes through concepts such as communicative, bio-linguistic capitalism, and social factory, and how it therefore offers several convergence points with political economy of communication. In this section, I also note we are witnessing new enclosures via recurrent processes of primary accumulation, which make possible incorporation of different spheres under capital. This brought about a possibility for a further expansion and intensification of commodification throughout society. In the last part of the chapter (Section 5.2), I build on the preceding sections and conceptualize *a seeping commodification* as a historically novel type of commodification, which trickles throughout society. This concept indicates we are witnessing a qualitative transformation

---

2 Dallas W. Smythe initiated this debate in 1977 with his article *Communications: Blindspot of Western Marxism*, which was followed by several replies and corrections, most notably by Murdock (1978) a year later and Smythe's (1978) rejoinder to Murdock in the same year.

in the commodification processes that is, in part, owed to an overwhelming capitalist enclosure of the wider communicative field, which accompanied its increased economic importance. Even though commodification of communicative and informational resources must be seen as a *long revolution*, to use Williams's (1961/2011) term, these processes have been considerably enhanced by political interventions occurring in the wider field of communication(s) in the last decades.

The main presupposition of this text will be that there is an increasing significance of communication in post-Fordist capitalism. Communication spreads into, and emanates from, all nooks of the social fabric; this notion, however, seems especially crucial in the current historical epoch, which seems to be completely permeated by communication on all levels of human and social life (i.e. notions regarding the mediatisation of society). At the same time, however, communication is also becoming almost fully commodified. Post-operaist thought claims that communication, or even language-capacity as such, gained hegemonic primacy in contemporary society, while also constituting a new source of capitalist accumulation. Several of the assertions pointed out by Marx, his early successors, and authors contributing to the "blind-sport debate" therefore need to be raised again because of the significantly (but not fundamentally) changed social context and technological changes that are enabling further expansion of commodification.

2 Conceptualizing Commodity-Form and Commodification

They know the price of everything and the value of nothing.
OSCAR WILDE

According to Lukács (1971), it was not a coincidence that Marx began his major works with an analysis of the commodity when he decided to lay out the totality of capitalist society. The problem of commodities should, according to Lukács, in fact be regarded "as the central, structural problem of capitalist society in all its aspects" (Lukács 1971, 83). It should therefore not be seen either in isolation or even as a central problem of only economics, which consequently means it is difficult to ignore this issue when providing a critique of the *really existing* social relations. For Marx (1990/1976, 90), the commodity-form, in which abstract human labour materialises itself (both being historical categories bound to capitalist societies), is one of the economic cell-forms of the current historical epoch. These categories enabled Marx to analyse capitalism in its most abstract form, but also at its most fundamental level. It is worth mentioning that he saw abstraction as a chief (and perhaps only possible) means of a scientific analysis of society, which, together with dialectics, enables the enquirer to go beyond mere appearances of things.[3]

This crucial role of the commodity can be seen from Marx's earliest writings on political economy to his later conceptualisations, and many authors believed this to be the pre-eminent starting point for any analysis of society under capitalism (e.g. Lukács 1971; Sohn-Rethel 1978; Postone 2003/1993). In Marx's early writings, for example in *The Poverty of Philosophy*, published in French in 1847 (Marx and Engels 1976, 105–212), he dealt with the use and especially exchange-value of commodities, the latter being an inexorable part of commodity production in the societies of producers who exchange their commodities. It is around this time that he defined the law of value of commodities as being determined by the labour time inherent in them (he still wrote of labour and not labour power, which is a more precise conceptualisation also present in his later writings). Labour time is therefore the measure of value, and labour, as Marx pointed out (Marx and Engels 1976, 130), was itself a commodity: labour-commodity, bought and sold in the market. If there is an exchange of two products (commodities), there is an exchange of equal quantities of labour, or more precisely, exchange of labour time (Marx and Engels 1976, 126). As he famously put it: "Time is everything, man is nothing; he is, at the most, time's carcase. Quality no longer matters. Quantity alone decides everything; hour for hour, day for day" (Marx and Engels 1976, 127). This, of

---

3   Experiments in natural sciences are replaced by the power of abstraction in social sciences. Theory is, for example, always an abstraction from empirical reality, even if it must inevitably build on this same reality. Marx furthermore pointed out that "all science would be superfluous if the form of appearance of things directly coincided with their essence" (Marx 1991/1981, 956). It is precisely here, according to him, that "vulgar economics feels completely at home, these relationships appearing all the more self-evident to it, the more their inner connections remain hidden." (ibid.) According to Eagleton (1996, 6), there is always a hiatus between how things actually are and how they seem; there is, so to say, a difference between essence and appearance, because the latter needs to be penetrated or bypassed to understand reality (see Barbalet 1983, 23f.; Postone 2003/1993). It could therefore be claimed that one of the central goals of both dialectics and abstraction is to take analysis beyond sole appearances of things, which is impossible with a mere analysis of concrete reality (where several mechanisms operate at the same time). In most cases, things are not simply opaque or what they seem on the surface. Barbalet (1983, 24) points out it is exactly the role commodity fetishism (which is dealt with later in this text) plays in society that demonstrates this point in its entirety. For a more detailed analysis of contradictions between appearances and reality (and questions concerning transphenomenality and counter-phenomenality) see also Collier's (1994, 6f.) interpretation of the meta-theoretical position of critical realism.

course, is a historical specificity of capitalist societies and not some eternal justice, as Proudhon at the time thought it was.

According to Murdock, it was already in the time when Marx wrote *The Poverty of Philosophy* that he identified "commodification as the central driving force propelling capitalism's expansion" (Murdock 2006a, 3). It was consequently only a matter of time before all things, from physical to moral, which might never have been sold or acquired before in the history of humankind are brought to the market and exchanged (ibid.; see also Marx and Engels 1976, 113). The role of the commodity-form in the Marxian critique of political economy can therefore hardly be overstated even in Marx's earliest writings. It can be regarded as an indispensable part of capitalism, the blood in its cycle of accumulation, which is essential for its continuing reproduction.[4] This also demonstrates that the commodity-form is an unavoidable part of a serious critique of capitalism, the line of thinking which was considerably extended by critical communication studies, especially by authors following Smythe's path. For Mosco, for example, the commodification process, defined as "the process of transforming use-values into exchange-values" (Mosco 2009, 129, ch. 7), is one of the central processes that make up the starting point for the political economy of communication.

Even though Marx had already analysed the commodity-form in his earliest writings, it is especially in his later works that he provided a detailed overview of the role it has, not only in the reproduction of capitalism, but also in social life as such. His perhaps most detailed account was in *A Contribution to the Critique of Political Economy* (see Marx and Engels 1987, 257–417), which was written between 1858 and 1859, and served as a basis for his elaboration of the commodity in the first volume of *Capital* (Marx 1990/1867). In these two works, all of the so-called cell-forms of capitalist economy are fully laid out, including the difference between abstract labour, which is the source of exchange-value, and concrete labour, which can produce an infinite variety of different use-values and is the source of actual material wealth. Both exchange-value, or simply value, and abstract labour, can be seen as such historical cell-forms, and

---

4 Seeing commodities as being the blood cells in capitalist accumulation cycle is not only an analogy or a metaphor. In his analysis of the primitive accumulation, Marx in fact points out that "a great deal of capital, which appears today in the United States without any birth-certificate, was yesterday, in England, the capitalized blood of children" (Marx 1990/1976, 920). This, at least implicitly, touches on another important part of his analysis of the commodity-form, namely commodity fetishism. I deal with this issue later in the text (especially in the Section 2.4).

both are indispensable parts of commodity-form.[5] All of these categories form the basis of the capitalist economy in the most abstract sense. According to Marx, the key difference between abstract and concrete labour is that "labour positing exchange-value is *abstract universal* and *uniform* labour," whereas "labour positing use-value is concrete and distinctive labour, comprising infinitely varying kinds of labour as regards its form and the material to which it is applied." (Marx and Engels 1987, 277) Abstract labour is, so to say, socially useful labour, but one which is without particular use-value to an individual. According to Marx, "universal labour is consequently not a ready-made prerequisite but an emerging result" (Marx and Engels 1987, 286); it exists in commodities in a latent state and only becomes universal as the result of the exchange process. The subject matter of political economy is only the abstract labour and (exchange-) value, while all commodities, regarded as exchange-values, "are merely definite quantities of *congealed labour time*" (Marx and Engels 1987, 272). This later led Marx to note that "moments are the elements of profit" (Marx 1990/1867, 352), something that the Taylorist management doctrine developed to the full in the production process.

What seems important here is that even though "exchange-value is a relation between persons; it is however necessary to add that it is a relation hidden by a material veil" (Marx and Engels 1987, 276). This enduring mystification can be seen as one of the most important premises pointed out by Marx and it was later on fully developed through the concept of fetishism. The core ideas of this important presupposition have been developed much earlier though:

> It is a characteristic feature of labour which posits exchange-value that it causes the social relations of individuals to appear in the perverted form of a social relation between things. [...] Only the conventions of everyday life make it appear commonplace and ordinary that social relations of production should assume the shape of things, so that the relations into which people enter in the course of their work appear as the relations of things to one another and of things to people. This mystification is still a very simple one in the case of a commodity. Everybody understands more or less clearly that the relations of commodities as exchange-values are really the relations of people to the productive activities of one another. The semblance of simplicity disappears in more advanced relations of production. All the illusions of the monetary system arise from

---

5   The fact that this particular type of labour is specific only for capitalism and at the same time also fundamental for its functioning, led both Marcuse (1955, 287–295) and Postone (2003/1993) to call for abolition of labour (as known in capitalist societies).

the failure to perceive that money, though a physical object with distinct properties, represents a social relation of production.

MARX AND ENGELS 1987, 275F.

There are several important consequences arising from these findings, perhaps most notably the following: While Marx's approach presupposes a need for abstraction to understand how capitalism works (as already pointed out), there is also a real abstraction going on all the time in the existing historical epoch dominated by commodity exchange. "An abstraction is made every day in the social process of production," Marx stresses (Marx and Engels 1987, 272). It is a prerequisite for the constitution of equivalents between factually unequal things. For example, a reduction of different kinds of useful labour into homogeneous abstract labour is unavoidable, because it makes possible monetary exchange between different use-values, which are inherent in commodities. Secondly, these findings have enormous consequences for how social life is constituted in existing societies. Most notably, what is the wider social role of the commodity-form in the concept of commodity fetishism, but also what role does exchange of commodities play in the individualisation of human beings and what types of instrumental rationalisation are developed? These issues will be more thoroughly analysed in the following subsections.

2.1   *Historical Changes and the Social Relations in Capitalist Societies*
Commodities contain abstract labour and their production is carried out in the context of the worldwide division of labour. They obtain definite social character and mediate between individuals and their private labour through the market. As already pointed out, it is not the physical nature of the commodity that matters when it comes to exchanging it, but its social character: what is central is its relation to the other commodities available for exchange (as products of various kinds of useful labour). This relationship between commodities and consequent equivalence between different kinds of labour is constituted through the market. Not only is there a unity of use-value and exchange-value in every commodity, but a commodity can only exist in relation to other commodities through a *series of equations*. "The *exchange process* of commodities is the *real* relation that exists between them. This is a social process which is carried on by individuals independently of one another" (Marx and Engels 1987, 282). As Marx so famously puts it in *Capital*, this creates a very special social relation that is established through things and forms the basis for commodity fetishism:

It is nothing but the definite social relation between men themselves, which assumes here, for them, the fantastic form of a relation between things. [...] In other words, the labour of the private individual manifests itself as an element of the total labour of society only through the relations which the act of exchange establishes between products, and, through mediation, between the producers. To the producers, therefore, the social relations between their private labours appear as what they are, i.e. they do not appear as direct social relations between persons in their work, but rather as material [dinglich] relations between persons and social relations between things.

MARX 1990/1867, 165F.

It is thus social relations between things that mediate between people, consequently producing the key mystification of contemporary social life. Social relations between people are displaced by (and to) something else, in this case, into relations between commodities, simultaneously creating a material veil (which will lead us directly to the questions of individualisation later in the text). The general idea behind both this displacement and commodity fetishism as a whole is relatively simple, but at the same time, it is notoriously difficult (Balibar 2007, 57). This is especially so because this concept produces such immensely far-reaching consequences on how we live our lives in (post) modern societies.

The key abstract historical arguments made by Marx, which are of crucial importance for the analysis of these consequences for society, have been succinctly presented by Hobsbawm (2011, 130–132). He points out that Marx's theory of social and economic evolution is based on his analysis of (wo)man as a social animal.[6] This can be seen as Marx's fundamental ontological position regarding human nature. Marx's quite abstract account of particular phases of social-economic formations, as depicted in *Grundrisse*, starts with human beings that labour in nature, changing it and taking from it. This is the basis and natural condition for creation and reproduction of their existence. Taking and changing a part of nature can be seen as perhaps the first kind of appropriation. This type of appropriation, however, is merely an aspect of human labour, a material interchange between nature and human beings, which is necessary for their survival. Appropriation is also expressed in the concept of property, but one that is very much different from historically specific *private* property, which is distinctive of capitalist societies (see Hobsbawm 2011, 130; May 2010). As social animals, human beings develop both co-operation and social division of labour, the latter being nothing else than specialisation of functions, enabling people to produce a *surplus* over what is needed to maintain and reproduce the individual and the community. Furthermore, "the existence of both the surplus

---

6   See also Barbalet (1983).

and the social division of labour makes possible *exchange*. But initially, both production and exchange have as their object merely *use*" (Hobsbawm 2011, 131). As human beings emancipate themselves from nature and start to "control" it (simultaneously also changing the relations of production), significant changes happen to the social relations into which they enter. A more detailed account of these changes will be looked at later and was partially already pointed out. In a historical sense, however, these changes are a result of both the aforementioned specialisation of labour, and furthermore, of the invention of the money form, and, with it, of the commodity production and market exchange. This provides "a basis for procedures unimaginable before, including capital accumulation" (Hobsbawm 2011, 131). In the latest phase, which occurred under capitalism, the worker was consequently reduced to nothing more than labour power. In the production process a total separation is made between use-value, exchange-value, and accumulation, which can be seen as a very distinct feature of this epoch. Reproduction is in fact separated from – or even opposes – production (of commodities), where unity used to exist in the pre-capitalist social formations (Fortunati 1989, 8). The economic aims of capitalism, as one can see, are radically different from those of preceding modes of production that focused on the production of use-values in relation to the reproduction of human lives. For Fortunati, this means that commodity production can be posited as "*the* fundamental point of capitalist production, and the laws that govern it as the laws that characterise capitalism itself" (Fortunati 1989, 8). The main goal becomes an endless accumulation of still more capital, an accumulation for accumulation's sake – this rational intent to maximise accumulation is a "law" that governs all economic activity in capitalism (Wallerstein 1983).

It can be claimed that there is a whole complex of different categories, which need to be developed (producing a qualitative social change) to make capitalist society what it is: from abstract labour, commodity-form and commodification, which presuppose production with the sole intent of exchange (and consequently dominance of exchange-value) (see Marx 1990/1867, 733), to the expropriation of surplus-value in the production process, the social (and finally worldwide) division of labour, accumulation for accumulation's sake and also a historically novel possibility of an endless accumulation. And for the latter to be possible, accumulation of a capitalist presupposes valorisation, constant increasing of the value of the commodities bought, which is done through the production process (see Marx 1990/1867, 711). This complex also needs a specific capital relation and its reproduction, namely the capitalist on the one hand and the wage-labourer on the other (Marx 1990/1867, 724).

I will focus on these changes in more detail in the next subsections. For a more detailed analysis of the historically specific capitalist epoch, as delineated by Marx, we are first bound to turn to the first volume of *Capital* (Marx 1990/1867). Looking at capitalism on its surface, one is quickly able to see there is an apparent rupture between the capitalist class and the proletariat, the latter being defined as those who do not own the means of production or are prevented direct access to (and thus divorced from) them. This crucial separation is constituted especially through the so-called primitive (or primary) accumulation, which can be seen as being an inherently extra-economic process and thereby has little to do with how the economy is supposed to reproduce itself "normally."[7] It is exactly primitive accumulation that historically and momentarily enables enclosures of the common lands, expropriation of the commoners, expulsion of peasants from their lands, incorporation of different activities and spheres into exchange relations, and finally, also incorporating these spheres into capitalist social relations (in the words of Sohn-Rethel, society of private appropriation in contrast to the previous societies of production). Amongst others – and one which is of indispensable importance for the existence of capitalist production – this process crucially contributes to the production of labour power as a commodity. It effectively prevents people from accessing the means of production and therefore also the means of their own subsistence, consequently pushing them into waged-labour (at the same time producing a very much changed constitution of society). Murdock (2011, 18–20) was one of the authors from the field of political economy of communication that constantly stressed the historical role of enclosures and processes of accumulation as dispossession for the march of commodification, which also forced people to start selling their labour power for a wage.

This factual inability to access the means of production is the key characteristic of the proletariat and its development in time contributes to ever larger proletarianisation of the labour force in capitalism as a historical system (see Wallerstein 1983, ch. 1). As people are (often quite forcefully) rejected access to

---

7   Primitive accumulation has (in most cases) been also an extremely violent process. There has been an increased interest into the problems of primary (or primitive) accumulation in recent years, demonstrating this is still a very much contested topic in the critique of political economy. It also demonstrates that this topic is gaining relevance in the existing historical epoch. One of the key arguments made in the reinterpretations of this concept has been that primitive accumulation is not a historically limited process, which would be significant only as a starting point of the capitalist accumulation. It is in fact constantly reproduced and therefore a permanent part of capitalism, helping both to constitute and expand capitalist social relations. On these issues see writings of Perelman (2000), Bonefeld (2001), De Angelis (2007, ch. 10), Prodnik (2011), or Mezzadra (2011). Harvey (2003, 144–152) coined the term *accumulation by dispossession* to clearly denote permanence of this process in capitalist societies. On the privatization of the commons, which is connected to these same issues, see Bollier (2002) and Boyle (2008).

the means of production, they need to sell their labour-power on the labour market to survive, which is a historical novelty of capitalist societies (and took a long time to actually develop, initially pushing many people into extreme pauperism) (see Polanyi 2001/1944). People sell their labour-power on the market in a free and apparently fair exchange between the buyers (capitalists) and sellers (labourers) of this commodity. In most cases, this is in fact the only commodity proletarians own: their own body and capacities inherent in it, which can (or rather must) now be exchanged as a commodity on the market. The capitalist, as the buyer of the labour-power commodity, is only able to "hire" the labourer, or to be more precise, his capacity to labour, for a particular period of time.[8] The latter can be seen as one of the key tenets of both the liberal political economy and liberal take on human freedom in society. It enables both apparently free exchange between two consenting parties, which is carried out in the market, and development of the labour market itself. But as Marcuse pointed out, the fact that an individual is free to sell his labour-power is actually the prerequisite for labour-power to even become a commodity. The labour contract thus "epitomizes this freedom, equality and justice" (Marcuse 1955, 308) (and of course also necessity to be exploited) in the context of liberal capitalism. As Marx himself puts it, "labour-power can appear on the market as a commodity only if, and in so far as, its possessor, the individual whose labour-power it is, offers it for sale or sells it as a commodity. In order that its possessor may sell it as a commodity, he must have it at his disposal, he must be the free proprietor of his own labour-capacity, hence of his person." (Marx 1990/1867, 271) As the capitalist temporarily buys the labourer's labour-power, he (or she) is able to employ him (or her) in the production process, where he (or she) can directly control him (or her), making sure the work he (or she) was hired for is done. Finally, in the production process, the labourer produces both (exchange-) value and surplus-value, the latter being the source of capitalist exploitation.[9]

---

8   It has not been stressed often enough, but individuals as such have no (exchange) value whatsoever in capitalist society and cannot have it. It is a commodity that is contained within the individual that potentially holds value: their capacity for production – labour-power. Capitalist therefore does not appropriate labourer as such, but *his labour*, and in concrete reality this exchange cannot happen in any other way but between the *individual-as-capacity-for-production* and capital (see Fortunati 1989).

9   This can be seen as one of the key findings that Marx successfully proved in the first volume of *Capital* on an abstract level (Marx 1990/1867, 293–306): exchange between buyers and sellers of the labour-power commodity is, in fact, *not* fair. But not on the market, which is the surface of capitalist social order. This inequality develops in the production process, where labourer as a rule produces more value with his labour-power than he gets paid for: "The

2.2   *The Exchange of Commodities and Social Totality*

This short summary might seem superfluous to those who are sufficiently acquainted with Marx, but it is crucial for the understanding of the roles that exchange, equivalence, and commodity have in his total argument. Products made in the capitalist production process are necessarily commodities. And they are also necessarily put into an exchange relation with other commodities, which can only be done through the market. This is, after all, what makes them commodities: their social character, their ability to be exchangeable because of their social desirability, and the market is the only way to compare these commodities. If this was not the case, they would be just some useful products for their actual producer, while the focus in the production process

---

value of labour-power, and the value which that labour-power valorizes [*verwertet*] in the labour-process, are two entirely different magnitudes; and this difference was what the capitalist had in mind when he was purchasing the labour-power" (Ibid., 300). This is called surplus-value and, in the first instance, it should be seen as a technical and not a moral term (as it is often both interpreted and used). Labour-power is also the only commodity from which more value can be extracted than it has been paid for in the market. According to Negri (1991/1984, 79), behind the appearance of exchange, a theft is thereby taking place. Furthermore, because labourer temporarily sold his labour-power to the capitalist before he entered the production process, the products he produced are alienated from him by the capitalist at the end of the working day (alienation is another concept that had vast influence in Marxism, but its conceptualization went through drastic changes even in Marx's own writings when his thought was developing). Final products of the labour process are therefore a property of the capitalist and not of its immediate producer, the labourer. Labourer waived away his right to the products when he temporarily sold his labour-power to the capitalist. Instead of retaining these products, he gets paid wages for his labour, which are of lower value than what he actually produced (hence, exploitation). The exchange between the worker and capital is therefore only formally an exchange of equivalents between equals. As Fortunati (1989, 9) points out, it is in fact an exchange of non-equivalents between unequals. The abstract argument made by Marx also presupposes that wage that labourer receives is no higher than living wages. He already came to this finding in 1847, saying that "labour, being itself a commodity, is measured as such by the labour time needed to produce the labour-commodity. And what is needed to produce this labour-commodity? Just enough labour time to produce the objects indispensable to the constant maintenance of labour, that is, to keep the worker alive and in a condition to propagate his race" (Marx and Engels 1976, 125). Several authors claimed this was a nice example of how Marx was historically completely wrong. But they (perhaps intentionally) forgot this was an abstract argument, building on a rational *tendency* of how a capitalist will operate. There are, of course, several other tendencies and mechanisms at work in a concrete and complex social reality, amongst others political interventions made by the state (regulation of working hours, minimal wage), which are often a result of class antagonisms and power relations in a specific society.

would simply be on the use-value of the products for their actual producer.[10] But the whole importance for the capitalist selling these products in fact lies in the production of exchange-value, which is, in most cases, expressed in the form of price on the market (i.e. through the money form, which is the universal equivalent and the measure of exchange-value). The ability to exchange these articles for the universal equivalent, which also makes extraction of surplus value fairly simple, is the sole reason the capitalist is employing labourers who produce these commodities. If something might be very useful for the society, but would at the same time (directly or indirectly) lack exchange-value, it, as a rule, could not be of any particular importance for the capitalists.[11] In the best-case scenario, it will be different *support systems* in the capitalist society (e.g. welfare state) that will take care of this – or not.

Furthermore, because it is the capitalist class that sells products (commodities) on the market, it is incidentally (also) the labourer that needs to buy these products as the means of his subsistence. Doing so, he inadvertently assists with the reproduction of the capitalist accumulation cycle and capitalist system as a whole; the labourer consequently inadvertently perpetuates his own exploitation (see Marcuse 1955, 309; Hobsbawm 2011). The labourer thus unintentionally helps with the preservation of the existing class relations, because he is reaffirming labour's separation from the means of production. The working class (i.e. proletariat) is therefore integral to capitalism, its unavoidable part (Postone 2003/1993, *cf.* Marx 1990/1867, 716, 724), which is based on the property relation of private ownership of the means of production. What is of crucial importance here is that even though the history of modern society and capital is of course socially constituted, it nevertheless "possesses a quasi-autonomous developmental logic" (Postone 2003/1993, 31). How the capitalist

---

10   Again, it is exactly this social character that is the main characteristic of the commodity. The commodity *must* be exchanged on the market. It is paradoxical that a specific commodity would in fact not be a commodity, if it were a mere use-value for its owner. "For its owner it is on the contrary a *non-use-value,*" Marx (Marx and Engels 1987, 283) writes in the *Critique*. Commodity is "merely the physical depository of exchange-value, or simply a *means of exchange.* [...] The commodity is a use-value for its owner only so far as it is an exchange-value. The commodity therefore has still to *become* a use-value, in the first place a use-value for others." (ibid.).

11   This is not because capitalist is somehow morally corrupt (even though he might be), but because in competitive market system he is pressured by the *coercive laws of competition*. If every individual capitalist did not follow his own self-interest he would quickly go bankrupt. Capitalists therefore cannot set boundaries to their own activities in a competitive system. This is, for example, a very significant notion when ecological issues are debated.

system actually works is therefore more or less independent and automated, as it generates a dynamic that is beyond the control of any individual actor constituting it (but not necessarily of the coalition of subjectivities, multitude or a whole social class, which can collectively resist its domination, but these questions will not occupy us in the present text). This becomes especially clear when Marx talks about (exchange-) value, which is an "immaterial" appendage to the commodity. Even if it is immaterial, that does not make it subjective: it is both (socially) objective and at the same time constantly changeable in space and time, because a commodity is a result of a socially useful (and also socially necessary) labour, which varies between specific types of society (e.g. because of rise and fall of productivity connected to technological developments, natural circumstances etc.).[12] As Marx puts it, "exchange-value appears to be something accidental and purely relative, and consequently an intrinsic value, i.e. an exchange-value that is inseparably connected with the commodity, inherent in it, seems a contradiction in terms" (Marx 1990/1867, 126). But as he develops his argument further, one can see that this is an argumentation distinctive of vulgar economics. The price of commodities indeed fluctuates, but neither value nor its market representation (via price and money) can be seen as arbitrary. Their common denominator is quantity of objectified (abstract) labour, put in the context of the whole capitalist economy. The labour time, "objectified in the use-values of commodities is both the substance that turns them into exchange-values and therefore into commodities, and the standard by which the precise magnitude of their value is measured" (Marx and Engels 1987, 272). Nevertheless, labourers themselves have little actual influence regarding how much labour time is socially necessary to produce a certain commodity – it is market forces that govern these relations in the world of commodities – and neither do they, of course, necessarily enter into direct personal relations with other labourers in the market. All these relations appear as

---

12   It is sensible to quote Marx here at length, because this is an important and often misunderstood presupposition: "The labour time expressed in and exchange-value is the labour time of an individual, but of an individual in no way differing [...] from all other individuals in so far as the perform equal labour; the labour time, therefore, which one person requires for the production of a given commodity is the *necessary* labour time which any other person would require to produce the same commodity. It is the labour time of an individual, his labour time, but only as labour time common to all; consequently it is quite immaterial *whose* individual labour time this is. This universal labour time finds its expression in a universal product, a universal equivalent [...] Only as such a *universal* magnitude does it represent a *social* magnitude. [...] The labour time of the individual is thus, in fact, the labour time required by society to produce a particular use-value, that is to satisfy a particular want" (Marx and Engels 1987, 272).

objective quantitative relations between commodities (usually represented via the money form) and only by looking behind this material veil is it possible to see that they are in fact antagonistic relations of production, where a conflict can emerge.

Marx's argumentation here is very complex and it can be argued that a coherently dialectical approach needs to be employed to sufficiently encompass it in its entirety. This would make it possible not to overlook any of the aspects of the capitalist order as a whole. What I have in mind here is a need to look at the social totality to adequately comprehend even the most abstract categories such as the commodity, value, or abstract labour. They are all constitutive cell parts of the system that influences and conditions them, meaning they cannot be adequately analysed when taken in isolation from one another or from the wider economic and social system. This need for totality is also one of the demands of dialectics; in this sense Marx's argument can be seen as a *global* and an all-encompassing one (see Lefebvre 1968; Harvey 1996, 48–57; Jameson 2009, ch. 1; Harvey 2010, 195f.). What seems important to note at this point is that looking at the commodity-form by itself would indeed be missing what it actually stands for: it is in fact an objective social relation. Not only does it make sense when it enters into exchange relations with other commodities and becomes a part of the *world of commodities*, thus presupposing a fully developed social division of labour,[13] other parts of the accumulation process also need to be taken into account: the circulation sphere, where exchange-value of these commodities is both realised and "measured" (it cannot be measured "directly" because, again, it needs to be put into a relation with other commodities; there is no way of knowing what the socially necessary labour time to produce a certain commodity is before they enter into this relation), while the sphere of production is where waged labour produces these commodities. As we are able to see, there is a certain societal structure that needs to be in place and functioning for a fully commodified society, where exchange of commodities takes place in a very automated fashion. In the words of Balibar: "The structure of production and circulation which confers an exchange-value on the products of labour [i.e. commodities] forms a single whole, and the existence of money, a 'developed' form of the general equivalent of commodities, is one of the necessary functions of that structure" (Balibar 2007, 61). All these categories and relations must be developed and functionally in place.

---

13   "But though it is correct to say that private exchange presupposes division of labour, it is
      wrong to maintain that division of labour presupposes private exchange" (Marx and
      Engels 1987, 299).

2.3 *Equivalence and the Real Abstraction*

The appearance of the commodity-form in pre-capitalist societies is essentially episodic. As Lukács (1971, 84) pointed out, this is when exchange-value does not yet have a form of its own and is directly bound to the use-value. The purpose of production in this context is to create use-values and they become means of exchange merely when supply exceeds the needs. It is only after the commodity successfully penetrates society to the extent that it becomes dominant that the qualitative change occurs and the endless (capitalist) accumulation becomes possible. This is why, for Lukács, "the commodity can only be understood in its undistorted essence when it becomes the universal category of society as a whole" (Lukács 1971, 86). This development does not take place before the advent of modern capitalism, when (wo)man's own activity and labour become objective and fully independent of him (her) and his (her) wants, "something that controls him by virtue of an autonomy alien to man" (Lukács 1971, 87). The necessary abstraction of human labour is at this point incorporated in commodities and the process of abstraction in the economy is completed. While in the previous modes of production the aim was the production of use-values, which would serve the reproduction of the individual within specific communal relations, under capitalism the sole aim thus becomes "the production of exchange-values, i.e. the creation of value for value" (Fortunati 1989, 7). According to Fortunati, this leads directly "to the *commodity*, to *exchange-value*, taking precedence over the-individual-as-use-value, despite the fact that the individual is still the only source of the creation of value" (Fortunati 1989, 7).

This development needs a specific kind of rationalisation, which, according to Lukács (1971, 88), is based on *what is and can be calculated*, so to say on instrumentally rationalistic measuring, which is the only way to enable equivalence (exchange-value) between factually unequal things (use-values). Sohn-Rethel (1972, 54) saw this as a type of mathematical reasoning, which can be traced also to the exchange abstraction (while he also connected it to objective knowledge and "exact" sciences). A consequence of this finding is that if the exchange process is to work effectively and reproduce itself in a society, it is obvious that a full-blown universalisation of equivalence needs to be carried out. A fully developed equivalence in fact has to be established between unequal things, making them measurable and thus comparable via some basic characteristic (in the case of Marx's labour theory of value these are abstract labour and labour time), if they are to be exchanged on the market. This leads us back to the cell-forms of capitalism, to the fundamental and most abstract categories in Marx's analysis, namely the commodity, abstract labour, and value, all being inherent parts of capital. All three categories are inexorable parts of capitalist societies in the most abstract sense.

It is quite clear that an abstraction is not only a thought process for social analysis, but is also a real, factual abstraction, "abstraction not by thought but by action and operating in time and space" (Sohn-Rethel 1972, 51). It is an abstraction developing through several fundamental categories: exchange abstraction, commodity abstraction, labour abstraction, time abstraction etc. (see Sohn-Rethel 1972; 1978). As Marx points out, "equality in the full sense between different kinds of labour can be arrived at only if we abstract from their real inequality, if we reduce them to the characteristics they have in common, that of being the expenditure of human labour-power, of human labour in the abstract" (Marx 1990/1867, 166). This argument can of course be extended further on to other categories, beyond only abstract labour. According to Marcuse:

> [Abstraction] is imposed upon the dialectical method by the structure of its subject matter, capitalist society. We may even say that the abstraction is capitalism's own work, and that the Marxian method only follows this process. Marx's analysis has shown that capitalist economy is built upon and perpetuated by the constant reduction of the concrete to the abstract labour. This economy step by step retreats from the concrete of human activity and needs, and achieves the integration of individual activities and needs only through complex of abstract relations in which individual work counts merely in so far as it represents socially necessary labor-time, and in which the relations among men appear as relations of things (commodities). The commodity world is a 'falsified' and 'mystified' world, and its critical analysis must first follow the abstractions which make up this world, and must then take its departure from these abstract relations in order to arrive at their real content. The second step is thus the abstraction from the abstraction, or the abandonment of a false concreteness, so that the true concreteness might be restored.
>
> MARCUSE 1955, 313

This notion was further developed by some of the aforementioned authors, amongst others such as Sohn-Rethel, who points out that abstractness takes shape in different social institutions, primarily in that of money form. Sohn-Rethel also stresses that "at the time and place where it happens the abstraction passes unnoticed" (Sohn-Rethel 1972, 51–52), not least because in most cases transactions involve physical objects, while the commodity exchange is no less real than anything else; but abstraction still has a form of thought, even if it does not spring from thought, but from actual practical activities (check, for example, the abstraction developing in exchange process: no actual material change to the commodity happens, physical events are at absolute minimum, no quantitative differentiation to the exchanged commodity is allowed etc.; what changes is the social status of ownership of the commodity). The sole fact that abstraction passes unnoticed is perhaps the most important practical outcome of what develops in everyday life activities.

2.4   The Fetishism of the Commodity

Marx's notion of fetishism[14] is a culmination of the processes mentioned in previous subsections. His conceptualisation was fully expanded in the chapter Fetishism of commodities in the first volume of *Capital* (Marx 1990/1867, 163–177). Harvey believes the concept of fetishism is an "essential tool for unravelling the mysteries of capitalist political economy" (Harvey 2010, 38). One of the consequences of fetishism, which is inseparable from the production of commodities, is in the fact that structural characteristics of capitalist production process are hidden. As noted by Fuchs (2011, 153), "commodity character of goods conceals that these goods exist only because they are produced by human labour within class relations." Several fundamental arguments, which are crucial for the conceptualisation of commodity fetishism, have already been implicitly noted earlier in the text and one is able to see what an immensely complex issue this is. It is thus not surprising when Marx notes that fetishism is inseparable from the production of commodities, while commodity is full of "metaphysical subtleties and theological niceties," transcending sensuousness as soon as it emerges; it can be both a sensuous and a suprasensible or social thing (Marx 1990/1867, 163, 165).

As stressed by Jhally (1987, 29), there are two major reasons for how and why fetishism arises: firstly, because of exchange of commodities; and secondly, because of the relationship between capital and labour (or to be more precise, between capitalists as a social class and the proletariat), which centres around

---

14   Balibar (2007, 63) points out how Marx realized that the money (as the general equivalent or universal commodity that can be exchanged for any other commodity) fetish is in fact nothing else than commodity fetish. This was only possible with a careful analysis of the commodity-form and the role of exchange-value in it, which was not present in Marx's earlier works. In these earlier works this particular social role, which he later ascribes to commodity, is in fact often attributed directly to money: "The complete domination of the estranged thing *over* man has become evident in *money*, which is completely indifferent both to the nature of the material, i.e., to the specific nature of the private property, and to the personality o the property owner. What was the domination of person over person is not the general domination of *thing* over the *person*, of the product over the producer. Just as the concept of the *equivalent*, the value, already implied the *alienation* of private property, so *money* is the sensuous, even objective existence of this *alienation*" (Marx and Engels 1975, 221).

waged labour and is constitutive of wider capitalist social relations. Both of these reasons have been thoroughly analysed already. Several critical communication scholars have dealt with commodity fetishism in their work (e.g. Jhally 1987; Maxwell 1991; Murdock 2006a; 2011; Fuchs 2011, 152–154). Jhally wrote about fetishism the following:

> In short, fetishism consists of seeing the meaning of things as an inherent part of their physical existence when in fact that meaning is created by their integration into a system of meaning. [...] For Marx, commodity fetishism consists of things seeming to have value inherent in them when in fact value is produced by humans: it is to naturalise a social process. Thus things appear to have value inherent in them. The essence however is that humans produce value. [...] It is quite clear that, for Marx, commodity fetishism and the mystery of the commodity concerns the false appearance of the commodity as possessing value in itself rather than as the result of labour. The theory of fetishism is indeed a theory of mystification.
>
> JHALLY 1987, 29, 39

With universalisation of the commodity-form in society, production of commodities is performed by individuals or groups that labour independently of each other because of the social division of labour. This means that the inherently social relations of production are only manifested in exchange (Jhally 1987, 29, 39); but, as already stressed, these relations are in fact hidden behind a material veil, behind the commodity itself. This material veil not only hides the social relations, but also abstract labour, which produces commodities in the production process (which is the site of an antagonistic relation between the owners and the expropriated labourers). Murdock (2011, 19) believes it is a crucial characteristic of the fetishism that people (understood as consumers of commodities) forget where commodities came from, instead thinking these issues away and enjoying the convenience and pleasure these commodities are supposed to bring. The final effect is abolishment of any talk of exploitative working conditions, of the labour process or of the environmental degradation. All attention when buying commodities and consuming them is focused solely on the commodity as the object of pleasure. This was for example identified as one of the key ideological elements in Disney comic books by Dorfman and Mattelart:

> The process of production has been eliminated, as has all reference to its genesis; the actors, the objects, the circumstances of the process never

existed. What, in fact, has been erased is the paternity of the object, and the possibility to link it to the process of production. [...] Objects are cleansed of guilt. It is a world of pure surplus without the slightest suspicion of a worker demanding the slightest reward. The proletariat, born out of the contradictions of the bourgeois regime, sell their labour 'freely' to the highest bidder, who transforms the labor into wealth for his own social class. In the Disney world, the proletariat are expelled from the society they created, thus ending all antagonisms, conflicts, class struggle and indeed, the very concept of class.

DORFMAN AND MATTELART 1975, 64–65

Commodity fetishism is therefore a prime example of what is usually defined as ideology (see also subchapter Media and ideology by Fuchs/2011, 152–154/), but it is an actually existing ideology that cannot simply be ignored or thought away, not an illusion. Commodity fetishism has an objective reality that is inevitable in capitalist societies, because it attaches itself to the commodity in the moment it is produced (Marx 1990/1867, 165). This is so, especially in the present context of the world division of labour and the global market. This *material* fetishistic construct veils what is in fact happening behind the market: specific social relations of labour exploitation. The aforementioned difference between appearance (the world of commodities) and essence (social relations of production) develops here in its entirety. It is thus especially through the fetish character of commodities that Marx's claim of the power of abstraction and dialectics is able to demonstrate its strength: He claimed their crucial characteristic is an ability to go beyond mere appearances of things.

An important consequence of commodity fetishism is that commodities thus exist independently of human beings, of those that in fact produce them, and assume a life of their own. But not only do they acquire independence from human beings, they become active and objective agents of their oppression (see Marx 1990/1867, 175; Barbalet 1983; Postone 2003/1993). As Harvey stresses, it is "market forces, which none of us individually control, [that] regulate us" in capitalist society. (Harvey 2010, 42).

The issue of commodity fetishism is in fact an "alternative" approach to the enduring problem of ideology. At least two diverging (to an extent, even conflicting) strands of critical analysis of ideology have developed in twentieth century Marxism. One is taking as a starting point commodity fetishism, taking commodity-form as an actually existing material veil that develops at the material level (in the base-superstructure model of society schemata) and amongst others includes theoreticians such as Lukács, Adorno, Sohn-Rethel or Postone (some of these authors developing from this point of departure concepts like reification or alienation). In critical communication studies such an approach to the base-superstructure formula has been taken especially by Smythe (1977; see Meehan 1993) and the authors participating in the audience commodity debate. In the other strand, in which one could include, for example Althusser or Žižek, the focus has been almost solely on the ideological level and apparatuses that produce ideology. It presides and develops through the level of superstructure, while being determined by the base, but in a different sense of the ownership of the means of production (i.e. the class in power is able to define ideology at the level of superstructure). Let us remember, Marx (see Marx and Engels 1987, 263) includes in the superstructure "the legal, political, religious, artistic or philosophic – in short, ideological forms" of life. Even though there is a relational approach between base and superstructure, in the latter approach, it is very much different from the former and leaves out questions concerning commodity fetishism. While for the latter ideology, it is solely a question of superstructure, the former sees ideology as the material veil produced by exchange of commodities; it is therefore a constitutive part of the material base from which it emerges (it can thus be seen as an immanent approach).

It is not the purpose of this chapter to present a detailed overview of these two approaches, but the former approach seems much closer, for example to Williams' (1973) reinterpretation of base and superstructure models or to Gramscian's (1971) concept of hegemony, which offers a viable alternative to the concept of ideology (both are close to Fuchs's (2011, 48–53) reconsideration of base and superstructure). In a Gramscian sense, one could claim that commodity fetishism is reproduced through everyday activities of human beings whether they want to or not, but it also demonstrates how the base is far from being static and without conflicts.[15] This approach largely encompasses material base, so to say production forces, production relations and conflicts and antagonisms emerging from this level of society. This is so, because the base is a precondition of the superstructure and also more fundamental than superstructure (to a large extent, base also restricts how superstructure functions, but it cannot determine it). This material level therefore in a significant sense forms and influences consciousness at the level of superstructure, which arises on this "real foundation," the material base; this seems to be much closer to what Marx himself claimed is actually happening in society, at least in comparison to where Althusser puts his focus. In his famous definition, given in the preface of *A Contribution to the Critique of Political Economy*, Marx points out that "the mode of production of material life conditions the general process of

---

15   This was most forcefully pointed out by Williams (1973) in his critique of mechanistic
      interpretations of the (often contradictory) relation between base and superstructure.

social, political and intellectual life," and furthermore, "it is not the consciousness of men that determines their existence, but their social existence that
determines their consciousness" (Marx and Engels 1987, 263).

Significantly, Sohn-Rethel's goal is precisely to research this relationship
between base and superstructure and to build a staircase between "productive
forces and production relations which together form the material basis for
consciousness as superstructure [...] The staircase must be given a firm anchor-
age in the basement, and this, for commodity-producing societies, can only be
found in the formal analysis of commodity itself" (Sohn-Rethel 1978, xi). For
the former approach, it is the material veil that is crucial to understand mystification in society and this material veil in fact exists (it cannot not exist in
capitalist societies, not least because social relations can never be direct,
unmediated (see Postone 2003/1993, 167)). It is obvious that people might
become conscious of class antagonisms at the level of ideology and fight out
this conflict by overtaking apparatuses in the superstructure, but this might
not change much if some of the basic categories at the material level stay the
same (for example dominance of the commodity-form and private ownership
of the means of production). This is also significant in the context of the really
existing socialisms.

2.5   Exchange as the Key Agent of Individualisation

Even though Marx's fundamental ontological position was that human beings
were social animals,[16] he was not naïve. In his time, a full-blown individualisation already took place and he acknowledged this was a society of free competition, where individuals seem detached from the natural bonds and are
emancipated from nature (in Marx's words, "the dissolution of the bondage
relations which fetter the worker to land and soil and to the lord of land and
soil" (Marx 1993/1858, 502)). Social relations already changed significantly and
individuals were largely independent from each other, at least in comparison
to the earlier historical periods, when they were a *part of a definite and limited
human conglomerate* (Marx's 1993/1858, 83–85; see also Barbalet 1983, ch. 3).

However, according to Marx, individualisation was not a natural condition
of human beings emerging from their human nature, which seemed to be a

---

16   Marx (1973/1993, 84) in fact speaks of a *political animal* (zoon politikon, πολιτικόν ζῷον).
        Hannah Arendt (1998/1958) was correct when she pointed out that Marx in fact conflated
        social with political realm, reducing Aristotles's notion of zoon politikon simply to social
        animal (for Arendt, there was a complete victory of society over political realm and public
        action in modern societies). Even though differences between these two conceptualiza-
        tions are important, they are not central for this text.

predominant philosophical position since the seventeenth century. It was a result of a definite historical process. According to him, a human being is, paradoxically, "an animal which can individuate itself only in the midst of society. Production by an isolated individual outside society [...] is as much of an absurdity as is the development of language without individuals living *together* and talking to each other" (Ibid., 84). For Hobsbawm, "this process of the emancipation of man from his original natural conditions of production" can thus be seen as "one of human *individualisation,*" exchange being one of its crucial agents (Hobsbawm 2011, 132). Human beings can thereby individualise themselves only through the process of commodity exchange and this is a self-reinforcing process.

As demonstrated by Barbalet (1983, 69f.; 89f.), Marx's claim in his earlier writings was that relations of human beings in capitalist societies were in fact unsocial; he claimed that in the capitalist epoch, they become external relations of independent and unsocial beings (which was a presupposition that was not far from that of liberal individualism).[17] When Marx's thought developed further, however, he changed his opinion, stating these relations "are merely a particular form of social relation, different in content from the relations of feudal society" (Barbalet 1983, 89). The capitalist historical epoch can in fact be seen as still having the most highly developed social relations, especially because of the nature of exchange and the role commodity plays in society (as mentioned earlier). It does however produce spatial rather than direct relations, while also functioning completely beyond the will or control of actors themselves (Barbalet 1983, 90f.).

Commodity transactions of course carry no particular social or reciprocal obligations, as was the case with preceding divergent types of moral economies that were dominant before the rise of political economy (see Thompson 1991, ch. 4; ch. 5; Murdock 2011). Crucially then, the commodity-form is "not only the basis of individualised society, it is also the root of the view that the individual is without social relations" (Barbalet 1983, 92), a predominant ontological presupposition especially in liberal, libertarian and other individualist outlooks on the world.

---

17   In his *Comments on James Mill* Marx (1975, 220) for example claims that "the greater and the more developed the social power appears to be within the private property relationship, the more *egoistic*, asocial and estranged from his own nature does man become. Just as the mutual exchange of the products of *human activity* appears as *barter*, as trade, so the mutual completion and exchange of the activity itself appears as *division of labour*, which turns man as far as possible into an abstract being, a machine tool, etc., and transforms him into a spiritual and physical monster."

3   The Global Commodification of Everything: The Long History

> What is open about capitalism is its dynamic of expansion (of accumula-
> tion, of appropriation, of imperialism). But this dynamic is also a doom
> and a necessity: the system cannot not expand; if it remains stable, it
> stagnates and dies; it must continue to absorb everything in its path, to
> interiorize everything that was hitherto exterior to it.
>
>   FREDRIC JAMESON (2011, 146)

The history of capitalism has, amongst other things, also been a history of a
never-ending (global) commodification. As noted by Marx (1993/1858, 408),
"the tendency to create the world market is directly given in the concept of
capital itself. Every limit appears as a barrier to be overcome." Nowadays, issues
connected to the sustained processes of commodification are not limited to the
supposedly radical margins of social sciences as they were in the past. Awareness
of these on-going transformations became important both in the more popular
media discourse and in mainstream academic research. According to Wittel:

> There seems to be a broad consensus that commodification is a fact, the
> capitalist market has become increasingly powerful, pervasive and hege-
> monic, the logic of the capitalist market colonises and destroys the logic
> of community, and that the market swallows more and more areas and
> aspects of life that hitherto have not been regulated by monetary mea-
> surement and monetary exchange.
>
>   WITTEL 2013, 315

However, the term commodification has, in many of these analyses, been
replaced by euphemisms such as *financialization, marketization, monetization*,
or simply "the reign of money." Martin (2002), for example, deployed the concept of the *financialization of everyday life*, claiming that money has become
both the means and the final goal of human lives. Because financialization
broke beyond the corporate world into the households of the ordinary people,
this forces them continuously to act and think like capitalists, even though
they have little to no capital (Ibid, 12). Simultaneously, they are accepting risk
(formerly dealt with by professionals) into their homes and into their everyday
activities. The lives of many people, claimed Martin (Ibid, 5), are becoming an
endless business school course, and every possible moment consequently
needs to be turned into an opportunity to make money.

Martin is not alone in his observations. Sandel (2012) has recently posited
very similar questions. Seemingly endless expansion of market relations prompts

him to ask the question, "What money can't buy?" Leaving capitalism to its own expansionary logic, any strict limits to its penetrating abilities seem illusory, and it seems Sandel agrees with this notion. Economics "is becoming an imperial domain," because it "increasingly governs the whole of life" (Ibid, 6), he laments. This is because "almost everything can be bought and sold," and markets "have come to govern our lives as never before." (Ibid., 5).

What seems equally important to the findings is the fact that both Martin and Sandel say these new "marketized" relations were not arrived at by any conscious or autonomous decision of the people that succumbed to it. These conditions in fact slowly but surely became a part of individuals' lives and encroached upon their everyday activities without any visible coercion. What would never be considered self-evident a couple of decades ago, today seems almost beyond dispute, an unquestionable imperative of human agency fully subjected to market forces. Because of an overwhelming intensification of social commodification, rationalistic calculation and measurement have become part and parcel of human activities and relations, while exchange-value equivalence and factual abstraction have simultaneously become the norm for many individuals in their everyday operations.[18]

Critical communication and social studies have, in fact, long been aware of this social transformation. Herbert Schiller (1984, xiv) observed three decades ago that "the penetration of corporate power and corporate thinking is now so extensive that the calculus of business performance has become the almost automatic measurement of individual purpose and achievement." In Marxist and other radical political-economic approaches – including those in the field of critical communication studies (e.g. Murdock 2006a; Mosco 1989; 2009, ch. 7; D. Schiller 2007; Fuchs 2014, 52–53) – these processes have fallen under the umbrella of theories that analyse the role of the commodity-form and commodification in capitalist societies.[19]

---

18   Livant's (1979, 105) lucid observation speaks volumes in this case. He points out that "the main impetus to the rise of measurement is the rise of commodity production. Where something begins to be measured it is an almost sure sign it is being traded."

19   Both Bettig (1996, 34) and Gandy (1992) write about *radical* political economy of communication, which is a similar differentiation to the one that is made by Winseck in his own typology (see: Winseck 2011, 21–25). While it is mostly Marxist approaches that fall under the umbrella of radical and critical political-economic approaches, some authors are not using an *explicitly* Marxian theoretical framework, but can nevertheless be considered as critical scholars, because they reflect on the social inequalities and provide a critique of the capitalism, adopt a deeply historical perspective, use dialectics to discern key structural developments in the society, while at the normative level they argue for a *better and more equitable world that could fulfil human potentials.* Such authors were either influenced

The concept of commodification, contrary to the commonly used euphemisms mentioned earlier, necessarily looks beyond appearances, into the structural causes of the existing capitalist relations in wider society, which makes it a more extensive concept (Mosco 2009, ch. 7). Commodity-form is one of the *cell forms* of capitalism, as Marx (1990/1867, 90) put it, and only in capitalism is a "collection of commodities" considered an "elementary form of wealth" (Heinrich 2012, 39–41). Commodification of diverse social processes and spheres, which enables an endless global accumulation of capital, is consequently the defining characteristic of historical capitalism: it enables its further expansion and reproduction (Wallerstein 1983, ch. 1). At the same time, one should not overlook that one of the defining characteristics of the commodity-form is that it is necessarily produced in the capitalist production process, which necessarily puts focus on the (un)waged labouring processes, the relations of production, and exploitative practices (Marx 1990/1867). Furthermore, commodities are necessarily produced *for* the market and exchanged *on* the market in the capitalist production (D. Schiller 2007, 21).

3.1   *Capitalism: The Many-Headed Hydra*

The capitalist system can only have one objective when operating, i.e. to accumulate capital (and even more capital). This is done by the holders of capital. A specific type of society with certain relations between people had to be established for this to be possible. Even though capitalism has been naturalised and one usually finds it difficult to think of alternatives, especially as this system has been fully embedded for so long, its development was difficult and full of obstacles.[20] In his attempt to explain why capitalism emerged as a social system, Wallerstein (1983, 40) writes that it is not so easy to provide answers to this question, as it might seem at first. Far from being a natural system, as its

---

somehow by Marxist thinking, see themselves as neo-Marxists, or adopt a theoretic framework that is similar to the one used by Marx. The most obvious example is perhaps Herbert I. Schiller, who was not explicitly a Marxist because of practical reasons (namely McCarthyian and other anti-communist witch-hunts), but also took his inspiration from other approaches (Maxwell /2003, 4/ for example writes about "radical eclecticism") (see: Maxwell 2003; Murdock 2006b). Fuchs (2014, 52–53) provides a somewhat more strict definition of the approaches that can be defined as being critical. In his opinion there were two main schools that provided a critical insight to the media, communication and culture: Critical Political Economy of the Media and Critical Theory, first one being rooted in economic theory, and the second one in philosophy and social theory.

20   Wallerstein (1983, 18) writes how an endless accumulation of capital has been the sole objective that prevailed in economic activities, but as penetration of these processes entered the social fabric, so did the opposition to these processes grow greater and louder.

apologists claim, it is in fact a patently absurd one: "One accumulates capital in order to accumulate more capital. Capitalists are like white mice on a treadmill, running ever faster in order to run still faster" (Wallerstein 1983, 40). As he stresses (Wallerstein 1983, 15), the whole circuit of capital was only seldom completed before modern times; several links were missing, meaning several processes were not yet transacted through the market, which means they were not yet commodified. For Wallerstein (1983, ch. 1), historical capitalism thus, first and foremost, presents itself as a process of a widespread commodification of different social processes, with it forming complex commodity chains (that in time become global). It is not merely a question of exchange processes, but also of commodification of production, distribution, and investment processes.[21]

As Jameson (2011) lately pointed out, commodity is not only a prerequisite to capitalist processes of accumulation, it actually constitutes "pre-history" of capital and is therefore strictly speaking "not yet about capital." Even though Jameson's contribution is an important one, this statement seems at least partially problematic. The commodity-form is not only an enduring prerequisite of capitalist accumulation, but also its ever-present and constitutive part (similarly to primitive accumulation), which on the most fundamental level enables extraction of surplus value. Looking at the process of capitalist accumulation from a dialectical point of view, which Jameson himself strongly supports, it is impossible to separate the commodity from exchange and surplus value (historically speaking, they ought to develop simultaneously). The commodity-form is a crucial cell-form in every sphere of the cycle of capital accumulation (for a good overview of the expanded reproduction of capital and cycle of capitalist accumulation see Fuchs's overview (2011, 137–141)) and even though the

---

21   It might be appropriate to distinguish between commercialization, commodification and objectification, three processes that are, as pointed out by Mosco (2009, 132f.), usually associated. Commercialization could also be called marketization and it is the narrowest of the three processes. It refers to what is happening on the surface of the capitalist economy, so to say, on the transparently visible market: in the exchange process, the sphere of circulation. In communication studies commercialization/marketization would for example refer to the relationship created between audiences and advertisers (ibid.). Capitalist market necessarily encompasses a lot more that just exchange relations of this kind; as already pointed out, it for example presupposes commodification of labour that produces commodities and should therefore also encompass the production process. In this sense commodification, which is the main focus of political economy of communication, is a much broader notion. Lastly, objectification refers especially to specific process of dehumanisation. Lukács (ibid.; 1971) for example used the word reification to denote how human beings and personal relations become *thing-like* (ibid.). Not everything that is objectified is necessarily a commodity of course.

production process, for example, might seem primary, capitalism cannot exist without reproducing itself via commodification, which enables its further expansion, and without commodity-form as one of its integral parts.

Whether one agrees with him on the mentioned issue or not, Jameson also acknowledges that in a social period, which is dominated by commodification, this process plays a crucial political role for an enduring critique of existing society. While Murdock (2006a) wrote about the *commodification of almost everything*, both Wallerstein and Jameson went further, stating it is in fact *everything* that can be commodified. According to Jameson (2011, 16, 26), in a capitalist society, commodification becomes tendentially universal and one can speak of the tendential dominion of the commodity-form. Similarly, Wallerstein points out that "the process of global accumulation is developing via the commodification of everything" (Wallerstein 2001/1991, 24f.).

Murdock explains how "only in a fully developed capitalist system is the production and marketing of commodities the central driving force of growth and profit" (Murdock 2011, 18). The world market is thereby a crucial development in capitalism (Hobsbawm 2011, 145) and we can claim that in the last decades it finally developed in its entirety, constructing a universalised totality where everything can become subsumed under the rule of capital (Hardt and Negri 2001). Processes of commodification are crucial for this expansion of capitalism together with primitive accumulation (or *accumulation as dispossession*). This constant expansion is also one of its unavoidable necessities, because without constant expansion, a capitalist system is in crisis. It is thus fair to say that commodification is reshaping the world in its own image, which led Huws to state that this process can be seen as central in understanding social changes. With commodification, she has in mind "the tendency of capitalist economies to generate new and increasingly standardised products for sale in the market whose sale will generate profits that increase in proportion to the scale of production" (Huws 2003, 17).

As stressed by Polanyi (2001/1944, ch. 6), there is, however, also a constant need for *commodity fiction* to legitimise the selling of different types of commodities on the market, which can serve as a constant reminder of the extreme artificiality of the capitalist market economy. This is especially obvious when market relations in certain spheres are still in the process of being established and have not been subordinated to commodity exchange beforehand. The great transformation from a feudalist to a capitalist society, as Polanyi called it, required new fictitious commodities for the successful functioning of new economic relations, most evidently labour force, money, and land. In an ongoing transformation to postmodernity, one can, on the other hand, establish that we are experiencing a historical epoch that is increasingly void of non-commodified

products, processes, or activities, which can all be willy-nilly subsumed and sub-
dued under *economistic* rationalisation.[22] In their chapter on culture industry,
Horkheimer and Adorno (2002/1947, ch. 4) anticipated such a development of
capitalist societies, pointing at the commodifying processes taking place. But
even their analysis could hardly be ascribed with the prediction that capital will
be able to colonise almost all spheres of society, meaning that nearly all aspects
of human life can be comprehended as a possible investment or a market opportunity. Capitalism has therefore not incorporated only cultural production, public places and creativity, or, more widely speaking, social symbols, into its
accumulation cycle. At first, it really made an industry out of culture and human
artistic creativity (Adorno 2001/1991; Horkheimer and Adorno 2002/1947, ch. 4).
But in time, it was not only symbols, public expression and ideas that were (as
today) constantly being commodified, but also knowledge and information as
such, while both categories are becoming an integral part of capitalism in postmodern societies (see Schiller 1989, Parker 1994, Fleissner 2009, May 2010). And
as Marazzi (2008) points out, information and communication are not only raw
materials, but also a labour instrument (*cf.* Williams 2005/1980, ch. 2). Information
and knowledge became commodities as any other, bought and sold, producing
aggregation of resources in the cultural and information sphere. Herbert Schiller
called this the *consciousness industry*, while indicating "the entrance of the profit
motive into fields, which for different reasons, historically had escaped this now
pervasive force" (Schiller 1989, 91). Entirely new private industries have been
developed and, in most cases, these same industries are exerting vast influence
on how we think and act in our everyday lives (see also Jhally 1987, Hardt 2004).
These privatisation and commodification processes on the other hand also constitute new monopolies of knowledge that have historically been typical of all
human societies (see Innis, 2008/1951).

  Debord's (1970, ch. 2) account of the role played by commodity-form in postmodern societies, fully submerged in the spectacle, remains one of the most
powerful accounts of the world, in which we live, ever written. He touches on
the domination of the commodity over the totality of human living and presents spectacle as a permanent opium war, which feeds itself in, and through,
the world of commodities. Everything is incorporated into the world market

---

22   What Polanyi failed to notice was that it was not only land, labour, and money that were
      fictitious commodities. *All* commodities are fictitious. There is no such thing as a "natu-
      ral" commodity. The simple difference is that some commodities quite obviously need
      some sort of an ideological underpinning (or an underlying fiction) to socially legitimize
      them as commodities that are bought and sold, while commodity-status of others is
      rarely questioned, especially when they are already successfully legitimized as commodi-
      ties in a specific society.

and changed in the way it satisfies the rules made by the capitalist type of economy and its instrumental rationalisation. Because commodity is independent of anything, it can autonomously rule over both the entire economy and society; social life thereby becomes completely colonised. The spectacle is, for Debord in fact "the moment when the commodity has attained the total occupation of social life. The relation to the commodity is not only visible, but one no longer sees anything but it: the world one sees is its world." (Debord's 1970, ch. 2, par. 42) Everything is submerged in the spectacle and the complete rule of the world of commodities fulfils itself through the spectacle. Debord's focus was at least indirectly pointed towards the mass media and a society flushed with images – and it is only after decades that most theoreticians admit that we live in fully mediatised societies. To put it in Debord's words, yet again, we have to recognise in these symptoms "our old enemy: the commodity." (Debord's 1970, ch. 2, par. 35).

It is quite possible that Debord's critique of contemporary life was (perhaps even rightly so) seen as an exaggeration when it was written almost five decades ago. But most of Debord's observations look increasingly obvious in the fully developed postmodern society where human sociability, affects and communication as such are transformed into commodities and exchanged. Expansion of commodification has now extended work and exploitation well beyond the factory floors and into the other spheres of everyday human lives (Smythe 1977; Terranova 2004; Marazzi 2008; Fuchs 2012a; Crary 2013; Fuchs and Sevignani 2013).[23] This expansion of commodification to communication in its widest sense therefore also means that these issues must become central topics of the political economy of communication, which simultaneously also needs to widen its scope of inquiry as much as possible and provide a critique of these invasive processes.

3.2   The Dialectics of Social Transformation and the Information Revolution

The mark of some successful dialectic is shock, surprise, and the undermining of preconceived notions.

FREDRIC JAMESON (2007, 196)

---

23   Several authors have extensively written on this topic (see Section 5). In Marazzi's (2008, 50) opinion "today the capitalist organization of work aims to overcome this separation, to *fuse* work and worker, to *put to work the entire lives* of workers." Crary (2013) has similarly pointed out there is a 24/7 logic in contemporary capitalism: non-stop consumption, exploitation, and commodification, an idea of constant work without any pauses or limits, spreading throughout society.

Historical accounts tracing the emergence of culture, information, and communication as somehow relevant parts of capitalist production and accumulation (the *material base*) usually extend only as far back as the second half of the twentieth century. In this historical period, there was supposedly a radical socioeconomic transformation, a clean break with the past that brought about the *information society*, which would abolish the antagonistic class relations and thoroughly alter the labour-capital relationship. Theories that developed the notion of an information society and a *post-industrial society* pointed at several mechanisms that contributed to this radical historical break, but the sharply increasing social and, especially, economic importance of the information resources was, in all likelihood, crucial. This was the so-called *information revolution*, which supposedly resulted from the new ICTs.[24]

Significantly, this historical period, as Herbert Schiller (1973, 13) pointed out at the time, was in fact "one of the most spectacular decades of social conflict and manipulative control in the United States' history." The end of the 1960s and the beginning of the following decade saw an almost worldwide rise of the New Left, persistent student protests, and new social movements that brought to the fore new political issues and conflicts (Offe 1987). These perturbations can, at least to an extent, also be seen in the light of the on-going process of decolonization that exposed serious worldwide inequalities and continuing dependencies of the nations that were now formally independent, these dependencies being implemented through both cultural imperialism and neo-imperialist practices (H. Schiller 1969; 1976; Harvey 2003, ch. 2; Thussu 2006, 24–37, 46–55). Cultural imperialism and cultural dependency were not a question of conspiracy or manipulation, but a structural fact according to Mattelart (2000, 67), main reason being unequal information and communication exchange on a world-scale.

It was this antagonistic social context that made Bell's proclamations of the "end of ideology" even more incomprehensible (or, perhaps, revealed it to be wishful thinking). What today seems plausible is that the primary (even if implicit and unintentional) consequence of the information society theories was to legitimize a comprehensive political-economic and wider societal reorganisation, which would provide a new social stability in the time of political perturbations and looming systemic economic crisis, as the existing mode of capitalist accumulation process reached its limits (Offe 1984). Critical authors, after all, promptly demystified key presuppositions contained in these theories and successfully demonstrated that societies will remain deeply embedded in the inequalities and asymmetries that are distinctive of capitalism, *even if*

---

24   For a critical account see for example Mosco (1989), May (2002), D. Schiller (2007, ch. 1),
       Fuchs (2012b).

information resources are in fact gaining in importance (Dyer-Witheford 1999, 77; cf. Dupuy 1980; Splichal 1981; Mosco 1982; 1989). Several authors today agree that the last few decades have, in fact, brought about a consolidation of capitalism and a deepening of commodification, consequently increasing economic inequalities and prompting new antagonistic conflicts between capital and labour.[25]

Looking at the surface of things, it therefore seems that we are confronted with a considerable contradiction. On the one hand, we are forced to acknowledge that, in the past few decades, there has indeed been an important reconstruction, not only of the existing mode of capitalist production and accumulation (new one often being labelled as *post-Fordist*), but also of the wider social fabric and of our everyday lives. This change is in large part owed to the increasing role played by information resources, communication, and knowledge, all of which have gained in economic importance. Mosco (1982; 1989), for example, was in the 1980s already debunking fantasies about the radically different social order that had supposedly originated from the changes brought by the new ICTs. However, at the same time, he also indicated that information had indeed become "vital to corporate capital accumulation" (Mosco 1982, 46). Similarly, Dan Schiller (2007, 24), another author who is very critical of the information society theories, points out that "Often supported by telecommunications infrastructures, information has become an increasingly significant factor of production across all economic sectors."

The insights that would simultaneously theorize both social continuity and discontinuity seem in stark opposition to the popular discourse in which *everything* has changed in the last decades because of the rise of the new technologies. They also go against some of the more orthodox authors in the field of critical political economy who even today often claim there was *no* relevant change *at all* in society and in how capitalism operates in the present historical phase.[26] Eran Fisher (2010) analysed the celebratory discourse connected to the network technologies and new ICTs and called it the *digital discourse*,

---

25   See Dyer-Witheford (1999), May (2002, ch. 2), Mosco (1989; 2009, 75, 120), McChesney, Wood and Bellamy Foster (1998), D. Schiller (2000; 2007), Fisher (2010), Fuchs (2008; 2011; 2012b) and other authors writing in the broad field of political economy of communication.

26   Fuchs (2012b, 2–6) provides a detailed critical assessment of the discontinuity and continuity theories of information society. As he points out: "In its extreme form, the continuity hypothesis is the claim that contemporary society does not differ in any significant way from nineteenth-century capitalism." (Ibid., 6) Both discontinuity and continuity approaches are intellectually close to techno-deterministic theories that disregard the ever-present power relations in specific social context.

pointing out that *the spirit of networks* embedded in it is dominant in academia, political and economic circles and especially in the popular jargon (he analysed the hyper-celebratory discourse of the *Wired* magazine) (cf. Mosco 2009). This hyper-optimistic discourse can be contrasted with a diametrically opposite one, which is, for example, present in Doogan's (2009) work. He provides a critique of what he terms the *new capitalism* on "the ideological, methodological and empirical basis of the societal transformation" (Doogan 2009, 4). While one can agree with his main argument that there is a need to provide a critique of the theories of radical discontinuity, for Doogan even using concepts such as knowledge, *informationalism* or networks is "nebulous," because they are "difficult to pin down and [are] resistant to close scrutiny, while globalization is a term whose usage is perhaps inversely proportional to the precision of its meaning." (Ibid., 5) It seems that for Doogan every theory which even suggests there was *any* relevant social change "rests upon an idealized representation of contemporary society." (Ibid., 6) It is "devoid of the materialist iconography," (Ibid.) and this holds true whether one is reading insights by Harvey, Bell, Castells, Beck, Bauman, Boltanski and Chiapello, or Sennet; their theories are all the same in the way they privilege discontinuity and "over determine the role of technological change." In Doogan's (Ibid.) view we thus need to "*rematerialize* an understanding of social change."

Such a generalizing and overarching assessment of even those approaches that are very critical in analysing the present social changes seems far-fetched and (indeed) *nebulous*. However, even if we concede that there were important changes in capitalist accumulation, we must also inevitably recognize that the system in its essence has remained capitalist. There was consequently no drastic change in the basic political economic organization of the social order – unlike what affirmative apologists claimed would happen – a conclusion most authors writing in the field of political economy of communication were (and still are) in full agreement. The changes in the new technologies therefore brought about a deepening, expansion, and acceleration of the capitalist accumulation and commodification on the one hand, and an intensification of control on the other, and not some kind of social revolution (Mosco 1989, 34–35).

One possible way of resolving this apparent contradiction between social continuity and discontinuity is by adopting the historical method of thinking from critical theory. We must radically historicize the key categories we are investigating, demonstrating that they are historically transitive and malleable. As Bonefeld (2009, 125) would have put it, echoing Marx and Engels, "historical materialism is the critique of things understood as dogmatic. It melts and dissolves all that appears solid." Furthermore, we must also turn to dialectics, which will help us to (re)think these internal contradictions related to the complex mutual relationship between social change and continuity. Fredric Jameson (1998, 171; cf. Marx 1973/1990, 103) pointed out that it enables us to simultaneously think two faces of history "which we otherwise seem ill-equipped to think: namely identity and difference all at once, the way in which a thing can both change and remain the same, can undergo the most astonishing mutations and expansions and still constitute the operation of some basic and persistent structure."

Fuchs (2012b; cf. 2014, 53–55) has in a way similar to Jameson's account of dialectics used Adorno's dialectical approach for his critique of both the approaches that see societal changes in the terms of radical discontinuity on the one hand, and on the other hand those that see no changes at all (theories of radical continuity). As Fuchs points out we live *both* in capitalism and in an informational society: "In terms of critical, dialectical theory, contemporary society is an information society according to the state of its *forces* of production. In contrast, however, contemporary society is capitalist in its *relations* of production." (Fuchs 2012b, 18; 2014, 55) A similar distinction was made earlier by Douglas and Guback (1984) and by May (2002, 42–43). They all pointed out that even if one can talk about a technological revolution (in the forces of production), the relations of production could not only remain the same, but could in fact be consolidated even further. But as Fuchs (2012b, 16) furthermore notes, even if informational character of global companies is increasing in importance, it remains "a non-dominant trend," as both finance and fossil fuels for example remain more important. It is thus, in his opinion (Ibid.), "financialization, hyperindustrialization, and informatization [that] characterize contemporary imperialist capitalism."

By adopting a materialist perspective, the concept of the so-called information revolution must therefore be connected to the increased *social* need for information in the current historical epoch. A key characteristic that has accompanied this emerging social need in the last few decades – which was, in its essence, a result of the existing social relations of power – is that information and communication have finally and completely constituted themselves as commodities that are bought and sold on the market. Two decades ago, Melody (1993, 75; cf. Hesmondhalgh 2008, 97) pointed out how "information that previously was outside the marked and not included as economic activity has now been drawn into the market." In May's (2002, 129) view, similarly, the *age of information* therefore "does not change the character of capitalism," it does however "require the renewal of certain aspects of property law, most importantly the reconfiguring of intellectual property rights. The information age has prompted the extension of intellectual property into areas previously unavailable for commodification." (cf. May 2010) New ICTs that were developed and also made possible this technological infrastructure can be seen as influential, but by no means determining factors, contributing to the social changes as information is produced, processed, and transmitted through these new communication channels.

It is, however, a historical fact that commodification of communication, information, and culture commenced long before the emergence of the so-called post-industrial/information society and also long before the constitution of the heavily enlarged cultural industries. Information has therefore for a long time been produced for the capitalist market, but never to such an extent as in the current historical context. Alas, *even if* communication and information have now fully constituted themselves as key commodities inside the capitalist accumulation process and the capitalist market, neither their social influence nor commodification started with the rise of the information society, as ideologically biased ahistorical theories claim. (see Headrick 2000; D. Schiller 2007).

3.3   *Commodifying Communication and Information in the Longue Durée*

> Each 'current event' brings together movements of different origins, of a different rhythm: today's time dates from yesterday, the day before yesterday, and all former times.
>
> FERNAND BRAUDEL (1980, 34)

Human societies have always been based on both communication and information. Language-capacity and communication can, in fact, be seen as defining characteristics of human societies. Hardt (1979, 19) points out that communication is "a basic social process involving individuals. In fact, communication becomes the sine qua non of human existence and the growth of society." Similarly for Mosco (2009, 67), "communication is a social process of exchange, whose product is the mark or embodiment of a social relationship. Broadly speaking, communication and society are mutually constituted." As noted by Melody (1993, 75), "detailed investigation certainly would show that societies have always been information based," which consequently means that "the changes of recent years have been primarily in the market characteristics of information."

Because both communication and information have always been fundamental parts of human societies, Headrick (2000, ch. 1) wrote it is consequently also impossible to define when *the information society* in fact started. We are, however, able to define different historical epochs in which the wider importance of information in a certain social context has been intensified, both in the sense of the amount of information to which people have access, and in the sense of the changes in the information systems that are crucial for the management, organization, transformation, and storing of information. At most it is therefore possible to define *several* information revolutions according to Headrick (2000), not only one that supposedly started in the middle of the twentieth century. These revolutions have always been put in motion by cultural, political, and economic upheavals of the times and were closely connected to existing social needs; undoubtedly they were responses to the demands for information (and their overall organization), echoing the wider power relations in societies.

The so-called information revolution we have been witnessing in recent decades should, therefore, only be seen as a long revolution, as Williams (2011/1961) named the long-term processes of transformation. The changes he analysed were happening in different spheres of culture, politics and economy, and in his view could not be considered as being separate from each other, as they dialectically intertwined. For Williams (2011/1961, 10) long revolution should be considered as "a genuine revolution, transforming men and institutions," yet it is at the same time "a difficult revolution to define, and its uneven action is taking place over so long a period that it is almost impossible not to get lost in its exceptionally complicated process." (Ibid.) The changes that accompanied the not-so-recent rise in the importance of communication, culture and information resources, points at a similar long-term change, one that developed as a part of an ever-changing capitalist economic system, while simultaneously overlapping with contradictory and deep structural transformation in the wider social order.

The latest information revolution can, according to Headrick (2000, ch. 7), quite possibly be traced back several centuries into the past, or at least to the second part of the nineteenth century, if we follow Winseck's and Pike's (2007) analysis. They point out how this was the historical period when global communications infrastructure was developed and first utilized, mostly owing to the emergence of deep globalization: that is, the expansion of the world markets, the rise of multinational companies and financial institutions, and the intensification of capital flows and global commodity exchange (Ibid.). At the time, global communication infrastructure was closely connected to these globalizing tendencies, including the development of new technologies. International commodity exchange and the increasingly global division of labour propelled the need for fast international communication, as successfully overcoming time-space constraints was often of fundamental importance (because it could also mean an important competitive advantage in the market). These tendencies had already been noted by Marx (see Melody 1993,

68–70; Dyer-Witheford 1999, 38–42; Fuchs 2011, 141–160) and were especially closely observed by another German political economist, Karl Knies, who wrote detailed analyses of communications and transportation systems, including two monographs, addressing, respectively, railroads and the telegraph, which were both published in the 1850s (see Hardt 2001, ch. 4).

The close connection between communications infrastructure, information and communication flows, media and culture, and the underlying economic transformation was closely observed by several other authors long before the formal emergence of communication studies in the twentieth century. In his historical analysis of journalism, Bücher (1893/1901, 241), one of the founding fathers of the German *Zeitungswissenschaft*, for example, pointed out that "The sole aim of this cursory survey of the modern development of journalism" was "to show how the gathering of the news has been conditioned at each epoch by general conditions of trade." His materialist and historical approach to the analysis of newspaper even today provides us with several important insights.[27] Bücher (Ibid, 225–226) was, in fact, one of the first authors to demonstrate that news-agencies and journalism first developed as businesses in Venice and Rome in the fifteenth century. This would mark the starting point of the historical period when transmission of the news via commercial correspondence became a source of profit. As historians in the field of media and communication studies have indicated, Venice was in fact the first city in Europe in which printing and publishing became an important type of business, and this development also included laws regulating the printing and publishing trade, which can be considered as precursors to the copyright system (Bettig 1996, 15–16). Even more importantly, it is crucial to note that the emergence of a *news-for-profit* rationale historically and spatially overlapped with Arrighi's (1994) and Braudel's (1977) account of the historical rise of capital. According to their analyses, the "first great phase" of capitalism as a social system started in the northern Italian city-states around the fifteenth century, and this included Venice as one of the key financial centres of the time.

As pointed out by Dan Schiller (2007, 35), "Cultural and informational commodification commenced not after, but within, the acute social struggles marking the transition to capitalism." These processes were, therefore, a part and parcel of structural changes and social struggles that accompanied the social transformation into capitalism (Smythe 1954, 31–34; H. Schiller 1996, 35;

---

27 Bücher was not a Marxist and his approach cannot be defined as historically materialist in the Marxian use of this term. His analysis however was both deeply historical and also materialist in the sense of a long-standing philosophical split between idealist and materialist approaches to the social ontology (see for example Hay 2002, ch. 6).

Hardt 2001, ch.1; D. Schiller 2007, 34–35). But these developments were neither self-evident nor indispensable; in many cases, they were accompanied by social conflicts and opposition, and were actively countered by more or less unsuccessful uprisings against the capitalist enclosure. Williams (2011/1961, 191), for example, noted that there were already several publishing houses in England in the sixteenth century, however commodity exchange of books was still considered vulgar at that time and there was consequently significant resistance against the publishing market.

The emergence of modern IPRS was, at least from today's point of view, one of the more important changes, with vast (and unplanned) consequences that we are still in the process of fully comprehending. In their historical analyses of the gradual transformation of information and culture into a special type of commodity, both Dan Schiller (2007) and Bettig (1996, 22–23) have pinpointed the eighteenth century as a crucial historical moment, when legal regulation of IPRS first appeared in England (cf. Hesmondhalgh 2009, ch. 5). Because these rights spread to human creativity, they also enabled its commodification. But, even before that, at the end of the seventeenth century, there was a considerable growth in the size of the reading public, which dialectically contributed to an expansion of the production and circulation of newspapers, books, magazines, and, consequently, also constituted a considerable expansion in the commodification of information and media (Williams 2011/1961, 192–193; Headrick 2000, ch. 1). The newspaper is, for example, often considered to be a product of the commercial middle class in the eighteenth century, since it provided them with crucial business information essential for their activities (Williams 2011/1961, 208, 222; Mosco 1989, 50). Because these early newspapers were still limited to a relatively narrow circle of people, a real reading revolution in England, which was followed by a vast market expansion of the press, only happened in the nineteenth century, especially between 1830 and 1850, when the first market speculators emerged. Writing became an important part of commodity exchange in England at that time and also led to a transformation of the media and press into typical capitalist industries; a process that was fully consolidated only at the start of the twentieth century (see Williams 2011/1961, 200; 1962).

A very similar historical development of the press to that which occurred in England could be observed in most developed capitalist countries, for example, in the US, where business imperatives in the media prevailed in the nineteenth century; this meant that both news and, later, advertising space, became important commodities (Schudson 1978). At around the same time, the first modern press agencies were founded around the world (Thussu 2006, 9–10) and there were also vast changes in postal services and telecommunications throughout the nineteenth century, which provided infrastructure for the distribution of communication and information as commodities (see Headrick 2000, ch. 6; Pike and Winseck 2007). According to Mattelart (2000, 23–24) it was exactly the rise of the major European news agencies and their international orientation throughout the 1870s that ultimately marked the rise of the market in information on a global scale.[28]

Hesmondhalgh (2007, 57) distinguished between three stages in which texts have been commodified: *First* stage occurred in the fifteenth century and was connected to the commodification of tangible objects, such as books; *Second* stage has been occurring from the eighteenth century onwards with the emergence of IPRs and is connected to the information contained *within* tangible object as 'the work'; *Third* stage, which we are currently witnessing and which first emerged with the late twentieth century, is commodification of the *access* to the information (e.g. via electronic databases). Commodification of access prompted Mosco (1989) to write about *Pay-Per Society*, whereas Rifkin (2000) labelled the present historical context as *the age of access*. As one can see, further restrictions to access and its commodification intensified, when the importance of intangible goods as such increased; this mainly happened because it became easier to reproduce them, which became particularly evident with digitalization.

Authors writing about the rise of the so-called information society in most cases have failed to grasp this longer historical genealogy because of the implicit technological determinism that was a part of their theories (Dyer-Witheford 1999; D. Schiller 2007). Because of historical ignorance, they failed to notice that information resources had been subject to capitalist economic relations much earlier. What was happening throughout the twentieth century was, in fact, a long-term and continuous expansion of commodification in this field, which was closely connected to the development of capitalism.

> Against those accounts that see the information society in terms of technological revolution, it is also important to emphasise that the appropriation of information and information resources has always been a constitutive aspect of capitalist societies quite outside of any technological context. [...] The gathering, recording, aggregation, and exploitation of information can be – and has been – achieved on the basis of minimal technological support.
>
> ROBINS AND WEBSTER 2004, 63

---

28   At the time three major European news agencies—German Wolff, British Reuters, and French Havas—were also the only agencies that were international in their scope. They made a cartel pact (treaty of alliance) in 1870s, through which they divided the world into territories of influence. This cartel lasted for over fifty years. (Mattelart 2000, 23–34).

Instead of directing our focus on the rise of the new ICTs as the main incentive that supposedly produced changes in society, we are therefore bound to point to the diverging and changing types of access to the management and control of information (Ibid,), which nowadays are mainly dependent on financial considerations and are going through new encosures. These continuing changes have established new economic – and with them social – inequalities; for example an unequal access to formerly public information and culture, *information poverty*, and an intensification of global dependencies because of the concentration of communication capacity and information is in the hands of the biggest capitalist conglomerates and corporations.[29] In any case, communication, culture, and information were being produced as commodities centuries ago, but their role in the overall capitalist production and wider accumulation process only slowly became as influential as it is today.

3.4 *"It's politics, Stupid!"*

> The information sphere is becoming the pivotal point in the American economy. And, as the uses of information multiply exponentially by virtue of its greatly enhanced refinement and flexibility – through computer processing, storing, retrieving, and transmitting data – *information itself becomes a primary item for sale.*
> HERBERT I. SCHILLER (1984, 33, emphasis by author)

Deep globalization was, as already mentioned, one of the important factors contributing to the infrastructural development of global communication systems. However, there were several other causes and processes contributing to the exceptional expansion of the wider field of communication (and, consequently, its commodification within capitalist societies) throughout the nineteenth and the start of the twentieth century. Amongst others were the emergence of the popular press and, later, a vast expansion of the culture and media industries. For Williams (2011/1961, 211) and Herbert Schiller (1984, 77), improvements in the productive and distributive methods that were propelled by industrialization were of considerable importance in these changes.

---

29   See for example Mosco (1989; 1993, 117–120), H. Schiller (1989; 1996), Bettig (1996), Perelman (2002), McChesney (2013). According to Perelman (2003b, 32; cf. 2002) "stronger intellectual property rights contribute to the unequal distribution of income and property, have destructive consequences for science and technology and the university system, inundate society with legal disputes, and reduce personal freedoms through intrusive measures to protect intellectual property."

Likewise, one should not overlook the expansion of the basic democratic freedoms that were an important process accompanying the struggle for democratization, connected to the rise of liberalism, liberal democracy and urbanization
(cf. Williams 2011/1961, 211; Hardt 2001, ch. 1; Jhally 2006, 50). Urban industrialization – which was, in fact, closely linked to the primary (primitive) accumulation and enclosure of the commons (Marx 1990/1867, part 8; Perelman 2000) – for
example, significantly eroded the older (rural) cultural forms, which opened up
the space for mass culture, which could now be produced as a commodity (Jhally
2006, 50). As Smythe (1954, 34) noted over half a century ago, "The mass media
now supply entertainment which more than fills the quantitative void left by the
displacement of the older rituals for entertainment." There was also an explosion
of advertising, which radically changed the economic organization of the press
at the start of the twentieth century and greatly contributed to its expansion (see
Park 1922, 360–365; Williams 1962, ch. 2; Baker 1994; Curran 2002, ch. 3).

Even if we take all of these different social processes into consideration it
remains impossible to explain what exactly contributed to such a considerable
qualitative change that communication, culture, and information (as commodities) have been turned into crucial resources in the existing capitalist
mode of production (even to the extent that, in some cases, they are now defining other political economic processes in the current historical epoch). North
American political economists of communication are in full agreement that
the key transformation was in fact led by political incentives and state interventions in this field. Herbert Schiller (1969; 1984; 1998; 2000, 49–54), Dan
Schiller (2000; 2007), Michael Perelman (2002), Vincent Mosco (1982; 1989;
1993), Nick Dyer-Witheford (1999) and Christopher May (2002, ch. 5; cf. 2010)
are amongst the authors pointing out that the political interventions were the
ones that led to what is often labelled as the information society and information revolution.

The increasing social, economic and political significance of information
and communication systems and resources (both the infrastructure and the
content) was ascertained in the US in the 1950s and, especially, in the 1960s.
Key political administrators and decision-makers have, together with the biggest corporations and conglomerates, and in co-operation with the military-
industrial complex, realized that controlling communication and information
resources and infrastructure is of prime importance if the US wants to expand
its economic interests beyond their own borders in the areas that were beyond
their immediate political control, defining the terms of global hegemony. The
goal was not an old-fashioned imperial control through military might and
interventions (even though the possibility of this could not be excluded), but
was aimed at providing opportunities to the biggest conglomerates and

commencing what Harvey (2003, ch. 2) called the "capitalist imperialism." At the same time, as Herbert Schiller (1984, 48) indicated, development of the information sector was intended to help in the revitalization of capitalism, both nationally and internationally, and to provide a solution to the enduring economic crisis.

It was the key decision-makers, therefore, that acted according to these pre-suppositions and goals by deploying international policies, enacting different state interventions in the field and providing the industry with huge govern-mental funding for research and development (R&D). National and interna-tional policies in the wider field of communication became an important part of the neo-imperialist tendencies in American politics and economics, and were coupled with cultural imperialism, which (perhaps often quite uninten-tionally) spread the vision of the American dream around the globe. They were implemented in the so-called military-industrial-communication complex that was most closely analysed by Herbert Schiller (1998; cf. Maxwell 2003, ch. 2). Schiller had already analysed these tendencies in his first major work, *Mass Communications and American Empire* (1969), and further developed his anal-ysis in his key work *Communication and Cultural Domination* (1976).[30] He pointed out that the imperial expansion of American power could be carried out only in parallel with the expansion of technological and communication "industrial" complexes. They helped to spread the media content and, with it, a very specific ideology, which would help to sustain American hegemony and incorporate new areas into the world capitalist economy. The crucial underly-ing objective of Washington's international communication policies was therefore "to secure as large a part as possible of the ex-colonial world for the world market system." (H. Schiller 2000, 42).

These imperial intentions helped to build an international system that suited American political and, especially, economic interests in the territories that were formally outside of their immediate control. This is perhaps best exemplified by the *free flow of information* doctrine that promoted a global free market in media, culture and information resources (H. Schiller 1976, ch. 2). Its political objective was, to put it in the words of Hardt (2004, 53–54), to ease "unrestricted trade, including the flow of cultural goods through channels of mass communication, for purposes of creating favourable social or political conditions of controlling the production of everyday realities." It helped to expand capitalism around the globe and develop markets in non-capitalist ter-ritories. The free flow doctrine in turn directly produced new international

---

30   These issues remained amongst his major research interests until his death (see H. Schiller 2000).

dependencies, especially in the field of information and communication (see Thussu 1998; 2006). With this intention in mind, "the free flow doctrine has been elevated to the highest level of u.s. foreign policy," Herbert Schiller (1984, 56) noted in 1980s (cf. H. Schiller 1969; Mosco 1993; Mattelart 2000, 50; Perelman 2002).[31] Only a couple of years later the free flow of information doctrine became fully united with its more wide-reaching big brother, the neo-liberal political economic doctrine of a full-blown *laissez-faire* free market capitalism, which consolidated itself in the 1980s in the US and the UK and since the 1990s spread throughout the globe (cf. Thussu 2005; Hesmondhalgh 2007).

The free flow of information doctrine attempted to present commodification and privatization of communication and information resources and their global exchange as natural and beyond-dispute, even though there were manifest struggles against incorporation of these fields into the capitalist market. The main intentions of the doctrine were ideologically presented as if the free market commodity exchange is a completely neutral, fair and unbiased exchange between equally powerful actors.[32] In fact it served especially those corporations (and countries helping them) that were already the most powerful on the capitalist market.[33] To put it in the words of Herbert Schiller (1976, 45), "when

---

31   As Herbert Schiller stressed at the end of the 1990s (see H. Schiller 2000, 76–87), this doctrine remains crucial in governmental documents of the United States together with an imperative of private property (e.g. over information via patents and intellectual property rights) right to this day. Its fundamental principles are enforced through international agreements and different bilateral arrangements between nation states.

32   As it is comprehended in the liberal theories. To put it in the words of Marx (1990/1867, 280), commodity exchange in the sphere of circulation "is in fact a very Eden of the innate rights of man. It is the exclusive realm of Freedom, Equality, Property and Bentham. Freedom, because both buyer and seller of a commodity, let us say of labour-power, are determined only by their own free will. They contract as free persons, who are equal before the law. Their contract is the final result in which their joint will finds a common legal expression. Equality, because each enters into relation with the other, as with a simple owner of commodities, and they exchange equivalent for equivalent. Property, because each disposes only of what is his own. And Bentham, because each looks only to his own advantage. The only force bringing them together, and putting them into relation with each other, is the selfishness, the gain and the private interest of each. Each pays heed to himself only, and no one worries about the others. And precisely for that reason, either in accordance with the pre-established harmony of thing, or under the auspices of an omniscient providence, they all work together to their mutual advantage, for the common weal, and in the common interest."

33   Nordenstreng and Varis (1974, 54) noted in the conclusion of their influential report for UNESCO, which focused on the international flows of television programme and was entitled *Television traffic – a one way street?*, that Western exporters (unlike other exporters

there is an uneven distribution of power," a free hand of the market "serves to strengthen the already-powerful and weaken further the already-frail." In his opinion "freedoms that are formally impressive may be substantively oppressive when they reinforce prevailing inequalities while claiming to be providing generalized opportunity for all." (Ibid.) Or as he emphasized years later:

> The free flow of information doctrine, undeniably beneficial to the already powerful, is a fraudulent construct. The flow of information it promotes is free in one respect only. The flow is expected to be freely admitted to all the spaces that its providers desire to transmit it to. Otherwise, there is nothing free about the information. Quite the contrary. Information and message flows are already, and continue to be, priced to exact the highest revenues extractable. Recent decades have witnessed the steady transformation of public information into saleable goods. Improved electronic information processing facilitates greatly the ability to package and charge for all kinds of messages and images.
>
> H. SCHILLER 2000, 85

---

around the world) were able to reach across the globe with their programmes. "Consequently, exports of TV programmes to other countries seem to be associated with the wealth and size of a country," (Ibid.) they pointed out. This also meant that "the free flow of TV material between nations means in actual fact that only those countries with considerable economic resources have taken advantage of the freedom to produce, while those with scarce resources have the 'freedom' to choose whether or not to take advantage of the material made available to them." (Ibid.) Empirical results of the analysis done by Nordenstreng and Varis led to a conclusion that television traffic indeed was a one way street at the time. As a consequence, there was no need for question marks anymore: "there is no need – in fact, no justification – for a question mark after the title of this publication. Globally speaking, television traffic does flow between nations according to the 'one way street' principle: the streams of heavy traffic flow one way only." (Nordenstreng and Varis 1974, 52) Mowlana (1985, 27) came to similar conclusions in his report in the 1980s, which synthesized previous analyses done for UNESCO in the field of media, culture, and communications. He pointed out there is an obvious vertical flow of international news from the most developed countries to the rest of the world. While horizontal flows existed, they represented only a fraction of the entire flow of information. This pattern was repeated in all other forms of information: "With virtually all types of information flow, whether it is news or data, educational, scientific or human flow, the pattern is the same. The cycles are quite similar to cycles in other trade areas: industrially less developed countries export raw materials to highly industrialized countries for processing and then purchase back the more costly finished products. Notably lacking is the exchange of data, news, information, cultural programmes and products, and persons among developing countries." (Mowlana 1985, 64).

According to Dan Schiller (2007, 39–48), the key role played by political interventions in the rise of the information and communication commodities and
systems can be recognized in several different areas, including: (1) Funding
research and development in telecommunications; (2) "Liberalization" of the
communication market; (3) Changing global trade and investment regulations
to favour services; (4) Privatization of formerly public and freely accessible
information; and (5) Strengthening legal rights to private property in information. Most of the funding went directly to the military establishment. As indicated by Mosco (1982, 49–51), the US budget for telecommunications in 1982
that went directly to the Pentagon was US$14.5bn, which was about the same
as the revenue from all the radio and TV stations in the US that year. Mosco saw
the Pentagon as "a major force for capital accumulation" that "exerts a substantial influence on the shape of the electronics industry." (Ibid, 49, 50) Herbert
Schiller (2000, 53) was certain that the rapid development of computers and
other new technologies, information industries and the underlying infrastructure of the *information age* would never have happened without vast amounts
of government money. His estimate of the subsidies and outlays for state-
funded research and development in this field since the Second World War was
over US$1trln (Ibid).

The last two areas of political interventionism that Dan Schiller mentions
are closely connected to the proliferation of IPRs, which since the 1980s, and
especially from the 1990s onward, played a very important part in the new
capitalist enclosures and the rise of the so-called digital/informational capitalism (Thussu 2005, 52–54; Thussu, 2006, ch.3; D. Schiller 2000). IPRs were
embedded in supranational free-trade agreements, such as the General
Agreement on Trade in Services (GATS), which made possible a global harmonization of private ownership of information and imposed this onto
national legislatures (cf. Marshall and Frith 2004). The long-time present
American interests became a part of the World Trade Organization (WTO),
which saw the free flow of information doctrine as essential for capitalist
expansion (see H. Schiller 2000, 41–44; Thussu 2005, 53). "With its growing
commodification, information acquired the status of a 'key strategic resource'
in the international economy," Thussu (2005, 54; cf. Berry 2008) pointed out.
Consequently "its distribution, regulation, marketing and management
became increasingly important." (Ibid.)

As pointed out above, the rise of new ICTs and commodification of the
wider field of communication should not, therefore, be seen as an inevitable
consequence of the continuing expansion of global capitalism, neither were
they an outcome of the infamous (supposedly neutral and somehow benign)
transformation towards the post-industrial/information society. They can only
be seen as a long-term development, which was excessively accelerated

through politically orchestrated interventions since the middle of the twentieth century: on the one hand through the global expansion of new ICT s that were actively promoted by the US with huge financial investments and international policymaking, and, on the other hand, through the transnational agreements that globally deployed IPRs and promotion of the free flow of information doctrine (where information was comprehended as a commodity), which helped globally to expand communication and cultural conglomerates.

The fact there was indeed nothing unavoidable in this transformation was perhaps best exemplified by the oppositional attempts of the actors within the international movement for *the New World Information and Communication Order* (NWICO). This geopolitical initiative, which ran under the patronage of the Non-Aligned Movement (NAM) and UNESCO, criticized the increasing global information inequalities and further commodification of culture, information, and communication. It vigorously attempted to provide an alternative developmental pattern in this field by promoting a more just international order, albeit with little actual political success.[34] It nevertheless successfully brought these issues to the fore in international decision-making arenas and explicitly called into question unequal communication and information flows by providing a critique of the structural causes for their emergence. Its proponents connected these cultural inequalities, which were often labelled under the term cultural imperialism, to the wider economic dominance present in world-wide capitalism. According to Nordenstreng (1993, 258), the issue of class inequalities and antagonisms was present in NWICO from its start, and for the first time in the international community, voice was given to those actors that were rarely heard before. An important influence on the initiative also came from the civil society and critical media and communication scholars (Nordenstreng 2013). An alternative to the exploitative and unequal international order based on structural dependencies was suggested by the MacBride commission, which promoted innovative proposals to democratize communications via the right to being informed, the right to communicate, a conceptualization of the freedom of the press, and so on (Osolnik 2005). A novel understanding of these concepts was only partly based on their traditional

---

34   For a detailed account of NWICO see Herbert Schiller (1976; 1978; 1984, ch. 4), Maxwell
      (2003, 39–40), Nordenstreng (1993; 2013), Osolnik (2005), Thussu (2005; 2006, 24–37),
      Mosco (2009, 72–75), and Mattelart (2011). NWICO was a part of a wider initiative for a
      New International Economic Order (NIEO) promoted by countries that formed NAM (see
      H. Schiller 1978, 36–38; Nordenstreng 1993, 268). It promoted *the right to communicate* in
      opposition to the free flow of information doctrine. It intellectually culminated in the
      MacBride report entitled *Many Voices, One World*, which was released under the patronage of UNESCO in 1980 (see also the special issue of journal *Javnost – the Public*, vol. 12, no.
      3; e.g. Osolnik 2005; Thussu 2005).

definitions, which often reduced those rights to an abstract and individual level (which in a capitalist society ultimately means a freedom to run a business, to paraphrase Marx). Instead, it connected them to certain concrete rights, for example a right to have an access to the means of mass communication, and to the wider social-economic and cultural rights. Even though NWICO was ultimately unsuccessful, its findings and proposals remain of crucial importance to this day.

4   The Political Economy of Communication and the Audience Commodity Thesis

Global expansion of capital into previously non-commodified spheres indicates that political economy of communication in many ways started to overlap with inquiries made by other fields originating in the critical theory of society. The critical (e.g. neo-Marxist) approach to political economy (and critical theory of society more generally) has of course been regarded as essential for media and communication research from its beginnings. Even though Smythe (1960) is usually considered as the founder of the political economy of communication, deeper origins of the critical approach toward media and communication can be found much earlier; at least as early as in Adorno and Horkheimer (2002/1947; Adorno 2001/1991) on the one hand, or Innis (2008/1951) on the other. Both cultural studies and political economy in fact shared similar origins that can be derived from these authors, while also sharing basic agreement regarding the critical analysis of capitalism and the cultural processes therein (see Babe 2009, ch. 1; Wasko 2005, 42f.). The increasingly important role of communication in postmodern societies produced several new convergence points between critical theory and the political economy of communication (e.g. Fuchs 2010).

Focusing on how the commodification process is considered in the political economy of communication, we can see that there are at least two general aspects significant for this relationship (Mosco 2009, 12f., 130). On the one hand, both communication and technology support commodification processes in the economy and throughout society. The role of technology in instrumental rationalisation that is necessary for commodification is becoming particularly transparent with digitalisation. On the other hand, however, commodification also penetrates institutions related to communication and starts to encroach on everyday social practices that have their foundations in communication. Both aspects are also stressed by Fuchs, who gives a close reading of Marx's thoughts on communication and media (Fuchs 2011, ch. 4). According to Fuchs, Marx establishes that communication media are, on the most basic level, important in co-ordinating production across distances, accelerating transmission of messages and co-ordinating the transport of commodities between different establishments. They are furthermore crucial also in a more fundamental sense, helping to widen the expansion of capital into non-commodified spheres where accumulation and consumption could be developed (but were not yet). This process therefore supports the whole circulation process of capital. Mosco (2009, ch. 8) terms this process "spatialization," which denotes overcoming of the constraints of space. As we are able to see, the spatialisation process is directly connected to commodification. In a more narrow sense of the media infrastructure and media contents, Fuchs also points out that for Marx, transmission technologies are operated by corporations. This means not only that the media themselves are commodities (and so is the infrastructure), but they consequently also transmit commodities. Media can be seen "as carriers of advertising messages that advance commodity sales" (Mosco 2009, 149), consequently accelerating the circulation of commodities.

Two other categories crucial for the political economy of communication and critical communication studies have been labour and audiences. As noted earlier in the text, selling labour power on the labour market is one of many important preconditions of the capitalist economy. A significant novelty is that in the information society, knowledge and information became fully commodified, which created a need for new types of labour that would be able to satisfy this "social" need. In the political economy of communication, labour has thus been analysed especially in its varying communicative-forms (as knowledge labour, information labour, labour of journalists etc.) and most of the work was done by Mosco and McKercher (2008). However, my focus in this section of the chapter will be especially on the second category, audiences. Their commodification is also a relative novelty in the capitalist economy, while the conceptualisation of audiences as commodities raises several important questions regarding the pervasiveness of commodification in society.

4.1 Audiences in the (Critique of the) Political Economy of Communication

The critical political-economic approach toward audiences is a heterodox and alternative approach that is in most cases overlooked in mainstream and celebratory communication studies focusing on this topic.[35] This is so despite

---

35   Perhaps most striking is the fact that "representative" literature neglects critique of political economy when it comes to audiences. A four-volume collection on audiences released by Sage in 2009, entitled Media Audiences, offers no valuable insights from the political-economic point of view, even though it contains many texts on this topic, encompassing 1320 pages (see: www.uk.sagepub.com/books/Book233064). The same, for example, holds

the fact that the so-called "blind spot debate" was one of the most heated debates in the historical development of the political economy of communication and provided several useful insights that seem crucial in understanding how audiences are instrumentalised by capital. This long-lasting debate, which at least indirectly continues in a much different technological and social context of today's society (see Bermejo 2009; Napoli 2010; Fuchs 2010; Caraway 2011; Biltereyst and Meers 2011; Kang and McAllister 2011), is an invaluable source for practices and ideas connected to Marxian-inspired critical communication studies. Perhaps even more importantly, it also provides several insights into how commodification spreads throughout the social fabric and how we are able to analyse these processes in postmodern society, which is completely permeated with communication. Insights provided by (the critique of) political economy in communication studies can thus offer a wide reflection on the current historical epoch by going beyond narrow affirmative approaches.

With the "blind spot debate," the issue of commodification in the media and communication has been extended beyond content and media labour to audiences. Audiences became the key media "goods" towards which scholarly

---

true for the journal *Participations: International Journal of Audience Research*, now renamed into *Participations: Journal of Audience & Reception Studies*, that "welcomes contributions from different fields," like "sociology, psychology, anthropology, linguistics, folkloristics, cultural and media studies" (see: www.participations.org). As it can be seen, the journal states basically every possible approach, perspective, and discipline, one of the rare exceptions being political economy. The same thing can be observed in respect to the recently published *Handbook of Media Audiences*, edited by Virginia Nightingale (2011), which almost completely avoids political economy (with perhaps an exception of Napoli's contribution) and only by a mere coincidence (if at all) touches at questions such as power relations, private ownership, exploitation, or class relations. Political economy, and especially its critique, is often neglected and concealed when it comes to audiences; they are often seen as proactive and empowered "consumer-citizens." Little to none reflection is given to the vast discrepancies between the owners of the means of production and the "consumers." This means questions concerning wider structural issues and social totality are quite possibly completely overlooked and taken for granted. To state it differently: in these approaches, capitalism is something that stays in the background as an irrelevant or presupposed factor, its influence not being worthy of any deeper analysis. When Marx and critique of political economy are used, they are often seen as outdated and reductionist or even deliberately misinterpreted (I thank the reviewer of this chapter for his comments on this issue, see also the critique provided by Biltereyst and Meers 2011). This is for example quite obvious in Fiske's influential book *Introduction to communication studies* (1990), which describes Marx's theory as "economistic." It also reduces it to the issues concerning ideology and gives very simplistic accounts of complex Marxist arguments.

attention could and should be aimed. Before this debate, media content has commonly been viewed as the vital commodity sold by the media to its readership. The recognition that "the mass media are first and foremost industrial and commercial organisations which produce and distribute commodities" (Murdoch and Golding 1973, 205f.), has already been widely accepted amongst critically engaged theorists. This important rethinking of the role of critical communication studies was initiated by Smythe (1977). Both Mosco (2009, 12) and Meehan (1993) have pointed out that Smythe's article, in which the audience commodity thesis was first proposed, has produced a fundamental shift in critical communication research. It could now include in its scope all communication companies that advertise, not only the media themselves. This can in fact be interpreted as an early and radical widening of the possible areas for analysis that can be carried out by the political economy of communication and this scope was, furthermore, extended by Smythe's belief that political economy can, in its widest meaning, be defined as "the study of control and survival in social life" (Mosco 2009, 3). According to this interpretation, political economy can be seen as the most holistic, and all-encompassing approach, while in many ways resembling the critical role it should in fact provide in its analysis of society.

In many ways Smythe's findings almost prophetically predicted some of the topics that would later become important in the framework of changes concerning immaterial work and post-Fordist production, which are well demonstrated by Gorz (2010) (in this text they are dealt with in Section 5). It is thus of the utmost importance to assess some of Smythe's key provocative statements and their continuing (in)validity in light of the rise of new media technologies, especially the Internet.

4.2   *Smythe's Audience Commodity Thesis and Technological Changes*
It is possible to derive a few key theses from Smythe's (1977) original article that initiated the audience commodity debate. His theses are not only still pertinent, they have been in fact reinforced by the technological and social changes ever since they were first proposed.[36]

---

36   One of the initial claims by Smythe (1977) was that critical theory, for example Western Marxism, had more or less ignored communication (hence "the blindspot"). One could claim so forty years ago, but it is hardly the case today. And it was a problematic thesis even then (both in the case of Austro-Marxism and some of the authors working in SFR Yugoslavia), which Murdock (1978) sufficiently pointed out in his reply to Smythe. Nowadays we have a developed field of study in political economy of communication,

Firstly, audiences are crucial commodities, which are manufactured and sold on the market. And not only this, audiences in fact labour! These were the main starting-points of the debate on the "audience as commodity." Smythe argued that the most important commodity produced by the media industry is the audience itself, which is constructed and then sold to the advertisers. This thesis not only survived the test of time, but has escalated in importance since it was proposed, which is demonstrated by several other critical approaches dealing with similar issues (one of them is dealt with in Section 5). This seems especially interesting because when Smythe wrote the article, his notion of audiences as commodities was often dismissed as a return to vulgar Marxism and he was accused of reductionist *economism* by his critics (Meehan 1993). The resurrection of the idea of media as a business, bound by the logic of profitability, even seemed old-fashioned at the time when Cultural Studies reigned supreme. In the early nineties, Meehan (1993) argued that Smythe could have in fact even been more radical in his analysis and subsequent claims. According to her, the validity of the theses he proposed were proven to be completely correct by history and actual practice.[37] Indeed, according to Biltereyst and Meers (2011), who recently took a fresh look at this debate, media content becomes secondary, a *free lunch* at best. Media in fact first and foremost produces audiences, not programmes or content! This means media as tendency become mere *hunter-gatherers of the audience*, while leisure time becomes an increasingly important component of capitalism, which is able to expand and commodify previously unknown territories. What is comprehended as leisure time, non-work time, is subsumed under capital, monetised and valorised.

Interestingly, Adorno (2001/1991, ch.8) indicated these processes as already happening in the year 1969, when the essay *Free time [Freizeit]* was published. He states that free time is becoming its own opposite, a parody of itself, because it is only a continuation of profit-oriented life; it becomes subjugated to similar norms and unfreedom distinctive of the production process. He demonstrates this through the hobby ideology. Everyone must have a hobby now, possibly one that can be supplied by the "show business" or "leisure industry" (both terms losing all of their irony). Free time is thus subject to much social control. It was therefore only a matter of time, before all of the living time became commodified in its entirety. Similarly to Adorno, Williams (2005/1980) pointed

---

while some of the radical neo-Marxist positions, for example autonomism, presuppose it is basically communication that is the main category in post-Fordist capitalism.

37   It is the contradictory (almost antagonistic) three-folded relationship between audiences (living beings that are again being reduced to commodities), content in the media, and advertisers (representing capital), that is crucial here.

out a decade later how the means of communication must be seen as a means of production, and this is especially so in modern societies, where communication significantly develops and becomes an important (both direct and indirect) productive force.

Secondly, an even more important and radical thesis was derived by Smythe on the basis of these initial findings. As if he simply continued Adorno's and Williams' line of thought, he claimed that today, "work time for most people is twenty-four hours a day" (Smythe 1981a, 121). Consequences of these findings are radical and wide-ranging and even more importantly, Smythe's observations are proven day-by-day. Even if one disagrees with Smythe's observation of how labour should be defined, which is indeed a complex issue, his thesis in its fundamental demonstrates the radical expansion of commodification throughout new spheres of society.

Both of Smythe's theses suggest that what can be considered as labour time has been radically extended into non-work time, when labour power is usually reproduced. Jhally and Livant (in Jhally 1987, 83–90) extended this notion further, while firmly basing their view in the critique of political economy as outlined by Marx. They pointed out that watching (as a form of labour) is in fact just an extension of factory labour and this should not be seen as a metaphor. It is a specific form of labour that is vital in the whole media economics process; similarly to how labourers sell their labour power to capitalists, so audiences sell their *watching power* to media owners. Leisure thereby becomes an increasingly important component in the workings of contemporary capitalism; it is subsumed under capital, monetised, and valorised, while audiences are viewed instrumentally, with the sole goal of (surplus) value extraction. Activities of audiences (listening, watching, browsing, "clicking") produce value, which is appropriated by the capitalist, which in exchange offer an apparently *free lunch* (various types of content).

Smythe's theses, as already pointed out, also indicate that all aspects of social and individual human life can be fully commodified and be drawn into the capitalist accumulation cycle, whether one wants and knows this or (preferably) not. There are basically no human activities left, from which a certain magnitude of exchange value could not be extracted and appropriated. This is possible also because of the rise of digital technologies that started to play a crucial role in these very processes, providing unprecedented detail and further rationalisation of measuring, quantification, and control (see Napoli 2010; 2011). Napoli (2011, 10) even goes as far as to claim that a broad array of options for data gathering, which the media corporations are able to use today, make the Internet almost too measurable. These techniques make it possible to record an unprecedented level of detail of its users (or in the discourse of marketers:

individual consumers). In this sense, Castells's notion that the Internet is *the fabric of our lives*, could hardly be taken more seriously, when it comes to the encroachment upon people's privacy.

The key changes brought by new digital technologies that offer new ways of controlling and measuring the audiences are: (a) fragmentation; (b) formally increased autonomy, participation and engagement of audiences; (c) unprecedented control over consumption; and (d) unprecedented detail of measuring users and audiences (Napoli 2011). Fragmentation of the media environment and consequently audiences brings an increasing prominence of the "long tail" scenarios, which break audiences into smaller and smaller pieces. There is a historical development from broadcasting, distinctive of the early mass media, to "narrowcasting," which was enabled by satellite TV and infrastructure privatisation and deregulation, and finally to "pointcasting," which is made possible by digitalisation and the Internet. The latter enables a radical "rationalisation of measuring" and full quantification of every activity that potentially becomes monetisable through several different techniques and methods (e.g. via data mining, see Gandy 2012, Andrejevic 2012, Fuchs *et al.* 2011, Prodnik 2012a). It is true that Internet users (also called "cybernauts") can be more engaged and have more influence over how they use the new media than before, but from the perspective of the political economy of the Internet, this enables the owner of the platform they are using an even more detailed measurement of their activities and preferences, possibly also their social status and other personal information. It is an idealist notion to speculate blindly on the revolutionary possibilities that have supposedly been opened up by the Internet. A more materialist approach should take into account the wider social context and recognise that the asymmetries have been growing in the last couple of decades and the Internet unfortunately did little to mitigate this. On the contrary, it could even be claimed that digitalisation to some extent helped to widen these gaps and intensify concentration and discrepancies between those in power and the disempowered many (see Hindman 2009, Bellamy Foster and McChesney 2011).

An exemplary case of the mentioned characteristics is, without any doubt, Google (see Kang and McAllister 2011). This corporation derives most of its profit from advertising (especially its main advertising product Google AdWords), by extensively commodifying its users, fragmenting them into niche audiences and then selling them to prospective advertisers that offer specific types of commodity that relate to these audiences. One of the theses, regarding the post-Fordist economy, proposed by Marazzi (2008), points precisely at such key duties of corporations: differentiation of products becomes one of the ways of getting the attention of the consumers. Production, in this light, steps into the background, at least to a certain extent, while the previously less noteworthy *attention economy* increases in importance. In fact, Google's yearly profit is levelled with annual budgets of some smaller nation-states (e.g. Slovenia, with a population of 2 million people), while (formally!) employing 30 000 people. This is only possible by severe infringement into the privacy of the users, a process in most cases denoted as economic surveillance (see Fuchs *et al.* 2011; Prodnik 2012a). Several authors, amongst them Pasquinelli (2009) and Fuchs (2012c), point out that one of the most important sources in the process of capital accumulation by Google is the unpaid labour of the people using its platform, with the World Wide Web content-producers being the other. Both can consequently be exploited, because Google Corporation is able to extract surplus value from their activity. This brings us directly to the definitions of the social factory and general intellect provided by the autonomia (post-operaist) movement, which are discussed in Section 5.

4.3 Caraway's Critique of Smythe and the Subject Matter of Political Economy

One of the more forceful recent critiques of Smythe's findings came from Caraway (2011), who quite vigorously argued against several of the basic presuppositions which Smythe put forward in his seminal study. While his critique is in no way representative for a quite long series of different rebuttals – they came especially from the field of Cultural Studies and were often directed against political economy in general (for an overview see Biltereyst and Meers 2011, especially 417–424) – it does offer a fruitful ground in the context of this text. This is especially so, because Caraway claims he is giving a Marxian revisiting of this issue. His text thereby deserves a short excursus that will fit well into the problems and issues that have already been raised.

One can wholeheartedly agree with Caraway on several points raised against the scholars dealing with the audience commodity. Firstly, he claims this approach overstates the degree to which co-optation of audiences as a source of value and free labour is in fact realised, because the activities of audiences are not under the direct control of the capitalist (the audience commodity transaction). His second notion is connected to the first, namely that this approach and especially Smythe himself, completely lacks focus on subjectivities and their agency (theses of audience power and of media content as free lunch). Thirdly, there is a lack of focus on use-value. It is, however, crucial to ask, what is the epistemological approach of political economy and what is the subject matter these authors employ? – answers to which might clarify some of the dilemmas. Let us look at his arguments more closely, starting with the last one.

Caraway claims that "an exploration of the use-values derived by audiences from media products would have demonstrated the limits to capitalist domination in the sphere of production" (Caraway 2011, 700). As mentioned earlier in this text, there are hardly any observations of use-value in the first volume of *Capital*. On the contrary, Marx focuses almost solely on exchange-value. He finds use-value as an almost irrelevant appendage, even talking about exchange-value simply as value. This is not because he *personally* feels use-value is irrelevant, but because this is how the capitalist economy operates. In *A Contribution to the Critique of Political Economy*, Marx even goes as far as to simply state that "use-value as such, lies outside the sphere of investigation of political economy," mainly because it is "a necessary prerequisite of the commodity" (Marx and Engels 1987, 270). And "since the use-value of the commodity is postulated, the specific utility and the definite usefulness of the labour expended on it is also postulated; but this is the only aspect of labour as useful labour which is relevant to the study of commodities" (Marx and Engels 1987, 277). Commodity must always posses some socially useful value, but its actual content is absolutely indifferent (Jameson 2011, 35–37).[38] It is exactly this *social* (or socially relevant) character of use-value of a certain commodity that makes it an exchangeable commodity, while at the same time, this characteristic also makes its actual content quite irrelevant as long as it has its consumers; basically anything can become commodified, as far as it has some use-value and as long as other people want it. Use-values provide commodities with commercial content, which makes them "material bearers of exchange-value." But "clearly, the exchange relation of commodities is characterised precisely by its abstraction from their use-values. Within the exchange relation, one use-value is worth just as much as another, provided only that it is present in the appropriate quantity" (Marx 1990/1867, 126f.). Exchange-value is a quantitative relation based in proportions and measurement, and for all we care, this can also be gossip on Lady Gaga's latest extravagance... So far as society deems such use-values relevant enough to consume them.

Other authors, most notably Jhally (1987), have focused on the role of use-value in relation to commodity fetishism and the social construction of symbolic code (thus how meaning is produced for commodities), even though retaining a firmly materialist epistemological paradigm. Just because Smythe himself does not focus on this aspect (neither did Marx, for that matter), does not mean that his approach is not correct (he is just giving a certain perspective) or even that he saw no value in other perspectives, such as Jhally's. There were quite a number of attacks directed at Marx, claiming that he naturalised

---

38   Or to put it in Sohn-Rethel's words: "Commodity exchange requires, as a condition of its
      possibility, that the use of the commodities be suspended while they are subject to a
      transaction of exchange." (Sohn-Rethel's 1972, 51).

use-value and produced a fetishism of exchange. Such critiques are nothing new (for an overview and a defence of Marx, see, for example, Jhally 1987, 35), but could hardly be more unfair. Just because political economy does not concern itself with use-value does not mean use-value is socially irrelevant (quite the contrary).

Let us now turn to Caraway's two other points of critique: to what degree subjugation of audiences under capital is actually possible and what the role of agency is. He claims that neither in Smythe's nor in Jhally's and Livant's analysis can one find any "demonstration that the labour process described here [audience-labour] is under the control of the capitalist; nor is there any attempt to show that the use value is alienated from the audience" (Caraway 2011, 697). He then presents new technologies of surveillance, but stresses it is necessary "to continually reassess the degree to which capital is able to bring these activities within the logic of accumulation. [...] The effectiveness of those efforts should be treated with a high degree of scepticism" (Caraway 2011, 698). He goes on to say that "the exact and dispassionate measurement of audiences is fiction" (Caraway 2011, 699).

It seems to me that Caraway is wrong in most of the issues raised. He is to an extent correct in saying that in the media relation, the capitalist does not directly control the labourer. That is of course true, but *neither* is the capitalist in the traditional production process able to fully control the labourer; the media owner is able to "buy" the interest of audiences with content and in both cases the labourer does not have that much of a choice if he wants to consume (there is of course always an option to turn off the TV, but it is an idealistic presumption that this somehow magically increases the power of audiences). In comparison to the labour process, the relationship here is definitely not so different. Labourers, much like audiences, can formally choose who they will work for; in reality however, their options are very limited in both cases. And owners in the media industry, much like traditional capitalists, know very well what they will be able to sell and how much they are able to spend so they remain profitable. If that was not the case, they would go out of business. The calculation is a pretty simple one and if it does not work out, the business cannot survive. No mystification is needed here; a capitalist will adapt his operation to the circumstances in which he has to operate. It is also leading readers astray by saying that in Smythe's formulation, "the audience does not appear as a seller of a commodity" (ibid., 697). Their commodity is the abstract time they are "selling" to the media owner in exchange for the content they receive, so to say their "free-time," leisure time. The use-value involved in this transaction is in fact irrelevant, but to go into detail, the use-values in the digitalised era are the personal characteristics (social status, interests, etc.) of the audiences that the media owner is able to sell to the advertiser (or quite simply, he sells their attention if these audiences are less differentiated) and most notably the content produced by audiences in digital environments. There is nothing unusual here that would not correspond to the Marxian analysis, neither is it completely true that "there is no formal contract, negotiation or discussion of terms between audience and advertiser" (Ibid.), which Caraway seems to feel is the crucial aspect of labour to appear as commodity (which is not the case; the sole precondition is the ability of the labourer to choose freely his exploiter when he puts his labour power in the labour-market). Everything Caraway mentions in fact does happen, mostly informally, true, but on the Internet often also formally; for example via terms of use and privacy statements (see Sandoval 2012), while the negotiations are happening with mouse clicks or on the remote control. The consumer of the media content is able to change his "employer," and on the Internet, a person can easily self-employ himself by building his own website that will in real-life circumstances of course have immense difficulties of surviving against dominant actors such as Google or Facebook (just like it happens in the real-world economy).

Caraway's major problem throughout the text is that he fails to distinguish between two very different levels of argumentation: the abstract level and the concrete level. Both levels are of course of immense importance and the abstract argumentation, with its focus on tendencies, is built with the sole purpose of explaining the movement of concrete reality. The abstract argumentation however, which abstracts away particular cases and several mechanisms that operate in actually existing everyday life, can never fully explain concrete reality and particular cases, because its insight is limited (intentionally so). Causes for Marx's use of abstraction have been laid out earlier in this text, but one perhaps most obvious reason is that there is no way of analysing *everything*, dropping to the level of concrete reality, because this leaves the analyst with the sole focus on particular cases (such an analysis can bring a lot of new knowledge, but then again, also very little). As Collier (1994, 255–259) points out, apprehending the concrete whole is impossible and failing to realise this often makes us overlook crucial mechanisms and determinations (or we, at best, construct generalisations with little explanatory power).[39]

Caraway's inability to comprehend that political economy necessitates abstraction (together with focus on tendencies) is seen through his statement that "advertisers are not buying audience power but a fabricated image of an audience – and it is this fabrication which needs to be challenged by critical

---

39 While it is true that the further away theory gets from the concrete toward the abstract, more prone to error it is, it should be noted that "in order to explain the concrete conjuncture we have to unravel by analysis (in thought) the multiple mechanisms and tendencies which make it what it is" (Collier 1994, 255).

scholarship." Does he really believe advertisers do not know that? They are buying an approximation, an abstraction, a statistical construct of an audience and not "real" audiences: there is a relevant tendency (because of all the data they have) that the fabricated construct of an audience they bought will in large part behave in a way they planned that they will. In the abstract argument, they *have to* behave like that, otherwise the advertiser goes bankrupt; in the abstract reasoning this approximation *must* be close enough to reality in the long run to make it a reasonable purchase (it is not critical scholarship that factually risks its money by buying these fabrications; if this was not an economic practice that enhanced capitalists profitability, they would quite simply abandon it). It is very similar to a capitalist that is never able to know *in advance* whether he will be able to extract enough surplus value from the labour power he bought, so he is able to succeed on the market with the commodities which he plans to produce (the capitalist needs to *speculate* that he will be wily enough to control the labourer and extract enough surplus value). Similarly, looking at concrete examples, a capitalist in the production process *never* has complete control over the labourers he hired; in the worst case scenario (for him), labourers will go on strike. Or in the worst case scenario for the media owner, audiences will stop watching the content he is producing (which means he will either: put something else on-air, reduce costs so they correspond to the money brought in by the advertising, or go out of business). The abstract approach, of course, de-subjectivises, but this is what capitalism *in fact* does: rationalising, objectifying, abstracting (see Section 2.3).

It is worth asking ourselves whether anyone, besides now mostly deceased Stalinist dialectical materialists, genuinely believes that Marx's quite apparent lack of interest in subjectivities and working-class power in some of his later writings, point at his disinterest in progressive changes in the world by these subjects? This would contradict much of his actual conduct throughout his whole life. It is, on the contrary, exactly because of his lack of attention toward subjectivities that he was able to analyse abstractly how the capitalist system in fact works (again, only at the abstract, not necessarily concrete level, where several other tendencies come into play, most importantly human agency that can resist this subjugation). He had to abstract from other aspects of concrete reality that are of prime importance to fight capitalism, to demonstrate how the capitalist exploits the worker in the production process if one accepts the ideal typology of the capitalist market constructed by classical political economists.[40] Abstraction offers both Marx and Smythe a specific perspective on

---

40   Let us take an obvious example, that of Adam Smith and his construction of social reality
      in *The Wealth of Nations*. The sheer fact his arguments are mostly abstractions tells us they
      cannot be refuted with practical examples (e.g. of the reputed failings of his theory when

how capitalism operates in an abstract form and it is obvious that this perspective is not complete; it leaves out vast parts of social life. It is an abstraction, a very important one, but still it is limited in its scope, which is a characteristic of any abstraction. Still, as Fuchs, for example, points out, Smythe in fact *does not* neglect agency, even if he finds no *automatic* resistance.[41] As Smythe points out in *Dependency Road*:

> True, people are subject to relentless pressures from Consciousness Industry; they are besieged with an avalanche of consumer goods and services; they are themselves produced as (audience) commodities; they reproduce their own lives and energies as damaged and in commodity form. But people are by no means passive or powerless. People do resist the powerful and manifold pressures of capital as best as they can. There is a dependable quantum of individual and group resistance, reproduced every day, arising out of people's innate capacity and need for love, respect, communal relations, and creativity. That is, the principal contradiction in the core area (as in the whole world) is that between people and capital. And presently people are the principal aspect of that contradiction.[42]
>
> SMYTHE 1981B, 270F.

Caraway's notion on Smythe's purported ignorance of agency therefore does not seem valid. But even if it was, criticising an author who is deriving his research from a political economic perspective (consequently adopting a specific epistemological position) for not focusing on subjectivities, would seem similar to criticising a physician on the ground that he is not a chemist (or a carpenter, because he is not a plumber). One *could* give additional perspectives, but if he does not, why *blame* him because of it? Even though social

---

they are applied to concrete reality); even though we are yet to see such a perfectly competitive market, which is at the fundaments of his theory (arguably, there has never been such an example, especially not in the last century or so). (see also Harvey 2010).

41 This thesis was raised in his plenary talk entitled *Critique of the Political Economy of Social Media*, which was given on 3rd of May 2012 at the *Critique, Democracy and Philosophy in 21st Century Information Society* conference in Uppsala (Sweden). As he also pointed out in a private debate, Smythe's focus is, amongst others, on labour – and *labour is an activity*, it is inherently a place where *active human subject comes in*.

42 This Smythe quote about agency was presented Fuchs in this talk at the Uppsala conference and taken from his presentation, see: http://www.scribd.com/doc/92818866/Christian-Fuchs-Critique-of-the-Political-Economy-of-Social-Media-and-Informational-Capitalism. See also Fuchs (2012a).

sciences necessarily include several different perspectives, especially if they are critical, and must be aware of diverging analyses from different disciplines, distinction between different approaches and their subject matter is still important; in my opinion, it would be a mistake to simply conflate one approach with another, even if their contributions to the analysis of society may vary significantly.

Many authors – and Marx would probably be one of them, especially if one accepts Jameson's (2011, 37f.) central observation that *Capital* is in fact *not* a work of political action – would probably concur that focus on agency (e.g. resistance by differing subjectivities and possibilities of (counter) power produced by social movements) is simply not a subject matter of political economy (or its critique). In any case, political economy *can* or even *must*, however, be seen as one of the central preconditions for successful political action, touching on the need for redistribution of wealth and providing foundation to see clearly where wealth in fact originates from (human labour).[43] There is no reason not to complement such a political-economic perspective with radical political theory if one wishes (without seeking straw-man arguments or simple failings that are a consequence of abstraction). This is an approach of Negri and Hardt (2001; 2004; 2009) and the whole autonomist line of thought (see Section 5). But agency and subjectivities are not a subject matter *par excellence* of political economy and in fact never were. They are a subject matter of (radical) political theory. Personally, I find it confusing when people for example claim Negri and Hardt have taken an easy path by ignoring the proletariat, instead focusing on the multitude, like it is an either-either choice. That is not the case. Similarly to the political-economic writings of Marx, in Negri and Hardt's works, the proletariat can be seen as a technical concept (just like several other concepts in Marx's writings are, for example commodity fetishism or exploitation, see also Harvey 2010). It is the type of reading that transforms them into political concepts. Autonomism for example offered a political reading of the concepts that were technical and constructed at the level of political economy (ibid.; Negri 1991/1984; Cleaver 2000/1979). Multitude (see Virno 2004; Hardt and Negri 2005) can on the other hand be seen as a concept derived from radical political theory that not by any chance contradicts or opposes the proletariat, but simply compliments one concept (derived from a certain field of study) with another. And neither does it exclude the other. My goal here is of course not to blindly defend the approach of political economy as the only

---

43 Barbalet (1983, 29–30) stresses that for Marx, abolition of social forms (such as commodity fetishism) requires social and political action, not scientific enquiry. Critical science is however an integral part of a wider revolutionary framework.

correct one. On the contrary, I feel in many cases it has in fact been highly detrimental, providing only an "objectivistic" account by focusing on tendencies and mechanisms. Its basic premises should, however, be accepted as being valuable and credit should be given where credit is due: political readings of the central concepts in political economy would for example be impossible if Marx would not first provide us with a stringently technical, abstract, non-subjectivist and non-political reading.

5 Communicative Capitalism and the Social Factory: Towards a Seeping Commodification?

The key difference between the presented strands of the political economy of communication and post-operaist/autonomist neo-Marxism is that the latter expands its scope beyond media and communication (even if in some cases it takes examples from the Internet as case studies). It also puts a much larger focus on the subjective agency; it is individual subjects that produce value and because value production has spread into wider society (e.g. the "social factory"), this offers a radical expansion for the political possibilities and human resistance against these processes.

Several findings and ideas on audience as commodity can be directly connected to this line of thought. Authors basing their approach in this neo-Marxist "school" claim that communication, or even language-capacity as such, gained hegemonic primacy in contemporary society, therefore providing only one of the several possible links to political economy of communication. The concept of "social factory," which discloses how work has expanded beyond places commonly intended to host the production process (i.e., factory, manufacture ...) into wider society (see Negri 1984/1991; Negri 1992; Terranova 2004 etc.), also indirectly points at a full-fledged commodification of society, a thesis quite similar to those of Smythe and authors participating in the audience commodity debate.

Several authors such as Agamben (2000, 109–120), Virno (2004), Terranova (2004), Marazzi (2008), Negri (1991/1984; 1992; 1999) Negri and Hardt (2001; 2004; 2009), Dean (2008), Pasquinelli (2009), Gorz (2010), Fumagalli and Mezzadra (2010), Moulier Boutang (2011) and others have recently been writing on variations of communicative, cognitive or even semio and bio-linguistic capitalism, where communication and language capacity are gaining in importance. They can even be seen as a *deeper*, ontological proposition on the species-being of human beings (see Dyer-Witheford 2004). Similar findings were applied before that by Lazzarato (1996), who wrote of immaterial labour.

Later-on this type of labour was most carefully analysed by Gorz (2010). Gorz demonstrated how immaterial work has become the hegemonic form of work and the source for value creation in contemporary societies. Because of this transformation, people are totally subsumed under capital, where they must become the *enterprises that they are*, self-entrepreneurs, and must hold as much human capital as possible. "With self-entrepreneurship, whole persons and entire lives can, at last, be put to work and exploited. Life becomes 'the most precious capital'. The boundary between work and non-work fades, not because work and non-work activities mobilise the same skills, but because time for living falls, in its entirety, into the clutches of value" (Gorz 2010, 22; for an overview see Brophy and de Peuter 2007).

This is quite peculiar. It is important to note such an intertwinement between the time of labouring and non-labouring is very far from being common to capitalist societies. Quite on the contrary, with the rise of capitalism there was a radical separation between what was deemed productive (by capital), and what was unproductive, merely adequate for reproduction of human life. As Thompson (1967, 59f.; 1991, ch. 6) demonstrates, task-orientated work and a hardly noticeable demarcation between "work" and "life" is distinctive of pre-capitalist communities, "where social intercourse and labour are inter-mingled – the working-day lengthens or contracts according to the task – and there is no great sense of conflict between labour and 'passing the time of day'" (ibid., 60). Labour in capitalist societies, on the other hand, has historically always been stringently measured and timed by the clock (with far-reaching consequences). Thompson not only demonstrated that apprehension of time is socially constructed, but that linear measurement of time is crucial for capitalism. One of the pre-requisites of Marxian labour theory of value, which is constitutive for capitalist and exploitation of labour, is therefore being able to measure the labourers work. This is what abstract time is all about – even though capitalists have developed several new techniques of measuring, leading some authors to write about neo-Taylorism or digital Taylorism (e.g. Brown et al. 2011, ch. 5). Nevertheless, this has important consequences, especially if we acknowledge there is an increasing number of jobs, where labour cannot be easily measured (see Gorz 1989). This often means neo-Taylorist practices are close to a mere façade, because they fail to measure anything of particular relevance. They are, however, effective means of surveillance and control over the workforce, as they were in the past. This difficulty is of course furthermore accentuated with the increasing blurring between time of labour and free-time. As noted by Postone (2003/1993, 26f.), "in the course of development of capitalist industrial production, value becomes less and less adequate as a measure of the 'real wealth' produced. [...] Value becomes anachronistic in terms of the potential of the system of production to which it gives rise; the realisation of that potential would entail the abolition of value." This means that "the abolition of value would signify that labour time no longer would serve as the measure of wealth and that the production of wealth no longer would be effected primarily by direct human labour in the process of production." For Postone it is therefore clear that "overcoming capitalism, according to Marx, entails a fundamental transformation of the material form of production, of the way people work."

It is not a historical novelty that much labour is done outside the production process or the places traditionally denoted as places for production (e.g. factory, manufacture). Such labour is however considered unproductive by capital and was often denoted as such also by "progressive" socialist movements, which excluded all but the "real proletariat," which was constituted by white men (see Huws 2003). These places were however at the same time crucial for reproduction of the lives of the labourers. This was especially the case with the unproductive labour done by women in the household, where this division was based on gender (for the role of this labour in the wider accumulation process see Wallerstein 1983, 22–28; Fortunati 1989; Huws 2003). According to Fortunati (1989, 9) the capitalist mode of production has a dual character, divided between production and reproduction. While the latter is deemed as a non-value (it is also non-waged and carried out in the home), the former supposedly produces value in the production process. Fortunati however twists this logic and demonstrates that reproduction is an integral part of the production process; in fact, "it clearly contributes to the creation of value as a crucial, integral part of the capitalist cycle" (Fortunati 1989, 8). It is an indirectly waged labour that is engaged in the reproduction of labour power, which is crucial for the production as such and simultaneously enables that two workers are exploited with one wage. This notion is today extended even further. Huws (2003, 27; 45f.; 68f.) for example uses terms "unpaid consumption labour" and "consumption workers" to denote many unprofitable tasks that are forced back on the consumer, adding to the unpaid labour common people must do to reproduce their labour power (and consequently their lives). This type of work has usually been done by women, who are disproportionately affected by these demands, reproducing the gender relations. The key novelty is that capital has been able to include this type of (what is known as) "economic externalities" into its accumulation cycle.

What is of particular interest to me here is not so much through what changes the conceptualisation of labour has gone and what the category of labour even means today. These can be indeed seen as crucial difficulties that political economy must face today. Neither do we want to focus on the structural transformations of capitalism in perhaps an entirely new phase of capitalism. What we want to consider here seems to be an equally important question, namely, "how far" commodification has been able to spread into lives of human beings, where and what it is able to colonise and under what conditions. We are able to see striking convergence points between early findings of Smythe and observations made by several strands of neo-Marxist critique of political economy when analysing not only the role of commodification in present historical moment, but also where capital is able to extract surplus value. There is no limit to the commodification process according to these two strands of thought and it is not a coincidence many critical communication scholars have integrated Autonomist perspective in their theoretical apparatus. It seems both strands fully demonstrate the real value of George Gerbner's statement from 1983 that "if Marx were alive today, his principal work would be entitled Communications rather than Capital" (cited in: Nordenstreng 2004, 13).

What is presently novel in contemporary societies is, as claimed by Autonomist authors, that capital is attempting to include in the capitalist accumulation circuit the sole human capabilities to produce knowledge, communicate, quickly adapt to changed conditions (flexibility), participate, or cooperate. These are capabilities that are specific to human beings, who, as open animals, are capable of constructing political and social institutions. These characteristics are being directly "employed" by contemporary capital through different techniques and apparatuses, which serve to extract value from living labour. This claim could even be seen as a naturally tendential development of capitalism, which cannot set itself any limits when colonising different spheres from which value can be extracted.

This is directly applicable to Virno's (1996; 2004) reinterpretation of the concept of *general intellect*, derived from the "Fragment on the machines" in Marx's Grundrisse. Virno argues that post-Fordist capitalism mobilises all the faculties that characterise our species (i.e. language, abstract thinking, plasticity), a thesis that is derived from his social ontology. For Virno, for example, these capabilities can be seen as generically human: "post-Fordism mobilises all the faculties that characterise our species: language, abstract thinking, disposition toward learning, plasticity, the habit of not having solid habits" (Virno 2005, 29f.). It is these characteristics that are probably used in all professions and occupations (in the sense of the given definition communication is a necessary social manifestation of human language-capacity). Pasquinelli (2009) instead uses the term "common intellect," which demonstrates how capital is in fact exploiting human capabilities common to all people, while at the same time appropriating our common social production without paying for it (see also Hardt and Negri 2009).

As pointed out by Chicchi (2010), Marazzi (2010), or Vercellone (2010) financial capitalism has been able spread over the entirety of the economic accumulation cycle. In its fundamentals this means that finance is now present in all of the phases of economic cycle, from its start (production), to its end (consumption). This is the main reason why finance capitalism is able to extract value beyond areas that were traditionally meant for producing value (i.e. production of exchange value behind the borders of a factory). This simultaneously means commodification has been able to spread into all areas of life.

5.1   *The Second Enclosure Movement: "...and all that is Solid Melts into a Commodity"?*

> In capitalism, that is to say, all that is solid melts into PR, and late capitalism is defined at least as much by this ubiquitous tendency towards PR-production as it is by the imposition of market mechanisms.
> MARK FISHER (2009, 44)

The vast expansion and intensification of commodification, which has developed through recent decades, opened up new possibilities for the extraction of profit from everyday activities and the new forms of labour. However, it seems that a full-blown commodification of communication, information, culture, creativity, innovation, knowledge, research and science, everyday activities, and even human affects – to name just a few – produced a novel way of carrying out commodification. A subjugation of the wider field of communication, which has been commodified in the latest wave of historical enclosures, must be separated from the things and areas that were produced and exchanged on the market earlier.

Communication and information are peculiar commodities. The basic characteristics of information and communication, after all, make them non-excludable and non-rivalrous public goods, which could even be defined as *meta-public* goods, because they can become more valuable when used (Perelman 2003a). This is the sole reason why they have to be enclosed through political intervention (IPRs), as, otherwise, they could not be sold as commodities. In May's (2010, 12) view, commodification in these cases is therefore directly linked to (new) enclosures.

Enclosures and privatization in the areas that were once a part of the public domain and constituted the society's commons (see H. Schiller 1984; 1989) was what James Boyle (2008, ch. 3) called "enclosing the commons of the mind." He defined this as the *second enclosure movement*, which, in a very similar manner to the earlier enclosures of the commons centuries earlier, has had extra-economic incentives. The key difference is that these enclosures are now also aimed against information and cultural resources (cf. Bollier 2002; Hesmondhalgh 2008; Berry 2008; May 2010). The width of the enclosures is exemplified by Perelman (2002, 5), who is certain that IPRs "have contributed to one of the most massive redistributions of wealth that has ever occurred." Several authors wrote about new imperial and colonial practices (see Bettig 1996; Bollier 2002; Perelman 2002; Berry 2008, 49, 92), while Harvey (2003, 144–152; 2009, 67–70, 73–74) conceptualized these processes of privatization under the term *accumulation by dispossession*, which he used to demonstrate that primary (primitive) accumulation is a recurrent process of an often violent incorporation of different spheres into a capitalist accumulation cycle. Primary accumulation is, for Harvey, a process that does not take place only with the emergence of capitalism, but also when the system is already in place (cf. Perelman 2000). It denotes "predatory accumulation practices" that are typical of neoliberal order and commodification of divergent types of commons. This also includes, amongst others, people's histories, culture and cultural heritage, personal and intellectual creativity, genetic materials and so on (especially via patents and IPRs) (see Harvey 2003, 147–148; 2009, 68–69). In Berry's (2008, 53) view "the rapid enclosure of ideas and expressions that has intensified in the past decade" could even be labelled as "new feudalism," because it can lead to the emergence of a rentier class.

Hesmondhalgh (2008; cf. D. Schiller 2007, 43) was one of the authors that systematically applied Harvey's concept to the IPRs system, which made possible to own creativity and knowledge, bringing about a new type of imperialism. According to him "capital has shown an unprecedented interest in culture" (Ibid., 101) in the last decades, and strong IPRs were a key dimension of neoliberalism that made commodification of this sphere possible. As McChesney (2013, 80, emphasis by author) recently pointed out, copyright "protects corporate monopoly rights over culture and provides much of the profits to media conglomerates. *They could not exist without it.* Copyright has become a major policy encouraging the wholesale privatization of our common culture."

These new enclosures in the field of information, communication, culture, and creativity should not be taken lightly. These are the spheres of social life that are crucial for how we, as human beings, think, comprehend, normalize, reflect, rationalize, institutionalize, research, create, consolidate, question, preserve, and critically deal with our society, with its political and economic order, and, consequently, with our lives. Their commodification, therefore, has a direct influence on the quality of democracy, democratic participation and the public sphere in our society.

As noted above, anything can be commodified in a capitalist social context and be subjected to the particular interests of accumulation and profitability.

This is the only possible underlying goal of capital in the production and exchange of commodities. Exchange value predominates in this relationship and universal equivalence and instrumental rationality are preliminary conditions of the commodity-form. Even declaratively, the central goal of these tendencies can hardly be the benefit of human beings and the promotion of democracy. Just to take an example, even the commodification of information today creates new social and economic inequalities and deepens existing ones, often influencing whole societies and communities, not "only" individuals (see H. Schiller 1996; Bettig 1996). And because IPRs can cover almost anything (Perelman 2002), especially with the help of new ICT s, everything can be commodified, a fact that has important repercussions for wider society. This was already noticed by Jameson (1991, 37), when he observed that ICT s "are themselves but a distorted figuration of something even deeper, namely, the whole world system of a present-day multinational capitalism." He saw the communication network as closely connected to capital and the global capitalist system. In this way, the commodification of communication and the seeming openness of the Internet are a perfect reflection of neo-liberal values, in which everything must operate as a business and the market should have the final word about everything (cf. Fisher 2010).

These early observations by Jameson are very close to those by Dan Schiller (2000), who closely connected computer networks to the rise of neo-liberal capitalism and the continuing global expansion of the capitalist marketplace. He used the notion of *digital capitalism* to denote the fact that the Internet is now one of the focal communications points of the supranational market system. It is its underlying and unavoidable infrastructure, which makes possible information sharing within and among transnational corporations. These findings should not come as a surprise, in Mattelart's (2000, 77) opinion communication *must* be omnipresent and offer completely free interaction if transnational corporations want to function properly. Otherwise the spatially separated and mutually dependent parts of the "network-firm" (its strategy is necessarily both global and local at the same time) cannot serve the whole. "Any shortcoming in the interoperability between the parts, any lack of free interaction, is a threat to the system," he points out (Ibid.).

It is exactly demands of the corporate business that were crucial for the development of the Internet, which made possible digital commerce. Dan Schiller's (Ibid., xvi) statement that "cyberspace not only exemplifies but today actually shapes the greater political economy of which it has become a critical part," in many ways underlines Jameson's earlier observations and supports them with a clear materialist historical account. Eran Fisher (2010) provided a similar account when he pointed out that digital discourse follows the same logic as neoliberalism and is in fact essential in comprehending society *as* market. Mosco (2004, 156–157) was one of the first authors to *directly* connect digitalization to commodification. For him the emergence of cyberspace should in fact be apprehended in light of commodification of the whole communication process. Communication and technology help to support the expansion of commodification throughout society according to Mosco (2009, 12–13, 13), and this has become especially manifest with the emergence of digitalization.

An important aspect of communication is its lack of solid boundaries. Communication is more often a fluid *process*, rather than a constant and solidified *thing*. This fact is perfectly encompassed in the term *information flow*. Communication is a constant flow that can seep through and gradually break down anything solid. Authors writing in critical communication studies learnt about this the hard way, through observing practices of cultural imperialism, as formally sovereign states had enormous difficulties constructing anything resembling impenetrable boundaries against the international communication flows organized by capital. According to Terranova (2004, 2, 8), it is in fact difficult to think about cultural formations as completely separate entities, the key reason being the mutual and interacting connection of communication processes. This is not necessarily down to a technological interconnectedness, which is enabled by new communication channels and ICTs, but to the "nature" of the informational flows that spill over networks and circulate beyond them, constituting an informational *milieu*. Marazzi (2008), similarly, writes that economic relations trickle into every pore of the flexible post-Fordist society. They are now pervasive and absolutizing, and according to Marazzi (Ibid., 43), this reflects the fact that language is similarly pervasive.[44]

Already at the end of the 1980s Robins and Webster (1988) paid attention to the penetration of commodification into all (even the most intimate) parts of human lives, which included the sphere of reproduction and of (formally) "free time." Mosco (1982, ch. 4, cf. Martin 2002; Wittel 2013, 315–316) similarly pointed out at that time that capital entered the sphere of intimate human relations. Also in the 1980s, Gorz (1982) noted that with the expansion of capital into "free time" profits could now also be extracted from those human activities that were previously left to human imagination. Mosco (1989, 26) separated between extensive and intensive commodification when he wrote

---

44 In fact, language has become central in the production and exchange of things in the current phase of capitalist accumulation; communication is now both a raw material and an instrument of work according to Marazzi (2008, 49). We could thus write about *semiocapital*, because of "the semioticization of the social relations of production. The private has become public, and the public has become economic." (Marazzi 2008, 44).

about expansion of commodification to the areas that were previously outside capitalist markets. If extensive commodification denoted its extension from local to global markets, the key characteristics of intensive commodification meant that the commodity-form has now also expanded into the field of social reproduction: into home, school, entertainment and so on. There has been an obvious increase in both types of commodification, leading to till then unprecedented levels of market penetration. Because he saw commodification and new enclosures (mainly of information) as the key forces leading to social transformations at the time, Mosco (1989) would write about "the Pay-Per Society" rather than about "the information society."

5.2   A Seeping Commodification

> The total absorption in commercial translations that permeates the tightest echelons of the social order filters down to all levels.
> HERBERT I. SCHILLER (2000, 45)

Overwhelming communicative enclosures and both intensive and extensive commodification of these fields lead us to the final observation of this chapter, namely, that we have been witnessing a qualitative transformation in the way commodification continues to expand. The key reason for this qualitative transformation seems to be in the characteristics of communication itself, which has been incorporated into capitalist accumulation process in all its phases. Communication inevitably runs throughout all the spheres of society, which is especially true with the new ICTs and concurrent expansion of digital networks that are able to permeate the most insignificant micro-practices of our lives. Some very similar characteristics that hold for communication can therefore be attributed to commodification when it fully encroaches upon information, communication, and culture (including their production, distribution, and consumption). Murdock (2014, 140) recently came to a similar conclusion in his critique of the celebratory observers of digital technologies. According to him, such non-critical authors "are apt to forget that this increasing mediatization of everyday life is not an abstract movement. It is part of a generalised, and very concrete, process of intensified integration into commodity culture."

The expansion of communication networks and digitalization have provided an important infrastructure that helped both to extend and intensify commodification throughout places that have hitherto been untouched by capitalist market. On this basis, it is possible to propose a concept of *a seeping commodification*, a qualitatively novel type of the commodification process.

The key characteristic of a seeping commodification is the fact that, in the current historical epoch, commodity-form is able to trickle down to all the niches and activities of society and human lives. A seeping commodification is able to more or less successfully mimic the activities that are distinctive of communication, which has (in the recent decades) been completely absorbed into the capitalist accumulation circuit.

Because of these characteristics, commodification is nowadays able literally to *seep* into the spheres that seemed completely impenetrable (even unimaginable) to the market exchange in the past. For example, one only needs to think of the importance of the (commodified) *genome* in the rise of biotechnology (Rifkin 2000) or the statistical collections of personal data, which presuppose novel and intrusive forms of (amongst other types especially economic) surveillance with the new ICTs (see Allmer 2012; Fuchs et al. 2012; Sandoval 2012). Or let us consider the increasing intrusiveness of the corporate branding, which now also covers branding of nations (see Kania-Lundholm 2012, ch. 3), whole communities (Prodnik 2012b), or even faculty departments at universities. One of the most absurd cases of the latter is provided by the IEDC-Bled School of Management (Slovenia), which today includes *The Coca-Cola Chair of Sustainable Development*.[45] No less absurd are Amazon's patent on the single-click buying method (see Berry 2008, 34), U.S. Olympic Committee's trademark over the word "Olympic" (see Boyle 2008, xi–xii), Microsoft's double-clicking patent,[46] or copyright claim over football match fixtures in the English Premier League, which lasted for a few years and has later been removed by the European Court of Justice.

One of the consequences of the process of a seeping commodification is that many boundaries are starting to disintegrate before our eyes, leaving the door open for further expansion of capital. It is not only that communication and information do not pay regard to any solid boundaries; they also became a constituent part of almost every institution, process, and thing in society, including a crucial part of the (post-Fordist) production process (Marazzi 2008). It is significant that an important characteristic of postmodernity is, precisely, fluidity. Bauman (2000), for example, used a very suitable metaphor of "the liquid modernity" to demonstrate that society on the one hand has remained the same (*modern capitalism*) and, on the other hand, that there are constant changes occurring throughout society (*liquidity*): this is the persisting continuity and change, which is occurring simultaneously, and has been mentioned earlier in the text. The liquidity of communication is accompanied by a

---

45   See: http://www.iedc.si/about-iedc/history (1. 2. 2014).

46   See: http://www.wired.com/techbiz/media/news/2004/06/63707 (1. 2. 2014).

strict rigidity, which is required by commodity-form, market exchange, and capitalist social relations.

Since communication is now an integral part of all aspects of human lives, commodification can spill across all society and quietly seep into formerly intact areas and relations. This constant problem of setting boundaries and limitations was closely observed by Dan Schiller (2007, 24–27). He stressed it has become near-impossible for communication scholars to focus only on the narrow field of media under informationalized digital capitalism. The areas that have traditionally been of interest to the media and communication research have now started to overlap with other spheres, such as the (increasingly commodified) field of biotechnology.

> The transition to information capitalism does not depend on or equate with a narrow sector of media-based products. It is coextensive with a socio-economic metamorphosis of information across a great (and still-undetermined) range. As commodity relations are imposed on previously overlooked spheres of production, new forms of genetic and biochemical information acquire an unanticipated equivalence with other, more familiar genres.
>
> D. SCHILLER 2007, 25

As mentioned, an important epiphenomenon of these processes is a continuous disintegration of many boundaries and their transformation into indefinable, malleable and constantly changeable areas and processes (cf. Deleuze 1992). There has been, for example, a disintegration of the dividing line between the spheres of the intimate, the private and the public, and of the formerly clearer distinctions between journalism and PR (see Dahlgren 2009, 49). Public communication and advertisement have likewise started to merge, while the dichotomy between the *virtual* and the *real* is falling apart and becoming more and more irrelevant (see Prodnik 2012b). One could also point to the formerly strict separation lines between the sovereign nation states and the wider global order that now dissipated because of the disintegration of the national borders for capital flows.[47] Similarly, separation between public and private ownership has started disintegrate both in the form of public-private ownerships and in recent socializations of private debts. There has also been an incorporation of our most intimate information into the circuit of capital

---

47   Herbert Schiller (1996, 113, 114) pointed out it was already satellite technology that "has largely made national borders irrelevant." In his view "global corporations and media-cultural conglomerates [...] are indifferent to formal communication boundaries."

via digital surveillance, which makes possible new types of quantification and amassment of data (the so-called "big data") that via economic surveillance lead to commodification of personal characteristics of the Internet users and their everyday life activities (see Allmer 2012; Fuchs et al. 2011; Sandoval 2012). The same disintegrative process, as already mentioned above, is happening between the formerly very distinct spheres of production and reproduction, or between leisure time and work time (Gorz 2010). While none of these boundaries were ever impenetrable and their slow disintegration is evident for several decades now, they are becoming increasingly porous and vague as somehow clear demarcation lines.

Herbert Schiller (1989) already noticed these changes decades ago, when he pointed out how different spheres and parts of society have started to blur. Amongst the key reasons for this transformation was an offensive of the corporate capital, which started to permeate all social spaces. Furthermore, "deregulation, privatization, and the expansion of market relationships have affected all corners of the economy" (H. Schiller 1996, 46).

What seems of prime importance is not only that commodification has encompassed new spheres of social life, but that even the spheres that are not (or, at least not yet) subjugated to these tendencies, are being remodelled in the ways to reflect the rules of the capitalist market. Even the projects and activities not driven directly by market considerations are now compelled to justify their existence through neoliberal categories such as efficiency, the real "use-value" of some public project (which is in fact the exchange-value on and for the market), economistic rationale and so on. As pointed out by Crouch (2004, 40) governments around the world are increasingly incapable of drawing the line between public-service and commercial entities. They heedlessly try to imitate the *modus operandi* of private firms and require from its own departments to act as if they were firms. In Crouch's view, this contributes to the arrival of what he calls post-democracy, which is devoid of egalitarianism and fundamentally flawed because of the increasing power of corporate elites. The instrumentalized quantifying logic is distinctive of neoliberal capitalism, where the legitimation for doing something must be either directly – or at the very least indirectly – connected to the underlying logic distinctive of the capitalist market.

With a general commodification of communication, there is an emergence of several new dilemmas, contradictions, conflicts, and antagonistic relations – from the rise in rent capitalism to the new forms of labour and the ways in which value is created. These contradictions perhaps indicate a fundamental structural crisis of capitalism, which could be transforming into a new phase of its development. There seems to be no doubt, as Wallerstein (2001/1991, 167) warns, that "The bourgeoisie of today are already in the process of trying to survive their structural crisis by transforming themselves into 'x' reigning over a new mode of production." This takeover, however, is neither inevitable nor completely unstoppable. The multifacetedness and contradictory nature of these intrusive social processes lies primarily in the fact that singularities and political subjectivities – such as alternative social movements – are struggling to create common spaces of living and acting that oppose total capitalist colonization (e.g. Hardt and Negri 2009).

The lessons of the past teach us that the bulldozing power of capital should not be naively underestimated, as the seemingly unstoppable expansion of capitalism marches forward, rarely being systematically opposed. But, even though there is a tendency to commodify everything, capital can never subjugate all social spheres. It cannot colonize human language-capacity, which makes possible creativity and virtuosity, even if it can commodify everything that originates in, and results from, communication. With its expansion into all spheres and areas commodification also "moves inexorably toward an asymptote of 100 percent. Once we are in the upper ranges of this curve, each further step begins to put a squeeze on global profit and hence renders very acute the internal competition among the accumulators of capital." (Wallerstein 2001/1991, 24–25) This leads to the limits of growth, to economic crisis, and consequently to new political turmoils, when alternatives to the present social order seem more pressing and feasible.

Even though there has been a more or less successful capitalist colonisation of many areas that have so far not been subordinated to the reign of the commodity-form, it should be noted that a seeping commodification is not an unequivocal process; it is, rather, a very ambivalent and contradictory one, in large part owing exactly to its mutability and lack of boundaries. Conflicts and contradictions can emerge at all levels of social reality and what seems like an opportunity for capital, can quite often be subverted against it. Holloway (2010) metaphorically wrote about "crack capitalism" as a way of radically transforming the world. In Holloway's *new grammar of revolution*, cracks are spaces that defy logic of capitalism and produce oppositional social relations. They are often simple and small acts of rebellion that produce small ruptures to the dominant dynamic of social totality, which attempt to turn these processes in the opposite way.

Communication can be both commodified and, at the same time, be a tool against oppression; its liquidity and lack of boundaries may be both a liability and an opportunity. Similarly, digital sphere is extremely commodified, but also offers rejection of capitalist social relations and offers new spaces of oppositional practices. Political movements are establishing active forms of rebellion, and there are both theoretic alternatives and practical applications that go beyond capitalist organization of communication, culture, and information. Together with these alternatives, new forms and possibilities for organization emerge. Williams (1980/2005, 33–35) forcefully argued that contradictions are not present only at the level of super-structure, where there are ideological conflicts are being played out. They are also present at the level of political-economic base, where capitalist relations of production are currently dominant, but are also opposed with alternative organization of production. Base in a concrete historical context should therefore not be seen as uniform or static; on the contrary, it is dynamic and contradictory. This means that alternative relations of production can both emerge or already be present within the wider capitalist context. Such antagonist struggles are best exemplified by movements that fight for (the/a) common(s). They present one possible alternative vision of the future that counters commodification, goes against capitalism and beyond public/private dichotomy (see Mosco 1989, 24; Bollier 2002; Dyer-Witheford 2007; Berry 2008; Hardt and Negri 2009; Murdock 2011; Wittel 2013). To put it in the words of Dyer-Witheford (2007, 28): "If the cell form of capitalism is the commodity, the cellular form of a society beyond capital is the common."

6   Conclusion

Several unresolved dilemmas have been posed throughout the text and more questions have been raised than answered. One of these is certainly in the category of labour: what does it encompass in the current historical context? It might be difficult for many to contemplate the idea that what is commonly considered as 'leisure time' can today be defined as a specific type of labour. My goal here was not to seek transhistorical, anthropological or essentialist definitions of a necessarily historical phenomenon – namely, labour in the context of a capitalist society. What should interest us is *what capital deems as labour*, no matter how implausible that particular type of labour or its products might seem to us personally. Both political economy and its critique need, first and foremost, technical rather than moral definitions, which can enable a radical political resistance against capitalist subjugation. Can one go so far as to claim that any activity producing additional exchange-value for the owner of the commodity could be considered as some sort of labour (no matter what the magnitude of this added value might be)? This is not far from Marcuse's definition, which he derives from Marx's writings. He is defining the term labour "to mean what capitalism actually understands by it in the last analysis, that activity which creates surplus value in commodity production, or, which 'produces capital'" (Marcuse 1955, 293). Productivity in this sense is always something that is defined by the capital alone.

More detailed answers will have to wait for now, but what is important here is to acknowledge that big shifts, both at the social and at the economic level, have happened in the last decades and we lack acceptable answers and thorough analyses for many of them. Some indicators of these transformations have been given, through the problems and dilemmas raised in this text. We might therefore be able to provide a working thesis with regard to the all-encompassing, seeping commodification, which runs throughout different spheres and parts of society, permeating all levels of human and social life. This thesis needs to be further substantiated, but can offer a solid ground for a continuation of several ideas already raised regarding this issue:

> The structural tendency of capitalism, which has developed into a world-integrated economic system, is not only to commodify and valorise all material and social aspects of life, but also to incorporate human life as such (i.e. species-being) into its accumulation cycle: not only speech, but our ability to speak [logos], not only our feelings and emotions, but our generic human abilities for these activities. This tendency dictates that not a second of human life should be wasted by falling out of this economistic circuit of instrumental rationalisation and detailed calculation; every human act must be encompassed and every aspect of social life carefully measured.

Marx has been able to demonstrate the importance of the commodity-form and exchange for our social lives. The current phase of commodification goes much further than this however; it starts to erode and change almost all human contacts and relations. It not only instrumentalises communication in the media, but also infringes interpersonal communication. Where commodity starts to reign supreme over society, any possible independence of use-value is eradicated; anything socially useful that lacks exchange-value becomes worthless, dispensable, and irrelevant (what else is the *real* meaning of the draconian austerity cuts throughout the European Union?). What should worry us is not only social communication, which is possibly a somewhat abstract notion, but also the fundamental categories of democratic life. Information and communication cannot be seen just as *one of the many types of commodities*. They are crucial components of what we deem as free and democratic societies.

As Hanno Hardt (2004, 74) stressed, communication is central in most of the definitions of democracy with cogent reason. But can we really claim a right to communicate exists for everybody if the whole communication process is turning into a big, interrelated and world-wide commodity chain, which has to play under "the coercive laws of competition" (Marx 1990/1867, 433): from the production (knowledge labour), to the content, infrastructure, and finally audiences – human beings? Is there any freedom when "creative, intellectual work turns into mass production, while individual ideas undergo ideological scrutiny to fit the demands of the market, where predictability and repetition are the key to commercial success" (Hardt 2004, 34)? In a time when the key communication channels and freedom of expression are in fact monopolised (or at best oligopolised) and owned by the smallest elite possible (McChesney 2008)?[48] When social inequalities are at one of its historical peaks?

It is possible to claim that from its outset, critical theory has fought against instrumental reasoning and against positivist outlook on the world that does not reflect or critique this instrumentalisation of human beings and their relations (see Fuchs 2011, 11–26). Our task as critical theorists is to continuously provide a cogent critique of these processes. This is so especially because of the enduring instrumentalisation and economistic rationalisation, which is a consequence of total and seemingly unprecedented commodification in the history of capitalism. If we believe Wallerstein, however, there is at least one positive consequence of these processes: "Total commodification eventually removes the veils of the market." (Wallerstein 2001/1991, 25).

References

Adorno, Theodor W. 2001/1991. *The Culture Industry: Selected Essays on Mass Culture.* London, New York: Routledge.

Agamben, Giorgio. 2000. *Means Without Ends: Notes on Politics.* Minneapolis, London: University of Minnesota Press.

---

48 McChesney goes even further, stressing that "the media have become a significant antidemocratic force in the United States. The wealthier and more powerful the corporate media giants have become, the poorer the prospects for participatory democracy." (McChesney 2008, 426) For Hardt, similarly, "the media have become part of the corporate domain of the American society which converts economic domination into political power. Thus, the media shape consciousness and help reinforce the dominant corporate ideology, which becomes the reigning political ideology". (Hardt 2004, 48).

Allmer, Thomas. 2012. *Towards a Critical Theory of Surveillance in Informational Capitalism*. Frankfurt am Main [...]: Peter Lang.

Andrejevic, Mark. 2012. Exploitation in the Data Mine. In *Internet and Surveillance: The Challenges of Web 2.0 and Social Media*, edited by Christian Fuchs, Kees Boersma, Anders Albrechtslund, and Marisol Sandoval, 71–88. New York: Routledge.

Arendt, Hannah. 1998/1958. *The Human Condition*. 2nd ed. Chicago, London: The University of Chicago Press.

Arrighi, Giovanni. 1994. *The Long Twentieth Century: Money, Power, and the Origins of Our Times*. London, New York: Verso.

Babe, Robert E. 2009. *Cultural Studies and Political Economy: Toward a New Integration*. Lanham, Boulder, New York: Lexington Books.

Baker, Edwin C. 1994. *Advertising and a Democratic Press*. Princeton, New Jersey: Princeton University Press.

Balibar, Étienne. 2007. *The Philosphy of Marx*. London, New York: Verso.

Barbalet, Jack M. 1983. *Marx's Construction of Social Theory*. London, Boston [...]: Routledge and Keegan Paul.

Bauman, Zygmunt. 2000. *Liquid Modernity*. Cambridge, Malden: Polity.

Bellamy Foster, John and Robert McChesney. 2011. The Internet's Unholy Marriage to Capitalism. *MRZine* 62 (10). Available via: http://monthlyreview.org/2011/03/01/the-Internets-unholy-marriage-to-capitalism (March 17, 2012).

Bermejo, Fernando. 2009. Audience Manufacture in Historical Perspective: from Broadcasting to Google. *New Media and Society* 11 (1–2): 133–154.

Berry, David. 2008. *Copy, Rip, Burn: The Politics of Copyleft and Open Source*. London: Pluto Press.

Bettig, Ronald V. 1996. *Copyright Culture: The Political Economy of Intellectual Property*. Boulder: Westview Press.

Bilureyst, Daniel and Philippe Meers. 2011. The Political Economy of Audiences. In *The Handbook of Political Economy of Communications*, edited by Janet Wasko, Graham Murdock and Helena Sousa, 415–435. Malden, Oxford: Wiley-Blackwell.

Bollier, David. 2002. *Silent Theft: The Private Plunder of Our Common Wealth*. New York, London: Pluto Press.

Bonefeld, Werner. 2001. The Permanence of Primitive Accumulation: Commodity Fetishism and Social Constitution. *The Commoner* 2: 1–15.

Bonefeld, Werner. 2009. Emancipatory Praxis and Conceptuality in Adorno. In *Negativity and Revolution: Adorno and Political Activism*, edited by John Holloway, Fernando Matamoros and Sergio Tischler, 122–150. London: Pluto Press.

Boyle, James. 2008. *The Public Domain: Enclosing the Commons of the Mind*. New Haven, London: Yale University Press.

Braudel, Fernand. 1979. *Afterthoughts on Material Civilization and Capitalism*. Baltimore, London: The John Hopkins University Press.

Braudel, Fernand. 1980. History and the Social Sciences: The Longue Durée. In Fernand Braudel, *On History*, pp.: 25–54. Chicago: Chicago University Press.

Brophy, Enda and Greig de Peuter. 2007. Immaterial Labour, Precarity, and Recomposition. In *Knowledge Workers in the Information Society*, edited by Catherine McKercher and Vincent Mosco, 177–192. Lanham: Lexington Books.

Brown, Phillip, Hugh Lauder, and David Ashton. 2011. *The Global Auction: The Broken Promises of Education, Jobs and Incomes*. Oxford, New York: Oxford University Press.

Bücher, Carl Wilhelm. 1893/1901. *Industrial Evolution*. New York: Henry Holt.

Caraway, Brett. 2011. Audience Labor in the New Media Environment: A Marxian Revisiting of the Audience Commodity. *Media, Culture & Society* 33 (5): 693–708.

Chicchi, Federico. 2010. On the Threshold of Capital, At the Thresholds of the Common. In *Crisis in the Global Economy* edited by Andrea Fumagalli Sandro Mezzadra, 139–152. New York: Autonomedia.

Cleaver, Harry. 2000/1979. *Reading Capital Politically*. Leeds: Anti/Theses.

Collier, Andrew. 1994. *Critical Realism*. London, New York: Verso.

Crary, Jonathan. 2013. *24/7: Late Capitalism and the Ends of Sleep*. London, New York: Verso.

Crouch, Colin. 2004. *Post-Democracy*. Cambridge, Malden: Polity.

Curran, James. 2002. *Media and Power*. London: Routledge.

Dahlgren, Peter. 2009. *Media and Political Engagement: Citizens, Communication and Democracy*. Cambridge, New York [...]: Cambridge University Press.

De Angelis, Massimo. 2007. *The Beginning of History: Value Struggles and Global Capital*. London: Pluto Press.

Dean, Jodi. 2008. Communicative Capitalism: Circulation and the Foreclosure of Politics. In *Digital Media and Democracy: Tactics in Hard Times*, edited by Megan Boler, 101–121. Cambridge, London: MIT Press.

Debord, Guy. 1970. *Society of Spectacle*. Detroit: Black and Red Press.

Deleuze, Gilles. 1992. Postscript on the Societies of Control. *October* 59: 3–7.

Doogan, Kevin. 2009. *New Capitalism? The Transformation of Work*. Cambridge, Malden: Polity Press.

Dyer-Witheford, Nick. 1999. *Cyber-Marx: Cycles and Circuits in High Technology Capitalism*. Urbana: University of Illinois Press.

Douglas, Sarah and Thomas Guback. 1984. Production and technology in the communication/information revolution. *Media, Culture and Society* 6: 233–245.

Dorfman, Ariel and Armand Mattelart. 1975. *How to Read Donald Duck: Imperialist Ideology in the Disney Comic*. New York: I. G. Editions.

Dyer-Witheford, Nick. 2004. 1844/2004/2044: The Return of Species-Being. *Historical Materialism* 12 (4): 3–26.

Dyer-Witheford, Nick. 2007. Commonism. *Turbulence* 1 (1): 28–29.

Eagleton, Terry. 1996. *The Illusions of Postmodernism*. Malden, Oxford: Blackwell.

Fisher, Eran. 2010. *Media and New Capitalism in the Digital Age: The Spirit of Networks.* New York: Palgrave Macmillan.

Fisher, Mark. 2009. *Capitalist Realism: Is There no Alternative?* Winchester, Washington: Zero Books.

Fiske, John. 1990. *Introduction to Communication Studies.* 2nd edition. London, New York: Routledge.

Fleissner, Peter. 2009. The "Commodification" of Knowledge in the Global Information Society. *tripleC – Cognition, Communication, Co-operation: Open Access Journal for a Global Sustainable Information Society* 7 (2): 228–238.

Fortunati, Leopoldina. 1989. *The Arcane of Reproduction: Housework, Prostitution, Labour and Capital.* New York: Autonomedia.

Frith, Simon and Lee Marshal (eds.). 2004. *Music and Copyright.* New York: Routledge.

Fuchs, Christian. 2008. *Internet and Society: Social Theory in the Information Age.* New York, London: Routledge.

Fuchs, Christian. 2010. Labor in Informational Capitalism and on the Internet. *The Information Society* 26 (3): 179–196.

Fuchs, Christian. 2011. *Foundations of Critical Media and Information Studies.* London, New York: Routledge.

Fuchs, Christian. 2012c. Google Capitalism. *tripleC – Cognition, Communication, Co-operation: Open Access Journal for a Global Sustainable Information Society* 10 (1): 42–48.

Fuchs, Christian. 2012a. Dallas Smythe Today – The Audience Commodity, the Digital Labour Debate, Marxist Political Economy and Critical Theory. Prolegomena to a Digital Labour Theory of Value. *TripleC – Cognition, Communication, Co-operation*, 10(2): 692–740.

Fuchs, Christian. 2012b. Capitalism or information society? The fundamental question of the present structure of society. *European Journal of Social Theory* 16(4): 1–22.

Fuchs, Christian. 2014. Critique of the Political Economy of Informational Capitalism and Social Media. In Christian Fuchs and Marisol Sandoval (eds.), *Critique, Social Media and the Information Society*, 51–65. New York, Oxon: Routledge.

Fuchs, Christian, Kees Boersma, Anders Albrechtslund, and Marisol Sandoval, eds. 2012. *Internet and Surveillance: The Challenges of Web 2.0 and Social Media.* New York: Routledge.

Fuchs, Christian and Sebastian Sevignani. 2013. What is Digital Labour? What is Digital Work? What's their Difference? And why do these Questions Matter for Understanding Social Media? *TripleC – Cognition, Communication, Co-operation*, 11(2): 237–293.

Fumagalli, Andrea and Sandro Mezzadra, eds. 2010. *Crisis in the Global Economy.* New York: Autonomedia.

Gandy, Oscar H. Jr. 1992. The political economy approach: A critical challenge. *Journal of Media Economics* 5 (2): 23–42.

Gandy, Oscar H. Jr. 2012. Matrix Multiplication and the Digital Divide. In *Race After the Internet*, edited by Lisa Nakamura and Peter A. Chow-White, 128–145. New York, London: Routledge.

Gorz, André. 1989. *Critique of Economic Reason.* London, New York: Verso.

Gorz, André. 1982. *Farewell to the Working Class: An Essay on Post-Industrial Socialism.* London: Pluto Press.

Gorz André. 2010. *The Immaterial.* London: Seagull Books.

Gramsci, Antonio. 1971. *Selections from the Prison Notebooks.* London: Lawrence and Wishart.

Hardt, Hanno. 1979. *Social Theories of the Press: Early German and American Perspectives.* Beverly Hills, London: Sage Publications.

Hardt, Hanno. 2001. *Social Theories of the Press: Constituents of Communication Research, 1840s to 1920s.* 2nd edition. Lanham, Boulder, New York, Oxford: Rowman & Littlefield Publishers.

Hardt, Hanno. 2004. *Myths for the Masses: An Essay on Mass Communication.* Malden, Oxford, Victoria: Blackwell Publishing.

Hardt, Michael and Antonio Negri. 2001. *Empire.* Cambridge: Harvard Univ. Press.

Hardt, Michael and Antonio Negri. 2004. *Multitude: War and Democracy in the Age of Empire.* New York: The Penguin Press.

Hardt, Michael and Antonio Negri. 2009. *Commonwealth.* Cambridge, Massachusetts: The Belknap Press of Harvard University Press.

Harvey, David. 1996. *Justice, Nature and the Geography of Difference.* Cambridge: Blackwell.

Harvey, David. 2003. *The New Imperialism.* Oxford, New York: Oxford University Press.

Harvey, David. 2009. *Cosmopolitanism and the Geographies of Freedom.* New York: Columbia University Press.

Harvey, David. 2010. *A Companion to Marx's Capital.* London, New York: Verso.

Hay, Colin. 2002. *Political Analysis: A Critical Introduction.* New York: Palgrave.

Headrick, Daniel R. 2000. *When Information Came of Age: Technologies of Knowledge in the Age of Reason and Revolution, 1700–1850.* Oxford, New York: Oxford University Press.

Heinrich, Michael. 2012. *An Introduction to the Three Volumes of Karl Marx's Capital.* New York: Monthly Review Press.

Hesmondhalgh, David. 2008. Neoliberalism, Imperialism and the Media. In David Hesmondhalgh and Jason Toynbee (eds.), *The Media and Social Theory*, pp. 95–111. Abingdon and New York: Routledge.

Hesmondhalgh, David. 2007. *The Cultural Industries.* 2nd ed. London: Sage

Hindman, Matthew. 2009. *The Myth of Digital Democracy.* Princeton in Oxford: Princeton Press.

Hobsbawm, Eric. 2011. *How to Change the World: Reflections of Marx and Marxism*. New Haven, London: Yale University Press.

Holloway, John. 2010. *Crack Capitalism*. London, New York: Pluto Press.

Horkheimer, Max and Theodor Wiesengrund Adorno. 2002/1947. *Dialectic of Enlightenment: Philosophical Fragments*. Stanford, California: Stanford University Press.

Huws, Ursula. 2003. *The Making of a Cybertariat: Virtual Work in a Real World*. New York: MR Press.

Innis, Harold Adams. 2008/1951. *The Bias of Communication*. 2nd ed. Toronto: Univ. of Toronto Press.

Jameson, Fredric. 1991. *Postmodernism, or, The Cultural Logic of Late Capitalism*. Durham: Duke University Press.

Jameson, Fredric. 1998. *The Cultural Turn: Selected Writings on the Postmodern, 1983–1998*. London, New York: Verso.

Jameson, Fredric. 2007. *Jameson on Jameson: Conversations on Cultural Marxism*. Durham, London: Duke University Press.

Jameson, Fredric. 2009. *Valences of the Dialectic*. London, New York: Verso.

Jameson, Fredric. 2011. *Representing Capital: A Reading of Volume One*. London, New York: Verso.

Jhally, Sut. 1987. *The Codes of Advertising: Fetishism and the Political Economy of Meaning in the Consumer Society*. New York: Routledge.

Jhally, Sut. 2006. *The Spectacle of Accumulation: Essays in Media, Culture & Politics*. New York: Peter Lang Publishers.

Kang, Hyunjin and Matthew P. McAllister. 2011. Selling You and Your Clicks: Examining the Audience Commodification of Google. *tripleC – Cognition, Communication, Co-operation: Open Access Journal for a Global Sustainable Information Society* 9 (2): 141–153.

Kania-Lundholm, Magdalena. 2012. *Re-Branding a Nation Online: Discourses on Polish Nationalism and Patriotism*. Uppsala Universityt: Uppsala.

Lazzarato, Maurizio. 1996. Immaterial Labour. In *Radical Thought in Italy: A Potential Politics*, edited by Paolo Virno and Michael Hardt, 133–147. Minneapolis and London: Minnesota University Press.

Livant, Bill. 1979. The Audience Commodity: On the Blindspot Debate. *Canadian Journal of Political and Social Theory* 3 (1): 91–106.

Lefebvre, Henri. 1968. *The Sociology of Marx*. New York: Pantheon Books.

Lukács, Georg. 1971. *History and Class Consciousness: Studies in Marxist Dialectics*. Cambridge, Massachusets: The MIT Press.

Marazzi, Christian. 2008. *Capital and Language: From the New Economy to the War Economy*. Los Angeles: Semiotext(e).

Marazzi, Christian. 2010. *The Violence of Financial Capitalism*. Los Angeles: Semiotext(e).

Marcuse, Herbert. 1955. *Reason and Revolution: Hegel and the Rise of Social Theory.* 2nd ed. London: Routledge & Keegan Paul Ltd.

Martin, Randy. 2002. *Financialization of Daily Life.* Philadelphia: Temple University Press.

Marx, Karl. 1993/1858. *Grundrisse: Foundations of the Critique of Political Economy (Rough Draft).* London: Penguin Books.

Marx, Karl. 1990/1867. *Capital: A Critique of Political Economy, Volume One.* London: Penguin Books.

Marx, Karl and Frederick Engels. 1975. *Collected Works, Volume 3 (1843–1844).* London: Lawrence & Wishart.

Marx, Karl and Frederick Engels. 1976. *Collected Works, Volume 6 (1845–1848).* New York: International Publishers.

Marx, Karl and Frederick Engels. 1987. *Collected Works, Volume 29 (1857–1861).* New York: International Publishers.

Mattelart, Armand. 2000. *Networking the World, 1794–2000.* Minneapolis, London: University of Minnesota Press.

Mattelart, Armand. 1978. The Nature of Communications Practice in a Dependent Society. *Latin American Perspectives* 5 (1): 13–34.

Mattelart, Armand. 2011. New International Debates on Culture, Information, and Communication. In Janet Wasko, Graham Murdock and Helena Sousa (eds.), *The Handbook of Political Economy of Communications*, pp. 501–520. Malden, Oxford: Wiley-Blackwell.

Maxwell, Rick. 1991. The Image is Gold: Value, The Audience Commodity, and Fetishism. *Journal of Film and Video* 43 (1–2): 29–45.

Maxwell, Richard. 2003. *Herbert Schiller.* Lanham: Rowman and Littlefield.

May, Christopher. 2002. *The Information Society: a sceptical view.* Malden, Cambridge: Polity Press.

May, Christopher. 2010. *The Global Political Economy of Intellectual Property Rights: The New Enclosures.* 2nd ed. New York: Routledge.

McChesney, Robert W. 2008. *The Political Economy of Media.* New York: Monthly Review Press.

McChesney, Robert W. 2013. *Digital Disconnect: How Capitalism is turning the Internet against Democracy.* New York: The New Press.

McChesney, Robert W., Ellen Meiksins Wood and John Bellamy Foster (eds.). 1998. *Capitalism and the Information Age: The Political Economy of the Global Communication Revolution.* New York: Monthly Review Press.

Meehan, Eileen. 1993. Commodity Audience, Actual Audience: The Blindspot Debate. In *Illuminating the Blindspots: Essays Honoring Dallas W. Smythe*, edited by Janet Wasko, Vincent Mosco, and Manjunath Pendakur, 378–400. New Jersey: Ablex.

Melody, William H. 1993. On the Political Economy of Communication in the Information Society. In Janet Wasko, Vincent Mosco and Manjunath Pendakur (eds.), *Illuminating the Blindspots: Essays Honoring Dallas W. Smythe*, pp.: 63–81. New Jersey: Ablex.

Mezzadra, Sandro. 2011. The Topicality of Prehistory: A New Reading of Marx's Analysis of "So-Called Primitive Accumulation". *Rethinking Marxism* 22 (3): 302–321.

Mosco, Vincent. 1982. *Pushbutton Fantasies: Critical Perspectives on Videotext and Information Technology.* Norwood, New Jersey: Ablex.

Mosco, Vincent. 1989. *The Pay-Per Society: Computers & Communication in the Information Age.* Toronto: Garamond Press.

Mosco, Vincent. 1993. Free Trade in Communication: Building a World Business Order. In Kaarle Nordenstreng and Herbert I. Schiller (eds.), *Beyond National Sovereignty: International Communication in the 1990s*, pp.: 193–209. New Jersey: Ablex.

Mosco, Vincent. 2004. *The Digital Sublime: Myth, Power, and Cyberspace.* Cambridge, London: The MIT Press.

Mosco, Vincent. 2009. *The Political Economy of Communication.* 2nd edition. Los Angeles, London: Sage.

Mosco, Vincent and Catherine McKercher. 2008. *The Laboring of Communication: Will Knowledge Workers of the World Unite?* Lanham, Boulder, New York: Lexington Books.

Moulier Boutang, Yann. 2011. *Cognitive Capitalism.* Cambridge, Malden: Polity Press.

Mowlana, Hamid. 1985. *International Flow of Information: A Global Report and Analysis.* [Unesco Reports and Papers on Mass Communication, No. 99]. Pariz: Unesco.

Murdock, Graham. 1978. Blindspots about Western Marxism: A Reply to Dallas Smythe. *Canadian Journal of Political and Social Theory* 2 (2): 109–119.

Murdock, Graham. 2000. Peculiar Commodities: Audiences at Large in the World of Goods. In *Consuming Audiences? Production and Reception in Media Research*, edited by Ingunn Hagen and Janet Wasko, 47–70. Cresskill: Hampton Press.

Murdock, Graham. 2006a. Marx on Commodities, Contradictions and Globalisations Resources for a Critique of Marketised Culture. *E-Compós* 7: 1–23.

Murdock, Graham. 2006b. Notes from the Number One Country: Herbert Schiller on Culture, Commerce, and American Power. *International Journal of Cultural Policy* 12 (2): 209–227.

Murdock, Graham. 2011. Political Economies as Moral Economies: Commodities, Gifts, and Public Goods. In *The Handbook of Political Economy of Communications*, edited by Janet Wasko, Graham Murdock, and Helena Sousa, 13–40. Malden, Oxford: Wiley-Blackwell.

Murdock, Graham. 2014. Producing Consumerism: Commodities, Ideologies, Practices. In *Critique, Social Media and the Information Society*, edited by Christian Fuchs in Marisol Sandoval, 125–143. New York, London: Routledge.

Murdock, Graham and Peter Golding. 1973. For a Political Economy of Mass Communications. *The Socialist Register* 10: 205–234.

Napoli, Philip M. 2010. Revisiting 'Mass Communication' and the 'Work' of Audience in the New Media Environment. *Media, Culture and Society*, 32 (3): 505–516.

Napoli, Philip M. 2011. *Audience Evolution: New Technologies and the Transformation of Media Audiences.* New York: Columbia University Press.

Negri, Antonio. 1991/1984. *Marx Beyond Marx: Lessons on the Grundrisse.* London: Pluto Press.

Negri, Antonio. 1992. Interpretation of the Class Situation Today: Methodological Aspects. In *Open Marxism, Volume 2: Theory and Practice*, edited by Werner Bonefeld, Richard Gunn, and Kosmas Psychopedis, 69–105. London: Pluto Press.

Negri, Antonio. 1999. Value and Affect. *Boundary 2* 26 (2): 77–88.

Nightingale, Virginia, ed. 2011. *The Handbook of Media Audiences.* Malden, Oxford: Wiley-Blackwell.

Nordenstreng, Kaarle. 1993. New Information Order and Communication Scholarship: Reflections on a Delicate Relationship. In Janet Wasko, Vincent Mosco and Manjunath Pendakur (eds.), *Illuminating the Blindspots: Essays Honouring Dallas W. Smythe*, pp.: 251–273. New Jersey: Ablex.

Nordenstreng, Kaarle. 2004. Ferment in the Field: Notes on the Evolution of Communication Studies and its Disciplinary Nature. *The Public – Javnost* 11 (3): 5–18.

Nordenstreng, Kaarle. 2013. How the New World Order and Imperialism Challenge Media. *TripleC – Capitalism, Communication & Critique* 11 (2): 348–358.

Nordenstreng, Kaarle and Tapio Varis. 1974. *Television traffic – a one-way street? A survey and analysis of the international flow of television programme material.* [Unesco Reports and Papers on Mass Communication, No. 70]. Paris: Unesco.

Offe, Claus. 1984. *The Contradictions of the Welfare State.* The MIT Press: Cambridge.

Offe, Claus. 1987. Challenging the Boundaries of Institutional Politics: Social Movements since the 1960s. In Charles S. Maier (ed.), *Changing Boundaries of the Political*, pp.: 63–105. Cambridge: Cambridge University Press.

Osolnik, Bogdan. 2005. The MacBride Report – 25 Years Later. *Javnost – The Public* 12 (3): 5–12.

Park, Robert Ezra. 1922. *The Immigrant Press and Its Control.* New York, London: Harper & Brothers Publishers.

Parker, Ian. 1994. Commodities as Sign-Systems. In *Information and Communication in Economics*, edited by Robert E. Babe, 69–91. Boston Dordrecht, London: Kluwer Academic Publishers.

Pasquinelli, Matteo. 2009. Google's PageRank Algorithm: A Diagram of Cognitive Capitalism and the Rentier of the Common Intellect. In *Deep Search: The Politics of Search Beyond Google*, edited by Konrad Becker and Felix Stalder. London: Transaction Publishers. Available via: http://matteopasquinelli.com/docs/Pasquinelli_PageRank.pdf (April 1, 2012).

Perelman, Michael. 2000. *The Invention of Capitalism: Classical Political Economy and the Secret History of Primitive Accumulation*. Durham, London: Duke University Press.

Perelman, Michael. 2002. *Steal This Idea: Intellectual Property Rights and the Corporate Confiscation of Creativity*. New York: Palgrave.

Perelman, Michael. 2003a. Intellectual Property Rights and the Commodity Form: New Dimensions in the Legislated Transfer of Surplus Value. *Review of Radical Political Economics*, 35(3): 304–311.

Perelman, Michael. 2003b. The Weakness in Strong Intellectual Property Rights. *Challenge*, 46(6): 32–61.

Polanyi, Karl. 2001/1944. *The Great Transformation: The Political and Economic Origins of Our Times*. Boston: Beacon Press.

Postone, Moishe. 2003/1993. *Time, Labor, and Social Domination: A Reinterpretation of Marx's Social Theory*. Cambridge: Cambridge Univesity Press.

Prodnik, Jernej. 2011. Permanentnost primitivne akumulacije, ali: o privatni lastnini, komodifikaciji in povratku rente [eng.: The Permanence of Primitive Accumulation, or: On the Private Property, Commodification and Return of the Rent]. *Casopis za kritiko znanosti* 244: 89–109.

Prodnik, Jernej. 2012a. Toward a Critique of Surveillance in the Age of the Internet: A Reflection on the "Internet and Surveillance" Volume Edited by Fuchs, Boersma, Albrechtslund, and Sandoval. *tripleC – Cognition, Communication, Co-operation: Open Access Journal for a Global Sustainable Information Society* 10 (1): 92–99.

Prodnik, Jernej. 2012b. Post-fordist communities and cyberspace: a critical approach. In Harris Breslow and Aris Mousoutzanis (eds.), *Cybercultures: mediations of community, culture, politics*, pp. 75–100. Amsterdam, New York: Rodopi.

Rifkin, Jeremy. 2000. *The Age of Access: The New Culture of Hypercapitalism, Where All of Life Is a Paid-for Experience*. New York: Penguin.

Robins, Kevin and Frank Webster. 1988. Cybernetic Capitalism: Information, Technology, Everyday Life. In Vincent Mosco and Janet Wasko (eds.), *The Political Economy of Information*, 44–75. Wisconsin, London: The University of Wisconsin Press.

Robins, Kevin and Frank Webster. 2004. The Long History of the Information Revolution. In Frank Webster (ed.), *The Information Society Reader*, pp.: 62–80. Routledge: London.

Sandel, Michael. 2012. *What Money Can't Buy: The Moral Limits of Markets*. London: Allen Lane.

Sandoval, Marisol. 2012. A Critical Empirical Case Study of Consumer Surveillance on Web 2.0. In *Internet and Surveillance: The Challenges of Web 2.0 and Social Media*, edited by Christian Fuchs, Kees Boersma, Anders Albrechtslund, and Marisol Sandoval, 147–169. New York: Routledge.

Schiller, Dan. 2000a. *Digital Capitalism: Networking the Global Market System*. Cambridge, London: The MIT Press.

Schiller, Dan. 2007. *How to Think about Information*. Urbana, Chicago: University of Illinois Press.

Schiller, Herbert Irwing. 1969. *Mass Communications and American Empire*. Boston: Beacon Press.

Schiller, Herbert Irwing. 1973. *The Mind Managers*. Boston: Beacon Press.

Schiller, Herbert Irwing. 1976. *Communication and Cultural Domination*. New York: International Arts and Sciences Press.

Schiller, Herbert Irwing. 1978. Decolonization of Information: Efforts toward a New International Order. *Latin American Perspectives* 5 (1): 35–48.

Schiller, Herbert Irwing. 1984. *Information and the Crisis Economy*. New Jersey: Ablex Publishing Corporation.

Schiller, Herbert I. 1989. *Culture, Inc.: The Corporate Takeover of Public Expression*. New York, Oxford: Oxford University Press.

Schiller, Herbert Irwing. 1996. *Information Inequality: The Deepening Social Crisis in America*. London, New York: Routledge.

Schiller, Herbert Irwing. 1998. Striving for communication dominance: a half-century review. In Daya Kishan Thussu (ed.), *Electronic Empires: Global Media and Local Resistance*, pp.: 17–26. London: Arnold.

Schiller, Herbert Irwing. 2000. *Living in the Number One Country: Reflections from a Critic of American Empire*. New York, London, Sydney: Seven Stories Press.

Schudson, Michael. 1978. *Discovering the News: A Social History of American Newspapers*. New York: Basic Books.

Smythe, Dallas W. 1954. Some Observations on Communications Theory. *Audio Visual Communication Review*, 2(1): 24–37.

Smythe, Dallas W. 1960. On the Political Economy Of Communications. *Journalism Quarterly* (Fall), 563–572.

Smythe, Dallas W. 1977. Communications: Blindspot of Western Marxism. In *Counterclockwise: Perspectives on Communication*, edited by Thomas Guback, 266–291. Boulder, San Francisco, Oxford: Westview Press.

Smythe, Dallas W. 1978. Rejoinder to Graham Murdock. In *Counterclockwise: Perspectives on Communication*, edited by Thomas Guback, 292–301. Boulder, San Francisco, Oxford: Westview Press.

Smythe, Dallas W. 1981a. Communications: Blindspot of Economics. In *Culture, Communication, and Dependency: The Tradition of H.A. Innis*, edited by William H. Melody, Liora Salter and Paul Heyer, 111–126. New Jersey: Ablex.

Smythe, Dallas W. 1981b. *Dependency Road: Communications, Capitalism, Consciousness, and Canada*. New Jersey: Ablex Publishing.

Sohn-Rethel, Alfred. 1972. Mental and Manual Labour in Marxism. In *Situating Marx*, edited by Paul Walton and Stuart Hall, 44–71. London: Human Context Books.

Sohn-Rethel, Alfred. 1978. *Intellectual and Manual Labour: A Critique of Epistemology*. London, Basingstoke: The MacMillan Press Ltd..

Splichal, Slavko. 1981. *Množično komuniciranje med svobodo in odtujitvijo* [*Mass Communication Between Freedom and Alienation*]. Maribor: Obzorja.

Terranova, Tiziana. 2004. *Network culture: Politics for the information age*. London: Pluto Press.

Thompson, Edward Palmer. 1967. Time, Work-Discipline, and Industrial Capitalism. *Past and Present* 38: 56–97.

Thompson, Edward Palmer. 1991. *Customs in Common*. London: Merlin Press.

Thussu, Daya Kishan (ed.). 1998. *Electronic Empires: Global Media and Local Resistance*. London, New York: Arnold Publ.

Thussu, Daya Kishan. 2005. From MacBride to Murdoch: The Marketisation of Global Communication. *Javnost – The Public* 12(3): 47–60.

Thussu, Daya Kishan. 2006. *International Communication: Continuity and Change*. 2nd Edition. London: Hodder Arnold.

Huws, Ursula. 2003b. *The Making of a Cybertariat: Virtual Work in Real World*. New York: Monthly Review Press.

Vercellone, Carlo. 2010. The Crisis of the Law of Value and the Becoming-Rent of Profit. In *Crisis in the Global Economy* edited by Andrea Fumagalli and Sandro Mezzadra, 85–118. New York: Autonomedia.

Virno, Paolo. 1996. Notes on the "General Intellect". In *Marxism beyond Marxism*, edited by Saree Makdisi, Cesare Casarino and Rebecca E. Karl, 265–272. New York, London: Routledge.

Virno, Paolo. 2004. *A Grammar of the Multitude: For an Analysis of Contemporary Forms of Life*. Semiotext(e), Los Angeles and New York.

Virno, Paolo. 2005. Interview with Paolo Virno (by Branden W. Joseph). *Grey Room* 21: 26–37.

Wallerstein, Immanuel. 1983. *Historical Capitalism*. London: Verso.

Wallerstein, Immanuel. 2001/1991. *Unthinking Social Science: The Limits of Nineteenth-Century Paradigms*. 2nd ed. Philadelphia: Temple University Press.

Wasko, Janet. 2005. Studying the Political Economy of Media and Information. *Communicaçao e Sociedade* 7: 25–48.

Williams, Raymond. 1962. *Communications*. Baltimore, Maryland: Penguin Books.

Williams, Raymond. 2011/1961. *The Long Revolution*. Cardigan: Parthian Books.

Williams, Raymond. 1973. Base and Superstructure in Marxist Cultural Theory. *New Left Review* 82: 3–16.

Williams, Raymond. 2005/1980. *Culture and Materialism*. London: Verso.

Winseck, Dwayne R. and Robert M. Pike. 2007. *Communication and Empire: Media, Markets, and Globalization, 1860–1930*. Durham, London: Duke University Press.

Winseck, Dwayne R. 2011. The Political Economies of Media and the Transformation of the Global Media Industries. In Dwayne R. Winseck and Dal Yong Jin (eds.), *The Political Economies of Media: The Transformations of the Global Media Industries*, 3–48. London, New York: Bloomsbury Academic.

Wittel, Andreas. 2013. Counter-commodification: The economy of contribution in the digital commons. *Culture and Organization* 19(4): 314–331.

CHAPTER 10

The Construction of Platform Imperialism in the Globalisation Era*

Dal Yong Jin

1   Introduction

In the early 21st century, notions of imperialism have gained significance with the rapid growth of platform technologies. Platforms, such as social network sites (SNS s, e.g., Facebook), search engines (e.g., Google), smartphones (e.g., iPhone), and operating systems (e.g., Android) are known as digital intermediaries, which have greatly influenced people's daily lives. The digital platform has emerged "as an increasingly familiar term in the description of the online services of content intermediaries, both in their self-characterizations and in the broader public discourse of users, the press and commentaries" (Gillespie 2010, 349). Due to the importance of platforms – not only as hardware architecture but also as software frameworks that allow software to run – for the digital economy and culture, several countries have developed their own SNS s and smartphones; however, only a handful of Western countries, primarily the U.S., have dominated the global platform market and society.

The hegemonic power of American-based platforms is crucial because Google, Facebook, iPhone, and Android have functioned as major digital media intermediaries thanks to their advanced roles in aggregating several services. The U.S, which had previously controlled non-Western countries with its military power, capital, and later cultural products, now seems to dominate the world with platforms, benefitting from these platforms, mainly in terms of capital accumulation. This new trend raises the question whether the U.S., which has always utilized its imperial power, not only with capital and technology, but also with culture, to control the majority of the world, actualizes the same dominance with platforms.

The primary goal of the chapter is to historicize a notion of imperialism in the 21st century by analyzing the evolutionary nature of imperialism, from 1) Lenin's imperialism, through 2) cultural imperialism, 3) information imperialism, and finally 4) platform imperialism. It then addresses whether or not we

* This research was supported by the Social Sciences Humanities Research Council, Canada.

are experiencing a new notion of imperialism by mapping out several core characteristics that define platform imperialism, including the swift growth and global dominance of SNS s and smartphones. It especially examines the capitalization of platforms and their global expansion in the digital age. It eventually endeavors to make a contribution to the discourse of platform imperialism as a new form of imperialism, focusing on the nexus of great powers encompassing nation-states and transnational corporations (TNC s), such as Google and Apple. The chapter finally discusses whether platform imperialism is useful for explaining the current power relations between the U.S. and non-Western countries.

2   The Evolution of Imperialism in the 20th and the 21st Centuries

The contemporary concept of imperialism is much different from the discourse developed in the early 20th century when it had been primarily advanced by classical, Marxist-inspired theories of imperialism (e.g., Kautsky, Lenin, and Luxemburg). From a Marxist perspective, imperialism is what happens when two forms of competition – the economic struggle among capitals and geopolitical rivalries between states – fuse (Callinicos 2007, 70). One of the central arguments of the Marxist tradition of thinking on imperialism is that there is an intrinsic relation between capitalism and expansion, and that capitalist expansion inevitably takes the political form of imperialism (Marx 1867).

Building on and modifying the theories of Karl Marx, there are several renditions of imperialism in the critical theory tradition, and Lenin's pamphlet, *Imperialism, the Highest State of Capitalism* (1917) provides an excellent place to start discussing imperialism, because the Leninist theory of imperialism has exerted a considerable impact on the current era. What Lenin emphasized almost one hundred years ago cannot be applied directly to the contemporary era due to vastly different social and economic conditions, as well as a different technological milieu. However, it is certainly worth trying to see whether Lenin's concepts can be applied to the 21st century situation.

Most of all, Lenin argued that modern imperialism (or capitalist imperialism) constitutes a different stage in the history of capitalism. "The first stage was the competitive form of capitalism characterized by relatively small-scale enterprises, few of which dominated their market. That is the form of capitalism that mostly existed in Marx's day" (Harrison 2007). The newer stage of capitalism, however, is characterized by huge monopolistic or oligopolistic corporations (Lenin 1917). In his pamphlet, Lenin remarked, "if it were necessary to give the briefest possible definition of imperialism, we should have to say that imperialism is the monopoly state of capitalism" (Lenin 1917, 265). The key to understanding is that it was an economic analysis of the transition from free competition to monopoly. For Lenin, imperialism is the monopoly stage of capitalism, and imperialism is a new development that had been predicted but not yet seen by Marx. What Lenin wanted to emphasize was that, at the fundamental economic level, what had most changed was that there were major aspects of monopoly in this new stage of capitalism, and that whether or not the consolidation of companies had reached the point of there being a single survivor in each industry. That is, even if there still are several huge companies in each industry, they tend to collude and jointly control the market to their mutual benefit (Harrison 2007, 1, 10).

Later, he gave a more elaborate five-point definition of capitalist imperialism, which emphasizes finance-capital – the dominant form of capital. The criteria are; 1) the concentration of production and capital developed to such a stage that it creates monopolies which play a decisive role in economic life; 2) the merging of bank capital with industrial capital, and the creation, on the basis of finance capital of a financial oligarchy; 3) the export of capital, which has become extremely important, as distinguished from the export of commodities; 4) the formation of international capitalist monopolies which share the world among themselves; and 5) the territorial division of the whole world among the greatest capitalist powers (Lenin 1917, 237). Based on these five characteristics, Lenin defined imperialism as:

> "capitalism at that stage of development at which the domination of monopolies and finance capital is established: in which the export of capital has acquired pronounced importance; in which the division of the world among the international trusts has begun; in which the division of all the territories of the globe among the biggest capitalist powers has been completed."
>
> LENIN, 1917, 237

As Lenin's five-point definition of imperialism explains, finance capital uses the state machinery to colonize the periphery. In the periphery, capitalists would use oppressed peripheral labour to produce primary commodities and raw materials cheaply and create an affluent stratum (peripheral elite) to consume expensive commodities imported from the core, and undermine indigenous industry (Galtung 1971). For Lenin, imperialism is the power struggle for the economic and political division of the world, which gives rise of a transitional dependence between rentier states and debtor states:

the epoch of the latest stage of capitalism shows us that certain relations between capitalist associations grow up, based on the economic division of the world; while parallel to and in connection with it, certain relations grow up between political alliances, between states, on the basis of the territorial division of the world, of the struggle for colonies, of the struggle for spheres of influence.

LENIN 1917, 239

Indeed, Lenin himself implicitly discussed the role of the nation-state; and his notion of state was part of strong power, which included also transnational capitals, and his argument for a strong state was a Commune worker state. The Commune was an armed and organized revolutionary section of the Parisian working class, but it was not a state (Lenin 1964; Rothenberg 1995). What Lenin described was that both economic rivalry and military conflicts are indicative as conflicts for hegemony between great powers that constitute essential features for imperialism. In his statement, great powers are not necessarily nation-states, because great powers are powerful actors, meaning that they can also be corporations as well as nation-states (Fuchs 2011a, 198). Though, in Lenin's conceptualization imperialism is essentially associated with a system of relations and contradictions between nation states (Liodakis 2003, 4).

Several new-Marxists (Galtung 1971; Doyle 1986) have also emphasized nation-states as major actors in imperialism theory. For them, imperialism involves the extension of power or authority over others in the interests of domination and results in the political, military, or economic dominance of one country over another (Wasko 2003). In other words, imperialism would be conceived of as a dominant relationship between collectivities, particularly between nations, which is a sophisticated type of dominant relationship (Galtung 1971, 81). Imperialism or empire can be therefore defined as "effective control, whether formal or informal, of a subordinated society by an imperial society" (Doyle 1986, 30). Therefore, while admitting that Lenin's definition has greatly influenced our understanding of global capitalism, we should update theoretical arguments in order to re-engage with Lenin's theory of imperialism today (Fuchs 2010b). One way to do so is to take Lenin as a theoretical impetus for the contemporary theorization of platform imperialism.

3   Cultural Imperialism from Lenin's Fourth Characteristic

Beginning in the early 20th century, media scholars have developed imperialism theory in the contexts of several different areas, including culture and technology. Media theoreticians have especially developed Lenin's fourth point of imperialism, primarily focusing on the major role of big companies that dominate the economy. As Lenin (1917) argued, these big corporations, cartels, syndicates, and trusts first divided the home market among themselves and obtained more or less complete possession of the industry in their own country. "But under capitalism the home market is inevitably bound up with the foreign market. As the export of capital increased, and as the foreign and colonial connections and spheres of influence of the big monopolist associations expanded in all ways, things naturally gravitated towards an international agreement among these associations, and towards the formation of international cartels" (Lenin 1917, 266). Information industries and services, including both audiovisual and information and communication technologies (ICTs) industries, are no exception from this inequal economic geography (Fuchs 2010a). Therefore, one can say that theories of communication imperialism and cultural domination have described Lenin's fourth characteristic of imperialism in relation to media and culture: the domination of the information sphere by large Western corporations (Fuchs 2010a; Said 1993; Galtung 1971; Schiller 1969). Such concepts focused on the ownership and control, structure and distribution of media content (and the media industries) in one country by another country (Fuchs 2010a; Boyd-Barrett 1977) or primarily by the U.S. (Schiller 1976). This updated version is suited for theoretically describing Lenin's dimension of corporate economic domination in the attempt to apply imperialism theory to informational capitalism.

The debate over imperialism in media studies intensified beginning in the mid-1970s.

Several media scholars, including H. Schiller (1976), debated the dominance in international cultural exchange when the international communication system mainly expanded by supplying television programs and motion pictures. They argued that "the international communication system was characterized by imbalances and inequalities between rich and poor nations, and that these imbalances were deepening the already existing economic and technological gaps between countries" (UNESCO 1980, 111–115). Schiller (1976) identified the dominance of the U.S. and a few European nations in the global flow of media products as an integral component of Western imperialism, and dubbed it cultural imperialism in the following way:

> "the concept of cultural imperialism describes the sum of processes by which a society is brought into the modern world system and how its dominating stratum is attracted, pressured, forced, and sometimes bribed

into shaping social institutions to correspond to, or even promote, the values and structures of the dominant center of the system" (1976, 9–10).

Guback (1984, 155–156) also argued, "the powerful U.S. communication industry, including film and television as well as news, exerts influence, sometime quite considerable, over the cultural life of other nations." These scholars defined cultural imperialism as the conscious and organized effort taken by the Western, especially U.S. media corporations to maintain commercial, political, and military superiority. Those Western multinational corporations exerted power through a vast extension of cultural control and domination, and thus saturated the cultural space of most countries in the world, which was claimed to have eliminated and destroyed local cultures by installing a new dominant culture in their place (Jin 2007).

What is also important in the cultural imperialism thesis is the major role taken by the U.S. government. As discussed, media scholars have developed cultural imperialism primarily based on Lenin's fourth characteristic of imperialism, which emphasized the primary role of big corporations, in this case, major U.S. media and cultural companies; however, the push by the large cultural, media and information industries corporations into markets and societies around the world was also propelled by strong support from the U.S. government. The U.S. government's initiative and support for its culture industry has a long history, and this strategy has emphasized the importance of information-based products, making the U.S. State Department a powerful government agent on behalf of the cultural sector (Miller et al. 2001). Given that much of the enormous revenues generated by the U.S. cultural industry have come from foreign markets, "the liberalization of the global cultural market is very significant for the U.S. government" (Magder 2004, 385).

The U.S. government has extensively supported Hollywood by driving other countries to open their cultural markets, which means the US government has been deeply involved in the cultural trade issue by demanding that other governments should take a hands-off approach in the cultural area. Several non-Western economics have been targeted by the U.S. due in larger part to the increasing role of emerging markets, such as China, Russia, Korea, Brazil, and India. For example, *Avatar's* – a Hollywood movie released in 2010 – overseas income of $915 million significantly outpaced comparable domestic action, more than doubling its $430.7 million domestic take in the U.S. and Canada (*Hollywood Reporter* 2011).

The restructuring of the global film sector was conducted through the use of larger power relations and patterns after World War II, with initial moves beginning prior to WWII. Since World War II, U.S. policy has generally supported

the liberalization of international trade – that is, the elimination of artificial barriers to trade and other distortions, such as tariffs, quotas, and subsidies that
countries use to protect their domestic industries from foreign competition
(Congressional Budget Office 2003). The U.S. government sought and eventually
secured the liberalization of the audiovisual sector in the first General Agreement
on Tariffs and Trade (GATT) negotiations in 1947. As Western countries began to
settle on the arrangements that would govern the post-war world, cinema was
high on the list of outstanding issues, and Hollywood wanted to restore its overseas markets (Magder 2004). The U.S. government alongside major film/
TV corporations has intensified its dominance in the global cultural market, and
cultural imperialism has been one of the primary practices of Lenin's imperialism in different contexts in the 20th century, of course, until recent years.

The new media sector is not much different. Facebook has rapidly increased
its revenue from advertising in foreign countries, including several emerging
markets, due to the soaring number of users in those markets (more than 1.3
billion in the world as of March 2014), as will be detailed later. Western-based
game corporations have also enjoyed profits from the global markets. Nnew
media corporations alongside cultural industries corporations have benefited
from global capitalism paved by the nexus of the U.S. government and mega
media TNCS.

4   The Nexus of Globalisation and Information Imperialism

Since the early 1990s, two historical developments – the rapid growth of new
technologies and the development of globalization – have greatly influenced
the concept of imperialism. To begin with, as globalization theory has evolved
over the last decade or so, contemporary theories of imperialism and global
capitalism can be categorized on a continuum that describes the degree of
novelty of imperialism (Fuchs 2010a). At the end of the continuum there are
theoreticians who argue that imperialism, including cultural imperialism no
longer exists today and that a post-imperialistic empire has emerged. Several
media scholars have indeed made a case against the cultural imperialism thesis. Straubhaar (1991) emphasizes that national cultures can defend their ways
of life and, in some respects, even share their images with the rest of the world.
Sparks (2007, 119) points out, "in the place of a single, U.S.-based production
center dominating the whole of the world trade in television programs, it was
increasingly argued that technical and economic changes were rendering the
world a more complex place, in which there were multiple centers of production and exchanges flowing through many different channels."

Several other scholars also convincingly stress the discontinuity between globalization in the 21st century and times past (Negri 2008, Robinson 2007, Hardt and Negri 2000). Hardt and Negri (2000) point out that imperialism, which was an extension of the sovereignty of the European nation-states beyond their own boundaries, is over, because no nation could ever be a world leader in the way modern European nations were in the midst of 19th and early-20th centuries versions of globalization. Hardt and Negri develop the term empire instead of imperialism to describe the contemporary form of the global order and argue that empire is a system of global capitalist rule that is altogether different from imperialism:

> "in contrast to imperialism, empire establishes no territorial center of power and does not rely on fixed boundaries or barriers. It is a decentered and deterritorializing apparatus of rule that progressively incorporates the entire global realm within its open, expanding frontiers."
>
> HARDT AND NEGRI 2000, xii-xiv

Robinson (2007, 7–8) also argues, "capitalism has fundamentally changed since the days of Lenin due to the appearance of a new transnational capitalist class, a class group grounded in new global markets and circuits of accumulation, rather than national markets and circuits." Robinson claims, "the imperialist era of world capitalism has ended" (2007, 24). He believes that TNCs are much different from national corporations because TNCs have been free from nation-states.

More importantly, in the midst of the globalization process, some theoreticians claim that the core-periphery dichotomy by Lenin and new Marxists does not work anymore because it is too simplistic. Hardt and Negri (2000, xii) especially argue that "theories of imperialism were founded on nation states, whereas in their opinion today a global empire has emerged, and imperialism no longer exists with the demise of nation-states," although they do not explain in detail as to why they think that Lenin limited his concept of imperialism to the extension of national sovereignty over foreign territory (Fuchs 2010b). In fact, "the nation state-centeredness of their own narrow definition of imperialism as the expansive process of the power of the nation state through policies of export of capital, export of labour power and constitution-occupation of areas of influence" (Negri 2008, 34) bears little resemblance to Lenin's definition (Fuchs 2010b, 841), because Lenin's emphasis is on finance capital, which is capital controlled by banks and employed by industrialists. Again, Lenin discussed the significant role of nation-states as colonizers and rentier states. However, economic interdependence and de-colonization do not mean the demise of nation-states, nor automatic de-territorialization.

Meanwhile, others argue that contemporary capitalism is just as imperialistic as imperialism was 100 years ago or that it has formed a new kind of imperialism (Fuchs 2010a; Harvey 2007; Wood 2003). As Ellen Wood (2003, 129) points out,

> the new imperialism that would eventually emerge from the wreckage of the old would no longer be a relationship between imperial masters and colonial subjects but a complex interaction between more or less sovereign states. While the u.s. took command of a new imperialism governed by economic imperative, however, this economic empire would be sustained by political and military hegemony.

The stress is, therefore, on continuity rather than fundamental change (Harvey 2003, 2007; Wood 2003). Unlike the emphasis on the coercive power of nation-states that Hardt and Negri focus on, "the harmonization of capitalist space relies on the soft power of consent and the emulation of models of development" (Winseck and Pike 2007, 8). Although contemporary aspects of imperialism cannot be considered in the same way as set out in Lenin's understanding of imperialism, contemporary critical scholars believe that "the notion of imperialism still functions as a meaningful theoretical framework to interpret the world which was globalized neo-liberally" (Fuchs 2010a, 34).

Many theoreticians have especially argued that the differential power relations associated with globalization are a continuation of past forms of Western imperialism that created the persistent differentiation between the First and Third Worlds (Miller 2010; Amin 1999). Harshe (1997) describes globalization and imperialism as intertwined and characterized by unequal cultural and intellectual exchanges. Grewal (2008, 7) also points out, "the assertion that globalization is imperial has lately become the subject of mainstream discussion in the u.s. and elsewhere; it is no longer a charge made by anti-globalization activists alone."

Alongside globalization, the rapid growth of ICTs has influenced the change and continuity of the notion of imperialism. The connection of imperialism and the information sector is not peculiar for a new form of imperialism. Boyd-Barrett (1980, 23) has shown that "already in the 19th and early 20th century the big news agencies Havas, Reuters and Wolff were based in imperial capitals, and their expansion was intimately associated with the territorial colonialism of the late nineteenth century." At the time of Lenin, they served as government propaganda arms in the First World War. Later, Winseck and Pike (2007) discuss with the example of the global expansion of cable and wireless companies (e.g. Western Union, Eastern Telegraph Company, Commercial Cable

Company, Anglo American Telegraph Company or Marconi) in the years 1860–1930 that at the time of Lenin there was a distinct connection between communication, globalization, and capitalist imperialism. They argue:

> the growth of a worldwide network of fast cables and telegraph systems, in tandem with developments in railways and steamships, eroded some of the obstacles of geography and made it easier to organize transcontinental business. These networks supported huge flows of capital, technology, people, news, and ideas which, in turn, led to a high degree of convergence among markets, merchants, and bankers.
>
> WINSECK AND PIKE, 2007, 1–2

It is clear that the notion of imperialism has gained a new perspective in the midst of the rapid growth of new technologies. While the importance of the global flow in capital and culture has arguably changed, several recent theoreticians have emphasized the importance of the dominance of ICTs. Dan Schiller (1999) has specifically developed a theory of digital capitalism that emphasizes the changing role of networks for capital accumulation:

> the networks that comprise cyberspace were originally created at the behest of government agencies, military contractors, and allied educational institutions. However, over the past generation or so, a growing number of these networks began to serve primarily corporate users. Under the sway of an expansionary market logic, the Internet began a political-economic transition toward digital capitalism.

Castells (2001) also cautions against the socially and functionally selective diffusion of technology. He identifies one of the major sources of social inequality as the differential timing in access to the power of technology for people, and thus acknowledges, in contrast to the laudatory rhetoric about the globalization of technological systems, that its outcome is instead large areas of the world, and considerable segments of population, switched off from the new technological system. Boyd-Barrett emphasizes (2006, 21–22), "the emergence of microprocessor-based computer network technology and the U.S. dominance of ICT are crucial for U.S. economy and imperialism." Meanwhile, Fuchs (2010a, 56) points out, "media and information play a pivotal role in the new concept of imperialism, which the U.S. has dominated based on its advanced digital technologies, although they are subsumed under finance capital in the 21st century."

However, with the swift transfer of power to platforms, the situation has recently changed, although of course, not without periodic setbacks for traditional ICT companies. Previously powerful ICT corporations have increasingly been subordinated to platforms due to the latters' ascendant role and power in digital media economies. For example, in August 2011, Google acquired Motorola Mobility for $12.5 billion in order to give the platform giant a presence in smartphone hardware while also bringing it thousands of new patents (Efrati and Ante, 2011). Almost at the same time, Hewlett-Packard Co., the world's largest personal-computer maker, is simultaneously exploring a spinoff of its PC business as profits slide, but buying U.K. software firm Autonomy Corp., for about $10.25 billion (Worthen et al., 2011). It is presumptuous to say that the hardware era is gone; however, these two recent events and the increasing role of U.S.-based platforms in capital accumulation and culture (Facebook and Google) are arguably clear examples of the rise of platform imperialism.

5   Great American Powers and Platform Imperialism

5.1   *What is Platform Imperialism?*

The term platform has recently emerged as a concept to describe the online services of content intermediaries, both in their self-characterizations and in the broader public discourse of users, the press and commentaries (Gillespie 2010, 349). While people associate platforms with their computational meaning (Bodle 2010), which is an infrastructure that supports the design and use of particular applications or operating systems, the concept of platform can be explained in three different, but interconnected ways. First, a platform is not only hardware architecture, but also a software framework that allows other programs to run (Tech Coders.com 2012). Second, platforms afford an opportunity to communicate, interact, or sell. This means that platforms allow code to be written or run, and a key is that they also enhance the ability of people to use a range of Web 2.0 technologies to express themselves online and participate in the commons of cyberspace (Gillespie 2010). Platforms also can be analyzed from the corporate sphere because their operation is substantially defined by market forces and the process of commodity exchange (van Dijck 2012, 162). Finally, it is crucial to understand the nature of platforms because a platform's value is embedded in design. As several theoreticians argue (Ess 2009; Feenberg 1991), technology is not value neutral but reflects the cultural bias, values and communicative preferences of their designers. Likewise, platforms often reinforce the values and preferences of designers, either explicitly or implicitly, while sometimes clashing with the values and preferences of their intended users (Ess 2009, 16). As Bodle (2010, 15) points out,

> the technological design of online spaces, tools, and operating systems constitutes a contested terrain where the imposition of designers' values and preferences are at odds with the values and preferences of the intended user base.

All three of these areas are relevant to why platforms have emerged in reference to online and mobile content-hosting intermediaries. Drawing these meanings together allows us to see that platforms emerge not simply as indicating a functional computational shape, but with cultural values embedded in them.

Since platforms are crucial for people's everyday information flows and capitalism, not only on a national level, but also on a global level, it is important to measure whether platforms suggest a progressive and egalitarian arrangement, promising to support those who stand upon them in the contemporary global society (Gillespie 2010). Arguably, global flows of culture and technology have been asymmetrical, as theories of cultural and media imperialism have long asserted, and thus the focal point here is whether asymmetrical relationships between a few developed and many developing countries exist in the case of platforms. Accepting platforms as digital media intermediaries, the idea of platform imperialism refers to an asymmetrical relationship of interdependence between the West, primarily the U.S., and many developing powers – of course, including transnational corporations as Lenin and H. Schiller analyzed. Characterized in part by unequal technological exchanges and therefore capital flows, the current state of platform development implies a technological domination of U.S.-based companies that have greatly influenced the majority of people and countries. Unlike other fields, including culture and hardware, in which a method for maintaining unequal power relations among countries is primarily the exportation of these goods and related services, in the case of platform imperialism, the methods are different because commercial values are embedded in platforms and in ways that are more significant for capital accumulation and the expansion of power.

5.2 Internet Platforms: The American Dominance in Platform Imperialism

American-based platforms, including search engines and social media, are dominant in the global Internet markets. According to Alexa.com (2012), over the three-month period between September and November of 2012, among the top 100 global sites on the Web based on page views and visits, 48 websites were owned by U.S. corporations and 52 websites were non-U.S. Internet firms. Other than the U.S., 16 countries had their own websites on the list, and among them, China had the largest number of websites (18), followed by Japan (6), Russia (5), India (4) and the UK (4). A few non-Western countries, including Indonesia, Turkey, Brazil, and Mexico also had one website each. This data seemingly explains that the U.S. is not a dominant force in the Internet market. However, when we consider the origins of the websites, the story is not the same, because the websites that belong to these non-Western countries are of U.S.-origin, including Google, Yahoo, and Amazon. Other than a handful of countries, including China and Russia, developing countries have no websites that they originally created and operated themselves. Based on the origin of the websites, U.S. companies comprised 72% of the list, which means that only one country controls three-fourths of the top Internet market.

More importantly, 88 of these websites, such as Google, Yahoo, and YouTube, accumulate capital primarily by (targeted) advertising, and they prove that U.S.-origin platforms are symbols of global capitalism. In fact, among the top 100 list, only two websites (Wikipedia and BBC Online) are operated with a non-profit model. Ten websites make revenues through other business models, including pay-per-view and subscription, although a few websites (Amazon and eBay) developed several business models, such as product and service sales and marketing. Among these, Craigslist.com makes money through a handful of revenue streams. The website charges some fees to post a job listing in several U.S. cities, while charging fees to list an apartment rental in New York, USA. The revenues cover only the operating expenses; the company has not made a profit since its inception (Patrick 2012). Meanwhile, WordPress. com is run by Automatic which currently makes money from the aforementioned upgrades, blog services, Akismet anti-spam technology, and hosting partnerships. What is most significant about the contemporary Internet is the swift growth of capitalist platforms, such as Facebook, Google, and Twitter. As Baran and Sweezy (1968) argued, in a capitalism dominated by large corporations operating in oligopolistic markets, advertising especially becomes a necessary, competitive weapon. No matter whether Western or non-Western, these websites and platforms are major engines appropriating advertising for global capitalism.

Specifically speaking, while there are many U.S-based platforms that have increased their global influence, three major American-based platforms – Google, Facebook, and YouTube (also owned by Google) – made up the top three websites in November 2012 (Alexa.com, 2012). Except for two Chinese-based platforms (Baidu.com and QQ.com), the other eight platforms in the top 10 were all American-based platforms. Among these, Google is the world's most accessed web platform: 46% of worldwide Internet users accessed Google in a three-month period in 2010 (Fuchs 2011b). Among search engines only, Google's dominant position is furthermore phenomenal. As of November 2012, Google accounted for as much as 88.8% of the global search engine market, followed by Bing (4.2%), Baidu (3.5%), Yahoo (2.4), and others (1.1%) (Kamasnack 2012). Google even launched google.cn in 2006, agreeing to some censorship of search results to enter the country, to meet the requirements of the Chinese government. In China, Google's market share stood at 16.7% as of December 2011, down from 27% in June 2010, while local web search engine Baidu's market share increased from 70% as of June 2010 to 78.3% in December 2011 (La Monica 2012; Lee 2010; Lau 2010). Due to the fact that Baidu is limited mainly to Chinese language users, though, it can't surmount Google's global market share.

SNSs have also gained tremendous attention as popular online spaces for both youth and adults in recent years. American-based SNSs have rapidly penetrated the world and enjoyed an ample amount of capital gains. Several local-based SNSs, such as Mixi (Japan), Cyworld (Korea), and QQ (China), as well as VK (Originally VKontakte) – a European social network site that Russian-speaking users use around the world (VK was established in 2006 by Pavel Durov, a Russian entrepreneur, who is still the co-owner alongside the Mail.ru Group–the Russian Internet giant that owns a 39.9% stake in Vkontakte; *East-west Digital News*, 2012) – are competing with American-based SNSs. For example, Russian Cyberspace, including the Commonwealth of Independent States (CIS), such as Azerbaijan, Armenia, and Georgia, known as RUNET, is a self-contained linguistic and cultural environment with well-developed and highly popular search engines, web portals, social network sites, and free e-mail services. Within RUNET, Russian search engines dominate with Yandex (often called the Google of Russia), beating out Google (Deibert et al. 2010, 17–19). The market share of Yandex was 60.3% in November 2012, while Google's share was 26.6% in November 2012, according to LiveInternet (2012). However, outside these few countries, the majority of countries in the world have increased their usage of Facebook and Twitter. These Western-based platforms have managed to overtake some local incumbent SNSs and search engines in the past few years (Jin forthcoming). The U.S. has continued an asymmetrical relationship of interdependence between a few developed countries and the majority of developing countries up to the present time.

Among these, Facebook, which was founded in the USA in 2004, is organized around linked personal platforms based on geographic, educational, or corporate networks. Given that the general concept of platform means any base of technologies on which other technologies or processes are built, Facebook is a platform that plays an advanced role in aggregating several services. When Netscape became a platform in the 1990s, their flagship product was the web browser, and their strategy was to use their dominance in the browser market to establish a market for high-priced products (O'Reilly 2005). However, for Facebook, 'usage' is more important than other functions. "People as consumers and producers flock to Facebook to socialize with their friends and acquaintances, to share information with interested others, and to see and be seen" (boyd 2011, 39). The site can be understood as an online communication platform that combines features of e-mail, instant messaging, photo-sharing, and blogging programs, as well as a way to monitor one's friends' online social activity. Since May 2007, members have been able to download and interact with Facebook applications, programs and accessories developed by outside companies that now have access to Facebook's operating platform and large networked membership (Cohen 2008).

Facebook is indeed maintaining its rate of growth and generating thousands of new user registrations every day. The number of total users has grown from 585 million in December 2010 to 1.3 billion in March 2014., These numbers are significant because they have contributed to the high valuation assigned to the company. Facebook's value reached $50 billion in January 2011 (McGirt 2007; Rushe 2011). Right after its public offering on May 18, 2012, the capital value of Facebook was as much as $104 billion (*AP* 2012).

Interestingly enough, before its public offering, Zuckerberg emphasized that "Facebook's social mission was to make the world more open and connected," and he stated that "the primary goal was not making money" (*Channel 4 News* 2012). This might be true and it will not always be easy to separate economic and social values as motives, but the public offering of Facebook clearly proves that the development of new technology cannot be understood without its value embedded in design for commodity exchange, as van Dijck (2012) points out. At the very least, the technological design of online spaces and operating systems constitute a contested terrain where the imposition of designers' values and preferences are at odds with the values and preferences of the intended user base (Bodle 2010).

Meanwhile, Facebook has rapidly expanded its dominance in many countries. According to the World Map of Social Networks, showing the most popular SNSs by country, which is based on Alexa and Google Trends for Websites traffic data (2012), Facebook is the market leader in 126 countries out of 137 (92%) as of June 2012, up from 87% in June 2010, and up from 78% in December 2009 (Vincos Blog 2012). Although several local-based SNSs are still market leaders in Asian countries, such as China, Japan, and Korea as well as Russia, which is very significant because these are some of the largest IT markets, Facebook has managed to overtake local incumbent SNSs, and has rapidly penetrated the majority of countries in the world. Facebook has positioned itself as the leader of interactive, participant-based online media, or Web 2.0, the descriptor for websites based on user-generated content that create value from the sharing of information between participants (Hoegg et al. 2006, 1; O'Reilly 2005).

The dominant positions of several social media, including Facebook and Google have been considered as clear examples of platform imperialism. While these sites can offer participants entertainment and a way to socialize, the social relations present on a site like Facebook can obscure economic relations that reflect larger patterns of capitalist development in the digital age. The connection of SNSs to capitalism is especially significant. SNS users provide their daily activities as free labour to network owners, and thereafter, to advertisers, and their activities are primarily being watched and counted and eventually appropriated by large corporations and advertising agencies (Jin forthcoming). As the number of SNS users has soared, advertisers, including corporations and advertising agencies, have focused more on SNSs as alternative advertising media. According to Facebook's S-1 filing with the U.S. Securities and Exchange Commission (SEC), Facebook's ad revenue in 2013 was $6.98 billion, up from $1.9 billion in 2010. Approximately 56% of Facebook's 2011 ad revenue of $3.1 billion came from the U.S. alone, according to the company's regulatory filings (Facebook 2014). However, the proportion of the U.S. significantly decreased from 70.5% in 2010 to 56% in 2011 (eMarketer 2010), meaning Facebook has rapidly increased its profits from foreign countries.

As Grewal (2008, 4) emphasizes, "the prominent elements of globalization can be understood as the rise of network power." The notion of network power consists of the joining of two ideas: first, that coordinating standards are more valuable when greater numbers of people use them, and second, that this dynamic as a form of power backed by Facebook, which is one of the largest TNCS, can lead to the progressive elimination of the alternatives, as Lenin (1917) and H. Schiller (1991) emphasized. Facebook as the market leader in the SNS world has eliminated competitors as the number of users exponentially soars. "In the digital era, one of the main sources of social inequality is the access to technology" (Castells 1996, 32–33). Even when the issue is no longer that of lack of material access to technology, a power distribution and hegemonic negotiation of technologically mediated space is always at play (Gajjala and Birzescu 2011). The powers that can be marshaled through platforms are not exclusively centered in the U.S. However, as Lenin argued, the conflicts for hegemony between great powers, in this case, U.S-based SNSs and local-based snss have been evident, and Facebook and Twitter have become dominant powers. In other words, a few u.s.-based platforms dominate the global order, which has resulted in the concentration of capital in a few hands within major tncs and start-ups. This is far from a globalization model in which power is infinitely dispersed. Capital and power are not the form of monopoly; however, a handful of u.s.-owned platforms have rapidly expanded their dominance in the global market, which has caused the asymmetrical gap between a few Western countries and the majority of non-Western countries.

6   The Role of Nation-States in the Construction of Platform Imperialism

While tncs have developed and advanced new technologies, it is important to understand that nation-states, both the u.s. government and other governments, including China, support the growth of their own platforms, and these new political agendas certainly construct the new form of media imperialism in tandem with platforms. The u.s. government, based on its state power, has greatly supported American-based platform owners in global politics. The involvement of the u.s. government and the Chinese government in the wake of China's attacks on Google services has become a recent case in this regard. In the midst of the conflicts between the Chinese government and Google, the Chinese government has restricted Google discussion topics that the government finds objectionable, such as independence drives in the regions of Tibet and Xinjiang and the banned religious movement Falun Gong. For the tens of thousands of censors employed by the Chinese government, blocking access to restricted information both at home and abroad is an ongoing struggle. Search engines are prevented from linking to sensitive content (Ramzy 2010). As discussed, Google launched google.cn in 2006, agreeing to some censorship of search results, as required by the Chinese government; however, due to the restrictions and some cyberattacks allegedly targeting Gmail, Google warned that it might end its operations in China (bbc News 2010). Interestingly enough, the u.s. as a nation-state has strongly supported Google. u.s. Secretary of State Hillary Clinton especially gave two major speeches in 2010 and 2011, respectively. Clinton gave the first significant speech on Internet freedom around the world, making it clear exactly where the u.s. stood in January 2010;

> on their own, new technologies do not take sides in the struggle for freedom and progress, but the u.s. does. We stand for a single Internet where

all of humanity has equal access to knowledge and ideas. And we recognize that the world's information infrastructure will become what we and others make of it. This challenge may be new, but our responsibility to help ensure the free exchange of ideas goes back to the birth of our republic.

U.S. SECRETARY OF STATE 2010

In her speech, Clinton cited China as among a number of countries where there has been "a spike in threats to the free flow of information" over the past year, and she also named Tunisia, Uzbekistan, Egypt, Iran, Saudi Arabia and Vietnam (U.S. Secretary of State 2010). Of course, China rejected a call by Clinton for the lifting of restrictions on the Internet in the communist country, denouncing her criticism as false and damaging to bilateral ties. Foreign Ministry spokesman Ma Zhaoxu said in a statement posted on the ministry's Web site:

regarding comments that contradict facts and harm China-U.S. relations, we are firmly opposed. We urged the U.S. side to respect facts and stop using the so-called freedom of the Internet to make unjustified accusations against China. The Chinese Internet is open and China is the country witnessing the most active development of the Internet.

MUFSON 2010, A14

Ma added that China regulated the Web according to law and in keeping with its national conditions and cultural traditions.

It is evident that the Chinese government understands the vast size of the Chinese Internet market, and it has taken measures to cultivate the growth of local information technology, including Google's competitor, Baidu.cn. The Chinese government has maneuvered to protect its own technology-driven corporations due to their significance for the national economy. China's English-language *Global Times* therefore characterizes Clinton's speech as a disguised attempt to impose [U.S.] values on other cultures in the name of democracy. The newspaper then dragged out another snarling phrase to denounce Clinton's overtures on freedom of speech: information imperialism (*Global Times* 2010).

The second round of debate between the U.S. and China occurred in February 2011. Hillary Clinton again warned repressive governments, such as China, Cuba and Syria, not to restrict Internet freedom, saying such efforts will ultimately fail. Calling the Internet the public space of the future, Clinton enumerated all the reasons that freedom of expression must be the overriding ethos of this worldwide landscape (Goodale 2011). As expected, the Chinese government also warned the U.S. not to use the issues to meddle in China's internal affairs. The government expressed that Internet freedom in China is guaranteed by law, and stated "we are opposed to any country using Internet freedom as a pretext for interference in Chinese affairs" (States News Service 2011).

As such, in the 21st century, the U.S. government has intensified its efforts to penetrate the global information market. As Panitch and Gindin (2003, 35–36) succinctly argue,

> neoliberal globalization is the acceleration of the drive to a seamless world of capital accumulation, and the mechanisms of neoliberalism may have been economic, but in essence it was a political response to the democratic gains that had been previously achieved by subordinate classes and which had become, in a new context and from capital's perspective, barriers to accumulation.... Once the American state itself moved in this direction, it had a new status: capitalism evolved to a new form of social rule that promised, and largely delivered, a) the revival of the productive base for American dominance; b) a universal model for restoring the conditions for profits in other developed countries; and c) the economic conditions for integrating global capitalism.

Direct government intervention and support by the State Department have developed and expanded U.S. platforms throughout the world. As the U.S. government has continuously supported Hollywood backed by the Motion Picture Association of America and major film producers (Wasko 2003), the U.S government has been actively involved in the discourse of the free flow of information, and of course, one of the primary backgrounds is Google. The company lobbied 13 government agencies in 2009, spending just under $6 million in the process, and Google chiefly focused on freedom of speech on the Internet in 2010, particularly because of its highly publicized battles with the Chinese government. Google urged lawmakers to adopt policies that assure a neutral and open Internet at home and put pressure on foreign governments that censor the Web (Goldman 2010). The U.S. campaign for uncensored and free flow of information on an unrestricted Internet backed by Google and other platforms, including Microsoft has been a clear proof of the collaboration between the government and TNCs, two major powers, in the global market.

Since the early 1990s, as H. Schiller (1999) criticized, several theoreticians have insisted that the market is the solution to all problems, that private enterprise is the preferred means to achieve solid economic results, and that government is the enemy. However, as the case of Google in China proves, as well as

IP rights related global politics, the last several decades' record is of government initiative, support, and promotion of information and communication policies. The principle – vital to the worldwide export of American cultural product and American way of life – of the free flow of information has arguably become a universal virtue to both the information industries and the U.S. government (H. Schiller 1999), and this fundamental political agenda continues in the Obama government. The U.S. government has become a primary actor in tandem with TNCs, which also applies to platform imperialism. The U.S. is not the only country to actualize neoliberal policies. The Chinese government also capitalizes on neoliberal globalization, meaning the role of China in global capitalism has rapidly increased. One needs to be very careful, though, because "China is not capitalist despite the rise of a capitalist class and capitalist enterprises" (Arrighi 2007, 331).

> The capitalist character of marked-based development is not determined by the presence of capitalist institutions and dispositions but by the relation of state power to capital. Add as many capitalists as you like to a market economy, but unless the state has been subordinated to their class interest, the market economy remains non-capitalist.
>
> ARRIGHI 2007, 331–332

The Chinese state in Arrighi's view still retains a high degree of autonomy from the capitalist class and is therefore able to act in the national rather than in a class interest (Robinson 2010).

Since the late 1970s, the Chinese state has undergone a radical transformation in order to pursue substantive linkages with transnational capitalism. Neoliberal ideas have been influential in China as the post-Mao leadership embraced the market system as a means to develop the country (Zhao, 2008). In *A Brief History of Neoliberalism*, David Harvey (2005, 120) clearly points out that "the outcome in China has been the construction of a particular kind of market economy that increasingly incorporates neoliberal elements interdigitated with authoritarian centralized control." As The Top 100 Sites on the Web show, Chinese platforms, including Baidu, QQ, and Taobao, utilize the targeted advertising capital business model, which is not different from US Internet capitalism. Of course, this does not imply that China has entirely adopted neoliberal capitalist reform. Although China's transition from a planned economy to a socialist market economy is substantial, China also poses an alternative to the Washington Consensus, which emphasizes the continuing role of the government in the market. As Zhao (2008, 37) aptly puts it, the Chinese government has developed both "neoliberalism as exception" and "exceptions to neoliberalism" for the national economy and culture. The Chinese government has developed a market-friendly economy; however, at the same time, it continues to play a primary role in the market.

In sum, when society looks to regulate an emerging form of information distribution, be it the telegraph or radio or the Internet, it is in many ways making decisions about what that technology is, what it is for, what sociotechnical arrangements are best suited to help it achieve that and what it must not be allowed to become (Benkler 2003). This is not just in the words of the policymakers themselves. Interested third parties, particularly the companies that provide these services, are deeply invested in fostering a regulatory paradigm that gives them the most leeway to conduct their businesses, imposes the fewest restrictions on their service provision, protects them from liability for things they hope not to be liable for and paints them in the best light in terms of the public interest (Gillespie 2010, 356). In fact, Google, in its newly adopted role of aggressive lobbyist, has become increasingly vocal on a number of policy issues, including net neutrality, spectrum allocation, freedom of speech and political transparency (Phillips 2006, Gillespie 2010). Platform imperialism has been developed and influenced by sometimes cooperative and at other times conflicting relationships among the government, domestic capital and TNCs. TNCs are valuable players to platform technologies; the nation-states are also primary actors in international negotiations. As Marx stated (1867), the capitalist expansion of TNCs inevitably takes the political form of imperialism, and it is further evident in the case with the development of platform imperialism.

7   Conclusion

This chapter has analyzed the evolutionary development of various theories of imperialism and examined whether we might be moving towards a situation of platform imperialism. It examined whether Lenin's analysis continues to explain what is happening in the world during these early years of the 21st century. Since the new concept of imperialism functions through digital technologies, first information and second platform technologies in the 21st century, which were not seen in Lenin's imperialism, it is crucial to understand whether such technologies play a primary role in changing the notions of imperialism.

At a glance, the massive switch to the digital economy has provided a surplus for several emerging powers, including China, India, and Korea with which to challenge the longer-term U.S. dominance, unlike the old notion of imperialism developed by Lenin (Boyd-Barrett 2006, 24). These countries have presumably competed with Western countries, and they are supposed to build a new global order with their advanced digital technologies. However, there are doubts as to whether non-Western ICT corporations have reorganized the global flow and constructed a balance between the West and the East. The panacea of technology may reduce imperialism and domination to vestiges of the past; however, technology will always be the reality of human hierarchy and domination (Maurais 2003, Demont-Heinrich 2008), and digital technologies have buttressed U.S. hegemony.

In particular, when the debates reach platforms, non-Western countries have not, and likely cannot, construct a balanced global order, because Google (including its Android operating system), Facebook, Twitter and Apple's iPhones (and iOS) are indices of the dominance of the U.S. in the digital economy. These platforms have penetrated the global market and expanded their global dominance. Therefore, it is not unsafe to say that American imperialism has been continued with platforms. As in the time of Lenin between the late 19th century and the early 20th century, there has been a connection between platform and capitalist imperialism. Platforms have functioned as a new form of distributor and producer that the U.S. dominates. Arguably, therefore, we are still living in the imperialist era.

A critical interrogation of the global hegemony of platforms proves that the dominant position of the U.S. has intensified an increasingly unequal relationship between the West and the East. In the 21st century, the world has become further divided into a handful of Western states, in particular, the U.S., which have developed platforms, and a vast majority of non-Western states, which do not have advanced platforms. Therefore, it is certain that American imperialism has been renewed with platforms, like the old form of American imperialism supported by politics, economy, and military, as well as culture.

At the time of Lenin, there was certainly a connection between communication – cable and telegraph systems – globalization and capitalist imperialism (Winseck and Pike 2007, 1). In the 21st century, again, there is a distinct connection between platforms, globalization, and capitalist imperialism. Unlike the old notion of imperialism, though, the contemporary concept of imperialism has supported huge flows of people, news, and symbols, which, in turn, leads to a high degree of convergence among markets, technologies, and major TNCs in tandem with nation-states. Platforms can be situated within more general capitalist processes that follow familiar patterns of asymmetrical power relations between the West and the East, as well as between workers and owners, commodification, and the harnessing of user power.

References

Alexa.com. 2012. Top 500 Sites on the Web. Accessed November 17, 2012. http://www
.alexa.com/topsites.

Amin, Samir. 1999. Capitalism, imperialism, globalization. In *The political economy of imperialism*, edited by Ronald Chilcote, 157–168. Boston: Kluwer Academic.

Arrighi, Govanni. 2007. *Adam Smith in Beijing: Lineages of the Twenty-First Century*. London: Verso.

Arthur, Charles. 2012. Samsung Galaxy Tab'does not copy Apple's iPad designs. *The Guardian*. October 18. Accessed November 18, 2012. http://www.guardian.co.uk/technology/2012/oct/18/samsung-galaxy-tab-apple-ipad.

Associated Press (AP). 2012. Facebook set to begin trading after $16 billion offering. May 22.

Baran, Paul and Paul M. Sweezy. 1968. *Monopoly Capital: An Essay on the American Economic and Social Order*. New York: Monthly Review Press.

BBC News. 2010. Google may end China operations. January 13.

Benkler, Yochai. 2003. Freedom in the Commons. *Duke Law Journal* 1245.

Bodle, Robert. 2010. Assessing Social Network Sites as International Platforms. *Journal of International Communication* 16 (2): 9–24.

boyd, danah. 2011. Social Network Sites as Networked Publics: affordances, dynamics and implications. In *NetworkedA Self: identity, community and culture on social network sites*, edited by Zizi Papacharissi, 39–58. London: Routledge.

Boyd-Barrett, Oliver. 1977. Media imperialism: towards an international framework for the analysis of media systems. In *Mass Communication and Society*, edited by James Curran and M. Gurevitch, 116–135. London: Edward Arnold.

Boyd-Barrett, Oliver. 1980. *The International News Agency*. London: Constable.

Boyd-Barrett, Oliver. 2006. Cyberspace, globalization and empire. *Global Media and Communication* 2(1): 21–41.

Callinicos, Alex. 2007. *Social Theory*. Cambridge: Polity.

Castells, Manual. 1996. *The Rise of the Network Society*. Cambridge, MA: Blackwell.

Castells, Manual. 2001. *The Internet Galaxy: Reflections on the Internet, Business, and Society*. New York: Oxford University Press.

Channel 4 News. 2012. Facebook's not only for money says Zuckerberg. Accessed April 29, 2012. http://www.channel4.com/news/facebook-set-for-biggest-ever-Internet-flotation, February 2.

Cohen, Nicole. 2008. The Valorization of Surveillance: towards a political economy of Facebook, *Democratic Comunique* 22 (1): 5–22.

Congressional Budget Office. 2003. The Pros and Cons of Pursuing Free-Trade Agreements. Accessed September 17, 2012. http://www.cbo.gov/ftpdoc.cfm?index=4458&type=0&sequence=0.

Deibert, Ronald, John Palfrey, Rafal Rohozinski, and Jonathan Zittrain. 2010. Access Controlled: the shaping of power, rights and role in cyberspace. Cambridge, MA: MIT Press.

Demont-Heinrich, Christof. 2008. The Death of Cultural Imperialism-and Power too? International Communication Gazette 70 (5): 378–394.

Dijck, José van. 2012. Facebook as a tool for Producing Sociality and Connectivity. Television and New Media 13 (2): 160–176.

Doyle, Michael. 1986. Empires. Ithaca, NY: Cornell University Press.

East–west Digital News. 2012. Vkontakte's IPO postponed indefinitely: shareholder Mail.ru Group yields control to founder. Accessed January 2, 2013. http://www .ewdn.com/2012/05/30/vkontaktes-ipo-postponed-indefinitely-shareholder-mail -ru-group-yields-control-to-founder/.

Efrati, Amir and Spencer Ante. 2011. Google's $12.5 billion Gamble. The Wall Street Journal. August 16. Accessed November 21, 2011. http://online.wsj.com/article/SB100 01424053111903392904576509953821437960.html.

eMarketer. 2010. Advertisers to Spend $1.7 Billion on Social Networks in 2010. Press Release. August 16.

Ess, Charles. 2009. Digital Media Ethics. Cambridge: Polity Press.

Facebook. 2014. Annual Report 2013. Menlo Park, CA: Facebook.

Feenberg, Andrew. 1991. The Critical Theory of Technology. London: Oxford University Press.

Fuchs, Christian. 2010a. New Imperialism: Information and Media Imperialism. Global Media and Communication 6(1): 33–60.

Fuchs, Christian. 2010b. Critical Globalization Studies and the New Imperialism. Critical Sociology 36 (6): 839–867.

Fuchs, Christian. 2011a. Foundations of Critical Media and Information Studies. London: Routledge.

Fuchs, Christian. 2011b. A Contribution to the Critique of the Political Economy of Google. Fast Capitalism 8 (1). Accessed August 17, 2012. http://www.fastcapitalism .com/.

Gajjala, Rrdhika and Anca Birzescu. 2011. Digital Imperialism through Online Social/ Financial Networks. Economic and Political Weekly, 95–102.

Galtung, Johan. 1971. A Structural Theory of Imperialism. Journal of Peace Research 8 (2): 81–117.

Gillespie, Tarleton. 2010. The Politics of Platforms. New Media and Society 12 (3): 347–364.

Global Times. 2010. The Real Stake in Free Flow of Information. January 22.

Goldman, David. 2010. How Google plays the angles in Washington. CNN Money. Accessed March 30, 2011. http://money.cnn.com/2010/03/30/technology/google_washington/#.

Goodale, Gloria. 2011. Hillary Clinton champions Internet freedom, but cautions on WikiLeaks. *The Christian Science Monitor*. February 15. Accessed March 25, 2011. http://www.csmonitor.com/USA/Foreign-Policy/2011/0215/Hillary-Clinton -champions-Internet-freedom-but-cautions-on-WikiLeaks.

Google. 2012. Facts about Google's acquisition of Motorola. Accessed March 29, 2012. http://www.google.com/press/motorola/.

Grewal, David. 2008. *Network Power: the social dynamics of globalization*. New Haven: Yale University Press.

Guback, Thomas. 1984. International Circulation of U.S. Theatrical Films and Television Programming. In *World Communications: A Handbook*, edited by George Gerbner and Marsha Siefert, 155–156. New York: Longman.

Hardt, Michael and Antonio Negri. 2000. *Empire*. Cambridge, MA: Harvard University Press.

Hargittai, Eszter. 2008. Whose Space? Differences among Users and Non-Users of Social Network Sites. *Journal of Computer-Mediated Communication* 13: 276–297.

Harrison, Scott. 2007. *Lenin on Imperialism*. Accessed March 1, 2012. http://www .massline.org/PolitEcon/ScottH/LeninOnImperialism.pdf.

Harshé, Rajen. 1997. *Twentieth century imperialism: Shifting contours and changing conceptions*. New Delhi: Sage.

Harvey, David. 2003. *The New Imperialism*. New York: Oxford University Press.

Harvey, David. 2005. *A Brief History of Neoliberalism*. New York: Oxford University Press.

Harvey, David. 2007. In What Ways is the New Imperialism Realty New. *Historical Materialism* 15 (3): 57–70.

Hoegg, Roman, Robert Martignoni, Miriam Meckel, and Katarina Stanoevska-Slabeva. 2006. Overview of business models for Web 2.0 communities Proceedings of GeNeMe 2006.

Jin, Dal Yong. forthcoming. Critical Analysis of User Commodities as Free Labor in Social Networking Sites: A Case Study of Cyworld. *Continuum: Journal of Media and Cultural Studies*.

Jin, Dal Yong. 2007. Reinterpretation of Cultural Imperialism: Emerging Domestic Market vs. Continuing U.S. Dominance. *Media, Culture and Society* 29 (5): 753–771.

Kamasnack. 2012. Nov 2012 update. Search engine market share. Accessed November 17, 2012. http://www.karmasnack.com/about/search-engine-market-share/.

La Monica, Paul. 2012. Baidu: Is China's Google better than Google? *CNN Money*. February 13. Accessed November 17, 2012. http://money.cnn.com/2012/02/13/technology/ thebuzz/index.htm.

Lau, Justin. 2010. Baidu profits from Google's China woes, *Financial Times*. July 22. Accessed November 1, 2011. http://www.ft.com/cms/s/2/c8fe238e-9542-11df-b2e1 -00144feab49a.html.

Lee, Micky. 2010. Revisiting the 'Google in China' Question from a Political Economic Perspective. *China Media Research* 6 (2):15–24.

Lenin, Vladimir. 1917. Imperialism, the Highest Stage of Capitalism. In *Essential Works of Lenin*, 177–270. New York: Dover.

Lenin, Vladimir. 1964. State and Revolution. Vol. 25.

Liodakis, George. 2003. The New Stage of Capitalist Development and the Prospects of Globalization. Paper presented for the Conference: Economics for the Future Cambridge. 17–19 September, 2003.

LiveInternet. 2012. Report from Search Engines. Accessed November 25, 2012. http://www.liveInternet.ru/stat/ru/searches.html?slice=ru;period=week.

Lu, Jia and Ian Weber. 2009. Internet Software Piracy in China: a user analysis of resistance to global software copyright enforcement. *Journal of International and Intercultural Communication* 2 (4): 296–317.

Magder, Ted. 2004. Transnational Media, International Trade and the Ideal of Cultural Diversity. *Continuum: Journal of Media and Cultural Studies* 18 (3): 385–402.

Marx, Karl. 1867. *Capital*. Volume I. London: Penguin.

Maurais, Jacques. 2003. Towards a New Linguistic Order. In *Languages in a Globalizing World*, edited by Jacques Maurais and Michael Morris, 13–36. Cambridge: Cambridge University Press.

McGirt, Ellen. 2007. Facebook's Mark Zuckerberg: hacker, dropout, CEO. Accessed September 17, 2012. http://www.fastcompany.com/magazine/115/open_features -hacker-dropout-ceo.html.

Miller, Toby. 2010. Holy Trinity: Nation Pentagon, Screen. In *Communication the Nation: national Topographies of Global Media Landscape*, edited by Anna Roosvall and I. Salovaara-Moring, 143–162. Nordicom.

Miller, Toby, Nitin Govil, John McMurria and Richard Maxwell. 2001. *Global Hollywood*. Bloomington: Indiana University Press.

Mufson, Steven. 2010. Chinese government sharply criticizes Clinton's speech urging Internet freedom. *The Washington Post*, January 23, A14.

Negri, Antonio. 2008. *Reflections on Empire*. Cambridge: Polity.

O'Reilly, Tim. 2005. What is Web 2.0. Accessed March 6, 2012. http://oreilly.com/web2/archive/what-is-web-20.html.

Pang, Laikwan. 2006. *Cultural Control and Globalization in Asia: Copyright, Piracy, and Cinema*. London: Routledge.

Panitch, Leo and Sam Gindin. 2003. Global Capitalism and American Empire. In *SocialistThe Register 2004: the new imperial challenge*, edited by Leo Panitch and Sam Gindin, 1–43. New York: Monthly Press.

Patrick, Keith. 2012. How Craigslist Makes Money. *The Houston Chronicle*. Accessed January 2, 2013. http://smallbusiness.chron.com/craigslist-money-27287.html.

Phillips, Kate. 2006. Google joins the Lobbying Herd. *The New York Times*. March 29. Accessed March 1, 2012. http://www.nytimes.com/2006/03/28/politics/28google .html?pagewanted=all.

Ramzy, Austin. 2010. The Great Firewall: China's Web Users Battle Censorship. *Time*. April 13. Accessed March 1, 2011. http://www.time.com/time/world/article/0,8599 ,1981566,00.html.

Robinson, William. 2007. Beyond the Theory of Imperialism: global capitalism and the transnational state. *Societies Without Borders* 2: 5–26.

Robinson, William. 2010. Giovanni Arrighi: Systemic Cycles of Accumulation, Hegemonic Transitions, and the Rise of China. *New Political Economy* 16 (2): 267–280.

Rothenberg, Mel. 1995. Lenin on the State. *Science and Society* 59 (3): 418–436.

Rushe, Dominic. 2011. Facebook's value swells to $50 billion after Goldman Sachs Investment. *Guardian*. January 3. Accessed February 22, 2011. http://www.guardian .co.uk/technology/2011/jan/03/facebook-value-50bn-goldman-sachs-investment.

Said, Edward. 1993. *Culture and Imperialism*. New York: A.A. Knopf.

Schiller, Dan. 1999. *Digital Capitalism: networking the global market system*. Cambridge, MA: MIT Press.

Schiller, Herbert. 1969. *Mass Communications and American Empire*. Oxford: Westview Press.

Schiller, Herbert. 1976. *Communication and Cultural Domination*. White Plains, N.Y.: International Arts and Sciences Press.

Schiller, Herbert. 1991. Net Yet the Post-Imperialist Era. *Critical Studies in Media Communication* 8(1): 13–28.

Schiller, Herbert. 1999. *Living in the Number one Country*. New York: Seven Stories Press.

Sparks, Colin. 2007. *Globalization, Development and the Mass Media*. London: Sage.

Straubhaar, Joseph. 1991. Beyond Media Imperialism: Asymmetrical Independence and Cultural Proximity. *Critical Studies in Mass Communication* 8 (1): 39–70.

Tech Coders. Com. 2012. Platforms for Software Development. Accessed March 2, 2012, from http://www.techcoders.com/platforms-for-software-development.html/.

The Hollywood Reporter. 2011. Avatar' still dominating overseas boxoffice. January 10. Accessed November 17, 2012. http://www.hollywoodreporter.com/news/avatar-still -dominating-overseas-boxoffice-19321.

U.S. Secretary of State. 2010. Remarks on Internet Freedom. Accessed March 1, 2012. http://www.state.gov/secretary/rm/2010/01/135519.htm.

UNESCO. 1980. *Many Voices, One World: Communication and Society Today and Tomorrow*.

Vincos Blog. 2010. World Map of Social Networks. Accessed September 3, 2011. http:// www.vincos.it/world-map-of-social-networks/.

Vincos Blog. 2012. World Map of Social Networks. Retrieved from http://vincos.it/ world-map-of-social-networks/.

Wasko, Janet. 2003. *How Hollywood Works*. London: Sage.

Winseck, Dwayne and Robert Pike. 2007. *Communication and Empire*. Duke University Press.

Wood, Ellen. 2003. *Empire of Capital*. London: Verso.

Worthen, Ben, Justin Scheck, and Gina Chon. 2011. H-P explores quitting computers as profits slide. *The Wall Street Journal*. August 19. Accessed November 1, 2011. http://online.wsj.com/article/SB10001424053111903596904576516403053718850.html.

Zhao, Yuezhi. 2008. Neoliberal Strategies, Socialist Legacies: Communication and State Transformation in China. In *Global Communications: toward a transcultural political economy*, edited by Paula Chakravartty and Yuezhi Zhao, 23–50. New York: Rowman & Littlefield.

CHAPTER 11

Foxconned Labour as the Dark Side of the Information Age: Working Conditions at Apple's Contract Manufacturers in China

Marisol Sandoval

Information and Communication Technologies (ICTs) have played a double role in the restructuring of capitalism since the 1970s. On the one hand they enable fast transnational communication that is needed for organising international markets and value chains. On the other hand the production of these technologies is itself based on an international supply network (Dyer-Witheford 2014; Hong 2011, 9). Nick Dyer-Witheford therefore describes the value chain as "the dirty secret of the digital revolution" (Dyer-Witheford 2014). Part of this "dirty secret" is that "the global information economy is built in part on the backs of tens of millions Chinese industrial workers" (Zhao and Duffy 2008, 229).

The clean, immaculate and advanced surface of modern computer products hides the dirty reality of their production process. Concepts such as "digital sublime" (Mosco 2004) or "technological sublime" (Maxwell and Miller 2012, 7) suggest that certain myths and utopian ideals are attached to media and communication technologies. Maxwell and Miller argue that this has as a consequence that the "way technology is experienced in daily life is far removed from the physical work and material resources that go into it" (Maxwell and Miller 2012, 7).

The tendency even of critical scholarship to focus on how the usage of ICTs as production technologies is transforming work, perpetuates the technological sublime rather than unmasking it. In this vein Hardt and Negri for example highlight that the "contemporary scene of labour and production [...] is being transformed under the hegemony of immaterial labor, that is labor that produces immaterial products, such as information, knowledge, ideas, images, relationships, and affects" (Hardt and Negri 2004, 65). Even if they recognize that the rise of "immaterial labour" does not lead to the disappearance of industrial labour the term tends to mystify the actual impact of ICTs and digital technologies on work and workers on a global scale. Before and after ICTs serve as the instruments of the mental labour of software developers, journalists, designers new media workers, prosumers etc. their production and disposal is shaped by various forms of manual work such as the extraction of minerals, the assembly of components into the final product and the waste work needed for their disposal. Conceptualizing digital labour only as mental and immaterial labour misrepresents the character of ICTs and digital technologies as it tends to downplay the physical and manual labour that goes into them.

The notion of immaterial labour only focuses on the bright side of the expansion of communication, interaction and knowledge, while leaving its dirty counterpart in the dark. What is rather needed is demystification by fostering "greater transparency in working conditions throughout the ICT/CE supply chain" in order to shed light on the work and life realities of "workers who disappear in the twilight zone of the technological sublime" (Maxwell and Miller 2012, 108). As Vincent Mosco argues, only if computer technologies "cease to be sublime icons of mythology [...] they can become important forces for social and economic change" (Mosco 2004, 6).

This chapter contributes to this task of demystification as it looks at the working conditions in Chinese assembly plants of one of the world's most dominant and most admired computer companies: Apple Inc. Studying Apple is important because the company represents both the mental and the manual side of digital labour: For many years Apple's products have been known as the preferred digital production technologies for the knowledge work of designers, journalists, artists and new media workers. iPhone, iPod and Co are symbols for technological progress that enables unprecedented levels of co-creation and sharing of knowledge, images and affects as well as interaction, communication, co-operation etc. At the same time during the past years Apple has become an infamous example for the existence of hard manual labour under miserable conditions along the supply chain of consumer electronics. In this chapter I therefore use the example of Apple for highlighting that an adequate conceptualization of digital labour must not ignore its physical and manual aspects.

In the first section I give a brief overview of the developments that led to the rise of China as the "workshop of the world." In Section 2 I contrast Apple's business success with allegations from corporate watchdogs regarding bad working conditions in the company's supply chain. In order to examine these allegations in greater detail I then introduce a systematic model of working conditions (Section 3) and apply it to Apple's contract manufacturers in China (Section 4). Finally, I discuss Apple's response to labour rights violations (Section 5) and conclude with some reflections on solidarity along the global value chain (Section 6).

1   The Rise of China as "Workshop of the World"

The rise of neoliberal globalization and international value chains is generally considered as a reaction to the crisis of Fordist capitalism in the 1970s (Fröbel,

Heinrichs and Kreye 1981; Smith 2012, 40; Harvey 2005, Munck 2002, 45). Part of the restructuring of capitalism was the gradual relocation of large parts of production activities from the industrialized core of the world economy to the former periphery. In this context Fröbel, Heinrichs and Kreye coined the concept of the "new international division of labour" (NIDL). They argue that: "The development of the world economy has increasingly created conditions (forcing the development of the new international division of labour) in which the survival of more and more companies can only be assured through the relocation of production to new industrial sites, where labour-power is cheap to buy, abundant and well-disciplined; in short, through the transnational reorganization of production" (Fröbel, Heinrichs and Kreye 1981, 15). As a consequence, commodity production became "increasingly subdivided into fragments which can be assigned to whichever part of the world can provide the most profitable combination of capital and labour" (Fröbel, Heinrichs and Kreye 1981, 15). The result was the emergence of global value chains and production networks in various industries including the electronics sector.

This development had a substantial impact on labour relations and working conditions around the world. As the global labour force expanded (Munck 2002, 109) the protection of labour rights was weakened. McGuigan argues that neoliberal restructurings and the rise of post-Fordism led to "an attack on organized labour in older industrialised capitalist states and devolution of much manufacturing to much cheaper labour markets and poor working conditions of newly industrialising countries" (McGuigan 2005, 230).

The rise of China as the "workshop of the world" needs to be seen in the context of these developments. Hung stresses that "China's labour-intensive takeoff coincided with the onset of an unprecedented expansion of global free trade since the 1980s" (Hung 2009, 10). The integration of China into global capitalist production networks was made possible by a number of policy reforms pursued by the Chinese state. David Harvey highlights that the Chinese economic reform programme initiated in the late 1970s coincided with the rise of neoliberalism in the US and the UK (Harvey 2006, 34). This reform program included the encouragement of competition between state owned companies, the introduction of market pricing as well as a gradual turn towards foreign direct investment (Harvey 2006, 39). The first Special Economic Zones (SEZ) in China were established in 1980 (Yeung et al. 2009, 223). The first four SEZ were located in the coastal areas of south-east China: Shantou, Shenzhen and Zhuhai in Guangdong province and Xiamen in Fujian Province (Yeung et al. 2009, 224). By 2002, David Harvey argues, foreign direct investment accounted for more than 40 percent of China's GDP (Harvey 2006, 39).

Hong highlights that China was particularly interested in entering the market for ICT production. In order to boost exports, tax refunds for the export of

ICT commodities were set in place In the 1990s (Hong 2011, 37). In 2005 import tariffs for semiconductor, computer and telecommunication products were removed (Hong 2011, 37). These policies proved effective: Hong argues that "In the global market China has emerged as leading ICT manufacturing power-house: In 2006, China became the world's second largest ICT manufacturer, and ICT products manufactured in China accounted for over 15 percent of the international trade of ICT products" (Hong 2011, 2).

The fact that attracting foreign direct investment was made possible by granting tax exemptions means that foreign companies could make use of Chinese land area and exploit Chinese labour, while paying only little back to the Chinese public through taxes. Hong shows that by 2005 40.4 percent of ICT companies in China were foreign enterprises, which controlled 71.1 percent of all profits from the industry, but due to tax benefits these foreign invested ICT enterprises only made up 42.3 percent of the total tax contribution of the sector (Hong 2011, 38).

An effect of the shift towards pro-market policies and the privatization of state enterprises was the massive commodification of labour (Su 2011, 346). The newly established market for labour power replaced the previous system in which workers were guaranteed employment as well as social welfare including medical care, education opportunities, pensions and housing (Friedman and Lee 2010, 509). Zhao and Duffy point out that the adoption of a policy towards foreign direct investment in the ICT sector and the privatiza-tion of industries also meant a weakening of the power of the Chinese working class. Older industrial workers were replaced by young, often female migrant workers (Zhao and Duffy 2008, 230).

Low wages and cheap production costs made China attractive for compa-nies in search for outsourcing opportunities. Hung argues that the prolonged stagnation of wages resulted from Chinese government policies that neglected and exploited the rural agricultural sector in order to spur urban industrial growth (Hung 2009 13f). This situation forced young people to leave the coun-tryside in order to find work in the city, creating a "limitless supply of labour" (Hung 2009, 14) while reinforcing "a rural social crisis" (Hung 2009, 14). Among the companies that are taking advantage of the cheap labour supply in China is the computer giant Apple.

2   Apple: Clean Image Versus Dirty Reality

Steve Wozniak, Steve Jobs and Ronald Wayne founded Apple in 1976 (Linzmayer 2004, 6). However, it was not until the mid 2000s that Apple joined the elite of

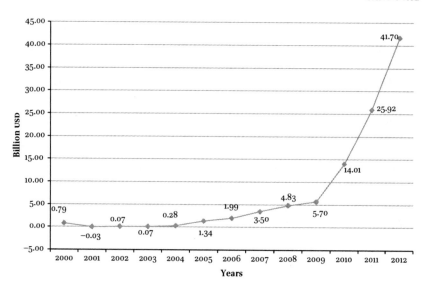

FIGURE 11.1   *Apple's Profits from 2000 to 2012 (Apple SEC-filings, 10-k forms 2010–2012)*

the most profitable companies in the world. In 2005 Apple's profits for the first time exceeded 1 billion USD and during the following years continued to increase rapidly until they reached 41.7 billion USD in 2012 (Apple SEC-Filings. 10-k form 2012[2]), which made Apple the second most profitable company in the world.[1] Between 2000 and 2012 Apple's profits on average grew 39.2% each year[2] (Apple SEC-Filings, 10-k form) (see Figure 11.1).

In 2012 Apple's total net sales amounted to 156.51 billion USD. The largest share of it was derived from hardware, whereby the iPhone was Apple's most successful product (see Figure 11.2).

In addition to its economic success Apple is also successful in building its reputation. Fortune Magazine, for six years in a row (2008–2013), has ranked Apple the most admired company in the world.[3] According to a survey among 47,000 people from 15 countries that was conducted by the consultancy firm Reputation Institute, Apple is the company with the 5th best Corporate Social Responsibility (CSR) reputation worldwide (Reputation Institute 2012, 19).

---

1   Forbes Magazine. The World's Biggest Public Companies. Retrieved from http://www.forbes
    .com/global2000/#page:1_sort:4_direction:desc_search:_filter:All%20industries_filter
    :All%20countries_filter:All%20states on April 24, 2013.

2   Compound Annual Growth Rate CAGR.

3   Fortune. 2013. World's Most Admired Companies. Retrieved from http://money.cnn.com/
    magazines/fortune/most-admired/ on April 24, 2013.

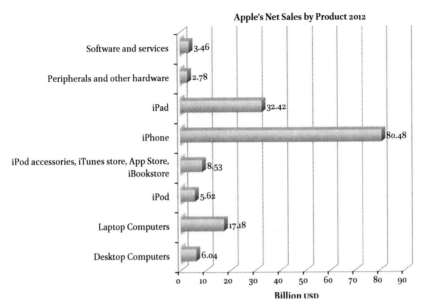

FIGURE 11.2   *Apple's Net Sales by Product 2012 (Apple SEC-filings, 10-k form 2012, 30).*

This image does not correspond to the company's actual business practices. The production of Apple's hardware products, on which its economic success is built (see Figure 11.1), is largely outsourced to contract manufacturers in China. In May and June 2010 many major Western media reported about a series of suicides at factory campuses in China. The factories, at which 17 young workers jumped to death between 2007 and May 2010[4] belong to the Taiwan-based company Hon Hai Precision Industry Co. Ltd, better known as Foxconn, which is a major supplier for computer giants such as Apple, Hewlett-Packard and Nokia (Finnwatch, SACOM and SOMO 2011, 8).

Hon Hai Precision is a profitable company itself. According to Forbes Magazine it is the 113th biggest company in the world. In 2012 its profits amounted to 10.7 billion USD.[5] Nevertheless the company strongly depends on orders from consumer brands such as Apple. Finnwatch, SACOM and SOMO describe this situation as follows: "These companies often drive down the

---

4   Wired Magazine. 2011. 1 Million Workers. 90 Million iPhones. 17 Suicides. Who's to blame? By Joel Johnson on Februar 28, 2011. Retrieved from http://www.wired.com/magazine/2011/02/ff_joelinchina/all/1 on October 23, 2011.

5   Forbes Magazine. The World's Biggest Public Companies. Retrieved from http://www.forbes.com/global2000/list/#page:1_sort:0_direction:asc_search:_filter:Electronics_filter:All%20countries_filter:All%20states on May 1, 2013.

price they pay their suppliers, which then makes the suppliers less or no longer profitable. To get back in the game, suppliers reduce costs, often at the cost of workers, violating labour laws in the process" (Finnwatch, SACOM and SOMO 2009, 44). Competition between contract manufacturers such as Foxconn is also high, which is why profit rates can often only be achieved by keeping cost low (SOMO 2005a, 41). Although some Foxconn factories are exclusively producing for Apple, such as for example three plants in Zhengzhou, Henan (SACOM 2012, 3), Foxconn is not the only company that is manufacturing Apple products. Other Apple suppliers include Pegatron Corporation, Primax Electronics, Quanta Computers, Wintek or Foxlink.[6] Working conditions are similar throughout these factories (SACOM 2010, 2012, 2013). SACOM argues that "illegal long working hours, low wages and poor occupational health and safety are rooted in the unethical purchasing practices of Apple" (SACOM 2012, 1).

The losers in this corporate race for profit are the workers. When young Foxconn workers decided to end their lives by jumping from their employer's factory buildings, Western media for some weeks were looking behind the surface of bright and shiny computer products. For example, The New York Times published a story about the *String of Suicides Continues at Electronics Supplier in China*;[7] the BBC reported on *Foxconn Suicides: 'Workers Feel Quite Lonely'*;[8] Time Magazine published an article entitled *Chinese Factory Under Scrutiny As Suicides Mount*;[9] The Guardian headlined *Latest Foxconn Suicide Raises Concern Over Factory Life in China*,[10] and CNN reported *Inside China Factory Hit By Suicides*.[11]

---

6   Apple. List of Suppliers. Retrieved from http://www.apple.com/supplierresponsibility/
     our-suppliers.html on May 1, 2013.

7   The New York Times. 2010. String of Suicides Continues at Electronics Supplier in China.
     By David Barboza on May 25, 2010. Retrieved from http://www.nytimes.com/2010/05/26/
     technology/26suicide.html on October 24, 2011.

8   BBC. 2010. Foxconn Suicides: 'Workers Feel Quite Lonely'. On May 28, 2010. Retrieved from
     http://www.bbc.co.uk/news/10182824 on October 24, 2011.

9   Time Magazine. 2010. Chinese Factory Under Scrutiny As Suicides Mount. On May 26,
     2010. Retrieved from http://www.time.com/time/world/article/0,8599,1991620,00.html on
     October 24, 2011.

10   The Guardian. 2010. Latest Foxconn Suicide Raises Concern Over Factory Life in China. By
     Tania Branigan on May 17, 2010. Retrieved from http://www.guardian.co.uk/world/2010/
     may/17/foxconn-suicide-china-factory-life on October 24, 2011.

11   CNN. 2010. Inside China Factory Hit By Suicides. By John Vause on June 1, 2010. Retrieved
     from   http://articles.cnn.com/2010-06-01/world/china.foxconn.inside.factory_1_foxconn
     -suicides-china-labor-bulletin?_s=PM:WORLD on October 24, 2011.

However, these suicides are only the tip of the iceberg. For several years NGOs have stressed that computers, mp3 players, game consoles, etc are often produced under miserable working conditions (ICO, Finnwatch and ECA 2005; SOMO 2005b, SOMO 2007a). Far away from shopping centres and department stores, workers in factories in Asia or Latin America produce consumer electronics devices during 10 to 12 hour shifts, a minimum of 6 days a week for at best a minimum wage. Apple's suppliers are no exception. In the next sections I develop a systematic account of working conditions (Section 3), which I will subsequently apply to the situation in the workshops of Apple's contract manufactures in China (Section 4).

3 A Systematic Model of Working Conditions

A suitable starting point for a systematic model of different dimensions of working conditions is the circuit of capital accumulation as it has been described by Karl Marx (1967/1990, 248–253; 1885/1992, 109). According to Marx, capital accumulation in a first stage requires the investment of capital in order to buy what is necessary for producing commodities, the productive forces: labour time of workers (L or variable capital) on the one hand, and working equipment like machines and raw materials (MoP or constant capital) on the other hand (Marx 1885/1992, 110). Thus, money (M) is used in order to buy labour power as well as machines and resources as commodities (C) that then in a second stage enter the labour process and produce (P) a new commodity (C') (Marx 1885/1992, 118). This new commodity (C') contains more value than the sum of its parts, i.e. surplus value. This surplus value needs to be realized and turned into more money (M') by selling the commodity in the market (Marx 1885/1992, 125). The circuit of capital accumulation can thus be described with the following formula: $M \rightarrow C \dots P \dots C' \rightarrow M'$ (Marx 1885/1992, 110).

According to Marx, surplus value can only be generated due to the specific qualities of labour-power as a commodity. Marx argued that labour power is the only commodity "whose use-value possesses the peculiar property of being a source of value, whose actual consumption is therefore itself an objectification of labour, hence a creation of value" (Marx 1867/1990, 270).

Labour is thus essential to the process of capital accumulation. The model I constructed thus takes this process as its point of departure for identifying different dimensions that shape working conditions (see Figure 11.2). The purpose of this model is to provide comprehensive guidelines that can be applied for systematically studying working conditions in different sectors.

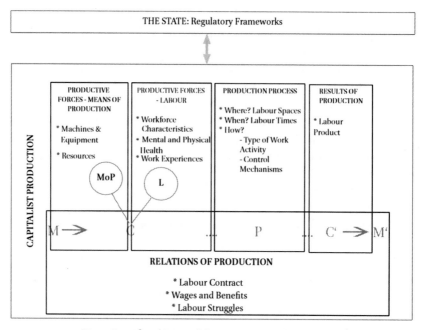

FIGURE 11.3   *Dimensions of working conditions*

The model pictured in Figure 11.3 identifies five areas that shape working conditions throughout the capital accumulation process: means of production, labour, relations of production, the production process and the outcome of production. Furthermore this model includes the state's impact on working conditions through labour legislation:

- **Productive Forces – Means of Production:** Means of production include *machines and equipment* on the one hand and *resources* that are needed for production on the other hand. The question whether workers operate big machines, work at the assembly line, use mobile devices such as laptops, handle potentially hazardous substances, use high-tech equipment, traditional tools or no technology at all etc. shapes the experience of work and has a strong impact on work processes and working conditions.
- **Productive Forces – Labour:** The subjects of the labour process are workers themselves. One dimension that impacts work in a certain sector is the question how the *workforce* is composed in terms of gender, ethnic background, age, education levels etc. Another question concerns worker *health and safety* and how it is affected by the means of production, the relations of production, the labour process and labour law. Apart from outside impacts

on the worker, an important factor is how workers themselves *experience* their working conditions.

- **Relations of Production:** Within capitalist relations of production, capitalists buy labour power as a commodity. Thereby a relation between capital and labour is established. The purchase of labour power is expressed through *wages*. Wages are the primary means of subsistence for workers and the reason why they enter a wage labour relation. The level of wages thus is a central element of working conditions. *Labour contracts* specify the conditions under which capital and labour enter this relation, including working hours, wages, work roles and responsibilities etc. The content of this contract is subject to negotiations and often *struggles between capital and labour*. The relation between capital and labour is thus established through a *wage relation* and formally enacted by a *labour contract* that is subject to negotiations and *struggles*. These three dimensions of the relation between capital and labour set the framework for the capitalist labour process.

- **Production process:** Assessing working conditions furthermore requires looking at the specifics of the actual production process. A first factor in this context is its *spatial location*. Whether it is attached to a certain place or is location independent, whether it takes place in a factory, an office building, or outdoors etc. are important questions. A second factor relates to the *temporal dimension of work*. Relevant questions concern the amount of regular working hours and overtime, work rhythms, the flexibility or rigidness of working hours, the relation between work time and free time etc. Finally working conditions are essentially shaped by how the production process is executed. This includes on the one hand the question which *types of work activity* are performed. The activities can range from intellectual work, to physical work, to service work, from skilled to unskilled work, from creative work to monotonous and standardized work tasks, etc. On the other hand another aspect of the production process is how it is *controlled and managed*. Different management styles can range from strict control of worker behaviour and the labour process to high degrees of autonomy, self-management or participatory management etc. *Space, time, activity* and *control* are essential qualities of the production process and therefore need to be considered when studying working conditions.

- **Product:** Throughout the production process workers put their time, effort and energy into producing a certain *product*. This actual outcome of production and how it relates back to the worker thus needs to be considered for understanding work in a certain sector.

- **The state:** Finally the state has an impact on working conditions through enacting *labour laws* that regulate minimum wages, maximum working hours, social security, safety standards etc.

Table 11.1 summarizes the dimensions of working conditions that I described above.

Based on research that has been conducted by corporate watchdogs I will now take a closer look at all of the described dimensions in Apple's manufacturing factories in China.

4   Working Conditions at Apple's Contract Manufacturers in China

Corporate watchdogs such as Students and Scholars Against Corporate Misbehaviour (SACOM), China Labour Watch and the organisations involved in the European project makeITfair have collected comprehensive data about working conditions in Apple's supply chain. SACOM is a Hong-Kong based NGO that was founded in 2005. It brings together concerned labour rights activists, students, scholars and consumers in order to monitor working conditions throughout China and elsewhere.[12] SACOM's research is largely based on undercover investigations and anonymous interviews with workers, conducted outside of factory campuses. Its research results are documented in reports such as *iSlave behind the iPhone* (2011b) or *New iPhone, Old Abuses* (2012) that are made available online. China Labour Watch (CLW) is another independent NGO that was founded in 2000. Since then it has collaborated with workers, unions, labour activists and the media in order to monitor working conditions in different industries in China. CLW's Shenzhen office works directly with local workers and factories, while CLW's New York based office produces investigation report and makes them available to an international audience.[13]

The project makeITfair,[14] funded by the European Union (2006–2012), focuses on working conditions and environmental impacts throughout the live-cycles consumer electronics such as computers, mobile phones, photo cameras or mp3 players. The research that was conducted within the project is based on anonymous interviews with workers outside factory buildings and sometimes also includes interviews with management officials. Workers tend

---

12   SACOM. About Us. Retrieved from http://sacom.hk/about-us on July 22, 2013.
13   China Labour Watch. Who We Are. Retrieved from http://www.chinalaborwatch.org/aboutus.html July 22, 2013.
14   MakeITfair: http://makeitfair.org/en?set_language=en.

TABLE 11.1   *Dimensions of working conditions*

Productive forces – Means of production	Machines and equipment	Which technology is being used during the production process?
	Resources	What resources are used during the production process?
Productive forces – Labour	Workforce characteristics	What are important characteristics of the workforce for example in terms of age, gender, ethnic background etc?
	Mental and physical health	How do the employed means of production and the labour process impact mental and physical health of workers?
	Work experiences	How do workers experience their working conditions?
Relations of production	Labour contracts	Which type of contracts do workers receive, what do they regulate?
	Wages and benefits	How high/low are wage levels and what are other material benefits for workers?
	Labour struggles	How do workers organize and engage in negotiations with capital and what is the role of worker protests?
Production process	Labour spaces	Where does the production process take place?
	Labour times	How many working hours are common within a certain sector, how are they enforced and how is the relationship between work and free time?
	Work activity	Which type of mental and/or physical activity are workers performing?
	Control mechanism	Which type of mechanisms are in place that control the behaviour of workers?
Results of production	Labour product	Which kinds of products or services are being produced?
The state	Labour law	Which regulations regarding minimum wages, maximum working hours, safety, social security etc are in place and how are they enforced?

to be hesitant to answer questions about their working conditions as they depend on their jobs and are afraid of negative consequences, especially if the investigators are foreigners. Therefore the European project partners such Swedwatch, Germanwatch, SOMO, Finnwatch or Danwatch co-operate with local NGOs and researchers who approach and interview workers without the knowledge of factory managers. MakeITfair informs the electronics brand companies such as Apple, Dell or HP of its research results and invites them to comment on the findings. Based on its research makeITfair aims at raising awareness among consumers, activists and policy makers about the work and life reality of workers in the manufacturing of consumer electronics and to pressure electronics companies to improve working conditions in their supply chains.

I will in the following use data provided by these corporate watchdogs in order to shed light on the work reality of those who are manufacturing Apple's products in China.

4.1   *Productive Forces – Means of Production*

According to Marx, means of production consist of tools and instruments on the one hand and raw materials on the other hand (Marx 1867/1990, 284f). The fact that in capitalism means of production are privately owned lays the foundation for exploitation and the domination of man by man: "modern bourgeois private property is the final and most complete expression of the system of producing and appropriating products, that is based on class antagonism, on the exploitation of the many by the few" (Marx and Engels 1848/2011, 18). For the majority of people private ownership of means of production in fact means non-ownership. Being deprived from the necessary capital to buy means of production that are needed to engage in a production process, workers have to sell their labour power in order to earn their means of subsistence. Private ownership of machines and equipment as well as resources is thus the starting point of the capitalist labour process. I will now consider which instruments (see Section 4.1.1) and resources (see Section 4.1.2) are needed for producing Apple's products.

4.1.1   Machines and Equipment

Compared to other manufacturing sectors such as apparel or toys, electronics manufacturing is relatively capital intensive and requires high-tech equipment (Plank and Staritz 2013, 4; Lüthje 2006, 22). This is even more the case as computer products are becoming more sophisticated smaller in size and lower in weight (WTEC 1997, 16). However the consultancy firm McKinsey & Company classifies the final assembly of high-tech products as labour-intensive (McKinsey

& Company 2012, 64). One reason for this is that the fragmentation of the production process allows to separate "labour-intensive and more capital- and knowledge-intensive parts" so that "there is a considerable amount of low-value and thus low-skill and low-wage activity, which is often combined with advanced production technologies in this 'high-tech' sector" (Plank and Staritz 2013, 9). Electronics manufacturing is thus characterized by both high-tech equipment and high demand for labour.

Electronics manufacturing is among those industries that account for the most robot purchases. According to McKinsey and Company "in 2010, automotive and electronics manufacturing each accounted for more than 30,000 robot units sold globally, while industries such as food and beverage, rubber and plastics, and metal products each bought only 4,000 to 6,000 new robots" (McKinsey & Company 2012, 88).

A technology that Apple's contract manufacturers employ for the automated part of assembly is Surface Mount Technology (SMT) (WTEC 1997, 16; Lüthje 2012). SMT uses programming to automatically solder electronics components such as chips or connectors onto circuit boards.[15] Boy Lüthje argues that as labour costs in China are low not the entire potential of automation is realized, thus "the degree of automation in most factories in China and Asia is lower than it would be in Europe or the United States" (Lüthje 2012). This means that labour is sometimes cheaper than high-tech equipment. It also means that making use of the full range of available automation technology could eliminate parts of the repetitive and standardized work activities that are now part of electronics production.

4.1.2   Resources

Among the resources needed for the production of consumer electronics such as Apple's Mac's, iPads, iPhones and iPods are minerals such as tin, beryllium, gallium, platinum tantalum, indium, neodymium, tungsten, palladium, yttrium, gold, and cobalt (SOMO 2007b, 10–12, Friends of the Earth 2012, 7;). Often these minerals are sourced in conflict areas (SOMO 2007b, 13). The mining activities usually take place under extremely poor health and safety conditions, are extremely low paid, require the resettlement of local villages, threaten the environment and the livelihood of local communities (SOMO 2007b; 2011; Swedwatch 2007; Finnwatch 2007).

---

15   Surface Mount Technology Association. Glossary of Acronyms Relevant to Electronics Manufacturing. Retrieved from http://www.smta.org/files/acronym_glossary.pdf on May 18, 2013.

Cobalt for example is mainly extracted in the so-called copperbelt in Zambia and the Democratic Republic of Congo (DRC) (Swedwatch 2007, 7). It is needed for the production of rechargeable batteries for laptops, mobile phones etc as well as for speakers, headphones and the coatings of hard drives (Swedwatch 2007, 12). Swedwatch in an investigation of mining activities in the Katanga province in DRC found that worker are risking their lives for an income of about 2–4 USD per day (Swedwatch 2007, 29,33). Many of the miners are children: An estimated number of 50,000 children between the age of 7 and 18 are working in the mines of Katanga and thus form a large part of the total workforce of 10,000–14,000 miners (Swedwatch 2007, 7).

The DRC is rich on mineral resources but has been shaped by poverty as well as colonial violence, civil war and armed conflict. A report by Free the Slaves shows that in DRC mines are often controlled by armed rebel groups that force local people into slavery (Free the Slaves 2011, 11). Many women and girls, who are often not allowed to work in the mines, are forced into sexual exploitation (Free the Slaves 2011, 17f).

It is difficult to determine where exactly and under which conditions the minerals contained in a product of a certain electronics brand were soured. However sometimes watchdogs successfully trace the supply chain of a brand back to the point of mineral extraction. In 2012 Friends of the Earth published a report that traces the tin used in Apple's iPhones back to mines in Bangka, an island in Indonesia. The report reveals that Foxconn and Samsung, which are Apple's direct suppliers, buy their tin from the middle companies Shenmao, Chernan and PT Timah, which obtain their tin from Indonesia. 90% of Indonesian tin is mined at Bangka island (Friends of the Earth 2012, 21). The report shows how tin mining destroyed forests and farmlands, killed coral, seagrass and mangroves and led fish to disappear, contaminated drinking water (Friends of the Earth 2012, 13). The destruction of the ecosystem deprives local farmers and fishermen of their livelihood, forcing them to become tin miners themselves (Friends of the Earth 2012, 15f). Tin mining at Bangka island is dangerous and security standards are low. Friends of the Earth reports that that in 2011 on average one miner per week was killed in an accident (Friends of the Earth 2012, 9).

Conflict minerals are used for producing electronics parts such as researchable batteries (cobalt), magnets (cobalt), speakers (cobalt), power amplifiers (gallium), camera flashes (gallium), high efficiency transistors (Indium), flat screens (indium, platinum), lead frames (palladium), plating connectors (palladium), chip resistors (ruthenium), capacitors (neodymium, lanthanum, tantalum) or circuit boards (tin) (Finnwatch 2007, 9f).

Long before minerals enter the final assembly process of consumer electronics, they have passed through a process framed by destruction and exploitation.

It is important to recognize this history of the components that are assembled in Apple's manufacturing factories. Threats to workers and the environment connected to these minerals however continue: Due to the toxic qualities of many minerals they can potentially harm workers in electronics manufacturing. Furthermore the fact that toxic minerals are contained in electronics products can cause problems at the point of disposal. Toxic electronic waste often ends up in waste dumps in the global South where it contaminates the environment and threatens the health of waste worker (Danwatch 2011).

4.2   *Productive Forces – Labour*

Focussing on the subjective side of the labour process, at workers themselves, shows that work on Apple's manufacturing sites is often performed by young female migrant workers (see Section 4.2.1), who are exposed to serious health hazards (see Section 4.2.2) and experience their daily work life as alienating and exhausting (see Section 4.2.3).

4.2.1   Workforce Characteristics

The majority of production workers in China are young female migrant workers (Bread for All 2007, 6; FinnWatch, SACOM and SOMO 2009, 17). Estimates show that in the Chinese Guangdong province, for example, migrant workers make up 65 percent of the workforce in the manufacturing sector (Finnwatch, SACOM and SOMO 2009, 17).

Migrant workers are a particularly vulnerable group of workers. Far away from their hometown they lack social contacts and are therefore prone to isolation. Migrant workers also receive less social benefits. According to the FLA investigation migrant workers at Shenzhen – which constitute 99% of the total workforce – are not covered by unemployment and maternity insurance systems because they do not have a Shenzhen residence card (FLA 2012, 9). Even if migrant workers have unemployment insurance they often cannot claim benefits in their hometown due to lacking transfer agreements between provinces (FLA 2012, 9). Chinese laws prevent migrant workers to officially become urban citizens who are entitled to education and medical care in the city. They remain always dependent on their social networks in their hometowns especially in times of unemployment, illness or pregnancy. This situation keeps many workers trapped as permanent migrants (Friedman and Lee 2010, 516).

Many workers in the electronics industry are young women, who leave their families on the countryside to find work in an industrial area and provide some financial assistance for their relatives. Often factories prefer to hire female workers because they are considered to be good at performing detail-oriented work and to be more obedient and less likely to engage in protests (Swedwatch, SACOM and SOMO 2008, 11).

Workers often have no other choice than to find employment in a factory in order to be able to earn enough money to support themselves and their families. This dependency increases the power of companies over workers. The lack of alternatives makes it likely that workers feel forced to accept bad working conditions.

4.2.2 Mental and Physical Health

Threats to health and safety in electronics factories result from the usage of hazardous substances, insufficient information of workers about the substances they are using, a lack of protection equipment and unsafe work routines. During the last couple of years a number of serious incidents occurred at Apple's supplier factories.

For example between July 2009 and early 2010, 47 workers at United Win, a subsidy of Wintek Corporation that produces Apple products, were hospitalized because of being poisoned with n-hexane (SACOM 2010, 2). If inhaled, n-hexane can cause nerve damage and paralysis of arms and legs. The poisoned workers were using n-hexane for cleaning iPhone touch screens (SACOM 2010, 2). When the first poisoning occurred workers organized a strike. As a result United Win organized health examinations. However, no poisoning was diagnosed during these examinations. The affected workers therefore went to a hospital outside the factory, in which the poisoning was finally diagnosed (SACOM 2010, 2). Similar health hazards were also found at Futaihua Precision Electronics, a Foxconn subsidiary in Zhengzhou, where around 52,500 workers are producing 100,000 iPhones per day. Workers were exposed to chemicals such as n-hexane without adequate protection equipment. Some workers suffered from allergies (SACOM 2011b, 7).

In 2011 SACOM monitored Foxconn's Chengdu factory that produces exclusively for Apple. The investigation revealed an alarming occupational health and safety situation. SACOM found poor ventilation, insufficient protection equipment and noisy workplaces. Workers were using chemicals, without knowing whether they were harmful. At the milling and the polishing department – in which the iPads's aluminium cover is polished until it is untarnished and shiny – workers were constantly breathing in aluminium dust. Several workers were suffering from a skin allergy after working with glue like substances without wearing gloves (SACOM 2011a, 14). Shortly after SACOM's report was published, aluminium dust triggered an explosion at the polishing department at Chengdu that killed 3 workers and left 15 injured (SACOM 2011b, 1; Friends of Nature, IPE, Green Beagle 2011, 36). The Chengdu campus, which consists of eight factory buildings, was built in only 76 days in order to meet growing demand from Apple. Furthermore workers were insufficiently trained and not aware of the dangers connected to aluminium dust (Friends of Nature, IPE, Green Beagle 2011, 37f).

A similar incident occurred at the iPhone polishing department at a Pegatron factory in Shanghai in December 2011. 61 workers were injured (SACOM 2013, 8). SACOM furthermore reports that weak ventilations system at Pegatron's polishing department creates high levels of dust that cover worker's faces and penetrate their masks entering their noses and mouths (SACOM 2013, 8).

Working conditions at electronics manufacturing factories are not only threatening workers' physical health but also creating psychological problems. Social life at Foxconn is deprived. Workers do not have time for any free time activities. Their life consists of working, eating and sleeping. Often they do not even find enough time to sleep. When asked what they would like to do on holiday most interviewees said that they would like to sleep (SACOM 2011a, 12). Workers lack social contacts. SACOM's research shows that workers were not allowed to talk during work. They live in rooms with workers from different shifts, which they therefore hardly ever meet (SACOM 2011a, 12f, FinnWatch, SACOM and SOMO 2011, 30).

Work and life at factory campuses have severe impacts on the bodies and minds of workers. The example of Apple's supplier factories in China illustrates that for many workers selling their labour power also means selling their mental and physical health.

4.2.3   Work Experiences

During the past five years corporate watchdogs have interviewed numerous workers at Apple's supplier factories. These interviews reveal that workers experience their work as exhausting and alienating. They feel stressed and under pressure in order to achieve production targets (FinnWatch, SACOM and SOMO 2011, 30) as well as exhausted due to extremely long working hours, long hours of standing, and stress during meal breaks (SACOM 2011a, 15).

One worker told SACOM that workers they feel that Apple's demand dictates their entire lives. Workers are torn between the need to increase their salary by working overtime and the need to rest:

> The daily production target is 6,400 pieces. I am worn out every day. I fall asleep immediately after returning to the dormitory. The demand from Apple determines our lives. On one hand, I hope I can have a higher wage. On the other hand, I cannot keep working everyday without a day-off.
>
> Foxconn worker quoted in SACOM 2012, 5F

Workers furthermore experience their work environment as unsafe and unpleasant. They are worried about their health due to a lack of protection equipment:

> In my department, the working conditions are unbearable. I'm a machine operator, producing the silver frame for the iPhone. We have to put some oil into the machines in the production. I don't know what kind of substance it is and the smell is irritating. The frontline management confided to us that we should not stay in the department for over a year because the oil could cause problems to our lungs. Although the shop floor has air conditioning, it is very hot and the ventilation is poor. For me, the installation of the air-conditioners is just a tactic to avoid paying high temperature subsidy to the workers.
>
> Worker quoted in SACOM 2011B, 9

Furthermore workers describe the way they are controlled and managed as humiliating and exhausting:

> We have to queue up all the time. Queuing up for bus, toilet, card-punching, food, etc. During recess, we don't have a place to sit. We can only sit on the floor. We get up in early morning and can only return to the dorm in late evening. I am really worn out.
>
> Worker quoted in SACOM 2011A, 15

Workers are aware of the alienating character of their work situation, which expressed by the fact that they are not able to own the products that they are themselves producing every day: One worker told SACOM:

> Though we produce for iPhone, I haven' t got a chance to use iPhone. I believe it is fascinating and has lots of function. However, I don't think I can own one by myself.
>
> Worker quoted in SACOM 2011A, 19

These descriptions show that workers find themselves in a state of exhaustion and alienation. Karl Marx in 1844 in the *Economic and Philosophic Manuscripts* described the alienation of worker as his/her labour becoming an external object that "exists outside him, independently, as something alien to him" (Marx 1844/2007, 70). The more life the workers puts into his/her product, the more alienated s/he becomes: "The worker puts his life into the object; but now his life no longer belongs to him but to the object. [...] The greater this product, the less is he himself" (Marx 1844/2007, 70).

Workers in Apple's manufacturing factories have put their labour power into these products while producing them. Many workers left their families, gave up their free time and their health for producing products, which they will never be able to own. The finished products, although containing the workers' energy and labour, suddenly turn out of their reach. Workers are inside Apple's products, but at the same time insurmountably separated from them.

4.3   *Relations of Production*

The relation between capital and labour needs to be understood as a relation of domination. In capitalism the only commodity workers possess is their labour power. In order to make a living they thus have no other choice but to sell it by entering into a wage labour relationship (Marx 1867/1990, 272). Research conducted by corporate watchdogs shows that the relation between capital and labour in Apple's supplier factories in China is largely based on precarious labour contracts (see Section 4.3.1), characterized by low wages (see Section 4.3.2) and occasionally contested through labour struggles (see Section 4.3.3).

4.3.1   Labour Contracts

Labour contracts that offer weak protection for workers are an expression of the unequal power relation between employers and workers. In 2004 the Institute for Contemporary Observation (ICO), FinnWatch and the Finnish Export Credit Agency (ECA) investigated the Shenzhen Foxconn campus. They found that workers could be dismissed anytime. If dismissed, employees had to leave immediately without any financial compensation. If a worker decided to quit and to leave immediately s/he would not receive her/his outstanding wage (ICO, Finnwatch and ECA 2005, 17).

Watchdogs found instances where workers in Apple supplier factories did not receive any contract at all (ICO, Finnwatch and ECA 2005, 17, Swedwatch, SACOM and SOMO 2008, 42; Bread for All and SACOM 2008, 19). Without a signed contract workers are deprived of the possibility of taking legal steps in the case of labour law violations.

The majority of labour contracts in Apple's supplier factories are precarious. Short-term contracts allow supplier companies to remain flexible and to quickly respond to fluctuations of Apple's demand. Another measure Foxconn uses in order to cover sudden increases of labour demand is to recruit workers from labour agencies, or to relocate workers from other cities and provinces to another factory that has a heightened demand for workers (SACOM 2012, 8). So-called dispatch or agency workers are hired by labour agencies rather than being employed directly by the contract manufacturer. According to SACOM around 80% of the total workforce of the Apple supplier factories Foxlink in

Guangdong, Pegatron in Shanghai and Wintek in Jiangsu are agency workers (SACOM 2013, 4). Often social insurance schemes do not cover agency workers (SACOM 2013, 4).

New workers often have a probationary period between three and six months during which their wages are lower than those of permanent workers For example, the wage increases Foxconn implemented after the suicide tragedies were only granted to workers that had been working in the facility for more than six months (Finnwatch, SACOM, SOMO 2011, 28).

Another common practice among Apple's contract manufacturers is the employment of student interns. Especially during peak season students are hired in order to cover the sudden labour demand (SACOM 2012, 6). Students are cheaper to employ since they do not receive regular social security benefits and are not covered by labour law. They however have to work night shifts and overtime like regular workers. Student workers complain that the work they have to perform in Apple supplier factories is unskilled labour that is unrelated to the subject of their studies. Although students officially are not allowed to work more than eight hours per day, they are treated like regular workers and have to work overtime as well as night shifts (SACOM 2011a, 18). They also feel forced to work at these factories, as they are afraid that they will not be able to graduate if they refuse to complete the internship (SACOM 2013, 6). Su argues that the internship programs led to the commodification of both student's labour and education (Su 2011, 342). Internship programmes allow factories such as Foxconn to exploit student labour for a profit. In return for sending students to factories technical schools receive equipment and funding (Su 2011, 350).

Finnwatch, SACOM and SOMO found that large numbers of 16-to 18-year old students were employed in Foxconn factories for periods between four and six months (Finnwatch, SACOM and SOMO 2009, 36; Finnwatch, SACOM an SOMO 2011, 5 see also Su 2011, 345). SACOM quotes reports form Chinese media according to which in 2010 100,000 vocational school students from Henan province were sent to work at a Foxconn plant in Shenzhen to complete a 3-month internship (SACOM 2011b, 3). An investigation by the Fair Labour Association (FLA), that Apple had requested, confirmed that Foxconn did not comply with the standards regarding maximum working hours for student interns. Like regular workers, students had to work overtime and nights shifts (FLA 2012, 10).

Short-term precarious contracts and weak protection against dismissal increase factory management's power over workers. It makes workers vulnerable and serves as a means for controlling their behaviour by threat of dismissal. Because workers need to fear loosing their jobs they are more likely to agree to higher production targets or increased overtime. Precarious contracts make long-term life planning difficult. Short notice periods leave workers hardly any time to rearrange their lives after a dismissal. Furthermore different types of contracts create divides between workers with fixed contracts, short-term contracts, agency contracts or internship contracts. The fact that different types of contracts confront workers with different kinds of problems makes it more difficult to formulate collective demands.

4.3.2   Wages and Benefits

Among the most pressing problems that occur throughout Apple's supplier factories is the low wage level. Already in 2007 the Dutch non-profit research centre SOMO (2007a) interviewed workers at five Apple supplier factories in China, the Philippines and Thailand: Workers in all investigated factories reported that their wages were too low to cover their living expenses. Wages at the Chinese factory of Volex Cable Assembly Co. Ltd. were found to be below the legal minimum (SOMO 2007a, 21). However, even if wages comply with minimum wage regulations they are often hardly enough to cover basic living expenses. In 2008 for example FinnWatch, SACOM and SOMO monitored buildings C03 and C04 of Foxconn's Shenzhen campus, in which 2,800 workers at 40 assembly lines are producing black and white models of the iPhone 8G and 16G (FinnWatch, SACOM and SOMO 2009, 35). Wages corresponded to the legal minimum wage of around 980 yuan, which however is not an adequate living wage (FinnWatch, SACOM and SOMO 2009, 36, 44). A living wage should cover expenses for food, housing, clothes, education, social security and health care for a family, and allow for some savings.[16]

After the suicide tragedies, Foxconn announced significant wage raises.[17] FinnWatch, SACOM and SOMO in 2010 did a follow up study at Apple's production line at Foxconn's Shenzhen campus in order to investigate how the promised

---

16   The Asia Floor Wage Campaign (2009) suggested a method for calculating the living wage. According to this calculation a living wage needs to cover the costs for food, equivalent of 3000 calories per adult family member multiplied by two, in order to cover also other basic need such as clothing, housing, education, healthcare, and savings. The living wage should provide for a family of two adults and two children. It thus should cover the cost for food worth 3000 calories for three consumption units (two adults and two children) multiplied by two. It is thus calculated as follows: price for food worth 3000 calories x 3 x 2 (Asia Floor Wage Campaign 2009, 50). A worker should be able to earn a living wage within a working week of a maximum of 48 hours. This calculation of a living wage was developed with specific regard to the garment sector, but is also applicable for other sectors such as electronics manufacturing.

17   Reuters 2010. Foxconn to Raise Wages Again at China Plant. Retrieved from http://www .reuters.com/article/2010/10/01/us-foxconn-idUSTRE6902GD20101001 on April 28, 2013.

wage raises[18] were implemented. 30 workers were interviewed. The investigation showed that Foxconn in June 2010 increased monthly wages from 900 Yuan to 1,200 Yuan (137 EUR). In October 2010 wages were further raised to 2,000 Yuan (229 EUR), but only for workers who had been working at the factory for more than six months. However, only estimated 50% of the workforce actually worked longer than 6 months in this factory (FinnWatch, SACOM and SOMO 2011, 28). Furthermore the wage increases only applied to Shenzhen and not to newly established upcountry factories to which Foxconn is increasingly relocating its production (FinnWatch, SACOM and SOMO 2011, 8).

In 2011 SACOM conducted a similar investigation at three other Foxconn campuses in order to evaluate once more how effective the proposed changes really were and whether they improved working and living conditions of employees. SACOM visited Foxconn campuses at Shenzhen, Chengdu and Chongqing and found that Foxconn had increased wages, but at the same time cancelled food and housing subsidies. This means that despite Foxconn's claims there was no actual wage increase (SACOM 2011a, 6). Foxconn was not paying a living wage. Figure 11.4 shows SACOM's estimations regarding the gap between actual basic wages and living wages in April 2011.

SACOM argues that one strategy Foxconn employs to avoid wage increases is to send workers away from cities with higher wage levels, such as Shenzhen, to ones with lower wages levels such as Chengdu (SACOM 2011a, 5–6).

The investigation conducted by the Fair Labour Association (FLA) confirms that workers at Apple suppliers perceive their wages as too low. In a survey that assessed the work satisfaction of 35,166 workers at two Foxconn campuses in Shenzhen and one Foxconn campus in Chengdu 64.3% of all respondents and 72% of respondents working at Foxconn's Chengdu campus reported that their wages do not cover their basic needs (FLA 2012, 9).

Apple is the second most profitable company in the world. These high profits are made possible at the cost of workers. According to calculations made by Kraemer, Linden and Dedrick in 2010 Apple kept 58.5% of the sales price of an iPhone, the costs of materials amounted to 21.9% of the sales prize while only 1.8% were spent for the labour cost for final assembly in China. For the iPad Chinese labour costs amount to 2%, input materials to 31% and Apple's profits to 30% of the sales price (Kraemer, Linden and Dedrick 2011, 5). The less Apple has to spend for paying wages the higher are the company's profits. While Apple could certainly afford spending more money for the manufacturing of its products, this would have a negative impact on its profit goals.

---

18   Reuters 2010. Foxconn to Raise Wages Again at China Plant. Retrieved from http://www
       .reuters.com/article/2010/10/01/us-foxconn-idUSTRE6902GD20101001 on April 28, 2013.

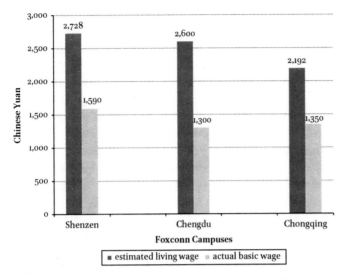

FIGURE 11.4   *Actual basic wages in comparison to estimated living wages at Foxconn*
campuses in April 2011 (SACOM 2011a, 6, 9)

Marx stressed that capitalism is based on a contradiction between capital and labour: "Political economy starts from labour as the real soul of production; yet to labour it gives nothing, and to private property everything" (Marx 1844/2007, 81). The example of Apple illustrates this fundamental injustice: Apple's success would be impossible without the work performed in its supplier factories. This work allowed Apple to become the second most profitable company in the world, while it left workers impoverished.

4.3.3   Labour Struggles

The low wage level is only one of the reasons why workers engage in strikes and protests. For example on January 15, 2010, 2,000 workers at United Win that produce Apple's iPad organized a strike (SACOM 2010, 1). On November 15, 2011 several thousand workers of the Foxconn facility in Foshan were protesting against low wages.[19] In January 2013 over 1,000 workers protested at Foxconn facility in Fengcheng held demonstrations against low wages and bad working conditions.[20]

---

19   M.I.C. Gadget. 2010. More Problems With Foxconn; Workers Protest Against Their Wages. Retrieved from http://micgadget.com/9620/more-problems-with-foxconn-workers-protest-against-their-wages/ on October 27, 2011.

20   SACOM. 2013. Strike Erupted Over Dire Working Conditions at Foxconn. Retrieved from http://sacom.hk/archives/971 on May 14, 2013.

Such protests are not without risks for factory workers. In 2011 during an investigation at Foxconn's Zhengzhou factory some interviewees told SACOM about workers being dismissed after attempting to strike (SACOM 2011b, 10). In January 2011 the police arrested around 20 workers at another Foxconn facility while protesting against miscalculations of wages (SACOM 2011a, 8).

Labour unions only play a limited role in these protests. The only official trade union in China is the All China Federation of Trade Unions (ACFTU), which is subordinate to the Chinese Communist Party (Friedman and Lee 2010, 521). Friedman and Lee argue that the ACFTU acts like a government agency that represents workers in a top-down process, promotes the introduction of labour laws, provides legal consultation to workers but is opposed to widespread worker mobilization (Friedman and Lee 2010, 521f).

Often workers either do not know what a union can do for them or do not even know that a union exists at their factory (Finnwatch, SACOM, SOMO 2009 & 2011). Similarly FLA in 2012 found that worker had very little knowledge about the function and activities of worker representatives. Furthermore the FLA found that unions at Foxconn often consist of supervisors or mangers (FLA 2012, 11).

In response to the findings of the FLA Foxconn in February 2013 announced that it will hold democratic union elections.[21] However a study conducted by a corporate watchdog shows that in March and April 2013, 90.2% of 685 questioned Foxconn workers had not heard about any election plans (The New Generation Migrant Workers Concern Programme 2013, 6). The results show that more than 50% of the respondents did not know that union members can democratically elect their representatives and that they can themselves come forward as a candidate. 82.5% of the workers did not know who the leader of their union group was. 16.9% of the respondents reported that they are union members. Further 24.6% said that they think that they are members of a union. These numbers show that actual union enrolment is much lower than 86.3%, the number given by Foxconn officials (The New Generation Migrant Workers Concern Programme 2013, 4f).

Despite these low levels of awareness regarding the existing union the survey results show that workers nevertheless think that unions could potentially help to improve their situation. 45.8% of the interviewed Foxconn workers think that a union can play a "very important" role in achieving wage increases,

---

21   Financial Times. February 3, 2013. Foxconn plans Chinese Union Vote. Retrieved from http://www.ft.com/cms/s/0/48091254-6c3e-11e2-b774-00144feab49a.html#axzz2TFz9DeNG on May 14, 2013.

while only 3.4% think that unions are "not important" in this context (The New Generation Migrant Workers Concern Programme 2013, 7). Fostering awareness among workers regarding their rights and strengthening their right to choose union representatives thus seems crucial to support the struggle of workers over their working conditions.

There is the potential that Chinese workers become important agents of labour struggle in the 21st century. In this context Zhao and Duffy highlight: "The fact that tens of thousand of Chinese workers are engaging in daily struggles over hand-to-mouth issues must qualify any sweeping post-Marxist formulations by Western-centric scholars about the disappearance of the working class as historical agents of struggle in the information age" (Zhao and Duffy 2008, 244). In this context Time Magazine in March 2013 reported that "Resentment is reaching a boiling point in China's factory towns. [...] Facing long hours, rising costs, indifferent managers and often late pay, workers are beginning to sound like true proletariat".[22] Rather than regarding Chinese workers at Apple's suppliers and elsewhere as mere victims of capitalist exploitation it is important to recognize that collectively organized they can cause severe disruptions to the global value chain.

On several occasions activists around the world have supported the struggle of Chinese workers. NGOs and labour rights activists have been protesting against Apple tolerating unbearable working conditions in its supplier factories. For example on May 7, 2011 an international day of action against unacceptable treatment of workers was held. MakeITfair, a project of a group of European corporate watchdog organizations, under the slogan "Time to bite into a fair Apple; Call for sustainable IT!" organized protest events throughout Europe,[23,24] SACOM organized a protest street theatre in Hong Kong.[25] Such international solidarity from activists can support worker struggles by raising awareness within Western civil society regarding the work and life reality of Chinese factory workers.

---

22   TIME Magazine. Karl Marx's Revenge.

23   SOMO. 2011. Time to Bite Into a Fair Apple. Call for Sustainable IT! Join Action Day on May 7th. Retrieved from http://somo.nl/events-en/time-to-bite-into-a-fair-apple-call-for -sustainable-it-join-action-day-on-may-7th on October 27, 2011.

24   A video that docments one camaign activitiy can be watched here: http://www.youtube .com/watch?v=kaiXni3h2Ug&feature=player_embedded Retrieved on October 27, 2011.

25   ChinaWorkers. 2011. Rotten Apple – Worldwide Protests Against IT Giant's Labour Abuses. Retrieved from http://chinaworker.info/en/content/news/1451/ on October 27, 2011.

4.4   *Production Process*

In the production process labour power and means of production are employed in order to produce a commodity (Marx 19867/1990, 284). Taking a closer look at the production process in the factories of Apple's contract manufacturers reveals a predominance of unpleasant and unsafe labour spaces (see Section 4.4.1), long working hours (see Section 4.4.2), standardized and repetitive production steps (see Section 4.4.3) and strict and often humiliating control mechanisms (see Section 4.4.4).

4.4.1   Labour Spaces

Work at Apple's contract manufacturers takes place within the boundaries of the factory. Shopfloors often lack proper ventilation systems, which means that the work environment is hot, dusty and has a strong chemical smell (SCAOM 2011b, 7). The behaviour of workers within their work spaces is strongly controlled: Workers at Foxconn have to pass through security checks with metal detectors when entering or leaving the shopfloor as well as bathrooms (FinnWatch, SACOM and SOMO 2011, 31). Most of the life of electronics workers takes place on factory campuses. Many workers live in dormitories provided by their employer. Factory dormitories are often crowded and provide only little privacy. In 2009 Finnwatch, SACOM and SOMO for example reported that on Foxconn campuses in Shenzhen the dormitory consists of a five storey building with 25 rooms per floor, each shared by eight to ten 10 workers (Finnwatch, SACOM and SOMO 2009, 39). The strict discipline and control of the workshop also enters the dormitory. Ngai Pun argues that "The dormitory labour system ensures that workers spend their off-hours just preparing for another round of production" (Ngai, 23).

Most factory campuses are based within Special Economic Zones (SEZ) that traditionally are located in urban costal areas. A recent trend in China's manufacturing sector is the relocation of production to inland provinces where wage levels are still lower. Foxconn has been relocating parts of its production from costal areas such as Shenzhen to inland provinces (SACOM 2011b, 3). Foxconn workers are forced to relocate to production facilities even farther away from their hometowns (SACOM 2012, 8). Among the new inland campuses are Foxconn production sites in Zhengzhou, Henan province. Because of growing demand new factories are often built and opened in a rush. SACOM reports that the new Zhengzhou factory was operating even before the construction work was finished. For workers this means that basic facilities such as bathrooms or grocery stores are not available (SACOM 2011b, 4). At unfinished factory campuses the environment is dusty on dry days and flooded on rainy days (SACOM 2011b, 4). Likewise Friends of Nature, IPE, and Green Beagle report that Foxconn's Chengdu campus was built in on 76 days, which created a number of security risks (Friends of Nature, IPE, Green Beagle 2011, 37f).

Labour spaces at Apple's supplier factories are unpleasant and dangerous. The fact that work takes place in centralized factory spaces makes it possible to exert strict control over working hours and behaviour of workers even in their "free" time.

4.4.2 Labour Times

Workers are not only underpaid (see Section 4.3.2), but also overworked. SOMO in its 2005 investigation of the Foxconn campus in Shenzhen found: "On average, a worker that works 27 days a month and 10–11 hours a day will receive about RMB 1000 a month including all the subsidies and OT [overtime] compensation" (SOMO 2005b, 26). In 2005 1,000 RMB were equivalent to about 100 EUR or 120 USD (SOMO 2005b, 27). Workers at Foxconn complained that during peak season they would not receive a single day off in four months (SOMO 2005b, 15). Another investigation of five Apple supplier factories conducted in 2007 confirmed that overtime between 2.5 and 4 hours per day in addition to the regular working hours of 8 to 9.5 hours were common. In four out of five investigated factories total working hours exceeded 60 weekly hours and at one factory workers even had to work up to 80 hours per week (SOMO 2007a, 22). In 2008 Finnwatch, SACOM and SOMO found similar conditions at Apple's production line at Foxconn's Shenzhen campus. Employees had to work compulsory excessive overtime of up to 120 hours per month, which resulted in a total of 70 hours per week (FinnWatch, SACOM and SOMO 2009, 37).

After the suicides tragedies Finnwatch, SACOM and SOMO conducted a follow up investigation of working conditions at Foxconn. The results show that while at the beginning of 2010 excessive compulsory overtime was still the same as in 2008, the situation changed after June 2010. From then on workers were granted one day off per week and overtime was reduced from 120 hours to between 75 and 80 hours per month, with still exceeded the legal maximum of 36 hours (FinnWatch, SACOM and SOMO 2011, 29).

Low wage levels and the problem of long working hours are connected to each other: Low wages force workers to work overtime in order to earn enough money to be able to cover their living expenses. A 19-year worker who was producing iPhones at Guanlan, Shenzhen told SACOM: "We do not have much overtime work this month. Our department has 3 shifts a day now. I can only receive a basic salary at CNY 1600 this month. It' s really not enough for a living but I believe the 8-hour shift is just a temporary measure for the low season" (Worker quoted in SACOM 2011a, 9). SACOM's investigation of Foxconn campuses in Shenzhen, Chengdu and Chongquing furthermore showed that workers in

Chengdu, where the gap between actual and living wage was highest (see Figure 11.1), also worked most overtime, between 80 and 100 hours per month (SACOM 2011a, 10). In 2012 the FLA found that at the three monitored Foxconn plants in Shenzhen and Chengdu workers during peek season worked more than 60 hours per week. Despite these very long working hours 48% of the interviewed workers stated that their working hours were reasonable, 33.8% said that they would like to work more in order to earn more money and 17.7% reported that their working hours were too long (FLA 2012, 8). In September 2012 SACOM investigated three Foxconn plants in Zhengzhou, Henan Province that are only producing iPhones. The results show that working hours vary strongly depending on Apple's demand. During low season overtime work was as low as 10 hours per month, while during peak season 80–100 hours monthly overtime were common (SACOM 2012, 3). During low season workers thus struggle to earn enough to cover their living expenses, while during high season they are exhausted due to a lack of free time.

Even if overtime work is officially labelled voluntary, low wages often force workers into working excessive overtime. While companies comply with legal minimum wage standards, compliance with regulations for maximum working hours is often insufficient. The fact that minimum wage levels are too low makes compliance relatively easy for companies, while it creates the need for workers to work overtime to earn extra money. The relation between low wages and high overtime rates is a basic structural characteristic of contemporary electronics manufacturing. It allows companies to keep their payroll low at the expense of workers, and at the same time meet high production targets.

4.4.3   Type of Work Activity

Work at Chinese contract manufacturers in the electronics sector in general is characterized by a strong segmentation of the labour process into small, standardized production steps (Lüthje 2008, 67). Low skilled assembly line labour and uniform work procedures therefore dominate work in electronics factories (Lüthje 2008, 73; 2005, 342). Workflows are fragmented and repetitive. One worker told China Labour Watch: "We finish one step in every 7 seconds, which requires us to concentrate and keep working and working. We work faster even than the machines" (Worker quoted by China Labour Watch 2010). Reports from corporate watchdogs show that machines dictates work procedures: SACOM reports that machines at Foxconn's factories have to run 24/7, therefore some workers always have to remain at the shopfloor during meal breaks. These continuous shifts require workers to skip meals. One worker complained:

> The machines in our department are in operation 24/7. If some colleagues go out for dinner, then the workers who stay in the workshop have to take care of 3 machines at the same time. It is hard work but we do not have additional subsidy for that. Workers can only have dinner after the work shift ends. Continuous shift occurs everyday.
>
> Worker quoted in SACOM 2011a, 11

The work activities workers perform in Apple's supplier factories are monotonous, repetitive and dictated by machines. Their activity can therefore be described as an alienated labour process, as "an activity which is turned against" the worker (Marx 1844/2007, 73). Marx argued that in capitalism the production process turns against the worker because "it is not the worker who employs the conditions of his work, but rather the reverse, the conditions of work employ the worker" (Marx 1867/1990, 548).

Work in Apple's supplier factories is characterized by a separation between mental and manual labour as it is associated with Taylorist production methods. Each step of the labour process is defined and controlled by management, while executed by the worker: "The physical processes of production are now carried out more or less blindly [...] The production units operate like a hand, watched, corrected and controlled by a distant brain" (Braverman 1974/1998, 86).

The computer industry furthermore illustrates the division between manual and mental labour on a global scale. While highly skilled engineers that design computer software and hardware tend to be located in the global North, the physical production and assembly of computer products largely takes place in the global South.

4.4.4   Control Mechanisms

Harsh and humiliating management styles are used to control the behaviour of workers at Apple's contract manufacturers. In 2009 Finnwatch, SACOM and SOMO reported about strict disciplinary measures in Apple's production line at Foxconn. No personal belongings were allowed in the factory and procedures of how to start work and leaving the shopfloor were strictly regulated. Workers reported that if asked how they felt they had to shout: "Fine! Very fine! Very, very fine!" Talking, giggling, and crossing legs was forbidden while sitting at the assembly line. Talking might be punished with shopfloor cleaning. Due to time-consuming security checks at toilets and short breaks workers often had to chose between using the bathroom and having lunch (Finnwatch, SACOM and SOMO 2009, 37f).

A follow-up investigation in 2011 showed that disciplinary measures at Foxconn were less strict after the suicides had occurred on the campus, than they were in 2008. However security checks at toilets did still exists and workers still had to collectively reply "Fine! Very fine! Very, very fine!" when asked how they felt (Finnwatch, SACOM and SOMO 2011, 31). At a Foxconn plant in Chengdu new workers for example had to participate in a one to two day long military training which only consisted of lining up and standing (SACOM 2011a, 16). Workers furthermore had to stand up to 14 hours per day. During breaks they were sitting on the floor often without talking to each other because they were too exhausted (SACOM 2011a, 16). If workers made mistakes they had to write confession letters to their supervisors and sometimes even read them loud in front of other workers (SACOM 2011a, 17). Supervisors were under pressure too. If one of the workers they were supervising made a mistake they had to face punishment themselves (SACOM 2011a, 17). The strict supervision and control mechanisms are a means for factory management to demonstrate its power over workers. It attempts to reduce human behaviour such as talking, eating or using the toilet and to force machine-like qualities onto the workers.

4.5   *Labour Law*

Several laws are in place to regulate work and employment in China including the Chinese Labour Law (1994), the Trade Union Law (1992, 2002), the Labour Contract Law (2007) and the Labour Dispute Mediation and Arbitration Law (2007) (Friedman and Lee 2010, 515). The Labour Contract Law for example entitles workers to a non-fixed term contract after their fixed term contract has been renewed twice and requires employers to pay higher severance payments in case of layoffs (Friedman and Lee 2010, 526). However, a major problem is that these laws often remain unenforced (Friedman and Lee 2010, 515). This is for example the case in regard to maximum hours overtime work. Chinese labour law limits maximum overtime to 36 hours per month (FinnWatch, SACOM and SOMO 2011, 29).

While Apple's contract manufacturers regularly exceed the legal maximum working hours, they mostly comply with minimum wage regulation. However, studies have shown that minimum wages in China are often too low (e.g. SACOM 2011a, 6, 9), which provides an excuse for companies to pay wages that are below the living wage level.

Although a number of labour regulations are in place in China, they often are either too lax (e.g. minimum wages) or not well enforced (e.g. maximum working hours). China furthermore has not ratified the core conventions of the International Labour Organization (ILO) on Forced Labour[26] and Freedom of

---

26   Forced Labour Convention (CO29) and the Abolition of Forced Labour Convention (CO105). Source: ILO. 2013. Retrieved from http://www.ilo.org/dyn/normlex/en/f?p =1000:11210:0::NO:11210:P11210_COUNTRY_ID:103404 on May 14, 2013.

Association.[27] Without the ratification of these conventions the legal obligation to protect these fundamental labour rights is weaker. Hong argues that in order to stay competitive in global capitalism the Chinese state "shares the interest with transnational capital to further tap into the reserves of cheap and disciplined labour and to keep down the cost of production" (Hong 2011, 6). Through tax benefits China was successful in attracting foreign enterprises (Hong 2011, 38). The result of these policies is an economic dependency on multinational companies, exports and consumer markets in the global North (Hung 2009, 14). It is therefore important not to underestimate the power multinational corporations have on influencing government policies in China as well as elsewhere.

4.6   Results of Production

Apple's products are at the forefront of technological innovation. They are symbols for modern 21st century lifestyle and progress. The conditions under which these products are produced on the contrary resemble the early days of industrial capitalism. The fact that for example an iPhone costs often twice as much as the average monthly salary of a worker in electronics manufacturing, reveals a deep separation between workers and the fruits of their labour.

Computer technology has the potential to alleviate work, to increase productivity and to reduce the amount of necessary labour time. It entails the potential that especially unqualified, monotonous, repetitive, and mechanical assembly line labour, which reduces workers to extensions of machines without human intellect or creativity, could in the future increasingly be taken over by machines. The way computers are produced today contradicts this potential.

Apple's 2011 marketing campaign praised the design, premium materials and high-quality manufacturing of Apple's products. Apple advertised the iPad as "Amazingly thin and light"[28] as a "Technology so advanced, you'll forget it's even there".[29] According to Apple's ads, "A Mac is as good as it looks. It's made from strong, beautiful materials like aluminium and glass":[30] "Take

---

27   Freedom of Organisation and Protection of the Right to Organise Convention (CO87) and the Right to Organise and Collective Bargaining Convention (CO98). Source: ILO. 2013. Retrieved from   http://www.ilo.org/dyn/normlex/en/f?p=1000:11210:0::NO:11210:P11210 _COUNTRY_ID:103404 on May 14, 2013.

28   Apple. 2011. Retrieved from http://www.apple.com/ipad/ on October 25, 2011.

29   Apple. 2011. Retrieved from http://www.apple.com/ipad/features/ on October 25, 2011.

30   Apple. 2011. Retrieved from http://www.apple.com/why-mac/better-hardware/ on October 25, 2011.

MacBook Air, for example. Its unibody enclosure is machined from a solid block of aluminium. The result is a notebook that is thin and light, looks polished and refined, and feels strong and durable".[31] This marketing strategy pictures Apple's products as trendy, clean, sophisticated, elegant and of high quality – a technology that is so advanced that it will expand the capacities of its users and fit their needs so neatly, that they will "forget it's even there."

Apple's marketing slogans present its products as technological marvels without history. They divert attention away from the fact that underpaid Chinese workers are producing these products during 10 to 12 hour shifts at least 6 days a week, in exhausting and repetitive working procedures, while jeopardizing their health. Once displayed on posters, magazines and TV-spots, iPad, MacBook and Co have lost any trace of the conditions under which they were produced.

4.7   *Summary*

Table 11.2 summarizes working conditions at Apple's contract manufacturers in China.

The results of the analysis provided here show that labour rights are systematically undermined in the factories of Apple's contract manufactures. The next section discusses Apple's response to the bad working conditions in the factories of its Chinese contract manufacturers.

5   Defending the Myth: Apple's Response to Labour Right Violations

Apple's response to labour right violations in its supply chain is very reactive. The company published its first Supplier Responsibility document as a reaction to ongoing criticism of its supply chain management. It starts with the following sentence: "In the summer of 2006, we were concerned by reports in the press alleging poor working and living conditions at one of our iPod final assembly suppliers in China" (Apple 2006, 1). Since then Apple published one Supplier Responsibility Report per year. These reports promise that Apple "is committed to the highest standard of social responsibility in everything we do. We are dedicated to ensuring that working conditions are safe, the environment is protected, and employees are treated with respect and dignity wherever Apple products are made" (Apple 2006, 4).

---

31   Apple. 2011. Retrieved from http://www.apple.com/why-mac/better-hardware/ on
         October 25, 2011.

TABLE 11.2 *Working conditions at Apple's contract manufacturers*

Productive forces – Means of production	Machines and equipment	High-tech equipment, e.g. Surface Mount Technology
	Resources	Minerals such as tin, beryllium, gallium, platinum tantalum, indium, neodymium, tungsten, palladium, yttrium, gold, and cobalt; often sourced from conflict areas
Productive forces – labour	Workforce characteristics	A majority of young, often female migrant workers
	Mental and physical health	Instances of injuries and deaths due to unsafe work environments, lack of protection equipment and insufficient information of workers Psychological problems due to social isolation and exhaustion, instances of suicides
	Work experiences	Workers describe their experiences as exhausting, humiliating and alienated
Relations of production	Labour contract	Dominance of precarious short term contracts and agency labour
	Wages and benefits	Low wage levels despite compliance with minimum wage regulation, no living wage
	Labour struggles	Several instances of strikes and protests but low awareness of and support from unions
Production process	Labour spaces	Unpleasant and unsafe factory environments, crowded factory dormitories, instances of forced relocation of workers to production facilities in other provinces
	Labour times	Long working hours of more than 60 hours per week during peak seasons. Working hours highly depend on shifts in demand
	Work activity	High workflow segmentation, uniform and repetitive production steps, separation of manual and mental work
	Control mechanism	Harsh, military management styles and harassment of workers
Results of production	Labour product	High-tech computer products and consumer electronics: computers, mp3players, mobile phones, tablet computers
The state	Labour law	Insufficient enforcement of labour laws, low minimum wages and missing ratification of ILO core conventions on forced labour and freedom of association

Based on Teun A. van Dijk's (2011) concept of the ideological square I in the following analyse the arguments Apple puts forward in its Supplier Responsibility Reports in order to demonstrate its efforts to improve working conditions. The ideological square identifies four possible ideological strategies that describe different ways of how the relation between in-groups and out-groups, between "us" and "them" is represented in talk or text (Van Dijk 2011, 397). These strategies are: "Emphasize *Our* good things," "Emphasize *Their* bad things," "De-emphasize *Our* bad things," "De-emphasize *Their* good things" (Van Dijk 2011, 396). Three of these strategies are present in Apple's response to watchdog criticism: Apple is de-emphasizing its own wrongdoings by downplaying the extent of the problem of labour rights violations (see Section 5.1), while at the same time emphasizing its achievements by using a rhetoric of continuous improvement (see Section 5.2). The company furthermore emphasizes the wrongdoings of others by blaming Chinese managers and workers for the persistence of bad working conditions (see Section 5.3).

5.1   *De-Emphasize Our Bad Things: Downplaying the Extent of the Problem*

The strategy that is most dominant in Apple's response to labour rights allegations is to de-emphasize the extent of the problem. While watchdog reports document the persistence of serious labour rights issues (see Section 4), Apple's Supplier Responsibility reports suggests that the problems are much less severe.

In its reports Apple defines "core violations" of its Code of Conduct, which require immediate improvements. These include physical abuse, child labour, forced labour, false audits, severe threats to worker safety and intimidation of workers that are interviewed during audits (Apple 2007, 7; Apple 2012, 10). Apple stresses that it considers core violations "as contrary to the core principles underlying Apple's Supplier Code of Conduct and require immediate corrective actions" (Apple 2007, 7).

Apparently it is not a "core principle" of Apple's business practices that workers who are producing the products that are the basis for Apple's profits, are paid for their work and have reasonable working hours. As neither underpayment nor overwork are considered a core violation, no immediate solution needs to be found if these problems occur. Apple thus de-facto tolerates, that workers receive wages that hardly suffice for paying basic living expenses, while working up to a point of complete exhaustion. By not regarding these issues as core violations Apple downplays how severe these problems are for workers.

Apart from this general downplaying of the problem of low wages and long working hours Apple's Supplier Responsibility reports furthermore hide the full extent of labour rights violations behind statistics and numbers and describe the problem as the result of minor shortcomings while ignoring structural causes:

- **Fetishism of statistics:** Throughout Apple's Supplier Responsibility reports hardly any descriptions about how working conditions in its supplier factories actually look like can be found. Apple only provides statistical data that actually tells little about the daily work and life experiences of workers. According to Apple's own audits, the non-compliance rate in regard to payment of at least minimum wages and transparent wage calculations was 46% in 2007, 41% in 2008, 35% in 2009, 30% in 2010, 31% in 2011 and 28% in 2012 (Apple 2007–2012). Although these figures show an improvement, it still means that a large number of workers in Apple's supplier factories are paid below the legal minimum. Considering that the even the legal minimum is often below a living wage, these numbers are even more troubling. Apple's figures on working hours give a similar picture. Non-compliance with a maximum 60 hours per week was 82% in 2007, 59% in 2008, 54% in 2009, 68% in 2010, 62% in 2011 before it suddenly dropped to 8% in 2012 (Apple 2007–2012). As an explanation for this sudden decrease of non-compliance in regard to weekly working hours Apple sates: "In 2012, we changed our measurement on working hours to one that is more meaningful and effective" (Apple 2012, 29). This explanation suggests that the sudden decrease in working hours stems from changes in measurement rather than actual changes in working conditions. Furthermore it is problematic that Apple considers a 60-hour working week as desirable. In fact, a 60-hour working week violates Chinese labour law. In China a regular working week must not exceed 44 hours. In addition maximum overtime according to the law is 9 hours per week. This means that including overtime, Chinese labour law limits working hours to 53 hours per week.[32] By calculating compliance with maximum working hours based on a 60-hour working week, which exceeds the legal maximum, Apple's audits misrepresent the extent to which workers are working excessive overtime. Without any descriptions of the work realities of workers the statistics Apple presents furthermore remain abstract and therefore hide how severe low wages, long working hours or the lack of health protection can be for the lives of individual workers and their families.

- **Ignoring root causes:** Apple has a strong business interests in keeping production costs low. In a 2012 financial statement Apple highlights that it has to deal with strong prize competition: "The markets for the Company's products

---

32   China.org. Labour Law of the People's Republic of China. Retrieved from http://www
      .china.org.cn/living_in_china/abc/2009-07/15/content_18140508.htm on May 15, 2013.

and services are highly competitive and the Company is confronted by aggressive competition in all areas of its business. [...] The Company's competitors who sell mobile devices and personal computers based on other operating systems have aggressively cut prices and lowered their product margins to gain or maintain market share" (Apple SEC-Filings, 10-k form 2012, 6).

This structural contradiction between Apple's need to reduce labour costs in order to stay competitive, and low wages, low safety standards and long working hours is not addressed in Apple's Supplier Responsibility reports. Furthermore Apple's response to the suicide tragedies ignores connections between bad working and living conditions and the suicide tragedies. In its 2010 report Apple highlighted that it is "disturbed and deeply saddened to learn that factory workers were taking their own lives at the Shenzhen facility of Foxconn" (Apple 2010, 18). Apple stressed that as a reaction to the suicides it launched "an international search for the most knowledgeable suicide prevention specialists – particularly those with experience in China – and asked them to advise Apple and Foxconn" (Apple 2010, 18). A team of suicide prevention experts was formed which conducted a questionnaire survey among 1,000 Foxconn workers, face to face interviews with workers and mangers, investigated each suicide individually and evaluated Foxconn's response to the suicides (Apple 2010, 18). The result of this evaluation was that Foxonn's reaction to the suicides was ideal: "Most important, the investigation found that Foxconn's response had definitely saved lives" (Apple 2010, 19). Suggestions for further improvement were only made regarding the training of hotline and care centre stuff (Apple 2010, 19).

Both the measures taken by Apple and the improvement suggestions made by the "most knowledgeable suicide prevention specialists" seem rather limited. They do not include any improvement of working conditions, which according to different labour rights groups had been bad for many years (SOMO 2005b; FinnWatch, SACOM and SOMO 2009; FinnWatch, SACOM and SOMO 2011; SACOM 2011a,b, 2012, 2013). The anti-suicide team's findings suggest that the suicides had nothing to do with working conditions at Foxconn. A study conducted by China Labour Watch (2010) tells a different story. On May 17, 2010 China Labour Watch asked 25 Foxconn workers about what they believed were the reason for the suicides of Foxconn workers. 17 said that high pressure at work was the main reason. Five workers argued that a lacking sense of community at Foxconn has led to the suicides, as even workers that were living in the same room would not know each other. Three workers doubted that the reasons for the deaths actually were suicides (China Labour Watch 2010).

Apple, by failing to discuss the connection between the suicides of workers and problems such as low wages, excessive working hours, humiliation, work pressure, social isolation etc, de-emphasizes the extent to which workers are suffering from bad working conditions.

5.2   *Emphasize Our Good Things: A Rhetoric of Continuous Improvement*
Apple's Supplier Responsibility Reports put forward a story of continuous improvement. They are officially labelled as "Progress Report." In the 2009 report Apple for example states: "In general, annual audits of final assembly manufacturers show continued performance improvements and better working conditions" (Apple 2009, 15). The 2007 report states: "By aggressively auditing our suppliers and pursuing corrective actions, Apple has improved living and working conditions for tens of thousands of employees in our supply chain" (Apple_SR 2007, 14). Similarly in the 2010 report Apple highlights "Our repeat audits showed continued performance improvements and better working conditions" (Apple_SR 2010, 15).

This rhetoric of improvement detracts from the fact that working conditions are bad, as independent research shows (see Section 4). Evidence for these alleged improvements is provided by reference to statistics form Apple's own audits. Apple claims that treatment of workers is "fair" in more than 90% of all monitored factories (Apple 2007–2012). By pointing at improvements and stressing that workers are treated in a fair way in the majority of cases Apple's is putting forward a positive image about working conditions in its supply chain.

This focus on good things also characterized Steve Job's response to the suicide at the Foxconn factory cafmpus. He stated that "Foxconn is not a sweatshop". "You go in this place and it's a factory but, my gosh, they've got restaurants and movie theatres and hospitals and swimming pools. For a factory, it's pretty nice" (Jobs 2010). Considering the descriptions of unacceptable working realities at Foxconn campuses provided in watchdog reports (see Section 4) as well as the low compliance rates according to Apple's own audits (see Section 5.1), this statement sounds overly euphemistic. The cynical character of Job's statement becomes evident when it is compared to a quote from a worker that appeared on a blog after the 12th suicide at Foxconn: "Perhaps for the Foxconn employees and employees like us – we who are called nongmingong, rural migrant workers, in China – the use of death is simply to testify that we were ever alive at all, and that while we lived, we had only despair" (Foxconn worker quoted in Chan and Ngai 2010).

5.3   *Emphasizing Their Bad Things: Blaming Others*
Apple's Supplier Responsibility Reports frame the problem of labour rights violation in a way that puts the entire blame on Chinese contract manufacturers.

SANDOVAL

This rhetoric suggests that the existence of bad working conditions is solely due to a lack of management skills of suppliers, and has nothing to do with Apple. Apple presents itself as a benevolent saviour that is bringing knowledge to developing countries. According to its Supplier Responsibility reports Apple seems to believe that its only responsibility consist in telling suppliers what they have to do. In the 2009 report Apple for example highlighted: "Apple's approach to supplier responsibility extends beyond monitoring compliance with our Code. We help our suppliers meet Apple's expectations by supporting their efforts to provide training in workers' rights and occupational health and safety" (Apple 2009, 3). At no point Apple mentions how much money it is paying for the production of its products in these supplier factories and whether this amount is enough for ensuring adequate working conditions. By blaming its suppliers Apple detracts attention away from the fact that these workers are in fact working for Apple and Apple therefore is responsible for ensuring that at least their working environment is save, that they receive a wage which allows them to pay their living expenses and that their working hours do not extend beyond certain limits. Blaming contract manufacturers detracts from the fact that Apple keeps almost 60% of the sales prize of an iPhone as a profit while spending less than 2% for labour cost of final assembly in China (Kraemer, Linden and Dedrick 2011, 5).

Apple's response to labour rights allegations follows certain ideological patterns: It downplays the severity of the problem of low wages and long working hours, avoids descriptions of actual work and life realities of workers by only referring to statistics and numbers, and ignores structural causes of the labour rights problem (de-emphasizing Apple's wrongdoings). The company stresses that the situation is continuously improving although independent research shows that problems persist (emphasizing Apple's achievements); and describes suppliers, rather than Apple itself, as the ones actually responsible for labour rights violations (emphasizing the wrongdoing of others).

Apple's rhetoric tends to downplay the scope of labour rights violations, mystifies their relation to Apple's business interest in cheap labour and attempts to deny the company's responsibility for bad working conditions in its supply chain. It defends Apple's business practices by detracting attention away from structural contradictions and social irresponsibilities that are connected to them.

6   Conclusion

In this chapter I first showed that neoliberal globalization, the transformation of international production networks together with Chinese policy reforms allowed multinational corporations to gain access to millions of Chinese workers (Section 1). Apple is an economically successful and admired company. Most of its profits are based on hardware products such as iPhone, iPad, iPod, Laptops and Desktop Computers. While for Apple these products mean success, for the workers in the factories of Apple's contract manufacturers they mean misery (Section 3). Their labour and lives often remain invisible, hidden behind the shiny surface of modern high-tech products. In order to shed light on this dark side of computer products I constructed a systematic model of working conditions based on the circuit of capital as it has been described by Karl Marx. This model starts with the productive forces including means of production one hand and the labour power of workers on the other hand. It then addresses the relations of production as they are expressed in a particular relation between capital and labour that determines wages, labour contracts and is subject to struggles. In order to produce a commodity, labour and means of production enter the production processes, which is shaped by labour spaces, labour times, the type of work activity and control mechanisms. The model also includes the produced commodity and the question how it relates back to the worker. Finally, it includes labour legislation and its impact on working conditions (Section 2).

This model of working conditions can be applied to study and compare working conditions in a variety of different industries. In this chapter I used it for describing the "Foxconned labour" of workers in Chinese workshops of Foxconn, Wintek, Pegatron and others where Apple's products are assembled. The results show that workers are partly dealing with high-tech equipment when assembling parts of computers that often contain conflict minerals. The relation between capital and labour is characterized by low wages, precarious contracts and occasionally contested by labour struggles. The production process is shaped by work and live in the factory, long working hours, repetitive and monotonous manual work and strict control. Mostly young migrant workers are risking their health and safety and experience of alienation, exhaustion and despair. They are producing high-tech computer products that they are unlikely to ever own themselves. Labour laws often remain unenforced and therefore offer little protection for workers.

Finally, in discussing Apple's response to the problem of bad working conditions I identified three ideological patterns that deflect attention away from the structural irresponsibility of Apple's business practices by using a rhetoric of improvement, hiding behind statistics, blaming others, looking at symptoms rather than root cause, or downplaying the problems (Section 5).

The example of Apple illustrates that there is a wide gap between the qualities of the products workers are producing and the conditions under which they are produced. While working conditions resemble the early days of industrial capitalism, the produced-high tech computer products build the foundation for 21st century knowledge work. Apple thus represents progress and regression at the same time. Karl Marx described this contradictory quality of capitalism when he stressed:

> It is true that labour produces for the rich wonderful things-but for the worker it produces privation. It produces palaces – but for the worker hovels. It produces beauty – but for the worker, deformity. It replaces labour by machines – but some of the workers it throws back to a barbarous type of labour, and the other workers it turns into machines. It produces intelligence – but for the worker idiocy, cretinism.
>
> MARX 1844/2007, 71

The labour performed in Chinese workshops produces profits for Apple and marvellous computer products for those who can afford them, while for workers it produces monotony and despair.

However, ICTs at the same time do not only mean misery for workers, but can also be a means of empowerment: Jack Qiu (2009) points out that the Internet and wireless communication is increasingly available to members of the Chinese working class. He stresses that rather than describing Chinese low-income groups as "information have-nots," they should be regarded as "information have-less" as they increasingly have access to the Internet and to inexpensive "working-class ICTs" that are produced for the Chinese market (Qiu 2009, 3f). These "working class ICTs" such as mobile phones or computers can be used "in order for the concerns of the have-less to reach across social divisions and have a general impact on society" (Qiu 2009, 243). Information about labour rights violations or protest can sometimes reach the mass media via online forums or self-made videos (Qiu 2009, 243). Qiu highlights that in the context of the spread of working-class ICTs there are "important instances of working-class cultural expression and political empowerment using tools as blogs, poetry, and mobile phones, which serve as the substance of new class dynamics in the twenty-first century" (Qiu 2009, 232). ICTs can thus be used as tools to support struggles for worker rights.

Although this chapter focuses on Apple it is important to be aware that similar working conditions as described here can be found throughout the electronics industry as well as other manufacturing sectors such as garment or toy production. Apple thus is more than a "bad apple." It is an example of structures of inequality and exploitation that characterize global capitalism. In order to confront these structural problems it is not enough to rely on corporate self-regulation, Codes of Conduct and promises of Corporate Social Responsibility. It is important to recognize that cheap production costs that result in bad working conditions are an important competitive advantage for companies. Raising wages, reducing working hours, improving health and safety protection etc would increase expenditures and thus negatively impact profit goals. Without international laws and regulations that force companies to meet certain standards it is unlikely that working conditions will improve.

However desirable stricter regulation might be, rather than waiting for top-down changes to occur, workers need to organize and struggle for their rights. In times of international value chains increasing pressure on governments and corporations requires international solidarity.

Pointing at the need to study the industrial labour of those who produce computer technologies in factories does not mean to idealize the working life of engineers, designers or media professionals. It rather seems important to highlight connections between these different forms of labour: what unites them is not only that they all, in different ways, deal with new information and communication technologies, but also that they are all subject to exploitation, high work pressure and often precariousness. Rather than using concepts such as "immaterial labour" (Hardt and Negri 2004) that reinforce the separation of manual and mental work it seems more useful to extend concepts such as knowledge work or digital labour to include the manual work of those who are producing computer technologies, electronic equipment and media technologies. I therefore agree with Hong who argues that "in the context of information and communications, we actually need to extend the concept of the 'knowledge worker' to include manual and industrial workers who are also essential to this industry" (Hong 2011, 11). Digital labour likewise includes both the mental and manual labour of workers who use ICT s and digital technologies as means of production and of those who produce and dispose them. Such extended notions can provide a conceptual framework for analysing the international division of digital labour. Broad understandings of digital labour can furthermore be a starting point for building connections and moments of solidarity along the global value chain of computer technologies from mineral miners and production workers to call centre agents, software engineers, and the labour of unpaid prosumers, back to waste workers in electronics dumping grounds.

References

Apple. 2006–2012. *Supplier Responsibility. Progress Report.* Accessed May 2013. http://www.apple.com/supplierresponsibility/reports.html.

Apple SEC-Filings. 10-k forms 1994–2012. In *Edgar Database*. Accessed May 20, 2013. http://www.sec.gov/cgi-bin/browse-edgar?action=getcompany&CIK=0000320193& type=10-k&dateb=&owner=exclude&count=40.

Braverman, Harry. 1974/1998. *Labor and Monopoly Capital: The Degradation of Work in the Twentieth Century*. New York: Monthly Review Press.

Bread for All and SACOM. 2008. *High Tech – No Rights*. Accessed May 13, 2013. http://sacom.hk/wp-content/uploads/2008/07/report-high-tech-no-rights-may2008.pdf.

Chan, Jenny and Pun Ngai. 2010. Suicide as Protest for the New Generation of Chinese Migrant Workers: Foxconn, Global Capital, and the State. *The Asia-Pacific Journal*. http://japanfocus.org/-Jenny-Chan/3408.

China Labour Watch. 2010. *"We are extremely tired, with tremendous pressure" A follow-up investigation of Foxconn*. Accessed October 20, 2011 http://www.chinalaborwatch.org/pro/proshow-100.html.

Danwatch. 2011.*What a Waste*. Accessed May 16, 2013. http://makeitfair.org/en/the-facts/reports/reports/2011.

Dyer-Whiteford, Nick. 2014. The global worker and the digital front. In *Critique, Social Media and the Information Society*, edited by Christian Fuchs and Marisol Sandoval. New York: Routledge.

Finnwatch. 2007. *Connecting Components, Dividing Communities*. Accessed May 14, 2013. http://makeitfair.org/en/the-facts/reports/2007-2009/reports-from-2009/Connecting-Components-Dividing-Communities.pdf/at_download/file.

Finnwatch, SACOM and SOMO. 2009. *Playing With Labour Rights*. Accessed October 19, 2011. http://makeitfair.org/the-facts/reports/playing-with-labour-rights/at_download/file.

Finnwatch, SACOM and SOMO. 2011. *Game Console and Music Player Production in China*. Accessed October 19, 2011. http://makeitfair.org/the-facts/reports/game-console-and-music-player-production-in-china.

FLA. 2012. *Independent Investigation of Apple Supplier, Foxconn*. Accessed April 10, 2012. http://www.fairlabor.org/sites/default/files/documents/reports/foxconn_investigation_report.pdf.

Free the Slaves. 2011. The Congo Report. Accessed May 13, 2013. http://www.freetheslaves.net/Document.Doc?id=243.

Friedman, Eli and Ching Kwan Lee. 2010. Remaking the world of Chinese labour: A 30-year retrospective. *British Journal of Industrial Relations* 48 (3): 507–533.

Friends of Nature, IPE, Green Beagle. 2011. *The Other Side of Apple II*. Accessed October 23, 2011. http://www.ipe.org.cn/En/about/notice_de_1.aspx?id=10281.

Friends of the Earth. 2012. *Mining for Smartphones. The True Cost of Tin*. Accessed April 12, 2013. http://www.foe.co.uk/resource/reports/tin_mining.pdf.

Fröbel, Folker, Jürgen Heinrichs and Otto Kreye. 1981. *The New International Division of Labour*. Cambridge: Cambridge University Press.

Hardt, Michael and Antonio Negri. 2004. *Multitude*. London: Hamish Hamilton.

Harvey, David. 2005. *A Brief History of Neoliberalism*. Oxford: Oxford University Press.

Harvey, David. 2006. *Spaces of Global Capitalism*. London: Verso.

Hong, Yu. 2011. *Labor, Class Formation, and China's Informationized Policy and Economic Development*. Lanham, MD: Rowman & Littlefield.

Hung, Ho-Fu. 2009. America's head servant? THe PRC's dilemma in the global crisis. *New Left Review* 60: 5–25.

ICO, FinnWatch and ECA. 2005. *Day and Night at the Factory*. Accessed October 19, 2011. http://www.corporatejustice.org/IMG/pdf/en_kiina-raportti.pdf.

Jobs, Steve. 2010. *Interview at the 2010 D8 conference*. Accessed May 10, 2013. http://www.youtube.com/watch?v=KEQEV6r2l2c.

Kramer, Kenneth L, Greg Linden and Jason Dedrick. 2011. *Capturing Value in Global Networks: Apple's iPad and iPhone*. Accessed May 14, 2013. http://pcic.merage.uci.edu/papers/2011/Value_iPad_iPhone.pdf.

Linzmayer, Owen W. 2004. *Apple Confidential 2.0: The Definitive History of the World's Most Colourful Company*. San Francisco: No Starch Press.

Lüthje, Boy. 2006. The Changing Map of Global Electronics: networks of Mass Production in the New Economy. In *Challenging the Chip. Labour Rights and Environmental Justice in the Global Electronics Industry*, edited by Ted Smith, David A. Sonnenfeld and David Naguib Pellow, 17–30. Philadelphia: Temple University Press.

Lüthje, Boy. 2008. *Arbeitspolitik in der Chinesischen IT Industrie – neue Perspektiven in der Diskussion um internationale Arbeitsstandards*. Accessed May 13, 2013. http://www.boeckler.de/pdf_fof/S-2007-14-1-1.pdf.

Lüthje, Boy. 2012. Interview. Accessed May 20, 2013. http://www.cultofmac.com/153784/heres-what-working-conditions-at-chinese-electronics-plants-are-really-like-exclusive-interview/.

Marx, Karl. 1844/2007. *Economic Philosophic Manuscripts*. Mineola, New York: Dover Publications.

Marx, Karl. 1867/1990. *Capital Vol I*. London: Penguin.

Marx, Karl and Friedrich, Engels. 1948/2011. *Communist Manifesto: Penguin Classics Deluxe Edition*. London: Penguin.

Marx Karl 1885/1992. *Capital Vol II*. London: Penguin.

Maxwell Richard and Toby Miller. 2012. *Greening the Media*. Oxford: Oxford University Press.

McGuigan, Jim 2005. Neoliberalism, Cultural and Policy. *International Journal of Cultural Policy* 11 (3): 229–241.

McKinsey & Company. 2012. *Manufacturing in the Future: The Next Era of Global Growth and Innovation*. Accessed May 18, 2013. http://www.mckinsey.com/insights/manufacturing/the_future_of_manufacturing.

Mosco, Vincent. 2004. *The Digital Sublime*. Cambridge: The MIT Press.

Munck, Ronaldo. 2002. *Globalisation and Labour*. New York: Palgrave.

Ngai, Pun. *Apple's Dream and Foxconn's Nightmare*. Accessed May 15, 2013. http://burawoy .berkeley.edu/Public%20Sociology,%20Live/Pun%20Ngai/PunNgai.Suicide%20 or%20Muder.pdf.

Plank, Leonhard and Cornelia Staritz. 2013. *Precarious Upgrading' in Electronics Global Production Networks in Central and Eastern Europe: The Cases of Hungary and Romania*. Accessed May 18, 2013 http://www.capturingthegains.org/pdf/ctg-wp-2013-31.pdf.

Qiu, Jack. 2009. *Working-Class Network Society*. Cambridge: MIT Press.

Reputation Institute 2012. *Is CSR Dead or Just Mismanaged*. Accessed February 14, 2013. http://www.reputationinstitute.com/thought-leadership/complimentary -reports-2012.

SACOM. 2010. *Apple Owes Workers and Public a Response over the Poisoning*. Accessed October 16, 2011. http://sacom.hk/wp-content/uploads/2010/05/apple-owes-workers -and-public-a-response-over-the-poisonings.pdf.

SACOM. 2011a. *Foxconn and Apple Fail to Fulfil Promises: Predicaments of Workers after the Suicides*. Accessed October 20, 2011. http://sacom.hk/wp-content/ uploads/2011/05/2011-05-06_foxconn-and-apple-fail-to-fulfill-promises1.pdf.

SACOM. 2011b. *iSlave behind the iPhone. Foxconn Workers in Central China*. Accessed October 20, 2011. http://sacom.hk/wp-content/uploads/2011/09/20110924-islave -behind-the-iphone.pdf.

SACOM. 2012. *New iPhone, Old Abuses. Have Working Conditions at Foxconn in China Improved?* Accessed May 13, 2013. http://www.waronwant.org/attachments/ SACOM%20-%20%20New%20iPhone,%20Old%20Abuses%20-%2020-09-12.pdf.

SACOM. 2013. *Apple Fails in Its Responsibility to Monitor Suppliers*. Accessed May 13, 2013. http://makeitfair.org/en/the-facts/reports/apple-fails-in-its-responsibility-to- monitor-suppliers/at_download/file.

Smith, John. 2012. Outsourcing, Financialization and the Crisis. *International Journal of Management Concepts and Philosophy* 6 (1/2): 19–44.

SOMO. 2005a. *CSR Issues in the ICT Hardware Manufacturing Sector*. By Irene Schipper and Esther de Haan. Accessed October 17, 2011 http://somo.nl/publications-nl/ Publication_476-nl/at_download/fullfile.

SOMO. 2005b. *ICT Hardware Sector in China and Corporate Social Responsibility Issues*. By Monina Wong. Accessed October 16, 2011. http://somo.nl/publications-en/ Publication_624/at_download/fullfile.

SOMO. 2007a. *Apple. CSR Company Profile*. By Michiel van Dijk and Irene Schipper. Accessed October 17, 2011. http://somo.nl/publications-en/Publication_1963/at_ download/fullfile.

SOMO. 2007b. *Capacitating Electronics. The Corrosive Effects of Platinum and Palladium Mining on Labour Rights and Communities*. Accessed May 13, 2013. http://makeitfair

.org/en/the-facts/reports/2007-2009/reports-from-2009/Capacitating-Electronics -november-2007.pdf/at_download/file.

SOMO 2011. *Unheard Voices*. Accessed May 13, 2013. http://makeitfair.org/en/the-facts/ reports/unheard-voices/at_download/file.

Su, Yihui. 2011. Student Workers in the Foxconn Empire. The Commodification of Education and Labour in China. *Journal of Workplace Rights* 15 (3–4): 341–362.

Swedwatch. 2007. *Powering the Mobile World*. Accessed May 13, 2013. http://makeitfair. org/en/the-facts/reports/2007-2009/reports-from-2009/Powering-the-Mobile -World-Swedwatch-November-2007.pdf/at_download/file.

Swedwatch, SACOM and SOMO. 2008. *Silenced to Deliver*. Accessed May 13, 2013 http:// makeitfair.org/en/the-facts/reports/2007-2009/reports-from-2009/silenced-to -deliver/at_download/file.

The New Generation Migrant Workers Concern Programme. 2013. *The Report on Foxconn Trade Union Research*. Accessed May 13, 2013. https://www.dropbox.com/s/ qzwo85nzly5u8wh/2013.05.01%20-%20English%20excerpt%20on%20 Foxconn%20union%20research%20report.pdf.

van Dijk, Teun. 2011. Discourse and ideology. In *Discourse Studies. A Multidisciplinary Approach*, edited by Teun van Dijk, 379–407. London: Sage.

WTEC. 1997. *Electronics Manufacturing in the Pacific Rim*. Accessed May 18, 2013. http:// www.wtec.org/loyola/pdf/em.pdf.

Yeung, Yue-man, Lee, Joanna, Gordon, Kee 2009. China's Special Economic Zones at 30. *Euresian Geography and Economics* 50 (2): 222–240.

Zhao, Yuezhi and Robert Duffy. 2008. Short-Circuited? The Communication and Labor in China, In *Knowledge Workers in the Information Society*, edited by Catherine McKercher and Vincent Mosco, 229–248. Lanham: Lexington Books.

CHAPTER 12

The Pastoral Power of Technology. Rethinking Alienation in Digital Culture

Katarina Giritli Nygren and Katarina L Gidlund

1   Introduction

Applying a Marxist approach to twenty-first-century information society is demanding and rewarding in equal measure; demanding in terms of the complex lines of argument required to unpick largely hidden phenomena, yet rewarding for its fine-grained analytical tools that uncover the power structures in any historical materiality. We will draw particularly on the early writings of Marx (Marx, 1963, 1986) and recent poststructuralist developments concerning hegemony and superstructure, and argue that such an endeavour provides a better understanding of the practices of digital technology in our time. In a classical Marxian analysis of technology in twenty-first century information society, digital technology could almost be seen as reinforcing the principles of automation, exploitation, and rationalization, for example in the context of electronic performance monitoring systems that are enhancing many of the Tayloristic thoughts on productivity, division of labour, and surplus value (Aiello and Kolb 1995; Carayon 1993). However, we would like to draw attention to another side of technological development – digital practices operating in the private sphere – where we suggest a Marxian analysis is relevant if we are to understand the new ways of reproducing capitalism.

To this end, we revisit a Marxian understanding of alienation and technology in the light of Foucault's concept of pastoral power, so capturing the new ways of distributing power in the digital era. Pastoral power as such does not displace other conceptions of power, but provides an additional level of analysis with which to examine the forging of subjects willing and able to sustain an all-encompassing social practice. To view alienation within digital cultures as a ramification of pastoral modalities of power makes it possible to discuss technology as operating in structures of thinking and action that often seem to be devoid of power relations in the digital era, such as for example the creation of surplus value by willing consumers (Humpreys and Grayson, 2008).

While there are contradictions between Marx's and Foucault's theories (see for example: Barrett 1991; McDonald 2002), we would argue that it is precisely because of these tensions that it is rewarding to analyse alienation in digital cultures. One of the most frequently mentioned contradictions between these two giants of theory concerns the possibility of causal explanations or the differences between why questions and how questions are posed. Marx's position is as follows:

> The ideas of the ruling class are in every epoch the ruling ideas: i.e. the class, which is the ruling material force in society, is at the same time its ruling intellectual force. The class which has the means of material production at its disposal, consequently also controls the means of mental production, so that the ideas of those who lack the means of mental production are on the whole subject to it. The ruling ideas are nothing more than the ideal expression of the dominant material relationships, the dominant relationships grasped as ideas.
> MARX AND ENGELS 1976, 59

Marx and Engels's interest was primarily the material relationships that constitute ruling ideas. This line of reasoning implicitly creates an ontological explanation for the causal relationship between the ruling material forces, the ruling class, and the ruling ideas. Foucault, on the other hand, goes to lengths to avoid raising ontological questions, and instead focuses on epistemological questions, which here mean analysing how technology is intertwined with political prescriptions, power, and knowledge, and is embedded in socio-cultural practices. Socio-cultural practices are understood as the institutional and organizational circumstances in which the making of technology is situated. Since information society, like all kinds of societal transformations in history, is multidimensional, involving technological, economic, social, cultural, and political changes, it is necessary to analyse the strong image of information technology in relation to its twofold nature.

The implications of the differences in Marx's and Foucault's focus are here presented as a challenging way to move our understanding forward. We argue that this unconventional way of situating both thinkers in a theorization of digital culture provides an important avenue to re-evaluating the contribution they might make. Using pastoral power as a lens, our discussion begins with an outline of the new modalities of power in digital culture, before moving on to a more analysis of alienation and reification in digital culture by revisiting Marx's early writings. We conclude with a discussion of objectification and subjectification. We argue that alienation and objectification are definitely still valid in digital culture, but have to be enriched by an understanding of the modalities of power in digital culture working in the processes of reification that produce objectified, subjectified, and subjectifying subjects.

2   Modalities of Pastoral Power in Digital Culture

Our starting-point is an analytical separation between the practices of industrial and digital technology, where industrial technology is closely related to
the labour sphere and ideas of rationalization (see for example: Habermas
1970; Feenberg 2010). Digital technology, in addition to being related to the
labour sphere as industrial technology, is also related to the private sphere and
ideas of individualization. Such an additional understanding assists in the
analysis of the distribution of power under the historical conditions surrounding digital culture. Furthermore, it provides an analytical approach to digital
practices operating as ideologies or norms, while at the same time retaining
the material historicity of locality and everyday life practices.

We will base our analysis of technology in general, and digital culture in
particular, on an epistemological rapprochement between "practices" (see for
example: Pacey 2001). In order to address digital practices in relation to alienation, we make an analytical distinction between the two different operations
of technology practices, in part following Pacey (1999), who writes of the two
faces of technology practice: an object-centred, mechanistic approach that
dominates science, engineering, and technology, and which marginalizes
everyday experiences and leads to a compartmentalized and alienated practice; and a more people-centred, convivial approach in which social meanings
co-exist and interact with the personal responses and existential experiences
of individuals. We use this dichotomy to understand technology's close relation to labour power distribution and rationalization, in line with many
updated Marxian analyses of technology (Feenberg 2010), but we also view
digital technology as being linked to individualization, where the subject is
part of the power distribution process. This is not a bald statement of the fact
that technology and humans are separable in modern society (since they are
linked in many ways) – the task is rather to retune the analysis of power
distribution.

Consequently, we understand digital technology as an analytical object
"on the threshold of materiality" (Dunne 2005, 11), a view informed by the
philosophical view of technology as being underdetermined. The undeter-
mination of technological artefacts "leaves room for social choice between
different designs," and these "have overlapping functions but better serve
one or another social interest" (Feenberg 2010, 7). According to Feenberg this
means that "context is not merely external to technology, but actually penetrates its rationality, carrying social requirements into the very workings of
gears and levers, electric circuits and combustion chambers" (Feenberg 2010,
7). Digital technology has a material existence without defined tangible

qualities, and as such could be adhered to in almost all possible future scenarios. The symbolic logic is translated into a form that is characteristic of the digital artefact, and it is both the acceptance of the symbolic logic and the performed practices themselves that become the object of analysis (see for example: Löwgren and Stolterman 2004). Technology is nothing but a mirroring of hegemonic social concepts (such as rationalization or individualization), but we need to create, update, and recreate tools to analyse its interaction with the distribution of power. Thus the opaqueness of digital technologies in twenty-first-century information society calls for a deeper understanding of alienation and capitalism, analysing and criticizing the uniqueness of things digital.

Here, Marxist theories and concepts are exceptionally well placed, especially where the ambition is to unveil cultural production in relation to marketization. However, we think that such an analysis is not enough. The opaqueness of digital technologies calls for a more complex conceptualization that allows a deeper, more structural analysis of the ways in which power is displayed. It is necessary to analyse an understanding of power that goes beyond power as a relation between oppressors and oppressed, between worker and owner, or as an effect of the State, and it is to this end we advance a theoretical framework that draws on both Marx and Foucault. We argue that a Foucauldian analysis of power is needed if Marx's concepts of alienation and dialectical analysis are to have full rein in a critical analysis of the distribution of power in digital culture.

Foucault's concept of pastoral power was coined in his genealogical discussion of the historical development of the Christian Church and its gradual assimilation into modern State apparatuses. Its primary focus is the technologies and modalities of power as first developed in a Christian context (Foucault 1982, 2007). He shows that during the eighteenth century, pastoral power found a new way of distributing this kind of individualizing power. The modern State developed as a sophisticated structure into which individuals could be integrated, given one condition: that their individuality would be shaped in a new form and submitted to a set of very specific patterns. The State, according to Foucault, should be seen as modern matrix of individualization – a new form of pastoral power. Foucault argues that pastoral power is reproduced by human beings themselves; the human being turns himself into a subject. At first the subjects were "the body of the religious soul," then "citizens," then "workers," and now they are "cultural beings" (see Touraine 2007). In the transformation from Christian to State modalities of pastoral power, Foucault characterized pastoral power as follows (Foucault 1982, 784):

(i)   It is a form of power whose ultimate aim is to assure individual salvation in this world.

(ii)   It is not merely a form of power that commands, it must also be prepared to sacrifice itself for the life and salvation of the flock.

(iii) It is a form of power that does not look after just the whole community, but each individual in particular, during his/her entire life.

(iv)   It is a form of power that cannot be exercised without knowing the inside of people's minds, without exploring their souls, without making them reveal their innermost secrets. It implies knowledge of the conscience and an ability to direct it. We argue that pastoral power has once again found a new way of distributing individualizing, and subjectifying power – this is what we call the pastoral power of technology.

We are addressing the process of subjectification, not as "the subject," but as "the storying of the self" (see for example: Rose 1996; Deleuze 1990; Derrida 1978). Subjectification is seen as arising from a regime, and this regime is tied to assemblages of power – in the present case, the pastoral power of technology, making the logic that of performing our multiple selves as commodities. The proposition is that this is an expression of our own will. So we the authors, for example, are performing ourselves as "elitist intellectuals" resistant to the possibilities of the market to attach lifestyle commodities to our performances. These performances are what is sayable, audible, operable, and performable, while other phenomena are not. Digital technologies effectively mask the origin of the relevant discursive practices, which are located in particular sites and procedures even though pastoral power disguises them effectively as logics of individualization and self-performance. The practices are pre-personal, structured into relations that grant power to some and limit the power of others. As such, the self is understood not as a mental mechanism, but as conversations, grammar, and rules. We *must* perform this way (see for example: Rose 1996).

It is also this dialogic character of self-narrative that demands a closer analysis when it comes to digital technology. Self-narratives are culturally provided stories about selves that serve as the resources with which individuals can interact with one another and with themselves (Rose 1996). By a combination of training and technological possibilities, we are becoming more and more skilled in performing ourselves (our multiple self-narratives). As a result, pastoral practice is increasingly being honed. The dialogic character of our self-narratives is also strengthened by digital technologies, since the responses (the interactional nature of subjectification) are more easily amplified (for example, by "liking" on Facebook, leaving blog comments, etc.). It is therefore also important to turn to the techniques and apparatuses of the regime. The pastoral power of digital technology adds to this by convincing individuals that the choices they make in the staging of their selves is their own, and that they are making these choices as expressions of their individuality. We are becoming willing and efficient self-governing subjects. By addressing things digital as a means of persuasion, exposure, amplification, and transmission, and as subjectification processes and performances, these circumstances are made more visible. The opaqueness of digital technology is exposed and made an object of study,and the masked two-fold performance by individuals as both consumer and producer of invidualization is possible to analyse. The specific historical conditions of digital technology allow the process of individualization to colonize the lifeworld in a very effective manner:

(i) Digital technologies amplify the exposure of our self-narratives (our performances).
(ii) Digital technologies speed up the transmission of self-narratives (our performances).
(iii) Digital technologies amplify the number of responses, so strengthening interactional subjectification.
(iv) Digital technologies speed up the response time for interactional subjectification.
(v) Digital technologies enable multiple self-narratives in a more efficient manner.
(vi) Digital technologies (software such as photoshop, hardware such as digital cameras or smartphones) facilitate the creation of multiple self-narratives.
(vii) Digital technologies enable congruent self-narratives.

Drawing on the arguments Foucault presents, we propose that digital technology can be viewed as a modern matrix of individualization or as a specific form of pastoral power. Foucault writes of the State modalities of power, yet consider the following quotation when the term "the State" is replaced by "digital technology":

> I don't think we should consider [*digital technology*] as an entity which was developed above individuals, ignoring what they are and even their very existence, but on the contrary as a very sophisticated structure, in which individuals can be integrated, under one condition: that this individuality would be shaped in a new form, and submitted to a set of very specific patterns.
>
> FOUCAULT 1982, 783

Digital technology allows the subject to individualize, to stage the self, and, as such, the technological (digital) potential seduces the subject with the idea that with digital technology we can construct and display individuality. In the same way as automated technologies are embedded with rationalization (the social concept of a rationality that co-constructs society), digital technologies are embedded with individualization (individualization as an equally social concept co-constructing society). Pastoral modalities of power involve the entire history of processes of human individualization; saying that one does not want to express individuality with the help of digital technology sounds as awkward in our digital society as refusing to act in a rational way sounded in industrial society. Because this individualization is left unquestioned, it appears all members of society find it of interest – universal, neutral, natural, and inevitable. Yet where Foucault talks about "the mad and the sane, the sick and the healthy" (Foucault 1982, 778), our argument turns on pre-censorship versus the censured, what is staged versus what is behind the scenes, the performed versus the unscripted, and the displayed versus "the dislocated" and "the localized."

3   Marx Revisited

In modern societies, knowledge is conjoined with power and together they produce individual subjectivity and the social order. Marx's works offers excellent tools to analyse objectifying practices, but when it comes to analysing subjectifying practices, they have some shortcomings. There are also clear connections between Marx's analysis of capitalism and Foucault's conception of disciplinary power. For example, Foucault clearly states that the rise of disciplinary power was a central feature of modern society that went hand in hand with the development of the capitalist mode of production, which needed a labour force both subjected to and better utilized by its system (see Marsden, 1999). Foucault also contrasts Marx's economics of untruth with the politics of truth – the first focuses on the relation between economic, material praxis, and ideology, while the second focuses on the relationship between knowledge, discourse, truth, and power. To capture the opaqueness of digital technology, we think it is necessary to keep both theories in mind, especially as Foucault's concept of pastoral power speaks to the subjectifying practices of digital technology, not only its objectifying practices. Foucault's notion of pastoral power is based on the metaphor of the relationship between the shepherd and his flock (Foucault 2007, 125–130), where the shepherd gathers and defines his flock and each member of the flock is saved by the shepherd's individualized goodness – the shepherd, in other words, takes control of the individuals through individualizing techniques. Pastoral modalities of power are based on people's freedom of choice, but have a controlling function that makes them choose what is deemed necessary. Humans are as much controlled when they are created as objects as when they are created as subjects, at least as long as their subjectivities confirm hegemonic practices (Foucault 1988).

Digital technologies can be understood as an institution producing and sustaining new forms of transnational material relationships that make the ruling classes even more invisible, as well as an institution that produces new subjectivities and new forms of governing that involve the activating rhetoric of neoliberalism. Neoliberalism is discussed by researchers in a variety of ways, such as being an economic doctrine, policy, ideology and/or political rationality. In this chapter, we move between several of them. Our starting point is that we understand neoliberalism as both a capitalist system and an ideological rationality. To consider neo-liberalism as a kind of ideology includes more principles than an expanding market. In neoliberalism new types of techniques of governing have emerged, and we will use the concept of neoliberalism following Foucault (2007), that is, as a certain development of liberal governmentality during the second half of the twentieth century. It is thus neither reduced to mere political ideology nor raised to the status of a new epoch. Instead it is thought in the plural but still marked by certain traits, such as marketization and competitiveness, 'a way of doing things', as Foucault put it, that today can be seen in technologies of governing such as New Public Management and audit culture (Dean 2010: 73). The penetration of market relations and of abstract systems into every aspect of the life-world compels the individual to choose. At the same time these processes promote forms of market and institutional dependency. Each individual is to be her own political economy, an informed, self-sufficient prosumer where, by the use of digital technologies even the private self may be commodified, at least from a structural point of view (Ritzer 2014).

Foucault (2007) describes the pastoral modalities of power as a power linked to the production of truth and a unique combination of individualization and totalization. As such, the conceptual advantages of situating pastoral modalities of power within the understanding of alienation in digital culture offers a clearer view of how the practices of power become processes of subjectification within digital cultures: it offers a dialectical understanding of reification and individualization.

Certainly, digital technologies in twenty-first-century information society are of an opaqueness that calls for a greater understanding of alienation and capitalism, and the question of their uniqueness should be analysed. Marxist theories and concepts are exceptionally well placed to unveil cultural production in relation to marketization, but equally, such an analysis is not enough, for the opaqueness of digital technologies calls for a more complex conceptualization, which allows a more detailed, structural analysis of the ways in which power is displayed. It is necessary to analyse an understanding of power that goes beyond that of power as a relationship between oppressors and the oppressed where the individual himself/herself could stage his/her individualization as creating value for himself/herself while at the same time being exploited and creating surplus value for capitalism, and defend their actions in terms of identity creation (subjectification). Moreover, we see the opaqueness of digital technology as something different and more complex than industrial technology, where ideal expressions of dominant material relationships, not to mention the material distribution of hegemonic, neo-liberal ideas, have to be taken into account. While Marx focuses on material conditions rather than ideas, Foucault focuses on ideas as material conditions (see for example: Foucault 1982).

There is much to revitalize thinking about twenty-first-century information society in the works of Marx. The concepts of alienation and reification offer good starting-points in better understanding the "digital" element in digital cultures. As is well known, Marx articulated his theory of alienation most clearly in the *Economic and Philosophic Manuscripts* (1988) and *The German Ideology* (1976). His critique extends to both Feuerbach and Hegel, while discussing and acknowledging other forms of alienation such as political alienation and religious alienation. For Marx, the alienation of labour is the most basic form of alienation (Marx and Engels 1976): built on a particular form of wage labour, is for him a systematic result of capitalism (Marx and Engels 1976, 1988).

Alienated individuals have to be alienated from *something*, as a result of certain objectifying and dualistic practices that manifest themselves in the historical framework. Alienation is then a consequence of human totality and human self-consciousness standing in opposition to each other. As such, religious alienation is connected with the dualistic construction of body and soul, or the empirical life on earth and the spiritual life in heaven, whereas political alienation is connected with the (bourgeois) dualistic creation of the individual as abstract citizen and private human being (Marx 1963). In his analysis of the alienation of labour, Marx stresses two points:

(i)   In the process of work, and especially work under the conditions of capitalism, man is estranged from his own creative powers, and,

(ii)   The objects of his own work become alien beings, and eventually rule over him; they become powers independent of the producer (Marx 1963).

This form of alienation means, for Marx, that individuals do not experience themselves as the acting agents, but that the world (Nature, others, and he himself) remains alien to them. They become reified and appear as objects, even though they may be objects of their own creation. In a capitalist society, workers can never become autonomous, self-realized human beings in any significant sense, except in the way the ruling class wants the workers to be realized. They can only express this fundamentally social aspect of individuality through a production system that is not publicly social, but privately owned; a system for which each individual functions as an instrument, not as a social being (Marx 1963).

When differentiating industrial from digital technology, it becomes apparent that Marx's theory of alienation is very much based upon his observation of emerging industrial production (for a similar discussion, see Feenberg 2010). Marx developed his theories during the era of modern industry, when workers were assembled in large factories or offices to work under the close supervision of a hierarchy of managers who were the self-appointed brains of the production process. Workers could be seen as extensions of machines rather than machines being the extensions of workers. This type of analysis of alienation is still valid in the twenty-first-century information society. Digital technologies also enhance many of the industrial phenomena of productivity, division of labour, and surplus value (Aiello and Kolb 1995; Carayon 1993), which shows that information society is not only, if at all, a post-industrial society. But, if we return to the question of digital technology and its opaqueness, we take our lead from Marx in suggesting that it is necessary to talk of a new form of alienation that has emerged with the Internet and information society – "digital alienation," which with its dislocated virtual life constructs a dualistic relation between for example dislocated and located forms of being (online/offline identities). The life situation (whether digital or virtual) is still located; the image of liberation, disengagement, and loss of stability is (to paraphrase Marx) part of this epoch's "ruling ideas," meaning the ideas of the ruling class. It is a widespread contemporary belief that increased economic globalization, together with online communication, will reduce the importance of geographical sites as a base for people's identity (see, for example, theorists such as Giddens 1990; Virilio 1993; Negroponte 1995). The construction of "placelessness" and a possible dissolution of space and time give rise to a new form of alienation – digital alienation – that reproduces and hides class conflicts in contemporary global societies. Another example of digital alienation is customization and digital design where individuals design their own product (being it sneakers or t-shirts) under the pretens of expressing their individuality and interpreting others' copying ones design as strengthening ones identity creation (short-term celebrity status) without allocate their action as a part of the creation of exchange value for capitalists (Humphreys and Grayson, 2008). Bloggers are performing their lives contributing to product placement, experiencing identity creation (Tynan, McKechnie, and Chhuon. 2010).

According to Marx, the alienation of labour occurs when the worker is alienated from the product of his work and therefore becomes alienated from work itself. His argument is that it is essential to human beings to express ourselves creatively, but that we lose contact with ourselves if this is not the case in our own working conditions. In industrialized society, working conditions deny us control of our work and the world we live in. The line of argument for digital alienation is similar, but based on the process of individualization. We position digital alienation alongside the alienation of labour, in much the same way as religious and political alienation are positioned alongside the alienation of labour: as an objectifying and dualistic practice. Human totality is alienated from self-consciousness, and the digital "self" becomes a commodity. The subject might resist, but is constantly undermined by the relation to the "screen." We are "seduced" by the world of consumption into performing our self on the digital stage. Here the individual is merely a screen onto which the desires, needs, and imaginary worlds manufactured by the new communications industries are projected. Those who no longer find the guarantee of their identity within themselves are ruled, indistinctly, by what escapes their consciousness (see Touraine 2007, 101).

Individuals perform themselves on the stage of digital culture, and their control of the performance is lost because of the conditions of the digital performance (Facebook, Twitter, blogs, etc.). We are no longer in control of the "self" we perform. We censor our thoughts and our images in relation to the expected (the life-styling logic) and the product/the self becomes alienated. We lose control of our digital selves and the world we live in, and it is hard to feel committed to the self since the analogue or localized life is separated from the digital. Neo-liberal subjects become dependent on the labour market, and ultimately on education, consumption, welfare state regulations and support, consumer supplies, and on possibilities and fashions in medical, psychological, and pedagogical counselling and care. This all points to the institution-dependent control structure of capitalist hegemony. With the advent of digital technology and neo-liberalism, the norms and hierarchies governing the processes of capitalistic hegemony tend to be hidden, and the processes themselves become mystified as nothing but the outcome of free individual choice (see Mosco 2004).

According to Marx, it is not until real individuals, in their individual circumstances, become one with their empirical lives that they can realize themselves as authentic social beings (Marx and Engels 1976). This line of thought is not unproblematic, since it is based on certain fundamental assumptions concerning the conditions for the self-realization of a possible, total, and authentic self, which is clearly related to Hegel and the *Bildung* tradition (for a more detailed discussion, see for example: Levine 2012). This is why the understanding of alienation in digital culture would be better redirected towards the analysis of processes of reification embedded within the pastoral modalities of the power of technology, where reification specifies the dialectic relationship between social existence and social consciousness. What we want to avoid is the social structural dimension disappearing, reducing alienation and reification to the level of a psychological characteristic of an abstract individual. To focus on the processes of reification means that we need to understand relations of power, recognizing that it is more important to analyse the processes that lead to alienation rather than the alienated condition as such. The concept of reification is used by Marx to describe a form of social consciousness, in which human relations come to be identified with the physical properties of things, thereby acquiring an appearance of naturalness and inevitability. To focus on processes of reification then means analysing how human relations operate and what they signify, which is, we argue, a theoretical standpoint very similar to Foucault's theory.

The multidimensionality of both the concepts of alienation and reification, and specifically the insights they provide into the inner structure of capitalist relations, show how capitalist social relations are materialized in the shape of the Internet. As such, they are built into information and communication technologies, and, because of the pervasiveness of commodity relations, they provide a fertile ground for reified forms of social consciousness. Based on the growth of digital technologies, new forms of reification have emerged.

Bringing the pastoral power of technology to an analysis of underlying social relations that produce alienation and reification provides a model for a more general analysis of the nature of technological and ideological mystification in contemporary neo-liberal and capitalist societies. This means that alongside the fetishism of commodities we also have the fetishism of technology. Where once the worker employed the instruments of production, now the instruments of production employ the worker.

4   A Multifaceted Analysis of the Distribution of Power

At the start of this chapter, we proposed rethinking alienation and power in digital cultures. By proposing a dialectical analysis of digital technologies in relation to superstructure and base, hegemony and everyday practices, we have reappraised the understanding of alienation in twenty-first-century digital culture by viewing it in terms of the pastoral power of technology in order to analyse the opaqueness of digital practices. Pastoral power not only directs our focus to the relation between power and technological practices, but also to the making of individuals who willingly take on the responsibilities of power. This shows that it is necessary to focus on the notion of the effective power of ideologies and their material reality.

In talking about alienation in digital culture, we suggest it is crucial to note the specific type of alienation that arises in the era of digital technologies. It is of the outmost importance to analyse alienation in digital culture as a result of certain objectifying and dualistic practices when using Marx's theory. For the fundamental alienation of labour, Marx emphasizes that we do not experience ourselves as the acting agents in our grasp of the world; with digital technology, we *do* experience ourselves as acting agents. However, it does not matter how virtual the subject might be, there is always a positioned and localized body of experience and everyday life attached to it, from which the virtual subject is alienated. In this way, digital technologies are able to cause an illusionary feeling of subjectification and agency without having any empirical consequences – it is possible to voice opinions and thoughts without anyone listening. In similar vein, Fuchs (2008, 2009, 2010) states that social networking platforms are ideological expressions of individual creativity that create the illusion that individual expression counts in capitalism because they can be published online. Furthermore, he discusses the complex connections between the objectifying and subjectifying practices of digital technologies that are based on instrumental reason, but driven by active play labour (ibid.). This form of alienation results in what Fuchs (2010) calls a "total commodification of human creativity" (see also Smythe's original analysis of audience commodification (2006)). This is very much in line with a Foucauldian power/knowledge dystopia, in which even moral and practical knowledge are transformed into cognitive and technical systems that normalize and regulate what was previously private (see Lash 2007). And here the reason to adduce Foucault's theory becomes obvious since it permits a more flexible exploration of digital cultural and subjective phenomena. A Marxian approach to analysing the distribution of power is still needed in the twenty-first century. It provides analytical tools that not only expose alienation and reification in terms of material conditions of labour (extreme Taylorism), but also reveal alienation and reification in terms of material and objectifying practices in digital culture. Furthermore, an analysis of the subject as a target for commodification and dislocation allows us to see how reification is performed and operates today. For a better understanding of reification in digital culture, we have supplemented Marx's concept of reification with Foucault's concept of pastoral power to reveal the subjectifying practices. The analysis shows that the subject is an object of different modalities of pastoral power, for example in the ideology that holds that there are unique opportunities to express individuality in digital practices. Digital practices enable the subject to perform individualization, to stage the self, and, as such, they seduce the subject with the thought that with digital technology it is possible to construct and display individuality.

This theoretical construct draws attention to another level of analysis: the multifaceted analysis of the distribution of power in terms of the sublime equilibrium of objectified, subjectified, and/or subjectifying subjects. Neither Marx's nor Foucault's analysis is completely dystopian, as both leave room for resistance and action. By adding a careful analysis of the distribution of power, subjectification, and subjectifying processes (see, for example, Touraine 2007), another balance is struck. When Touraine address the image of a self and the subject, he draws a clear distinction between the notion of a subjectified subject and the subject in Foucault's pastoral power, and adds the idea of the subjectifying subject who has the ability to resist and to reflect. In the pairing of subject and subjectifyer, creator and created, liberator and imprisoned, the subjectification-reflecting subject resists the subjectifying practices. By focusing on processes of reification, the combined framework of Marx and Foucault successfully addresses both the procedures of objectification and subjectification in digital practices: objectification as an extension of competitive rationalization and domination (in other words, an extension of industrialization with the help of digital practices) and subjectification as commodification of the subject (or the marketization of the self), where, for example, the naturalization of certain capitalist values that turn the consumer into the ideal citizen takes place across national borders. Moreover, digital technologies have also been employed as modes of surveillance. As a consequence, control and power in digital culture manifest an increasing tendency towards the total surveillance and administration of society conducted through globally gathered and sorted digital information. Citizens, thanks to digital technologies, are becoming increasingly transparent to private and public monitoring agencies. The leading companies such as Apple, Google, Amazon, and Facebook have integrated data about our locations, preferences, or life events that are already put to use in various economic, political, and social contexts (see Andrejevic 2009). This chapter has shown how the relationship between the distribution of power in digital practices in terms of *objectification* as a prolonged modernity, where everything is objectified and shaped according to commercial, rational and instrumental thinking, and *subjectification* as the expression of ultra-modernity, where instrumentality is supported by the illusory and ideological image of individual self-choice, could simultaneously be analysed as processes of reification within the digital pastoral modalities of power.

Reification then refers to two contemporary regulatory digital practices:

(i)   processes of domination by others and/or subordination to an alien system of power, and

(ii) processes of being invented as a subject of a certain type.

Digital technologies have made it possible to govern in an advanced, liberal manner, providing a surplus of indirect mechanisms that translate the goals of political, social, and economic authorities into individual choices and commitments.

The task of global chains of production within digital societies is as much about producing subjects as it is about providing jobs and generating profit. However, it is important to also note that such a multifaceted analysis also touches on the transcendent balance between dystopia and utopia. We are not arguing for one or the other, but for revealing the full extent of the distribution of power and the potential for practices of resistance. Online activities, after all, also hold the promise of new forms of citizenship, communities, and political practice (see, for example, Bernal, 2006).

References

Aiello, John R. and Kathryn J. Kolb. 1995. Electronic Performance Monitoring and Social Context: Impact on Productivity and Stress. *Journal of Applied Psychology* 80 (3): 339–353.

Andrejevic, Mark 2009. *ISpy: Surveillience and Power in the Interactive Era*. Kansas: University Press of Kansas.

Barrett, Michele 1991. *The Politics of Truth: From Marx to Foucault*. Cambridge: Polity Press.

Bernal, Victoria. 2006. Diaspora, Cyberspace and Political Imagination: The Eritrean Diaspora Online. *Global Networks* 6 (2): 161–179.

Carayon, Pascale 1993. Effect of Electronic Performance Monitoring on Job Design and Worker Stress: Review of the Literature and Conceptual Model. *Human Factors: Journal of the Human Factors and Ergonomics Society*,35 (3): 385–395.

Dean, M. (2010) *Governmentality: Power and Rule in Modern Society*. 2nd ed. Thousand Oaks, CA: SAGE Publications.

Deleuze, Gilles 1990. *Entretien sur Mille Plateaux.*, translated by S.-O. Wallenstein. Paris: Minuit (originally published in *Libération*, 23 October 1989).

Derrida, Jacques. 1978. *The Dangerous Supplement. Of Grammatology*. Translated by Gayatri Spivak, 141–164. Baltimore, MD: John Hopkins University Press.

Dunne, Anthony. 2005. *Hertzian Tales, Electronic Products, Aesthetic Experience, and Critical Design*. Cambridge, Mass.: MIT Press.

Feenberg, Andrew. 2010. Marxism and the Critique of Social Rationality: From Surplus Value to the Politics of Technology. *Cambridge Journal of Economics* 34 (1): 37–49.

Foucault, Michel. 1982. The Subject and Power. *Critical Inquiry* 8 (4): 777–795.

Foucault, Michel. 1988. *Politics, Philosophy, Culture. Interviews and Other writings 1977– 1984*. New York: Routledge.

Foucault, Michel. 2007. *Security, Territory, Population: Lectures at the Collège de France, 1977–1978*. New York & Basingstoke: Palgrave Macmillan.

Fuchs, Christian 2008. *Internet and Society: Social Theory in the Information Age*. New York: Routledge.

Fuchs, Christian. 2009. Information and Communication Technologies and Society: A Contribution to the Critique of the Political Economy of the Internet. *European Journal of Communication* 24 (1): 69–87.

Fuchs, Christian. 2010. Class, Knowledge and New Media. *Media Culture and Society* 32 (1): 141–150.

Giddens, Anthony. 1990. *The Consequences of Modernity*. Oxford: Polity Press.

Habermas, Jürgen. 1970. Technology and Science as 'Ideology'. In *Toward a Rational Society: Student Protest, Science, and Politics*, translated by Jeremy Shapiro, 81–127. Boston: Beacon.

Humpreys, A. and Grayson, K. 2008. The Intersecting Roles of Consumer and Producer: A Critical Perspective on Co-production, Co-creation and Prosumption. Sociology Compass 2 (2008):

Lash, Scott. 2007. Power after Hegemony: Cultural Studies in Mutation? *Theory, Culture & Society* 24 (55): 55–87.

Levine, Norman 2012. *Marx's Discourse with Hegel*. Basingstoke: Palgrave Macmillan.

Löwgren, Jonas and Erik Stolterman. 2004. *Design av informationsteknik, materialet utan egenskaper*. Lund: Studentlitteratur.

Marsden, Richard 1999. *The nature of capital: Marx after Foucault*. London: Routledge.

Marx, Karl. 1963. *Early Writings*, translated and edited by T. Bottomore. London: C.A. Watts.

Marx, Karl 1986. *Karl Marx: The Essential Writings*, edited by F.L. Bender. Boulder: Westview.

Marx, Karl and Friedrich Engels. 1976. *The German ideology. Marx and Engels Collected Works, V.* 19–539. Moscow: Progress.

Marx, Karl and Friedrich Engels. 1988. *Economic and Philosophic Manuscripts of 1844: and the Communist Manifesto.* London: Prometheus Books.

McDonald, Bradley J. 2002. Marx, Foucault, Genealogy. *Polity* 34 (3): 259–284.

Mosco, Vincent. 2004. *The Digital Sublime: Myth, Power and Cyberspace.* Cambridge: MIT Press.

Negroponte, Nicholas. 1995. *Being Digital.* London: Hodder & Stoughton.

Pacey, Arnold 2001. *Meaning in Technology.* Cambridge: MIT Press.

Ritzer, G. (2014) 'Prosumption: Evolution, revolution, or eternal return of the same?' *Journal of Consumer* 14:1:3–24.

Rose, N. 1996. *Inventing Our Selves: Psychology, Power and Personhood.* Cambridge: CUP.

Smythe, Dallas W. 2006. On the Audience Commodity and its Work. In *Media and Cultural Studies: Keyworks*, edited by Meenakshi G. Durham and Douglas M. Kellner, 230–256. Malden: Blackwell.

Touraine, Alain. 2007. *A New Paradigm for Understanding Today's World.* Cambridge: Polity Press.

Tynan, C. McKechnie, S, and Chhuon, C. 2010. Co-creating value for luxury brands. Journal of Business Research. Vol. 3 Issue. 11.

Virilio, Paul 1993. The Third Interval: A Critical Transition. In *Rethinking Technologies*, edited by Verena Andermatt-Conley, 3–10. London: University of Minnesota Press.

CHAPTER 13

The Problem of Privacy in Capitalism and Alternative Social Media: The Case of Diaspora*[1]

Sebastian Sevignani

In 2010, four young New York university students were listening to a speech by law professor and free software foundation advocate, Eben Moglen, entitled: "Freedom in the Cloud: Software Freedom, Privacy, and Security for Web 2.0 and Cloud Computing" (2010). Moglen, also known as the author of the dot-Communist Manifesto (Moglen 2003), a document where he, inspired by Marx, propagates a contradiction between free information and multi-national capitalism in the age of the Internet, describes in his speech the surveillance-based heteronomy that users face within an Internet controlled by large corporate monopolists. Corporations, such as Facebook and Google, are able to dictate "take-it-or-leave-it" terms and provide users with a dubious but working privacy-threatening deal: "I will give you free web hosting and some PHP [personal home page tools] doodads and you get spying for free all the time" (Moglen 2010). Moglen challenges the status quo by stressing that the situation need not be the way it currently is. Technological means that are currently available, he points out, provide us with a potential alternative to an Internet controlled by powerful centres. He calls upon his audience: "We're technologists, we should *fix it* [...]. You know every day that goes by there's more data we'll never get back. Every day that goes by there's more data inferences we can't undo. Every day that goes by we pile up more stuff in the hands of the people who got too much" (Moglen 2010).

The four students were inspired by Moglen's call to start developing an alternative social networking site (SNS), Diaspora*, that was soon and – as we know in retro-perspective – too soon celebrated as the potential Facebook-Killer. The euphoria comes, on the one hand, from Diaspora*'s quick success in fundraising. Via an Internet platform, they were able to raise 200,000 USD to get their project running. On the other hand, Facebook, the world's biggest SNS and one of the globally most frequented websites, has faced several privacy problems as well as growing user discontent.

---

1   The research presented in this chapter was conducted in the project "Social Networking Sites in the Surveillance Society" (http://www.sns3.uti.at), funded by the Austrian Science Fund (FWF): project number P 22445-G17. Project co-ordination: Prof. Christian Fuchs.

After Diaspora* initially has been released to a broader publichas ensured itself further funding, and has built up an organizational structure, the further development of its software slowed down. In May 2012, the founders participated with the project in a commercially oriented startup programm but acknowledged shortly thereafter that they will backtrack from their leading role in the further development and Diaspora* will be fully released to the community.

Although, Diaspora* certainly failed challenging Facebook and other commercial social media, we can learn from this example what potentials, limitations, and threats might come along with building privacy sensitive alternatives to a corporate Internet. There are comparable approaches to building and establishing alternative SNS, such as Friendica, Libertree, and identi.ca, however, Diaspora* is an particularly interesting example since it focused on the privacy discourse to pronounce its alternative quality and has attracted public attention therefore. This is interesting because, as I will try to show, privacy issues are a problem that contemporary commcercial social media cannot really escape.

In the course of this chapter, I describe Diaspora*'s way of production by pointing out its alternative character as part of the free software and copyleft movement. Second, dominant theories of privacy related to individual control, exclusion, and property are introduced. Third, the problem of privacy in capitalism is described wherein dominant concepts of privacy will be contextualised on behalf of a critical political economy analysis that refers to the Marxian concept of ideology critique, Marx's differentiation between a societal sphere of production and a societal sphere of circulation, and his analysis of capitalist fetishisms. Fourth, taking into account the problem of privacy in capitalism, the alternative potential of Diaspora* is evaluated. Finally, a brief outline of a Marxist theory of privacy is proposed.

1   The Alternative Social Networking Site Diaspora*

Diaspora* looks similar and provides features akin to those of well-known commercial SNSs. In terms of social privacy, i.e. privacy relative to other SNS users (Raynes-Goldie 2010), Diaspora* allows users to specifically assign to different groups various access opportunities in terms of their own activities on the SNS. Diaspora* cannot be described as an alternative to existing SNSs in terms of these elaborate settings for social privacy, but one the one hand in its funding model, which was initially based on donations instead of advertising and is now completely based on voluntary free work of the free software community. On the other hand and particularly, in the fact that the site is fundamentally different in its infrastructure and mode of production. This difference holds important alternative consequences for its users. In describing this alternative SNS, it is useful to distinguish between two levels. One is the code level; here, we are interested in how Diaspora*'s software is produced, what the means to produce SNS looks like, and in which social relations they are embedded. The other level is the user level; here, we are interested in the use value of Diaspora*, such as its ability to satisfy users' need for privacy. We will see that on Diaspora* the user level interacts with the code level in an important manner.

Diaspora* is a distributed SNS, which means that uploaded user data are not stored and managed centrally. Unlike Facebook and Google+, which process user data in huge server parks, Diaspora* consists of a potentially unlimited number of interoperating servers that are locally distributed and not controlled by a single organisation. Theoretically, it is possible for everyone to operate such a "pod." Therefore, the Diaspora* project should be seen in the context of initiatives that seek to empower users to run personal, self-controlled servers easily. For instance, the Freedom Box initiative describes itself as "a project that combines the computing power of a smart phone with your wireless router to create a network of personal servers to protect privacy during daily life [...]. The basic hardware and software components already exist. Our job is to assemble the right collection of social communication tools, distributed services, and intelligent routing in a package anyone can use to get the freedoms we all need right out of the box" (Freedom Box Foundation n.d.). Practically, however, there are a limited number of servers,[2] hence the social network is not yet distributed widely. Nevertheless, the principle behind Diaspora* is aimed at this direction: "Get started on a community pod and then move all of your social data to a pod you control. Diaspora*'s distributed design means that you will never have to sacrifice control of your data" (Diaspora* n.d.a). The effect of this structure is that "as soon as it becomes public that a company is exploiting the data of the users of its pod, they move away and the company is dead (in that sector). So the product shifts from you being the product to the software being the product" (Diaspora* 2012).

Chopra and Dexter (2006) describe the traditional capital strategy to make profit in the informational economy: capital is closing the source code and this means excluding others from this code on behalf of private property rights. "In this model then, the 'means of production' remain with the corporate owner of the software, because the worker is unable to modify the code" (Chopra and

---

2 See list at http://podupti.me/.

Dexter 2006, 8). Due to the specific quality of the means of production, however, the production of informational goods, such as software code, comes potentially in conflict with capital interest for the following reasons:

- Information is produced and diffused by networks,
- information is hard to control in terms of accessibility and ownership,
- and as information is intangible, it can easily be copied and owned by many, which consequently undermines individual private property (Fuchs 2009, 76f.; see also Benkler 2006, 60).

Marx argues that the "social relations between the producers, and the conditions under which they exchange their activities and share in the total act of production, will naturally vary according to the character of the means of production" (Marx 1849/2006, 28). The Diaspora* software is produced and developed according to a mode of production that can be called "peer-production" (Benkler 2006, Bauwens 2006), which is a way of producing goods and services that relies on self-organizing communities of individuals who come together to produce a shared and desired outcome. Instead of being exchanged, outcomes and inputs of the working process are shared. Goods and services in peer-production are therefore not commodities, because "only the products of mutually independent acts of labour, performed in isolation" can become commodities (Marx 1867/1976, 57).

In terms of forces and modes of production, Marx argues further that "at a certain stage of their development, the material forces of production in society come in conflict with the existing relations of production, or – what is but a legal expression for the same thing – with the property relations within which they had been at work before" (Marx 1859/1909, 12). The Diaspora* software, to which access is needed for users to set up their own pods, is (mainly) licensed under the GNU's Affero General Public License (AGPL). This license, provided by the Free Software Foundation, follows a principle called "copyleft." Copyleft says that code must be free software and works like this: "I make my code available for use in free software, and not for use in proprietary software, in order to encourage other people who write software to make it free as well. I figure that since proprietary software developers use copyright to stop us from sharing, we cooperators can use copyright to give other cooperators an advantage of their own: they can use our code" (Stallman 2010, 129). Copyleft uses existing property regimes to subvert them and uses the power of the right to property to avoid exclusive appropriation of software code (de Laat 2005; Wolf, Miller, and Grodzinsky 2009). It can be understood as a self-protecting measure for a specific mode of production and as an expression of the conflict that Marx has denoted. It is self-protecting for it requires any adaption of the free software code to be free software and licensed under the copyleft principle again. This clearly runs contrary to the capital strategy of excluding others in order to make profit. Copyleft suspends the capitalist logic within a limited realm because "the capital relation presupposes a complete separation between the workers and the ownership of the conditions for the realization of their labour" (Marx 1867/1976, 874).

In the case of Diaspora* and other free software, contributors really own the conditions for the realisation of their programming, thereby ensuring that work and the realisation of their work cannot be torn apart and alienated from each other. The distinction between being a consumer and producer is blurring within the realm of the Internet and SNS (Toffler, Alvin. 1984. The Third Wave. New York: Bantam, Bruns 2008). So, users can become productive and contribute to the social network because they can, due to the freely available software, run their own pod or migrate from non-trustworthy pods to trustworthy ones. In the case of Diaspora*, we can see that the quality of the code level affects the user level and enables greater user control.

The previously quoted famous and controversial preface to *A Contribution to the Critique of Political Economy* also claims that "the sum total of these relations of production constitutes the economic structure of society – the real foundation, on which rise legal and political superstructures and to which correspond definite forms of social consciousness [...]. With the change of the economic foundation, the entire immense superstructure is more or less rapidly transformed. In considering such transformations, the distinction should always be made between the material transformation of the economic condition of production [...] and the legal, political, religious, aesthetic or philosophic – in short ideological forms in which men become conscious of this conflict and fight it out" (Marx 1859/1909, 11f.). It is important to comment further on this quote. Marx says that the *entire relations of production* correspond with the social consciousness and ideas in different life spheres. He makes such claims from a very high level of abstraction; for him the passage is a guiding principle or a "leading threat" of investigation (Marx 1859/1909, 11). It is obvious that Diaspora*'s mode of production, apart from perhaps being a germ form of an alternative society (Fuchs 2009, 77), does not represent contemporary society's entire relations of production. Furthermore, Marx points in this quote to a potential asynchrony between economic foundation and ideological superstructures. Both constraints denote the importance of analysing these very ideological structures.

Commercial SNSs consistently come into conflict with privacy. This is, as I have showed elsewhere in detail (Sevignani 2013; 2015), because in a commercially organised Internet there is an logical internal self-contradiction between the burgeois value of privacy and profit-oriented Internet services that are based on user surveillance. On the practical level, this contradiction is expressed in public outcries and privacy struggles, such as complaints against the leading SNS, Facebook, such as the complaints by the Electronic Privacy Information Center, the complaints by Austrian students addressed to the Irish Data Protection Commissioner (Europe versus Facebook 2011), or the investigation by the Nordic data inspection agencies (Datatilsynet 2011). From this perspective Diaspora*'s apparent initial quick success and distinctive self-understanding as a result of its focus on privacy becomes understandable. Diaspora* describes itself as "the privacy-aware, personally controlled, do-it-all open-source social network" (Diaspora* 2010). Its self-understanding distinguishes Diaspora* from the practices and the nature of dominant SNSs such as Facebook and Google+, and highlights how the site frames itself as an alternative SNS.

In order to be able to evaluate which role privacy can play in an alternative SNS project, I need to explain what privacy commonly entails (Section 2) and how it fits into capitalist society (Section 3).

2   Dominant Theories of Privacy: Individual Control, Exclusion, and Property

The starting point of the modern privacy debate was an article by Samuel D. Warren and Louis D. Brandeis published in 1890. The motive for writing this article was an infringement during the wedding of Warren's daughter by the press. In this article, privacy is defined as the "right to be left alone" (Warren and Brandeis 1890/1984, 76). "The right to be left alone" is identical with the liberal core value of negative freedom (Rössler 2001, 20f.), and as such it determines most of the subsequent theoretical work on privacy and situates it within the liberal tradition. The plethora of values that are associated with privacy, such as the value of freedom, autonomy, personal well-being and so forth, mostly stem from this very kind of thinking. Serving these values, informational privacy is today most often defined either as control over the flow of information or over the access to information. For Alan F. Westin, "privacy is the claim of individuals, groups, or institutions to determine for themselves when, how, and to what extent information about them is communicated to others" (Westin 1967, 7). Westin focuses on the control of information, which makes him a prototypical proponent of "control-theories" of privacy (Tavani 2008, 142f.). On the other hand, there are "access-theories" of privacy (Tavani

2008, 141f.). Gavinson, for instance, relates privacy "to our concern over our accessibility to others: the extent to which we are known to others, the extent to which others have physical access to us, and the extent to which we are the subject of others' attention" (Gavinson 1980/1984, 347). If we combine these two major strands of privacy approaches, one can speak of privacy as individual control over access to personal information (Moor 1997; Tavani 2008). Some authors challenge the non-determination of "privacy as control" definitions (e.g., Wacks 2010, 40f.; Solove 2008, 25); they argue that these theories fail to define the content of privacy. In fact, control theories deal with the "freedom to choose privacy" (Wacks 2010, 41), rather than a determination of the content to be deemed private. Here, privacy is what is subjectively seen as private; such theories, therefore, foster individuals' exclusive control over their data, and do not want to and cannot lay claim to privacy within a good society and a happy fulfilled life (Jaggar 1983, 174). Access theories differ on this point; these theories can denote a realm of privacy that is not at the disposal of the individual's choice by any means (Fuchs 2011b, 223). For instance, such determinations of privacy could include the agreement that individuals' bodies, homes or financial issues such as bank secrecy, are inherently private. In access theories, privacy is what is objectively private and, therefore, theories as these can conjure up constraints to individuals' control over their data in terms of certain values. It is crucial to understand that access theories may allow thinking about what privacy should be in a good society, but not as a matter of necessity. In fact, access theories of privacy are also most often situated within the liberal tradition and have a limited notion of societal issues as the stress is on the individual control aspect.

A resemblance between privacy and property is often noted in the literature (Lyon 1994, 186; Laudon 1996, 93; Brenkert 1979, 126; Habermas 1991, 74; Goldring 1984, 308f.; Lessig 2002, 250; Hettinger 1989, 45; Geuss 2001, 103; Sofsky 2008, 95f.; Solove 2008, 26–28; Moore 2008, 420; Kang 1998; Litman 2000; Westin 1967, 324–325; Varian 1997; Samuelson 2000), but has rarely been analysed critically (exception: Fuchs 2011b).

A broad notion that expresses its fundamental character for human life and fits in with various kinds of property, understands property as a social relation with regard to (tangible and/or intangible) things (Pedersen 2010b). Macpherson speaks about three possible forms: private property, state property, and common property. He points out that private property and state property are of similar structure, since in both the social relation with regard to things is exclusionary (Macpherson 1978, 5). Macpherson further remarks upon three shifts in the property notion, which took place when capitalism and market society appeared (Macpherson 1978, 9f.). These shifts include relevant

– and, as we shall see, ideological – identifications: private property, based on a relation of exclusion, is taken for property as such; property in the consumable means of life is identified with property in producing these means of life; and property in producing the means of life is identified with a specific property in producing the means of life, namely property of the labour force. These shifts are not arbitrary; rather, Macpherson argues that they are needed by market society and capitalism (Macpherson 1978, 9). Nowadays, private property is commonly associated with four aspects: the right to use, to abuse, to alienate or exchange something, as well as the right to receive the fruits that the usage of something generates (Munzer 2005, 858). Private property can be or probably has always been constrained by state or society (Christman 1994). However, "it may be called an absolute right in two senses: it is a right to dispose of, or alienate, as well as to use; and it is a right which is not conditional on the owner's performance of any social function" (Macpherson 1978, 10).

A relation of exclusion lies behind privacy as well as in the case of private property. I will now point to some similarities between both concepts on a phenomenological level. In the next section, the resemblance is then explored more systematically using Marxian theory.

Most often, privacy is defined as an individual's right against others and society (ensuring negative freedom), so one may conclude that an opposition against 'the common' lies behind the privacy discourse. In the age of the Internet, "just as the individual concerned about privacy wants to control who gets access to what and when, the copyright holder wants to control who get access to what and when" (Lessig 2002, 250). Consequently, there is much discussion about how, on the one hand, to understand, justify, and criticize intangible private property, and on the other hand, to analyse, welcome, or mourn the blurring between the public and private realm online (with respect to SNS: boyd 2007). Further similarities between privacy and private property can be found in their dependence on people's class status (Goldring 1984, 313; Papacharissi 2010). It makes an important difference if one has private property only in things that one needs for life, or if one has much more private property than he or she needs for life. There are rich private property owners who possess far more housing space than they can ever use. On the other hand, there are poor private property owners, being on welfare, who only possess their labour power. In terms of privacy, there are, for instance, people who rely on sharing the flat with other people that brings along several constraints in temporarily withdrawing from other people, or they may be forced to report their whole private life to state authorities (Gilliom 2001). However, there are people who have far more privacy. For instance, people who live in castles are well protected from any unappreciated intrusions, be they from other people, noise, or anything else. These people may be able to circumvent reporting their financial status to state authorities, using the law effectively on their behalf by means of tax and investment consultants. As much as private property, privacy is also good for different things depending on one's class status. In capitalism, all people rely on having private property in order to satisfy their material and cultural needs. For the rich and powerful, private property ensures that they have the right to own the means of production and use them for their own purpose. For the poor, private property is essential because only via private property can they reproduce their labour power and ensure that they will make ends meet. In capitalism, all humans also rely on having privacy in order to be competitive within a society that forces them to compete, and at the same time to allow for spaces of escape from that competition (Geuss 2001, 88). Rich and powerful people's call for privacy is not only about individuation, but moreover about ensuring the sanctity of their wealth while hiding its origin (one thinks of bank secrecy, for instance). The poorer people also call for privacy in order to protect their lives against overexploitation and other forms of powerful abuse by the rich (Demirović 2004).

Not surprisingly, we know of theories that draw consequences from the outlined close connection between the individualistic control theory of privacy and private property by conceptualising the right to privacy as a right to property (Laudon 1996, 93; Lessig 2002; Kang 1998; Varian 1997). Property, according to the previously outlined identifying processes, is for these authors always to be understood as private property. Privacy as property would strengthen the individual control of personal data (Laudon 1996, 93; 97) and would prevent privacy invasions that occur when personal data is accessed non-consensually (Laudon 1996, 99). The "privacy as property"-approach demands that "everyone possesses information about themselves that would be valuable under some circumstances to others for commercial purposes. Everyone possesses his or her own reputation and data image. In this sense, basing privacy on the value of one's name is egalitarian. Even the poor possess their identity. In the current regime of privacy protection, not even the wealthy can protect their personal information" (Laudon 1996, 102). Admittedly, with other political implications in mind, Lessig says, in the context of privacy as property, that "property talk [...] would strengthen the rhetorical force behind privacy" (Lessig 2002, 247). If privacy is property, then it becomes possible to speak about theft regarding the non-consensual usage of personal data (Lessig 2002, 255).

3   Privacy as Ideology and Privacy as Private Property: A Marxian
         Critique

In this section, I will use Marxian theory to analyse dominant notions of privacy. Thereby I refer to Marx's concepts of ideology critique, commodity fetish,
and his differentiation between a societal sphere of production and a societal
sphere of circulation. Marx's concept of ideology critique is used as an umbrella
theory that includes his analysis of fetishisms as well as the differentiation
between a sphere of production and a sphere of circulation.

First, I must clarify what I mean by ideology. In general, ideology has different meanings. The term can be used neutrally to denote a worldview or a system of ideas. It can be used positively as a class struggle concept in order to
mark positions within a struggle of beliefs. It can also be used denunciatively
to dismiss ideas as negative or dogmatic, and the term can be used in the sense
of the Enlightenment to point to an objectivity that is not yet present or known.

3.1 Marx's Concept(s) of Ideology

Marx has never outlined what he exactly understands by ideology; rather, there
are different concepts of ideology notable in Marx's texts. Consequently,
Marxist theory has developed different notions of ideology (Rehman 2007;
Koivisto and Pietilä 1996; Žižek 1995; Eagleton 1991). I think that Marx's complete works show that he is committed to a concept of ideology that wants to
enlighten through criticism (Rehmann 2007, 215), and I want to suggest a critical notion of ideology that includes three interacting aspects: a sociological, an
epistemological, and a political dimension. All these aspects can be found in
Marx. I propose that the problem of ideology consists of a specific form of
human association that evokes a false consciousness as well as a structure of
political domination.

Ideology as false consciousness is often associated with Marxist theory and
its interest in enlightenment. Frederick Engels wrote in a letter to Franz
Mehring that "ideology is a process accomplished by the so-called thinker consciously, indeed, but with a false consciousness" (Engels 1893). Obviously, ideology has to do with falseness and this is its epistemological aspect. However,
it is often forgotten that Marx connects the question of truth strictly to human
practice. Within the *Theses on Feuerbach* he expressed this very well: "The
question whether objective truth can be attributed to human thinking is not a
question of theory but is a practical question" (Marx 1845–46/1998, 569). If the
point is not only to interpret the world but to change it, as Marx suggested in
the same manuscript (Marx 1845–46/1998, 571), then it becomes clear that ideology stops existing only if its societal preconditions cease to exist. For society,

this demands changing practices and cannot be achieved solely through alternative "true" thinking. Marx interlinks epistemological questions of truth to sociological questions of human association and practice. In *The German Ideology,* Marx and Engels investigate forms of ideology along the modern division of labour between brain and hand. They introduce the societal role of the ideologist. Ideologists are removed from material production and can therefore imagine a "false" thinking which is detached from these processes (Marx and Engels 1845–46/1998, 67f.). Regarding *The German Ideology*, Terry Eagleton points towards a curious fusion of that epistemological aspect of ideology and a political definition (1991, 79f.), because Marx and Engels situate the labour division also in the context of class society and political domination. They argue that:

> The ideas of the ruling class are in every epoch the ruling ideas: i.e., the class which is the ruling material force of society is at the same time its ruling intellectual force. The class which has the means of material production at its disposal, consequently also controls the means of mental production, so that the ideas of those who lack the means of mental production are on the whole subject to it. The ruling ideas are nothing more than the ideal expression of the dominant material relations, the dominant material relations grasped as ideas; hence of the relations which make the one class the ruling one, therefore, the ideas of its dominance. The individuals composing the ruling class possess among other things consciousness, and therefore think. Insofar, therefore, as they rule as a class and determine the extent and compass of an historical epoch, it is self-evident that they do this in its whole range, hence among other things rule also as thinkers, as producers of ideas, and regulate the production and distribution of the ideas of their age: thus their ideas are the ruling ideas of the epoch
>
> MARX and ENGELS 1845–46/1998, 67

Marx's talk of social relations here again points to the sociological aspect of ideology, and so we can reasonably claim that Marx's concept of ideology stems from a form of human association that evokes false consciousness and a structure of political domination.

3.2   *Objective Forms of Thought as Societal Impingement Structures of Privacy Ideologies*

If we do not assume a break in Marx's works but rather recognize a certain continuity, then we can understand his most important work, *Capital*, as a clarifying application of previously developed categories, such as ideology and others. At the same time, it might also be seen as a narrowing since it focuses on the field of economy. In terms of ideology, we can indeed find narrowing clarifications of that concept. Within *Capital*, as I shall outline and contextualise in terms of privacy, the specific form of sociological association is commodity exchange which gives rise to epistemological falseness and political domination. The epistemological falseness consists of naturalising human-made relations, where political domination is maintained through the appropriation of societal-produced surplus by the capitalist.

In *Capital*, Marx analyses "forms of thought which are socially valid, and therefore objective, for the relations of production belonging to this historically determined mode of social production, i.e. commodity production" (Marx 1867/1976, 169). These forms of thought tend to be dominant patterns of thinking, since commodity production and exchange are dominant in society. The process of commercialization of ever more spheres of life and human activities, such as education, media, ecology, human biology, and personality, is ongoing today and this means that ever more knowledge, content, natural resources, (genetic) codes, and personal data appear as exchangeable commodities. Critical philosopher Theodor W. Adorno argues that it is the principle of commodity exchange that determines the whole development of society (Adorno 2002, 31f.; 43; 112) or even human fatality (Adorno 1972, 209). Marx himself states that specific capitalist forms of thought influence "all the notions of justice held by both the worker and the capitalist, all the mystifications of the capitalist mode of production, all capitalism's illusions about freedom, all the apologetic tricks of vulgar economics" (Marx 1867/1976, 680). At the same time, one has to be careful not to universalise these forms of thought too much; it is important to stress that Marx highlights those forms of thought that have relevance for people in their role as marketers. While commodification plays a key role within ever more fields of activity, we are not only marketers. A second limitation of Marx's assertion is that we cannot expect to know everything about ideologies by only analysing forms of thought. Wolfgang Fritz Haug has suggested understanding Marx's investigations in *Capital* as societal impingement structures that are taken as a basis by and interact with the concrete work of ideologists (Haug 1987). I will try to mark points of intersection where objective forms of thought meet ideological privacy theories. Both privacy and property theories build on basal premises which are unquestioned because they originate from the marketer's common sense behaviour. Such forms of thought affect privacy and property theories, but the opposite is also true: privacy and property theories contribute to maintaining these forms of thought and the related forms of capitalist association. In the following, what objective forms of thought look like is explained and how they can be related to privacy and property.

3.3   Marx's Fetish Argument: Deciphering Objective Forms of Thought

Fetishism is used to denote inversions between subject and object, between humans and human-made things or relations. According to Haug (2005, 161), investigating fetishisms means examining where man-made things exercise force over man. Marx addresses several fetishisms within *Capital*, starting with *commodity fetishism*. Marx observes that today, "the wealth of societies in which the capitalist mode of production prevails appears as an 'immense collection of commodities'" (Marx 1867/1976, 125), so that "only the products of mutually independent acts of labour, performed in isolation" are meaningful to be exchanged (Marx 1867/1976, 57). Commodity exchange presumes a certain historical development of the division of labour. Obviously, there are different companies producing essential things, to which I do not contribute. The way to get these things is to exchange them for money. In this sense, we are all marketers. Marx asks the question of why an exchange of so many different things, such as shoes, video games, personal data, etc. is possible at all: what makes them comparable and exchangeable? He finds an answer while analysing the specific sociality of private and isolated production that, however, appears as strictly non-social because there is no direct agreement or planning among producers over what and how much to produce.

Marx speaks of the differentiation between "abstract" and "concrete" labour as the crucial point for understanding the sociality of commodity production (Marx 1867/1976, 131–137). Any labour, however spent in isolation or in cooperation, produces use value that is valuable because it satisfies human needs. Such labour can be named "concrete" labour, as it contributes immediately to that end. However, when things are produced for exchange, then they have also an exchange value. Where does this exchange value come from? There must be a kind of labour, he named it "abstract" labour, that produces this value. As Marx's term suggests, abstract labour and the value that it produces are not tangible; rather, he argues that it originates from an abstraction: when two products are exchanged, a third moment, namely the exchange value that makes them comparable, arises. This happens just as one can speak of apples and strawberries as fruits, where the term "fruits" has the role of the mediating third that makes apples and strawberries comparable. The term "fruits" is an abstraction for apples and strawberries. In contrast to apples and strawberries, which are eatable and embody use value, the category "fruits" has no concrete use value. Marx says that exchange value originates within an abstraction;

however, this abstraction is of an uncommon quality. It is not an abstraction in mind; rather it is an abstraction that evolves from the marketers' activities. The exchange process then can consequently be called "abstraction in reality," in contrast to common abstractions in mind. The "comparable becoming" of isolated and private workers within the exchange process, or in other words the value creation, is only possible because societal standards assert themselves within the exchange process. Otherwise, without comparison, no exchange would be possible at all. Such standards can be found in the amount of labour that is, on average, necessary to be spent to produce something (Marx 1867/1976, 129f.). The average necessary amount of labour, of course, clearly depends on the state of technology and the machines that are available for production. For instance, company A produces umbrellas and it takes 45 minutes to produce a piece, while company B has introduced new machines and is able to produce the same piece in 15 minutes. If both companies would exchange their products then both of them would recognize that the value of umbrellas consists of 30 minutes labour time. But the companies do not know the value of their umbrellas before the exchange takes place, because they do not cooperate. Value does not appear before the exchange takes place; it can never be predicted beforehand (Marx 1867/1976, 166). The labour that is spent privately with a company has value only in relation to labour spent in the whole society (in all companies), and there is no institution that organizes the labour that is spent in the whole society. Companies A and B recognize the value of their products (30 minutes average necessary labour time) when they are exchanging their umbrellas. They receive the value in exchange for the umbrellas. For them, to be concerned with "how much of some other product they get for their own" (Marx 1867/1976, 167), it is obvious that their umbrella *has* this value as a property instead of it being built within a societal abstraction process (Marx 1867/1976, 187). The fact that labour creates value and that value is only recognisable in exchange and then determines further production is what Marx means when he speaks of the "phantom-like quality of value" (Marx 1867/1976, 128). He says:

> The mysterious character of the commodity-form consists therefore simply in the fact that the commodity reflects the societal characteristics of men's own labour as objective characteristics of the products of labour themselves, as the socio-natural properties of these things. Hence it also reflects the social relation of the producers to the sum total of labour as a social relation between objects, a relation which exists apart from and outside the producers.
>
> MARX 1867/1976, 164f

The societal dimension of value creation is thus effectively "hidden" for marketers, but asserts itself behind people's backs (Marx 1867/1976, 135), because exchange value must be in the marketers' interest. They have exchange value and selling in mind when they start to produce and enter markets. Therefore, they adjust their activities according to the expected exchange value (Marx 1867/1976, 167).

The commodity fetish, which means that value is objectified in things, breaks the ground for a more highly developed fetishism, the *money fetish*. When value appears as a property of things, it is possible to imagine a specific commodity that objectifies value: money. Within money, exchange value and use value fall into each other; the use value of money is the exchange. The transition to independence of the law of value then becomes very concrete, and at the same time, the social quality of value becomes more "hidden." The fetish is thus perfected, and in fact, it is increasingly perfected in the further establishment of the capital relation. Ultimately, it appears that invested money itself begs money (capital fetish). I will come back to the capital relation in the following discussion.

3.4 *Privacy and the Mutual Recognition of Private Property Owners*
According to the premises of Marx's ideology theory, specific practices are related to specific forms of thought. In terms of the idea of a universal right to private property, Marx argues that marketers must "recognize each other as owners of private property. This juridical relation, whose form is the contract, whether as part of a developed legal system or not, is a relation between two wills which mirrors the economic relation" (Marx 1867/1976, 178). In the *Grundrisse,* Marx outlines this in detail. The mutual recognition of private property owners implies equality and freedom that are "not only respected in exchange based on exchange values but, also, the exchange of exchange values is the productive, real basis of all *equality* and *freedom*. As pure ideas they are merely the idealized expressions of this basis; as developed in juridical, political, social relations, they are merely this basis to a higher power" (Marx 1857–58/1983, 170).

Freedom is given within commodity exchange, as "individual A feels a need for the commodity of individual B, he does not appropriate it by force, nor vice versa, but rather they recognize one another reciprocally as proprietors, as persons whose will penetrates their commodities. Accordingly, the juridical moment of the Person enters here, as well as that of freedom, in so far as it is contained in the former. No one seizes hold of another's property by force. Each divests himself of his property voluntarily" (Marx 1857–58/1983, 169). Equality is given, since "only the differences between their needs and between their production give rise to exchange and to their social equation in exchange; these natural differences are therefore the precondition of their social equality in the act of exchange, and of this relation in general, in which they relate to one another as productive" (Marx 1857–58/1983, 168).

From the mutual recognition as private property owners, only formal equality between people can be deduced; the social status is not affected here. Also, freedom appears as very formal here. In *Privacy: A Manifesto*, Wolfgang Sofsky puts it this way:

> Exchange among private individuals is the basis for equality and freedom. Trading partners recognize each other as equals. Each accepts the other as a subject with his own will. The sales contract that they agree to does not establish equality of status or property but rather a voluntary relationship between peers. We should not expect more from a society that shields people from the pressure of the community and is supposed to put a protective distance between them.
>
> SOFSKY 2008, 85f

In addition to freedom and equality, a third aspect is set within the commodity exchange, namely self-interest: "Individual A serves the need of individual B by means of the commodity a only in so far as and because individual B serves the need of individual A by means of the commodity B, and vice versa. Each serves the other in order to serve himself; each makes use of the other, reciprocally, as his means [...] That is, the common interest which appears as the motive of the act as a whole is recognized as a fact by both sides; but, as such, it is not the motive, but rather proceeds, as it were, behind the back of these self-reflected particular interests, behind the back of one individual's interest in opposition to that of the other" (Marx 1857–58/1983, 169f.).

In summary, Marx's differentiation between two societal spheres that are necessarily interwoven (Marx 1885/1992, 131f., 139, 190) may be helpful also for the theory of ideology. One sphere is about producing things and the labour that has to be spent on it. The other sphere is where the produced things circulate among people, i.e. the market. Equality, freedom, and self-interest appear in the latter.

"It is the exclusive realm of Freedom, Equality, Property and Bentham. Freedom, because both buyer and seller of a commodity, let us say of labour power, are determined only by their own free will. They contract as free persons, who are equal before the law. Their contract is the final result in which their joint will finds a common legal expression. Equality, because each enters into relation with the other, as with a simple Owner of commodities, and they exchange equivalent for equivalent. Property, because each disposes only of what is his own. And Bentham, because each looks only to his own advantage. The only force bringing them together, and putting them into relation with each other, is the selfishness, the gain and the private interest of each. Each pays heed to himself only, and no one worries about the others. And precisely for that reason, either in accordance with the pre-established harmony of things, or under the auspices of an omniscient providence, they all work together to their mutual advantage, for the common weal, and in the common interest" (Marx 1867/1976, 280).

By employing Marx's theory, I have thus far shown that the properties of the dominant privacy notion – competitive individualism, exclusive control, exchangeable private property – have their very origin in the commodity exchange. The commodity exchange hides human sociality. Value appears as property of things and not as a social relation. Hence, it is important to own things for realising their value. But sociality asserts itself behind people's back and establishes pressures to perform that are not controlled by the individuals. They perceive themselves as competitors.

C.B. Macpherson (1962) detected the great influence of the outlined objective forms of thought within the most influential philosophical and political thinking, from Hobbes to Locke, and labelled it "possessive individualism." Possessive individualism denotes a kind of thinking *and* a social practice. Within capitalism it is useful and necessary that the individual perceives herself or himself as essentially "the proprietor of his own person and capacities, for which he owes nothing to society" (Macpherson, 1962, 263) and enters "into self-interested relations with other individuals" (Macpherson 1962, 263). The value associated with privacy comes from these kinds of objective forms of thought. Admittedly, there has been much critique of this kind of privacy (Habermas 1991, 74; Lyon 1994, 186, 196; Etzioni 1999, 194), but for the evaluation of these critiques, it is important to keep in mind that privacy's origin in possessive individualism is not arbitrary; rather, this style of privacy originates from material, capitalist practices. There are also several newer privacy theories that do not proceed from the liberal individualistic point of view (for instance: Solove 2008, 91–98); however, the dominant mode of production in society remains bound to that point of view. We cannot simply define privacy differently without leaving social practices as they are.

3.5 *The Political Aspect: Privacy and Class Domination*

Ideology was defined as a specific form of human association that evokes a false consciousness and a structure of political domination. I have shown that it is in the associational form of commodity exchange that ideology is falsified and thus makes privacy one-sided and individualistic. But what about the political dimension of ideology? I am stuck for an answer that addresses why ideology and therefore ideological notions of privacy are tied to implicit class domination and are therefore problematic. Marx gives an answer to this question within his capital theory. It is important to stress that there is a logical unity between the value theory and capital theory in Marx. The unity exists because commodity exchange and exploitation take place in capitalist reality at the same time. This means that commodity exchange and its objective forms of thought are necessarily interwoven with capitalism, i.e. we cannot separate them. And it also means that the dominant notion of privacy is related to the maintenance of political domination.

Marx describes capital as self-processing value (Marx 1867/1976, 257); in short, 'M-C-M': in the sphere of circulation, money (M) is invested for a specific commodity production (C) and results then, if the sale was successful, in more money (M'). Why are investments profitable? Marx gives the following answer. Self-processing value is possible due to the commodification of the workforce. The workforce is a certain commodity as it is able to produce more value than it costs to reproduce. For instance, food and opportunities for regeneration, such as free time, sleeping, etc. that have to be produced, are reproduction costs of the workforce. The difference between these costs and the surplus produced by workers is appropriated by the buyers of the workforce. In this manner, capitalists are steadily able to appropriate the societally-produced surplus by workers. They become therefore richer and more powerful than workers. Consequently, a structural class division in society becomes inevitable.

Why is such appropriation legitimate? It is legitimate because the principle of equivalence, "do ut des," "I give that you may give," no one cheats anyone, remains intact and therefore the mutual recognition as private property owners is not affected. On the contrary, fair commodity exchange – and therefore the ideological notion of privacy – is presupposed for a capitalist class society. Not surprisingly, class society affects the privacy issue, as argued in Section 2.

Marx argues that besides commodity exchange, i.e. labour performed privately and in isolation, capitalism needs to work out "a complete separation between the workers and the ownership of the conditions for the realization of their labour" (Marx 1867/1976, 874). In the prehistory of capitalism, this separation took place through a violent process of expropriation of great segments of the population, to which Marx refers as "primitive accumulation of capital" (Marx 1867/1976, part eight). Thereby, workers were set free, but this "liberation" was of ambiguous character. It resulted in a dual sense of freedom (Marx 1867/1976, 270–272), namely, workers are free of personal dependences, for instance, from their overlords in feudalism, but also free from the ownership of the condition for the realisation of their labour. Workers are on the one hand free to engage in contracts. This freedom is precisely the freedom of commodity exchange. On the other hand, workers are forced to engage in contracts and to sell their labour power on the markets to make ends meet. This freedom is also set in commodity exchange as it is a freedom to choose regardless of one's social status. Hence, workers are forced to maintain their status as a subaltern class because the capitalist can steadily appropriate the societal surplus that is produced by the workers (Marx 1867/1976, 729f.). This fair exploitation process is, according to Marx, a structural reason for domination in society.

The capitalist quality of society as class society is expressed by the right to have others work for you and the right to private property in labour's terms of realisation. These rights are identified with the right to private property in general in an ideological manner (Macpherson 1978). Today's unitary legal frameworks for different sorts of private property are only possible because commodity exchange and appropriation of societally produced surplus are not divisible (Römer 1978, 140). The universal right to private property, to use, abuse, alienate or exchange something, and the right to receive the fruits that the usage of something generates, does not matter if only the things owned are needed for life, or the conditions within which labour can be realised (means of production) are private property, or if private property is extended to the labour force (Munzer 2005, 858).

In terms of privacy, Niels van Dijk (2010, 64) points to an interesting difference in legislation between Europe and the u.s. While in the u.s. tradition, personal data is predominantly seen as a commodity and therefore exchangeable (privacy as property), in Europe there is "little room for propertization of personal data" (van Dijk 2010, 64), because privacy is conceptualized as a persona right and important for the individual's dignity (McGeveran 2009; Shepherd 2012). But human dignity is generally seen as inalienable. In the discussion on the question whether privacy should or should not be alienable, exchangeable, and tradable on the markets, it is crucial to understand that in capitalism any commodification process presupposes rights that cannot be alienated or exchanged. The labourer must not become a slave, cannot alienate his or her whole person because this would reverse the double freedom of the labourer (Pateman 2002, 33). This is a feature of capitalist progress in comparison to previous forms of society. According to Marx, this means that domination, which still exists, is mediated through basic freedoms of the individual. Macpherson (1962, 264; see also Pateman 2002) argues that alienability of the labour force presupposes itself a universal, inalienable right of self-ownership that originates from the practice of commodity exchange and contains, as already outlined, the circulation sphere-based rights of freedom, equality,

property, and self-interest (Marx 1867/1976, 280). In terms of privacy, I conclude that approaches to privacy as an inalienable right may be helpful but are
ultimately not sufficient to be an alternative to capitalist class domination particularly if they operate with the notion of autonomy and privacy as
self-possession.

Carole Pateman argues that the double freedom assigned to the worker in
capitalism is a "political fiction" (Pateman and Mills 2007, 17f.) since the inalienable part of the individual that enters into employment contracts cannot be
separated from the individual's alienable aspects. When employers buy work
force, it is demanded that the worker brings in his or her knowledge, skills, etc.,
which in fact is his or her person. Labour cannot be separated from person-
being and person-becoming (Marx 1976, 283). The same applies to privacy and
personal data. It is a fiction to assume that users can exchange their personal
data and that this exchange would not affect their person, which also has to be
conceptualised as non-alienable in order to speak meaningfully of free and
voluntary exchanges on privacy markets. Pateman argues that contracts,
although entered voluntarily, enable superiority and subordination. Hence,
there is also a subordination of the users at stake when they accept commercial SNSS' terms of use. Such subordination is a precondition for exploitation
and class domination ultimately. Ellerman refers to this fiction as a "person-
thing mismatch" (Ellerman 2005, 463) as if aspects of personality could be
alienated like things. The political fiction of severability of person and work
force or person and personal data can easily be understood as ideology and
fetishism in the sense that I have outlined it here.

Whereas privacy can, though ought not, be seen as an inalienable right, private property reasonably cannot (Andrew 1985, 529; Pateman 2002, 20–21;
Litman 2000, 1295–1297). The closer privacy comes to private property, the
more privacy is alienable or exchangeable, becoming itself a commodity. It
does then not only contribute to the capitalist ideology, but also directly to
exploitation. In Table 13.1, I summarise what we can learn from Marx in terms
of understanding privacy in (informational) capitalism.

Dominant theories of privacy, focussing on individual control and exclusion
of others, are ideological as they originate from commodity exchange while
hiding individuals' sociality. They are part of circulation sphere-based objective forms of thought that contain the mutual recognition of marketers as free
and equal private property owners. Such freedom, equality, and lastly privacy,
however, do not contradict exploitation and class division in society that take
place in the sphere of production. In a circular movement, class status has then
again a constraining effect on freedom, equality, and privacy. If privacy may be
seen as exchangeable private property, privacy itself can in addition to labour

TABLE 13.1   *Ideological privacy and privacy as commodity in capitalism*

ideology societal sphere of circulation	privacy as aspect of self-ownership/privacy as inalienable right equal and free private property owners	
	labour force commodity	privacy as private property/privacy commodity
societal sphere of production	classical exploitation	new forms of exploitation
	appropriation of societally produced surplus and class domination	

force become a commodity and therefore part of the exploitation process. It contributes then directly to class divisions in society. Such newer forms of exploitation, based on economic surveillance, are described shortly in the next section, where Diaspora* is compared to profit-oriented SNSs, such as Facebook and Google+.

4   Evaluating Diaspora*'s Alternative Potential

As the privacy issue is a core issue in Diaspora*'s self-image, evaluating Diaspora*'s alternative potential must include not only evaluating its mode of production, but also a critical evaluation of privacy as a whole. In the following, I will interlink both issues.

Christian Fuchs has outlined how we can analyse capital accumulation on SNSs in Marxian terms (Fuchs 2012, 143–146). Facebook's and others' capital accumulation strategy is mainly based on the targeted advertising business model, which means that they engage in exchange contracts with the advertising industry. The owner buys technical infrastructure, such as server parks and software components, as well as labour force, such as accountants, software developer, etc., and produces the SNS on which users can interact. While people use the site for different reasons, such as getting news, providing information, staying in touch with friends, making new relations, or organising events, they produce a wide range of data. These data, which include for instance socio-demographic information and consumer preferences deduced from users' browsing behaviour, are then sold to advertisers. Whereas traditional forms of advertising are directed to broad groups of potential buyers, targeted advertising is tailored for exactly defined and differentiated groups, or even single consumers. This demands more detailed, exact, and differentiated knowledge of the users' needs and (buying) behaviour, which can be provided by the owner of SNSS. The SNSS' business model is based on the secondary use of user interaction for commodification and valorisation purposes (Smythe 2006; Fuchs 2011a). The economic reason why profit-oriented SNSS develop massive systems of user surveillance and store "literally everything," as a Facebook employee has admitted (Wong 2010), lies therein. Users' interests in privacy can only be considered where the need for privacy does not inhibit SNSS' profit interests. In fact, commercial SNSS commodify users' privacy. They often do it without users' explicit consent, when they hide their profit-orientation behind the social value of networking. Today, SNSS are increasingly compelled to respect users' privacy through legal investigations, public pressure initiated by privacy movements, and alternative SNSS such as Diaspora*, but this does not mean that commercial SNSS have to abjure the targeted advertising model. Commercial and advertising funded SNSS need users who have control over their data and are able to exchange their privacy for the usage of the platform voluntarily by agreeing to the terms of use. For them, in order to maintain newer forms of exploitation, the challenge is not to fight against privacy at all; rather, they can support privacy if it is – as an analogy to labour force – related to private property, and hence alienable or exchangeable. It seems that simply upholding privacy is not the right move in order to challenge surveillance (Nock 1993, 1; Lyon 2005, 27; Stalder 2002).

Diaspora* breaks with this advertising model based on privacy as commodity; hence, it protects its users and their personal data from exploitation: "Yet our distributed design means *no big corporation will ever control Diaspora.* Diaspora* will never sell your social life to advertisers, and you won't have to conform to someone's arbitrary rules or look over your shoulder before you speak" (Diaspora 2011c; emphasis in original). Gary T. Marx reminds us that "privacy for whom and surveillance of whom and by whom and for what reasons need to be specified in any assessment" (Marx 2012, vii). Due to its distributed infrastructure and its funding model that is not based on advertising, one can argue that Diaspora* practically provides an alternative concept of privacy (Fuchs 2012, 153f.). Diaspora* sees "privacy as collective right of dominated and exploited groups that need to be protected from corporate domination that aims at gathering information about workers and consumers for accumulating capital, disciplining workers and consumers, and for increasing the productivity of capitalist production and advertising" (Fuchs 2011b, 232).

While I agree that Diaspora* practically avoids commodification of privacy and the exploitation of users, I nevertheless see some constraints for an alternative non-ideological notion of privacy that follows from my preceding analysis. Not only is treating privacy as commodity a problem but it should also be taken into account that conceptualising privacy as an aspect of self-ownership is ideological and cannot be separated from exploitation in capitalism. In fact, although Diaspora* is directed against newer forms of exploitation of users' privacy, its recourse to privacy remains bound to exploitation in general as it confirms exploitation's ideological premises – the possessive individualistic ideology. I shall provide evidence for such a claim.

In its various self-descriptions Diaspora* prominently states: It "is the social network that puts *you in control of your information.* You decide what you'd like to share, and with whom. *You retain full ownership of all your information,* including friend lists, messages, photos, and profile details" (Diaspora* n.d.b; my emphasis). Here, two aspects are intertwined: Diaspora* refers to a specific notion of privacy ("puts you in control of your information") and relates the promise of user control to property ("You retain full ownership of all your information").

Dominant privacy theories stress the individual's control over access to personal information and are deeply rooted in people's minds and their practical role as marketers. Privacy-aware users, who see commercial SNSs as associated with privacy invasive behaviour, are surely attracted by Diaspora*'s privacy statement. One consequence of privacy theories stressing the individual control aspect is that they avoid objective constraints of the individual's power to control and decide. The public good finds no consideration here. Another alternative SNS in the making, TheGlobalSquare, which is associated with the "occupy" movement (Roos 2011), also relates to the privacy discourse. It makes more substantial claims about what privacy is and what it is not: "Individuals have a right to privacy as part of the rights they brought from a state of nature [...]. Organizations and actions which affect the public are not protected by any such rights" (Marsh 2012). Here, individual control is not seen exclusively and this example proves that Diaspora* could also behave differently in its recourse to the value of privacy. As far as I can see, in its various self-descriptions, Diaspora* does not propose any qualification of privacy that can constrain exclusive individual control and is therefore likely to fit into the dominant theories of privacy. Diaspora* mobilises the power of the individuals and their privacy – for which they think that they owe nothing to society – against economic surveillance. So, it challenges successfully the economic foundations underlying privacy threats, but does not challenge privacy as a possessive individualistic concept.

On the contrary, Diaspora*'s focus on privacy is accompanied by stressing the relevance of ownership. Concepts of ownership or private property support the exclusive and individualistic notion of privacy. Here again, Diaspora* reacts to commercial SNSs. Facebook, for example, states in its terms of use that users grant Facebook "a non-exclusive, transferable, sub-licensable, royalty-free, worldwide license to use any IP [intellectual property] content that you post on or in connection with Facebook" (Facebook 2011). In the case of Diaspora*, such a license is not possible. However, in the same passage, Facebook also states that "you own all of the content and information you post on Facebook, and you can control how it is shared through your privacy and application settings" (Facebook 2011). Is the notion of ownership then so appropriate for an alternative to capitalist SNSs? I think it is not and the relationship between privacy as commodity (the Facebook license for instance) and privacy as an aspect of self-possession (Diaspora*'s notion), which has been outlined above, gives grounds for holding a sceptical view. Diaspora*'s vision of privacy protection is, as outlined in the first section, essentially based on the individual opportunity to change pods/SNS-provider. Users need ownership of their data in order to migrate them from pod to pod: "And because your information is yours, not ours, *you'll have the ultimate power* – the ability to move your profile and all your social data from one pod to another, without sacrificing your connection to the social web" (Diaspora 2011c; emphasis in original). Assuming that Diaspora* will never be able to outdo Facebook in terms of provided features and network effects in the view of the majority of SNSs users – and this assumption seems to be affirmed by Diaspor*'s history, users may then voluntarily decide to sell their privacy on Facebook or Google+ and they are indeed able to do this as they have exclusive control and ownership of their privacy. Exactly, these premises of the privacy commodity exchange are also propagated by Diaspora*. The dominant theoretical privacy concept cannot provide reasons why users should not behave like this.

At this point of Diaspora*'s evaluation, it may be useful to remember Marx's "leading threat" of investigation expressed in the previously quoted passage from the preface to *A Contribution to the Critique of Political Economy*, where he refers to the relation between the entire economic foundation of society and the more or less rapidly transforming superstructures within which humans become conscious of conflicts and fight them out. The focus on privacy, as it is dominant in capitalism, may result from Diaspora*'s multi-faceted embeddedness in capitalist structures.

There is capital accumulation related to copyleft. On the one hand, copyleft products can be used for free in order to produce non copyleft products. For instance, machines that produce umbrellas can be operated on behalf of free and copyleft software. The producer of umbrellas does not have to pay for that kind of software although it contributes as means of production to his or her capital accumulation. In this case, an intensive exploitation of the labour that was once spent on the copyleft product takes place. The producer of umbrellas saves the money that he or she would otherwise have to pay for the machine's operating software. On the other hand, copyleft products are attractive for users as they cheap, widely cheaply accessible and have a high quality since a huge pool of co-operative labour builds them. Copyleft products are also often more flexibly adaptable to specific purposes. This appeal can be used for capital accumulation indirectly. Commercial firms may offer services that are related to copyleft products. For instance, a producer of umbrellas pays another firm that collects and aggregates suitable copyleft components for running umbrella-producing machines. In this case, it is not the labour spent on producing the copyleft product that contributes directly to capital accumulation, but rather the labour spent on collection and service. I argue that copyleft production is indeed opposed to capital accumulation. However, at the same time, it allows for newer forms of exploitation that can be much more intensive – the producer of umbrellas pays nothing for the use of copyleft products, but these products enable him to realise surplus through selling the umbrellas.

A major problem in this context is that copyleft is not the dominant principle of production; rather, it can be understood as an expression of a transforming economic foundation in a partial realm and therefore capital accumulation can behave parasitical to copyleft production. Diaspora*'s mode of production is bound to the immaterial or informational realm. In terms of political economic theories of this realm, it can be differentiated in terms of three approaches, as Fuchs (2009, 79) argues. A neoliberal position wants to take back peer-production by enforcing intellectual private property rights and the principle of exclusion. A social democratic position sees advantages in initiatives such as Free Software and Diaspora*, but seeks to establish a kind of dual economy. Pedersen calls this position "information exceptionalism." Informational exceptionalists reject property rights in the intangible realm, but do not challenge them in the tangible realm: "The market is good for humanity, as long as it behaves nicely in cyberspace" (Pedersen 2010a, 105). A way to explain the difference between the two positions is to understand informational exceptionalists as representing a distinct group of capital interests. While there are corporations making profit by enforcing intellectual private property rights, there are other corporations, such as Google, which gain profits without enforcing intellectual property rights but are ultimately dependent of private property rights in the tangible realm (Söderberg 2002).

A third position mentioned by Fuchs (2009, 79) aims to transcend capital-ism and sees the intangible realm as a germ form of a new mode of production for the whole society – also within the tangible realm. At the same time, this position always stresses the fragility of peer-productions by pointing to their dependence on dominant capitalist social relations (Barbrook 1998/2005). In terms of Diaspora*'s mode of production, the following argument made by Söderberg can be applied. It is "a prerequisite of free programming [...] that those involved are sustained outside of market relations. Hackers are generally supported financially in diverse ways – by their parents, as students living on grants, as dropouts getting by on social benefits, or even employees within computer companies – and their existence is linked to the burgeoning mate-rial surplus of informational capitalism" (Söderberg 2002). Also, the donation funding system initially applied by Diaspora* remains embedded in capitalist structures. The value objectified in money donations has to be produced in capitalist structures. Capitalists themselves may donate out of idealistic rea-sons, but probably most of the donations stem from wage labourers. One can glean from an interview with the Diaspora* founders that there were different meanings among the project team on whether Diaspora* will and should make money in the future (Nussbaum 2010). When the founders brought Diaspora* into a commercially oriented start up programm in 2012, many were convinced that tis is the end of an truly alternative project. Full-time software contribu-tors to Diaspora* cannot live without an income and the project's fund of donations was finite (Diaspora* 2011a), which is a general problem that all alternative media are facing. Hence, "the team has spoken to venture capital-ists and others who want in on the project, although so far, they have remained independent," as reported in a New York Magazine article on Diaspora* (Nussbaum 2010).

Interestingly, in this context of capitalist embeddedness, at least Diaspora*'s initial mode of production, when the founders controlled the project, itself offers a gateway to suspend the copyleft principle and allows capital accumu-lation more directly. Besides using a copyleft license (GNU Affero General Public License), which makes it and all adoptions of it free software and ensures or even extends the alternative mode of production, Diaspora* also used a compatible but different kind of license (MIT/XII license). The differ-ence between both licenses is that the latter is not "viral" or self-protecting. That means Diaspora is allowed "to license general-use components of the Diaspora™ Software (e.g., parsers for standard formats, libraries implementing standard protocols, etc.)" not protected by copyleft (Diaspora* 2011b). Indeed, the software code cannot be used directly for proprietary and profit-generating reasons, although indirectly it can (Fitzgerald 2006, de Laat 2005).

The preceding evaluation of Diaspora* has shown that the project and its alternative mode of production are open to be exploited by capitalist modes of production and capital strategies in the informational age (Chopra and Dexter 2006).

Diaspora* performs practically an alternative concept of privacy that protects users from commodification, but at the same time does not aim at an alternative to a possessive-individualistic privacy notion. As such, this is not contradictory and may rest with Diaspora*'s multi-faceted – wilfully or not – embeddedness within capitalist structures that are dominant in society and remain dominant in people's minds. However, in order to strengthen the alternative quality of Diaspora* and other non-commercial SNSs, the privacy issue and its possessive individualistic capitalist coinage should be rethought and not simply be permitted to enter the discourse about social media.

5   Conclusion

Diaspora* challenges commodity production; hence, it challenges capital accumulation in the realm of SNSs. Its alternative and cooperative mode of production provides, according to ideology theory, a base for thinking about an alternative notion of privacy. I have argued that an alternative notion of privacy demands grounding in alternative material practices since the dominant notion of privacy is associated with commodity exchange. Thinking about an alternative notion of privacy instead of abandoning it is relevant and worthy as privacy, although predominantly occupied by possessive individualistic concepts such as exclusion and private property, also represents the basal human need of individuality that cannot be meaningfully denied by any alternative form of society. As far as I can see, there is no positive Marxist theory of privacy and I cannot provide one here. Marx's focus on a negative critique of capitalism first and foremost aims to abolish social structures that inhibit human potentials and creativity. Following this tradition, Fuchs (2011b) and Allmer (2011) provide some critical remarks for a socialist notion of privacy. I tried to apply myself Marx's negative critique on capitalist ideology and private property to privacy, following the often mentioned connection between both of the latter terms.

However, an alternative vision of privacy must contain more than an opposition to societal relations of inequality; rather it should constructively theorise the value of privacy alternatively and based on a "social conception of individuality" (Pateman 1989, 136). It is an important theoretical task to reflect on an alternative relation between the individual and society and various approaches that take seriously the critique of individualistic privacy notions are taking this path (for instance: Solove 2008, 91–98; Cohen 2012). Unfortunately, these approaches do not engage with Marx's profound analysis of capitalist domination structures. In his fetish analysis, Marx has shown that the individual, following the commodity exchange induced assumption that he or she owes nothing to society, cannot get rid of society. Society asserts itself behind individuals' backs and predetermines their behaviour. Accepting and consciously shaping sociality would be the better option. Taking privacy as an individual claim that excludes others and is raised against society from the outset thus makes no sense at all. Privacy can only be a "societal license" (Etzioni 1999, 196). It is a collective task on how best to satisfy individual privacy needs, such as a home, being alone, silence, reflection, recreation, freedom of expression and decision-making, personal and intimate relations, trust and respect, secrecy, and protection from harm. Pure subjective control theories of privacy should be rejected. Instead, comprehensive democratic structures are required to enable individuals to effectively shape their privacy license in association with others. However, privacy is then not my property and I cannot exchange it and contract it out; it is then a collectively achieved individual value that I can only claim as a member of society. Understanding privacy as an aspect of self-possession then makes no sense. It should be conceptualised as an inalienable collective right.

Objective notions of privacy as an outcome of conscious association are needed, and Diaspora* has practically developed one: it is based on the idea of privacy for SNS users that challenges economic surveillance. As a consequence, the idea of the exploitation of users and the commodification of data, as done by Facebook and Google+, is rejected. Contributors to Diaspora* are associating themselves consciously, not mediated by commodity exchange, but on behalf of copyleft. They have created an objective notion of privacy in and through their practices. This is vital since a basal assumption of Marx was that there would be no individuality, freedom, autonomy, and privacy as long as there is systematic exploitation and class domination in society. It turns out that what is easier to accept as a starting point for theory, i.e. a societal concept of privacy, is much harder to achieve for Diaspora*, although some consequences of this concept are already realised in Diaspora*'s opposition to exploitation. Diaspora* provides an alternative to privacy commodification and user exploitation, but its struggle is fought out on the ideological battlefield of privacy which is not a neutral one, and is rather predetermined by possessive individualistic thinking that objectively contradicts Diaspora*'s alternative goals. Diaspora* refers to ownership and individual control exactly because these are the most powerful means of action in capitalism. I have introduced views, such as informational exceptionalism, that welcome changes in the intangible mode of production, but do not challenge capital accumulation in general. Sticking to possessive individualistic premises, albeit in terms of privacy, may ultimately refer to an immanent transformation of capitalism that reproduces the overall system rather than to a real alternative to it.

The challenge for a Marxist theory of privacy and for alternative social media is to thoroughly disentangle privacy from private property (Goldring 1984, 321f.) in such a way that privacy neither appears as a commodity itself nor contributes to the ideological premises of commodity production and capital accumulation. A material base for such thinking can already be found in Diaspora*, copyleft, and projects of a similar nature.

References

Adorno, Theodor W. 1972. Society. In *The Legacy of the German Refugee Intellectuals*, edited by Robert Boyers. New York: Schocken.

Adorno, Theodor W. 2002. *Introduction to Sociology*. Stanford, CA: Stanford University Press.

Allmer, Thomas. 2011. A Critical Contribution to Theoretical Foundations of Privacy Studies. *Journal of Information, Communication and Ethics in Society* 9 (2): 83–101.

Andrew, Edward. 1985. Inalienable Right, Alienable Property and Freedom of Choice: Locke, Nozick and Marx on the Alienability of Labour. *Canadian Journal of Political Science* 18 (3): 529–550.

Barbrook, Richard. 1998. The Hi-Tech Gift Economy. *First Monday* Special Issue 3. http://www.firstmonday.org/htbin/cgiwrap/bin/ojs/index.php/fm/article/view/1517/1432.

Bauwens, Michel. 2006. The Political Economy of Peer Production. *Post-autistic Economics Review* 37: 33–44.

Benkler, Yochai. 2006. *The Wealth of Networks: How Social Production Transforms Markets and Freedom*. New Haven: Yale University Press.

boyd, danah. 2007. Social Network Sites: Public, Private, or What? *Knowledge Tree* 13. http://www.danah.org/papers/KnowledgeTree.pdf.

Brenkert, George G. 1979. Freedom and Private Property in Marx. *Philosophy and Public Affairs* 8 (2): 122–147.

Bruns, Axel. 2008. *Blogs, Wikipedia, Second Life, and Beyond: From Production to Produsage*. New York: Peter Lang.

Chopra, Samir and Scott Dexter. 2006. The Political Economy of Open Source Software. Accessed February 25, 2012. http://www.sci.brooklyn.cuny.edu/~sdexter/Pubs/chopra-dexter-TC05-paper.doc.

Christman, John. 1994. *The Myth of Property: Toward an Egalitarian Theory of Ownership.* Oxford: Oxford University Press.

Cohen, Julie E. 2012. *Configuring the Networked Self: Law, Code, and the Play of Everyday Practice.* New Haven: Yale University Press.

Datasilnet. 2011. Questions to Facebook from the Nordic DPA's. Accessed February 25, 2012. http://www.datatilsynet.no/upload/Dokumenter/utredninger%20 av%20Datatilsynet/Letter%20with%20questions%20to%20Facebook%20 from%20nordic%20countries%20endellig.pdf.

Demirović, Alex. 2004. Hegemony and the Paradox of Public and Private. Accessed February 25, 2012. http://www.republicart.net/disc/publicum/demirovic01_en.htm.

Diaspora*. n.d.aaaaaaaaaaaaaaaaaaaaaa. The Diaspora* Project. Accessed February 25, 2012. http://diasporaproject.org/.

Diaspora*. n.d.bbbbbbbbbbbbbbbbbbbbbb. JoinDiaspora* blog entry "What is Diaspora*." Accessed October 23, 2011. http://blog.joindiaspora.com/what-is-dias-pora.html.

Diaspora*. 2010. Flyer about Diaspora*. Accessed February 25, 2012. http://blog.joindi-aspora.com/2010/04/24/awesome-flyers-are-here.html.

Diaspora*. 2011a. Diaspora* blog entry "Diaspora* is Back in Action." Accessed February 25, 2012. http://blog.diasporafoundation.org/page/2.

Diaspora*. 2011b. Diaspora* Contributor Agreement. Accessed February 25, 2012. https://github.com/Diaspora/Diaspora/wiki/New-CLA-12-13-10.

Diaspora*. 2011c. Diaspora* blog entry "Diaspora* Means a Brighter Future for All of Us". Accessed March 6, 2012.http://blog.diasporafoundation.org/page/5.

Diaspora*. 2012. The Official Diaspora* Wiki entry "Why Client Side Encryption is a Bad Idea". Accessed February 25, 2012. https://github.com/Diaspora/Diaspora/wiki/ Why-client-side-encryption-is-a-bad-idea.

van Dijk, Niels. 2010. Property, Privacy and Personhood in a World of Ambient Intelligence. *Ethics and Information Technology* 12 (1): 57–69.

Eagleton, Terry. 1991. *Ideology: An Introduction.* London: Verso.

Ellerman, David. 2005. Translatio Versus Concessio: Retrieving the Debate About Contracts of Alienation with an Application to Today's Employment Contract. *Politics & Society* 33 (3): 449–480.

Engels, Frederick. 1893. Letter to Franz Mehring from July 14, 1893. Accessed February 25, 2012. http://www.marxists.org/archive/marx/works/1893/letters/93_07_14.htm.

Etzioni, Amitai. 1999. *The Limits of Privacy.* New York: Basic Books.

Europe versus Facebook. 2011. Complaints against 'Facebook Ireland Limited'. Accessed February 25, 2012. http://www.europe-v-facebook.org/EN/Complaints/complaints. html.

Facebook. 2011. Statement of Rights and Responsibilities. Accessed March 6, 2012. https://www.facebook.com/legal/terms.

Fitzgerald, Brian. 2006. The Transformation of Open Source Software. *Management Information Systems Quarterly* 30 (3): 587–598.

Fredom Box Foundation. n. d. Flyer about the FreedomBox. Accessed February 25, 2012. http://freedomboxfoundation.org/doc/flyer.pdf.

Fuchs, Christian. 2009. Information and Communication Technologies and Society: A Contribution to the Critique of the Political Economy of the Internet. *European Journal of Communication* 24 (1): 69–87.

Fuchs, Christian. 2011a. Web 2.0, Prosumption, and Surveillance. *Surveillance & Society* 8 (3): 288–309.

Fuchs, Christian. 2011b. Towards an Alternative Concept of Privacy. *Journal of Information, Communication and Ethics in Society* 9 (4): 220–237.

Fuchs, Christian. 2012. The Political Economy of Privacy on Facebook. *Television & New Media* 13 (2): 139–159.

Gavinson, Ruth. 1980. Privacy and the Limits of Law. In *Philosophical Dimensions of Privacy: An Anthology*, edited by Ferdinand Schoeman, 346–402. Cambridge: Cambridge University Press.

Geuss, Raymond. 2001. *Public Goods, Private Goods*. Princeton: Princeton University Press.

Gilliom, John. 2001. *Overseers of the Poor: Surveillance, Resistance, and the Limits of Privacy*. Chicago: University of Chicago Press.

Goldring, John. 1984. Privacy and Property. *The Australien Quarterly* 56 (4): 308–324.

Habermas, Jürgen. 1991. *The Structural Transformation of the Public Sphere: An Inquiry into a Category of Bourgeois Society*. Cambridge: MIT Press.

Haug, Wolfgang Fritz. 1987. Outlines for a Theory of the Ideological. In *Commodity Aesthetics, Ideology and Culture*, edited by Wolfgang Fritz Haug, 59–99. New York: International General.

Haug. 2005. Vorlesungen zur Einführung ins "Kapital". Berlin: Argument.

Hettinger, Edwin C. 1989. Justifiying Intellectual Property. *Philosophy and Public Affairs* 18 (1): 31–52.

Jaggar, Alison. 1983. *Feminist Politics and Human Nature*. Totowa: Rowman & Allanheld.

Kang, Jerry. 1998. Information Privacy in Cyberspace Transactions. *Stanford Law Review* 50 (4): 1193–1294.

Koivisto, Juha and Veikko Pietilä. 1996. Ideological Powers and Resistance: The Contribution of W. F. Haug and Projekt Ideologie-Theorie. *Rethinking Marxism* 9 (4): 40–59.

de Laat, Paul B. 2005. Copyright or Copyleft?: An Analysis of Property Regimes for Software Development. *Research Policy* 34 (10): 1511–1532.

Laudon, Kenneth C. 1996. Markets and Privacy. *Communications of the ACM* 39 (9): 92–104.

Lessig, Lawrence. 2002. Privacy as Property. *Social Research* 69 (1): 247–269.

Litman, Jessica. 2000. Information Privacy/Information Property. *Stanford Law Review* 52 (5): 1283–1313.

Lyon, David. 1994. *The Electronic Eye: The Rise of Surveillance Society*. Minneapolis: University of Minnesota Press.

Lyon, David. 2005. *Surveillance Society: Monitoring Everyday Life*. Buckingham: Open University Press.

Macpherson, Crawford B. 1962. *The Political Theory of Possessive Individualism: Hobbes to Locke*. Oxford: Clarendon.

Macpherson, Crawford B. 1978. The Meaning of Property. In *Property: Mainstream and Critical Positions*, edited by Crawford B. Macpherson, 1–13. Toronto: University of Toronto Press.

Marsch, Heather. 2012. A Proposal for Governance: Privacy and Transparency. Accessed February 25, 2012. http://wlcentral.org/node/2445.

Marx, Gary T. 2012. Foreword: Privacy Is Not Quite Like the Weather. In *Privacy Impact Assessment*, edited by David Wright and Paul de Hert, v–xiv. Dordrecht: Springer.

Marx, Karl. 1849/2006. Wage-labour and Capital. In *Wage-labour and Capital & Value, Price, Profit*. New York: International Publishers.

Marx, Karl. 1857–58/1983. Grundrisse der Kritik der Politischen Ökonomie. In *Marx Engels Werke (MEW)*, Band 43. Berlin: Dietz. English translation accessed February 25, 2012. http://www.marxists.org/archive/marx/works/download/Marx_Grundrisse.pdf.

Marx, Karl. 1859/1909. *A Contribution to the Critique of Political Economy*. Chicago: Charles H. Kerr & Company.

Marx, Karl. 1867/1976. *Capital: A Critique of Political Economy: Volume One*. Middlesex: Penguin.

Marx, Karl. 1885/1992. *Capital: A Critique of Political Economy: Volume Two*. Middlesex: Penguin.

Marx, Karl. 1845/1998. Theses on Feuerbach. In *The German Ideology Including Theses on Feuerbach and Introduction to the Critique of the Political Economy*, 569–571. Amherst: Prometheus.

Marx, Karl and Frederick Engels. 1845–46/1998. The German Ideology. In *The German Ideology Including Theses on Feuerbach and Introduction to the Critique of the Political Economy*, 27–658. Amherst: Prometheus.

McGeveran, William. 2009. Disclosure, Endorsement, and Identity in Social Marketing. *University of Illinois Law Review* 2009 (4): 1105–1166.

Moglen, Eben. 2003. The dotCommunist Manifesto. Accessed March 20, 2012. http://emoglen.law.columbia.edu/my_pubs/dcm.html.

Moglen, Eben. 2010. Freedom in the Cloud: Software Freedom, Privacy, and Security for Web 2.0 and Cloud Computing. Accessed February 25, 2012. http://www.software-freedom.org/events/2010/isoc-ny/FreedomInTheCloud-transcript.html.

Moor, James H. 1997. Towards a Theory of Privacy in the Information Age. *Computers and Society* 27 (3): 27–32.

Moore, Adam D. 2008. Defining Privacy. *Journal of Social Philosophy* 39 (3): 411–428.

Munzer, Stephen R. 2005. Property. In *The Shorter Routledge Encyclopedia of Philosophy*, edited by Edward Craig, 858–861. London: Routledge.

Nock, Steven. 1993. *The Costs of Privacy: Surveillance and Reputation in America*. New York: de Gruyter.

Nussbaum, Emily. 2010. Defacebook: Four Young Friends Who Are Out to Create a Very Different Sort of Social Network. *New York Magazine*, September 26, 2010. Accessed February 25, 2012. http://nymag.com/news/features/establishments/68512/.

Papacharisi, Zizi. 2010. Privacy as a Luxury Commodity. *First Monday* 15 (8). Accessed February 25, 2012. http://firstmonday.org/htbin/cgiwrap/bin/ojs/index.php/fm/article/viewArticle/3075/2581.

Pateman, Carole. 1989. *The Disorder of Women: Democracy, Feminism, and Political Theory*. Stanford: Stanford University Press.

Pateman, Carole. 2002. Self-ownership and Property in the Person: Democratization and a Tale of Two Concepts. *Journal of Political Philosophy* 10 (1): 20–53.

Pateman, Carole and Charles W. Mills. 2007. *Contract and Domination*. Cambridge: Polity.

Pedersen, J. Martin. 2010a. Free Culture in Context: Property and the Politics of Free Software. *The Commoner* 14: 49–136.

Pedersen, J. Martin. 2010b. Free Software as Property. *The Commoner* 14: 211–286.

Raynes-Goldie, Kate. 2010. Aliases, Creeping, and Wall Cleaning: Understanding Privacy in the Age of Facebook. *First Monday* 15 (1). Accessed February 25, 2012. http://firstmonday.org/htbin/cgiwrap/bin/ojs/index.php/fm/article/view/2775/2432.

Rehmann, 2007. Ideology Theory. Historical Materialism 15 (4): 211–239.

Römer, Peter. 1978. *Entstehung, Rechtsform und Funktion des kapitalistischen Privateigentums*. Köln: Pahl-Rugenstein.

Roos, Jerome. 2011. The Global Square: An Online Platform for Our Movement. Accessed February 25, 2012. http://roarmag.org/2011/11/the-global-square-an-online-platform-for-our-movement/.

Rössler, Beate. 2001. *Der Wert des Privaten*. Frankfurt am Main: Suhrkamp.

Samuelson, Pamela. 2000. Privacy as Intellectual Property? *Stanford Law Review* 52 (5): 1125–1173.

Sevignani, Sebastian. 2013. The Commodification of Privacy on the Internet. *Science and Public Policy* 40 (6): 733–739.

Sevignani, Sebastian. 2016. *Privacy and Capitalism in the Age of Social Media*. New York: Routledge.

Shepherd, Tamara. 2012. Persona Rights for User-generated Content: A Normative Framework for Privacy and Intellectual Property Regulation. tripleC 10 (1): 100–113.

Smythe, Dallas W. 2006. On the Audience Commodity and Its Work. In *Media and Cultural Studies: Keyworks*, edited by Durham G. Meenakshi and Douglas Kellner, 230–256. Malden: Blackwell.

Söderberg, Johan. 2002. Copyleft Vs. Copyright: A Marxist Critique. *First Monday* 7 (3–4). Accessed February 25, 2012. http://www.firstmonday.org/htbin/cgiwrap/bin/ojs/index.php/fm/article/viewArticle/938/860.

Sofsky, Wolfgang. 2008. *Privacy: A Manifesto*. Princeton: Princeton University Press.

Solove, Daniel J. 2008. *Understanding Privacy*. Cambridge: Harvard University Press.

Stalder, Felix. 2002. Opinion: Privacy Is Not the Antidote to Surveillance. *Surveillance & Society* 1 (1): 120–124.

Stallman, Richard M. 2010. Copyleft: Pragmatic Idealism. In *Free Software, Free Society: Selected Essays of Richard M. Stallman*, 129–131. Boston: Free Software Foundation.

Tavani, Herman T. 2008. Informational Privacy: Concepts, Theories, and Controversies. In *The Handbook of Information and Computer Ethics*, edited by Kenneth Einar Himma and Herman T. Tavani, 131–164. Hoboken: Wiley.

Varian, Hal R. 1997. Economic Aspects of Personal Privacy. In *Privacy and Self-regulation in the Information Age*, edited by National Telecommunications and Information Administration (NTIA). Washington: NTIA.

Wacks, Raymond. 2010. *Privacy. A Very Short Introduction*. Oxford: Oxford University Press.

Warren, Samuel and Louis Brandeis. 1890. The Right to Privacy. In *Philosophical Dimensions of Privacy: An Anthology,* edited by Ferdinand Schoeman, 75–103. Cambridge: Cambridge University Press.

Westin, Alan. 1967. *Privacy and Freedom*. New York: Atheneum.

Wolf, Marty. J., Keith W. Miller, and Frances S. Grodzinsky. 2009. On the Meaning of Free Software. *Ethics and Information Technology* 11 (4): 279–286.

Wong, Phil. 2010. Conversations About the Internet #5: Anonymous Facebook Employee. Accessed February 25, 2012. http://therumpus.net/2010/01/conversations-about-the-Internet-5-anonymous-facebook-employee/3/.

Žižek, Slavoj, ed. 1995. *Mapping Ideology*. London: Verso.

CHAPTER 14

"A Workers' Inquiry 2.0": An Ethnographic Method for the Study of Produsage in Social Media Contexts*

Brian A. Brown and Anabel Quan-Haase

1   **Web 2.0 and Critical Theory**

User-generated content (UGC) and Web 2.0 sites and services have unleashed a torrent of creativity, ingenuity, and generosity on the part of their participants, who daily post, comment, and update content on sites such as Facebook, Twitter, and Flickr. On Web 2.0 environments a shift has occurred in how individuals communicate with one another through the sharing of thoughts, ideas, likes, and dislikes. The rising popularity of Web 2.0 sites and services is at the centre of this shift and also shows no signs of abating. Data from 2010 indicates that email is being substituted – at least in Canada – for Web 2.0 services (Moretti 2010). In the 13–17 and 18–24 age groups, a total of 77% and 82%, respectively, are now using Facebook more than email. In these digital environments, 'users' become active participants, producing massive amounts of content free of the wage relation. What makes the study of unwaged immaterial labour, or what Bruns (2008) refers to as produsage, interesting is that 'users', a complete misnomer, are willing to produce content at no cost to the owners of these domains at the same time as these sites generate massive profits.

Bruns (2008) coined produsage in an attempt to differentiate between the industrial mode of production and the mode of 'production' responsible for the creation of digital content in Web 2.0 environments. According to Bruns (2008), the mode of produsage is "built on iterative, evolutionary development models in which often very large communities of participants make a number of usually very small, incremental changes to the established knowledge base,

*   The present study has benefitted from support given to Anabel Quan-Haase by the Academic Development Fund and Social Science Alumni Research Award, Western University and to Brian A. Brown by the Provincial Government of Ontario through two Ontario Graduate Scholarships 2009–2010 and 2010–2011. We thank Ahmad Kamal and two anonymous reviewers for their comments and suggestions.

thereby enabling a gradual improvement in quality which – under the right conditions – an nonetheless outpace the speed of production development in the conventional, industrial model" (1). Various terms have been proposed to describe the nature and dynamics of this new form of work. Building on contributions made by Lazzarato (1996) in his coining of the term 'immaterial labour' and Hardt and Negri's amplification of the concept in *Empire* (2000), Terranova offers the concept of "free labour" (2004) as a term meant to describe all of the unwaged immaterial labour undertaken by Internet 'users'. Immaterial labour 2.0 (Coté and Pybus 2007), and informational labour (Fuchs 2011) have also been introduced as new concepts to describe these changes. What these concepts emphasize is that the absence of the wage relation does not negate the productive capacities of Web 2.0 'users' nor does it preclude the presence of an exploitative relation. Expanding on the groundbreaking work of Smythe (1977), critical theorists Cohen (2008) and Fuchs (2009, 2011) argue that Web 2.0 sites and services are highly exploitative in that they profit from the work of 'users' and do not offer a wage in return for this labour. In fact, the above authors rightly stress that the absence of a wage actually intensifies these exploitative relations.

Part of the complexity of this situation and relationship is that we have yet to adequately grasp how the 'users' of Web 2.0 sites and services perceive their place in this socio-economic system. The study of the mode of produsage and of the unwaged immaterial labour taking place therein, then, requires an appropriate set of methods through which workers' perceptions and opinions might be uncovered. Such a method can serve as the starting point to increase produser awareness of how their contributions are part of a new relationship between owners and workers unique to social media environments, yet still based on the exploitation of labour prevalent in the industrial era. Current methodologies, however, do not do justice to the complex relations that exist between Web 2.0 produsers, the sense of community engendered by the mode of produsage, and the exploitative relations between these communities and the owners of the sites. Moreover, a new complexity emerges in the study of produsage through the intimate links that obtain between produsers and the artefacts they produse. Thus, this chapter suggests that with each modification to the mode of production, there arises a need to develop new methodologies adapted to the particularities of these changed circumstances. The mode of produsage characteristic of Web 2.0 signals the need for such alterations. In turn and below, we detail the adaptations required to one research method of particular importance to critical communications scholars working within the Marxist tradition.

We propose a new ethnographic method called "A Workers' Inquiry 2.0" for the study of the mode of produsage taking place in social media contexts. The proposed method is based on Marx's 'A Workers' Inquiry', the thinking and methods of Italian autonomists, and recent critical theory of Web 2.0. To show the applicability and usefulness of the proposed method, in Section 2 of this chapter we compare it to Marx's method of "A Workers' Inquiry." Section 3 demonstrates the alterations made by autonomists to Marx's original method and discusses the links between this method and participatory action research (PAR). In Section 4, we explain the theoretical lineage that underlies the mode of produsage and address some of the criticisms of one of its central tenets. In Section 5, we analyse how the proposed method of "A Workers' Inquiry 2.0" adapts Marx's and the autonomists' method to the Web 2.0 environment. This section consists of a case study and a critical examination of the mode of produsage as it occurs on Flickr, one of the largest photo-sharing communities on the Internet. In Section 6, we suggest that the mode of produsage – and the central place of the produser within it – necessitates a re-consideration of the value – economic, personal, and social – of the product or artefact created through labour. Central to this section is a discussion of the close and often personal link between produsers and the artefacts, or content, they contribute to these sites. Section 7 compares the proposed method with other approaches and outlines its strengths and weaknesses. Finally, in Section 8, we conclude with a discussion of the value of employing the tenets outlined in a 'A Workers' Inquiry 2.0' to concerns regarding the mode of produsage, cyber capitalism, and the processes of monetizing produser-generated content.

2   Marx's "A Workers' Inquiry"

In 1880, Karl Marx published a list of one hundred and one questions in *La Revue Socialiste*. *La Revue Socialiste* was a publication that served the industrial proletariat of France in the late nineteenth century. Known as "A Workers' Inquiry," (1938/1880) the questions were divided into four untitled subsections that dealt with different facets of the labouring context in that era. The questions Marx asked to the workers were designed to assess the level of exploitation within the industrial factories of France and to make workers conscious of their own exploitation. In this way, 'A Workers' Inquiry' was an attempt to obtain a holistic picture of the social, technical, and political dynamics occurring in the workplace (Wright 2002), so as to

> make the worker aware of his own predicament in capitalist society, to
> cut through the fog of illusions and habitual responses and fictions which
> prevent the worker from understanding his social world, and by thus
> making the worker conscious of his predicament giving him a chance to
> solve it.
>
> BURNHAM, SHACHTMAN, and SPECTOR 1938, 1

By making the worker aware of his predicament, Marx's questions were inherently political, drafted to rouse the anger of labourers, help the workers to realize the extent of their exploitation, and, as this realization grew, ultimately motivate them to take action.

The editors of *The New International*, which republished Marx's 'A Workers' Inquiry', argue that "[w]ith the changes in industrial production during the past half-century, certain of these questions in their given form have become archaic. But no one would find difficulty in modifying them in such a manner as to bring them up to date" (Burnham, Shachtman, and Spector 1938, 1). What the editors of *The New International* were signalling is not that the key tenets of the methodology were archaic, out-dated, or flawed, but rather that as the struggles between capital and labour change the form and content of our modes of production, our methods of study must change along with them. Hence, if our methodologies are to keep pace with the evident changes in the labour process, then they too must be adapted and updated so as to take into account these changed circumstances. In the mid-1950s, Italian autonomists did just that and it is to the modifications they made to Marx's 'A Workers' Inquiry' that we now shift our focus.

3   Autonomist Co-Research & Participatory Action Research

Beginning in the 1950s, Italian autonomist Marxists[1] had similar desires to that of Marx's, but found themselves in distinctively different historical circumstances. While the mode and relations of production had changed significantly (see: Bologna 1980; Wright 2002; Negri 1989), the need to speak with and consult

---

1   Autonomist Marxism is a branch of Marxist philosophy that emphasizes the priority, creativity, and initiative of labour in its relation to capital. While capital relies on labour as the source of profit, labour has the skill and knowledge to organize its productive activities free of the capitalist relation. It is, then, potentially autonomous. Nowhere is the potential autonomy of labour more evident than on the self-organized, self-managed, and self-directed networks of Web 2.0 sites and services.

workers so as to gain insight into the technical and political circumstances of
the workplace remained a central concern for autonomists. Adapting their
methods of gathering information regarding the level of exploitation in the
factories of Italy and the consciousness of the workers toiling therein was
therefore necessary. Taking a much more direct approach than Marx, autonomists infiltrated the industrial factories – sometimes even got jobs therein –
and conducted their research alongside the workers and from within the
factory itself.

To adapt the existing methods to the new circumstances, autonomist
Marxists developed co-research (Negri 2008, 162–163).[2] Like "A Workers'
Inquiry," the aim of co-research is to gather information about the conditions
of workers through surveys, observations, and interviews, to create awareness
in the workers themselves regarding their exploitation, and, by doing so, giving
them the opportunity to do something about it. One of the key advantages of
co-research is that it begins on the shop floor and is premised on the political
organization and radicalization of the workers' consciousness. By infiltrating
the factories, speaking with workers directly, asking them questions through
interviews, having them complete surveys, getting their impressions of their
working conditions, observing worker behaviour first-hand, and, finally, trying
to identify within it strategies or tactics that could be leveraged in the service
of liberating the workers from the exploitation exacted upon them, autonomists were following in the tradition established by Marx's "A Workers' Inquiry,"
but modified that tradition to suit the unique attributes of their time and
place.

Antonio Negri, one of the leading figures of autonomist Marxism, offers a
succinct summation of the practice of co-research. His is one of the clearest
treatments regarding the procedural aspects of the methodology and has the
advantage of drawing parallels between co-research and Marx's "A Workers'
Inquiry," while at the same time acknowledging the differences between them:

> In terms of practice, 'co-research' simply meant using the method of
> inquiry as a means of identifying the workers' levels of consciousness and
> awareness among workers of the processes in which they, as productive
> subjects, were engaged. So one would go into a factory, make contact with
> the workers, and, together, with them, conduct an inquiry into their con-
> ditions of work; here co-research obviously involves building a descrip-

---

2 For overviews of co-research, its contemporary uses, and the attempts to organize struggles
   against exploitation from a variety of perspectives see: Malo de Molina 2004a, 2004b;
   Situaciones Colectivo 2003, 2005; Precarias a la Derive 2004; Brophy 2006.

tion of the productive cycle and identifying each worker's function within that cycle; but at the same time it also involves assessing the levels of exploitation which each of them undergoes. It also involves assessing the workers' capacity for reaction – in other words, their awareness of their exploitation in the system of machinery and in relation to the structure of command. Thus, as the research moves forward, co-research builds possibilities for struggle in the factory.

NEGRI 2008,162–163

One of the central parallels between Marx's "A Workers' Inquiry" and co-research is the concentration on the factory as the central site of study. Both methods focus on conducting research with individuals who work within the physical infrastructure of a factory in the hopes of making the conditions of their exploitation overt and, ultimately, leading toward changing these conditions. Marx contacted the workers via a publication distributed to the factories. By contrast, co-researchers went directly to the sites of production and infiltrated the factory in order to obtain information regarding the level of exploitation and the preparedness of the workers to struggle against it. Because large numbers of workers were concentrated in geographically specific locations – working en masse at regular and predictable hours, and on jobs that could be observed or described first hand – the factory was the obvious place to start any inquiry into labour relations.

Co-research as practiced by autonomists closely resembles what has come to be known as participatory action research (PAR) or action research. Both methodologies emphasize the active role of the researcher and the individuals, groups, and communities that participate in the co-creation of actionable knowledge. One of the central differences, however, between the two is that co-research maintains its focus on the factory, while action research expands the scope of research locales into communities, schools, and clinics (Fals-Borda and Rahman 1991; Barnsley and Ellis 1992). Similar to co-research, in action research, individuals in the community or institution under investigation are actively involved in establishing the goals and directions of the research, but are also involved throughout the entire research process – including the presentation of the findings and the implications of these for the community or group. Action research is often contrasted with other research approaches, where research participants are not engaged in all phases of the study and members of organizations and communities are viewed as passive (Whyte et al. 1990). Another similarity between co-research and action research is that they both try to develop programs-based research findings acquired through direct interactions and conversations with individuals, groups, and institutions (Barnsley and Ellis 1992). Similar to co-research, the objectives of action research "go beyond the creation of knowledge. The litera- ture emphasizes that PAR includes an educative function which raises the consciousness of its participants and a plan for action to improve the quality of their lives" (Cassano and Dunlop 2005). Both co-research and action research are methods that recognize the importance of applying unique approaches to unique contexts so as to gain new insight and formulate rele- vant conclusions and actionable strategies (Whyte 1990). It is the problems presented by the contemporary labouring context that force us to once again change our strategies. "A Workers' Inquiry 2.0" draws inspiration from the above methodological lineages, but is focused on a unique productive locale. We discuss next how changes to the nature of labour itself and the locales where labour takes place impact where and how an inquiry into the social and political dynamics of a relatively new labouring context might occur. These changes are conceptualized under the heading of immaterial labour and the mode of produsage.

4   Immaterial Labour, the Mode of Produsage, and the Role of the Produser

Similar to, yet fundamentally different from, the owners of industrial factories, the owners of Web 2.0 sites and services also depend on legions of workers to produce the outputs that get turned into profit for them and their sharehold- ers. There exist, however, significant differences between these two exploit- ative relationships. The differences are best explained by recourse to a better understanding of the concept of *immaterial labour* (Lazzarato 1996) and what Bruns (2008) calls the *mode of produsage*. In what follows, then, we discuss the concept of immaterial labour, its critiques, and its relation to the mode of produsage. This theoretical lineage informs the proposed methodology of "A Workers' Inquiry 2.0" by placing an emphasis on the nature of the artefacts produced/prodused, the close and personal interrelationship between workers and these artefacts, and the conspicuous absence of the wage relation within the mode of produsage.

4.1   *Immaterial Labour*
Immaterial labour is a concept coined by Maurizio Lazzarato (1996) in an attempt to describe the changes in the nature of labour that were taking place at the end of the twentieth and beginning of the twenty-first century. For him, immaterial labour is split into two different kinds of labour related to, but

distinct from, industrial production. Lazzarato identifies as the defining characteristics of his concept on the one hand, the labour that produces the informational content of a commodity and on the other, the labour that produces the cultural content of the commodity. These two types of labour result in no physical or tangible end product, but rather create the language, symbols, images, and ideas that adhere to commodities (Lazzarato 1996). For instance, producing the informational content of a commodity refers to the activities that are needed to explain the functioning, purpose, and/or legalities of a particular product. The Terms of Service (TOS) for one of the popular social networking sites (SNSs),[3] or one of the dense and multilingual instruction booklets that accompany any digital gadget sold on the market, are good examples of the labour required to produce the informational content of a commodity. The labour required to produce the cultural content of a commodity is described by Lazzarato as "the kinds of activities involved in defining and fixing cultural and artistic standards, fashions, tastes, consumer norms, and, more strategically, public opinion" (Lazzarato 1996, 133). This work is done primarily by advertising agencies, public relations firms, institutions of the mass media, and all of the photographers, copy and film editors, technicians, engineers, etc. that support this kind of cultural production. In *Empire* (2000), Hardt and Negri expand upon Lazzarato's initial formulation of the theory of immaterial labour by adding "a third type of immaterial labour [that] involves the production and manipulation of affect and requires (virtual or actual) human contact, labour in the bodily mode" (Hardt and Negri 2000, 293). This form of immaterial labour is characteristic of those persons working in the service industries where producing a sense of satisfaction, a feeling of well-being, contentment, or frustration are the primary outcomes of one's labour.

Despite the importance of the concept in its description of a relatively new mode of production, from the beginning, the theory of immaterial labour has been wrought by controversy and debate. The major point of contention regarding the concept of immaterial labour revolves around the qualifier "immaterial." These criticisms mainly address two shortcomings of the theory as put forth by Lazzarato and amended by Hardt and Negri. The first is that the

---

3   The extent of the work needed to create the informational content of an immaterial commodity is exemplified by Facebook's privacy rules, which have been critiqued because of their length being comparable to that of the United States Constitution. Navigating the complexity of these rules and regulations is not made easier by Facebook's "Help Center," which is meant to assist members, in that it has more than 45,000 'explanatory' words (Privacy Commissioner of Canada 2009).

labour that produces the informational, cultural, and affective content of a commodity still requires the application of material body and mind to the tasks at hand. Immaterial labour, then, necessarily contains within it a material essence and this materiality requires more attention than the above authors have devoted to it. The second major criticism has to do with Hardt and Negri's (2004) characterization of immaterial labour as hegemonic in the contemporary era. That is, according to Hardt and Negri immaterial labour "has become *hegemonic in qualitative terms* [in that it] has imposed a tendency on other forms of labour and society itself. Immaterial labour, in other words, is today in the same position that industrial labour was 150 years ago" (Hardt and Negri 2004, 109; emphasis in the original).

In the above explanation, Hardt and Negri attempt to qualify their use of immaterial labour by defending it against the critiques that claim it all too quickly elides the persistence of material forms of industrial production, especially those pushed to areas of the 'global south'. In response to these criticisms, the authors argue that

> This does not mean that there is no more industrial working class whose calloused hands toil with machines or that there are no more agricultural workers who till the soil. It does not even mean that the numbers of such workers has decreased globally. What it means, rather, is that the qualities and characteristics of immaterial production are tending to transform the other forms of labour and indeed society as a whole.
>
> HARDT and NEGRI 2004, 65

While these debates rage on, there is no doubt that Lazzarato and Hardt and Negri have identified a number of core characteristics representative of a relatively new labouring context that is having an increasing impact on the working lives of many individuals.[4] While admittedly problematic, the concept of immaterial labour does go a long way in explicating some of the more consequential changes to have taken place in the nature and form of labour for large numbers of workers around the world. These changes should not be considered in isolation, but need to be thought of in their relationship to the industrial mode of production (Castells and Hall 1994). This necessitates that we further explore and continue to question the

---

4   Recent reports in the media on working conditions at electronics manufacturing facilities in Asia and Latin America highlight the close interplay between immaterial and material labour (Duhigg and Barboza 2012) as well as the political potentials that continue to exist within these industrialized domains.

meaning of the concept and examine more carefully how it is related not only to industrialized labour, but also to its unwaged variant known succinctly as produsage.

4.2   The Mode of Produsage, The Produser and The Wage Relation

Drawing inspiration from the work of Toffler (1981) and his concept of the prosumer, Bruns grasps the unique position of the misnomic 'user' and the work that s/he does on Web 2.0 sites and services via his hybrid concepts of the Prod-User and Prod-Usage. According to Bruns (2008),

> Produsers engage not in a traditional form of content production, but are instead involved in *produsage* – the collaborative and continuous building and extending of existing content in pursuit of further improvement. Participants in such activities are not producers in a conventional, industrial sense, as that term implies a distinction between producers and consumers which no longer exists; the artefacts of their work are not products existing as discrete, complete packages...; and their activities are not a form of production because they proceed based on a set of preconditions and principles that are markedly at odds with the conventional industrial model.
>
> BRUNS 2008, 21

By leveraging the "techno-social affordances" (Bruns 2008, 19) of distributed networks, the mode of produsage and the produsers responsible for the evident efficiencies made possible by these affordances, do not require, nor want, a boss to scientifically manage their labour (Taylor 1915), organize their activities from above, or hand down orders from on high. This capricious and fickle labour force shows up to 'work' when they want, they concentrate their energies on what they want, work with whom they want, and can walk away from these tasks at any time they see fit. Through these terminological innovations, Bruns emphasizes the produser's active and creative role in the creation and generation of digital *artefacts*. 'Artefact' is the term used by Bruns to describe the dynamic and iterative nature of digital creations in the contemporary era. This term better emphasizes the ephemeral and inherently dynamic qualities of digital creations than does 'end-product'. Bruns' concepts of produser, produsage, and the artefact are adopted herein because they emphasize the active and creative nature of the work done by content generators on Web 2.0 sites and services. This kind of work is fundamentally different than that done by industrial labourers, but, as is detailed below, there is a common feature that weaves them together.

The owners and shareholders of industrial manufacturing facilities exploit their workers by offering them a disproportionally low wage in exchange for their labour power and time. By paying a wage lower than the amount of capital it generates, the capitalist enterprise extracts a profit from the labour force. It is these profits and, reciprocally, the exploitative relationship that underlies them, which are the lifeblood of capitalist enterprises. Profitable Web 2.0 sites and services operate via recourse to a similar logic. They too are heavily reliant on a workforce to produse the artefacts (including content and site development) that draw a mass audience to the site and, in turn, make a profit. However, these individuals are not offered a wage in return for their labour power and time. This business model depends on selling advertising space to advertisers that are purchasing the ability to ply their wares to a consistent and quantifiable number of eyeballs. Via the concept of the audience commodity, Smythe (1977) filled in the so-called Blind Spot of Western Marxism by arguing that the straightforward "answer to the question – What is the commodity form of mass-produced, advertiser-supported communications under monopoly capitalism? – is audiences and readerships" (2). While this business model has undergone significant changes in the past few years, according to Fuchs (2011) and Cohen (2008), its core characteristics are easily identifiable in the Web 2.0 era. Moreover, the exploitative relationship between owners and workers typical of the industrial mode of production is intensified within the immaterial mode of produsage as a result of the absence of the wage relation. However, what makes this relationship more complex is the quasi-voluntary nature of the engagement in the exploitative relation. On the face of it, participating on social networks is a voluntary act that one enters into without being compelled by force. When the unique attributes of the contemporary communicative environment are taken into consideration, however, characterizing participation as voluntary becomes less convincing. Social networking sites and services have centralized the means of online communication to the extent that not participating in them runs the risk of missing important information and potentially feeling disconnected from certain social groups (Raynes-Goldie 2010). Individuals are compelled, then, to participate on these sites and services at the risk of decreasing their social capital (Ellison, Steinfield, and Lampe 2007), thus making the voluntary nature of them an illusion.

According to Fuchs and Cohen, when compared to the industrial mode of production, the mode of produsage should be considered hyper-exploitative because it does not even offer its legions of workers a wage in exchange for their labour power and time. The exploitation of this workforce is made palpable when the surplus value generated by produsers is considered. In 2005, Rupert Murdoch's News Corp purchased then popular MySpace for $580 million

(Brook 2005). Six years later and in response to a rapid decrease in membership, News Corp sold MySpace at a considerable loss for $35 million (Stelter 2011) – a telling indicator of the value generated by the Web 2.0 audience commodity. In the spring of 2011, LinkedIn, a professional social networking site, went public and netted its owners and investors a combined $8.8 billion (Levy and Spears 2011). Twitter, a micro-blogging service, is estimated to be worth roughly $7.7 billion by secondary markets (Reuters 2011). And finally, Facebook's rumoured initial public offering (IPO) in the spring of 2012 is reportedly valued at nearly $100 billion (Bilton and Rusli 2012; Cellan-Jones 2012). Clearly, the Web 2.0 'audience commodity' is in high demand. The above valuations are based on the vast stores of information prodused by produsers regarding their tastes, likes, predilections, habits, hobbies, and interests stored within these sites and services. All of this personal information results in a highly refined audience commodity. In turn, these sites sell this commodity to advertisers seeking a better return on their investment by micro-marketing their products or services to niches of eyes, ears, and minds that have shown previous interest in the products or services on offer. The pivotal role of the produser in this relationship is emphasized by Fuchs (2011) when he asks us to consider "what would happen if [produsers] would stop using platforms like YouTube, MySpace, and Facebook: the number of [prod-]users would drop, advertisers would stop investments because no objects for their advertising messages and therefore no potential customers for their products could be found, the profits of the new media corporations would drop, and they would go bankrupt" (Fuchs 2011, 298). Additionally, expanding the scope of this analysis to the World Wide Web (WWW) by focusing on Google and the commodities prodused by Google 'users', Fuchs (2012) argues "Google exploits Google users and WWW content producers because their work that serves Google's capital accumulation is fully unpaid" (Fuchs 2012, 44). Thus, when produsers begin generating content and, by doing so, generating value for the site, "in terms of Marxian class theory, this means that they also produce surplus value and are exploited by capital as for Marx productive labour is labour generating surplus" (Fuchs 2009, 30; see also: Cohen 2008; Kleiner and Wyrick 2007). Based on the work of Smythe and according to political economists of Web 2.0 and social media, the relationship between Web 2.0 owner and produser is, therefore, hyper-exploitative because it does not even offer the "user" a wage in exchange for their pivotally important work.

There is nascent evidence that this hyper-exploitative relationship is causing produsers to organize struggles against it. The frequent uproars occurring on social networking sites regarding the violation of one's privacy have time and again resulted in controversy, but these controversies are more often than not understood as having to do with the violation of one's privacy on social networks that are essentially public. The near-exclusive focus on the violation of one's privacy as the cause of these uproars is a mischaracterization and a mistake. A better understanding of these instances of produser uproar is provided by Brown (2013) when he argues that privacy and social networks are conceptually oxymoronic in that adherence to the principles of the former would render pointless the primary purposes of the latter. Therefore, the frequent occurrences of produser uproar regarding the violation of one's privacy on networks that are eminently social are better understood as instances of struggle against the exploitation of the highly personal artefacts prodused by and through the mode of produsage. Undergirding this characterization of these uproars are a long lineage of struggles fought by other unwaged, yet highly productive, groups of individuals such as female domestic labourers (Dalla Costa and James 1973; Huws 2003) and students (Wright 2002; Touraine 1971).

As Bruns (2008) notes above, the social and political dynamics of the mode of produsage are fundamentally different than the industrial factories that Marx and the autonomists concerned themselves with. Moreover, they are also different from the social and political dynamics of domestic labour as well as that of student labour. While exploitation remains an important and salient feature of the mode of production/produsage, the relationships between owner and worker and between workers themselves are fundamentally different in the Web 2.0 era than they were in the industrial era. These differences require that we once again modify our methodologies so as to better understand the unique social and political dynamics of the mode of produsage. While Marx's and the autonomists' goal of creating awareness and also rousing the ire of workers so as to enable them to put a stop to the exploitative circumstances they found themselves in remains a goal of "A Workers' Inquiry 2.0," the context within which this research takes place as well as the context from which the researcher conducts his/her research have changed substantially. The idiosyncrasies of the mode of produsage characteristic of sites like Flickr force us to approach the procedural elements of "A Workers' Inquiry 2.0" with caution and care. These idiosyncrasies must be considered when attempting to undertake a research project inspired by Marx's and the autonomists' methodological lineage. What follows, then, is our attempt to rethink these methods in light of the unique nature of Web 2.0.

In order to do so, three distinctive characteristics specific to the mode of produsage and its relationship to contemporary academic research need to be taken into consideration. The first characteristic of produsage that needs to be addressed in its relation to "A Workers' Inquiry" and co-research is the lack of a distinct, physical, and consistent location from which to recruit potential research subjects. The second characteristic addresses the challenges of subjecting an informal, casual, and leisurely domain such as any number of Web 2.0 sites and services to the formalities and rigid protocols required of academic research on human subjects. Reconciling the highly formal procedural requirements of ethical research boards at universities with the highly informal communicative norms and cultural practices characteristic of Web 2.0 sites and services necessitates a unique approach. The means and method by which these incongruities were successfully negotiated are addressed below in prong one of "A Workers' Inquiry 2.0." The third characteristic, addressed below in prong two of "A Workers' Inquiry 2.0," has to do with the nature of the artefacts prodused through the mode of produsage. The pivotal role occupied by the produser in the design, functionality, and evolution of these artefacts necessitates further methodological adaptation. It is to the details of these adaptations that we now focus our attention.

5   A Workers' Inquiry 2.0: Prong One – Factory Flickr

We discuss in this section the key tenets of 'A Workers' Inquiry 2.0' and show its applicability to the study of the mode of produsage taking place in social media contexts. We examine the unique challenges of Web 2.0 inquiry and employ a case study and a critical examination of the mode of produsage as it occurs on Flickr to illustrate how the proposed method functions in the field.

5.1   *Location of Contact with Research Participants*
The first characteristic of produsage that needs to be addressed in its relation to "A Workers' Inquiry" and co-research is the lack of a distinct, physical, and consistent location and time from which to recruit potential research subjects. Similar to Marx's and the autonomists' goal of gaining insight into how power relationships circulate throughout the industrial mode of production, in the Web 2.0 era, the need to get a sense of the social and political power relationships that underlie the mode of produsage remains undiminished. However, with no central and consistent geographic location acting as a primary meeting place from which to conduct the research, communicating and engaging with produsers in a similar fashion to Marx and the autonomists is more complex than simply turning up at the factory gates. The openness, highly social, and communicative qualities of Web 2.0 sites and services, though, make the lack of a consistent physical location to contact research participants less of a problem than it appears to be.

The Internet Protocol (IP) address of these sites (i.e., www.flickr.com) resembles the street address of the factories where Marx and the autonomists contacted workers. The IP address is the virtual, yet centralized, meeting place where the produsers responsible for building and maintaining these sites and services assemble. While workers in the industrial era had predefined and pre-dictable work hours, Web 2.0 sites and services consist of a fluid and loosely-connected network of produsers. In the example of Flickr, it is within this space that the work of coding the software via Flickr's open application pro-gramming interface (API), sharing photographs, participating in groups, chat-ting with friends, and commenting on others' images takes place. Vital to the virtual infrastructure of Factory Flickr are communicative channels that not only encourage, but also make natural the inclination to share one's thoughts, ideas, and opinions with other community members. Via internal messaging systems, such as FlickrMail or discussion forums, members chat about what-ever it is they deem to be important, thought provoking, or exciting at that particular moment in time.

Communication amongst Flickr members, then, is the social bedrock of the website. Predictably, the topics, focus, and concentration of the publicly accessible forums are as diverse as the interests and aptitudes of their mem-bers. Ranging from mundane discussions regarding photographic technique to well considered thoughts on the social, cultural, and political impact of digital photography, one thing is certain, for a website dedicated to sharing photographs, Flickr is replete with chatter and banter. "Finding" *some* Flickr members and getting them to talk about photographs, photography, and the various aspects or dimensions of them is not a problem. Finding all of them, however, is a challenge and it is to this challenge that portions of Section 7 of this chapter are focused. Conducting this kind of inquiry as an academic investigation, all the while adhering to the ethical protocols, standards, and formalities of this type of research is also challenging and a different matter entirely.

In sum, this first attribute of "A Workers' Inquiry 2.0" emulates one of the primary methodological features of the research conducted by Marx and the autonomists. Speaking to and with those responsible for produsing the ever-evolving artefacts on Flickr is an irreplaceable element in trying to assess and to dissect the social and political dynamics of Factory Flickr. The opin-ions, thoughts, impressions, ideas, and feelings of these individuals remain a pivotal ingredient in trying to understand the social and political dynam-ics of these domains at the same time as trying to grasp the subjective dimensions of the produsers working within them. The idiosyncrasies of the mode of produsage combined with the ethical requirements of non-medical research on human subjects, however, require a level of planning, strategizing, and understanding that Marx and the autonomists were never forced to consider.

5.2   *Codes of Research Ethics and Social Norms of Web 2.0 Sites*
The second central characteristic has to do with modifying one's methodology so that it remains congruent with the idiosyncrasies of the environment from which research participants are recruited. We suggest the following four steps as a good strategy for recruitment: 1) engage the community in discussion about the topic of interest; 2) approach a select group of participants for more in-depth data collection; 3) obtain informed consent for the interviews, and 4) determine the time and media over which the interview will take place. The goal of this recruitment process is to be inclusive so as to recruit as many respondents as possible, all the while leveraging the communicative advantages of Web 2.0 sites to its benefit. It should be noted that the method described below was developed for Flickr in particular but can be easily adapted to other Web 2.0 domains where produsage occurs as well.

One of the foremost challenges encountered when conducting research on human subjects online is the successful recruitment and retention of research subjects. This is an especially tricky process when Web 2.0 environments are the spaces upon and within which the research is conducted. Web 2.0 sites and services each have their own unique patterns of normalized behaviour that have developed over time and which characterize the quotidian behaviours of their membership. To obtain a better understanding of Flickr's unwritten norms and standards was, in fact, the primary purpose of the research project to which this method applies.[5]

Similar to Marx's method, "A Workers' Inquiry 2.0" asks produsers a list of questions in the hope of gaining insight into their thoughts, feelings, and consciousness regarding their place in the mode of produsage. At the same time and once again similar to Marx's method, this methodology aims to increase the awareness of produsers regarding their own exploitation. As well, much like the process of co-research where researchers would enter the industrial factory, sometimes get a job there, and conduct their research alongside

---

5   The research project for which the 'A Workers' Inquiry 2.0' was originally developed was designed to answer the following question: If, as Hardt and Negri claim (2004, 66), waged immaterial labour is biopolitcal, then what are the biopolitics of unwaged immaterial labour or produsage? Following the example set by Marx and the autonomists, the best way to evaluate the biopolitics of this environment is to try and understand the relationships of power that influence the ways in which individuals act and react within it.

the workers labouring therein, "A Workers' Inquiry 2.0" also encourages the researcher to become a member of the Web 2.0 site within which the research is taking place. This is advantageous because previous involvement in these domains increases familiarity with the unwritten behavioural norms that characterize them, greatly aiding in recruitment of research participants.[6] However, this element of the methodology raises another important ethical consideration that has to be managed with care. As a result of being both a community member and a researcher at the same time, the scholar/community member must negotiate these roles judiciously. The reason being that, if handled awkwardly, the trust of other community members in the scholar might be broken and along with it their willingness to further participate in the research.

Each and every step in designing the methodology and executing the research, therefore, needs to respect the idiosyncratic norms of the particular space if it is to be successful. The initial point of contact is, in this way, ultimately important. If one's initial message and approach is ill fitting, too blunt, or awkward in any way, the thousands upon thousands of potential research participants that populate Web 2.0 sites and services very quickly falls to none. For this particular design, the first step was to recruit research participants from three different groups on Flickr by posting a provocative question to their group discussion forums. The three groups used as sources for the recruitment of research participants were: Flickr Central, Flickr API, and Utata. All three of the chosen groups are designated as "Public – Anyone can join." Importantly, the vast majority of the groups on Flickr are created, administered, organized, and managed by members. They have their own self-authored guidelines that explain what the group is about, what it focuses on, and what one can expect if one were to join it. These guidelines were important elements in selecting the groups as potential sources of research participants because they describe the purpose of the group and by doing so allow the researcher a glimpse, albeit an obstructed one, into the norms of the group in question.

In the subject line of the initial message, a very simple, straightforward, yet suggestive question was asked: "Is Flickr Work?" In the body of the accompanying message, the purposes of the project, the researcher's identity, his institutional affiliation, and the broader contexts of the question were detailed. The provocative nature of the question, as well as the ensuing description, elicited a large number of responses from the members of two of the three chosen

---

6   In this particular instance, the lead author of this chapter had been a member of Flickr for five years before initiation of the research project.

groups.[7] The group that did not respond very well to the initial message is tell-ing of the importance of crafting this initial message so that it adheres to the norms of the group. This is one of the weaknesses of the present methodology and will be addressed more substantively in Section 7 of this article.

The other two groups were better suited to the contemplative nature of the original question and responded to it well. Flickr Central and Utata are both public groups within Flickr that address a plethora of topics, ideas, issues, and elements regarding digital photography and photo-sharing. Their members responded quickly, enthusiastically, and comprehensively to the research question. As with all discussion threads, however, there is a point in time when the conversation runs its course and members move on to different threads so as to think through different ideas and issues. This is the moment when the second step of recruiting research participants should take place. From our experience within these virtual and ever-shifting environments, it is important not to delay sending follow-up requests for interviews because doing so adversely impacts the readiness of potential research subjects to participate further in the project.

Like many social networks, Flickr has an internal email/messaging system called FlickrMail that allows members to contact each other via a more pri-vate form of communication than the group chat forums.[8] Very soon after the threaded discussion ran its course, a private message was sent via FlickrMail to all those persons that responded to the thread. In this private email, they were asked if they were willing to have a more in-depth conversation regarding whether or not the time they spent on Flickr can or should be considered a form of labour and if they ever felt it to be exploitative.

The third step consists of obtaining informed consent, which can be cum-bersome in the context of Web 2.0. Importantly, and somewhat frustratingly, FlickrMail does not allow one to attach files or documents to messages sent to other members making the procedural requirements of ethical research more involved and complicated than they would have been otherwise. The delivery and return of a Letter of Informed Consent that details the purposes of the research, the obligations of the researcher, and the rights of the research sub-ject is an important element to any ethical research. It is also, however, an

---

7 In the FlickrCentral group there was a total of forty-four unique respondents and one-hundred-and-one messages. In Flickr API there was a total of three respondents and three total messages and in Utata there were thirty-five individual respondents and forty-four total messages.

8 When one signs up for a Flickr account, one is automatically given a FlickrMail account as well.

obstacle that disrupts the casual, informal, and natural flow of communication on Web 2.0 sites and services in such a way that threatens the continuing participation of research participants. This is especially the case when the delivery and receipt of such a document is pushed beyond the immediate site of research. The inherently informal, casual, and relaxed norms and mores of Web 2.0 discussion forums – where punctuation, grammar, and sentence structure are often ignored – stand in opposition to the formal and often temporally taxing nature of ethical protocols. There exists a tension between these formal documents and the casual and informal communicative norms associated with Flickr and other Web 2.0 sites and services. It is this tension that threatens the success of conducting research of the sort proposed by "A Workers' Inquiry 2.0."

After a Flickr member agreed to participate in the research project, a second message was sent via FlickrMail asking them for an email address where a Letter of Informed Consent might be delivered. When, and if, this email address was received the Letter of Informed Consent was attached to a message and sent to the given address. This step is particularly sensitive because participants are asked to provide contact information outside of Flickr. Considering that participants may use pseudonyms, aliases, or other nicknames to protect their identity (Raynes-Goldie 2010), it is important to consider that participants may drop out of the study at this point. Upon its return, a third message was drafted and a convenient time and medium over which to conduct semi-structured, open-ended interviews was scheduled.[9]

Conducting the interviews, then, is the fourth and final step in the first prong of "A Workers' Inquiry 2.0." Following the suggestion of the editors of *The New International* which republished Marx's "A Workers' Inquiry" in 1938, these open-ended, semi-structured interviews were inspired by Marx's technique, questions, and goals, yet were adjusted and modified so as to reflect the idiosyncrasies of the mode of produsage characteristic of Flickr and Web 2.0. Interviews varied in length, lasting on average less than an hour and addressed a host of issues all involving the ways in which the Flickr member thought and felt about the time, effort, and energy they expended on the site, their consciousness regarding the exploitation of their labour time and power, and, similar to Marx and the autonomists, their preparedness to do something

---

9   In an attempt to accommodate as many research subjects as possible, it is advisable that each interviewee be given the option of conducting the interview via the media of their choice. In this case telephone, Voice-Over-Internet-Protocol, instant messaging, or email were all used by the researcher to communicate with research subjects.

about that exploitation.[10] As the above steps have detailed, the first prong of 'A Workers' Inquiry 2.0' emulates the methods used by Marx and the autonomists but modifies and adapts their procedures so as to bring them into the contemporary era. Focusing exclusively on the experiences, impressions, and affects of produsers, however, fails to acknowledge one of the most important pieces of information that reflects the members' subjectivity and consciousness. It is to this, or, rather, these artefacts that we now turn our attentions.

6   A Workers' Inquiry 2.0: Prong Two – A New Object of Study

Similar to other Web 2.0 sites and services that leverage the unwaged labour of members, nearly all of the labour required to produse Flickr is self-managed, self-organized, self-motivated, and, because of this, fundamentally different from the mode of industrial production that Marx and the autonomists were researching. From the perspective of business consultants, Tapscott and Williams appreciate the monumental changes that the mode of produsage responsible for Flickr evinces. They comment,

> Flickr provides the basic technology platform and free hosting for photos.... *Users do everything else.* For example, users add all of the content (the photos and captions). They create their own self-organizing classification system for the site.... They even build most of the applications that members use to access, upload, manipulate, and share their content.
>
> TAPSCOTT and WILLIAMS 2006, 38; emphasis added

Echoing the undercurrent of amazement identifiable in Tapscott and Williams' assessment of the mode of produsage, Caterina Fake, co-founder and former owner of Flickr, argues,

> the thing that really makes Flickr Flickr is that *the users invent what Flickr is*. ...[L]ike us, outside developers could build new features and give Flickr new capabilities. In fact, we used the same API as the outside developers, meaning that they had all the same capabilities we had. We hoped that people would build things that we didn't have the time or resources to

---

10   The results of this research project are too involved to adequately address in the available space and are oblique to the central purposes of this chapter. They are, however, dealt with briefly in what follows and in much more detail separately and elsewhere (Brown 2012).

build – like an uploader for Linux or plug-ins for desktop management software and blogging services – and they did. But we also hoped that they would build things that we hadn't thought of – and they definitely did that too.

TAPSCOTT and WILLIAMS 2006, xi; emphasis added

And finally, from the perspective of a Yahoo! executive involved in the purchase of Flickr in 2005 for an estimated US$30 million (Schonfeld, 2005), Bradley Horowitz gushes, "With less than 10 people on the payroll, they had millions of users generating content, millions of users organizing that content for them, tens of thousands of users distributing that across the Internet, and thousands of people not on the payroll actually building this thing,.... That's a neat trick" (Levy 2006). A neat trick indeed, but one predicated on the exploitation of an unwaged workforce that spans the globe. According to Fuchs, "this situation is one of infinite over-exploitation...[or] an extreme form of exploitation" (Fuchs 2011, 298). It is for this very reason that Flickr's produsers were consulted via the methodological foundations provided by Marx and the autonomists. The pivotal place occupied by the produser in the mode of produsage, however, also forces us to reconsider an element that Marx and the autonomists had no reason to contemplate with their investigations of the industrial mode of production.

By "Harnessing the Collective Intelligence" of its membership and by "Treating Users as Co-Developers" (O'Reilly 2005), the owners and administrators of Flickr were more than willing to relinquish their control over the process of developing their photo-sharing utility and let their members do the majority of the heavy lifting required to test, debug, develop new applications, code software, and, of course, upload photographs. As the quotes above suggest, the labour of produsers was (and continues to be) instrumental in the construction and creation of the website. Rather than trying to predict what their members wanted out of the website and devoting scarce temporal and financial resources to untested ends, the owners of Flickr released the source code to the developer community and by doing so enlisted them to hack and code Flickr into existence. They also granted their members a great deal of autonomy and latitude to build and grow the site in whatever way they saw fit. Additionally, the owners of Flickr actively encouraged their produsers to communicate with them via discussion forums and, in paying close attention to what their members were saying, many of the suggestions made by produsers were incorporated into the design and functionality of Flickr by its paid staff. According to one of Flickr's paid software developers, Eric Costello divulges that "User feedback...drove a lot of the decisions about features. We had user forums very early on and people told us what they wanted. ... We do look at numbers, but really we just keep our ears open. We listen to what people say to us on our forums" (Garrett and Costello 2005, 11–24). Hence, Flickr developed in the way it did not because of a corporate hierarchy dictating to wage labourers what was going to be built and scientifically managing the exact manner in which they were going to build it. Rather, by reversing the direction of this command and control structure, the owners and administrators of the site took a very hands-off approach and allowed produsers to build Flickr in their own image.

In short, then, Flickr is a reflection of the subjective wants, needs, desires, and labour of its membership more than it is that of its owners and administrators. While Marx and the autonomists considered the end products produced by industrial labourers as important ingredients in the overall mode of production, they never thought of them as a source of insight or knowledge regarding the social and political dynamics of the workplace or as a reflection of the subjective consciousnesses of those that produced them. For Marx or the autonomists, the end products, whether coal, cars, or typewriters, held no interpretive or hermeneutic value regarding the subjectivities of workers. As Flickr's developmental history indicates, however, the irreplaceable position, contribution, and place of the produsers' subjectivity in the design, functionality, and content stored on the website, indicates that continuing inattention to the artefacts of produsage is a mistake. Ignoring these artefacts omits from consideration valuable information regarding the social and political dynamics of the mode of produsage and the subjective dispositions of those produsers responsible for building Flickr.

We must, therefore, consider these ever-developing artefacts as important indices of the social and political dynamics of the workplace and of the workers' subjectivity, predispositions, inclinations, and consciousness. Marx and the autonomists rightfully ignored this dimension of the end products of industrial labour in their studies. Because the scientific management of an industrial workforce alienates and divorces the workers' head from the products of his/her hands, the links between the subjectivity of the worker and the end product were non-existent. Under these conditions, there was no justifiable reason for Marx or the autonomists to examine these end products with any hope of gaining further insight into the subjectivities of those persons following orders and doing the work of assembling them. The labour of generating the raw content for Flickr – of capturing, uploading, indexing, and annotating the billions of images found therein, of coding new applications and software, and of providing a constant stream of input, feedback, and direction – grants Flickr's membership much more agency in the overall structure and feeling of the website.

In sum, the history of the development of Flickr, much like many Web 2.0 sites and services, was not driven, directed, or scientifically managed in an hierarchical, top-down fashion by the owners or managers of the website. Rather, as the one-time owner of Flickr acknowledged above, the members and produsers of Flickr – their whimsical wants, idiosyncratic desires, playful hacks and remixes, their enthusiasm, but most of all their self-managed, self-organized, and autonomous labour – made Flickr what Flickr is. This photo-sharing social network is and would be nothing without the direction, guidance, and unwaged labour of its membership. Unlike the tedious, monotonous, and highly repetitive industrial production process where workers have no control over what gets built, when it gets built, how it is built, what these products are meant to do, and whose needs they satisfy, the mode of produsage responsible for produsing Flickr is diametrically different. It is this difference that confers upon the prodused artefacts a particularly important hermeneutic value.

One way of approaching this new object of study would be to examine the structure, dynamics, and motivational instruments used by particular groups within Flickr that have been successful in eliciting enthusiastic participation. Utata, for instance, one of the groups on Flickr used as a source of research participants for this project, is an excellent example. With a few simple guide-lines and a request that members be polite, the self-organized and self-motivated unwaged administrators of the group have managed to produse a vibrant and committed community built around the sharing of photographs, thoughts, and ideas. Utata has over twenty thousand members and more than three hundred and seventy-five thousand images uploaded to its group photo-stream. They organize weekly "photo-projects" built around thematically inspired topics combined with particular photographic techniques. Every Thursday, members go on a virtual "photo-walk" with each other. They capture images of the places, faces, and spaces they happen to be, see, or visit that day and upload their favourites to that week's dedicated photostream. There is a group discussion forum where ideas, problems, thoughts, and photographs are discussed politely and in detail. If the conversation gets heated, as it some-times does, there are offerings of virtual cake to one's interlocutor(s) as a ges-ture of good will and support. In short, Utata is a fascinating group that has managed to harness the creative activities of its membership to inspired ends.

Another artefactual corner of the Flickr-verse that merits attention in this regard is an area called The Commons. The Commons began as a joint endeavour between the U.S. Library of Congress (LOC) and Flickr in 2008. The LOC approached Flickr and asked if there was a way to share their archival photo-graphic collection with Flickr's membership and by doing so 'harness their col-lective intelligence' by asking them to add information to the photographs on display. The aim of this project was to augment and increase the profile of the LOC's collection at the same time as increasing the available information regarding this same collection. They did so by bringing their photographic archive to one of the largest groups of individuals interested in photography on the Internet and by simply asking for their assistance. According to the LOC, this project "resulted in many positive yet unplanned outcomes" (Springer et al. 2008, 2).

One of the benefits of using Flickr is that it has an inbuilt tagging system that allows produsers to add descriptive tags to the photographs shared by others. It is "important to note that for the purposes of this pilot, [the LOC] took a very 'hands off' approach to the tags, other than to check for blatantly inappropriate content. (...) There were exceptionally few tags that fell below a level of civil discourse appropriate to such an online forum – a true credit to the Flickr community" (Springer et al. 2008, 18).

The LOC's participation in The Commons was a massive success for both Flickr and the library. They conclude their internal report on the Flickr project by stating that "the overwhelmingly positive response to the digitized historical photographs in the Library's Flickr account suggests that participation in The Commons should continue" (Springer et al. 2008, 33). The success of this project as well as other aspects of Factory Flickr shed much needed light into the social and political dynamics of the space. Once again, unlike the automobiles rolling off the assembly line in the industrial era, the artefacts of produsage allow for a better-informed appreciation of the kinds of subjectivities being prodused and re-prodused via the mode of produsage.

The full results of the research project for which this method was designed are too involved to be dealt with in the available space. Briefly, however, the social and political dynamics of the Flickr-verse are such that, for the most part, those individuals responsible for Flickr's creation and evolution do not consider the time, effort, and energy they expend on the website as a form of labour, nor do they feel exploited by the owners of Flickr. As this article suggests, however, the relationship between the owners and members of Flickr is eminently exploitative. Via mechanisms and systems that tap into Flickr's "altruistic substratum" (Springer et al. 2008, 15), the owners of these sites and services enlist a legion of produsers to do the work of expanding the boundaries of the Flickr-verse by creating the social connections and relationships required to continue its growth. This paradox is one of the primary reasons that research focused on raising the consciousness of produsers regarding their own exploitation is important to undertake and accomplish on Web 2.0 sites and services.

We need to know much more about the virtual gears and cogs of the mode of produsage responsible for these kinds of produser generated artefacts, their

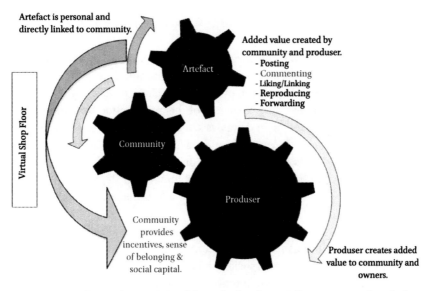

FIGURE 14.1   *Unique characteristics of the mode of produsage influencing research methods.*

inner-workings, and their social dynamics if we are to understand how this organization of labouring bodies and minds differs from its predecessors and the political potentials that these differences make possible. We need, in other words, to continue to engage in serious academic study of how they work, why they work, and where they might be replicated. The above method offers one such approach.

Figure 14.1 shows three key dimensions that lie at the centre of our methodological framework: 1) the artefact, 2) the community of produsers, and 3) the produser her/himself. While Marx and the autonomists took into consideration the worker him/herself, they had no reason to consider the end products (or artefacts) of industrial labour as important elements that contribute to a better understanding of worker subjectivity. As Figure 14.1 indicates, however, in the Web 2.0 era and regarding the mode of produsage, the artefact is an influential and consequential instrument that contributes significantly to the overall dynamics of the mode of produsage. In light of this, 'A Workers' Inquiry 2.0' adopts a two-pronged approach that, much like Marx and the autonomists, begins on the virtual 'shop floor' by speaking with the exploited workers responsible for the produsage of Web 2.0 sites and services, but goes one step further and beyond by also considering the community in which these workers operate, and the artefacts of their labour as hermeneutically significant objects of study that have important details to communicate regarding the social and political dynamics that imbue the means and relations of produsage.

7   Strengths and Weaknesses of "A Workers' Inquiry 2.0"

It is important to not only consider "A Workers' Inquiry 2.0" in the context of the Marxist tradition and methodology, but also to understand its relevance vis-à-vis other methodologies employed in the social sciences. In this section, we discern the strengths and weaknesses of the new method by comparing it with other data collection and analysis techniques available to scholars. Moreover, we show how 'A Workers' Inquiry 2.0' builds on ethnography as practiced by anthropologists, with its emphasis on lived experience and emergence in the field. We also show where 'A Workers' Inquiry 2.0' departs from Marx's 'A Workers' Inquiry' and uniquely addresses concerns that arise within Web 2.0 and produsage.

The Field: The experiences accumulated in the field are central to any ethnography. While ethnography usually consists of living in other cultures or immersing oneself in different social environments, in this case it consists of becoming part of an online community (Kendall 2002). A part of this consists of understanding social meanings and participating in what Brewer describes as "ordinary activities" (Brewe 2000, 10).

Multiple Sources: "A Workers' Inquiry 2.0" relies on multiple sources of information, to a large extent resembling qualitative methodologies employed in the social sciences. It not only collects data from those involved in the mode of produsage through discussions on the forum/groups, interviews, and surveys, but it attempts to go beyond these standard means of gathering information about a phenomenon. Figure 14.2 shows how a critical engagement with

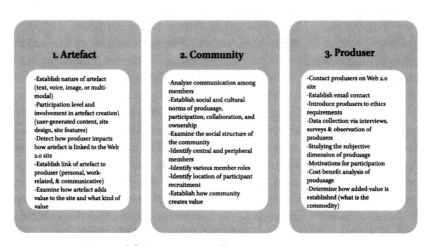

FIGURE 14.2   *Framework for Examining 'A Workers Inquiry 2.0'.*

the nature of the artefact and its link to the community and the produser are a central source of data.

Triangulation: Similar to qualitative research, triangulation becomes an integral part of the analysis. Triangulation in qualitative analysis refers to the study of data from sources in relation to one another. That is, data from one source is compared and contrasted with data from other sources to obtain a more rich and holistic picture of the individuals involved and their social relations. Triangulation also becomes important in light of the nature of online communities, where trolling and identity play are an inherent part of these communities.

Artefacts as Data: What really sets "A Workers' Inquiry 2.0" apart from other data collection techniques is a focus on the artefacts prodused by produsers within Web 2.0 environments. These artefacts represent a rich source of data in "A Workers' Inquiry 2.0" as they directly speak to the complex relations that exist between produsers, the rest of the community, and the norms and mores that characterize the site.

Worker Awareness: This is the primary goal of "A Workers' Inquiry 2.0" as it attempts to start a discussion around the uniquely exploitative relation that exists between produsers and those who own Web 2.0 sites and services. The juxtaposition here is between the benefits and costs associated with participation in these social media environments. On the one hand, there is no doubt that social media creates gains for those involved, including the pleasure of adding UGC, as well as being uniquely positioned to engage and contribute to a community (see Figures 14.1 and 14.2). In a study of uses and gratifications of Facebook, survey respondents indicated that their key gratifications were to pass time on the site (for example for entertainment, for relaxation, and to escape) (Papacharissi and Mendelson 2011; Quan-Haase and Young 2010), for social surveillance and social searching (for example to learn about friends and family without their knowledge) (Joinson 2008; Zhang et al. 2011), and for maintaining social ties (i.e., connecting with friends and family) (Dunne, Lawlor and Rowley 2010; Raacke and Bonds-Raacke 2008). On the other hand, produsers are not compensated for their time, effort, and overall added-value to the site. Indeed, produsers in many cases have no control over how the site manages content, as the example of Facebook and its constantly changing Terms of Service has clearly demonstrated. Similar to Marx and the autonomists, by making produsers aware that their labour is the source of the accumulated wealth of these websites, the present method seeks to raise the consciousnesses of these produsers regarding their own exploitation and their abilities to do something about it. As Figure 14.2 shows a detailed analysis of costs and benefits is also an integral part of understanding produsage in Web 2.0 environments.

Action and Social Change: One of the cornerstones of Marx's "A Workers' Inquiry" and the autonomists' method of co-research was the idea that the methodology should lead not only to workers' increased awareness of their exploitative labour conditions, but ultimately also to take action. As quoted above, the goal of the intervention was to "make the worker aware of his own predicament in capitalist society (...) and by thus making the worker conscious of his predicament giving him a chance to solve it" (Burnham, Shachtman and Spector 1938, 1). Even though "A Workers' Inquiry 2.0" ultimately has the same goals, it becomes quickly apparent that this is not a straightforward task. What complicates this endeavour is the quasi-voluntary nature of the engagement in the exploitative relation. While the industrial mode of production offered workers little choice regarding where they laboured, in Web 2.0 environments, participation in the mode of produsage is compelled not by the risks associated with a lack of income, but by the risk of social seclusion and communicative isolation. While easily transportable to other (often new) Web 2.0 sites and services, in the contemporary communicative context, produsers are concentrated in a very small number of sites and rely on these sites for their communication needs. This is where the method requires further elaboration as it develops and is utilized to study the quasi-voluntary mode of produsage within social media environments.

Central Strength and Weakness: In light of the above, it is possible to identify a central strength and weakness of "A Workers Inquiry 2.0." The central strength of "A Workers' Inquiry 2.0" is that rather than stopping at the identification of an exploitative relationship between the owners of Web 2.0 sites and services and the produsers of them, it follows the example set by Marx and the autonomists by going directly to the workers themselves and trying to better understand their thoughts regarding their own exploitation. It enables an examination of the social and political dynamics of the mode of produsage from "below" or from the perspective of the workers. However, "A Workers' Inquiry 2.0" goes beyond this revelatory function in its attempt to better understand the political potentials of produsage and the alternatives it posits regarding the autonomous labouring capacities of coordinated groups. While the valuations of Web 2.0 sites and services clearly indicate the presence of an exploitative relation, the existence of such a relationship, as well as the produsers opinions regarding the time and effort they expend on the site, should not overshadow the possibilities and potentials created by the mode of produsage. This method, then, enables an examination and appreciation of an organization of labouring bodies and minds that come together to work collaboratively, cooperatively, and autonomously, free of the wage relation. The original goal of Marx's and the autonomists' method was to provide workers with the intellectual and emotional tools required to struggle against their own exploitation. While produsage remains highly exploitative, Flickr produsers do not experience it as such. Making clear this exploitative relation, then, is vital. However, the self-organized, self-managed, and autonomous nature of the mode of produsage points to ways of living and working together beyond capital. It is by no means a perfect blueprint. It does, however, provide valuable information regarding some of the constituent elements of a mode of production/produsage that may play an important role in moving beyond the exploitative capitalist relation.

The central weakness of this iteration of "A Workers' Inquiry 2.0" is the relatively limited number of produsers consulted as research participants in proportion to the overall Flickr membership. With over fifty-one million members intermittently populating Factory Flickr, it is all but impossible to get in contact with each of them. This leaves particular areas of the Flickr-verse underexplored or completely unexplored. As the sparse reaction of the Flickr API group to the research question indicated, the voluntary nature of produsage and the specific focus of particular groups within Flickr, creates new challenges for researchers undertaking this kind of research. These challenges are directly related to accessing and recruiting Flickr members to participate in a research project oblique to their primary purpose of being on the site. Our experience with attempting to recruit participants from the Flickr API group is indicative of these new challenges.

The Flickr API Group is a place for unwaged hackers and programmers working with Flickr's code to share their experiences. While the API group is designated as 'public' and open to anyone, the focus of the group and the vast majority of the discussion threads found therein are overwhelmingly directed towards technical programming issues and their solutions. The question posed to them by this research project, then, has nothing to do directly with these core activities and was simply ignored by the majority of the group's membership. This is evidence of the potential problem alluded to above. Even if a researcher approaches his/her potential research participants on Web 2.0 sites and services with an informed understanding of the particular norms that circulate throughout the domain, the members of particular groups may not respond to the message, ignore the call for participation, and as a result the research project will stall before it is allowed to begin.

The amount of time, effort, energy, and work devoted to hacking the API is substantial. For this reason, a larger number of members from this group would have been interesting produsers to speak with regarding whether or not they considered their activities a form of labour and if they ever felt exploited by this process. Obtaining this perspective would have been of particular relevance as these produsers are engaged in creating highly specialized knowledge for Flickr, are responsible in part for how Flickr operates, and have one of the largest stakes in how Flickr makes use of their artefacts. While two research participants were in fact recruited from this group, the response to the original question was meagre compared to the response from Flickr Central and Utata. We believe this is due to the fact that the Flickr API discussion group is primarily a space for hackers/coders to discuss the intricacies, challenges, and opportunities of hacking the API. It is however not clear why this group, who is most involved with the development of the Flickr backbone, would be the most hesitant to engage in reflective practices about their labour. This remains a concern that needs to be addressed by subsequent iterations of the proposed methodology.

The difficulty of accessing produsers working within important corners of Factory Flickr is another reason why the artefacts of produsage are particularly important elements to consider when assessing the overall social and political dynamics of the mode of produsage. They do not replace the input provided by produsers, but they do assist in shedding some much-needed light into the obscure corners of Factory Flickr that might otherwise escape detailed scrutiny. While the weakness identified above merits recognition, it should not overshadow the information and data gleaned by the other members who did participate in the project.

8   Conclusions

The goal of Marx's and the autonomists' methods was to seek out workers, speak with them, evaluate the social and political dynamics of the workplace, gauge the workers level of exploitation, their cognizance of this exploitation, and, by doing so, provide them with the intellectual and emotional tools to do something about it. This remains the goal of "A Workers' Inquiry 2.0." In prong one of the research design detailed above, we describe one procedure for adapting Marx's and the autonomists' methods to the Web 2.0 era and the mode of produsage. In addition to the elemental step of seeking out produsers and speaking with them, we must, however, also examine the artefacts prodused by them in an attempt to better understand the intricacies and nuances of the social and political dynamics that animate the mode of produsage. This vital function was described in prong two of "A Workers' Inquiry 2.0" by arguing that the artefacts of produsage are valuable pieces of data because of their being conceived, directed, and prodused by produsers themselves and not by the owners or administrators of these sites and services.

These artefacts and the mode of produsage responsible for their creation are evidence of what self-organized and self-managed individuals can accomplish autonomously, in cooperation and collaboration with others, free of the wage relation, and when left to their own devices. They tell us things about how we might relate to one another when the naked self-interest characteristic of monetary gain is pushed into the background. Whereas industrial production fragments the worker and the workforce into so many scientifically managed, fractured, and frustrated shards (Braverman 1998; Lukács 1967), the mode of produsage allows a place for all these contributions in and to the whole. By holding these artefacts and accomplishments up to the light and learning as much as we can from them – examining their successes, failures, set-backs, and achievements – we provide produsers not only with proof of their exploitation, but, more importantly, with imperfect evidence of the nascent feasibility of an organization of labouring bodies and minds uninspired and unmotivated by the dictates of capitalist command and control. As a result, the artefacts are both a critique of the present and evidence of what may be possible in the future. In its own small way, then, Flickr provides the intellectual and emotional tools required to begin thinking about what it might mean to live and labour in a world beyond capital.

References

Barnsley, Jan, and Diana Ellis. 1992. *Research for Change: Participatory Action Research for Community Groups.* Vancouver, British Columbia: Women's Research Centre.

Bilton, Nick, and Evelyn Rusli. 2012. From Founders to Decorators, Facebook Riches. Accessed March 15, 2012. http://www.nytimes.com/2012/02/02/technology/for-founders-to-decorators-facebook-riches.html?_r=1andsrc=meandref=technology.

Bologna, Sergio. 1980. The Tribe of Moles. *Semiotext(e)* 3 (3): 36–61.

Braverman, Harry. 1998. *Labor and Monopoly Capital: The Degradation of Work in the Twentieth Century.* New York: Monthly Review Press.

Brewer, John D. 2000. *Ethnography.* Philadelphia: Open University Press.

Brook, Stephen. 2005. *Sale of Website to News Corp Branded a 'Giveaway'.* Accessed March 20, 2012: http://www.guardian.co.uk/technology/2005/sep/01/media.business1.

Brophy, Enda. 2006. System Error: Precarity and Collective Organizing at Microsoft. *Canadian Journal Of Communication* 31 (3): 619–638.

Brown, Brian A. 2012. Will Work For Free: Examining the Biopolitics of Unwaged Immaterial Labour. *University of Western Ontario - Electronic Thesis and Dissertation Repository.* Paper 620.

Brown, Brian A. 2013. Primitive Digital Accumulation: Privacy, Social Networks & Biopolitical Exploitation. *Rethinking Marxism.* 25 (3): 385–403.

Bruns, Axel. 2008. *Blogs, Wikipedia, Second Life, and Beyond: From Production to Produsage.* New York: Peter Lang.

Burnham, James, Max Shachtman, Max, and Maurice Spector. 1938. *Introduction to Marx's "A Workers' Inquiry."* Accessed March 15, 2012. http://www.marxists.org/history/etol/newspape/ni/vol04/no12/marx.htm.

Cassano, Rosemary, and Judith Dunlop. 2005. Participatory Action Research with South Asian Immigrant Women: A Canadian Example. *Critical Social Work 6* (1).

Castells, Manuel and Peter Hall 1994. *Technopoles of the World: The Making of Twenty-First-Century Industrial Complexes.* London: Routledge.

Cellan-Jones, Rory. 2012. Facebook's IPO – It's Up To You. Accessed March 15, 2012. http://www.bbc.co.uk/news/technology-16835116.

Cohen, Nicole. 2008. The Valorization of Surveillance: Towards a Political Economy of Facebook. *Democratic Communique: Journal for the Union of Democratic Communications* 22 (1): 5–22.

Coté, Mark, and Jennifer Pybus. 2007. Learning to Immaterial Labor 2.0: MySpace and Social Networks. *ephemera: theory and politics in organization* 7 (1): 88–106.

Dalla Costa, Mariarosa and Selma James. 1973. *The Power of Women and the Subversion of Community.* Bristol, England: Falling Wall Press.

Duhigg, Charles and Barboza, David. 2012, January 25. In China, Human Costs are Built into an iPad. Accessed March 15, 2012: http://www.nytimes.com/2012/01/26/business/ieconomy-apples-ipad-and-the-human-costs-for-workers-in-china.html?pagewanted=all.

Dunne, Áine, Lawlor, Margaret-Anne, and Rowley, Jennifer. 2010. Young People's Use of Online Social Networking Sites – A Uses and Gratifications Perspective. *Journal of Research in Interactive Marketing* 4 (1): 46–58.

Ellison, Nicole B., Charles Steinfield, and Cliff Lampe. 2007. The Benefits of Facebook "Friends": Social Capital and College Students' Use of Online Social Network Sites. *Journal of Computer-Mediated Communication* 12 (4): article 1. Retrieved from http://jcmc.indiana.edu/vol12/issue4/ellison.html.

Fals-Borda, Orlando and Muhammad Anisur Rahman, eds. 1991. *Action And Knowledge: Breaking the Monopoly with Participatory Action Research.* New York: The Apex Press.

Fuchs, Christian. 2009. Social Networking Sites and the Surveillance Society. A Critical Case Study of the Usage of studiVZ, Facebook, and MySpace by Students in Salzburg in the Context of Electronic Surveillance. Salzburg/Vienna: Research Group UTI.

Fuchs, Christian. 2011. Web 2.0, Prosumption, and Surveillance. *Surveillance and Society* 8 (3): 288–309.

Fuchs, Christian. 2012. Google Capitalism. *tripleC: cognition, communication, co-operation* 10 (1): 42–48.

Garrett, Jesse James, and Eric Costello. 2005. An Interview With Flickr's Eric Costello. Accessed March 15, 2012. http://www.adaptivepath.com/ideas/essays/archives/000519.php.

Hardt, Michael, and Antonio Negri. 2000. *Empire*. Cambridge, Mass.: Harvard University Press.

Hardt, Michael, and Antonio Negri. 2004. *Multitude: War and democracy in the age of Empire*. New York: Penguin Press.

Huws, Ursula. 2003. *The Making of a Cybertariat: virtual work in a real world*. London: Merlin.

Joinson, Adam. 2008. 'Looking at', 'Looking up' or 'Keeping up with' People? Motives and Uses of Facebook. In *Proceedings of CHI'08*, 1027–1036.

Kendall, Lori. 2002. *Hanging out in the Virtual Pub: Masculinities and Relationships Online*. Berkeley, CA: University of California Press.

Kleiner, Dimytri and Brian Wyrick. 2007. InfoEnclosure 2.0. Accessed March 15, 2012 from *Mute: Culture and Politics After the Net*: http://www.metamute.org/en/InfoEnclosure-2.0.

Lazzarato, Maurizzio. 1996. Immaterial Labor. In *Radical Thought in Italy: A Potential Politics*, edited by Paolo Virno and Michael Hardt, 133–147. Minneapolis, Minnesota: University of Minnesota Press.

Levy, Ari, and Spears, Lee. 2011. LinkedIn Retains Most Gains Second Day After Surging in Initial Offering. Accessed March 15, 2012. http://www.bloomberg.com/news/2011-05-18/linkedin-raises-352-8-million-in-ipo-as-shares-priced-at-top-end-of-range.html.

Levy, Steven. 2006. The New Wisdom of the Web. Accessed March 15, 2012 from Newsweek: http://www.newsweek.com/id/45976.

Lukács, Georg. 1967. *History and Class Consciousness*. London: Merlin Press.

Malo de Molina, Marta. 2004a. *Common Notions, Part 1: Workers-Inquiry, Co-Research, Consciousness Raising*. Accessed February 23, 2012: http://eipcp.net/transversal/0406/malo/en.

Malo de Molina, Marta. 2004b. *Common Notions, Part 2: Institutional Analysis, Participatory Action-Research, Militant Research*. Accessed February 23, 2012: http://eipcp.net/transversal/0707/malo/en.

Marx, Karl. 1938/1880. *A Workers' Inquiry*. Accessed March 15, 2012 from Marxists.org: http://www.marxists.org/history/etol/newspape/ni/vol04/no12/marx.htm.

Moretti, Stefania. 2010, November 2. Facebook using Canada as testing ground. London Free Press. Accessed March 15, 2012: http://www.lfpress.com/money/2010/11/02/15923106.html#/money/2010/11/02/pf-15923101.html.

Negri, Antonio. 1989. *The Politics of Subversion: A Manifesto for the Twenty-First Century*. Oxford, Great Britain: Polity Press.

Negri, Antonio. 2008. *Reflections on Empire*. Cambridge, U.K.: Polity Press.

O'Reilly, Tim. 2005. *What is Web 2.0? Design Patterns and Business Models for the Next Generation of Software*. Accessed March 15, 2012. http://oreilly.com/web2/archive/what-is-web-20.html.

Papacharissi, Zizi, and Andrew Mendelson. 2011. Toward a New(er) Sociability: Uses, Gratifications, and Social Capital on Facebook. In *Media Perspectives for the 21st Century*, edited by Stylianos Papathanassopoulos, 212–230. New York: Routledge: 212–230.

Precarias a la deriva. 2004. *Adrift through the Circuits of Feminized Precarious Work*. Accessed March 15, 2012: http://eipcp.net/transversal/0704/precarias1/en.

Privacy Commissioner of Canada. 2009. Facebook Agrees to Address Privacy Commissioner's Concerns. Retrieved from http://www.priv.gc.ca/media/nr-c/2009/nr-c_090827_e.cfm.

Quan-Haase, Anabel, and Alison Young. 2010. Uses and Gratifications of Social Media: A Comparison of Facebook and Instant Messaging. *Bulletin of Science, Technology and Society* 30 (5): 350–361.

Raacke, John and Jennifer Bonds-Raack. 2008. MySpace and Facebook: Applying the Uses and Gratifications Theory to Exploring Friend-Networking Sites. *CyberPsychology and Behaviour* 11 (3): 169–174.

Raynes-Goldie, Kate 2010. Aliases, Creeping, and Wall Cleaning: Understanding Privacy in the Age of Facebook. *First Monday*,15 (1), January. Accessed March 15, 2012: http://firstmonday.org/htbin/cgiwrap/bin/ojs/index.php/fm/article/viewArticle/2775.

Reuters. 2011. *Twitter Share Auction Suggests $7.7 Billion Valuation*. Accessed March 15, 2012. http://www.reuters.com/article/2011/03/04/us-twitter-idUSTRE7221JL20110304.

Schonfeld, Erick. 2005. *The Flickrization of Yahoo!* Accessed March 20, 2012: http://money.cnn.com/magazines/business2/business2_archive/2005/12/01/8364623/.

Situaciones, Colectivo. 2003. *On the Researcher Militant*. Accessed March 20, 2012. http://eipcp.net/transversal/0406/colectivosituaciones/en.

Situaciones Colectivo. 2005. Something More on Research Militancy: Footnotes on procedures and (in)decisions. *Ephemera* 5 (4): 602–614.

Smythe, Dallas. 1977. Communications: Blindspot of Western Marxism. *Canadian Journal of Political and Social Theory* 1 (3): 1–28.

Springer, Michelle, Beth Dulabahn, Phil Michel, Barbara Natason, David Reser, David Woodward, and Helena Zinkham. 2008. *For the Common Good: The Library of Congress Flickr Pilot Project*. The Library of Congress. United States Government.

Stelter, Brian. 2011. *News Corporation Sells MySpace for $35 Million*. Accessed March 20, 2012: http://mediadecoder.blogs.nytimes.com/2011/06/29/news-corp-sells-myspace-to-specific-media-for-35-million/.

Tapscott, Dan and Anthony Williams. 2006. *Wikinomics: How Mass Collaboration Changes Everything*. New York: Portfolio.

Taylor, Frederick Winslow. 1915. *The Principles of Scientific Management*. New York: Harper and Brothers.

Terranova, Tiziana. 2004. *Network Culture: Politics for the Information Age*. London: Pluto Press.

Toffler, Alvin. 1981. *The Third Wave*. New York: Bantam Books.

Touraine, Alain. 1971. *The May Movement, Revolt and Reform: May 1968-The Student Rebellion and Workers' Strikes-the Birth of a Social Movement*. New York: Random House.

Whyte, William F. 1990. Introduction. In *Participatory Action Research*, edited by William F. Whyte, 7–15. Newbury Park, CA: Sage.

Whyte, William F., Davydd Greenwood, and Peter Lazes, Peter. 1990. Participatory Action Research: Through Practice to Science in Social Research. In *Particpatory Action Research*, edited by William F. Whyte, 19–55. Newbury Park, California: Sage.

Wright, Steven. 2002. *Storming Heaven: Class Composition and Struggle in Italian Autonomist Marxism*. Sterling, Virginia: Pluto Press.

Zhang, Yin, Leo Shing-Tung Tang, and Louis Leung, Louis. 2011. Gratifications, Collective Self-Esteem, Online Emotional Openness, and Trait like Communication Apprehension as Predictors of Facebook Uses. *Cyberpsychology, Behavior, and Social Networking* 14 (12): 733–739.

CHAPTER 15

Social Media, Mediation and the Arab Revolutions*

Miriyam Aouragh

There is no doubt that the internet is an important medium for the simple fact that it offers alternative channels to disseminate counter-hegemonic content and instant mobilization. By hook or by crook, activists must experiment with the internet if they want to be effective. Since political engagement in the Middle East and North Africa (MENA) often operates in the context of media censorship, police oppression, war or colonial-occupation this claim requires a critical analysis though. Especially in times of (counter-) revolution many forms of online politics are rendered meaningless – unless organically related to offline street politics. The events shaking the region especially since 2011 have starkly demonstrated this. I wish to revisit these developments from a media, communication and (non-western) anthropological angle.

The Arab uprisings motivated a broad range of responses. But by simultaneously providing a publicity niche this focus has also resulted in facile analyses of the "Arab Spring" and a sense of "intellectual frustration" (Sabry 2012, 80). Sabry identifies four categories: *Muteness* (intellectual impotence); *Stammering*; *Tele-Techno-* (the 'experts'); *Subaltern* (the activists themselves) (81). In fact, a quick overview of the work published in communication and media disciplines responding to the 'Arab Spring' shows two remarkable features: the sheer volume of material produced (dozens of academic publications in several special issues dedicated to the topic)[1] and its lack of engagement with Marxist theory. The fact that recent years have seen a popular re-emergence of interest in Marxist critiques while Marxist theories are hardly engaged with in mainstream academia shows a widespread gap between established and new scholarship and probably an inherited prejudice regarding 'systemic' analyses, also for anthropology (Graeber 2001). Part of the reason is disagreement or

---

* I would like to thank Jamie Pitman and Jonny Jones for comradely advice concerning the Marxist theory of value helpful references with regards to immaterial labour; the anonymous reviewers for their valuable comments; and Rob Jackson for proof-reading.

1 Special issues related to internet activism and/or the Arab Spring between 2001 and 2013 are for instance: *International Journal of Communication* ["The Arab Spring and the role of ICTs," Volume 5]; *Communication Review* [Volume 14]; *Arab Media & Society* [Issue 14]; *Middle East Journal of Culture and Communication* [Volume 5]; *Globalizations* [Volume 9]; *Cyber Orient* ["The Net Worth of the Arab Spring," Autumn 2012]; *Journal of Communication* ["Social Media and the Arab Spring," Volume 62].

confusion at the very core of Marxist academia mostly centred on the dependency of superstructure.[2] This chapter intends to contribute to a critical conceptualisation of the Arab uprisings through the prism of the internet. The theoretical and political proposition regarding the potentials of social media, which underlies this chapter, rests on a radical critique of the liberal-capitalist internet-ecology. But revolutions cannot be simply studied through the prism of the internet: internet activism is here viewed through the prism of the revolutions, combining theory with ethnographic insights based on meetings and long discussions with activists in the summer of 2011 and their online testimonies over a longer period. This will help to push back the narrow presumptions about the universality of digital experiences and, by relying on a *grounded* empiricism, contribute to existing critical explorations. From this positionality follows a *rejection* of technological reductionism which distract from necessary material-political explanations, and an *inclusion* of the disempowering materiality of technology. Social movement theories popularised with the surge of anti-capitalist movements in the early 2000s and have become formative to internet studies, but to some extent became part of the problem.

Marxist theories of literature and art provided inspiring vantage points for a radical approach to social media and political change. Marxist studies about the dialectics of art and literature provide fruitful frameworks for the study of the social-political implications of online media productions, as I will argue. Such a Marxist-dialectic lexicon refers to non-material (non-economic) consequences whereby producers of culture (in whatever form or expression) are influenced by that material reality yet also relatively free.[3] How this relation is structured, the interdependence formed, is called mediation. Raymond Williams (1977) (following Adorno's *Theses on the Sociology of Art*) stressed that mediation is in the object itself. As this chapter shows,

---

2   This is probably related to a general anti-Marxist reflex but is quite common in the international academic field at large. As discussed by Graeber, many anthropologists (at Western universities) avoided Marxist theories in their work simply because Marxists were often persecuted. Even after WW2 and height of the Cold war, when there was more intellectual space, Marxist anthropology was absent or dominated by an orthodox Marxist (evolutionary) scheme. There was a break in the 1960s when most anthropologists' understanding of their discipline underwent a transformation, engaging more with a type of scrutiny exposing the workings of a system of inequality and injustice. A Marxist anthropologists' critique of non-Western social orders was not because it was different (the kind of relativism that was for long dominant in anthropology) from his or hers, but also to the degree that it was *similar* (2001, 24).

3   As Harman clarifies, ideology and consciousness is "a subjective link between objective processes"; ideas develop on the basis of material reality and feed back into that reality. Thus while they cannot be reduced to that reality, they can neither be divorced from it.

this corresponds to what is believed to be the core characteristic of internet media.

This chapter aims to shed light on the complex online-offline dynamics that have preceded and are shaping recent (counter-) revolutionary transformations, and to step away from the cheerful yet void 'Facebook Revolutions'. I will start by describing the Marxist concept of *mediation*, which offers a helpful tool to explore the pros and cons of the internet in revolutionary turmoil. The theoretical (sometimes dreary) propositions about base-superstructure need (and deserve) to be spelled out first. Especially in internet studies where the subject of investigation is also a powerful economic sector and condition of capitalist production, it is crucial to critique the economic context. Mediation unveils the relation between base and superstructure in the most illuminating ways. He internet is both a product of capitalist hegemony and simultaneously used to resist those logics. How internet-related conceptualisations have in due course redefined the very definition of activism and resistance shall be reviewed in the second section. And in the third section I discuss ICT imperialism and its potential impacts on political activism. In the final part of this chapter, I set out to deconstruct how political organising and internet technologies relate, avoiding the customary straw-man positions. As mentioned, the concept mediation because it allows me to engage with its dual nature for social media(tion) represents the nexus of political hegemony and liberation of internet politics.

1   Deconstructing Mediation

The reluctance to engage with Marxist concepts is partly due to the fact that 'base and superstructure' represents a combination of forces and relations of production, but one of these two dynamics will always seem more 'basic'. The confusion about 'superstructure' mostly arises from the definition of the 'base' as an over arching typology. An important correction given by Harman (1986), namely that Marx doesn't make a *single* distinction between 'base' and 'superstructure' because there are two distinctions; between the 'forces of production' and the relations of production; and between the relations of production and the remaining social relations. The *forces* of production can come into conflict with the (more static) *relations* of production. The relations of production correspond to the forces of production – hence, the forces of production (that have the agency and motivation) rebel against the relations of production – not the other way round. So the forces and organisation of labour are the economic structures (base) of capitalist society and from this emerge a certain polity and politics (superstructure), and these in turn merge in different ways, depending on the historical situation in which it occurs. If as Marx and Engels argued, the class which is the ruling material force of society is at the same time its ruling intellectual force, how does this dynamic occur in the realm of ideology – literature, art, media?

Literary work and art are a good example for they are (and aren't) embedded in state ideology. They are forms of perception related to the dominant (state) ideology (Eagleton 1976, 7). Which is why the *mediation* between these forms requires analyses, *Mediation* suggests the presence of normative representations of social relations, but it also depends on what form of mediation (books, newspapers, films, websites) is at stake. For Eagleton, literature is shaped by the means of production and is distribution. Therefore, to be able to understand its implications requires an awareness of the historical conditions (iv) as well as the social composition of the authors (1976, 2). This evokes the broader dialectic I am interested in exploring regarding social media. The (revolutionary) interconnected role of literature was originally outlined by Trotsky (1991) who stressed that literary forms should have, and in fact do have, a high degree of autonomy. This means that literature and art do not merely bend to ideology but evolve partly in accordance with it (Eagleton 1976, 26). Books are not just (structured) expressions of meaning but also commodities produced by publishers for profit. Literature as a part of 'superstructure' is in fact a highly mediated social product and part of the economic base (60). The superstructure functions as an ideological organiser of the social class that owns the means of economic production. Again, this double metaphor has suffered from distortion because the concept of the base (political-economy) is easily confused to mean 'essence' with superstructure (ideology/media) an extraction thereof. In reality, each technological transformation is both a continuation and a unique transformation, manifested in ways depending on a particular development. Every new technological force will also have implications for the balance of forces and the tools required.

This is where the Marxist roots of mediation are still relevant to current political (e.g. the superstructures of ideologies that prefer non-violent horizontal networks) – economic (a medium deeply embedded in neoliberal ICT corporations) ICT bases. As Engels himself anticipated "If therefore somebody twists this into the statement that the economic element is the only determining one, he transforms it into a meaningless abstract and absurd phrase" (in Eagleton 1976, 9).

Thus than its literal or aesthetic meaning, this chapter engages with mediation beyond dissemination and signifies the capitalist rules of engagement between base and superstructure. Mediation reveals these inner relationships

and lays down the patterns that obscure relations of exploitation; hence it represents both hegemonic and counter-hegemonic processes. The transformations regarding the availability and usage of communication and information
has always had political implications. Replacing the time-consuming technique of parchment with papyrus had important consequences for European
Protestantism and (via the upcoming bourgeoisie) for most other social classes
(Deibert 1997). Presenting social phenomena with the adjective 'new' tere-
foe does not acknowledge how everyday technologies have morphed with
each new stage of development (Briggs and Burke 2005). Armbrust (2007)
remind us of the need to historicise (new) media developments and suggest looking at the longer existing and still prevalent media culture (e.g.
oral mediation or tape-recordings) distributions. But historicising is more
than tracing technical forces in themselves, it also allow us to recognise a
common tension between historical continuity and change. In these
Marxist epistemologies is the place they occupy within a whole mode of
production matters in particular (Eagleton 1976, 74). Obviously, such transformations don't occur immediately. According to Peters (2009, 18), mass
media of any sort passes through five stages: the technical invention (which
is a combination of the old and new); cultural invention (thus how they are
linked to new social uses); legal regulation; economic distribution; and
finally, social mainstream.[4] The question remains how to apply this Marxist
exercise in the context of media technologies.

Wayne (2003, 128) identifies seven levels of mediation with regards to the
media: text; production process; production context; industrial context; the
state; modes of development; and mode of production. All these levels are related
but the most important levels in the context of social media are the production
process and production of context. The relationship between producer and
consumer is itself contained in the practices of communication.[5] So how can
we reconcile the apparent contradiction inhibited in mediation? The organized fashion of exploitation - through the concentration of workers into
workplaces, paradoxically - created deeper class consciousness and stronger
class-based ties and identities. This was something new and in addition to existing identity formations based on shared expectations, endurances, lifestyles,
and proximity. It is the reason behind the adagio that capitalism is a system

---

4 To the fifth phase can be added the register of ways new technologic inventions are countered, as is sometimes the case with dystopian deliberation about the internet, including by
   leftist progressives.

5 Williams engages here with Adorno's *Theses on the Sociology of Art*.

that creates its own gravediggers. Meanwhile, the absence of (free, accessible) communication technology (through the free-market privatisation of these means) weakens the social ties of the exploited classes. So what happens to the process of mediation when this gap is overcome in terms of 'authorship', when the user-generated content or products as well as the users' intentions are about artistic development, about social change, subversive acts? What happens to this process when the producer and consumer are the same, indeed: the most celebrated feature of Web 2.0?

The (power of the) author as producer is not a new idea only invented with social networking in he present decade. Discussed by Marxist cultural theorist Walter Benjamin in 1934 and later coined *prosumer* by Toffler (1980). Unlike the recent focus on participation by consumers within the capitalist system such as by Bruns (2010) with *produsage*,[6] Benjamin meant a revolutionary intervention to counter dominant bourgeois media and ideology. This is a far cry from the idea of consumers/users extraction empowerment by participating in corporations with the effect of further reducing investment costs (Fuchs 2009, 95), which doesn't signify democratization but commodification of human creativity which is actually a risky trade-off.

A related point is that ideological mediation is played out partly through the commodification of media sources and tools. Corporate operators and providers basically intensify users' exposure to the commodity propaganda of advertisements while online (Fuchs 2012,146). In this paradoxical arena the mediated base and superstructure approach was demonstrated clearly in the case of the Arab uprisings: the availability of ICT is a direct output of corporate structure and yet their ideology (consensual symbols) have helped frame the narrative about social media and the Arab revolutions. Of course we have to rethink if we really can draw conclusions about very different media environments – whether between Web 0 (pre-internet) and Web 2.0 or between, social media empowerment in California and mass uprisings. But the relatively similar underlying understanding here concern the ramifications of neoliberalism in an increasingly transformed capitalism sometimes described as an information-economy. It is important to engage with these shifts if only because it has been misunderstood. This will help uncover some flawed interpretations about the role of internet in the Arab uprisings.

---

6 For a helpful overview of the so-called 'democratic turn' and its introduction in the Knowledge Economy debate see Daniel Araya's review: <http://www.danielaraya.com/docs/ProsumerInnovation.pdf>.

2   From Das Kapital and Class to Das Empire and Multitudes?

Since the *Communist Manifesto* or *Das Kapital* the dominant corporate media has obviously restructured itself, morphed into different mode of production and capital. Technological innovations are often in par with new stages in capitalist societies. When focussing on distinctiveness of internet-economies in the new contexts (via post-war liberal welfare to a neo-liberal state), communication emerges as *the* force of change. According to Castells (2009) communication is the central (counter-)power in our times. This alludes to a transformative power by a technological development rather than a mode of production, in this scenario *base* can be understood as *informationalism*. This adaptation is similar to what became known as *immaterial labour*, characterising a type of capitalism. Hardt and Negri consider the 'immaterial' production of ideas by virtue of what it produces rather than the labour process (confusing the term 'labour' with 'work') with the internet as a qualitatively different commodity. In *Empire* Hardt and Negri understand immaterial labour as industrial production that has been 'informationalised' and therefore transformed "the production process itself," which is especially clear manufacturing is replaced by 'services', the new driving forces behind "the postmodernisation of the global economy" (2000, 293). According to Camfield (2007), these proposed alterations can't actually play the role assigned to it because they don't address how surplus value is extracted, this strangely enough underestimate the complex and deep exploitation that underlies it. The separation between consumption and production mysteriously dissolves with new technologies suggests that the internet can function outside the structures of capitalism, turning class into a different category altogether.[7] Meanwhile the global economy is somehow one entity, beyond inter-state competition, thus beside class (multitude) there is also a different role reserved for states (one dominant empire rather than competing capitalisms).

Ironically, while Hardt and Negri challenge his theory of value in reference to technology, Marx gives serious consideration to the social implications of technological development. He ascribes to technology the potential to *unlock*

---

7   Voluntarism in the blogger, open-source and hacker communities often comes to mind. A telling example is the recent case by former contributors against the much hailed Huffington Post. These bloggers had produced and helped disseminate Huffington content for free. It was the kind of immaterial labour praised indeed. But when the owner made a multi-million deal with AOL the philanthropy ended: they sued her and demanded a share in the proceeds. See: <http://www.politico.com/blogs/onmedia/0411/Unpaid:bloggers_sue_Huffington_Post_and_AOL.html>.

the free development of individualities and the *reduction of labour time to a minimum* in the service of *artistic and scientific development* (i.e. rather than only creating surplus labour).[8] The (old) term 'labour' challenges the question of (new) 'knowledge production', but for Marx labour represents action that both presupposes and propagates new knowledge. Far from ignoring the impact of the 'superstructure' on the 'base'. Marx builds his whole account of human history around it because knowledge and physical labour have always been continuous with one another, but the idea of the *informationalisation* of industrial production is problematic.

Perspectives about a *new* capitalism are associated with a restructuring of the labour market. Political and ideological struggles arise as a result of competition and exploitation, are decisive for whether a new rising class (based on new forces of production) displaces an old ruling class (Harman 1986). And yet the link between technology and postmodern or post-capitalist shifts keep resuming. For Hardt and Negri (2004, 140) history moves on and social reality changes, thus old theories are no longer adequate: new realities demand new theories. Globalization fuse transnational market systems with new technologies, the supposed 'dematerialisation' of the economy (Haug 2009). 'Old' forms of employment are replaced by new internet-formed discourses that aligned it mostly with knowledge ('cognitive') processes. It is now "biopolitical production" in which the economic, the political, and the cultural increasingly overlap (Sayers 2007, 444). Such, (re)definitions do not have a clear analysis of the exploitative mechanisms at work and have provoked fair critique, some describing these far-fetching propositions "the presence of left wing harmonies in the neoliberal chorus" (Doogan 2010, 29). Again, some are motivated by the idea that Marx didn't allow the absorption of knowledge and new technologies in the production process. Thus by substituting the 'classical' Marxist tradition with 'immaterial labour' the analysis is flipped. But the real challenge is to have a clear understanding of the social relations underpinning capitalist production "rather than fetishize its effects" (Fine & Saad-Filho 2010, 23). Marx obviously did not delve into a communication and information medium at the time, but he didn't overlook its role either. Whilst discussing technology as an alienating force of modern industry Marx observes that technology disclosing the process of production and thereby also "lays bare the mode of formation of his social relations, and of the mental conceptions that flow from them."[9]

---

8   These views can be found particularly in Chapter 14 of the *Grundrisse* (Marx 1857/1858).

9   From Capital Vol. 1, the rest of the paragraph in: <http://www.marxists.org/archive/lenin/works/1914/granat/cho2.htm>.

The material relations of production rely on production *and* information, this *dual* condition when applied on helps see why online communication *product* are *both* lucrative and genuine user-generated medium. This also means that besides catering for its users, social media also constitute the mechanism that strongly underlies capital accumulation (Fuchs 2009). This draws a different picture, one that makes space for assessing such techno-social dialectics in relation to theories about social movement and later allows a clearer view on how resistance is organised.

3   How the Internet Redefines Resistance

According to celebratory portrayals about the Arab revolutions the awakening of the people are helped by (Western) technology, such portrayals are not completely. Since the Zapatistas – an interesting appropriation in the early internet-resistance myth since they were not internet activists but mainly guerrillas in the mountains of Chiapas deploying the internet to ocassionally mediate their offline resistance – and the anti-capitalist protest movements such as WTO-Seattle and te World Social Forum's – especially its introduction alternative media platforms like *Indymedia* – academic interest in communication and technology joined these waves. This enthused debates about the internet as the new spaces of resistance, and a turn to politics into the realm of social networking sites developed considerably. As it turned out, mediating the message of protest came to be considered the protest itself, it introduced a *commoditization* of internet politics. To a certain extent . It is tis reading of politics that since communicating our demands and alternative analyses is fundamental. We *want* to construct (influence) meaning-making processes; we understand that the media are amongst the most fundamental spaces to achieve this on he broadest possible scale.

Social movement literature motivated the prominence of the internet for collective action while questioning the relevance of traditional collective action paradigms. This sounded reasonable, for many (traditional) theories discussing social movements emerged in different conditions after all. However, we should does this imply that certain (pre)conditions are no longer present in the realm of contemporary activism? The much cited work by Bimber et al. (2005) argues that "new forms of collective action *reliant* on certain technological aspects illuminate several fundamental aspects of all collective actions that so far have remained theoretically obscure" (366). The two most important changes challenge the binary choices of *participation* (in the past this is assumed to rely on strong ties and vanguards) and the role of *organisation* (conceived mainly as vertical structures of command and control) with explicit leadership and division of labour. Bimber et al. reframe collective action as "'a set of communication processes involving the crossing of boundaries between private and public life" (367). It is true that with the internet weak ties can contribute to political organising. The opposition between 'free riders' and 'vanguards' is partly a false dichotomy, caused and causing an error in the overall assessment. Firstly, a discrepancy between weak and strong ties is not only a matter of cost and benefit, as if people want to engage when has most to gain, a condition that the internet offered. Beneath its optimistic narrative there is a rather pessimistic outlook whereby motivation or political engagement is strongly dependent on 'low investment'. It misses factors like solidarity, camaraderie, unity and of course necessity. My second point has to do with the word 'reliant' in the previous quotation. The answer to the riddle can be found in this 'relative' condition as I will explain regarding the *unequal* effects of internet activism causing much of the confusion.

Bimber etal make the same point when considering the largest obstacle to be the nature of organisation (369) overcome during novel loosely coupled networks at anti-WTO protests (Seattle, WA, 1999), finally rid off outdated fixed structure of leadership, decision making processes or recruitment policies. There are two underlying premises I take issue with: everybody everywhere seems to be connected (otherwise it wouldn't be a democratic – representative – form of organising obviously); as if people value online commitment and community similarly as offline [physical] interaction. Illustrative is the following quote they cite "Right now, every time we do an action, we send out an e-mail and a hundred people show up. It's like magic. We couldn't do it without e-mail" (Bullert cited, 4; in Bimber, Flanagin and Stohl 2005, 370). But anyone who was or is involved in activism knows that it isn't so magical. When you mobilize and send out an email, that is *communicating*, just as calling, texting, fly-posting and standing on a soap box was and often still is. We hardly consider the turn-out in these cases as magical. More relevant in the context of this chapter: many people are not convinced enough to sacrifice their time, risk their jobs or accept bodily harm based on a passing message received via online platforms.

Technology has undercut some of the annoying requirements of organising and allows a broader circle of people to contribute, this are important improvements. But many of the examples have to do with dissemination (thanks to email, bulletin boards, SNS) and better ways of sharing. But how does the mobilization of new collective action now result from "largely uncoordinated efforts" (373)? What seems missing is the *content* and thus the question *how* the demands come about: who organised the initial or eventual calls/meetings/protests? There is certainly some truth to Bimber's suggestion but it is partial.

If there are, hypothetically, six crucial stages or spheres of political organising then the issue of coordination of dissemination covers two at most. Thus as activists we are relieved from some important burdens but most characteristics of political organising are not *overcome* or altered because they have to do with the power relations we depend on and the privilege we (because of our subversion) don't possess and wish to actually remove altogether. Nevertheless, as the authors note "new faces of collective action exhibit both formalized and informal structures" (374). And such groundbreaking phenomena "lie at the heart of new forms of technology based collective action, and they form the general class of which the traditional free-riding decision is one special albeit very important, subset" (377). Some of the same processes are found in non-technological spaces of interaction, how are we to reassess this if it turns out it underestimated previous and non-wired dynamics? That is why it so important to historicise our current modes of communication and embed these analyses in ethnographic realities. For instance, the networks of the *baqqal* (local grocer), the taxi driver, the mosque or *hammam* (public bath) includes an enormous amount of information flows. All of a sudden it seems less extraordinarily unique that boundaries between private and public domains can be crossed (Alexander and Aouragh 2011). But this is not a sufficient analysis, in the last section I will return to *when* exactly *what* matters in more detail.

The problem in our age is that revisions of concepts (such as resistance and revolution) are devied real-life practices behind those very concepts, results in a conceptual flattening. At best it connotes to myths about technology bringing modernity for Arabs (Aouragh 2012) an at worst it can and potentially weaken this very resistance when such assessments compromise the strategy and tactics on the ground. These redefinitions are neither novel nor autonomous but associated with earlier the altered meaning of class (considered to be defeated) and state (dissolved into flows of networks) by neoliberal globalisation; even replacing political-economy (Kellner 2002, 287). The techno-tunes stemming from these theoretical alterations resemble earlier ('post-colonial') shifts which contributed to analytical moves from politics to culture. Paradoxically, the subaltern-type reassessments, de-politicised the debate in the long term (removing some of the necessary conceptual tools), particularly in the context of the Middle East which comprises neo-colonialism and imperialism.[10] Social movement paradigms have internalized the possibility of creating new

---

10   In such anti-class definitions 'marginal' comes to mean 'the other' in the Third World, but the same conditions or accounts can be found in the 'First World'. To follow Eagleton: "The true scandal of the present is that almost everyone in it is banished to the margins" (2004, 19).

identities and in the process problemetized, 'old' struggles redefining tem as only interested in over access to resources and considering old identities based on class alliances, i.e. the (original) idea of collective identities and class struggle were deemed outdated, conservative and essentialist. The internet as representational activism (texts, visuals, online public spheres) sits comfortably with this new view where change matter at the level of representation and social movement theories that related to *narrative* or discursive practices – exercising power in and through discourses – was a further flattening and westernization of the concept of resistance. The theoretical shifts coincide with novel interpretations about the role of new online networking methods for political change because the internet offers democratised networks and the increasing power of the individual.[11] The main (Eurocentric) flaw here regards the recommendation to 'go beyond' the nation-state to those struggling for economic and territorial autonomy or (in the case of Palestine, Kashmir or Western-Sahara) an independent state.

Consequently, if labour and capital are both core forces in capitalism, the state is the mediator between (the exploitation of) the first and (the potential of) the second, the state is the metaphorical hyphen in political-economy. As noted earlier, mediation is not about representation in a figurative sense. I mean political and economic *regulation* through corresponding state structures and in turn and spontaneously through their ensuing ideologies. Gramsci developed the concept hegemony in a way to suggest that capitalism maintained control not just through violence and political and economic coercion, but through a dominant culture in which the values of the bourgeoisie became the 'common sense' (hegemony). Ordinary people identify with the bourgeoisie (consensus culture) and maintain the status quo but Gramsci set out to emphasize the importance of the superstructure in both maintaining and fracturing relations of the base.[12]

Similarly, the internet is not non-hierarchical but embedded in structural inequalities and the strong privileges of some media over others. Other forces of power set the rules for such fights. The strong effect of hegemony (of coercion and consent) in capitalist ideology, disseminated and shaped by state-institutes.

---

11   Often mentioned are the four versions of power according to Manuel Castells: Networking power; Network power, Networked power, and Network-making power. Castells is important to mention as he has had a great impact. He is the 5th most cited author and is susceptible for unintended re-conceptualised frameworks that continue to be associated to him.

12   For a collection of analyses see: <http://www.marxists.org/archive/gramsci/index.htm>, and see also International Socialism Journal (114, Special Issue on Gramsci): http://www.isj.org.uk/index.php4?s=contents&issue=114.

The overwhelming prominence of the narrative that Facebook and Twitter are crucial agents for change (besides being conceptually wrong) white-washes corporate capitalism (Mejias 2009).

For much longer debates about the internet coincided with the 'globalisation discourse' because neo-liberal globalisation had strongly shaped conventional modes of communication (Featherstone and Lash 1995). They were accompanied by extravagant suggestions about the internet creating gender equality, increasing economic development and other anticipations, but also doom-scenarios often articulated with postmodern theory about virtual reality. Take for instance this view by Baudrillard (from *Impossible Exchange*):

> Reality is growing increasingly technical and efficient; everything that can be done is being done, though without any longer meaning anything. [...] As for the sign, it is passing into the pure speculation and simulation of the virtual world, the world of the total screen, where the same uncertainty hovers over the real and 'virtual reality' once they go their separate ways. The real no longer has any force as sign, and signs no longer have any force of meaning
>
> BAUDRILLARD 2001, 5

Some new technologies were indeed revolutionary in the realm of everyday life (to refuse this new reality is basically to refuse progress). But it is precisely therefore that they involve new modes of fetishism and disseminate capitalist norms (Kellner 2002, 299). Insofar as social and economic relations are not egalitarian within society today, we need to expect the same for the economy of new media (Mansell 2004, 97). The political realities after 9/11 and the collapse of the housing market and subsequently the banking system itself in 2008 forcibly 'corrected' some of the premature propositions about the political impact of the internet downgrading the significance of nation-states in (temporarily) global networks. This is for instance tackled by Jones' (2011, 89–90) suggestion that the importance of class presents itself in the class nature of the internet (as a sector) which conditions our communication styles (open source FLOSS entrepreneurialism notwithstanding) and class in terms of the organisational consequences of the proponents of internet media (as opposed to independent left-wing publications sold face-to-face on streets and protests) which has real implications for political organising. The latter is important because, as Mejias (2009) argues, network theories rely heavily on being wired by technologically connected nodes, but the overwhelming majority are not, they are 'para-node'. Through this important critique Mejias shows the politics of inclusion and exclusion encoded in the network as they are embedded in global economic systems based on corporate interests. Most people in revolutions are non-nodes, excluded from the networks, those who have no access to technologically mediated networks of communication. Technology is *one of many* societal interactions. There are nodes in all networks. What matters is to differentiate between the quality of technological networks and social networks, and between each and when these two interact (Fuchs 2009, 96). They can organically interact through mediators, as I will explain. But what could Marxist theories contribute to my understanding of contemporary revolutionary activity and ICT?

As argued at the outset, reconciling differences between theories that start from social structure (top down) and individual motivation (bottom up) comes down to unveiling the mediation without ending up disregarding individual human action. This is not a new problem in social theory. Engaging with the theory of value is uncommon in anthropology because this discipline was wedged in the theoretical limbo of social theory (Graeber 2001, 2).[13] The very idea of applying grand theory was even seen as a contradiction since an anthropologist's place is in (the other's) ethnography. But ethnography is based on a ray of assumptions and *always* applies theories, the real choice is acknowledging and rethinking this epistemological challenge or not (Graeber 2001, 20). Marxist anthropology offered the opportunity to add a critical niche when it started to be more centred around the idea of 'mode of production', a focus that offered debates beyond (the classic anthropological) exchange but how societies continue to exist and "reproduces" itself. The questions are often about how a society's most basic forms of exploitation and inequality are rooted in the social relations through which people do so (24). These Marxist-inspired inquires introduced a series of powerful analytical terms – exploitation, fetishism, appropriation and inspired a whole series of academic approaches in what came knows as "critical theory" (25). The main motivation was to unmask the hidden structures of power, dominance, and exploitation that lay below even the most mundane aspects of daily life. But critical theory ended up *"sabotaging its own best intentions, making power and domination so fundamental to the very nature of social reality that it became impossible to imagine a world without it"* (30); losing its critical arguments altogether. Since

---

13 The Marxist theory of value considers that the value of commodities is derived from the human labour that went into producing them. This fact tends to be obscured when the object is bought and sold on the market so it seems that its value arises naturally, from the qualities of the object itself. In a way, is obfuscation can also be considered the trap in the reinterpretation of internet commodities.

we are stuck in a totalising system, as some in effect argued, resistance is futile.
A good example is this élan, following-up from the previous que

> [T]he economic sphere, the sphere of all exchange, taken overall, cannot
> be exchanged for anything. There is no meta-economic equivalent of the
> economy anywhere, nothing to exchange it for as such, nothing with
> which to redeem it in another world. It is, in a sense, insolvent, and in any
> event insoluble to a global intelligence. [...] Politics is laden with signs
> and meanings, but seen from the outside it has none. It has nothing to
> justify it at a universal level (all attempts to ground politics at a meta-
> physical or philosophical level have failed). It absorbs everything which
> comes into its ambit and converts it into its own substance, but it is not
> able to convert itself into – or be reflected in – a higher reality which
> would give it meaning.
>
> BAUDRILLARD 2001, 3–4

This mix of edgy yet abstract discourse explains the appeal of mass consumption not uncommon for upper-middle class academics. But Baurillard also
reminds us that these awkward preoccupations did not occur in a vacuum but
respond to the dissolution of the vast social movements in the '60s; the rise
of neoliberal ideologies; itself partly made possible by the failure of the left
to come up with plausible alternatives. The most influential impact on anthropologists' understanding of value came from Appadurai's "Commodities and
the Politics of Value" (1986). Anthropologists would do better, he suggests, to
forget Marx's approach (which has an emphasis on production and thus value
arises from human labour; a annoying focus on class in other words) and look
instead to value that is not rooted in human labour or a social system but arising from exchange, from individual desire. Unlike Marx's, his model can easily
be applied even where formal markets don't exist; there is always some form of
exchange after all. This approach has its advantages: it allows the analyst to
skip past the problem of social totalities (structures of meaning) and focus on
individual actors and their motivations as Graeber argues (2001, 30–31). It
leaves us with a doomed and static image of a self-interested, calculative universal human urge (33). It is not very surprising how this comes to fit with the
emphasis on consumption as a topic in cultural and communication studies.

  But there is also a critical 'realist' philosophy of a different kind, Bhaskar
managed to merge a Marxist theory adhered to the description of ideology in
mediation and base/superstructure analyses yet opening it up for contemporary debates and critical emancipatory inquiries in defence of against postmodernist analyses. One that sees reality operating at different levels, what is

happening at the surface does not tell us all. In a contribution written with political philosopher Callinicos, bot describe how, underneath that surface, one may find the very structures that could destabilise existing social relations. This approach suggests is that human agency is made possible by social structures, though themselves very conditioned, offer the potentiality to undermine it. Moreover, while doing so we are capable to (consciously) reflect upon the (changing) the actions that produce them (Bhaskar and Callinicos 2003). In other words, to bring them to the surface, deconstruct the systems in order to better dismantle it. These are not new discoveries but they do bring back some of the powerful radical philosophies that it has taken its cue from, for instance in the words of Karl Marx "All science would be superfluous if the outward appearance was the essence of things" (Volume III of Capital) and of course Gramsci's "philosophy of practice" (see also Harman 2007). This method inspired me to regard both the liberating and imprisoning implications of ICTs at once as well as to separate the internet as an entity between social media as space and tool.

This dual assessment echoes the agency-structure twin-approach where internet space refers to both the structural aspects of the internet and society, while internet tool represents the tactical aspects and political agency, I derive this distinction from the correlation between practice and theory (Figure. 15.1). Having made this deconstruction, it still requires a critical inclusion of the materiality of the internet as it *actually* exists, such as in terms of internet access. Actual penetration rates and other statistical evidence are important arguments against the celebratory and technophile claims cheerleading neoliberalism, but I argue that online and offline politics are actually unequal. A misunderstanding regarding the negative interpretations of the internet (also by progressive critics) stems from the fact that the total penetration rates are not equal for political penetration. We cannot assess the political impact of the internet in terms of 'the population' and should, instead, appreciate this (especially the 'tool' function) in terms of its meaning for 'the activists'. This allows me to get deeper into the matter and give affirmative assumptions where they are the case as I show in the final section.

To start with, we need more than the increase of communication and dissemination. I take from internet theorist Fenton (2006) that first and foremost political solidarity is the socio-political glue, and that social movements gain public legitimacy and political force through the embodiment of solidarity offline. Without an organised body with a centre, resistance is more likely to dissipate. The misconception of revolutionary organising comes down to centralism + hierarchy = authoritarianism. A Leninist understanding of democratic centralism therefore has two conditions: it has to be democratic because only through democracy can the best lessons be incorporated and the most advanced experiences internalised and if necessary generalised. Secondly, although consensus-style activism without a form of centralism may seem more acceptable (if not morally superior) it fails to guaranty accountability. Hence, a relevant problem is that no centralised structure deepens the lack of democracy, representation and – what Jo Freeman famously called the *tyranny of structurelessness*. It is certainly legitimate to disagree, to *not* reach consensus, but above all it is a method that can at times allow for a certain trial and error in our tactics and in turn improve (or disprove) the overall methods of struggle, this is why centralisation and (party) politics disproportionately focused on the instrumental (bureaucratic) issues is rarely a lasting project. That is precisely why in Gramsci's dialectical understanding of power and hegemony resistance is prepared and applied by an independent organised subaltern through a revolutionary party, not to act as a substitute but represents the organised body of the oppressed by the oppressed or exploited.

Perhaps more to the point in our discussion about activism and to arrive at the case of the Middle East and the internet: forms and choices of organizing are not autonomous but very determined by the territorial context and the balance of power therein. While the discourse (and to some extent practical manifestations) of capitalism and imperialism changed, its effects did not). There are changes in the economic practice in a globalized era; but it is not as if nation-states don't network. The question is where exactly power lies in those 'spaces' and 'flows'. Global political-economy, ICT and Middle East politics are more related than we think. The myth that ICT positively impacts the promotion of freedom is considered to be generated by the expansion of ICT, the tools and services enabling citizen participation in the decision-making process, and (peculiarly in the counter-revolutionary hindsight) democracy.

4   ICT Imperialism

Political-economy, which in the MENA region often entails (neo)colonialism and imperialism, is the elephant in the room in much of the earlier ICT analyses. There was much anticipation that the internet would increase 'development' (ICT4D) in the MENA. This narrative was partly the result of the ICT sector being at the front of a shift from state to liberal [privatised] economy on one hand and a more or less correlated experience of democratization processes and social political reform in the late 1990s on the other hand. Jordan and Egypt were hailed as the poster boys of this new experience. The ict sector is at the heart of neoliberal globalisation, if not its life-line. This whereas *development*, is often deployed as rhetorical tools to promote the internet and understood to bring economic prosperity and even peace, the imperialism that obstructs much of the potential justice-based prosperity in the MENA is hardly mentioned in ICT policy.

Ya'u (2004) referred to the merging of political-economy and ICT as the 'new imperialism' because economic participation depends on ICT, i.e. and if we zoom out, enforced institutionalised policies like the Free Trade Agreement (FTA) increased rather than prevented digital divides on national scales. The most important feature of this imperialism is control and ownership, very prevalent through what is called 'global governance' directed by powerful institutes that strongly privilege industrial-free market states. The infrastructures of the internet expose how powerful and centralised bodies like the internet Corporation for Assigned Names and Numbers (ICANN) are, demonstrated by their allocating of URL names and addresses. The argument could be that the sheer volume of information will transform policies (e.g. Shirazi 2008). But such analyses mostly depend on western-centred analysis where the internet facilitates the expression of liberal values such as individualism (e.g. Brinkerhoff 2005).

Ya'u makes an important contribution by reintroducing neo-colonialism and imperialism into our terminology. A weak ICT in MENA is related to the combined problem of 'late development' post-independence impediments itself stemming from colonial structures. In essence, these inherited structures hardly changed and continued in a neo-colonial fashion, and where the internet manages to grow it is bounded by neoliberal rules of engagement, this clearly disadvantaged Middle East countries (Saleh 2011). While the agenda for the 2003 WSIS conference in Tunisia was set by the private sector (the internet Telecom Union, ITU) and serves powerful conglomerates, its public goal was promoting ICT and bridge digital divides for the benefit of common people. As Costanza-Chock (2003, 4–5) argues, civil society and NGO actors were invited to such summits to mask the neoliberal agenda and also refer to this corporate behaviour as 'imperialist'. Furthermore, the Middle East is predominantly depicted as suffering from political social conflicts. So, of course there is also another definition of imperialism which is not sufficiently clear and cannot be solely explained through parasitical ICT firms.

While these conflicts are mostly portrayed as an essential characteristic of a volatile region always in conflict or at war, they are rarely identified as a result of external factors (settler-colonialism or major and violent invasions under the banner 'war on terror', or the arming and funding dictatorships). This is a far cry from space-less and border-less myths and the very point of struggle over self-determination and territorial autonomy. I agree with Terranova (2004) who argued against the notion of disconnection from particular places (virtual reality) but to see that internet power is (state) grounded. The overwhelming materiality of power over technology in capitalist nation states was practiced during internet shut-downs at the start of the revolutions in Egypt and Syria. Showing the world just how 'free' the free market is, Vodafone complied with Mubarak's orders to disconnect its clients. The internet provider Noor was the last one to operate but that was mainly because it hosted the stock exchange. The graphs offered by Renesys (listing all the ISPs) starkly visualise the day of the shutdown when all of a sudden there is a flat line. For Dan Mcquillan the sequenced-pattern (with short intervals) suggesting that the companies were probably being phoned one at a time and being told to take their connection off the air.[14] With this, we are also reminded that it is real people- managers and CEO's – with choices and decision-making power and not some abstract infrastructures that run the show. This implicates them as collaborators. Looking back, it seems quite extraordinary that internet connection was restored at the moment the fiercest and state-orchestrated crackdown (*the battle of the camels*) took place, suggesting there were also internal divisions at the heart of the regime. That can be explained by the fact the security apparatus was taken by surprise by people's well-organised and steadfast resistance, and that not being able to monitor their online communications hampered intelligence forces.

Imperialism is not just a label for Middle East politics, it lies at the centre of the nexus oppression-resistance precisely because this is a region where the most important natural resources for capitalism (oil, gas, phosphate) are found and its geography practically streamline most of the trade routes (including access to those very resources). On top of this: the region is an important source for the (state-sponsored) arms industry. In light of these realities the copy&pasted revolution discourses become more about wishful projections of liberal uprisings than they are about indigenous experiences. The unprecedented uprisings are driven by popular protest and cannot be understood without placing them in the years of preparations.

5   The Arab Revolutions and the Internet

Whereas they are widely debated and often treated with either awe or contempt, revolutions are "first of all a history of the forcible entrance of the masses into the realm of rulership over their own destiny" (Trotsky 1930). For long, collective self-emancipation through such revolutionary processes were deemed a part of the past. Hence, the Arab uprisings refute many of the social

---

14   The 'flat-line' graphs by *Renesys* are found in this online post: <http://www.renesys.com/blog/2011/01/egypt-leaves-the-internet.shtml>.

theories that considered revolution a outdated (Callinicos 2011, 5). The uprisings showed world-wide resonances through protest movements that centred around city squares such as the Spanish *Indignado* Movement and the Occupy Movement which started in New York but spread to 900 cities. Two of the most important factors of the uprisings are the changing political public landscape (flocked by an amalgam of new leftist, political, student groups and the re-surfacing of class struggle. The latter signified in Egypt through some of the largest workers strikes and the formation of independent unions the minute Mubarak was ousted. Class struggles and relations are a crucial element of the political struggle in Egypt (Al-Mahdi and Marfleet 2009), this is not unique, its rather more related to the objective condition that political uprisings crystallize in a 'periodic fertilisation'. It is through the spreading of the political struggle the economic struggle extends as theorised by Rosa Luxemburg (1970). The digital difference is a an additional third segment of the revolutionary political dynamics of and during the manifold political campaigns, strikes and new coalitions.

While the surprised responses unmasked a particular bias, the initial assessments seemed confused by the discovery that 'they' too use new technologies, it is these essentialist approaches that created the fantasy that the internet caused a "tipping point." it all seemed in any case to be a very new focus. Conversely, before 2011, foreign-policy and security experts were also very interested in the use of the internet in the Middle East with regards to counter-terrorism. In fact, to those following these debates for much longer, Ukraine's Orange Revolution, Lebanon's Cedar Revolution, Moldova's Twitter-Spring and Iran's Green-Twitter Revolution in the 5 years preceding the Arab revolts were a preview of the popular copy and pasting that were to emanate. They prepared the prominent 2011 markers-fetishized with colourful flora and fauna labels - of events in which the internet was elevated as a crucial player. Thus the Arab Spring/Facebook reference were simultaneously a continuation and a break of this narrative. When the struggles intensified, 'revolution' began to mean something else, more than the copy-and-paste demarcations.

The tipping-point moment in actual revolutions hardly depends on the tools at hand but predominantly on the social-class dynamics. That is why there are years where nothing happens with the same tools at hand (for instance, masses of young people were using the internet for over a decade); and suddenly there are weeks where decades happen, to paraphrase Lenin.[15] The digital difference is a. additional segment of the revolutionary political

---

15 This quote can be found in a 1920 text by Lenin and bundled in his Collected Works available online: <http://www.marxists.org/archive/lenin/works/1920/oct/20.htm>.

dynamics of and during the manifold strikes, political campaigns and new coalitions. The increasing importance of the internet is certainly not irrelevant. Revolutions do offer an important occasion study to understand the implications of the internet and even may open up a space for bottom-up analysis.

This space from below is also very welcome because overt fascination with social media gave the impression that the revolutions were mainly middle class and secular. In a way, the Arab uprisings evaluated through the lens of (western) modernity smoothly folded with the idea that social media plays an important role in developing a sense of modernity or, as this blustering description claims: "Much like Western societies, parts of Egyptian society are transforming away from traditional groups and towards more loosely structured "networked individualism" (Wellman et al. 2011, 6). The underlying assumption paradigm of these such modernity-technology paradigms such assumptions is that digital politics were crucial because they changed nature of mass communication platforms and new forms of organising, the old-fashioned hierarchic or class-based formations improved. In such digital worlds, ideologically 'recalcitrant' groups such as the Muslim Brotherhood are no longer the way to organize political opposition[16]. Obviously, this narrative is possible if firstly, the Muslim brotherhood is not seen as a legitimate (modern) actor while certain individuals (e.g. Google rep. Wael Ghonim, also the administrator of the much-discussed Khaled Said Facebook group) were greatly admired; helping projecting a certain wishful thinking about the birth to non-ideological (secular) generations via social media. This way Western liberal values are being injected into what are predominantly local ideals and efforts.

This critique notwithstanding, the revolutions uprisings still raise crucial questions about the role of communication technology in social movements, such as how political agency is mediated in and through cyberspace. I don't share the overtly negative outlook as the initial outburst of the "Facebook Revolution" commentary tended to but rather consider the internet as an additional segment that is tactically embedded in a broader political strategy. The uprisings initially represented an ideological melange of progressive socialists, liberal Islamists, capitalists, reactionary conservatives; including 'ideological' groups such as the active Revolutionary Socialists and huge Muslim

---

16   Philip Howard's comment "In a digital world, older ideologically recalcitrant political parties may not even be the most effective way to organize effective political opposition." In a commentary for Reuters, found at:<http://blogs.reuters.com/great-debate/2011/02/16/digital-media-and-the-arab-spring/>.

Brotherhood that might be seen as recalcitrant in many networked politics literature, were at the base of the uprisings. Many of the activists in Egypt's April 6, or 20 February (Morocco) and LCC's (Syrian Local Coordination Committees) and many grassroots networks that played a defining role, don't fit these liberal frameworks while they are actually extremely well versed in the digital world of politics.

As mentioned, while the preferred 'networks' are suppose to have less hierarchy and more autonomy, the paradoxical grounded context refutes the approach to political activism. One of the implications of imperialism its is protecting dictators for the sake of geopolitical hegemony ('stability'), those protesting did not forget, and a reminder of one of the causes for the mass outburst, it is a complicity that those protesting did not forget. Ben Ali and Mubarak were both Western backed rulers. Not until it became clear that the mass protests were indeed historical events with crucial (geo-political) ramifications did the needles of the political compass in Washington-London-Paris reversed. The reluctance of major Western powers with the regards to Syria is even worse, there the uprisings were a major opportunity to oust one of the most brutal dictators, yet people mostly received lip-service until the balance seemed to tip back to Bashar al Assad due to the rise of Daesh (isis). Many of those networks also work within online and offline networks and take internet serious without considering them causes.

For them online activism *facilitates* offline liberation strategies. The local specificities are crucial because the internet is shaped by a strong relation with the balance of force on the ground. Online activism *facilitates* offline liberation strategies. In other words, explaining the value of the internet can never make sense without political and historic contextualisation in terms of conditions and motives. Rather than a sudden 'awakening', the region was already in turmoil, protests had been accumulating for almost a decade, starting with the outbreak of the Second Intifada and Ariel Sharon's massacre of Palestinians; the invasion of Iraq; anger over leaders seen as the local lackeys of the US and Israel. A widespread and deep anger over the regional politics overlapped with domestic issues and grew deeper as the economic impact of the neoliberal (IMF/WB) privatisation combined with price increases caused by the global financial crisis. Wikileaks documents in 2010 illustrates that the extent of corruption and Arab collaboration were not a cause but a confirmation – a deepening – of the growing anger. In the face of these important and contentious events technology was of essential importance, probably projecting the everyday conditions of the authors of those narratives.

Inserting the internet corporations – Facebook, Twitter, Google – at the centre of analyses deny a genuinely popular Arab revolution and allows for orientalist discourse to represent (Aouragh 2015). That is why I protest the technophile production of knowledge through certain technophile mediation. The fallacy in much of the discourse is where the internet framing prefers non-violence and non-ideolog as the preferable form, thereby insinuating a negative undertone for the much more common grassroots activism that includes *all forms* (violent-non-violent, manifest-latent) of struggle when necessary. This bias is crucial because in reality.

Activists have to juggle between self-activity, destruction and the potential of being co-opted in these volatile dynamics; subversion of power is not easy in the face of the extreme asymmetrical relation, and the internet is not always a friend. Youmans and York (2012, 3) remind us that social media platforms were not designed to cater to activists in the first place. Information systems empower authoritarian regimes concretely in the prohibition of anonymity. There is a direct mismatch between the commercial logic and activist use of social media as public information infrastructures. Fuchs clarifies the matter by asking to what degree are users autonomous if 19 out of the top 20 Web 2.0 platforms are profit-oriented (2009, 99). Put differently, while the (user-generated) internet affects the material conditions, it also implicates political activism. This return to political-economy provides an answer to the earlier discussion about how (base and superstructure) dialectics defines mediation. Therefore political resistance should be treated as inhibiting the same dual power.

6   Online-Offline Dialectics

The MENA region at large has the world's highest internet penetration growth rates (1600 per cent for 2001–2009) in terms of internet usage; particularly the increase of social (user-generated) media in 2011 are indicative (asmr 2011). But instead of isolating 'the internet', they are part of new synergies. This was most clear in the way social networking and satellite broadcasters interacted such as when Al Jazeera became a temporary megaphone for activists in Tunisia and Egypt when it aired their YouTube content. According to well-known blogger Hossam al-Hamalawi, the strength of the internet is seen when mainstream media re-mediate activist sources or witness accounts. Such was the case with live-feeds in January and February. Re-dissemination from big or respected mediums added to the fame of these tools, which at the same time reminds of the indirect mediation. After this a new paragraph. It is important to distinguish what impact or effect we mean to address in potential scenarios where the internet might tip the scales of power. The internet shut down enforced debates about designing an independent survival mode, this is why it was important to experiment with pre/non-digital technologies were crucial (such as dial-up modems and fax-to-web bridges), so-called *analogue networks*.[17] I merge these suggestions with the earlier assessment that the internet has two sides, it is a *tool* for activists (survival, operational continuity) and a *space* for activism (expanding and deepening networks). Archiving, solidarity, technological cooperation and nurturing political conviction, these are some of the meaningful elements that reflect all these different sides.

Furthermore, when I deconstruct these abstract levels of interrogation we can connect them with ethnographic features of online politics. Borrowing from the semantics of *mediation* as discussed in first section I suggest interpreting the online/offline divide as a reflection of the *base-superstructure* separation and the space/tool separation as part of the overall political strategies and tactics. Moreover, the stage (timing) of certain interventions shapes the potential of the internet as previous fieldwork in Palestine and Lebanon and events in recent uprisings suggested. I thus distinguish between three revolutionary stages: pre-revolution (preparation and mobilization), moment of revolution (the actual tipping points), and post-revolution (successful continuation or dangerous escalation). This As shown in (Figure 15.1) the internet is not dominant but can be a factor of change. Illustrated in the Matrix of internet resistance, when merging these conceptual deconstructions we get a much more coherent understanding of internet resistance. Adding a hermeneutic separation based on stages allows us to escape the suffocating uniformity of generalising and appreciate the values of technology differently during the chaotic outbreak of revolt because it.

This reminds us that political networks and collective protest are, first and foremost, consolidated offline. Online spaces of interaction and tools of communication can amplify these agendas and opinions. Social media are the choice of most Arab activists simply because they are the spaces and tools which people *already* choose in their everyday lives. For a specific layer of activists and participants of the uprisings, internet spaces served as important counter-hegemonic spaces (Warner 2002). In the 'pre-revolutionary' period, critique of the existing political and social order were articulated on many such spaces, without this preparatory stage the maturation of the tipping point is hard to imagine. On the 25th of January it was critical to use

---

17   Internet Artizans, 10 Februari 2011: http://www.internetartizans.co.uk/socnets_with_old_tech_egypt#comment-8423.

Matrix of Resistance (Analytical Framework)		
Space Stage	Online	Offline
Pre-Revolution (Preparation & Mobilization) Space	Tool Space	Tool Space
Revolution (Tipping Point) Space	Tool Space	Tool Space
Post-Revolution (Continuation & Escalation) Space	Tool Space	Tool Space

With each stage of the revolution the existing balance of power(and the actors involved) changes.

FIGURE 15.1   *Matrix of internet Resistance*

real-time online updates in order to device the safest routes for marches or locate the most risky one's and avoid those. Kira Allmann (2012) shows the life and death significance of a functioning mobile technology in her research among activists in Cairo. And *during* the uprisings the internet was relevant as a vehicle for building global solidarity. The internet also became a parallel space for political identity formation: where people met other people who relate to their opposition and shared information about protests, or disseminate messages that further ignited their anger and determination. In this sense, social media platforms became more convenient online public spheres for political deliberation.

Within the social networking spaces of the *Shabaab 6 April* (April-6 Youth) and *Kuluna Khaled Said* (We are all Khaled Said) Facebook groups (the English and the Arabic one), as well as high-profile individuals (Alaa Abdel Fatta, 3arabawi, Sandmonkey) were important nodes. These were not only meeting points for activists themselves, they were also the *source* of much of the forwarded mobile text messages and emails, Tweets and Facebook posts, and as such instrumental in mobilizing a section of the wired-youth. As we have seen, in revolutionary moments *repetition* is important; so is agitation (for a march towards Tahrir); and of course the consolidation of general political analysis (the need to stay in Tahrir square); finally, the organization

of the acts themselves. These different engagements echo the inspiring adagio *Educate-Agitate-Organize:* the trio-characteristic of revolutionary political organising.

Those involved in these *online* realms are a selective segment of the protesters
– and we know that social movements are in themselves a small or selective
portion of society. In extraordinary times, the impact of these sub-scenes can
reach beyond their usual networks marking the digital-revolutionary difference. In revolutionary moments, when at a 'tipping point', emotional or cognitive power is crucial. Without the innumerable video files provided via
Facebook and YouTube by ordinary people, the revolutions would not have
been documented (and therefore: experienced) with the same intensity.
Massive reporting by mainstream sources has political repercussions too, giving activists the confidence to advance their agendas, reassure people that
they are not alone and thus further influencing the judgements and choices of
activists.

The internet archives bravery and resolve, and these recorded events are in
due course valuable for other activists (Naguib 2011, 17). The most empowering
impact of the internet can be found in this juxtaposition.

During a fieldwork visit in August 2011 several activists recalled how they
experienced the revolutionary upheavals in the early days (January/February).
I was told several times that being cut off didn't dismantle the revolt at all; that
the disruption of the mobile phone services was far more crucial for on the
ground politics. What I also learned was that the crucial tactics that finally led
to the occupation of Tahrir Square had little to do with Facebook, in fact: false
information was purposely posted to confuse the secret service. The fact that
the protests continued *and* increased despite the internet black-out is of monumental importance. It turned out that for weeks, activists had met often in
cramped living rooms. Ironically, it is precisely because the organising was
done offline that it was rarely noted by the internet-obsessed reporters. While
the technology was absent the people, and their physical resistance, were very
present. Paradoxically, it reduced distraction and gave focus during the five-
day blackout. Websites like Facebook are not a social networks in and off themselves but social-networking-tools. All *users*, including – those outside the
virtual structures of the 'nodes' what Mejias (2011) called the *para-nodal* – were
the networks. Thus not the technological networks but the people were the
organizational backbone.

Lastly, the impact of agitation and education cannot be underestimated. The
uprising of Egypt was beamed to millions via the now world-famous Kuluna
Khaled Said Facebook groups, Twitter and YouTube. With the verbally-graphic
narratives of Sandmonkey I aim to offer a slice of the (start of the) revolution as

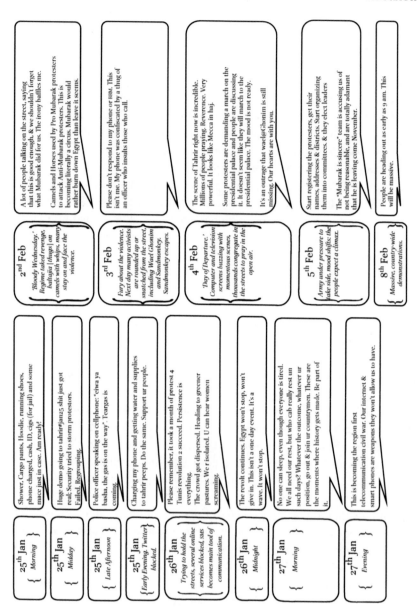

25th Jan
{ Morning }

Shower, Cargo pants, Hoodie, running shoes, phone charged, cash, ID, cigs (for jail) and some mace just in case. Am ready!

25th Jan
{ Midday }

Huge demo going to tahrir#jan25 shit just got real. Security tried to storm protesters. Failed. Regrouping.

25th Jan
{ Late Afternoon }

Police officer speaking on cellphone: "eiwa ya basha, the gas is on the way". Teargas is coming.

25th Jan
{ Early Evening, Twitter blocked. }

Charging my phone and getting water and supplies to tahrir peeps. Do the same. Support ur people.

26th Jan
{ Trying to hold the streets, several online services blocked, SMS becomes main tool of communication. }

Please remember, it took a month of protest 4 Tunis revolution 2 succeed. Persistence is everything.
The crowd got dispersed. Heading to greener pastures. We r isolated. U can hear women screaming.

26th Jan
{ Midnight }

The revolt continues, Egypt won't stop, won't give in. This isn't a one day event. It's a wave. It won't stop.

27th Jan
{ Morning }

No one can sleep, even though everyone is tired. We all need our rest, but who cab really rest un such days? Whatever the outcome, whatever ur position, go out & join ur countrymen. These are the moments where history gets made. Be part of it.

27th Jan
{ Evening }

This is becoming the region first telecommunication civil war. Our internet & smart phones are weapons they won't allow us to have.

2nd Feb
'Bloody Wednesday.' Regime took revenge. baltajia [thugs] on camels with whips, many stay on and face the violence.

A lot of people talking on the street, saying that this is good enough, & we shouldn't forget what Mubarak did for us. The irony baffles me.

Camels and Horses used by Pro Mubarak protesters to attack Anti-Mubarak protesters. This is becoming literally a circus. Mubarak would rather burn down Egypt than leave it seems.

3rd Feb
Fury about the violence. Next day many activists are rounded up or snatched from the street, including Wael Ghonim and Sandmonkey. Sandmonkey escapes.

Please don't respond to my phone or sms. This isn't me. My phone was confiscated by a thug of an officer who insults those who call.

4th Feb
'Day of Departure.' Computer and television screens buzzing with momentous scenes, thousands congregate in the streets to pray in the open air.

The scene of Tahrir right now is incredible. Millions of people praying. Reverence. Very powerful. It looks like Mecca in haj.
Some protesters are demanding a march on the presidential palace and people are discussing it. It doesn't seem like they will march to the presidential palace. The mood is not ready.
It's an outrage that wael@Ghonim is still missing. Our hearts are with you.

5th Feb
'Army under pressure to take side, mood shifts; the people expect a climax.'

Start registering the protesters, get their names, addresses & districts. Start organizing them into committees. & they elect leaders
The 'Mubarak is sincere' team is accusing us of not being reasonable, and are totally adamant that he is leaving come November.

8th Feb
Massive, country-wide demonstrations.

People are heading out as early as 9 am. This will be massive.

FIGURE 15.2   *Narrating the Revolution through Twitter by Sandmonkey*[18]

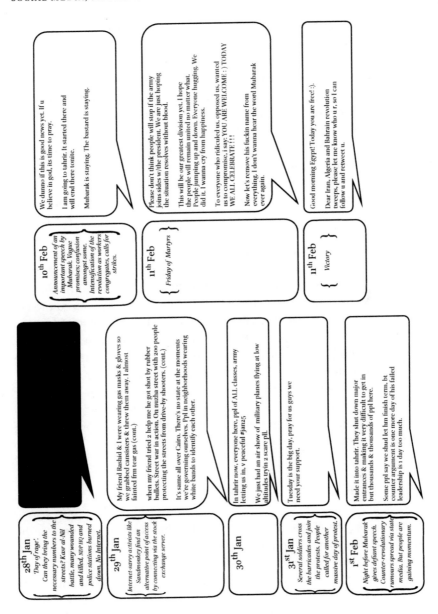

it unfolded (Figure 15.2). This digital footprint, coming straight from the epicentre of events, as documented in his own words on Twitter. The Twitter voices included activists who were very prominent in the physical movements.[19]

There are nevertheless several caveats about the prospects of the internet as a space or tool of activism. Firstly, the scale between hegemonic and counter-hegemonic use is not balanced, as demonstrated in the section about ICT and imperialism. Another important prospect is that activists in online social media spaces are operating in an online community that increasingly mirrors their own. The implication of a digital world filtered and dominated by the parasitical Facebook creates unrepresentative bubbles is a result of the fact that these platforms derived from corporate premises and thus marketing algorithms. This means that debating, sharing and inviting those already largely on your side and actually not reaching out to wider networks. Pariser (2011) remarked that with the rise of personalization (e.g. Google and Facebook customizing search results) internet users are sent down particular information tunnels and hence controlling-and limiting-the information we consume based on the motivation to predict what users are most likely to click, threatening the autonomy of how we consume or share information. Finally, archiving is important in itself, but with digital media this happens in real-time and en-masse, the downside clearly being updates are quickly buried under millions of other updates. Therefore, I argue that it is the very awareness of these techno-social power fields, as outlined in this article that will become increasingly crucial. This social capital has offline repercussions for activists – the difference between being arrested or intercepted online.

7   Conclusion

Hence at the start of this chapter I referred to the *relative* importance of the internet to help counter the difference between absolute and proportional representation. One of the signs of the relative importance of ICT was the particular empirical dynamic shared by activists in Cairo. There were interesting divisions of labour between techno-savvy activists, crackers and hackers; those able to communicate in different languages; those with well-established international networks; those who can reach large audiences (unions, football

---

18   Selections of Tweets were recited by Idle and Nunns (2011) in their joyful *Tweets from Tahrir.*

19   Graph-design made with help of Kira Allmann, Oxford University.

clubs, and student groups). Activists very consciously use different tools for different audiences. Two of the tents on Tahrir Square were manned by some of the most techno-savvy protesters with their laptops, tapping power from lamp posts while signs on the tent mark the point to gather videos and pictures; mobile phone footage recorded during the blackout was collected and posted online so as to be used by journalists. Activists who were not in Egypt would follow tweets from within Egypt, translate and re-tweet to non-Arabic speakers, and offer online critiques of misrepresentations.

I regard social media as *disproportionate* and *parallel* spaces because the internet is valued less than where/when one can meet face-to-face, such as the overlapping private-public places in the previous section signify. With regards to discussions about the importance of democratic centralism, physical meetings are better for political planning and organising and building trust; for conscripting personal sacrifice as the hundreds of martyrs testify. Another reason is that offline protest sites often included those connected to mosques in densely populated working-class neighbourhoods, and in university campuses.

The ultimate and recurring question for many of us is the following: would this have happened without the internet? One of the answers is that it would not have been exactly the same, i.e. we wouldn't be able to retweet and forward the amazing updates of people like Sandmonkey, or the YouTube footage from the ground and in response to many such mediations assemble at the Egyptian, Tunisian, Libyan embassies in protest of the complicity of our western governments and in support and celebration with the people rising up. And revolutionaries could not have countered many of the government lies as they came out.

Another answer could be that, *of course*, the revolution would have happened because the main conditions were there anyway, maybe it would not have been January but February or 80 days not 18 for Mubarak to be defeated. But the real answer is that this is an illogical question to begin with, we need to apply a historical materialist approach to the whole question. This is the stage we are at in the production and development of technology and it is a medium in the conditions we have not ourselves chosen.

That is why i discussed the internet as a tool of protest in the Arab revolutions as part of larger political-economic landscape in which political activists operate; they allude to an (orientalist) framing and reflect the deeper ideological meaning of the Marxist concept of mediation. I evoked the interplay between technology and Marxist politics and invoked examples from Arab activists. This multi-levelled investigation allows me to go beyond the dominant Euro-American focus that prevails in (mainstream) internet studies. I argued, echoing Rosa Luxemburg, that revolutionary change does not rely on spontaneous unorganized acts: it needs organizers, leaders, determination, and accountability. Discipline and structured organizing enables activists to generalize from complex and uneven realities and they are imperative for the survival of political movements. The activist networks do not confirm the view of leaderless swarms because it looked like it was a new, youth, non-ideological, online, horizontal movement it gained attention and for many disillusioned with mainstream politics they therefore gave it the benefit of the doubt. Clichés about the role of the internet don't help us understand the dual character of the internet, Invoking the notion of mediation made us see can empowers and disempowers. This chapter therefore offered a conceptual understanding of internet activism that integrates imperialism and political-economy with the possible value and contribution of the internet to grassroots social capital. This is important because "unless we can relate past literature, however indirectly, to the struggle of men and women against exploitation, we shall not fully understand our own present and so [will be] less able to change it effectively" (Eagleton 1976, 76). And such is not a contradiction after all but the *normalized* exception in the ultimate rule called 'capitalism', a paradox prominent in the opening of Marx and Engels' Communist Manifesto for a good reason.

References

Allmann, Kira C. 2012. Mind, Body and Phone: Mobility, Mobile Technology and Political Activism in the Context of the Egyptian Revolution. (Unpublished Master's Thesis). University of Oxford, Oxford, United Kingdom.

Aouragh, Miriyam. 2012. Framing the Arab Revolutions: Myth Meets Modernity. *Cinema Journal* (51) 4.

Aouragh, Miriyam and Anne Alexander. 2011. Sense and Nonsense of Facebook Revolutions. *International Journal of Communication* 5: 1344–1358.

Arab Social Media Report (ASMR). Vol. 1 (2). 2011. Civil Movements: The Impact of Facebook and Twitter. Accessed May 25, 2012. http://www.dsg.ae/NEWSANDEVENTS/UpcomingEvents/ASMRHome.aspx.

Armbrust, Walter. 2007. New Media and Old Agendas: The Internet in the Middle East and Middle Eastern Studies. International Journal of Middle East Studies. 39 (4): 531–533.

Bimber, Bruce., Andrew. J. Flanagin and Cynthia Stohl. 2005. Reconceptualizing collective action in the contemporary media environment. *Communication Theory* 15 (4), 365–388.

Baudrillard, Jean. 2001. Impossible Exchange. New York: Verso.

Brinkerhoff, Jennifer. 2005. Digital Diasporas and Governance in Semi-authoritarian States: The Case of the Egyptian COPTS, Public Administration and Development, 25, 193–204.

Bhaskar, Roy and Alex Callinicos. 2003. Marxism and Critical Realism: A Debate. *Journal of Critical Realism* (1(2).

Benjamin, Walter. 1970 (1934). The Author as Producer. Republished by New Left Review I/62 July-August. http://www2.warwick.ac.uk/fac/arts/theatre_s/postgraduate/maipr/teaching_1112/warwick/st2/kobialka_reading_-_benjamin_w_-_the_author_as_producer.pdf.

Briggs, Asa and Peter Burke. 2005. *A Social History of Media From Gutenberg to the Internet.* Cambridge: Polity Press.

Bruns, Axel. 2010. From Reader to Writer: Citizen Journalism as News Produsage. In *International Handbook of Internet Research,* edited by Jeremy Hunsinger, Lisbeth Klastrup, Matthew Allen, 119–134. Dordrecht, NL: Springer.

Camfield, David 2007. The Multitude and the Kangaroo: A Critique of Hardt and Negri's Theory of Immaterial Labour. *Historical Materialism* 15 (2): 21–52.

Callinicos, Alex. 2011. The Return of the Arab Revolution. *International Socialism* 130, April. Accessed May 25, 2012. http://www.isj.org.uk/?id=717.

Castells, Manuel 2009. *Communication Power.* New York: Oxford University Press.

Costanza-Chock, Sasha. 2003. WSIS, the Neoliberal Agenda, and Counterproposals from 'Civil Society'. *Journal of Communication Inquiry* 3 (2): 118–139. Paper presented for OURmedia III, Barranquilla Conference May, 30 2003.see also: http://mediaresearchhub.ssrc.org/wsis-the-neoliberal-agenda-and-counterproposals-from-civil-society/resource_view.

Deibert, Ronald. 1997. *Parchment, Printing, and Hypermedia: Communication in World Order Transformation.* New York: Columbia University Press.

Doogan, Kevin. 2010. *New Capitalism? The Transformation of Work.* Cambridge, MA: Polity.

Eagleton, Terry. 1976. *Marxism and Literary Criticism.* Berkeley, CA: University of California Press.

Eagleton, Terry. 2004. *After Theory.* London: Penguin Books.

El-Mahdi, Rabab, and Philip Marfleet, eds. 2009. *Egypt: The Moment of Change.* London: Zed Books.

Featherstone Mike and Scott Lash. 1995. Globalization, Modernity and the Spatialization of Social Theory: An Introduction. In *Global Modernities,* edited by Mike Featherstone, Scott Lash, and Roland Robertson, 1–24. London: Sage.

Fenton, Nathalie. 2006. Contesting Global Capital, New Media, Solidarity, and the Role of a Social Imaginary. In Reclaiming the Media. Communication Rights and Democratic Media Roles, edited by Bart Cammaerts and Nico Carpentier, 225–242. Bristol: Intellect.

Fine, Ben and Alfredo Saad-Filho. 2010. *Marx's Capital.* 5th ed. London: Pluto Press.

Fuchs, Christian. 2009. Some Reflections on Manuel Castells' Book "Communication Power." *tripleC – Open Access Journal for a Global Sustainable Information Society* 7 (1): 94–108.

Fuchs, Christian. 2011. Cognitive Capitalism or Informational Capitalism? The Role of Class in the Information Economy. In *Cognitive Capitalism, Education and Digital Labour*, edited by Michael A. Peters and Ergin Bulut, 75–119. New York: Peter Lang.

Fuchs, Christian 2012. The Political Economy of Privacy on Facebook. *Television & New Media* 13 (2): 139–159.

Graeber, David. 2001. Toward an anthropological theory of value: the false coin of our own dreams. Palgrave Macmillan, Basingstoke, UK.

Hardt, Michael and Antonio Negri. 2004. *Multitude. War and Democracy in the Age of Empire*. New York: Penguin Books.

Harman, Chris. 1986. Base and Superstructure. *International Socialism* 2(32): 3–44.

Harman, Chris. 2007. Dialectics of Morality. *International Socialism* 113.

Haug, Wolfgang Fritz. 2009. Historical–Critical Dictionary of Marxism: Immaterial Labour. *Historical Materialism* 17 (4): 177–185.

Idle, Nadia and Nunns, Alex 2011. *Tweets from Tahrir: Egypt's Revolution as it Unfolded, in the Words of the People Who Made It*. London: Or Books.

Jones, Jonny. 2011. Social Media and Social Movements. *International Socialism* 130.

Kellner, Douglas. 2002. Theorizing Globalization. *Sociological Theory* 20 (3): 285–305.

Mansell Robin. 2004. Political Economy, Power and New Media. *New Media & Society* 6 (1): 96–105.

Marx, Karl. 1857/1858. *Grundrisse*. http://www.marxists.org/archive/marx/works/1857/grundrisse/ch14.htm.

Mejias, Ulises. 2009. The Limits of Networks as Models for Organizing the Social. *New Media & Society* 12 (4): 603–617.

Mejias, Ulises. 2011. The Twitter Revolution Must Die. http://blog.ulisesmejias.com/2011/01/30/the-twitter-revolution-must-die.

Mitchell, Timothy. 2003. The Middle East in the Past and Future of Social Science. University of California International and Area Studies Digital Collection, MIT-IJMES (1).

Naguib, Sameh. 2011. *The Egyptian Revolution: A Political Analysis and Eyewitness Account*. London: Bookmarks.

Pariser, Eli. 2011. The filter bubble : what the Internet is hiding from you New York : Penguin Press.

Peters, Benjamin 2009. And Lead Us Not into Thinking the New is New: A Bibliographic Case for New Media History. *New Media & Society* 11 (1&2): 13–30.

Sabry, Tarik. 2012. On Historicism, the Aporia of Time and the Arab Revolutions. *Middle East Journal of Culture and Communication* 5 (1): 80–85.

Saleh, Nivien. 2011. *Third World Citizens and the Information Technology Revolution*. Basingstoke: Palgrave Macmillan.

Sayers, Sean. 2007. The Concept of Labour: Marx and his Critics. *Science & Society* 71 (4): 431–454.

Said, Edward W. 1997. *Covering Islam: How the Media and the Experts Determine How We See the Rest of the World*. New York: Vintage Books.

Shirazi, Farid. 2008. The contribution of ICT to freedom and democracy: an empirical analysis of archival data on Middle East. The Electronic Journal of Information Systems in Developing Countries. v35 i6. 1–24.

Terranova, Tiziana. 2004. *Network Culture: Politics for the Information Age*. London: Pluto.

Toffler, Alvin. 1980. The Third Wave. New York: Bantam Books.

Trotsky, Leon. 1930. *The History of the Russian Revolution*. http://www.marxists.org/archive/trotsky/1930/hrr/ch00.htm.

Trotsky, Leon. 1991. *Literature and Revolution*. London: Redwords.

Wayne, Mike 2003. Marxism and Media Studies: Key Concepts and Contemporary Trends. London: Pluto Press.

Warner, Michael. 2002. Publics and Counterpublics. *Public Culture* 14 (1): 49–90.

Youmans, William and Jillian York. 2012. Social Media and the Activist Toolkit: User Agreements, Corporate Interests, and the Information Infrastructure of Modern Social Movements. *Journal of Communication* 62 (2): 315–329.

Wellman Barry, Xiaolin Zhuo, and Justine Yu. 2011. Egypt: The First Internet Revolt? Peace, July–September, 2011, 8.

Williams, Raymond. 1977. *Marxism and Literature*. Oxford: Oxford University Press.

CHAPTER 16

Marx in the Cloud

Vincent Mosco

Nature builds no machines, no locomotives, railways, electric telegraphs, self-acting mules etc. They are organs of the human brain, created by the human hand; the power of knowledge, objectified. The development of fixed capital indicates to what degree general social knowledge has become a direct force of production, and to what degree, hence, the conditions of the process of social life itself have come under the control of the *general intellect* and been transformed in accordance with it; to what degree the powers of social production have been produced, not only in the form of knowledge, but also as immediate organs of social practice, of the real life process (Marx 1858).

1 The Digital World at a Critical Juncture

The digital world is at a critical juncture represented by two clashing visions of the information society. The first imagines a democratic world where information is fully accessible to all citizens as an essential service. This world manages information through forms of regulation and control that are governed by representative institutions whose goal is the fullest possible access for the greatest number of citizens. Governance might take multiple forms, including different combinations of centralized and decentralized approaches at local, regional, national, and international levels. The second imagines a world governed by global corporations and the surveillance and intelligence arms of national governments. Under this model, the market is the leading force shaping decisions about the production, distribution and exchange of information and those corporations with market power hold the most influence. This influence is tempered by the control needs of the state represented primarily by its security and intelligence agencies.

Neither of these approaches ever appears in its pure form but each has historical precedents in society and especially in communication and information technology. The democratic model of governance had the upper hand in the early years of the internet when early developers based primarily in universities organized the information network as an open, decentralized, and democratically managed system primarily interested in connecting active citizens rather than enlarging an audience of relatively passive consumers. This began to change in the early 2000s when companies began to recognize the profit potential in the new global information networks and governments determined that it would enable them to deepen traditional surveillance networks and create entire new ones.

This tension between these competing approaches takes many forms including, for example, policy disputes such as the emergence in 2013 of a conflict in the United States over network neutrality. Would the internet remain based on the principle, admittedly breached more often than its supporters would like, of equal access, or would the market and the need to deliver audiences to advertisers skew its shape in favor of those eager to build shareholder value (McChesney 2013)? Network neutrality attracted enormous interest with the U.S. Federal Communications Commission deluged with a record number of submissions attempting to sway decision-making on the issue. Important as it is, the net neutrality debate is merely symptomatic of the much larger issue of governing the digital world. Specifically, debates about this issue have grown considerably in importance with the rise of new digital systems including cloud computing, big data analytics, and the internet of things. Since the latter is less well developed than the first two, the chapter will address the cloud and big data and briefly return to the internet of things in the conclusion.

2   Cloud Computing

Cloud computing is a model for enabling on-demand network access to a shared pool of ubiquitous, configurable computing resources (e.g., networks, servers, storage, applications, and services) that can be rapidly provisioned and released with minimal management effort or service provider interaction. The cloud, as it is called, is the fastest growing segment of the IT sector and because it enables distant storage, processing, and distribution of data, applications, and services for individuals and organizations, industry observers view it as a disruptive and transformational technology. The cloud is actually housed in data centers, large information factories containing tens or hundreds of thousands of servers, that are linked to telecommunications systems that provide data and services to subscribers,who pay on demand for timely delivery to their individual smart phones, tablets and computers (Mosco 2014). Big data analytics is a term that refers to a form of research using data stored primarily in the cloud. The data centers that store and process information, emails, audio and visual files as well as software and apps for individuals and organizations can also analyze their large data sets, thereby adding value that is attractive to users for whom the provision of timely answers to questions is essential to meet their goals.

There are several critical problems associated with cloud computing and big data including growing concentration of power in a handful of companies and in the surveillance arms of the state with which they are closely associated. These technologies also create significant environmental problems including massive drains on the global electricity grid for powering and cooling data centers and in the use of backup systems essential for maintaining 24/7 access to data and services such as access to Gmail, Facebook, Twitter, and iCloud. Furthermore, the cloud and big data enable massive breeches of privacy and pervasive surveillance arising from widespread hacking but more significantly because there is significant value in cloud computing and data analytics from the profit to be made by selling information gathered in the cloud. In addition, organizations like the National Security Agency and the CIA use the cloud and big data analytics to carry out their mission as spy agencies. The cloud and big data also create enormous problems for labour as they make possible massive outsourcing of jobs in the specific fields occupied by information technology professionals and, more ominously, in the many occupations of knowledge workers, from teachers to journalists from lawyers to accountants, whose analytic skills can increasingly be moved to the cloud. The cloud and big data can also subject these jobs to deepening surveillance and control. Finally, the cloud and big data raise a significant epistemological issue. Lost in the enthusiasm surrounding the potential, especially of big data analytics, is the threat to the pluralism of long-established and successful ways of knowing. The singular reliance on the correlational analysis of quantitative data, to the exclusion of historical, theoretical, qualitative and causal analysis, what I term *digital positivism*, narrows the scope of research that is critical for addressing major social problems.

3 Digital Capitalism and the Surveillance State

Even though it is still young, in a pattern consistent with one Marx identified time and time again, the cloud computing industry is increasingly characterized by the concentration of power in a handful of companies and their allies in the surveillance state. The dominant company is Amazon Web Services, a subsidiary of the global online retailer. AWS uses its dominant position in online sales to undercut the competition in pricing cloud services. It has been so successful in this practice of predatory pricing, one that dominant companies have used since the beginnings of capitalism, that smaller companies have either been driven out of the marketplace or forced to concentrate on narrow niche positions. Remaining industry leaders include Google, Microsoft, Apple and Facebook, old powers in the computer industry such IBM, Cisco, and H-P, which are scurrying to shift from their traditional practices of supplying corporate IT departments to leading them into the cloud, and companies like Rackspace and Salesforce that came of age with cloud computing (Mosco 2014, 48–66).

In addition to using its success in the online world to build a dominant position in the cloud, Amazon demonstrates another well-worn tendency identified by Marx: the ability to use its political influence for economic advantage. AWS provided cloud and big data services to the Obama campaign organization in 2012 and its success in identifying and delivering voters to the Obama forces with the same success that it delivers online users to advertisers, is widely considered one of the most important reasons for the President's re-election (Cohen 2012; Hoover 2012). In a pivotal decision that some suggest was a reward for its campaign success, Amazon was awarded a $600 million contract to provide cloud and big data services to the CIA. Whatever the reasons for the award, which IBM formally challenged unsuccessfully, it brought together leaders in digital capitalism and the surveillance state to create a marriage that would certainly benefit both parties, but it also created a dangerous direct connection between anti-democratic forces in the United States. To further the role of the surveillance state in the cloud computing power structure, the National Security Agency is building one of the world's largest cloud computing facilities deep in a Utah mountain (Bamford 2012).

The US dominates cloud computing but China is rapidly developing its own industry with strong government support that extends to including the cloud in its latest five-year development plan. Government and business, with the investment of some US firms like IBM, have joined to develop entire cloud cities that feature data centers, research and development facilities, corporate offices, training facilities as well as the housing, shops and infrastructure that make up cities of all types. The company Alibaba is a leader in China's cloud industry and, along with Baidu, Tencent and a handful of other firms, makes use of government protection against foreign competition to rise in the global ranks. In 2014 Alibaba made its debut in the United States by launching the most lucrative IPO in history (Hardy 2014). Although it controls only three percent of the global cloud industry marketplace, China's firms are growing and represent threats to the global political economy that would not surprise Marx. Moreover, Alibaba is the leading online source of materials essential to produce fissionable material, a clear threat to global stability. Finally, China's data centers are subject to rules set by its authoritarian government which raises questions about what will happen when more of the world's digital information is stored and processed in that country (Clover 2014).

4   The Cloud and the Environment

In addition to representing the concentrated power of capital and the surveillance state, cloud computing presents significant environmental challenges. Data centers filled with always-on servers are major drains on the global electricity grid. Requiring both operational power and constant cooling, data centers even in these early years of the cloud industry, already consume about 3 percent of the global grid. Moreover, the pressure to provide uninterrupted service leads cloud companies to develop several layers of backup which create serious pollution issues. These include diesel generators that release known carcinogens, among other pollutants, into the air, and chemical batteries that are known to pollute ground water supplies. Some companies have responded to the pressures of investigative journalists and environmental organizations, especially Greenpeace, by introducing solar and other more sustainable forms of power (Mosco 2014, 123–137). Noticeably absent is Amazon which refuses to adjust its power supplies or to cooperate in any way with organizations concerned about the company's environmental record. But even with some adjustments possible, the entire cloud industry is under great pressure to cut costs and that includes making use of the least expensive power supply. It is therefore more likely that companies, in order to survive Amazon's ability to cut costs and make use of its political influence, will increasingly emulate the bleak environmental record of the industry leader (Cook 2014).

5   Hacking, Corporate Surveillance, State Surveillance

Just as ruthless competition reduces the likelihood that cloud companies will improve their environmental record without improvements in their bottom line, it also reduces the probability that companies will moderate their surveillance practices. On one level, the business model of a cloud computing company involves storing and processing data for individual and organizational customers who pay for on-demand access to their data and to services, such as managing and providing insights into sales records based on big data analytics. But, as Marx explained, companies need to maximize profit by making use of all available resources. Today, that means engaging in what some might see as questionable surveillance practices such as those that lead Google to read customer email to refine the advertising directed at them or Facebook to manipulate the newsfeed of users to increase the amount of time people spend with the social media site and to improve directed advertising. It is hard to imagine that Marx would be surprised to learn that Facebook has directed "bucket list" ads to people who share a cancer diagnosis on the site. Relentless invasion of privacy and deepening surveillance are essential elements of the basic business plans of cloud companies who profit by making the fullest possible use of the data stored in their servers to package and deliver valuable information on user identities to their paying clients. Since most legal constraints are minimal, the only significant way around these practices is to avoid using the cloud or to pay for extra security through the use of customized "private" cloud services (Mosco 2014, 137–155).

Similarly, it is fundamental to the missions of state agencies like the NSA, the CIA, and their counterparts throughout the world that they gather, store, process, and use as much information as possible about online users. Teaming with Amazon helps the CIA to deepen and extend its digital spy operations as do the accelerated expansion of the NSA's facilities and the continuing cooperation of the major cloud and social media firms in their activities. The military-information complex is strong and growing and the implications for personal and organizational privacy are profound. Nevertheless, while the revelations of Edward Snowden, Glenn Greenwald, and others have prompted some minor reforms, most media attention is directed at privacy and surveillance violations that emerge from the actions of criminal hackers who regularly demonstrate the relative ease with which they can break through the security that cloud companies allege protects the security of customer data. There is no denying the significance of the September 2014 attacks on ten financial institutions that affected 83 million consumer and business customers at JP Morgan Chase alone (Goldstein, Perlroth, and Sanger 2014). The regularity of such attacks, most of which are not reported by companies fearful of tarnishing their brand, demonstrates the porous nature of the cloud. Nevertheless, concentrating attention on these criminal acts alone detracts attention from the surveillance at the heart of the everyday business plans of cloud computing companies and the mission of government agencies. Eliminating or even dampening legal surveillance would diminish the profits of cloud companies and their business customers, as well as limit the ability of governments to gather data on everyone.

6   Cloud Computing and the Threat to Knowledge Labor

Cloud computing and big data pose threats to professional labour in IT and across the knowledge occupations. In fact, one expert consultant prefers to define cloud computing as "nothing more than the next step in outsourcing your IT operations" (McKendrick 2013). This is in keeping with a general tendency which one researcher for the major consulting firm Gartner Associates summarizes succinctly: "The long run value proposition of IT is not to support the human workforce – it is to replace it" (Dignan 2011a). This view remarkably echoes one that Marx himself and more contemporary neo-Marxists like Harry Braverman presented, to the effect that capitalism is driven to replace living labour with dead labor, that is, to replace the human workforce with machinery.

Cloud computing and big data analytics can advance this process in several ways. They create immediate opportunities for companies to rationalize their information technology operations. Again, from Gartner, "CIOs believe that their data centers, servers, desktop and business applications are grossly inefficient and must be rationalized over the next ten years. We believe that the people associated with these inefficient assets will also be rationalized in significant numbers along the way" (Dignan 2011a). Cloud computing companies maintain that their systems can break a pattern in business organization that began when the first large computers entered the workplace. Every business or government agency believed it was essential to operate their own IT department and, for the larger organizations, their own data centers. With the cloud, companies can move their IT and related business processes out of the organization. Why, they insist, is it necessary to build and operate thousands of organization-specific facilities when a few large data centers can meet the demand at lower costs with fewer professional personnel? This process has already begun and early studies demonstrate that even with limited downsizing of IT departments, organizations are saving between fifteen and twenty percent of their IT budgets (Howlett 2014).

The cloud also makes possible the widespread rationalization of all knowledge and creative labour because the work of these occupations increasingly involves the production, processing, and distribution of information. According to one observer, "In the next 40 years analytics systems will replace much of what the knowledge worker does today" (Dignan 2011b). A 2013 report concluded that 47 percent of the current U.S. workforce is directly threatened (Frey and Osborne 2013). The timing of this forecast may or may not be accurate but there is no doubt that the current trend is to move increasing amounts of the work that knowledge workers perform to the cloud, specifically through intelligent software systems. One study estimates the potential impact of this move by 2025 will total $5.2 to $6.7 trillion with additional labour productivity the equivalent of 110 million to 140 million knowledge workers (Manyika 2013, 40). Key applications include "smart learning in education," pioneered today in MOOCs (Massive Open Online Courses) and blended learning systems that include automated and classroom learning. Analytical systems in the cloud are also becoming prominent in health care, the law, accounting, finance, sales and the media. Thanks to the cloud, organizations in the private and public sectors are encouraged to outsource all but their core business processes to companies like Salesforce.com which specializes in managing the vast databases of customer information, a function that traditional marketing and client service departments within organizations once performed. The expansion of outsourcing to the cloud raises serious questions for the entire global system of shifting work outside the corporation or government agency. According to Gartner, "That outcome will hit all economies – especially emerging ones like India that now dominate technology outsourcing."

Cloud computing and big data also expand the range of potential outsourcing practices. It may not be the case that, as Forbes magazine declares, "We are all outsourcers now, thanks to Cloud," but it certainly makes feasible more kinds of outsourcing: "Outsourcing is no longer simply defined by multi-million-dollar mega-deals in which IT department operations are turned over to a third party. Rather, bits and pieces of a lot of smaller things are gradually being turned over to outside entities" (McKendrick 2014). Amazon is a leading force in this process with its Mechanical Turk service that charges individuals and organizations to outsource small tasks to an online army of piece workers. In essence, the cloud and big data make possible the expansion of labour commodification throughout the world.

They also make possible greater control over the workplace by expanding opportunities for surveillance and for the analysis of large data sets that facilitate rapid redeployment of workers to meet corporate needs. According to one leading business publication, "As Big Data becomes a fixture of office life, companies are turning to tracking devices to gather real-time information on how teams of employees work and interact. Sensors, worn on lanyards or placed on office furniture, record how often staffers get up from their desks, consult other teams and hold meetings" (Silverman 2013). Once again, as Simon Head notes, Amazon is a leader: "Amazon equals Walmart in the use of monitoring technologies to track the minute-by-minute movements and performance of employees and in settings that go beyond the assembly line to include their movement between loading and unloading docks, between packing and unpacking stations, and to and from the miles of shelving at what Amazon calls its 'fulfillment centers' ..." (Head 2014). Big data analytics enable companies to do more than just keep an eye on everything workers do. It provides new opportunities to actually make use of the data gathered in the course of monitoring the shop floor and the office. For example, Starbucks uses the data it gathers on customer flows through its stores to schedule worker shifts on short notice. This creates havoc for many workers, particularly those whose lives are tightly scheduled with child care, classes, and other jobs that make responding to constantly changing work times very difficult. Low-income workers are especially hard hit by a process that forces them to operate as flexible machines capable of responding to whatever logistical demands the companies that carry out big data analysis require.

7   Digital Positivism

The growing reliance on the cloud and especially on big data analytics raises a significant epistemological issue. One can observe a narrowing of what constitutes legitimate knowledge to the results of correlational methods applied to quantitative data. Big data is increasingly *the* model for examining not only scientific evidence but social science and humanities evidence as well. Big data enthusiasts take this to a striking, if not startling, extreme: "This is a world where massive amounts of data and applied mathematics replace every other tool that might be brought to bear. Out with every theory of human behavior, from linguistics to sociology. Forget taxonomy, ontology, and psychology. Who knows why people do what they do? The point is they do it, and we can track and measure it with unprecedented fidelity. With enough data, the numbers speak for themselves" (Anderson 2008). This view, and even considerably less strident perspectives on big data, embody a *digital positivism* that singularly valorizes one way of knowing above all others. It questions knowledge gathered through qualitative research that, for example, through in-depth interviews and close observation, seeks to understand subjective experience and intersubjectivity. It also devalues research grounded in historical, theoretical and disciplinary understandings of a field. If indeed the numbers speak for themselves then there is little need for these or for anything resembling the kind of thinking that has guided social science and humanities research for centuries. It is an approach congenial with capitalism because there is a close relationship between the quantification of everything, including the self, and the commodification of all things. As devices like the iWatch proliferate and make it possible to gather detailed quantitative data on each and every user, it is easier for Apple and its clients to profit from its sale. In this case the quantification of health states advances the commodification of the self.

There is no denying the methodological value of research based on the quantitative analysis of large data sets. But its usefulness does not justify sequestering other forms of research to lesser status. This is especially important because there is mounting evidence that big data can create big problems. In some cases, big data research produces remarkable results, as when Google succeeded in forecasting 2012 flu outbreaks across the United States by correlating search terms for flu symptoms with the incidence of flu. In beating the Centers for Disease Control with the speed and accuracy of its forecast, Google believed that it had the best predictive tool, that is, until 2013 when its model proved remarkably unreliable. It turns out that when the numbers speak, they often do so unreliably. It is also tempting for companies, most notably Facebook, to manipulate their very large data sets if such actions might boost ad revenue. Large data sets can also hide many errors that are not likely to be detected without time-consuming careful scrutiny. For example, if it were not for a hard-working PhD student, the critical errors in a paper that used large data sets to justify national economic austerity policies would not have been discovered. These and other examples document the problems associated with using big data analytics exclusively and the related difficulties of drawing conclusions based on correlations without taking into account theory, history, human subjectivity, and causality (Mosco 2014, 175–226).

8 Selling the Cloud

The importance of the cloud and big data for business and the state helps to explain why they are being promoted so vigorously. So too do the significant problems. Cloud promoters are using every available outlet and opportunity to convince individuals and businesses to move to the cloud. Advertising, social media, corporate and government reports, as well as lobbying and trade fairs are all used to demonstrate why the cloud and big data are essential. Promoters either ignore the problems or use this massive promotional space to downplay their significance. Whereas advertising gives promoters the opportunity to shout the message in a blunt and direct fashion; more legitimate sources, like the global public-private partnership of the World Economic Forum make it more subtle, as when the WEF concluded in a report on the cloud that experts believe "our society must move past the fear of data and privacy breaches" (World Economic Forum 2012, 99).

9   Chains of Accumulation and Chains of Resistance

Cloud computing and big data are vital for building and managing the global supply chains necessary to sustain the complex networks of transnational capital. There are enormous risks for business and the state in relying on these networks in a turbulent world. Private think tanks like Frost & Sullivan make it clear that the surveillance and analytic capabilities of the cloud and big data are essential for managing potentially disastrous risks to the many global chains of accumulation (Frost & Sullivan 2012). But neither promotion nor risk management can stop the chains of resistance that are also growing worldwide.

Where are the signs of resistance? First, supply chain disruptions make it more difficult to deploy cloud systems around the world and organized resistance from workers may alter the potential to profit from the cloud. The labour force in China, the base of global electronics supply chains, has grown restive in recent years, prompting tighter workplace controls and a redeployment of electronics manufacturing sites. It is unlikely these measures will do anything more than delay the inevitable choice between substantially raising the living standards, including the wages, working conditions and political freedom of China's workforce, or face escalating mass civil unrest. One can deploy suicide prevention curtains for just so long. The acknowledgment of unrest in China's once-placid factories has reached the mainstream Western press where an account in *Time* magazine offered this startling set of observations: "'The way the rich get money is through exploiting the workers', says Guan Guohau, another Shenzhen factory employee. 'Communism is what we are looking forward to'. Unless the government takes greater action to improve their welfare, they say, laborers will become more and more willing to take action themselves" (Schuman 2013). But this is no more startling than the kinds of protests that China's workers are mounting. In order to build data centers, the country will have to expand it electricity grid and this is especially disruptive in urban areas such as Wuhan where in the summer of 2014 people protested the development of new electrical substations. They did so by slowly parading their cars through the affected areas with clearly visible signs noting a naked inflatable doll of a female figure strapped to the back of one of them. The signs read: "we are giving you this inflatable doll so you don't have to rape our will" (Personal correspondence and photograph from a friend in Wuhan). Resistance in China is matched by similar upheavals in India where expected prosperity from the development of an information industry has stalled. As a result, the labour movement has grown with worker organizations like the New Trade Union Initiative building strong coalitions (Stevens 2014).

It is not only the base of the global supply chains created by major cloud companies that can create disruptions. Chains of resistance can also form in the advanced nations of the West where the labour process is certainly more humane than in Chinese electronic assembly plants, but very far from what applies in the headquarters of these companies. One hot spot for labour tensions is Germany where Amazon has established eight distribution centers employing 8,000 workers. Germany is important for the company because it is the source of 14 percent of its revenues (Wingfield and Eddy 2013). The country has not received a great deal of attention in struggles over global supply chains, but it has a long history of battles with Walmart which abandoned Germany in 2006 rather than bend its worldwide labour standards to meet the expectations of German workers and especially their union Ver.di which represents over two million employees in the service sector. German workers and their unions have considerably greater power than their counterparts in the United States and the UK. Mobilizing workers across the country, Ver.di's actions succeeded in ending Walmart's presence in the country. In 2013 a new battle erupted over Amazon which, in the view of German workers, is attempting to impose "American-style management" by relying on ruthless labour practices such as hiring thousands of low-wage and mainly foreign temporary workers and the security police necessary to maintain control. This has enabled the company to cut prices and drive out competition, including one German firm. According to a union leader, Amazon applies rigid controls to its workforce: "Everything is measured, everything is calculated, everything is geared toward efficiency. People want to be treated with respect" (Ewing 2013). The company denies these claims, arguing that it hires foreign temps because there are not enough local workers. But the online giant, now the largest cloud computing company in the United States, faced embarrassment when it had to fire a security firm hired to police one of its plants because some of the firm's employees, dressed in outfits associated with neo-Nazi groups, roughed up people trying to film activity outside the plant. The company maintains that it could not possibly know the backgrounds of all those it hires and insists that, while it refuses to negotiate with the union, it does pay workers well.

What will happen in this key node of Amazon's global supply chain is uncertain. Workers mount regular protests using mass mobilization, guerilla theater, and online global petition drives (37,000 signatures received by March 2013). But Amazon has refused to back down. In May 2013, workers at the giant Amazon distribution center in Leipzig walked off the job, marking the first reported strike at an Amazon facility (Wilson and Jopson 2013). The story continues to unfold with Ver.di leading another strike against the company in 2014.

It is not only in the material workplace that Amazon labour is restive. The company operates a global system of piecework in the cloud that critics have called a "digital sweatshop" (Cushing 2013). The Amazon Mechanical Turk (AMT) employs a large body of "crowdsourced" workers, which Amazon calls Providers (also known as Turkers), who carry out minute tasks online for Requesters who pay piece rates for writing descriptions of products, identifying individuals in images, or just producing spam (a 2010 study by NYU researchers determined that spam constitutes as much as 40 percent of the jobs) (Ipeirotis 2013). The system was originally set up by Amazon to carry out work that could be done online but required some human involvement. The typical job was sorting merchandise into categories based on color or style for the company's massive online warehouse. It was so successful that Amazon decided to become a job broker for corporations needing people to do things like look up foreign zip codes or transcribe podcasts.

For managing the service, Amazon receives 10 percent of the value of a completed job or, as it is called, a Human Intelligence Task (HIT). Although Turkers include professionals, the vast majority are semi-skilled workers who provide their credentials to Requesters, and, once cleared, choose among posted tasks. Workers in the United States are paid in cash but many foreign workers are primarily given the option to accept gift certificates. Exact figures are hard to pin down, but it is estimated that the industry employs over 200,000 workers, and by 2011 was earning about $375 million annually (Cushing 2013). There is also growing evidence that workers are less than happy with the system. It did not take long for them to realize, as one put it, "They make it sound like you can just do a few tasks in your free time in between other things, but if you worked like that, I believe you would make about a dollar a day" (Cushing 2013). Because companies have an enormous workforce to draw from, they can pay the lowest possible rates, a dollar or two an hour is not unusual, and demand swift and accurate completion of jobs. Workers who mess up a job are dropped or banned from applying again. In January 2013 Amazon stopped accepting new applications from international Turkers because of what the company concluded were unacceptable levels of fraud and poor worker performance. Since international workers are more likely to accept the low pay and constant demands, Requesters have begun to set up their own Turk operations.

Upset about the system, Turkers use their online world to vet Requesters and contact other Turkers. The result is Turkopticon, a piece of software that adds functionality to sites that post HITs by adding ratings, reviews of employers, and advice to exploited Turkers (http://turkopticon.differenceengines .com/). According to one scientist who has worked on AMT 28,000 times, "There's no sick leave, paid holidays, anything like that on Turk. There is no arbitration, no appeal if you feel that you have been unfairly treated, apart from a stinging review on Turkopticon" (Hodson 2013). Furthermore, worker complaints, fraud, and a host of negative consequences resulting from AMT's sweatshop in the cloud have encouraged other firms to set up somewhat more hospitable operations. For example, the firm MobileWorks pays the minimum wage in effect in the country where the work is being done, assigns each worker a manager whose job it is to deal with problems, and provides opportunities for worker mobility (Hodson 2013). It is uncertain whether the emergence of more worker friendly companies will restore some of the credibility to online piecework. Much will depend on whether big companies like Amazon respond to resistance by reforming the labour process in the cloud.

Worker organizations, especially trade unions, are not often discussed alongside cloud computing. Only a handful of cloud providers, mainly the older computer and telecommunications firms such as IBM and Verizon, have to deal with organized labor. But as we have seen in the case of Apple's experience with Foxconn in China and Amazon in Germany, cloud companies, as they become inextricably bound to global supply chains, face the resistance of organized labor. These are examples of a process at work in the broadly defined knowledge and cultural industries that brings together workers across what were once discrete sectors. As a result, unions that once represented only telecommunications workers, now include creative and technical talent in the audio-visual, writing, service, and technology sectors. The Communication Workers of America and its counterpart in Canada, which in 2013 merged its communications and power workers union with the union representing auto workers to form Unifor, are good examples of worker organizations that have followed the path of technological convergence in its organizing efforts. The 2012 merger of the Screen Actors Guild and the American Federation of Television and Radio Artists brings together the major Hollywood unions for the first time to face off more effectively against the increasingly integrated Hollywood media industry. Moreover, individual unions are not only expanding across the converging communication and information industries, they are forming large transnational organizations like Ver.di and UNI Global Union. These transnational unions are better equipped to deal with powerful multinational companies because they have enormous membership and because they are well funded. Furthermore, the scope of their membership enables them to better represent the convergences in both the labour process and the working conditions among information, cultural, and service workers. It also makes it possible to build bridges across the divide separating workers at different spatial and occupational points in the global division of labor.

Ver.di was founded in 2001 and by 2013 reached 2.3 million members, primarily in Germany but in other parts of the world as well. It represents workers in thirteen sectors, all of which are increasingly affected by the rollout of cloud computing including financial services, health and social services, education, science and research, media and culture, telecommunications, information technology, and data processing, postal, transport and commerce services. Its members work in government and business at almost every level of occupational skill and function. Not only can the union mobilize a large and diverse workforce, it can also draw on the specialized talents of its members who help the union to tighten and secure its internal communication and carry out guerilla theater protests that attract widespread media attention. UNI Global Union was created in 2000 when three international worker federations in the information, media, and service sectors came together to form a genuinely global federation of knowledge workers. Today, it gives voice to 20 million workers in 150 countries through 900 affiliated unions in a broad range of fields including information technology and services, media, entertainment and the arts, gaming and sport, finance, commerce and security, as well as the growing numbers of workers who toil for temporary employment agencies. Among its major activities is negotiating global agreements with transnational companies to address important issues such as child labor, discrimination, and the right to organize local unions. By early 2013 it had completed 48 such agreements with a wide range of companies, including a number in the communication and information technology sector. In 2014 it set its sights on negotiating fresh agreements with major transnational firms including IBM and Disney.

Ver.di and UNI are not alone among converging unions and international labour federations that are having an impact on global supply chains, including those central to the growth of cloud computing. But it is uncertain whether this development is the harbinger of a significant upsurge in global labour activism or a defensive posture that can at best slow down the inevitable decline and demise of organized labor. That depends, in part, on how one defines organized labour because another important trend is the growth of labour organizations that are not formal trade unions. These worker associations resemble unions but, either out of choice or necessity, remain outside the legal and political structures that govern the operation of trade unions. They operate all over the world and research has documented their importance in China, India, Europe, and the United States (Mosco, McKercher, and Huws 2010). They are especially active in the information, communication and cultural sectors where worker associations have represented employees in occupations ranging from call centers to software engineering. Worker associations have won major victories for contract employees at Microsoft and for telecommunications workers in India. While they do not typically negotiate contracts, they have provided workers with legal representation, group medical insurance, training, model contract language, counseling, and support for collective resistance without suffering from some of the bureaucratic entanglements that plague traditional trade unions. These associations are particularly active among contract and temporary workers where, for example, the Freelancers Union has signed up 200,000 members in a wide range of jobs including law, app and software development, graphic arts, accounting, writing, editing, and consulting. Worker associations do not just differ from trade unions in what they lack, a system of formal bargaining with employees, but in their emphasis on mutual assistance outside, as well as in, the workplace. They follow the social movement tradition of earlier trade unions, which provided workers with social support including family assistance, housing, and a source of collective power and community. As the head of the Freelancers Union puts it, "The social unionism of the 1920s had it right. They said: 'We serve workers 360 degrees. It's not just about their work. It's about their whole life'. We view things the same way" (Greenhouse 2013). As companies move to the cloud, it is likely that workers and their organizations will follow. Cloud computing and big data deepen the chains of accumulation that power digital capitalism. But they also produce chains of resistance, from China to Silicon Valley. The success of resistance will depend on how well workers, especially those in the knowledge workforce, are able to unite and develop strategies both locally and globally. Any successful plan of action needs to include a policy vision for the cloud that addresses its potential for public benefit and its serious flaws including corporate concentration, environmental damage, deepening surveillance from the NSA and its counterparts, the growing fetishization of big data analytics, and the many threats to labor. Can worker organizations join policy activists fighting for a democratic internet to make the cloud a public utility to serve democracy?

10   The Coming Computer Utility

The cloud and big data are important forces for global capitalism and for the surveillance state. But their shortcomings and the social problems they create are also significant. Building and maintaining global chains of accumulation in the cloud is not easy and certainly far from inherently stable (Huws 2014). The resistance from social movement and labour organizations adds stress to the tenuous nature of global networks. But it is far from clear what the challenges amount to beyond the inevitability of chronic disruptions. They certainly do not guarantee a fundamental change from a digital world governed by markets that are controlled by a handful of companies and the surveillance arms of governments.

One starting point is "ruthless criticism," of the sort that Marx (1843) described in his letter to Ruge as "ruthless both in the sense of not being afraid of the results it arrives at and in the sense of being just as little afraid of conflict with the powers that be." Empirical descriptions of resistance movements contribute a next step. Along with and beyond these strategies, we need a debate about alternatives to digital capitalism, digital positivism, and the surveillance state. Specifically, how can we move the digital world closer to the vision of the General Intellect where information is a resource available to all, where it is managed by citizens democratically, where the concept of a public cloud means a digital world subject to public control rather than one where rights are limited to the right to purchase digital services?

Given the power of the dominant cloud companies and the NSA, it is admittedly difficult to envision an alternative. It is hard to imagine that another digital world is possible. To bring it closer to home, it is important to uncover a subterranean history of computer communication, where the concept of delivering information publicly was not just open to debate but was also a lived reality. It is too soon in the debate to produce anything approaching a blueprint for the alternative but not too early to document and debate the range of historical possibilities that can provide the elements for one or more genuine alternatives to the status quo. These include the Soviet cybernetics program of the 1950s–60s which sought to use computers for national economic planning and which was viewed by adversaries, most notably the U.S. government, as a significant threat to American economic leadership (Gerovitch 2010). In the 1970s the socialist government of Chile initiated Project Cybersyn which was committed to a publicly controlled, decentralized system of computer-based planning that would help the country achieve workplace democracy (Medina 2011). In the 1980s the debate came to North America when policy makers discovered the work of Canadian analyst Douglas Parkhill who had advanced the idea of a computer utility, modeled after public utilities for water and power, which would deliver an equally essential resource, information (Parkhill 1966). These ideas were tested in the US, UK, Canada, and France with teletext and videotex systems that delivered information to kiosks located in public places like post offices and airports as well as to the home. In the 1990s they grew into the internet which began as a decentralized, self-managed network open to all those with access to the necessary technology. But at the turn of the new century, this burgeoning public network was challenged by companies aiming to shape it into a commercial profit machine and by governments that would use the internet to deepen their control over citizens within and outside their borders. The information revolution has met its counter-revolution. Nevertheless, the lessons from the ideas and experiences with genuinely public networks, including their successes and failures, live on and can provide building blocks for creating genuine alternatives that can help to envision and build a new General Intellect for the digital world.

References

Anderson, Chris. 2008. The End of Theory: The Data Deluge Makes the Scientific Method Obsolete. *Wired.* June 23. Accessed October 27, 2014. http://archive.wired.com/science/discoveries/magazine/16-07/pb_theory.

Bamford, James. 2012. The NSA Is Building the Country's Biggest Spy Center (Watch What You Say). *Wired.* March 15. Accessed October 25, 2014. www.wired.com/threatlevel/2012/03/ff_nsadatacenter/all.

Clover, Charles. 2014. Alibaba: Weapons of Mass Ecommerce. *Financial Times,* September 26. Accessed October 25, 2014. http://www.ft.com/intl/cms/s/0/2a19e07c-43ef-11e4-8abd-00144feabdc0.html?siteedition=intl.

Cohen, Reuven. 2012. "How Cloud Computing Helped Obama Win the Presidential Election." *Forbes.* Accessed October 25, 2014. www.forbes.com/sites/reuvencohen/2012/11/15/how-cloud-computing-helped-obama-win-the-presidential-election.

Cook, Gary. 2014. *Clicking Green: How Companies are Creating the Green Internet.* April. Accessed October 25, 2014. http://www.greenpeace.org/usa/global/usa/planet3/pdfs/clickingclean.pdf.

Cushing, Ellen. 2013. "Amazon Mechanical Turk: The Digital Sweatshop." *UTNE Reader.* Accessed October 27, 2014. www.utne.com/science-technology/amazon-mechanical-turk-zmoz13jfzlin.aspx.

Dignan, Larry, 2011a. Cloud Computing's Real Creative Destruction May be the IT Workforce. *ZDNet.* October 24. Accessed October 26, 2014. http://www.zdnet.com/blog/btl/cloud-computings-real-creative-destruction-may-be-the-it-workforce/61581.

Dignan, Larry. 2011b. Analytics in 40 Years: Machines will Kick Human Managers to the Curb. *ZDNet.* October 18. Accessed October 26, 2014. http://www.zdnet.com/blog/btl/analytics-in-40-years-machines-will-kick-human-managers-to-the-curb/61092.

Ewing, Jack. 2013. Amazon Labor Relations under Scrutiny in Germany. *New York Times.* Accessed October 27, 2014. www.nytimes.com/2013/03/04/business/global/amazons-labor-relations-under-scrutiny-in-germany.html.

Frey, Carl Benedikt and Osborne, Michael A. 2013. *The Future of Employment: How Susceptible are Jobs to Computerisation?* Oxford University. September. Accessed October 27, 2014. http://www.oxfordmartin.ox.ac.uk/publications/view/1314.

Frost & Sullivan. 2012. *How Cloud Computing can Reduce Supply Chain Risks.* Accessed October 27, 2014. http://www.cfoinnovation.com/white-paper/5541/how-cloud-computing-can-reduce-supply-chain-risks.

Gerovitch, Slava. 2010. The Cybernetic Scare and the Origins of the Internet. *Baltic Worlds.* Accessed October 27, 2014. http://balticworlds.com/the-cybernetics-scare-and-the-origins-of-the-internet.

Goldstein, Matthew, Perlroth, Nicole, and Sanger, David E. 2014. Hackers' Attack Cracked10 Financial Firms in Major Assault. *New York Times.* October 3, Accessed October 25, 2014. http://nyti.ms/1to7tnX.

Greenhouse, Steven. 2013. Tackling Concerns of Independent Workers. *New York Times.* Accessed October 27, 2014. www.nytimes.com/2013/03/24/business/freelancers-union-tackles-concerns-of-independent-workers.html.

Hardy, Quentin. 2014. Alibaba has a Computing Cloud, and It's Growing, Too. *The New York Times*, August 4, Accessed October 25, 2014. http://nyti.ms/1srRPLh.

Head, Simon. 2014. Worse than Walmart: Amazon's Sick Brutality and Secret History of Ruthlessly Intimidating Workers. *Salon.* February 23. Accessed October 27, 2014. http://bit.ly/1e726X6.

Hodson, Hal. 2013. "Crowdsourcing Grows Up as Online Workers Unite." *New Scientist.* Accessed October 27, 2014. www.newscientist.com/article/mg21729036.200-crowdsourcing-grows-up-as-online-workers-unite.html.

Hoover, J. Nicholas. 2012. "6 Ways Amazon Helped Obama Win." *InformationWeek.* Accessed October 25, 2014. www.informationweek.com/government/cloud-saas/6-ways-amazon-cloud-helped-obama-win/240142268.

Howlett, Den. 2014. Exclusive: Computer Economics Study – Cloud Saves 15 Percent. *diginomica.* February 13. Accessed October 26, 2014. http://diginomica.com/2014/02/13/exclusive-computer-economics-study-cloud-saves/.

Huws, Ursula. 2014. *Labor in the Global Digital Economy: The Cybertariat Comes of Age.* New York: Monthly Review Press.

Ipeirotis, Panos. 2013. "Mechanical Turk: Now with 40.92% Spam." *A Computer Scientist in a Business School.* Accessed October 27, 2014. www.behind-the-enemy-lines.com/2010/12/mechanical-turk-now-with-4092-spam.html.

Manyika, James, et al. 2013. *Disruptive Technologies: Advances that will Transform Life, Business, and the Global Economy.* New York: McKinsey and Co.

Marx, Karl. 1858. *The Grundrisse: Notebook VII.* Accessed October 27, 2014 https://www.marxists.org/archive/marx/works/1857/grundrisse/ch14.htm.

Marx, Karl. 1843. *Letters from the Deutsch-Französische Jahrbücher.* Accessed October 27, 2014. https://www.marxists.org/archive/marx/works/1843/letters/43_09.htm.

McChesney, Robert W. 2013. *Digital Disconnect: How Capitalism is Turning the Internet Against Democracy*. New York: The New Press.

McKendrick, Joe. 2013. In the Rush to Cloud Computing Here's One Question Not Enough People are Asking. *Forbes*. February 19. Accessed October 26, 2014. http://onforb.es/1yCk7UY.

McKendrick, Joe. 2014. We're All Outsourcers Now, Thanks to Cloud. *Forbes*. August 11. Accessed October 26, 2014. http://onforb.es/1mBuxgp.

Medina, Eden. 2011. *Cybernetic Revolutionaries: Technology and Politics in Allende's Chile*. Cambridge, MA: MIT Press.

Mosco, Vincent. 2014. *To the Cloud: Big Data in a Turbulent World*. New York: Paradigm.

Mosco, Vincent, McKercher, Catherine and Huws, Ursula. (eds.) 2010. *Getting the Message: Communications Workers and Global Value Chains*, London: Merlin Press.

Parkhill, Douglas. F. 1966. *The Challenge of the Computer Utility*. Reading, MA: Addison-Wesley.

Schuman, Michael. 2013. "Marx's Revenge: How Class Struggle Is Shaping the World." *Time*. Accessed October 27, 2014. http://business.time.com/2013/03/25/marxs-revenge-how-class-struggle-is-shaping-the-world.

Silverman, Rachel Emma. 2013. Tracking Sensors Invade the Workplace. *Wall Street Journal*. March 7. Accessed October 27, 2013. http://online.wsj.com/articles/SB10001424127887324034804578344303429080678.

Stevens, Andrew. 2014. *Call Centers and the Global Division of Labor*. New York: Routledge.

Wilson, James, and Jopson, Barney. 2013. "Amazon Hit by Old World Strike Action." *Financial Times*. Accessed October 27, 2014. www.ft.com/intl/cms/s/0/e4d3bdde-bc82-11e2-9519-00144feab7de.html.

Wingfield, Nick, and Eddy, Melissa. 2013. In Germany, Union Culture Clashes with Amazon's Labor Practices. *New York Times*. Accessed October 27, 2014. www.nytimes.com/2013/08/05/business/workers-of-amazon-divergent.html.

World Economic Forum. 2012. *Global Information Technology Report: 2012*. Geneva: World Economic Forum.

Index